TRENDS IN INNOVATION AND ENTREPRENEURSHIP RESEARCH

Ecosystems, Digital Technologies and Responses to Shocks

TRENDS IN INNOVATION AND ENTREPRENEURSHIP RESEARCH

Ecosystems, Digital Technologies and Responses to Shocks

EDITORS

ALEXANDER BREM
University of Stuttgart, Germany

JIN CHEN
Tsinghua University, China

World Scientific

NEW JERSEY • LONDON • SINGAPORE • BEIJING • SHANGHAI • HONG KONG • TAIPEI • CHENNAI • TOKYO

Published by

World Scientific Publishing Co. Pte. Ltd.
5 Toh Tuck Link, Singapore 596224
USA office: 27 Warren Street, Suite 401-402, Hackensack, NJ 07601
UK office: 57 Shelton Street, Covent Garden, London WC2H 9HE

British Library Cataloguing-in-Publication Data
A catalogue record for this book is available from the British Library.

TRENDS IN INNOVATION AND ENTREPRENEURSHIP RESEARCH
Ecosystems, Digital Technologies and Responses to Shocks

ISBN 978-981-127-328-5 (hardcover)
ISBN 978-981-127-329-2 (ebook for institutions)
ISBN 978-981-127-330-8 (ebook for individuals)

For any available supplementary material, please visit
https://www.worldscientific.com/worldscibooks/10.1142/13332#t=suppl

Desk Editor: Venkatesh Sandhya

Typeset by Stallion Press
Email: enquiries@stallionpress.com

Editorial

Since Joseph Schumpeter's theory, the field of technological innovation and entrepreneurship has grown considerably over the decades, even proving relevant to contemporary challenges such as the COVID-19 pandemic (Brem, 2021). It has had a huge impact on businesses and organizations in general, encouraging business leaders and policymakers to experiment with a variety of new approaches for creating and commercializing innovation. With the technical and social advances, however, new challenges emerge, such as (1) the importance of understanding the interaction between ecological actors and the dynamic evolution of ecosystems; (2) the increasing use of advanced digital technologies; and (3) the unprecedented external shocks resulting from the global COVID-19 pandemic. In light of these novel contexts, innovation and entrepreneurship research needs to consider and explore the emerging trends of novel frameworks and theoretical aspects.

The objective of this book is to shed light on recent trends in innovation and entrepreneurship research. This compilation comprises works that were chosen based on their relevance and rigor, and it presents, illustrates, and discusses novel results in the following areas:

— *Innovation and Entrepreneurial Ecosystems*
— *Digital Technologies and Digital Innovation*
— *Exogenous Shocks and Responses to Pandemics*

All chapters were carefully chosen from the International Journal of Innovation and Technology Management, of which Jin Chen is currently editing and Alexander Brem was previously Editor-in-Chief. Hence, this was an ideal setup to identify the best fitting and most insightful articles for this edited book.

The first part focuses on *Innovation and Entrepreneurial Ecosystems*. The open innovation movement, coupled with a rising consensus on the value of collaborative research and networks, has drawn special attention to ecosystem conditions that support and foster innovation and entrepreneurship. The creation of the ecosystem is to go beyond the traditional industrial border and to reach the wide boundary set by the purposed interdependence. New contexts highlight new avenues in innovation and entrepreneurship ecosystem studies. For example, with the growth and maturity of digital publishing technology, Open Access Ecosystem (OAE) has emerged, changing the prevailing business model in the scholarly communications ecosystem. To better understand the process of enabling OAE, Osorio-Sanabria *et al.* (2022) provide a literature review of the main components of an OAE, the essential roles of the different stakeholders, as well as relationships between them. Another emerging question concerns the factors pertaining to why China's solar photovoltaic (PV) industry can catch up so rapidly without radical technological innovation. Based on the grounded theory method, Ge and Liu (2022) illustrate that it was the industrial innovation ecosystem construction and the interactive relationship between ecological actors that made China's solar PV industry achieve a catch-up without radical technological innovation. Besides, digital platforms have revolutionized the service sector by not only introducing traditional services online but also continuously making frequent modifications to them in the form of incremental innovations. To better understand the level at which the users of digital platforms are adopting incremental innovations, Dutta and Sarma (2020) outline three categories of the adoption of incremental innovations in digital platforms, namely Beginner, Enhanced, and Advanced, based on a survey study conducted in India. With the increasing significance of university-based technology commercialization in economic development, further research is needed especially in relation to academic entrepreneurship. Using a sample of 160 UK higher education institutions, Prokop (2022) studies the composition of the university entrepreneurial ecosystems and recognizes its important role in academic entrepreneurship performance. Along the same vein, Rahim *et al.* (2021) focus on the characteristics of academic entrepreneurs and find that academics' opportunity recognition increases their academic entrepreneurship performances, and that the positive relationship is strengthened by self-regulated learning.

The second part concerns *Digital Technologies and Digital Innovation.* All facets of economic and social activities are being reorganized because of the permeation of digital technology. The increasing usage of advanced digital technologies is driving a paradigm shift and providing new insights for research in the innovation and entrepreneurship stream. For example, organizations across all sectors and industries are facing the need for structural change toward a digital future. To master this organizational task, Buck *et al.* (2021) develop an integrated framework for organizational digital transformation that is structured into eight building blocks and associated action items. Focusing on incumbent firms' competitiveness in the continually evolving digital world, Bosler *et al.* (2021) analyze the value creation from the multi-sided changes for the development and management of digital innovations based on multiple case studies. Although employees play a crucial role in developing innovations, little is known about their participation in the digital innovation process. Kaiser et al. (2021) find that employees must be integrated into digital innovation processes to reduce their resistance to change by engaging them in the change. How digital technologies such as digital platforms can be employed in innovative endeavors and crisis management presents another emerging trend. For instance, using the business model for dynamic capabilities and a case study, Okano *et al.* (2022) explore how digital platforms digitally innovate organizations by creating new business models and providing new value propositions, thus allowing new areas of activity, types of business, and organizational scenarios. Moreover, Marino and Pariso (2022) examine if the digital platform experience of a leading country in wine tourism can help to overcome COVID-19 and turn the sector. In the final chapter of this part, Steenhuis *et al.* (2020) investigate how additive manufacturing (AM) is spreading globally. They find that the early-stage diffusion of AM technology for industrial 3D printers is primarily in advanced economies and that most of the existing companies have expanded into AM as a related area or were corporate spin-offs, probably because of the complexity of AM which requires expert knowledge across a range of fields.

The last part of this book is about *Exogenous Shocks and Responses to Pandemics.* In 2020, the world had witnessed an unprecedented global pandemic with COVID-19, which left organizations, industries, and countries facing unprecedented challenges and difficulties. Considering the turbulence caused by the pandemic, organizations have to develop response strategies. For example, although the COVID-19 pandemic and social distancing entangled physical trading of products and services worldwide, the development of marketplace platforms has allowed for knowledge resources and knowledge sharing. In such contexts, Jorge et al. (2022) identify and analyze the influential aspects of knowledge sharing in marketplace platforms during the COVID-19 pandemic. Although there is a rising consensus on the value of social networks and concepts such as open innovation, the importance of social networks in the process of organizational innovation adoption (OIA) has not yet been fully addressed. Hence, Jacob and Teuteberg (2022) explore the nature of networks based on a case study and reveal four types of influence through which social networks influence the OIA on micro, meso, and macro levels. Another emerging topic is how to support Industry 4.0 (I4.0) technology adoption which facilitates innovative solutions to address the significant impacts of the COVID-19 pandemic. Drawing on insights from a case study, Kruger and Steyn (2022) find that innovation environments offer an agile platform to leverage innovation by streamlining certain critical success factors of I4.0 technology adoption. Another intriguing question involves whether the mobility patterns of inventors have changed after COVID-19 spread globally. Using patent data in the semiconductor industry, Fujiwara (2022) analyzes the factors affecting the international mobility of engineers before and after COVID-19. Researchers and practitioners also highlight the relevance of evaluating the opportunities to capitalize on technology for tackling the associated challenges of COVID-19. Guggenberger *et al.* (2021) investigate the innovative potentials of three emerging digital technologies, namely, the Internet of Things (IoT), artificial intelligence (AI) and distributed ledgers to tackle pandemic-related challenges. Although university–industry (UI) partnerships have captured increased managerial interest, as well as scholarly attention, systemic issues pose a challenge in selecting the appropriate mode of UI technology transfer. Focusing on UI relationships, Sharma (2022) investigates the value of such linkages that motivates firms to choose a particular mode to acquire university-generated research output.

To sum up, this book brings together rigorous research exploring and discussing recent developments in the field of technological innovation and entrepreneurship through empirical studies, case studies, systematic literature reviews, and grounded analyses. It covers three trending topics in the field, including *Innovation and Entrepreneurial Ecosystems*, *Digital Technologies and Digital Innovation,* and *Exogenous Shocks and Responses to Pandemics.* This book is ideally intended for academicians, researchers, firm managers, industry experts, entrepreneurs, practitioners, stakeholders, and the public who are interested in knowing about emerging trends in technological innovation and entrepreneurship and how firms and organizations pursuing innovation and entrepreneurship are going to evolve and progress in the near future.

We expect that this book will provide readers with a collection of inspiring ideas and stimulate promising research directions in the field of technological innovation and entrepreneurship. We would like to express our gratitude to all the authors for their contributions. Also, we would like to thank Sandhya Venkatesh from WSPC for her great support on this project.

Alexander Brem
University of Stuttgart, Germany

Jin Chen
Tsinghua University, China

References

Bosler, M., Burr, W., & Ihring, L. (2021). Digital innovation in incumbent firms: An exploratory analysis of value creation. *International Journal of Innovation and Technology Management,* **18**, 2: 1–22. https://doi.org/10.1142/S0219877020400039

Brem, A. (2021). Was würde Schumpeter tun? Entrepreneurship in Zeiten der Covid-Pandemie. *ZfKE–Zeitschrift für KMU und Entrepreneurship*, **69**, 2: 137–145. https://doi.org/10.3790/zfke.69.2.137

Buck, C., Marques, C. P., & Rosemann, M. (2021). Eight building blocks for managing digital transformation. *International Journal of Innovation and Technology Management,* **18**, 5: 1–31. https://doi.org/10.1142/S0219877021500231

Dutta, D., & Sarma, M. K. (2020). Adoption of digital innovation –formulating adopter categories and levels of adoption in a digital sphere in an emerging economy. *International Journal of Innovation and Technology Management,* **17**, 8: 1–21. . https://doi.org/10.1142/S0219877020500595

Fujiwara, A. (2022). Impact of the COVID-19 outbreak on engineers' mobility: Evidence from patent data in the semiconductor industry. *International Journal of Innovation and Technology Management,* **19**, 6: 1–18. https://doi.org/10.1142/S0219877022420032

Ge, S., & Liu, X. (2022). Catch-up in solar PV industry of China: A perspective of industrial innovation ecosystem. *International Journal of Innovation and Technology Management,* **19**, 6: 1–30. https://doi.org/10.1142/S0219877022420032

Guggenberger, T., Lockl, J., Rglinger, M., Schlatt, V., Sedlmeir, J., Stoetzer, J. C., Urbach, N., & Völter, F. (2021). Emerging digital technologies to combat future crises: Learnings from COVID-19 to be prepared for the future. *International Journal of Innovation and Technology Management,* **18**, 4: 1–27. https://doi.org/10.1142/S0219877021400022

Jacob, A., & Teuteberg, F. (2022). How social networks influence organizational innovation adoption. *International Journal of Innovation and Technology Management,* **19**, 8: 1–39. https://doi.org/10.1142/S0219877022500328

Jorge, C. F. B., Machad, J. G. D. C. F., Menegassi, C. H. M., Stecca, R. D. S., & Sutton, M. J. D. (2022). Influential aspects of knowledge sharing in the context of a marketplace platform during the COVID-19 pandemic: A Brazilian case study. *International Journal of Innovation and Technology Management,* **19**, 7: 1–31. https://doi.org/10.1142/S0219877022500225

Kaiser, L. F., Wehking, C., & Brocke, J. V. (2021). How to organize digital innovation? The role of involvement, structure, and technology. *International Journal of Innovation and Technology Management,* **18**, 3: 1–22. https://doi.org/10.1142/S0219877021500103

Kruger, S., & Steyn, A. A. (2022). Innovation environment's role in supporting Industry 4.0 technology adoption to address effects of COVID-19. *International Journal of Innovation and Technology Management,* **19**, 6: 1–25. https://doi.org/10.1142/S0219877022420019

López-Rubio, P., Roig-Tierno, N., & Mas-Tur, A. (2021). A research journey from national systems of innovation to national systems of entrepreneurship: Introducing the sextuple helix. *International Journal of Innovation and Technology Management,* **18**, 8: 1–23. https://doi.org/10.1142/S0219877021300081

Marino, A., & Pariso, P. (2022). The digital platform experience of a leading country in wine tourism: From COVID-19 to the new era. *International Journal of Innovation and Technology Management,* **19**, 7: 1–17. https://doi.org/10.1142/S0219877022500213

Okano, M. T., Santos, H. D. C. L. D., & Ursini, E. L. (2022). The digital platform as digital innovation: A study from the perspective of dynamic capabilities. *International Journal of Innovation and Technology Management,* **19**, 3: 1–23. https://doi.org/10.1142/S0219877021400149

Osorio-Sanabria, M. A., Jaime, A., & Amaya-Fernández, F. (2022). Roles and relationships among open-access ecosystem actors. *International Journal of Innovation and Technology Management,* **19**, 4: 1–23. https://doi.org/10.1142/S0219877022500079

Prokop, D. (2022). The composition of university entrepreneurial ecosystems and academic entrepreneurship: A UK study. *International Journal of Innovation and Technology Management,* **19**, 6: 1–23. https://doi.org/10.1142/S0219877022500201

Rahim, N. A., Mohamed, Z., Amrin, A., & Masrom, M. (2021). Impact of self-regulated learning on entrepreneurial opportunity recognition and academic entrepreneurship performance. *International Journal of Innovation and Technology Management,* **18**, 4: 1–30. https://doi.org/10.1142/S0219877021500164

Sharma, P. (2022). A framework to manage university–industry technology transfer. *International Journal of Innovation and Technology Management,* **19**, 8: 1–35. https://doi.org/10.1142/S021987702250033X

Steenhuis, H. J., Fang, X., & Ulusemre, T. (2020). Global diffusion of innovation during the fourth industrial revolution: The case of additive manufacturing or 3d printing. *International Journal of Innovation and Technology Management,* **17**, 1: 1–34. . https://doi.org/10.1142/S0219877020500054

Contents

Part 1

Innovation and Entrepreneurial Ecosystems

Roles and Relationships Among Open-Access Ecosystem Actors*

Mariutsi Alexandra Osorio-Sanabria*, Astrid Jaime[‡,§] and Ferney Amaya-Fernández[†]

*Fundación Universitaria María Cano (FUMC), Medellín, Colombia

[†]Universidad Pontificia Bolivariana (UPB), Medellín, Colombia

[‡]Corporación Universitaria Minuto de Dios, Bogotá, D. C., Colombia
[§]mireya.jaime@uniminuto.edu, astrid_jaime@yahoo.com

We aim to establish the relationship between the stakeholders who are part of the Open-Access Ecosystem (OAE). The study was developed from an ecosystem approach, analyzing the actors and their relationships. As a result, we proposed a simplified view of the main components of an OAE and the relationships between them, which could be useful for understanding the roles of the different stakeholders and the implications that current and new policies and mandates could have for them.

Keywords: Open access; ecosystem; open-access ecosystem; academic communication; scholarly communication.

1. Introduction

Access to scientific knowledge is at the cornerstone of scientific activity [Fosci *et al.* (2020)] and the basis of the knowledge society [Czerniewicz (2018)]. However, increasing publications and costs, as well as budgetary constraints, sometimes make it difficult to access all the necessary resources to develop research endeavors appropriately. This situation led to what has been called the "serials crisis".[a] For that reason, advocates of the Open Access (OA) movement defend it as the solution to it [Jurchen (2020); Saarti and Tuominen (2021)]. According to Fosci *et al.* [2020], OA has recently been fostered by "interventions from and policies of research funders, combined with the growth and maturity of digital publishing technology." (p. 43). On the other hand, Wessels *et al.* [2014] argue that the process of enabling open access to research data involves addressing four main areas: stakeholder roles and values;

[§]Corresponding author.

[a]For a brief explanation, see http://blogs.harvard.edu/openaccess101/what-is-open-access/what-is-open-access/ (accessed on 23/01/2021).

*This chapter was originally published in International Journal of Innovation and Technology Management, Vol. 19, No. 4, March 2018, published by World Scientific Publishing, Singapore. Reprinted with permission.

technological requirements for data management; legal and ethical regulations and procedures; and institutional roles and policy frameworks.

Some authors have even shown that OA combined with social media dissemination of scholarly articles appears to enhance its reach [Li *et al.* (2021)]. However, OA faces important challenges such as financial constraints [Jurchen (2020)], prestige [Eve (2014)], intellectual property barriers [Eve (2014); Czerniewicz (2018)], and impact on academic advancement [Zhu (2017)], among others.

One of the bigger challenges has been that OA has impacted the prevailing business model in the scholarly communications ecosystem [Fosci *et al.* (2020)]. The shift in this business model from "user-funded to author-funded changed the access barrier for readers into a publication barrier for authors" [Jurchen (2020, p. 166)]. To overcome these challenges, there have been different proposals, such as "a collectively funded publishing ecosystem" [Pooley (2019, The Library Solution, paragraph 11)], which could, at a smaller scale, correspond to "library consortial arrangements" [Eve (2014, p. 61)], which have led to initiatives such as "ArXiv, SCOAP, Knowledge Unlatched and the Open Library of Humanities" [Eve (2014, p. 61)]. However, according to [Eve (2014, p. 61)], "such models, though, do not sit harmoniously within the present, dominant business in the context of free-market competition".

For Jurchen [2020], academic libraries should collaborate to collectively influence the scholarly communications' ecosystem to "move beyond APC funding as the favored OA publishing approach and retain their traditional role in information accessibility" [b] [Jurchen (2020, p. 168)]. Such an influence, among others, could strengthen the OA Ecosystem — OAE by lowering both the access and publication barriers if permission barriers could also be reduced [Eve (2014)].

Although many of the OA advocates preconize the need of strengthening the OAE [Linde *et al.* (2015); Czerniewicz (2018); Smith and Dickson (2017); López-López (2019b)], not many works explicitly define what is the OAE or what are the relationships between its components.

This lack of understanding about the OAE has led us to wonder what the OAE is. For that reason, in this work, we provide an overview of the essential roles and relationships of OAE stakeholders based on a literature review on the subject. The review included a content analysis of documents found in the literature to identify the OAE stakeholders and map the roles and relationships among them. This proposal takes advantage of previous works on this subject [Osorio-Sanabria *et al.* (2020)] and advances on the understanding of the OAE by improving the identified roles and incorporating the main relationships we have found among the stakeholders identified in the literature. As far as we know, this is the first time an effort has been made to provide an overview of the OEA based on a literature review. The stakeholders and relationships identified and mapped in this paper constitute a first analytical basis for understanding the OAE and offer several possibilities for future analyses that consider them in greater depth. It is worth noting that limitations due to the abundance of stakeholders identified and lack of previous work on the matter led us to focus only on the roles and main relationships among stakeholders.

[b] APC stands for Article Processing Charges.

The rest of this work is organized as follows: We start by presenting a brief overview of the literature on OAE and then describe the methodology used, followed by the findings and the discussion of these findings, and we end with the conclusions of our work.

2. Theoretical Framework

The Systematic Literature Review (SLR) was created to support evidence-based medicine to obtain advice based on the accumulation of results from scientific experiments. Kitchenham *et al.* [2009] define evidence "as a synthesis of [the] best quality scientific studies on a specific topic or research question" (p. 53), and the main method of synthesis is a SLR. Kitchenham and Charters [2007] define SLR as "a means of evaluating and interpreting all available research relevant to a particular research question, topic area, or phenomenon of interest ... using a trustworthy, rigorous, and auditable methodology" (p. vi). SLR supports better decision-making, and it helps to synthesize and classify the literature under review and provides a framework to position new research activities [Kitchenham and Charters (2007)].

Tranfield *et al.* [2003] suggest a methodology for SLR studies that consists of three stages: (1) Planning the review, (2) Conducting a review, and (3) Reporting and dissemination. The first stage includes identification of the need for a review and the development of a review protocol. The second stage ranges from identification of research and selection of studies to data extraction and data synthesis. The last stage includes the report and recommendations and getting evidence into practice.

Another methodology that has been defined for reporting the SLR method and results is the Preferred Reporting Items for Systematic reviews and Meta-Analyses (PRISMA) statement [Page *et al.* (2021)]. This statement includes tools such as checklists, explanation, and elaboration, and a flow diagram. These tools show in sufficient detail the transparency and applicability of the SLR.

On the other hand, bibliometric analysis is used to validate findings and propose practices and tools to facilitate decision-making in the SLR process. One of the tools used is data visualization from a scientific perspective [Espinosa *et al.* (2020)]. These visualizations, supported by the graph logic, provide accessibility and support the confirmation or confrontation of knowledge and the identification emerging themes or topics of interest.

3. Literature Review

Although the ecosystem metaphor has had various detractors [Koenig (2012)], it is widely used in OA literature.[c] Linde *et al.* [2015] define ecosystem "as a way of describing a community of performers with different functions and drivers and heterogeneous interests but with overarching values and motivations. These values and motivations link the functions and performers together and form the boundaries of the ecosystem." (p. 9). [Elia *et al.* (2016)] define that this concept

[c] See, for example: Kiesewetter [2020], Becerril-García and Aguado López [2019], Czerniewicz [2018], and Linde *et al.* [2015] to name just a few.

has been used to indicate the network of complementary actors, resources, and relationships required to succeed in knowledge-related initiatives [Elia *et al.* (2016)]. Also, Van Schalkwyk *et al.* [2016], while discussing the possible impact of open data on the governance of South African public universities, establish that ecosystems are seen as

> ...consisting of mutually interacting organisms; complex in their arrangement; characterized by the interdependency of and between organisms and resources; dynamic rather than static — seeking equilibrium through motion rather than stasis; populated by keystone species that play a critical role in facilitating exchange in the ecosystem thereby ensuring dynamism and constant movement; movement tends to be cyclical and reinforcing making the system resilient (adaptable and restorative); but it is also vulnerable to exogenous forces which may disrupt or destroy the ecosystem. (p. 2)

Valkokari [2015] states that the limit of the ecosystem can be set, among others, according to the "types of flows (knowledge, value, material)" (p. 18), which implies a shared intention within the ecosystem. She distinguishes three types of economic ecosystems (referring to those that are "man-made"): business ecosystems, innovation ecosystems, and knowledge ecosystems. In the case of innovation ecosystems, Gastaldi and Corso [2016] suggest how to orchestrate innovation ecosystem communities to support and complement their innovation efforts. In the case of knowledge ecosystems, for Valkokari [2015, p. 18], they "have their main interest and outcome in creation of new knowledge through joint research work, collaboration, or the development of knowledge base." [Valkokari (2015, p. 18)]. For that reason, we posit that the OAE is immersed in the Scholarly Communications Ecosystem, which is immersed in the Knowledge Ecosystem and has actors common to these Ecosystems.

For Van Schalkwyk *et al.* [2016], "an ecosystem consists of at least three contextual conditions under which actors in the ecosystem function and which motivate, direct and/or constrain their actions as data providers, intermediaries or consumers." (p. 3) These three contextual conditions are the regulatory condition, the institutional context in which the actors operate, and current information and communications technologies. Furthermore, Fernández Flores and Hernández-Morales [2016] highlight the importance of building repositories (institutional and national) for digital content and developing OA learning ecosystems. They propose a model that consists of three elements:

(1) a freely available Learning Management System (LMS) (such as Moodle).
(2) a curricula-based index (Red Universitaria de Aprendizaje, RUA) that resides at Universidad Nacional Autónoma de México (UNAM), but it is open access, and
(3) a repository of open-access learning resources with learning activities, simulators, and lectures.

However, for Czerniewicz [2018], the OAE is emerging within "new legal and technological frameworks... which exist on continua from analog to digital, and from legal to illegal" (p. 4).

Several studies have mentioned the OAE. However, very few establish what it is or how it is conformed. Among the very few studies that propose an OAE or related ones, we find the work of Linde *et al.* [2015], which mentions the "RECODE project about the open access stakeholder ecosystem." (p. 3) and propose a "stakeholder ecosystem using a functional taxonomy consisting of five entities or functions with interconnected performers. It can be visualized as a layered cake in which stakeholders operate and interact in different layers at the same time. Creators can also be Users and Disseminators. Curators can be Disseminators and Users, and so on." (p. 7). These stakeholders form a "research data ecosystem", which is affected by external factors, such as "political, social, economic, scientific and cultural systems", and by internal factors such as "political will, economic and academic competition, social solidarity, technical infrastructures, laws, ethics, etc." (p. 9). They also propose an "Open Access Organization and Networks Ecosystem" (p. 24), where they outline the importance of networks for communication, "the transfer of norms and expectations" (p. 24) and joint actions. They group the identified networks in funders and initiators networks ("Research councils, Advocacy groups, Policymakers, Foundations, and Intergovernmental Organizations (IGOs)", p. 24), creator networks ("Universities and academies, research institutes, scholarly societies, IGOs, standard organizations, and service providers", p. 29), disseminator and curator networks ("stakeholders representing CSOs, Professional Associations, Data Centers, libraries, projects and publishers", p. 33), and user networks (the media and information aggregators, p. 37) (see Fig. 1).

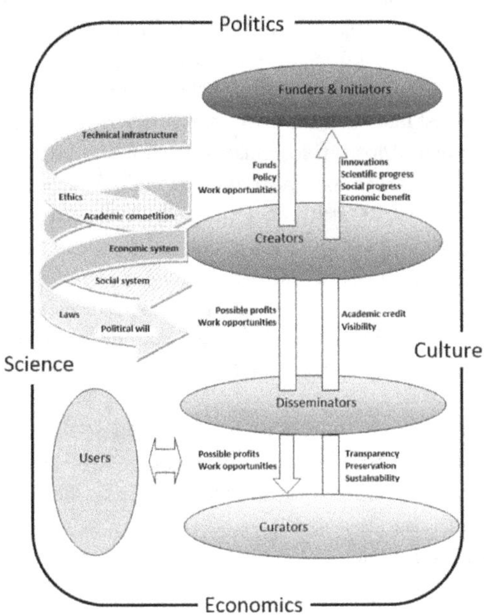

Fig. 1. RECODE research data ecosystem (taken from Linde *et al.* (2015, p. 10)).

Fig. 2. MedOANet Open Access Tracker (taken from http://www.medoanet.eu/browse?quicktabs_oatracker=0).

Tsoukala and Sachini [2013] describe the Mediterranean Open Access Network — MedOANet, which, according to the authors, "mapped the open access ecosystem" (p. 80) and "developed an online tool, the Open Access Tracker", which "tracks the development of open access policies and initiatives (such as funder policies, repositories, etc.)" (p. 80) in "six Mediterranean European countries: Greece, Italy, France, Spain, Portugal and Turkey" (p. 80). The authors mention that the Open Access Tracker "draws together information from directories of journals and repositories, institutional policies, funders' policies, and publishers' self-archiving policies from authoritative registries" (pp. 83–84). However, an actual OAE is not detailed. Figure 2 shows an image of the OA Tracker.

Becerril García *et al.* [2018] state that the Latin-American region "has an ecosystem where the nature of publication is conceived as the act of making public, of sharing and not as the publishing industry" (p. 5). There is a sort of "informal cooperative" in this region, where "each institution finances journals with its own faculty members, and then that content is made available through Open Access to other institutions." There are several platforms used for sharing these contents. This is shown in Fig. 3.

It is also worth noting that there is an initiative called Ameli, Open Knowledge for Latin America and the Global South (amelica.org), "which seeks a collaborative, sustainable, protected and non-commercial Open Access solution for Latin America and the Global South" [Becerril García *et al.* (2018, p. 17)], which corresponds to what Eve [2014] sees as a model for funding gold publishing (p. 73).

Fosci *et al.* [2020] state that, like AmeliCA, there is an initiative called AfricArXiv, a repository supported by African countries for African research that hosts manuscripts before peer review (preprints).

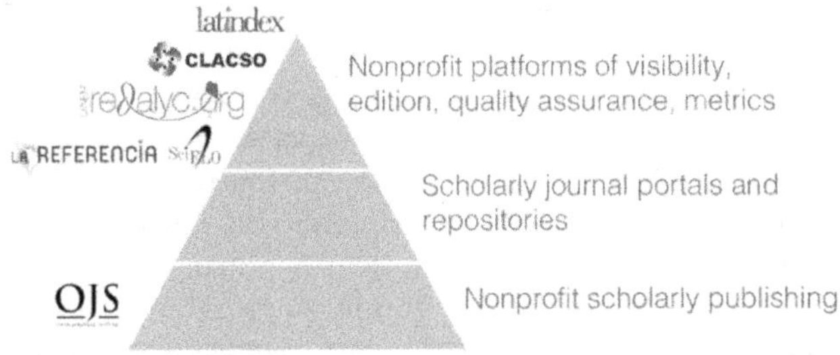

Fig. 3. Latin-American OAE (taken from [Becerril García *et al.* (2018)]).

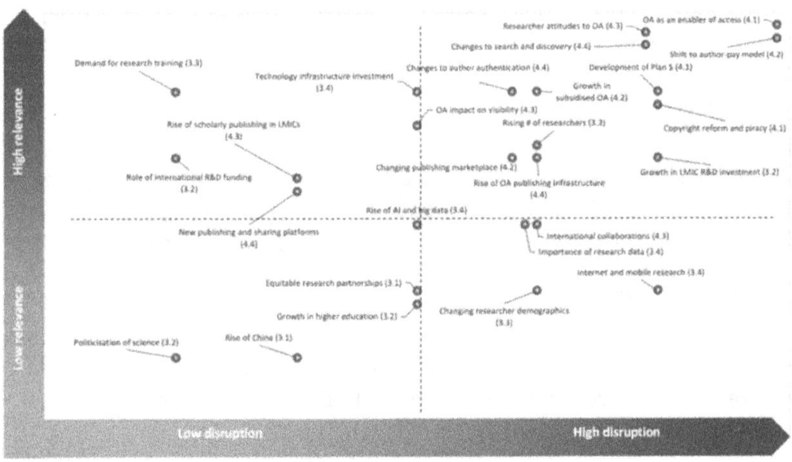

Fig. 4. Global trends in research and scholarly communication (taken from [Fosci *et al.* (2020, p. 68)]).

Fosci *et al.* [2020] center their attention on global trends in research and scholarly communication. As key political trends, they mention access to science and the United Nations Sustainable Development Goals, equitable research (given "the financial reality of researches and research organizations in LMICs,"[d] p. 5), and the OA policy push and Plan S. As key economic trends, they include: The Growth in R&D investment, the shift to author-pay model, and the changing publishing marketplace. As key social trends, they consider University growth, the importance of other actors such as governmental and non-governmental research organizations, and the slow growth in the number of researchers in LMICs. In terms of key technological trends, they establish Internet and mobile research (improvements in communication technology), the growing importance of research data and an increased ability to share it in large quantities, and changes to search and discovery (given the emergence of platforms such as ResearchGate or Sci-Hub). Fosci *et al.* [2020] try "to measure the likely impact (significance) of each trend over the next 5 years" (p. 64). The result is shown in Fig. 4.

[d]LMICs stands for Low-and-Middle-Income Countries.

As shown, several studies have worked on different aspects of the OAE and pointed out very important issues related to it. Linde *et al.* [2015] center their attention on research data, while Tsoukala and Sachini [2013] present the MedOANet Open Access Tracker, where very important information about OA is presented but not the relationships between the OAE actors. Becerril García *et al.* [2018] focus on the platforms available in Latin America. Finally, Fosci *et al.* [2020] work on tendencies in scholarly communication, identifying and classifying trends according to their relevance and level of disruption. As shown, these works do not identify the stakeholders in the OAE nor present the relationships between them. For that reason, we consider it necessary to shed light on the stakeholders participating in the OAE, on how they relate to each other, and on how the changes observed in the scholarly communication ecosystem, as a whole, translate into the OAE. In the next section, we present the methodology we have used to advance on this purpose.

4. Methodology

This paper aims to provide an overview of the essential roles and relationships of the OAE stakeholders identified in the literature. We attained this objective by conducting an exploratory investigation and by making use of the literature review method. Figure 5 shows the four stages carried out.

4.1. *Literature review*

We conducted a literature review to identify, map, and provide a better understanding of the roles and relationships between the stakeholders of the OAE. At this stage, we define the research review protocol. The four steps of the protocol are documented below.

4.1.1. *Research questions*

The research questions addressed are:

RQ1.What are the stakeholders of the OAE?
RQ2. What are the roles and relationships among the stakeholders of the OAE?

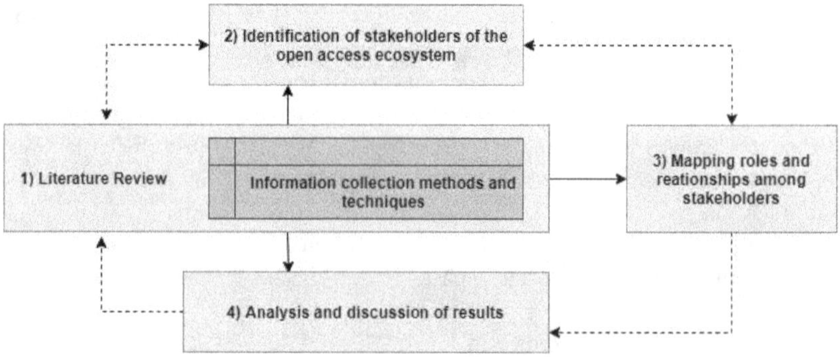

Fig. 5. Methodology.

4.1.2. *Search process*

The search process was based on digital sources searching for articles, governmental and non-governmental reports, and other information in the academic database Scopus and Publish or Perish (PoP), respectively. We increased and expanded the review using the backward snowball technique from the references cited in the articles we identified. The keywords "open access ecosystem", "open access", and "ecosystem" were used for searching in these databases.

4.1.3. *Inclusion and exclusion criteria*

We applied the inclusion and exclusion criteria to reduce documents that are directly aligned with the focus of the study and relevant for answering the research questions.

The inclusion criteria for documents are:

(1) Documents including open access or OAE conceptualization: the title or abstract explicitly mentions the terms Open Access or OAE.
(2) Documents published between 2010 and 2020.

The exclusion criteria applied to the documents, analyzing the titles and abstracts, are:

(1) Duplicate documents: documents that are reported in several sources.
(2) Document focus unrelated to OA or OAE: documents that were outside the field of OA.
(3) Documents related to OA but not related to stakeholders: studies within the area of OA but where stakeholders are not part of their contribution.
(4) Documents that focus on OA but with limited information about OAE's stakeholders are mentioned in a general manner in the abstract but are not part of the contribution.

Figure 6 shows the search results and filters for inclusion and exclusion criteria. We found 263 documents via databases and records in Scopus and PoP, 14 studies via other methods, and three previous studies.

4.1.4. *Document selection*

In this step, we examined the documents to filter the studies. In total, 54 documents relevant to this research were selected (these documents are shown in Appendix A). These documents are classified according to the source and the document type: article, blog, book, book chapter, conference proceedings, editorial, presentation, and report (Table 1).

4.2. *Identification of stakeholders in the Open Access Ecosystem*

At this stage, the objective was to determine the OAE stakeholders. The identification was made based on the content analysis of the documents. Initially, we made a term co-occurrences map based on text data of the studies found in the Scopus

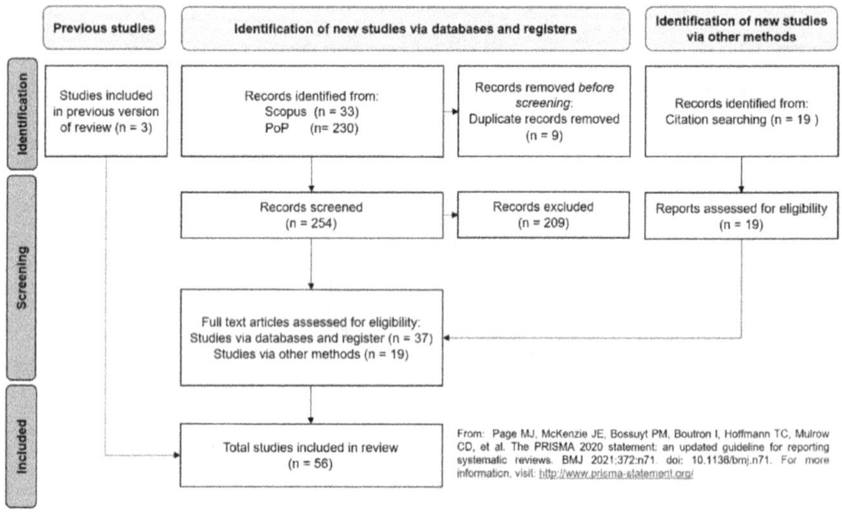

Fig. 6. Literature review process.

Table 1. Selected papers per document type.

Document type	Source				
	Previous studies	PoP	Scopus	Citation searching	**Total**
Article	2	6	10	11	**29**
Blog		3			**3**
Book		3			**3**
Book Chapter		2		1	**3**
Conference Proceedings	1	1	3	1	**6**
Editorial			1		**1**
Presentation		1		2	**3**
Report		7		1	**8**
Total	**3**	**23**	**14**	**16**	**56**

database. This analysis allowed us to observe terms related to actors, roles, or processes. Furthermore, we examined the complete documents to identify relevant information – specifically, we analyzed processes, perspectives, benefits, barriers, problems, and challenges related to the OAE or scholarly communication ecosystems. Subsequently, the main actors in the OAE were identified and then the roles. As a result of the two analyses, we identified four categories of stakeholder roles: associations, government, institutions, and individuals.

4.3. *Mapping of roles and relationships among actors*

Based on the identified stakeholders, at this stage, we carried out the mapping of actors according to their roles and the relationships between them. Initially, we performed a bibliometric network analysis through the VoSviewer tool, which uses bibliographic database files to create maps based on network data

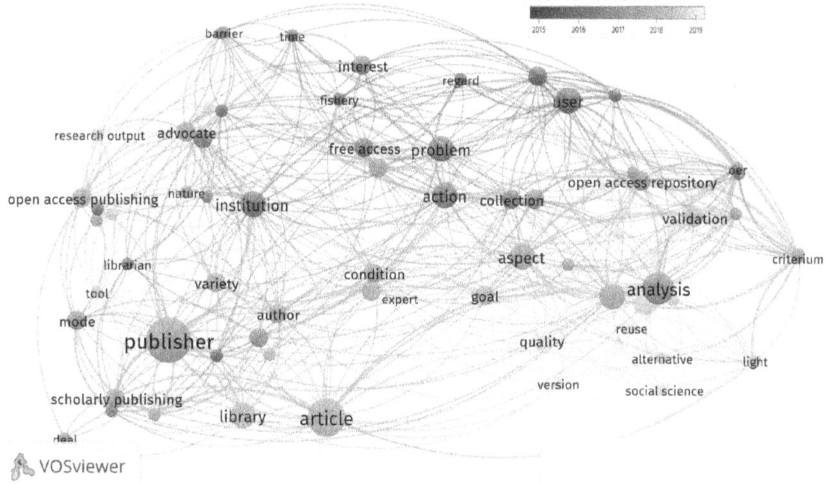

Fig. 7. Term co-occurrence map based on text data.

(Web of Science, Scopus, Dimensions, Lens, and PubMed files). Consequently, we used the 33 documents obtained in the SCOPUS search for the analysis by applying the equation presented below (1) and selecting the binary counting method and the number two as the minimum number of occurrences of a term. Figure 7 shows the results.

$$\text{(TITLE (“OPEN ACCESS”) AND ABS (“open access” AND ecosystem)) AND (EXCLUDE(SUBJAREA, “ENVI”) OR EXCLUDE (SUBJAREA, “AGRI”))} \tag{1}$$

Subsequently, based on the content analysis of the selected documents, a mapping of actors was carried out according to four categories and subcategories, and the associated macro-systems were identified.

4.4. *Analysis and discussion of findings*

At this stage, we analyze, compare, and discuss the mapping of stakeholders and their relationships concerning previous studies related to OAE.

5. Findings

The methodology previously described allowed us to obtain a corpus of literature pertinent to the study of OAE. Its analysis with the VoSviewer tool allows us to obtain a co-occurrences map (see Fig. 7) where the main terms and the strongest relationships can be observed.

By observing Fig. 7, it is possible to note that certain nodes show greater importance given their frequency [Assefa and Rorissa (2013)] and centrality [Hage and Harary (1995)]. These nodes are Institutions, Users, Publishers, and Analysis. By isolating these subnetworks, it is possible to better observe the terms to which these

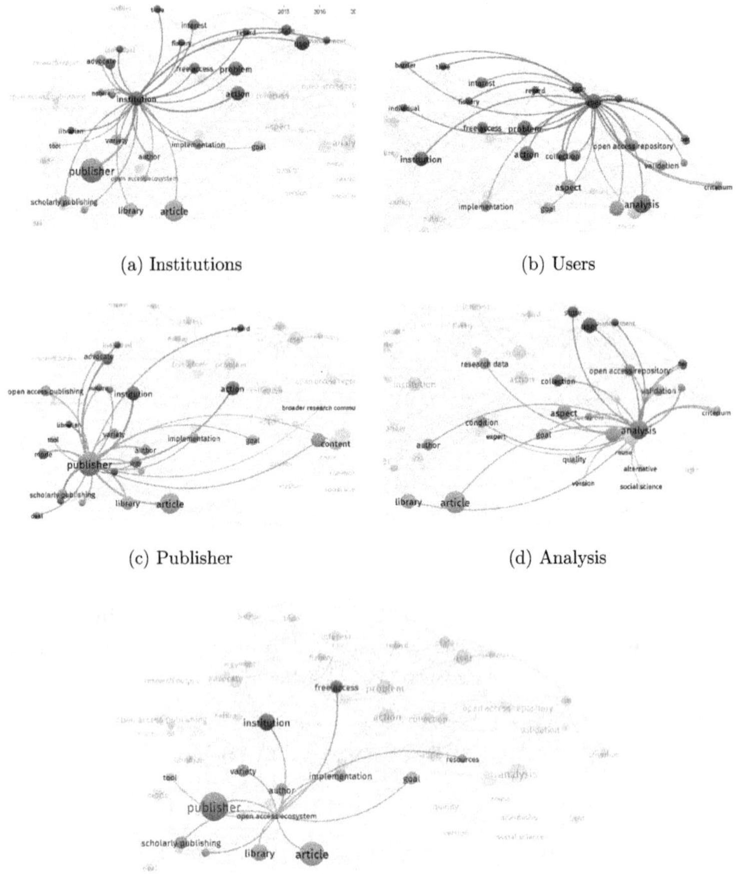

(a) Institutions (b) Users

(c) Publisher (d) Analysis

(e) OAE

Fig. 8. Subnetworks.

nodes relate. These subnetworks are shown in Fig. 8. It is worth noting that although the term "Open Access Ecosystem" appears explicitly, it does not emerge among the main nodes identified, although it is shown as being closely related to the "Publisher" and "Article" nodes, which seem to have greater importance.

These subnetworks show actors (such as institutions, publishers, and users), artifacts (such as articles, library, and repository), processes (such as management and validation), and even preoccupations emerging in the literature (such as quality or social science). Given the state of our research, we focus our attention on the stakeholders and artifacts present in these subnetworks. Taking advantage of the co-occurrence analysis, it is possible to extract the stakeholders identified in the corpus. Table 2 shows these stakeholders and the occurrences and relevance for each of them, where it is evident that the "research community" shows the greatest relevance.

Table 2. Co-occurrence and relevance of terms identifying actors.

Term	Occurrences	Relevance
Individual	2	0.84
Expert	2	0.88
Librarian	2	0.97
Research community	2	1.99
Author	3	0.61
Institution	4	0.46
User	4	0.65
Library	4	0.93
Publisher	7	0.76

With this information and the complete reading of all the articles in our corpus, we were able to identify the main categories of stakeholders in the OAE, complement the results obtained from the co-occurrence analysis, define the main relations identified, and establish the limits of the OAE. Figure 9 shows the result of our analysis.

As Fig. 9 shows, the main categories we were able to identify are Government, Associations, Institutions, and Individuals. Each one of these has a main kind of relationship with the others. For example, governmental stakeholders oversee the definition of national policies, while individuals may be ascribed to institutions or associations of different kinds. We are aware of the multiple relationships that remain to be shown, such as the publications made by members of the research community (authors) or the possibility that OA presents to the users to access knowledge. It is also clear that the interactions between the different stakeholders of

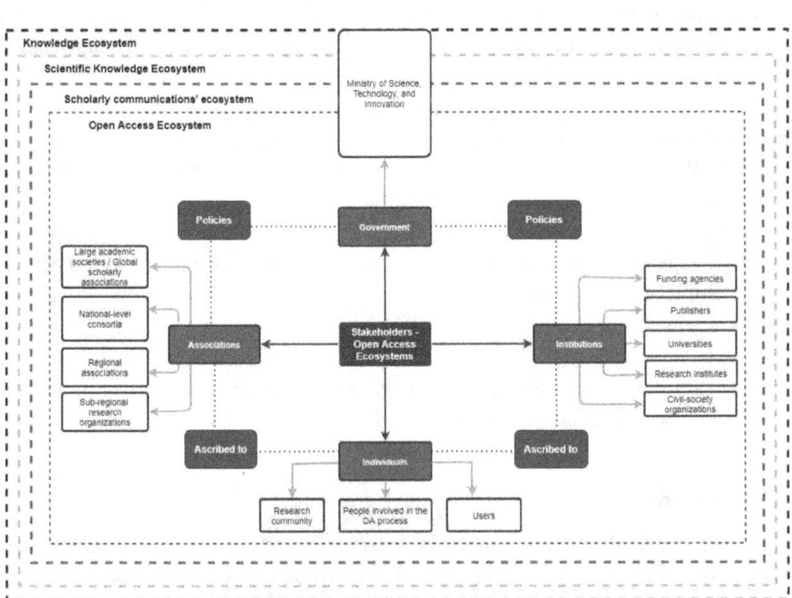

Fig. 9. Stakeholders in the OA Ecosystem.

the OAE are very varied and depend, among other parameters, on the main purposes of its stakeholders. What we are showing, for the moment, is an attempt to better understand the fundamental relationships of the Open Access Movement as a collaborative ecosystem.

6. Discussion

The OA movement has recently acquired great importance for academia. The number of publications on this subject has steadily increased in recent years, covering aspects such as the perception of OA by different stakeholders, the financial implications it has, the technologies supporting it, among other issues [Osorio-Sanabria *et al.* (2020)]. Furthermore, although progress is being made in the OA study, and specifically in the analysis of the stakeholders in OA, other studies, such as those discussed in this work, center their attention on research data [Linde *et al.* (2015)], tracking information about OA by country [Tsoukala and Sachini (2013)], the platforms available in Latin-America [Becerril García *et al.* (2018)] and the trends in scholarly communication [Fosci *et al.* (2020)]. However, much remains to be studied to understand who the OAE stakeholders are and how they relate to each other.

For this reason, our work tries to provide some insight into this subject, defining the main categories and relationships between stakeholders present in the OAE as a step towards a better understanding of it. To do so, we took advantage of the scope of the knowledge ecosystem defined by Valkokari [2015] to set the limits of the OAE, which is considered a subsystem of the Scholarly Communications Ecosystem. This, although may seem like a simple definition, was only achieved after carefully studying the corpus of the literature on the subject and serves to define what is included as part of the OAE and what is not. Later, when examining the objective of the studies on OA discussed in this work, it is clear that each one has a different scope of analysis regarding OA, its stakeholders, geographic scope, and tools to support it. We used this to identify specific stakeholders that were later classified into the categories we propose in the OAE.

Finally, OAE has participating stakeholders who establish relationships with each other. Stakeholder interactions include collaborations around the scholarly and scientific communication process, enabled by policies, dissemination practices, and technical elements in the ecosystem, such as institutional repositories. The main outcomes of interactions within this ecosystem include policies, regulations, applications, and organizational arrangements, all of which need to be studied in depth to achieve a better comprehension of the functioning of the OAE.

7. Conclusions

In this work, we analyze the open access movement from an ecosystem approach. It assumes that the OAE is a subsystem in the broader scholarly communication ecosystem, having access to contents without technological, economical, or legal barriers as a key driver.

Our review of OA studies found that it is common to include government actors, financing organizations, public or private, and individuals who are part of the generation, dissemination, and use of academic and scientific knowledge as main stakeholders of an OAE. We also found that different kinds of associations play a role in the OAE, either by fostering it or going against it. They are linked by policies (as well as mandates) that frame the activities they perform.

It is worth noting that although we do not pretend to have achieved an exhaustive map of the OA ecosystem, we strived to represent the main categories of stakeholders participating in it, as well as the main relationships we were able to extract from the literature review we conducted. As far as we know, this is the first effort to propose an OAE based on a literature review about the subject. As we have shown, previous efforts have focused on specific aspects of the OAE such as data (RECODE) [Linde *et al.* (2015)], the European regulatory framework and actors (MedOANet) [Tsoukala and Sachini (2013)], the platforms used in Latin-America to support OA processes [Becerril García *et al.* (2018)], or the global trends in research and scholarly communication [Fosci *et al.* (2020)]. For that reason, our purpose was to provide a comprehensive view of OAE, which could support a better understanding of what the OAE is.

An aspect that we consider an important contribution from our work is the definition of the limits of the OAE. As we mentioned earlier, we consider the OAE to be a subsystem of the Academic Communications Ecosystem within the knowledge ecosystem [Valkokari (2015)]. For Valkokari [2015], "interaction between the ecosystem actors strengthens the dependencies between them." (p. 21). For that reason, we consider that understanding the stakeholders present in the OAE and the way they relate to each other may be of great importance in analyzing the possible implications that the proposed regional, national, and institutional policies and mandates may have and how they support, if at all, OA efforts at different levels and locations. Furthermore, a clarification of the OAE can help different stakeholders to identify the roles and relationships they can play, as well as the networks each one should be building. This may help those stakeholders who do not fully understand their scope to do so and, hopefully, act according to the general principles of knowledge sharing, looking for the construction of a knowledge society even in locations where geographical frontiers and socioeconomic circumstances currently do not present the stronger conditions to do so.

It is important to acknowledge that, given the huge number of actors we have identified, we only aim to establish the main categories and relationships among the OAE stakeholders but not the whole universe of specific actors. The components and dynamics of OAE are very varied and may differ according to the discipline, region, and even infrastructure. Also, further analysis is still needed to identify a more complete set of relationships among the stakeholders identified.

For that reason, further research is necessary to explore the processes performed by the OAE, the relationships with other ecosystems, and the evolution the OAE may have in the short term, given the dynamics it is showing. It would also be interesting to explore the particularities that exist in different regions, where there are important initiatives such as AmeliCA or AfricArXiv, to name just two, that could foster the OAE in these regions and promote particularities that could lead to important learnings from which other regions could take advantage. In addition, it would be necessary to study the evolution of the OAE over time, given the important challenges and great dynamics observed in it. Finally, additional research ways are also open for related issues such as the impact OA may have on the knowledge ecosystem, especially on aspects such as scientific assessment, where frequent discussions are observed on the need to review how it is done [Nature (2021)].

Acknowledgment

This work was funded by the Corporación Universitaria Minuto de Dios and Universidad Pontificia Bolivariana.

Appendix A

Table A.1. Research papers.

Source	Title	Document type
Kiesewetter [2020]	A New Genealogy for Critical OA Publishing: Towards a Politics of Intersectional Transnationality	Article
Scherer *et al.* [2020]	Collaborative Approaches to Integrate Repositories within the Research Information Ecosystem Creating Bridges for Common Goals	Article
Czerniewicz [2018]	Ecologies of (Open) access: Towards a knowledge society	Book Chapter
Fosci *et al.* [2020]	Equitable access to research in a changing world: Research4Life Landscape and Situation Analysis	Blog
Aguado-López and Becerril-Garcia [2020]	Latin America's longstanding open access ecosystem could be undermined by proposals from the Global North [LSE Latin America and the Caribbean]	Blog
Huang *et al.* [2020]	Meta-Research: Evaluating the impact of open access policies on research institutions	Article
Lopez-Borrull *et al.* [2020]	Plan S and Ecosystem of Spanish Journals of Social Sciences Towards Open Access: Threats and Opportunities	Article
Debat and Babini [2020]	Plan S en América Latina: Una nota de precaución	Report
Machovec [2020]	Selected Tools and Services for Analyzing and Managing Open Access Journal Transformative Agreements	Article
Osorio-Sanabria *et al.* [2020]	Tendencias investigativas de acceso abierto en el sector de la educación: una revisión de literature	Conference Proceedings
Aguado-López and Becerril-Garcia [2020]	The commercial model of academic publishing underscoring Plan S weakens the existing open access ecosystem in Latin America	Blog
López-López [2019a]	Knowledge ecosystem in Latin America: Open access, metrics, paradoxes, and contradictions	Article
Luiz Appel and Albagli [2019]	OPEN ACCESS IN QUESTION: New agendas and challenges	Article
López-López [2019b]	Open access to knowledge, a universal right: The implications of the governance of open access ecosystems	Editorial
Mullen [2019]	Scholarly communication and open access in psychology: Current considerations for researchers	Report

Table A.1. (*Continued*)

Source	Title	Document type
Uribe-Tirado *et al.* [2019]	Situación del acceso abierto en las universidades. Caso y modelo de análisis Universidad de Antioquia	Article
Becerril-García and Aguado López [2019]	The End of a Centralized Open Access Project and the Beginning of a Community-Based Sustainable Infrastructure for Latin America	Conference Proceedings
Barbour [2019]	The future of academic publishing: disruption, opportunity and a new ecosystem	Article
Martone [and Aghazarian]	The Scholarly Commons	Presentation
Becerril García *et al.* [2018]	AmeliCA: A community-driven sustainable framework for Open Knowledge in Latin America and the Global South	Report
Okada [2018]	Polarization in the future journal publishing ecosystem: Selective subscription journals and open access mega-journals	Article
Rittman [2018]	Sustainability in Publishing: An Open Access Publisher's View	Conference Proceedings
Becerril García *et al.* [2018]	The End of a Centralized Open Access Project and the Beginning of a Community-Based Sustainable Infrastructure for Latin America: Redalyc.org after Fifteen Years. The Open Access ecosystem in Latin America	Article
Holzmeyer [2018]	Wider Worlds of Research for Health Equity: Public Health NGOs as Stakeholders in Open Access Ecosystems	Article
Welle Donker and van Loenen [2017]	How to assess the success of the open data ecosystem?	Article
Moreira *et al.* [2017]	Integrating a national network of institutional repositories into the national/international research management ecosystem	Conference Proceedings
Smith and Dickson [2017]	Open Access and the Future of Scholarly Communication	Book Chapter
Cornic [2016]	ROAD: The Directory of Open Access Scholarly Resources to Promote Open Access Worldwide	Conference Proceedings
Fernández Flores and Hernández-Morales [2016]	Towards an open learning ecosystem based on open access repositories, curricula-based indices and learning management systems.	Conference Proceedings
Tennant *et al.* [2016]	The academic, economic and societal impacts of Open Access: an evidence-based review	Article
Van Schalkwyk *et al.* [2016]	Viscous open data: The roles of intermediaries in an open data ecosystem. Information Technology for Development	Article
Waller *et al.* [2017]	The Open Textbook Toolkit: Seeding Successful Partnerships for Collaboration between Academic Libraries and University Presses	Article
Zubcoff *et al.* [2016]	The university as an open data ecosystem	Article
Linde *et al.* [2015]	Feasibility of using existing open access networks to support the harmonization of open access	Report
Hugelier *et al.* [2015]	Legal and IPR Management Framework for an Open Science Platform Services	Book
Tsoukala *et al.* [2015]	Policy guidelines for open access and data dissemination and preservation	Report
Wessels *et al.* [2014]	Issues in the development of open access to research data	Article
Clobridge [2014]	Open access progress, possibilities scholarly communications ecosystem	Article

Table A.1. (*Continued*)

Source	Title	Document type
Blanke [2014]	Open and closed digital asset ecosystems	Article
Elia *et al.* [2016]	An Operational Model to Develop Technology Entrepreneurship "EGO-System"	Article
Poblet *et al.* [2014]	Open-Access Grant Data: Towards Meta-Research Innovation	Article
Nafpliotis *et al.* [2014]	Open access policy guidelines by the MedOANet project: Facilitating open access policy development in Mediterranean Europe	Presentation
Sveinsdottir *et al.* [2014]	Policy recommendations for Open Access to research data in Europe-Stakeholder values and ecosystems	Article
Steele [2014]	Scholarly Communication, Scholarly Publishing and University Libraries. Plus Ça Change?	Article
Babini [2014]	The risk of open access becoming integrated into existing commercial publishing - the need of a global system of non-commercial open access scholarly communications	Article
Tsoukala and Sachini [2013]	MedOANet: Facilitating Coordinated Open Access Policies and Strategies in Mediterranean Europe	Report
Reinsfelder and Anderson [2013]	Observations and perceptions of academic administrator influence on open access initiatives.	Article
Wellen [2013]	Open access, megajournals, and MOOCs: on the political economy of academic unbundling	Article
MedOANet [2013]	The MedOANet Guidelines for Implementing Open Access Policies in Research Performing and research funding organizations	Report
Dillaerts and Chartron [2013]	'Héloïse': Towards a co-ordinated ecosystem approach for the archiving of scientific publications?	Article
Rodrigues *et al.* [2013]	Uma década de acesso aberto na UMinho e no mundo	Book
Harrison *et al.* [2012]	Creating Open Government Ecosystems: A Research and Development Agenda	Article
Webster [2012]	Evolving role of libraries in the scholarly ecosystem	Book Chapter
Holzman [2012]	From the University Presses-Open Access Monographs and the Scholarly Communication Ecosystem	Article
Bérard [2011]	Free-library-data	Article

References

Aguado-López, E. and Becerril-Garcia, A. (2020). The commercial model of academic publishing underscoring Plan S weakens the existing open access ecosystem in Latin America. *Impact of Social Sciences.* Available at https://blogs.lse.ac.uk/impactofsocialsciences/2020/05/20/the-commercial-model-of-academic-publishing-underscoring-plan-s-weakens-the-existing-open-access-ecosystem-in-latin-america/ [accessed on 26 January 2021].

Espinosa, A. M., Romero, E. R., Flórez, G. L. Y. and Guerrero, C. D. (2020). DANDELION: Propuesta metodológica para recopilación y análisis de información de artículos científicos. Un enfoque desde la bibliometría y la revisión sistemática de la literatura. *Revista Ibérica de Sistemas e Tecnologias de Informaçao*, **E28**: 110–122.

Assefa, S. G. and Rorissa, A. (2013). A bibliometric mapping of the structure of STEM education using co-word analysis. *Journal of the American Society for Information Science and Technology*, **64**: 2513–2536.

Babini, D. (2014). The risk of open access becoming integrated into existing commercial publishing — The need of a global system of non-commercial open access scholarly communications. *Revista Eletrônica de Comunicação, Informação e Inovação Em Saúde*, **8**, 4: 433–437.

Barbour, V. (2019). The future of academic publishing: disruption, opportunity, and a new ecosystem. *Medical Journal of Australia*, **211**, 4: 151–152.e1.

Becerril-García, A. and Aguado López, E. (2019). The end of a centralized open access project and the beginning of a community-based sustainable infrastructure for Latin America. *Connecting the Knowledge Commons form Projects to Sustainable Infrastructure*, OpenEdition Press, pp. 41–55.

Becerril García, A., Aguado López, E., Batthyány, K., Melero, R., Beigel, F., Vélez Cuartas, G., Banzato, G., Rozemblum, C., Amescua García, C., Gallardo, O. and Torres, J. (2018). AmeliCA: A community-driven sustainable framework for Open Knowledge in Latin America and the Global South, Editorial: Redalyc, Universidad Autónoma del Estado de México, CLACSO, Universidad Nacional de La Plata and Universidad de Antioquia. Available at http://sedici.unlp.edu.ar/handle/10915/90958 [accessed on 25 January 2021].

Bérard, R. (2011). Free library data?*Liber Quarterly*, **20**, 3: 321–331.

Blanke, T. (2014). Open and closed digital asset ecosystems. Digital Asset Ecosystems, 61–86.

Clobridge, A. (2014). Open access: Progress, possibilities, and the changing scholarly communications ecosystem. *Online*, **38**, 2: 42–52.

Cornic, N. (2016). ROAD: The directory of open access scholarly resources to promote open access worldwide. *Proceedings of the 20th International Conference on Electronic Publishing on IOS Press*, pp. 1–5.

Czerniewicz, L. (2018). Ecologies of (open) access: Towards A knowledge society. *Making Open Development Inclusive: Lessons from IDRC Researc*, eds. M. L. Smith and R. K. Seward. MIT Press, pp. 143–156.

Debat, H. and Babini, D. (2020). Plan S en América Latina: una nota de precaución. *Revista Iberoamericana de Ciencia, Tecnología y Sociedad - CTS*, **15**, 44: 279–292.

Dillaerts, H. and Chartron, G. (2013). "Héloïse": Towards a co-ordinated ecosystem approach for the archiving of scientific publications?. *Learned Publishing*, **26**, 3: 173–179.

Eve, M. P. (2014). Open access and the humanities: Contexts, controversies, and the future. Cambridge University Press. Available at https://www.cambridge.org/core/books/open-access-and-the-humanities/02BD7DB4A5172A864C432DBFD86E5FB4 [accessed on 25 January 2021].

Elia, G., Margherita, A. and Petti, C. (2016). An operational model to develop technology entrepreneurship "ego-system", *International Journal of Innovation and Technology Management* **13**, 5.

Fernández Flores, R. and Hernández-Morales, B. (2016). Towards an open learning ecosystem based on open access repositories, curricula-based indices and learning management systems. In *EDULEARN16 Proceedings*, Barcelona, Spain, 1, pp. 2826–2831.

Fosci, M., Ficarra, V., Chiarelli, A. and Johnson, R. (2020). Equitable access to research in a changing world: Research4Life Landscape and Situation Analysis. *Commonplace*. Available at https://commonplace.knowledgefutures.org/pub/fgm2pqu5 [accessed on 25 January 2021].

Gastaldi, L. and Corso, M. (2016). Academics as orchestrators of innovation ecosystems: The role of knowledge management. *International Journal of Innovation and Technology Management*, **13**: 1640009.

Granstrand, O. and Holgersson, M. (2020). Innovation ecosystems: A conceptual review and a new definition. *Technovation*, **90-91**: 102098.

Hage, P. and Harary, F. (1995). Eccentricity and centrality in networks. *Social Networks*, **17**, 1: 57–63.

Harrison, T. M., Pardo, T. A. and Cook, M. (2012). Creating open government ecosystems: A research and development agenda. *Future Internet*, **4**, 4: 900–928.

Holzman, A. (2012). From the University Presses — Open access monographs and the scholarly communication ecosystem. *Against the Grain*, **24**, 6: 56–57.

Holzmeyer, C. (2018). Wider worlds of research for health equity: public health NGOs as stakeholders in open access ecosystems. *The Journal of Community Informatics*, **14**: 1–16.

Huang, C.-K. (Karl), Neylon, C., Hosking, R., Montgomery, L., Wilson, K. S., Ozaygen, A. and Brookes-Kenworthy, C. (2020). Evaluating the impact of open access policies on research institutions. *ELife*, **9**: e57067.

Hugelier, S., Janssens, M.-C., van den Boom, F. and Verhenneman, G. (2015). Legal and IPR management framework for an open science platform services. KU Leuven.

Jurchen, S. (2020). Open access and the serials crisis: The role of academic libraries. *Technical Services Quarterly*, **37**, 2: 160–170.

Kiesewetter, R. (2020). A new genealogy for critical OA publishing: Towards a politics of intersectional transnationality intersectional transnationality. *Journal of International Women's Studies*, **21**, 7: 61–76.

Kitchenham, B., Brereton, O. P., Budgen, D., Mark, T., Bailey, S. and Linkman, S. (2009). Systematic literature reviews in software engineering — A systematic literature review. *Information and Software Technology*, **51**: 7–15.

Kitchenham, B. and Charters, S. (2007). Technical report: Guidelines for performing systematic literature reviews in software engineering. School of Computer Science and Mathematics, Keele University. Available at https://userpages.uni-koblenz.de/~laemmel/esecourse/slides/slr.pdf [accessed on 25 January 2021].

Koenig, G. (2012). Business ecosystems revisited. *M@n@gement*, **15**, 2: 208–224. Available at https://management-aims.com/index.php/mgmt/article/view/3962 [accessed on 25 January 2021].

Li, H., Liu, L. and Wang, X. (2021). The open access effect in social media exposure of scholarly articles: A matched-pair analysis. *Journal of Informetrics*, **15**, 3: 101154.

Linde, P., Wessels, B., Smallwood, R., Price, L., Noorman, M., Wyatt, S. and Sondervan, J. (2015). Feasibility of using existing open access networks to support the harmonization of open access. In *Seventh Framework Programme*. Available at http://urn.kb.se/resolve?urn=urn:nbn:se:bth-6421 [accessed on 25 January 2021].

Lopez-Borrull, A., Ollé-Castellá, C., García-Grimau, F. and Abadal, E. (2020). Plan S y ecosistema de revistas españolas de ciencias sociales hacia el acceso abierto: Amenazas y oportunidades. *El Profesional de la Información*, **29**, 2: 1–12.

López-López, W. (2019a). Knowledge ecosystem in Latin America: Open access, metrics, paradox, and contradictions. *Universitas Psychologica*, **18**: 1–3.

López-López, W. (2019b). Open access to knowledge, a universal right: The implications of the governance of open access ecosystems. *Universitas Psychologica*, **18**, 5: 1–3.

Luiz Appel, A. and Albagli, S. (2019). Open access in question: New agendas and challenges. *Informação & Sociedade; João Pessoa*, **29**, 4: 187–208.

Machovec, G. (2020). Selected tools and services for analyzing and managing open access journal transformative agreements. *Journal Transformative Agreements*, **60**, 3: 301–307.

Martone, M. and Aghazarian, M. (2019). The scholarly commons. *The Serials Librarian*, **76**, 1–4: 220–224.

Mediterraneo Open Access Network — MedOANet (2013). Directrices MedOANet para la implantación de políticas de acceso abierto para entidades financiadoras, universidades y centros de investigación. Available at http://medoanet.eu/sites/www.medoanet.eu/files/documents/GUIDLine_ES_ws.pdf [accessed on 26 January 2021].

Moreira, J. M., Laranjeira, C., Carvalho, J., Ribeiro, F., Lopes, P. and Graça, P. (2017). Integrating a national network of institutional repositories into the national/international research management ecosystem. *Procedia Computer Science* **106**, 146–152.

Mullen, L. (2019). *Scholarly Communication and Open Access in Psychology: Current Considerations for Researchers.* Rutgers University Libraries.

Nature (2021). Responsible research assessment faces the acid test. *Nature*, **595**: 471–472.

Nafpliotis, A., Tsoukala, V. and Kalatizi, V. (2014). Open access policy guidelines by the MedOANet project: Facilitating open access policy development in Mediterranean Europe. *The 8th Munin Conference on Scholarly Publishing 2013*, Vol. 1, pp. 1–12.

Okada, M. (2018). Polarization in the future journal publishing ecosystem: Selective subscription journals and open access mega-journals. *Journal of Self-Governance and Management Economics*, **6**, 3: 96.

Osorio-Sanabria, M. A., Alcántara-Concepción, T., Barreto Granada, P. L. and Jaime, A. (2020). Tendencias investigativas de acceso abierto en el sector de la educación: una revisión de literature. In *CISTI'2020 — 15th Iberian Conference on Information Systems and Technologies*, Sevilla, Spain, pp. 1–7.

Page, M. J., McKenzie, J. E., Bossuyt, P. M., Boutron, I., Hoffmann, T. C., Mulrow, C. D., Shamseer, L., Tetzlaff, J. M., Akl, E. A., Brennan, S. E., Chou, R., Glanville, J., Grimshaw, J. M., Hróbjartsson, A., Lalu, M. M., Li, T., Loder, E. W., Mayo-Wilson, E., McDonald, S., ... Moher, D. (2021). The PRISMA 2020 statement: An updated guideline for reporting systematic reviews. *BMJ Publishing Group*, **372**: 71.

Poblet, M., Aryani, A., Caldecott, K., Sellis, T. and Casanovas, P. (2014). Open-Access Grant Data: Towards Meta-Research Innovation. In *Frontiers in Artificial Intelligence and Applications Proceedings*, IOS Press, 271: pp. 125–130.

Pooley, J. (2019, September 3). The library solution: How academic libraries could end the APC scourge. Available at https://items.ssrc.org/parameters/the-library-solution-how-academic-libraries-could-end-the-apc-scourge/.

Reinsfelder, T. L. and Anderson, J. A. (2013). Observations and perceptions of academic administrator influence on open access initiatives. *Journal of Academic Librarianship*, **39**, 6: 481–487.

Rittman, M. (2018). Sustainability in publishing: An open access publisher's view. ELPUB 2018, pp. 1–7.

Rodrigues, E., Swan, A. and Baptista, A. A. (2013). Uma década de acesso aberto na UMinho e no mundo (Universida). Universidade do Minho, Servicos de Documentacão,

Saarti, J. and Tuominen, K. (2021). Openness, resource sharing and digitalization — An examination of the current trends in Finland. *Information Discovery and Delivery*, **49**, 2: 97–104.

Scherer, D., Byrne, K., Hahnel, M. and Valen, D. (2020). Collaborative approaches to integrate repositories within the research information ecosystem: Creating bridges for common goals. *Serials Librarian*, **78**, 1–4: 181–190.

Smith, K. L. and Dickson, K. A. (2017). *Open Access and the Future of Scholarly Communication*, eds. K. L. Smith and K. A. Dickson. Rowman & Littlefield, London.

Steele, C. (2014). Scholarly communication, scholarly publishing and university libraries. Plus Ça Change?*Australian Academic and Research Libraries*, **45**, 4: 241–261.

Suber, P. (2012). *Open Access*. MIT Press, Cambridge.

Sveinsdottir, T., Wessels, B. A., Smallwood, R., Linde, P., Kala, V., Tsoukala, V. and Sondervan, J. (2014). Policy recommendations for Open Access to research data in Europe-Stakeholder values and ecosystems. *Information Services & Use*, **34**: 331–333.

Tennant, J. P., Waldner, F., Jacques, D. C., Masuzzo, P., Collister, L. B. and Hartgerink, C. H. J. (2016). The academic, economic and societal impacts of Open Access: An evidence-based review. *F1000Research*, **5**: 632.

Tranfield, D., Denyer, D. and Smart, P. (2003). Towards a methodology for developing evidence-informed management knowledge by means of systematic review. *British Journal of Management*, **14**, 3: 207–222.

Tsoukala, V. and Sachini, E. (2013) MedOANet: Facilitating coordinated open access policies and strategies in Mediterranean Europe. Uma Década de Acesso Aberto na UMinho e no Mundo, Universidade do Minho, Servicos de Documentacão, eds. E. Rodrigues, A. Swan and A.A. Baptista. Available at http://hdl.handle.net/1822/26144. Retrieved January 25, 2021.

Tsoukala, V., Angelaki, M., Kalaitzi, V., Wessels, B., Price, L., Taylor, M. J., . . ., Wadhwa, K. (2015). Policy guidelines for open access and data dissemination and preservation. In *Seventh Framework Programme*. Available at https://zenodo.org/record/1297497#.YQWJGegzbIU [accessed on 30 January 2021].

Uribe-Tirado, A., Ochoa-Gutiérrez, J., Pallares, C., Restrepo-Quintero, D., Vélez-Cuartas, G., Robledo-Velásquez, J., . . ., Osorio-López, A. M. (2019). Situación del acceso abierto en las universidades. *Caso y modelo de análisis Universidad de Antioquia*, **9**, 1: e078.

Valkokari, K. (2015). Business, innovation, and knowledge ecosystems: How they differ and how to survive and thrive within them. *Technology Innovation Management Review*, **5**, 8: 17–24.

Van Schalkwyk, F., Willmers, M. and McNaughton, M. (2016). Viscous open data: The roles of intermediaries in an open data ecosystem. *Information Technology for Development*, **22**: 68–83.

Waller, M., Cross, W. M. and Rigling, L. (2017). The open textbook toolkit: Seeding successful partnerships for collaboration between academic libraries and university presses. *Journal of Scholarly Publishing*, **49**, 1: 53–65.

Webster, K. (2012). The evolving role of libraries in the scholarly ecosystem. In Academic and Professional Publishing, *Elsevier*, pp. 315–336.

Welle Donker, F. and van Loenen, B. (2017). How to assess the success of the open data ecosystem? *International Journal of Digital Earth*, **10**, 3, 284–306.

Wellen, R. (2013). Open access, Megajournals, and MOOCs: On the political economy of academic unbundling. *SAGE Open*, **3**, 4: 215824401350727.

Wessels, B., Finn, R. L., Linde, P., Mazzetti, P., Nativi, S., Riley, S., . . ., Wyatt, S. (2014). Issues in the development of open access to research data. *Prometheus*, **32**: 1, 49–66.

Zhu, Y. (2017). Who support open access publishing? Gender, discipline, seniority and other factors associated with academics' OA practice. *Scientometrics*, **111**, 2: 557–579.

Zubcoff, J. J., Vaquer, L., Mazón, J.-N., Maciá, F., Garrigós, I., Fuster, A. and Carcel, J. V. (2016). The university as an open data ecosystem. *International Journal of Design & Nature and Ecodynamics*, **11**, 3: 250–257.

Biography

Mariutsi Osorio-Sanabria, PhD student at the College of Engineering, Universidad Pontificia Bolivariana (UPB), Colombia. She holds a master's degree in the Information and Communications Technology (ICT). She is a member of ICT Applications Research and Development Team (GIDATIC) with UPB. She is also an Assistant Professor with the Engineering Faculty, Fundación Universitaria María Cano (FUMC), Colombia. Her main Research and Development interests include e-government, open government, open data, data governance, and information technology management.

Astrid Jaime, PhD in Industrial Engineering, with emphasis on Knowledge Management in Research. At present, working as Associate Researcher at the Corporación Universitaria Minuto de Dios — UniMinuto. Her research interests include Management of Knowledge, Science, Technology and Innovation, knowledge transfer, entrepreneurship, intellectual property, and University — Industry relationships, areas where she has professional and research experience.

Ferney Amaya-Fernández, Ph.D. in Engineering. He is currently a Professor with the College of Engineering, Universidad Pontificia Bolivariana (UPB), Colombia. He is a member of the Information and Communications Technology (ICT) Applications Research and Development Team (GIDATIC) with UPB. His main Research and Development interests include sustainable cities, telecommunications, fiber optic sensors, optical networks and communications, open data, and data mining.

Catch-Up in Solar PV Industry of China: A Perspective of Industrial Innovation Ecosystem*

Shuang Ge*,‡ and Xielin Liu†,§

*Business School
China University of Political Science and Law
Beijing, 100088, P. R. China

†School of Economics and Management
University of Chinese Academy of Science
Beijing 100190, P. R. China
‡geshuang17@mails.ucas.ac.cn
§liuxielin@ucas.ac.cn

This study explores how China's solar photovoltaic (PV) industry can catch up so rapidly without radical technological innovation. Through the grounded theory method, we found it was the industrial innovation ecosystem construction and industrial innovation ecological relationship maintenance that made China's solar PV industry gain competitive advantages. From the perspective of the industrial innovation ecosystem, clustering and colocation provided a foundation for industrial innovation ecosystem construction. China's solar PV enterprises maintain the ecological relationship among the actors of the industrial innovation ecosystem through several ecological strategies, including resource orchestration and co-opetition. Hub firms played an important role in overcoming the liability of newness and putting forward the vision of shared fate in the early stage of industry development. Local governments and industry associations provided institutional support, coordination, and intermediary to enterprises.

Keywords: Solar PV; industrial innovation ecosystem; grounded theory; catch-up; China.

1. Introduction

Solar energy is considered as one of the best solutions of global climate change and greenhouse gas emissions. Correspondingly, the number of deployments has increased sharply, and China is the main contributor [Schmela (2020)]. We argue that to evaluate whether an industry has successfully achieved catchup requires three outcomes: (1) whether the product is competitive in the global market; (2) whether the enterprise's technological capability is globally leading; and (3) whether the industry has a sustainable source of profit growth in the future. Among the top 20 companies in the photovoltaic (PV) industry by revenue in 2020, 15 are

‡Corresponding author.

*This chapter was originally published in International Journal of Innovation and Technology Management, Vol. 19, No. 6, March 2018, published by World Scientific Publishing, Singapore. Reprinted with permission.

Chinese enterprises.[a] In 2020, China's production capacity in polysilicon, silicon wafer, battery, and module sectors accounted for 75.2%, 97%, 80.7%, and 76.3% of the global total, respectively. Since 2014, the efficiency of crystalline silicon cell laboratories in China has broken records 35 times. In 2021, LONGi N-type TOPCon achieved a new world record of 25.09%, the monocrystalline double-sided P-type TOPCon achieved a world record of 25.02%, and the conversion efficiency of monocrystalline HJT battery reached a record of 25.26%.[b] In July 2020, Trina Solar of China officially released a new generation of ultra-high-power modules with a single-chip power of up to 600 W, leading the global PV industry to officially enter the PV 6.0 new era. According to our definition of successful catchup, China's PV industry has successfully achieved catchup from scratch in just 20 years.

In fact, the diamond wire cutting technology, which has a disruptive impact on the technology paradigm of the PV industry, was not invented by Chinese enterprises. Most of China's enterprises in the industry do not have disruptive, rare, inimitable, or irreplaceable technological competitive advantages, and the catchup of China's solar PV industry cannot be explained by the emergence of disruptive innovations [Zheng and Kammen (2014); de la Tour *et al.* (2011)]. Why can China's solar PV enterprises develop so rapidly without breakthrough technological innovations?

There have been some different theories explaining the rapid rising of China's PV industry, such as windows of opportunity [Perez and Soete (1988); Lee (2020); Dong *et al.* (2020)], industrial policy [Lee and Kim (2017); Stinchcome (1965)], and innovation ecosystem [Adner and Kapoor (2010); Hannah *et al.* (2016)]. We propose that the innovation ecosystem has a more explanatory power than other theories. We first concluded the key factors of China's solar PV industry are leapfrogging through the grounded theory method. Then, through the reflection of the literature review and the grounded theory results, we constructed a theoretical framework to analyze the dynamic change of China's solar PV industry. Based on the interviews of China's solar PV enterprises, we argue that it is more appropriate to analyze China's solar PV industry from the perspective of the dynamic evolution of the industrial innovation ecosystem. We found that (1) enterprises constructed the industrial innovation ecosystem based on clustering and colocation of industrial condition. (2) Hub firms played an important role in overcoming the liability of newness and establishing legitimacy in the early stage of solar PV industry development. (3) From the perspective of the industrial innovation ecosystem, Chinese solar PV enterprises strengthened the ecological relationship among the actors of the industrial innovation ecosystem through resource orchestration and co-opetition. (4) Local governments and industry associations also played an important role in the industrial innovation ecosystem construction and industrial innovation ecological relationship maintenance.

Our contributions are as follows: (1) Industrial innovation ecosystem provides a new research perspective that is between sectoral innovation system and the innovation ecosystem for the study of the development of emerging industries. We focus

[a] Data source: WWW.ChinaIRN.COM.
[b] Data source: China Photovoltaic industry association.

more on the interior of the industry but can analyze the dynamic evolution of interaction between ecological actors and the dynamic changes of ecological strategies. (2) Different from the traditional catch-up theory, we built a catch-up model with China's PV industry innovation ecosystem based on grounded analysis, which illustrates how emerging industries catch up in the absence of breakthrough technologies.

2. Literature Review

2.1. *Windows of opportunity and catching up*

The original catch-up theory from the perspective of the technological paradigm can be traced back to Gershenkron's idea of the latecomers' advantage (1962; 1963). The emerging technology paradigm provides a window of opportunity for latecomers who no longer rely on the old technology paradigm [Perez and Soete (1988)]. Later scholars concluded that windows of opportunity are the shortcut for latecomers to catch up [Freeman and Soete (1997)]. However, it was limited to catching up with mature technologies [Lee (2020)]. As a mid-tech industry, there is no new disruptive technological innovation nor emerging technological paradigm in China's solar PV industry; thus, the solar PV industry lacks significant latecomers' advantage. Therefore, it is inappropriate to analyze the catchup of China's PV companies from the perspective of the new technological paradigm and latecomers' advantage.

In addition to technological sectors, there are also other scholars studying China's solar PV industry from the perspective of market. Some scholars argued that China has taken the opportunity of demand shifts of international markets [Dong *et al.* (2020)]. But the fact is that Europe's demand for clean energy has shifted much earlier than Chinese, Germany started subsidies on a large scale in the 1990s. The solar PV industries in western countries also face this opportunity or even before China, and developed countries prepared for it much longer than China. However, Chinese solar PV enterprises have overtaken Europe's enterprises.

2.2. *Industrial policy and catching up*

Representing a new form of organization to China, solar PV enterprises overcame stronger "liabilities of newness" in the early stages of industry development compared with other mature industries [Scott (1995); Greenwood and Suddaby (2006); Zhang and White (2016)]. They had to face more significant challenges including establish legitimacy [Sine *et al.* (2007); Battilana *et al.* (2009)], acquire resources, and then gain their own competitive advantages to catchup [Venkataraman (1997); Shane (2000); Eckhardt and Shane (2003)].

Some scholars argued that in the process of overcoming the liability of newness, the government played a core role in industrial policies [Lee and Kim (2017)]. They claimed China used industrial policies to rise many successful new industries including the solar PV industry [Peng and Luo (2000); Li and Huang (2020)]. But we argue that China's solar PV industry is not created by a single large state-owned enterprise that is supported by the government [Shin (2016)] but catchup in the continuous market competition of countless private enterprises. Chinese first industrial policy of solar PV industry (Golden Sun Demonstration Project) came out in a very late stage: after the world had met a financial crisis in 2008 and the whole industry had fallen in big trouble [Binz and Anadon (2016)]. The fact is that, even before the industrial policy was promulgated, China's solar PV industry had been rapidly developing and catching up [Zhao *et al.* (2008); Zhang and White (2016)]. Furthermore, the policy may be inefficient in a short term [Hu *et al.* (2020)]. So, we claim that government may have some effect, but the industrial policy is not the key element of the catching up of China's solar PV industry [Kuik *et al.* (2019); Binz and Anadon (2016)].

2.3. *Innovation ecosystem and catching up*

Sectoral innovation system at the industry level is the traditional industrial analysis [Breschi and Malerba (1997)], while recently innovation ecosystem is used more to break the industrial boundary according to the concern of interdependence at the product level [Adner (2006)].

The concept of sectoral innovation system emphasizes that industrial innovation shows a clear sectoral pattern in terms of many aspects [Nelson and Winter (1982); Malerba (2002); Fukugawa (2016)]. But compared with the ecosystem, the sectoral innovation system does not provide a detailed and dynamic analysis of the specific interactions between the actors. What we want to focus on are the flow of elements, interaction between actors, and more specific system functions, which are more explanatory than sectoral innovation system.

Innovation ecosystem focuses on the innovation production level and the set of upstream suppliers, downstream users, complementors, and competitors, and they view ecosystem as "the collaborative arrangements" [Kapoor and Furr (2014); Adner and Kapoor (2010); Adner (2006)]. Co-opetition can explain the complex relationship between the hub firms and competitors in China's solar PV industry [Hannah and Eisenhardt (2017)]. We argue that the innovation ecosystem approach is particularly appropriate to understand the rising of solar PV in China, and it's a big progress to understand the rising of the emerging industry. In previous research, the creation of the ecosystem is to break the traditional industry boundary and to reach the wide boundary set by the purposed interdependence [Adner (2017)], and scholars like to refer the ecosystems to be a community that covers different industries. The essence of the ecosystem is to have a club advantage compared with other systems or no system. However, the innovation ecosystem is too broad for studying China's solar PV industry enterprises, and our research needs to focus more on "the industry club" inside the industry boundary. We emphasize that the solar PV industry is a shared-fate community and focus on the interaction between actors within the boundary of the industry [Iansiti and Levien (2004b)].

Through literature review, we found that the window of opportunity theory and the viewpoint of industrial policy are less sufficient than ecosystem view to explain the rapid catchup of China's PV industry. However, the theoretical research scope of the sectoral innovation system and innovation ecosystem is too narrow or too broad. A medium perspective is needed to explain the ecological behavior of Chinese PV

Table 1. Summary of relevant views.

Related views	Core argument	Our comments
Window of opportunity	The emerging technology paradigm provides a window of opportunity for latecomers [Perez and Soete (1988)] China has taken the opportunity of demand shifts of international markets [Dong *et al.* (2020)]	There is no new disruptive technological innovation nor emerging technological paradigm in China's solar PV industry. Solar PV industry in Western countries also faces this opportunity, and they prepared much longer than China.
Industrial policy	Government played a core role in industrial policy [Lee and Kim (2017)]	Chinese first industrial policy of solar PV industry came out very late.
Sectoral innovation system	Industrial innovation emphasizes a system in which actors perform market and nonmarket functions [Malerba (2002); Fukugawa (2016)]	Sectoral innovation system does not provide a detailed and dynamic analysis of the specific interactions between the actors.
Innovation ecosystem	Ecosystem is "the collaborative arrangements," which emphasize the set of upstream suppliers, downstream users, complementors, and competitors [Kapoor and Furr (2014); Adner and Kapoor (2010); Adner (2006)]	Innovation ecosystem tends to break the traditional industry boundary and is too broad for studying China's solar PV industry.

enterprises within the industry. Based on this, this paper puts forward two questions: How do Chinese solar PV enterprises construct an innovation ecosystem within the industry? What ecological strategies have actors adopted to maintain ecological relationships? In view of this, we try to analyze and answer the above questions mainly focusing on the ecological actions of solar PV enterprises and other actors at the industrial level.

3. Research Methodology and Data

3.1. *Case selection*

We selected 16 case enterprises, which are all core enterprises in various industrial chain links of China's PV industry over the years. The scale of them is at the forefront of the industry, and their technical capabilities, business levels, and brand influence are all at a relatively high level. We further selected 9 leading companies (or former industry leading companies) from these 16 companies to enter the research process. The remaining 7 enterprises serve as saturation test case enterprises. Table 2 presents an overview of the case enterprises. Table 3 presents an overview of saturation test case enterprises.

3.2. *Research methodology*

We used the case study method to analyze China's solar PV industry [Yin (2003)], which helps us explore dynamic relationships between enterprises that enable us to

Table 2. Case enterprises and investigation.

Num.	Enterprises	Establishment time	Data source	Interviewee	Business profile	2020 Operating income (million CNY)
1	LONGi	2000	2019 field interview	Strategy manager	Silicon wafers and PV cells	32897
2	GCL	2006	Since 2018 two field interviews	Deputy general manager and wisdom workshop manager	The whole industrial chain of silicon materials and equipment manufacturing	31349
3	Trina Solar	1997	2012 field interview	Chairman and CEO	Silicon wafers, PV cells, and module	23376
4	Canadian Solar	2001	2013 field interview	Director of president's office and R&D engineer	Module and solar-integrated solution provider	22324
5	JA Solar	2005	2012 field interview	Chairman and CEO	Silicon wafers and PV cells	21155
6	Zhonghuan	1999	Since 2019 two field interviews	General managers	Silicon material and silicon wafer	15439
7	Yingli	1987	2020 field interview	Heir to the founder	Module	Restructured debt
8	Suntech	2001	Secondary data	/	PV cells and module	Bankrupt
9	LDK	2005	Secondary data	/	Silicon wafer, PV cell, and module	Bankrupt

Table 3. Saturation test case enterprises and investigation.

Num.	Enterprises	Establishment time	Data source	Interviewee	Business profile	2020 Operating income (million CNY)
1	Talesun Solar	2010	2018 field interview	Chief scientist	PV cell, module, and solar power panel support	4765
2	Foster	2003	2018 field interview	Senior management	EVA and solar panel	6344
3	Sunlink	2004	2019 field interview	Vice chairman and technical manager	Module	/
4	AKCOME	2010	2019 field interview	Director of production and technical manager	PV cell and module	5126
5	Jingying	2009	2019 field interview	Deputy general manager	Complementary equipment	/
6	NAURA	2001	2019 field interview	Vice president	Integrated circuit	6056
7	JYT	2002	2019 field interview	Senior management	Silicon wafer and equipment	4056

Note: Financial data for delisted and unlisted companies were not available.

construct the theoretical model [Eisenhardt and Graebner (2007)]. The case study is inductive qualitative study with the grounded theory approach. We tried to find the factors of catching up of China's solar PV enterprises and build a systematic theoretical model from bottom to top [Glaser and Strauss (1967); Dougherty (2002)]. We first conducted semistructured interviews with 14 enterprises and collected secondary data of 2 enterprises. The interview questions are shown in Table A.1. Then, we began to data coding, define categories, and constantly revise the theoretical framework until saturated. Finally, we combined the conclusions of grounded theory with the literature review and management theory to construct the theoretical framework. The snapshots of the research steps we followed are shown in Fig. A.1.

3.3. *Data collection and validity assurance*

In order to ensure the validity of the research data, we used multiple data sources in the study, including primary data and secondary data. The interview materials (as primary data) of 14 enterprises include field interviews with chairman and CEO, general manager, strategy manager, and so on. The primary data of about 200,000 words were sorted out according to interview materials (about 20 h). In order to improve the reliability of our study, all interviews were conducted face-to-face. After recorded and transcribed by the authors, materials were sent to the interviewees for consent and confirmation. Two enterprises used secondary data for their analysis, including media reports, research papers, professional publication, and company websites. By triangulating data from different channels, the effectiveness of secondary materials can be ensured.

4. Data Coding and Analysis

On the basis of manual classification, this paper analyzes the data with the help of NVivo11 software and follows the (1) open coding, (2) axial coding, and (3) selective coding procedures. We collated primary data, and more than 213 original statements were obtained. In the open coding stage, coding units are "labeled" as a*** and conceptualized one by one, and then classified into the most suitable initial concepts as A**. AA** represents the subcategory. On the basis of 30 "initial concepts," 13 subcategories are summarized. In the stage of axial coding, the logical association between categories is sorted out until theoretical saturation, and 13 categories are integrated into 6 main categories. On the basis of axial coding, through the analysis of the connotation and nature of the 6 main categories, two core categories are further extracted by selective coding.

4.1. *Open coding*

In this study, we first sorted out the original materials of 9 case enterprises and eliminated the interference languages with no obvious academic use, and 213 initial concepts were obtained. After several times of code sorting and analysis, the similar concepts were systematically integrated, finally 30 initial concepts were formed, and 13 subcategories were further condensed and extracted. The initial concept and some

Table 4. Open coding categorization–conceptualization.

Initial concept	Frequency	Original statement is labeled (syntactically collated)
A^{01}: Team work (a^{001} a^{003} a^{005} a^{011} a^{041} a^{055} a^{067} a^{072} a^{095} a^{127})	10	Introducing auxiliary material suppliers into the industrial park (a^{001}), cultivating industry chain (a^{002}), team work in industrial parks (a^{003}), cooperate with suppliers who provide auxiliary materials (a^{004}), coordinate with each other in the industrial park (a^{005}), building comrade-in-arms relationships between suppliers and customers (a^{006}), cultivating listed complementary enterprises (a^{007}), cultivating local suppliers (a^{008}), helping enterprises in industrial chain operate (a^{009}), providing technical parameter requirements and theoretical suggestions to upstream enterprises (a^{010}), enhancing the team combat capability of enterprises in industrial parks (a^{011}), promoting the idea of co-prosperity and strengthening the ability to withstand risks (a^{012}), insisting efficiency monocrystal route (a^{013}), forming strategic partnership with competitors (a^{014}), cross-shareholding with competitors (a^{015}), establishing a fixed relationship between upstream and downstream (a^{016}), win-win and symbiosis against external forces (a^{017}), competing and cooperating with competitors (a^{018}), becoming each other's benchmarks (a^{019}), the industrial park offers a consistent value orientation (a^{020})
A^{02}: Industrial chain cultivation (a^{002} a^{007} a^{008} a^{009} a^{061} a^{101} a^{102} a^{162} a^{197} a^{198} a^{201} a^{202} a^{204} a^{205})	14	
A^{03}: Complementary joint R&D (a^{004} a^{034} a^{035} a^{068} a^{087})	5	
A^{04}: Industrial chain strategic cooperation (a^{006} a^{016} a^{028} a^{029} a^{053} a^{057} a^{060} a^{081} a^{082} a^{091} a^{105} a^{111} a^{132} a^{141} a^{158} a^{193} a^{194} a^{195} a^{207} a^{210})	20	
A^{05}: Industrial chain joint R&D (a^{010} a^{059} a^{094} a^{186} a^{199})	5	
A^{06}: Shared fate (a^{012} a^{020} a^{027} a^{144})	4	
A^{07}:Specialization strategy (a^{013} a^{031} a^{032} a^{044} a^{058} a^{077} a^{080} a^{093} a^{099} a^{150} a^{152})	11	
A^{08}: Alliance with competitors (a^{014} a^{074})	2	……
A^{09}: Taking equity stakes or acquiring competitors (a^{015} a^{066} a^{070} a^{163})	4	Industry associations organize enterprises to deal with antidumping and antibribery (a^{213}).
A^{10}: Industrial chain alliance (a^{017} a^{073} a^{078} a^{083} a^{085} a^{119} a^{120} a^{122} a^{123} a^{124} a^{136} a^{142} a^{143} a^{151} a^{154} a^{196} a^{203})	17	
A^{11}: Cooperate with competitors on projects (a^{018} a^{046})	2	
A^{12}: Take competitors as the benchmark for catching up (a^{019})	1	
A^{13}: User management (a^{021} a^{100} a^{107} a^{169} a^{170} a^{171} a^{172} a^{173} a^{174} a^{176} a^{177} a^{178} a^{179} a^{180})	14	
A^{14}: Collaborate with research institutions and collages (a^{022} a^{043} a^{065} a^{075} a^{098} a^{109} a^{110} a^{113} a^{115} a^{121} a^{164} a^{181} a^{182} a^{183} a^{184} a^{187} a^{188} a^{190} a^{191} a^{192} a^{209})	21	

Table 4. (*Continued*)

Initial concept	Frequency	Original statement is labeled (syntactically collated)
A^{15}: Participate in government projects (a^{023} a^{062} a^{135} a^{185})	4	
A^{16}: Adjacent to the upstream/downstream plant (a^{024} a^{056} a^{208})	3	
A^{17}: Geographic migration of each link of the industrial chain (a^{025} a^{042} a^{130})	3	
A^{18}: Industrial chain integration (a^{026} a^{033} a^{047} a^{050} a^{054} a^{076} a^{092} a^{104} a^{108} a^{112} a^{114} a^{116} a^{118} a^{125} a^{145} a^{153} a^{155} a^{156} a^{159} a^{165} a^{206})	21	
A^{19}: Local government support (a^{030} a^{040} a^{048} a^{063} a^{071} a^{103} a^{131} a^{133} a^{134} a^{137} a^{138} a^{139} a^{140} a^{147} a^{148} a^{149} a^{189})	17	
A^{20}: Linkage of industrial chain (a^{036} a^{037} a^{069} a^{079})	4	
A^{21}: Half a step ahead of the competition (a^{038})	1	
A^{22}: Users promotion (a^{039} a^{084} a^{166} a^{167} a^{168} a^{175})	6	
A^{23}: Set up factories abroad (a^{045} a^{096} a^{106} a^{128})	4	
A^{24}: Import equipment and mining talent (a^{049} a^{052} a^{086} a^{117})	4	
A^{25}: Joint venture with state-owned enterprises (a^{051})	1	
A^{26}: Free disclosure of patents/technologies (a^{064} a^{126} a^{146})	3	
A^{27}: Industry chain joint venture (a^{088} a^{089} a^{157})	3	
A^{28}: Industrial chain approaching (a^{090} a^{097} a^{129})	3	
A^{29}: Merger complementors (a^{160})	2	
A^{30}: Participation in association forum (a^{200} a^{211} a^{212} a^{213})	4	

Data sources: Field interviews and secondary data were collected. Due to space constraints, only some of the original statement labels are listed.

Table 5. Open coding categorization–subcategorization.

Subcategory	Initial concept
AA[01]: Supply chain partnership management	Industrial chain strategic cooperation(A[04]); industrial chain joint R&D (A[05]); industry chain alliance (A[10]); linkage of industrial chain (A[20]); industrial chain integration (A[18]); industrial chain joint venture (A[27]); merger complementors (A[29])
AA[02]: Value cocreation and sharing	Complementary joint R&D (A[03])
AA[03]: Legality	Set up factories abroad (A[23]); joint venture with state-owned enterprises (A[25])
AA[04]: User management	User management (A[13]); user promotion (A[22])
AA[05]: Industry-college-institute cooperation	Collaborate with research institutions and collages (A[14])
AA[06]: Competitive strategy	Specialization strategy (A[07]); taking equity stakes or acquiring competitors (A[09]); take competitors as the benchmark for catching up (A[12]); half a step ahead of the competition (A[21]); import equipment and mining talent (A[24]); free disclosure of patents to expand the market (A[26])
AA[07]: Cooperation strategy	Alliance with competitors (A[08]); cooperate with competitors on projects (A[11])
AA[08]: Industrial chain cluster	Geographic migration of each link of the industrial chain (A[17]); industrial chain approaching (A[28])
AA[09]: Industrial park	Team work (A[01])
AA[10]: Colocation	Adjacent to the upstream or downstream plant (A[16]);
AA[11]: Local government	Participate in government projects (A[15]); local government support (A[19])
AA[12]: Industry association	Participation in association forum (A[30])
AA[13]: Entrepreneurship	Industrial chain cultivation (A[02]); shared fate (A[06])

examples of each category are shown in Table 4. Open coding categorization and 13 subcategories are shown in Table 5.

4.2. *Axial coding*

We clustered the 13 subcategories obtained from open coding to extract the main categories in the axial coding stage. In this paper, 6 main categories are summarized through the interrelationships of 13 subcategories. The main categories obtained by axial coding and corresponding subcategories are shown in Table 6.

We coded the remaining seven case companies and found no new initial concepts, proving that the original theoretical framework was constructed reasonably.

4.3. *Selective coding*

Based on the original data, 30 initial concepts, 13 subcategories, and 6 main categories are re-examined and compared to analyze the catching-up factors of China's solar PV industry. Two core categories, which are related to all main categories — "industrial innovation ecosystem construction" and "industrial innovation ecological relationship maintenance," are obtained. The theoretical framework of this paper is finally determined, as shown in Fig. 1.

Table 6. Axial coding categorization–main categorization.

Main categories	Corresponding subcategory
Resource orchestration	AA^{01} Industrial chain management; AA^{02} value cocreation and sharing; AA^{04} user management; AA^{05} industry-college-institute cooperation
The role of hub firms	AA^{03} Legality; AA^{13} entrepreneurship
Co-opetition	AA^{06} Competitive strategy; AA^{07} cooperation strategy
Clustering	AA^{08} industrial chain cluster; AA^{09} industrial park
Co-location	AA^{10} Colocation
Local governments and associations	AA^{11} Local government; AA^{12} industry association

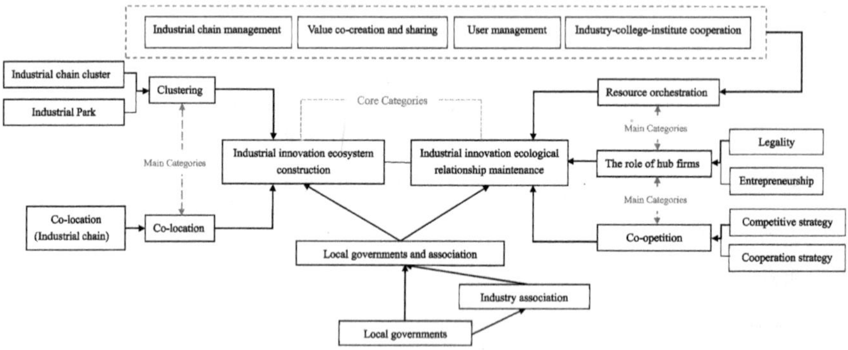

Fig. 1. Schematic diagram of coding structure.

5. Industrial Innovation Ecosystem Theoretical Model

Through the previous analysis, we found that the concept of industrial innovation ecosystem can effectively explain the internal mechanism of rapid catchup of China's PV industry. The theoretical framework of industrial innovation ecosystem takes a middle position between sectoral innovation system and innovation ecosystem. Industrial innovation ecosystem is more productive, dynamic, and coevolutionary than the sectoral innovation system. In some way, industrial innovation ecosystem is a subset of innovation ecosystem with an industrial bound, and many actions are in industrial shared-fate community.

Specifically, the path for the rapid catchup of China's PV industry can be summarized into the following two main categories: industrial innovation ecosystem construction and industrial innovation ecological relationship maintenance. Both actions are influenced by local governments and industry associations.

5.1. *Industrial innovation ecosystem construction*

Autio and Thomas [2014] argued that the competitiveness of an ecosystem is not only a question of the competitiveness of a single enterprise but also includes the construction and coordination of the ecosystem, the distribution and utilization of value, and the interactions between upstream and downstream in the value chain. Constructing and developing a well-functioning innovation ecosystem have become a new source of competitive advantage [Adner (2006)]. The actors of the industrial innovation ecosystem need to clarify the direction of innovation, common goals, and future challenges in the technical field and make joint commitments to the blueprint for the future of innovation and development [Autio and Thomas (2014); Dattée *et al.* (2018)]. In the early stage, PV core companies formed stable strategic partnerships with upstream and downstream companies through industrial clustering and colocation strategies and formed ecological relationships with complementary companies through the construction of value cocreation industrial parks [Kapoor and Furr (2014)]. The proposal of the shared fate constructed an industrial innovation ecosystem with themselves as the core. At this time, the industrial innovation ecosystem is affected by industrial parks, geographic distances, and regional policies and has obvious boundary characteristics.

5.1.1. *Clustering*

Porter [1998] proposed that through acquiring specialized information from employees, suppliers, and complementarities, enterprises can increase productivity and clustering benefits. Clustering lets enterprises benefit as if they had a greater scale but without sacrificing flexibility [Feser *et al.* (2008)]. Through the investigation of China's solar PV enterprises, we found that there are two clustering ways for China's solar PV enterprises. One is the clustering in the form of industrial parks with hub firms as the center [Monga (2011)]. Each industrial park is a small shared-fate ecosystem, and most of the actors are complementors to the hub firm. The other type is geographical and regional clustering with regional resources as the core, and enterprises form a whole industrial chain or a certain link of the industrial chain [Takeda *et al.* (2008)].

5.1.1.1. Photovoltaic industrial park

By forming a small ecosystem with hub firms as the center in the industrial park, a more stable ecological cooperative relationship can be formed among PV enterprises in various links, and more consistent behavior can be maintained in facing crises and risks. Industrial parks with a stable dependence relationship will unify the value vision of the hub firm and a large number of complementary SMEs, which is the basis for constructing the whole industrial innovation ecosystem.

In 2008, Changzhou National High-tech Zone and Trina jointly built Trina Solar Photovoltaic Industrial Park. The whole park has formed a complete regional PV industry cluster with Trina as the leader, integrating the upstream and downstream of the industry, equipment, and accessories and has created a PV industry demonstration base with high efficiency and low cost. An executive of Trina Solar said the following:

> *Here all the companies are the SMEs, which are supplier of components and complementary equipment only for Trina Solar. Trina Solar and all SMEs here are family. We collaborated for R&D and*

> *innovation. Trina is the final user. This can bring us innovation across the industrial supply chain.*

On July 18, 2019, the opening ceremony of the fifth-phase project of Inner Mongolia Zhonghuan-GCL Photovoltaic Material Co., LTD., which is jointly owned by Zhonghuan, GCL, and Hohhot government, was held. General Manager of Inner Mongolia Zhonghuan Asset Management Co., Ltd. said the following:

> *Based on the production of monocrystalline silicon materials, partners were introduced in the park, including our main auxiliary suppliers and some upstream and downstream companies. We deployed the matching suppliers of cutting, the suppliers of quartz crucible, and corresponding service providers of our downstream power station construction and component products. Whether cost reduction or response to major changes in the market, the actions will be consistency and timeliness.*

5.1.1.2. Regional clustering

Clustering within an area is an important factor to affect competition by increasing the productivity of companies, accelerating resource transfers, and enhancing regional knowledge diffusion [Porter (1998); Takeda *et al.* (2008)]. Firms enjoyed the advantage of proximity because of knowledge externality and sharing. Regional clusters with talents, knowledge, policies, and other resources as the core provide great competitive advantages for the development of early photovoltaic enterprises. In the industrial innovation ecosystem, geographical boundaries matter. The stable strategic relationships within the industrial clusters with geographical boundaries lay a foundation for the construction of the subsequent industrial innovation ecosystem.

China's Jiangsu province has formed the largest solar PV industry cluster in China, with a complete industrial chain and the largest number of PV enterprises. Several of the most famous companies in the PV industry, such as Suntech, Trina, and Linyang, are clustering in Jiangsu province. Our study found that the reasons for China's solar PV enterprises to cluster in Jiangsu include the following: (1) Jiangsu province has advantages in technology, capital, and talent. (2) The development of the internet and other emerging industries in Jiangsu province provides a good industrial foundation for the development of solar PV industry. (3) The flexible and loose industrial policy of Jiangsu government has provided a lot of support for the PV industry [Zhu *et al.* (2013)]. Through the flow of talents and frequent business cooperation between enterprises, a small regional ecosystem with geographical boundaries is gradually formed. The advantages of regional clustering and superior ecological conditions in Jiangsu province make solar PV enterprises in Jiangsu province more dynamic and innovative.

In addition, we found that different links of the entire industry chain tend to migrate to different directions in recent years, and the same or adjacent links of industry chain tend to cluster together. The upstream parts of industry chain tend to move to the provinces which have low cost of generating electricity, including Inner Mongolia and Xinjiang (pithead power), Sichuan province, and Yunnan province (hydroelectric power), while the downstream parts of the industrial chain tend to cluster in the Yangtze River Delta region for their entrepreneurial culture and the regional policies to support export-oriented industries [Binz and Anadon (2018)], including Jiangsu province and Zhejiang province. Cost is the main cause of industrial chain migration but gradually formed a unique industrial cluster divided by geographical boundaries. The enterprises in this kind of industrial cluster are no longer complementary but more competitive. Due to the homogeneity of knowledge, knowledge and talent flow between competitors are more rapid and frequent, gradually forming a knowledge network with talent as the link, which is more conducive to the construction of ecological relations between enterprises.

5.1.2. *Colocation*

Colocation strategy is a production strategy adopted by solar PV enterprises in order to maintain close cooperation with upstream or downstream and reduce transportation loss costs. GCL's colocation strategy is to maximize customers' convenience, which is one of the major reasons for GCL's continuous expansion of market shares. Vice general manager of GCL System Integration Technology Co., Ltd. said the following:

> *Silicon wafers are relatively thin and easy to be broken in long-distance transportation, we adopt a strategy-building factory next to the customers. In this way, our silicon wafers have the competitive advantage of low fragmentation rate and low transportation costs.*

Another typical case is the "just-in-time (JIT)" strategy of Canadian solar. By colocation with suppliers and planning the delivery time, Canadian solar reduces the inventory in the warehouse and thus reduces the cost. Figure 3 shows thatthe major suppliers of Canadian solar are GCL (located in Suzhou), ReneSola (located in Jiaxing), and CONCA solar (located in Wuxi), and Canadian Solar is located in the middle of the suppliers and has convenient transportation with them. Shen, director of the company's president office, said the following:

> *Our orders of customers are sent to upstream suppliers at the same time, then suppliers will arrange delivery according to our production strategies, just don't need a warehouse. We will start to product as soon as we have received the materials, and then send productions to customers when the goods are finished.*

This JIT of Canadian solar benefits from the fact that Jiangsu province and its surrounding areas have become a cluster with complete PV industry chain, which provides an ecological advantage. Through colocation strategy, GCL and Canadian Solar actively embed themselves in the industrial chain cluster and get huge

Fig. 2. Location map of Canadian solar and suppliers.

geographical advantages. Thus, stable strategic cooperative relationship with upstream and downstream enterprises of the industrial chain can be formed to make preparations for the further construction of self-centered ecosystem.

5.2. *Industrial innovation ecological relationship maintenance*

The interdependent ecological relationship between ecological actors is the potential source of the competitiveness of the innovation ecosystem [Jacobides *et al.* (2018)]. The value cocreation guided by the hub firms benefits all actors, thereby bringing new competitiveness to the ecosystem [Adner (2006)]. This requires hub firms to play an irreplaceable role in the maintenance of the innovation ecological relationship [Gawer and Cusumano (2014)], especially to initiate a common value vision within the innovation ecosystem through their own ecological connections, to efficiently orchestrate resources through ecological strategies [Sirmon *et al.* (2011)], and to promote the creating and sharing of resources among ecological actors [Alexy *et al.* (2013)]. The process of value cocreation emphasizes the relationship with the external environment, thereby embedding the competition and cooperation between competitors and changes in the institutional environment into the ecosystem [Chae (2019); Gawer and Phillips (2013)].

5.2.1. *The role of hub firms*

Ecosystem research studies have proposed the role of hub firms includes value creating [Teece (2007)], sharing, transforming, harmonizing [Baert *et al.* (2016)], stabilizing, and pioneering [Cai *et al.* (2016)]. Consistent with the theoretical analysis above, we found that hub firms played an important role in overcoming the liability of newness and expanding the industrial scale in the early stage of industrial development.

First, hub firms established legitimacy to gain enough critical resource for industry [Sine and Lee (2009)]. In the initial stage of China's solar PV industry, entrepreneurs were excluded from critical resources [Zhang and White (2016)]. At that time, some hub firms establish legitimacy through becoming "institutional entrepreneurship" [Sine and Lee (2009)], including listing in foreign capital markets, helping local infrastructure construction, and joint ventures with state-owned enterprises. GCL chose to establish legitimacy in domestic market through joint ventures with Poly — a large central enterprise with a wide range of main business areas. GCL deputy general manager said in an interview the following:

> *Private enterprises should learn to seek help from central enterprises, so that you may have more opportunities to get government projects. Now Poly has shares, but has been diluted to a few tenths of a percent. SOE is symbolic, but it has put GCL-Poly's name on the list of government cooperation.*

Second, they integrated and transformed resources to expand the scale of the industry [Zhang and White (2016)]. At the early stage of China's solar PV industry, in order to rapidly expand the industrial scale and construct ecosystem, many hub firms demonstrated their entrepreneurship and put forward the vision of the shared fate in the industry. They tried to share their technologies free of charge and cultivate upstream suppliers, downstream users, and complementary enterprises of the industrial chain. Hub firms gradually construct a complete industrial innovation ecosystem by cultivating other actors in the ecosystem. Yingli, as a leading enterprise at their time, has cultivated many small- and medium-sized equipment and material suppliers. Heir to the founder of Yingli said the following:

> *We have always cultivated material suppliers. A company called Angie Foster, which is now public, used to be a small business. We helped it and cultivated it, now it develops very well. We have cultivated too many SMEs of glass, silicon carbide and so on.*

5.2.2. *Resource orchestration*

From the theoretical perspective, the research studies on resource-based theory (RBT) have been deepened from the roles of resources [Barney (1991)] to the analysis of how enterprises gain competitive advantages through resource construction, integration, and utilization [Sirmon *et al.* (2007)]. Resource orchestration forms a response to the neglect of dynamics of RBT [Barney and Arikan (2001); Sirmon *et al.* (2007); Hannah and Piezunka (2014); Sirmon *et al.* (2011)], and it is to solve the problem of resource deficiency and ecosystem dynamic change from the perspective of resource strategies [Dhanaraj and Parkhe (2006); Sirmon *et al.* (2011)]. According to the resource orchestration, the resource will not appear itself and give enterprises the competitive advantages, and only the action of resources can create the value and make enterprises gain competitive advantages [Sirmon *et al.* (2007)]. The concept of resource orchestration includes several subprocesses, including acquiring, stabilizing, coordinating, and so on [Sirmon *et al.* (2011)]. Survival pressure pushes China's solar PV enterprises to flexibly adjust their ecological strategies dynamically according to the external environmental changes, and they have adopted different resource orchestration activities to maintain stable ecological relationships and gain more ecological resources [Iansiti and Levine (2004a); Teece (2012)].

First, Chinese solar PV enterprises acquired and coordinated resources through a set of actions including industrial chain partnership management, user management, industry-college-institute cooperation, and so on. Over the years, Suntech has been encouraging their suppliers to develop new materials, new technology, and new equipment related to Suntech's productions [Zhu *et al.* (2013)]. Through joint research and development of "wisdom solar PV modules" technology with National Semiconductor Corporation (NSC) and Suntech-embedded Solar Magic™ power optimizer chipsets in its solar PV components, greatly increasing the power generation of its solar energy system [National Semiconductor Corporation (2010)]. Ecological strategy of sharing scarce knowledge resources with ecological actors is common in China's PV industry ecosystem.

Second, Chinese solar PV enterprises acquired and stabilized resources through value cocreating and sharing with complementors. The value creating of solar PV module technological knowledge has to be combined with complementary knowledge, and the enterprises need expensive and complicated solar PV manufacturing equipment with embedded technology expertise [Kapoor and Furr (2014)]. Although key components and machinery were imported from abroad [Binz and Anadon (2018)], hub firms tend to gradually combine key machineries with domestic auxiliary materials to decrease the cost [Fu and Zhang (2011)]. Thus, in the process of equipment manufacturing, the hub firms have been engaged in helping domestic manufacturers increase their production capacity. Many local auxiliary material (wiring cables, steel frames, or welding materials) manufacturers lacked basic technical competence to produce high-quality auxiliary productions, and some hub firms directly trained them [Zhang and White (2016)]. Sometimes, hub firms provided free patent licenses or do joint R&D to increase the quality of complementary productions [Binz and Anadon (2018)]. We found that many enterprises have joint R&D strategies with equipment manufacturers. According to the director of president's office of Canadian Solar

> *After two years of joint R&D with equipment manufacturers, our domestic manufactured equipment, including laminating machine and welding equipment, have been success. First, we have priority to buy*

them and the price is relatively favorable. Second, the laminating machine can only be sold to us, it can be sold to the public after a year.

Through value cocreating and sharing, Canadian Solar formed a close strategic cooperative relationship with complementary enterprises to stabilize its own ecological strategic resources and position. On the one hand, joint R&D can reduce the cost of equipment procurement by sharing of knowledge and resources; on the other hand, the equipment is customized for Canadian Solar's newest production, thus greatly improving the iterative speed of innovation. The most important thing is to bind equipment manufacturing enterprises with hub firms through cooperative patent, forming an ecological relationship of value cocreation and shared fate.

5.2.3. *Co-opetition*

The importance of co-opetition for enabling access to knowledge and resources in technology industries has been emphasized by many scholars [Carayannis and Alexander (1999); Gnyawali and Park (2010)]. Solar PV industry changes rapidly, which lead the uncertainty [Binz and Anadon (2016)]. So, here, competition is fierce, and co-opetition is just as common. Co-opetition strategy helps the enterprises keep up with changes more easily, cushion the blow against the risks, and maintain ecological relationships [Carayannis and Alexander (1999)].

In China's solar PV industry, there is not only the traditional competition between various enterprises but also the competition between monocrystalline and polycrystalline camps, and the focus of the competition is how to capture more market share. Hub firms from their respective camps adopted a variety of strategies to compete for market share, including disclosing patented technologies for free, technical specialization, merging and acquiring of competitors, and so on. Hub firms' disclosing technology becomes a feature of China's solar PV industry, and some hub firms chose to disclose their new technologies rather than patent or keep trade secrets, in order to help enterprises in the same camp to compete for market share and maintain their ecological niche in the industrial innovation ecosystem. The competition between the monocrystal and polycrystal camps leads to the formation of co-opetition relationship between the enterprises producing the same product. Through technology sharing and patent layout, the ecological relationship of value cocreation is formed among the competitive enterprises.

On April 20, 2017, LONGi Solar (a wholly owned subsidiary of LONGi) disclosed its world-leading monocrystalline low-attenuation technology — light/carrier injection-induced regeneration (LIR) technology. In fact, LONGi opened the LIR technology that is aimed at further solving the light-induced degradation of monocrystalline silicon and rapidly promoting monocrystalline products to compete with polycrystalline products for market share. In addition, this co-opetition strategy stabilized the ecological relationships of LONGi with monocrystal enterprises. On the one hand, more enterprises using this technology increased the industrial scale of monocrystal, which can accelerate the cost reduction of products and lower the price of monocrystalline products. This has encouraged more companies to invest in monocrystal products and expanded strategic partner ecosystem of LONGi. On the other hand, multiple enterprises tried to further solve other bottleneck problems of low-attenuation technology based on LONGi's technology. Patent layout made LONGi occupy the core position of the industrial innovation ecosystem.

Of course, the polycrystalline camp enterprises are not willing to be outdone. On April 21, GCL-Poly Energy Holdings Limited announced the free transfer MCCE technology of TS products. MCCE technology can perfectly solve the technical problems of oversmooth surface and high reflectivity by texturing sub-micron-level suede on the surface of the silicon wafer, bringing further improvement in polycrystalline photoelectric conversion efficiency. This strategy also promoted the development of the black silicon market segment and stabilized polycrystalline ecological niche in the whole industrial innovation ecosystem.

5.3. *Local government and association*

As important actors in the innovation ecosystem of China's PV industry, local governments and industry associations have played a large role in financial support, policy support, and coordination in the process of constructing the innovation ecosystem and maintaining the ecological relationship.

5.3.1. *Local government*

China's PV industrial innovation ecosystem has some Chinese characteristics: It is the cochairing of hub firms with local government in the process of construction. Although central government guides the development direction of the entire solar PV industry by formulating policies, new enterprises still lack internal and external resources because of the liability of newness, so they need some extra support: local government. In earlier 2010 or so, Chinese local government is entrepreneurial and like to take the risk in new industries for the benefits of regional development. They generally do coordination work: attracting companies to local high-tech development zones, obtaining seed capital from local state-owned enterprises and regional banks, providing local policy support and financial support to solar PV startups, and cooperating with solar PV enterprises in an in-depth way [Corwin and Johnson (2019)], [Quitzow (2015)]. Suntech was founded on investment from 6 state-owned enterprises coordinated by the Wuxi government (Jiangsu province). The development of Trina Solar Energy Co., Ltd. is inseparable from the support of Changzhou municipal government. In Changzhou city, when the founder of Trina Solar, Mr. Gao, expressed the idea of the new industry, local government immediately allocated funds:

> *With the help of local government (Changzhou city, Jiangsu province), he (Mr. Gao) completed China's first model house with solar PV electricity. When other governments were questioning if he will succeed, Changzhou government encouraged him to "make something that people can actually see", and funded him 300,000 RMB as seed money for scientific research.*

Now, Trina has grown rapidly from one of the first solar PV enterprises in China to a global leader in PV technology innovation and product manufacturing. Trina Solar has built a Trina Industrial Park in Changzhou, becoming a core enterprise in Chinese sola PV industry innovation ecosystem.

Inspired by the successful story of Trina, many new solar enterprises were established by this wave and many of them, such as Canadian Solar, CLP, and Linyang Electronics, all have successively landed on the Nasdaq market and New York Stock Exchange. In 2019, the cumulative installed capacity of PV in Jiangsu province reached 14.86 million KW and Jiangsu became the largest base for solar PV in China [Zhu *et al.* (2013)]. The development of China's PV industry is closely related to the help and support of local governments.

Although local governments have played an important role in supporting the development, some local governments do have the problem of excessive intervention. Local protection has become an important source of serious excess production capacity. For local economic growth, local governments have given preferential policies such as low land prices and low water prices to some PV enterprises to promote the blind expansion of local companies. When losses are incurred, local governments use financial subsidies to keep enterprises afloat, which makes the withdrawal mechanism unsmooth and ultimately leads to overcapacity in the PV industry.

5.3.2. *Chinese photovoltaic industry association*

Chinese Photovoltaic Industry Association (CPIA) is a national first-level association that plays an important role of an intermediary between the government and enterprises. The role of CPIA is supporting the construction of innovation ecosystem and maintaining ecological relationship through improving the construction of standard system, carrying out technical exchange activities, and providing enterprise service platform. A CPIA staff member said the following:

> *We usually provide services to enterprises, mainly acting as an intermediary. If an enterprise has requests, we draft the opinions of the enterprise into a quarterly report to the government for feedback. We are also mainly engaged in industrial research to provide support for government formulation. In addition, we also provide supporting services, including formulating some standards and applying for patents.*

In 2018, when household-distributed PV market is under the condition of suffering defeat, association overcame all kinds of pressure to study in PV standards. CPIA standardization technical committee organization domestic mainstream household solar PV enterprises and experts established the "household PV standard working group," released CPIA standard system and household grid-connected PV power generation system standard in 2019, which make great contribution for solar PV industry.

At the same time, CPIA as an authoritative information exchanges platform for industry services and contributes to the healthy development of China's solar PV industry. CPIA holds two annual/semiannual review and outlook seminars at the beginning and middle of each year to report the latest development of the industry, analyzes the trend of the industry, and studies hot issues encountered in the development of the industry.

6. Conclusions

6.1. *Main findings*

Our research explores how China's Solar PV enterprises caught up so rapidly from the perspective of the industrial innovation ecosystem. We found that the rapid catchup of China's PV industry can be explained by industrial innovation ecosystem construction and industrial innovation ecological relationship maintenance. Emerging industries can rely on the interactive relationship between ecological actors to achieve catchup, rather than stick to breakthrough technological innovation. Chinese solar PV enterprises constructed industrial innovation ecosystem through industrial clustering and colocation strategies. With the help of local government, core companies formed stable strategic partnerships with upstream and downstream companies through industrial clustering and colocation strategies and formed ecological relationships with complementary companies through the construction of value cocreation industrial parks. The early small regional innovation ecosystems provided the foundation for the ecological construction of an innovation ecosystem covering the entire industry.

Hub firms played an important role in overcoming the liability of newness and proposing common vision in the early stage of solar PV industry development, which is consistent with the conclusion of Zhang and White [2016]. At that time, some hub firms established legitimacy of the industry through listing in foreign capital markets, helping local infrastructure construction, and joint ventures with state-owned enterprises [Sine and Lee (2009)]. In order to rapidly expand the industrial scale, many hub firms put forward the vision of the shared fate, shared their technologies free of charge, and cultivated actors in the industrial innovation ecosystem.

China's PV firms maintained the ecological relationship through resource orchestration and co-opetition [Sirmon *et al.* (2007, 2011); Carayannis and Alexander (1999)]. They acquired and coordinated resource through a set of ecological actions including industrial chain partnership management, user management, industry-college-institute cooperation, and so on. They also stabilized resource through value cocreating and sharing with complementors. The competition between the monocrystalline and polycrystalline camps leads to the formation of co-opetition relationship between the enterprises producing the same product. Through technology sharing and patent layout, the ecological relationship of value cocreation is formed.

Local governments and industry associations also played an important role in every stage of industry development. Local governments generally do coordination work, and industry association generally does intermediary work.

6.2. *Contributions and implications*

6.2.1. *Theoretical contribution*

First, we have expanded the theoretical thinking of catch-up research in emerging industries. From the perspective of the industrial innovation ecosystem, this paper explores the factors why China's solar PV enterprises can develop without radical technological innovation. Industrial innovation ecosystem is a new research perspective between sectoral innovation system and innovation ecosystem to analyzing emerging industry catchup. We focus more on the interior of the industry but can analyze the dynamic evolution of interaction between ecological actors and the dynamic changes of ecological strategies.

Second, different from the traditional catch-up theory, we illustrate emerging industries can catch up in the absence of radical technologies. The origin catch-up theory from the perspective of technological paradigm argued the emerging technology paradigm provides latecomers' advantage to catch up [Gerschenkron (1962, 1963); Perez and Soete (1988); Freeman and Soete (1997)]. But we found that emerging industries can rely on the interactive relationship between ecological participants to generate competitive advantages and then achieve catchup through product innovation. Catching up does not need to stick to breakthrough technological innovation.

6.2.2. *Managerial implications*

The conclusions of this article provided managerial guidance for the government and policy-makers. In addition to providing financial support, such as R&D subsidies, to enterprises, local governments should also pay attention to the construction of the local industrial innovation ecosystems and the maintenance of ecological relationships. Core enterprises should be given more legitimacy in the early stage of industrial development, such as government cooperation projects, local talents, and other scarce resources. In the operations of enterprises, governments should focus on promoting strategic cooperative relations between enterprises and guide enterprises to form diversified cooperation mechanisms. When enterprises suffer losses, governments should reduce intervention, establish a timely exit mechanism for poorly managed enterprises, emphasize market-based fair competition, and guide the healthy development of local industries.

6.3. *Limitations and future research*

The research samples in this paper only include large-scale enterprises in China's solar PV industry, and the research perspective is limited by the interview content of sample enterprises. Future research can include samples of small- and medium-sized suppliers in the industry to obtain more data from multiple perspectives from various types of enterprises in the industry or conduct long-term follow-up interviews to deeply explore the dynamic changes in the whole development process of solar PV enterprises. In terms of research methods, questionnaire surveys can be used to quantify and test the rationality of the industrial innovation ecosystem research framework in this paper.

Acknowledgment

This research was supported by the National Natural Science Foundation of China: No. 71932009.

Appendix

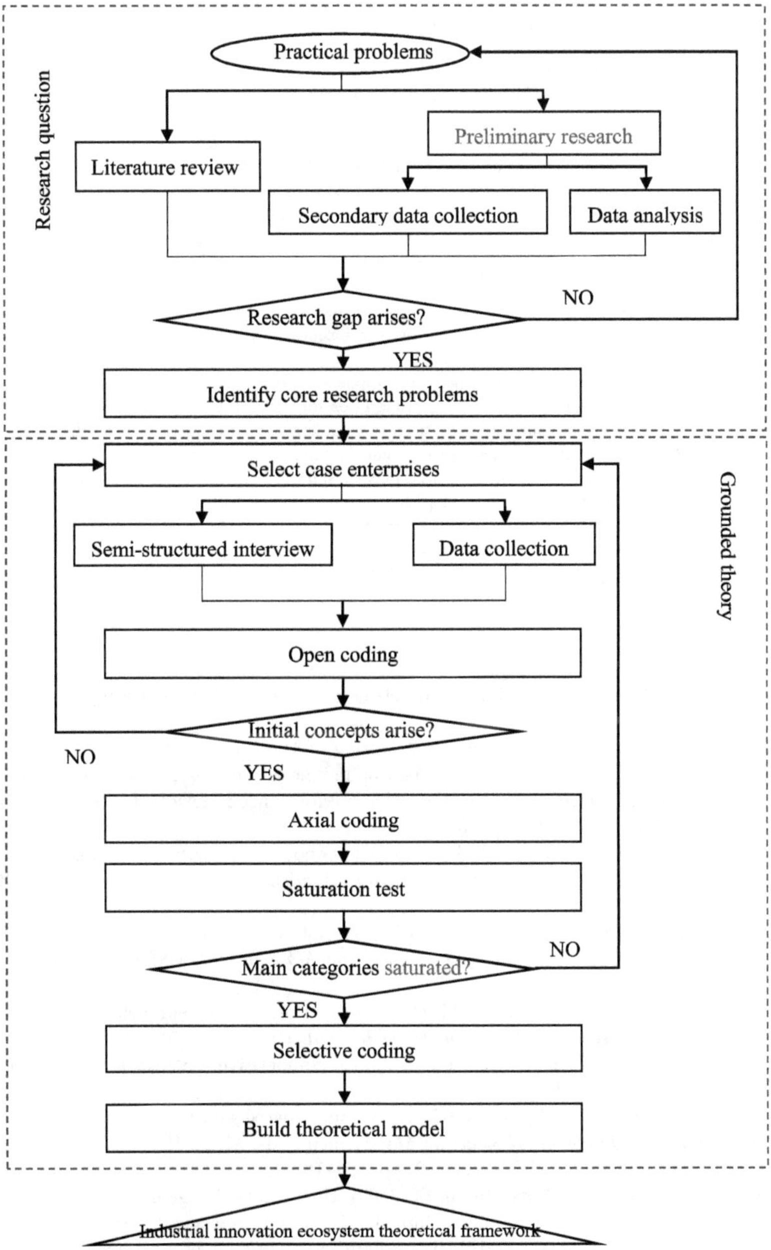

Fig. A.1. Research method snapshot.

Table A.1. Semistructured interview questions.

Num.	Interview questions
1	How did your enterprise get into solar PV industry? Why you choose monocrystalline or polycrystalline products?
2	How did your enterprise layout industry strategies in the initial stage of entering the market?
3	What do you think are the core competitive advantages for your enterprise to become a leading firm?
4	What types of partners do your enterprise have? What are the partnerships like?
5	Are the partners of your enterprise mainly located in the local area?
6	Are the goals and visions of your business aligned with those of your partners? How do you align your value propositions with those of your partners?
7	Did your enterprise communicate with your partners in a timely manner in the face of a crisis such as sudden changes in the industry?
8	Does your company develop products with partners? How did they work together?
9	Is the government or industry association helpful to your enterprises' development?
10	Will users provide advice and suggestions to business? Does it increase productivity of your enterprise?
11	Whether your enterprise and upstream suppliers are centrally located in the same area or address adjacent? Is there any consideration for the location?
12	Do the products of your enterprise need to complement and cooperate with other companies (providing equipment, accessories, technology, etc.) to form a complete product?
13	What role do you think your enterprise plays in solar PV industry? Are there any contributions of your enterprise to the development of the industry?

Note: The interview questions in Table A.1 are semi-structured interview outline. The actual interview content was adjusted according to the on-site situation.

References

Adner, R. (2006). Match your innovation strategy to your innovation ecosystem. *Harvard Business Review*, **84**, 4: 98–107.

Adner, R. (2017). Ecosystem as structure. *Journal of Management*, **1**, 39–58.

Adner, R. and Kapoor, R. (2010). Value creation in innovation ecosystems: How the structure of technological interdependence affects firm performance in new technology generations. *Strategic Management Journal*, **31**, 3: 306–333.

Alexy, O., George, G. and Salter, A. J. (2013). Cui bono? The selective revealing of knowledge and its implications for innovative activity. *Academy of Management Review*, **38**, 2: 270–291.

Autio, E. and Thomas, L. (2014). Innovation ecosystems: Implication for innovation management, *The Oxford Handbook of Innovation Management*. Oxford University Press, Oxford.

Baert, C., Meuleman, M., Debruyne, M. *et al.* (2016). Portfolio entrepreneurship and resource orchestration. *Strategic Entrepreneurship Journal*, **10**, 4: 346–370.

Barney, J. B. (1991). Firm resource and sustained competitive advantage. *Journal of Management*, **17**, 1: 99–120.

Barney, J. B. and Arikan, A. M. (2001). The resource-based view: Origins and implications. *The Blackwell Handbook of Strategic Management*, eds. M. A. Hitt, R. E. Freeman and J. S. Harrison, Oxford, UK, Blackwell, pp. 124–188.

Battilana, J., Leca, B. and Boxenbaum, E. (2009). How actors change institutions: Towards a theory of institutional entrepreneurship. *Academy of Management Annals*, **3**, 1: 65–107.

Binz, C. and Anadon, L. D. (2016). Transplanting clean-tech paths from elsewhere: The emergence of the Chinese solar PV industry. *Papers in Innovation Studies 2016/29*, Lund University, CIRCLE — Center for Innovation Research.

Binz, C. and Anadon, L. D. (2018). Unrelated diversification in latecomer contexts — the emergence of the Chinese solar photovoltaics industry. *Environmental Innovation & Societal Transitions*, **28**, 14–24.

Breschi, S. and Malerba, F. (1997). Sectoral innovation systems: Technological regimes, schumpeterian dynamics, and spatial boundaries. *Systems of Innovation Technologies, Institutions and Organisations*, ed. C. Edquist, Routledge, pp. 130–156.

Carayannis, E. G. and Alexander, J. (1999). Winning by co-opeting in strategic government-university-industry r&d partnerships: The power of complex, dynamic knowledge networks. *The Journal of Technology Transfer*, **24**, 2: 197–210.

Cai, L., Anokhin, S., Yin, M. *et al.* (2016). Environment, resource integration, and new ventures' competitive advantage in china. *Management and Organization Review*, **12**, 2: 333–356.

Chae, B. (2019). A General framework for studying the evolution of the digital innovation ecosystem: The case of big data. *International Journal of Information Management*, **45**, 83–94.

Corwin, S. and Johnson, T. L. (2019). The role of local governments in the development of Chinese solar photovoltaic industry. *Energy Policy*, **130**, JUL: 283–293.

Dattée, B., Alexy, O. and Autio, E. (2018). Maneuvering in poor visibility: How firms play the ecosystem game when uncertainty is high. *Academy of Management Journal*, **61**, 2: 466–498.

de la Tour, A., Glachant, M., Ménière, Y. (2011). Innovation and international technology transfer: The case of the Chinese photovoltaic industry. *Energy Policy*, **39**, 761–70.

Dhanaraj, C. and Parkhe, A. (2006). Orchestrating innovation networks. *Academy of Management Review*, **31**, 3: 659–669.

Dong, H., Zeng, B., Wang, Y. *et al.* (2020). China's Solar Subsidy Policy: Government Funding Yields to Open Markets. *IEEE Power & Energy Magazine*, **18**, 3: 49–60.

Dong, X. and Worthington, A. C. (2014). The impact of government financial assistance on the performance and financing of Australian SMEs. *Accounting Research Journal*, **30**, 4: 447–464.

Dougherty, D. (2002). Grounded theory research methods. *The Blackwell Companion to Organizations*, ed. J. A. C. Baum, Blackwell, Oxford, pp. 849–866.

Eckhardt, J. and Shane, S. (2003). Opportunities and entrepreneurship. *Journal of Management*, **29**, 333–349.

Eisenhardt, K. M. and Graebner, M. E. (2007). Theory building from cases: Opportunities and challenges. *Academy of Management Journal*, **50**, 1: 25–32.

Feser, E., Renski, H. and Goldstein, H. (2008). Clusters and economic development outcomes: An analysis of the link between clustering and industry growth. *Economic Development Quarterly*, **22**, 4: 324–344.

Freeman, C. and Soete, L. (1997). Development and the diffusion of technology. *The Economics of Industrial Innovation*, eds. C. Freeman and L. Soete, Pinter Publishers, London.

Fu, X. and Zhang, J. (2011). Technology transfer, indigenous innovation and leapfrogging in green technology: Solar-PV panel industries in India and China. *Journal of Chinese Economic & Business Studies*, **9**, 4: 329–347.

Fukugawa, N. (2016). Knowledge creation and dissemination by Kosetsushi in sectoral innovation systems: Insights from patent data. *Scientometrics*, **109**, 3: 1–25.

Gawer, A. and Cusumano, M. A. (2014). Industry platforms and ecosystem innovation. *Journal of Product Innovation Management*, **31**, 3: 417–433.

Gawer, A. and Phillips, N. (2013). Institutional work as logics shift: The case of Intel's transformation to platform leader. *Organization Studies*, **34**, 8: 1035–1071.

Gerschenkron, A. (1962). *Economic Backwardness in Historical Perspective*, Harvard University Press, Cambridge, Mass.

Gerschenkron, A. (1963). The early phases of industrialization in Russia: Afterthoughts and counterthoughts. *The Economics of Take-off into Sustained Growth*, ed. W. W. Rostow, Macmillan, London.

Glaser, B. G. and Strauss, A. L. (1967). *The Discovery of Grounded Theory: Strategies for Qualitative Research*, Aldine, Chicago.

Gnyawali, D. R. and Park, B. J. R. (2010). Co-opetition and technological innovation in small and medium-sized enterprises: A multilevel conceptual model. *Journal of Small Business Management*, **47**, 3: 308–330.

Greenwood, R. and Suddaby, R. (2006). Institutional entrepreneurship in mature fields: The big five accounting firms. *Academy of Management Journal*, **49**, 27–48.

Hannah, D. P., Bremner, R. P. and Eisenhardt, K. M. (2016). *Resource Redeployment in Business Ecosystems*, Emerald Group Publishing Limited.

Hannah, D. P. and Eisenhardt, K. M. (2017). How firms navigate cooperation and competition in nascent ecosystems. *Strategic Management Journal*, **39**, 12: 3163–3192.

Hannah, D. P. and Piezunka, H. (2014). Competition in the Search for Innovation: Getting Ahead by Falling Behind. Aca. of Manage. Meeting.

Hu, H., Tang, P., Zhu, Y. *et al.* (2020). The impact of policy intensity on overcapacity in low-carbon Energy Industry: Evidence from photovoltaic firms. *Frontiers in Energy Research*, **8**, 577515.

Iansiti, M. and Levine, R. (2004a). *The Keystone Advantage*, Harvard Business School Press, Boston.

Iansiti, M. and Levien, R. (2004b). *What the New Dynamics of Business Ecosystems Mean for Strategy, Innovation, and Sustainability*, Harvard Business School Press.

Jacobides, M. G., Cennamo, C. and Gawer, A. (2018). Towards a theory of ecosystems. *Strategic Management Journal*, **39**, 2255–2276.

Kapoor, R. and Furr, N. R. (2014). Complementarities and competition: Unpacking the drivers of entrants' technology choices in the solar photovoltaic industry. *Strategic Management Journal*, **36**, 3: 316–436.

Kuik, O., Branger, F. and Quirion, P. (2019). Competitive advantage in the renewable energy industry: Evidence from a gravity model. *Renewable Energy*, **131**, 2019: 472–481.

Lee, K. (2020). Economics of technological leapfrogging. *SSRN Electronic Journal*. DOI: 10.2139/ssrn.3549420.

Lee, K. and Kim, J. H. (2017). Rise of latecomers and catch-up cycles in the world steel industry. *Research Policy*, **46**, 2: 365–375.

Li, J. and Huang, J. (2020). The expansion of China's solar energy: Challenges and policy options. *Renewable and Sustainable Energy Reviews*, **132**. https://doi.org/10.1016/j.rser.2020.110002.

Malerba, F. (2002). Sectoral systems of innovation and production. *Research Policy*, **31**, 2: 247–264.

Monga, C. (2011). Cluster-based industrial parks: A practical framework for action. Policy Research Working Paper.

Nambisan, S. and Sawhney, M. (2010). *Innovating in a Connected World: Harnessing the Vast Creative Potential Outside Your Company*. FT Press.

National Semiconductor Corporation (2010). National Semiconductor and Suntech cooperate to develop "smart solar cell" technology. *Application of Electronic Technique*, **36**, 11: 18–18.

Nelson, R. and Winter, S. (1982). *An Evolutionary Theory of Economic Change*. Harvard University Press, Cambridge.

Peng, M. and Luo, Y. (2000). Managerial ties and firm performance in a transition economy: The nature of a micro-macro link. *Academy of Management Journal*, **43**, 486–501.

Perez, C. and Soete, L. (1988). Catching up in technology: entry barriers and windows of opportunity. *Technical Change and Economic Theory*, ed. G. Dosi, Pinter publishers, New York.

Porter, M. E. (1998). Clusters and the new economics of competition. *Harvard Business Review*, 77–90.

Quitzow, R. (2015). Dynamics of a policy-driven market: The co-evolution of technological innovation systems for solar photovoltaics in China and Germany. *Environmental Innovation and Societal Transitions*, **17**, 126–148.

Schmela, M. (2020). Global market outlook for solar power 2020–2024, Solar Power Europe. Technical Report.

Scott, W. R. (1995). *Institutions and Organizations*, Sage, Thousand Oaks, CA.

Shane, S. (2000). Prior knowledge and the discovery of entrepreneurial opportunities. *Organization Science*, **11**, 448–469.

Shin, J. (2016). Dynamic catch-up strategy, capability expansion and changing windows of opportunity in the memory industry. *Research Policy*, 404–416.

Sine, W., David, R. and Mitsuhashi, H. (2007). From plan to plant: Effects of certification on operational start-up in the emergent independent power sector. *Organization Science*, **18**, 578–594.

Sine, W. and Lee, B. (2009). Tilting at windmills? The environmental movement and the emergence of the US wind energy sector. *Administrative Science Quarterly*, **54**, 123–155.

Sirmon, D. G., Hitt, M. A., Ireland, R. D. *et al.* (2011). Resource orchestration to create competitive advantage: Breadth, depth, and life cycle effects. *Social Science Electronic Publishing*, **37**, 5: 1390–1412.

Sirmon, D. G., Hitt, M. A. and Ireland, R. D. (2007). Managing firm resources in dynamic environments to create value: Looking inside the black box. *Academy of Management Review*, **32**, 1: 273–292.

Stinchcome, A. (1965). Social structure and organization. *Handbook of Organizations*, Rand McNally, Chicago, IL.

Takeda, Y., Kajikawa, Y., Sakata, I. *et al.* (2008). An analysis of geographical agglomeration and modularized industrial networks in a regional cluster: A case study at yamagata prefecture in Japan. *Technovation*, **28**, 8: 531–539.

Teece, D. J. (2007). Explicating dynamic capabilities: Nature and microfoundation. *Strategic Management Journal*, **28**, 13: 1319–1350.

Teece, D. J. (2012). Dynamic capabilities: Routines versus entrepreneurial action. *Journal of Management Stu.*, **49**, 8: 1395–1401.

Venkataraman, S. (1997). The distinctive domain of entrepreneurship. *Advances in Entrepreneurship: Firm Emergence and Growth*, ed. J. A. Katz, 119–138.

Yin, R. K. (2003). *Case Study Research: Design and Methods*. Sage, Thousand Oaks, CA.

Zhang, W. and White, S. (2016). Overcoming the liability of newness: Entrepreneurial action and the emergence of china's private solar photovoltaic firms. *Research Policy*, **45**, 3: 604–617.

Zhao, Y., Wang, S., Wang, W. *et al.* (2008). Report on the development of the photovoltaic industry in China (2006–2007). *China Renewable Energy Development Project Office.*

Zheng, C. and Kammen, D. M. (2014). An innovation-focused roadmap for a sustainable global photovoltaic industry. *Energy Policy*, **67**: 159–69.

Zhu, J., Y. Wu and Han, C. (2013). *Visit to Suntech Solar Power Company.* Economy & Management Publishing House, Beijing.

Biography

Shuang Ge is a lecturer of China University of Political Science and Law, obtained Ph.D. degree from University of Chinese Academy of Sciences. Her research areas mainly cover innovative ecosystem, innovation policy and technological innovation. Over the years she has been committed to the research of China's solar PV industry and has been conducting follow-up interviews with China's solar PV industry enterprises. She has published paper in Technovation, Asian Economic and Financial Review.

Xielin Liu is a professor of University of Chinese Academy of Sciences, vice president of Chinese Association of Science of Science and Technology policy (1998–2010) and the main editor of Journal of Science of Sciences and Technology Management (since 2003). He has been selected for Chinese Most Cited Researchers in the business management category for many years (released by Elsevier). His research areas mainly cover innovation policy, management of technology and innovation, management of entrepreneurship. Prof. Liu has published a lot of papers in Research Policy, Technovation, Journal of Management Studies, International Journal of Innovation Management, International Journal of Technology Management, Science and Public Policy and so on.

Adoption of Digital Innovation — Formulating Adopter Categories and Levels of Adoption in a Digital Sphere in an Emerging Economy *

Dorothy Dutta* and Mrinmoy K. Sarma†

Department of Business Administration
Tezpur University, Assam, India
**duttadorothy1@gmail.com*
†drmrinmoysarma@gmail.com

Digital innovations are happening all over the globe with the advent of technology. The digital platforms are not only introducing the traditional services online but are also continuously engaged in making frequent modifications to them in the form of incremental innovations. In our quest of creating a time horizon for innovation adoption, and determining levels of adopters of incremental innovations 837 participants from India were asked about their level of adoption of digital innovations. While most of the respondents did not seem affected by the digital transition, amongst the ones adopting these innovations are mostly Early Adopters and Early Majority. The study arrived at an adoption score for the respondents based on the time from the introduction of the innovation and their adoption. The time horizon suggests the increase in adoption of innovation with each new digital innovation introduced. In the case of incremental innovations, ten levels of adoption, and three categories consisting of the ten levels of adoption are formulated based on the LoA model. The users in India fall majorly on the Beginner category in which maximum is aware of the incremental innovations but are skeptical about using them. The study further suggests certain measures for the digital platform providers for each category of users to make them accustomed to the process of incremental innovations.

Keywords: Adoption; incremental; innovation; digital; platforms.

1. Introduction

The concept of innovation has been defined in the literature differently. However, the basic idea behind innovation is mostly been its degree of newness. According to Ven de Ven [1986], innovation is a "perception of newness" in the concerned market (or geographical region), even if it "appears" to an imitation, which is going on presently somewhere else. Innovation has revolutionized both the manufacturing sector as well as the services sector. The most recent innovations are aided by the use of technology, mostly in the form of digital innovation. Digital innovation is a comprehensive term that signifies a combination of digital and physical components to produce new products that offer diverse services, which dissolve the product and

*This chapter was originally published in International Journal of Innovation and Technology Management, Vol. 17, No. 8, March 2018, published by World Scientific Publishing, Singapore. Reprinted with permission.

industry boundaries [Yoo *et al.* (2010)]. Digital innovation does not only imply a shift in technology but also indicates the shift in the dynamics of relationships within the business and markets [Akesson and Akram (2011)]. In this scenario, one important role that technology has played is enabling service innovations in the digital sphere at a faster pace. Sundbo [1997] categorized service innovations into two parts based on its degree of newness — radical and incremental innovations. Radical innovations are simply defined as innovations that are new to the world and incremental innovations are the ones that are new to the market. Hurmelinna-Laukkanen *et al.* [2008] mentioned citing Garcia and Calantone [2002] that radical innovations are responsible for making both marketing and technological discontinuities at a macro and micro levels. But incremental innovations are relatively smaller where certain changes or modifications are made to the already existing service which involves a lower rate of risk. Rather than waiting for radical innovations to take place, marketers are now adopting frequent incremental service innovations to keep updating their digital services until the next big disruption occurs [Pappenheim (2016)]. It has become important, therefore, to understand the level at which the users of digital platforms are adopting these incremental innovations occurring now and then.

2. Literature Review

Developing new services in business is a strategic procedure that require planning for it to be effective [Busagara *et al.* (2020)]. The involvement of consumers in the process of new service development is very beneficial. The study highlighted that post service interaction with customer show a positive link with the process of new service development. Another study by Chichkanov [2020] confirmed the positive role of client knowledge assimilation in the product and business process innovations in knowledge-intensive business services. Lopes and Godinho [2019] found that there is a relationship between implementation of innovation and productivity in a firm. Although there is a positive impact of innovation on labor productivity but its effect on innovation output could not be established. The relationship of the firm with its customers, suppliers and partners boost the probability of innovating. However, there are several shortcomings as well when organisations try to implement service innovations. As mentioned by 21 senior executives of differnet banks in a study conducted by Velayati *et al.* [2020], technological difficulties, deposit orientation of the innovations instead of market orientation, privatisation and legislative inefficiencies are the major trends in the industry that affect service innovation.

It is quite evident that service innovation process depends to a large extent on a firm's associate and mostly its consumers. To design an innovation around the need and want of their users could help in introducing a successful innovation. Service innovation literature pertaining to firms in India is rather few in numbers. In the following part, an overview of the situation of service innovation in India is discussed.

Alam [2010] studied the process of new service development (NSD) across various geographical locations. A comparative analysis of two countries, namely Australia and India, suggested the presence of a significant difference between the two. The involvement of customers in India in the NSD process is lower than that in Australia; the reason identified as the use of moderate innovative services in India, which is more than Australia, that is why Indian firms are said to be more driven towards commercialization and business analysis tactics. Alam [2012] studied the NSD process in India by considering 148 multinational and 126 local business-to-business financial service firms. The results showed that most of the local firms due to risk factors opted for moderately innovative services but the multinational firms were found to be highly innovative. While multinational firms are more rigorous in their idea generation and test marketing stages, the indigenous firms are more active in their business analysis stage. However, both rank low on the grounds of strategizing, they make it up by seriously investing in the launch activities and commercialization. Thakur and Hale [2013] conducted a comparative study between Indian and US service firms about their service innovation strategies. Indian firms are reported to have implemented service innovations due to competition in the market rather than focusing on the actual need and demand in the market and thus they implemented only those innovations which were seen to have successful results when applied by their counterparts overseas. Bharwani and Mathews [2016] in their study determined the customer service innovation scenario in the hospitality sector of India. Hospitality professionals in the sector were interviewed and it is reported that service innovation did enhance the consumer experience. It helped the hotels to connect with their guests at an emotional and personal level through the implementation of customer service innovations. Rautela and Mavale [2016] studied incremental innovations in the restaurant business in India, especially in a technologically advanced era. The restaurant owners realize the importance of having an online presence and have been reported to be better at handling food purposes of the restaurant as well as attracting and retaining the consumers by implementing various technological incremental innovations.

Extant literature supports the notion that Indian marketers are not willing to take risks in implementing innovations in their business. Hence, they are adapting to the idea of incremental innovations which help them to keep up with the competition in the market as well as earning their profits. The need to explore in detail the adoption rate of incremental innovations in India as well becomes important.

There are several well-established methods in the literature that determine the adoption of technological innovations among the masses. The first and the most prominent one is the Technology Acceptance Model or popularly known as TAM. TAM was developed by Davis [1989] that uses two factors, namely perceived usefulness (PU) and perceived ease of use (PEOU) to determine the behavioral pattern. TAM has been modified over time by various researchers by adding other relevant variables into the picture. Venkatesh and Davis [2000] extended TAM by adding the constructs of social influence and cognitive instrumental processes as the variable PU has always been seen to have stronger and consistent effects in determining the usage than that of PEOU. The two new constructs of social influence processes and cognitive instrumental processes were found to influence user acceptance significantly. Further, Venkatesh and Bala [2008] further extended the TAM 2 model and framed

TAM 3 to determine the adoption and use of information technology (IT) at an individual level. TAM 3 is formulated by adding new variables to moderate the relationship between PEOU and PU. The variables introduced are computer self-efficacy, perception of external control, computer-anxiety, computer-playfulness, perceived enjoyment, and objective usability. All three TAM models are extensively used to measure the adoption of technology. However, one of the earliest theories determining adoption and diffusion of technological innovations is the Diffusion of Innovation theory by Rogers [1983].

Diffusion is referred to as a type of communication that involves a new idea leading to a social change as alterations occur in the existing structural system. However, when technological innovation is involved, there is a certain kind of uncertainty in the minds of the potential adopters; but then it is the advantages that arise out of using these innovations makes them put in the effort to learn and adopt. The rate at which an individual picks up an innovation has been termed as "innovativeness" which is the time taken by an individual to finally adopt an innovation. Mostly, the rate of adoption is measured by the length of time required for a certain percentage of people to adopt an innovation. Rogers divided the adopter categories into five depending on the time taken. Innovators are the individuals most enthusiastic about innovation with wider networks either through mass media or in person and have the ability to cope up with higher levels of uncertainty. They are the first ones to adopt an innovation. Early Adopters are people who have an upper hand in opinion leaders in their respective social systems and adopt the innovations almost immediately after the innovators. They help in speeding up the diffusion process because people go to them in need of advice about the trial of a new idea. Early Majority takes longer in the decision-making process of adopting or rejecting an innovation compared to that of innovators and Early Adopters. They analyze the situation for some time and then finally make a decision. Late Majority are referred to as skeptical as they adopt an innovation only after the majority of the people in a society have adopted it. An innovation is acceptable to this category only when they see proven benefits in the social system and removal of any kind of uncertainty. Lastly, laggards are the last ones to adopt who represent traditionalists in a social system who is suspicious of the happenings. By the time laggards start using an innovation, another idea has already hit the market and the innovators start using it already!

Steiber *et al.* [2020] studied the analytical framework for the diffusion of innovations during the phase of digital transformation. They have found that it is important for the firm to combine their existing frameworks in a complementing way to the framework set up for this purpose. A blueprint designed by combining both these methods would help analyze the efficiency and effectiveness of the digital transformation of the firms. These adopter categories have been used across various disciplines to determine the adoption of innovations [Sahin (2006)]. However, as the rate of incremental innovations in the digital age is increasing it demands a faster rate of adoption due to its frequent nature of the occurrence. Pappenheim [2016] mentioned that the companies nowadays are using incremental innovations but the researchers are still focused on working for radical innovations. The findings of the study would help in understanding the acceptance of different types of innovations (*radical as well as incremental*) in the digital space.

3. Objectives

To know better about these innovations, the following objectives have been laid down for the study:

(1) To create a time horizon for the adoption of innovations in Digital Platforms.
(2) To set up levels of adoption to determine the influence of incremental innovations in Digital Platforms.

4. Research Methodology

A survey with a questionnaire was conducted to fulfill the objectives of the study. After screening out the incomplete responses, a total of 837 samples are finally considered for analyzing the beliefs laid down for the research. The respondents were selected based on judgment sampling where the criterion for selection was the use of any digital platform for availing service at least once in the past.

4.1. *Research instrument*

The survey instrument formulated is a structured questionnaire where two separate sections are constructed for each objective. For the first objective, the questionnaire has three questions where the first one is dichotomous (*Yes/No*) in nature enquiring if the respondent remembers any service that made his/her life easier when launched online. The respondents marking "Yes" to this question go on to answer the next two questions which are open-ended in nature. The respondents are required to mention the name of the service they recall *(as an answer to the first question)* and the approximate year in which they had started using the online service. While a respondent answering "No" to the first question automatically falls into the category of users who are not affected by the services going digital.

For the second objective, the respondents are presented with ten statements that represent each level of adoption, which are mutually exclusive. The respondent is required to select the statement that matches his/her situation the most. The ten statements are expanded from the "Level of Adoption" (LoA) scale constructed by Mrazek and Orr [2009]. LoA scale is a combination of the Levels of Use (LoU) matrix by Hall *et al.* [1975] and stages of concern indices created initially to understand the adoption of technologies in the educational sector. Hall *et al.* [1975] stress that innovation adoption is not merely a decision point but an entire process that individual experiences. The experience level of each individual during the entire process must be described behaviorally and systematically for the innovations to be used effectively. However, as individual experiences are subjected to high variations the LoU is capable of capturing each level appropriately. LoU consists of eight levels that are mutually exclusive and vary from being unaware of innovation to being actively involved in its use. It describes various states of innovation that an individual could be in. But the LoU does not explain the causes of attitudes responsible when a person is put on a particular level. The LoU adoption stages are "non-use", "orientation", "preparation", "mechanical use", "routine", "refinement", "integration", and "renewal". The difference between LoU and LoA seems to be in their methods. While the former uses focused interviews for collecting data, the latter is an instrument for collecting self-reported data; also the LoU uses the descriptors, LoA focuses mostly on designing easier statements for identification of the level. The authors suggest that the LoA could be used over time to collect information on the implementation of innovation across a population. Moreover, the same set of statements, if framed effectively, can be used for longitudinal research. The ten statements proposed for the current study are influenced by the LoA as self-reported data is sought here. They are mutually exclusive and are arranged in order of their level of occurrence. For example, if a respondent is at level 1 then his/her adoption level of the frequent changes made in digital platforms is lower than the respondent in level 2. These statements have been defined and calibrated into the adopter levels based on their state of adoption. A detailed discussion on this is offered in Sec. 7. We present the statements constructed for the study in Table 1.

4.2. *Sampling*

The nature of the objectives requires detailed self-reported data on their level of adoption of innovations in digital platforms. The respondents must have experience of using online modes for availing services, and it is important to select the study locale to seek the targeted respondents. We need a population that is somehow well off to use different services that might have added some innovation in the near past. Unlike developed regions of the world where this is not at all a concern, we faced the tough task of deciding about a cluster of populations who could offer us good and study-worthy data. Since the study is conducted in Assam (a state of India) we relied on the Employment Livelihood Quality Index (ELQI) of the Assam Human

Table 1. List of ten statements for measuring adoption level.

Level	Statement
1	I don't know anything about the frequent modifications made in the Digital Platforms
2	I think I have some information/idea about these improvements
3	I know about the improvements and I am thinking about whether it might be useful for me
4	I think I know enough about this kind of modifications made in the Digital Platforms
5	I think I know as much as necessary about these improvements and I am preparing to use it
6	I am already using the modifications in Digital Platforms while learning the skills necessary to use it properly and effectively
7	I use the modifications regularly without having much difficulty
8	I use such modifications regularly while finding out ways of changing its use to improve the results
9	I discuss with my friends to develop ways in which we can use these improvements to get better results
10	I still use these modifications but am exploring other technologies to replace it that will be better

Development Survey [2014]. The ELQI considers several socio-economic factors while listing the districts which include factors like the proportion of workers having regular salaried employment, percent of workers in non-agricultural sectors, average per capita income from different sources, the proportion of marginal social groups in the total population, level of education, etc. Per capita income, which happens to be one of the important components while formulating the index, is considered to be related to the greater use of technology [Pew Research Center (2014)]. After careful consideration, the top four districts are selected for collecting responses as they would ensure good quality data and of the desired number. Armed with the insight provided by the Report, we have decided to collect the samples from four relatively "well-off" districts of Assam, namely, Kamrup Metropolitan, Nalbari, Jorhat, and Sibsagar. Primary data collection in these districts was conducted during January–July 2019.

Statistical analyses of the collected data have been conducted using IBM Statistical Packages for Social Sciences (SPSS) and MS Excel.

5. Demographics of the Respondents

As per Statista [2017], in 2016, 74% of total internet users in India were below the age of 35 years, which is predicted to come down to 67% in the year 2020. The data collection follows this pattern of internet usage and hence sample respondents are skewed towards certain categories based on age, education, and income more than the others. Table 2 shows the demographic representation of the data collected. Done

Table 2. Demographic representation of the sample.

Demographics	Frequency	Percent
Residence		
Urban	418	49.9
Non-urban	419	50.1
Age		
15–24	482	57.6
25–34	292	34.9
35–44	36	4.3
45–54	17	2.0
More than 55	10	1.2
Gender		
Male	410	49.0
Female	427	51.0
Education level		
Undergraduate	292	34.9
Graduate	303	36.2
Post graduate	242	28.9
Income		
Non-earning	452	54.0
Earning	385	46.0

6. Developing a Time Horizon for Adoption of Innovations

The main aim of the work is to determine the proportion of innovators and consequently the largest adopter category from the categories given by Rogers [1983]. A total of 49% of the respondents went on to answer the name of the innovation that made the highest impact on their lives. The digital innovations mentioned are mostly seen to fall into eight broad categories and to make the innovations service-specific from this point on we move forward with these eight categories. The launch year of each of these eight innovations has been collected using reliable secondary sources.

Table 3 gives an overall picture of the eight categories with their launch year details and the frequency of responses in each of them. While most of the services are launched at the same time throughout the country, the state of Assam got its first online food delivery services operating from 2018. The launch years are generated from extant literature and dates are expected to be correct as the reference materials are found to be reliable.

Even though the total responses were 837, as much as 427 respondents have reported being "Unaffected" users and hence not considered as a part of Table 3. The most popular service is seen to be shopping (14.3%) followed by banking (11.9%) and online bookings (9.6%).

6.1. *Adoption score*

To fulfill the objective, we need to identify the number of respondents in each of the adopter categories, and to do that an adoption score needs to be calculated. We asked the respondents about their starting year of use of the specified services. We have assumed that starting to use the service through various platforms on the internet in itself is an indication of the adoption of innovation. Thus, we have decided to use the following formula for generating the adoption score.

$$\text{Adoption score} = D_U \div D_L,$$

where

D_U is the duration of using the mentioned online service in years,
D_L is the duration of the launch of the mentioned online service in years.

As an example, one respondent mentioned the services of the online shopping site Flipkart as helpful and she has been using Flipkart since 2015. The launch year of Flipkart is 2007 (refer to Table 3), thus

$$\text{Duration of launch in years} = 2019{-}2007 = 12 \text{ years},$$

$$\text{Duration of use in years} = 2019{-}2015 = 4 \text{ years},$$

$$\text{Adoption score of the respondent} = 4/12 = 0.333.$$

We have calculated the Adoption Score calculated for each of the 410 adopters. The score is inversely proportional to the time taken for adoption. That is, fast adopters shall score higher, while late one will be scoring less. We have used the Visual Binning process to categorize them into different segments. The process enables us to divide the value into a limited number of continuous distinct groups. We have taken

Table 3. List of services stated by respondents.

Service	Details	Launch year	Frequency	Percent
Banking	The first online internet banking platform was provided by ICICI bank [Iyengar and Belvalkar (2010)]	1996	100	11.9
Shopping	Flipkart started its operations in 2007 after which Amazon came to India in 2012 [Flipkart Stories (2017)]	2007	120	14.3
Information seeking	Here, the first launch of Google is taken as in most of the cases the term "Google" was mentioned for information seeking.	1998	32	3.9
Bookings	IRCTC first launched the online booking platform in India [Khandelwal (2019)]	2002	80	9.6
Bill payments	The first player to bring in online bill payments through e-wallets was Paytm [Kochar (2016)]	2013	15	1.8
Social media	Though the first social media was launched way back in 1997, the one that had gained popularity in India was Orkut [Mehra (n.d.)].	2004	22	2.6
Food delivery	Food delivery apps have very recently started its operation in the state of Assam. Swiggy ventured into the Assam followed by Zomato in the previous year [Financial Express (2018)]	2018	21	2.5
Wallets	India's first e-wallet was called "Wallet365.com" launched. The product was in association with Yes Bank for conducting the payment services. [CIOL Bureau (2006)]	2006	20	2.4
Total			410	49.0

+1 standard deviation as the cut-off point to generate the groups. The responses show a large number (51%) of users who could not remember any online service being influential in their lives. This category has been named as the "Unaffected" users. As more than half of the respondents fell into the Unaffected category of users, we decided to club two of the Rogers adopter categories into one namely — late majority and laggards. Both these categories by definition suggest similar situations like they use an innovation only after their benefits are proven and are adopted by the majority of the population.

Table 4 shows the modified adopter categories and their "strength" in terms of frequency.

It is seen that most of the respondents fall into the category of Early Majority (31.1%) followed by Early Adopters (10.5%). However, interestingly, the number of Innovators (6.1%) is seen to be more than that of the Laggards (1.3%). However, the fact remains that the Unaffected category (51%) is the largest, where the respondents could not think of any such innovation online that made their life easier.

Table 4. Adopter categories of innovations in digital platforms.

Adopter category	Range	Frequency	Percent
Innovators	0.52+	51	6.1
Early Adopters	0.28–0.51	88	10.5
Early Majority	0.05–0.27	260	31.1
Laggards	<= 0.04	11	1.3
Total		410	49
Unaffected	427	51	

It will be interesting to see if these adopter categories can be related to demography. Thus, we have conducted a few tests to compare the average scores of respondents across common demographic variables. Relevant hypotheses are reproduced in the following.

H_{01}: *The adopter category of a digital platform user doesn't depend on his/her gender.*
H_{02}: *The age of the user doesn't determine the adopter category of the individual.*
H_{03}: *The innovativeness of the user is irrespective of his/her level of education.*
H_{04}: *The adopter category of the user is regardless of his/her place of residence in the country.*
H_{05}: The *earning status of the user is irrelevant while acquiring his/her adopter category.*

6.1.1. *Interpretation*

For the four demographic variables, independent t-tests were conducted to find out if there exist differences in the means of the demographic sections for the adopter categories. There are almost equivalent numbers of responses in each of the demographic categories with a certain difference in their mean scores. The results of the t-test show that the p-value is greater than the significance level of 0.05 for the variables of gender, age, and place of residence. However, equality of variances is achieved in the case of income i.e. $p < 0.05$ (refer Table 5). Thus, we go on rejecting

Table 5. Mean and SD of demographic variables.

Demographics	N	Mean of each category	p-value	Decision on H_0
Male	185	0.2904		
Female	225	0.2537	0.089	Not rejected
Above 25 years	188	0.2642		
Below 25 years	222	0.2774	0.898	Not rejected
Urban	216	0.2797		
Non-urban	194	0.2598	0.070	Not rejected
Earning	184	0.2991		
Non-earning	226	0.2468	0.012	Rejected

Table 6. Mean and SD for education level.

Demographics	N	Mean of each category	SD	F	Sig. p-value
Education level					
Undergraduate	129	0.2124	0.1675		
Graduate	137	0.3077	0.2653		
Post graduate	144	0.2865	0.2473	60.137	0.002

Table 7. Summary of one way ANOVA conducted.

		Mean difference	Sig. p-value
Undergraduate	Graduate	−0.09523	**0.001**
	Post graduate	−0.07405	**0.011**
Graduate	Undergraduate	0.09523	0.001
	Post graduate	0.02118	0.769
Post graduate	Undergraduate	0.07405	0.011
	Graduate	−0.02118	0.769

Table 8. Linear regression analysis model summary

				Unstandardized coefficient		Standardized coefficient	
Model	R square	Adjusted R square	Sig	B	SE	Beta	Sig
Constant				−40.115	2.773		0.000
Launch year	0.342	0.340	0.000	0.020	0.001	0.585	0.000

by reporting that there is a statistical difference between the mean scores of earning users and non-earning users of digital platforms (Tables 6–8).

6.1.2. *Interpretation*

To determine the relationship of different adopter categories and the level of education, a one way ANOVA is conducted. The F statistic generated is found to be significant ($p < 0.005$) indicating significant differences between the level of education and the corresponding adopter categories. The *post hoc* test results show that there are significant differences between undergraduate–graduate users and undergraduate–postgraduate users in their adopter categories. However, the difference between the graduate–postgraduate users' adopter categories is not significant. The mean score for the graduate users is seen to be the highest followed by post-graduate users and undergraduate users respectively. The mean difference, however, from the two significant sets is seen to be more between that of the undergraduate and graduate users.

The adoption scores calculated have been used to generate an indicative graph depicting the time horizon for the adoption of innovations in digital platforms. We took the launch year in ascending order for the X-axis and put the resultant adoption

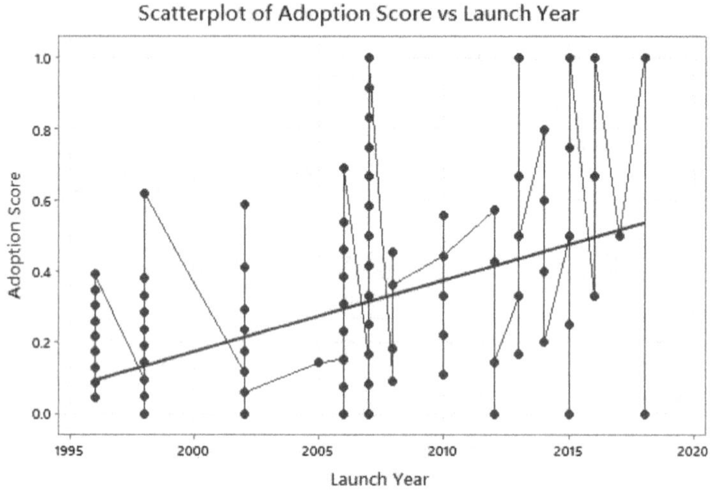

Fig. 1. Adoption score pattern against launch year.

scores on the Y-axis. It returns a zigzag path. The graph is shown in Fig. 1. However, the resultant trendline indicates a linear relationship between the two. To carry forward our quest, we have decided to conduct a linear regression analysis to generate an indicative equation for fitting the line from the data.

6.1.3. *Interpretation*

Table 9 shows the results from the analysis conducted and it can be seen that the launch year significantly explains 34.2% variance in the adoption score. When we look at the regression coefficient they are seen to be significant and we move forward to forming the regression equation:

$$\text{Adoption score} = -40.115 + 0.020 * \text{ Launch year.}$$

The regression equation illustrates that with recent launch years the adoption score of the user increases indicating that the innovations that are launched in recent times are being adopted at a faster rate. Though the figure does not give a strong fit of the line to the data, it strengthens the logic that the newer is the innovation, the higher will be the rate of adoption. When we look at the largest adopter category — Early Majority in the adoption score range of 0.05–0.27 it is seen that their number is more because the launch year of the innovations mentioned is as early as 1995–2005 whereas the mean year of use amongst all the users is found to be 2016. The laggards ($\leq$0.04) are found to be present in a certain number across all the periods — I ndicating the presence of such users over time. We have tried to generate a visual representation in Fig. 2 showing the proportion of each adopter category (*including the Unaffected*).

The fastest adopters of innovations (termed here as Innovators) are comprised of a small section of the total target population. They are followed by Early Adopters,

Table 9. Levels of adoption of incremental innovations in digital platforms.

Level number	Level of adoption	Definition
1	Non-user	This stage is a depiction of the ignorance of digital platform users about the frequent changes that are occurring The users of digital platforms who are not aware of who is not being able to recognize the changes occurring in the platforms
2	Aware	The users here are conscious of the frequently modified versions of the digital platforms they use.
3	Contemplative	They have serious contemplation before adopting any new modifications every time they are introduced on a digital platform by measuring every pros and cons of it. This stage involves the respondents thought process in whether to use the changes being offered to them regularly or not
4	Enlightened	The users have sufficient knowledge about these innovations. They are exposed to the modifications happening in digital platforms for an ample period and can grab the fundamental nature of it
5	Hot prospects	A user in this stage is indeed a hot prospect for adopting the incremental innovations in digital platforms as they are convinced of the advantages of frequently revising the platforms and are about to use it shortly.
6	Newbies	They are the new users of the incremental innovations occurring in the digital platforms who are enthusiastic about exploring better ways to use and utilize the new trend as they are getting used to it.
7	Adopters	The users here have fully adopted these changes and are comfortable using them daily without much difficulties and hesitation.
8	Utilisers	The users in this stage are well versed with the existing ways of modifications and are putting them to its best possible use
9	Restless	The stage represents the users of incremental innovations engaged in peer discussion and ideas to perform better using the ones provided in the digital platforms
10	User innovators	The respondent here is well informed and an expert in the digital field and is in a continuous process of adopting other improvements released in the digital sphere

and then by the Early Majority. Early Majority covers a relatively larger proportion. The main concern about the adoption of incremental service innovations in digital platforms is the target population's rate of instant adoption of frequent modifications. Looking at Fig. 1, we can conclude that as the chances of the users being innovators increase with its launch year, in the coming time, the adoption of incremental innovations in digital platforms can be expected to grow at a faster pace. The Laggards forming the least crowded group amongst all is a relatively good sign. But the major concern still lies with the majority of the population being covered by the Unaffected users (51%) who are least concerned about the services offering innovation. Are unaffected users more because of frequent incremental innovations? Well, there might be a possibility!

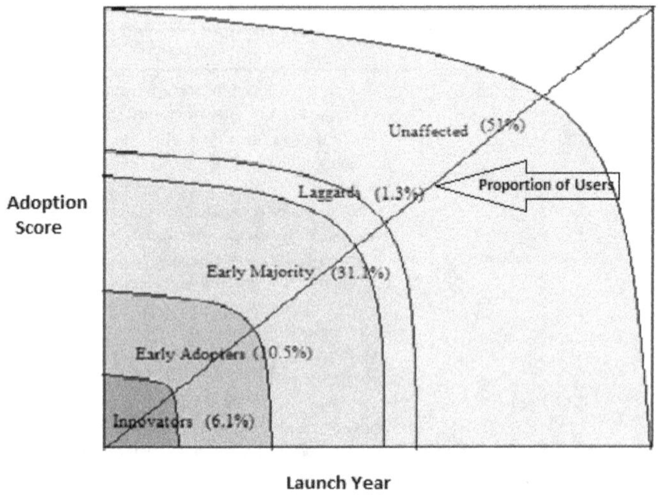

Fig. 2. Time horizon of adopter categories.

7. Formulating the Levels of Adoption of Incremental Service Innovations in Digital Platforms

As discussed in Sec. 1, incremental innovations reinforce the potential of the existing products or services with the help of different emerging technologies. Ringberg *et al.* [2019] state that an incremental innovation occurs when there is a new result created from the existing technology and mindset of the organization. Incremental innovations are iterative and most organizations fall into this category of innovation. The digital platforms continuously employ incremental innovations either in the form of marketing strategies like rewards (cashback, discounts, etc.) or in product enhancement like new features added with each upgraded version. While looking into the digitization situation in India, it made progress a few years back. With 560 million internet users in 2019, the internet penetration in India showed an increase from 7.5% in 2010 to 34% in 2017 [Diwanji (2019)]. The rapid growth in internet penetration, and the simultaneous incremental innovations in digital platforms by the service providers, might give rise to some confusion. Though the rate of internet use is seen to be increasing, there still exists the problem of the digital divide in India, which might demotivate the new users due to the constant changes in the digital canvas. This section discusses in detail the characteristics of each of the ten levels that one goes through in the process of adopting incremental innovations. The motive of the objective is to present an overview of the dynamic stage of digital platforms in an emerging economy like India.

The ten levels of adoption are based on the LoA by Mazrek and Orr [2009] due to the similarities like innovation. However, here, each of the ten levels has been individually named based on their characteristics to better identify them. Table 9 represents the stages in ascending order of adoption.

7.1. *Categorising the variables into levels*

The ten levels capture every transition a user makes in the process of adopting incremental service innovations in detail. Based on the richness of experience of the user, the levels are grouped into three categories — Beginner, Enhanced, and Advanced.

(1) Beginners — Non-users, Aware users, and Contemplative users fall into this category of adopters. The respondents corresponding to this section are beginners in the entire process of adopting incremental service innovation in digital platforms. They are yet to discover their intention to either use or adapt these kinds of frequent innovations or to discard the use of it completely.
(2) Enhanced — The second broad category of respondents refers to the ones who form the user base of the digital platforms which include the Enlightened users, Hot Prospects, Newbies, and the Adopters. These users are actively using all the frequent changes that the digital platforms are making without many difficulties. The users are content with the benefits arising out of the modifications.
(3) Advanced — The advanced level of users includes the Utilisers, Restless Users, and the User Innovators. These respondents are at a higher level in terms of understanding and using the various modifications made in the digital platforms. These categories of users are in constant search for better ways to make transactions in a digital platform and hence can give the marketers a tough time.

Table 10 shows the frequency of users in each of the categories

As discussed in Sec. 6, India is growing in terms of internet users every year, and the results are shown in Table 10 to validate the trend. As the concept of availing of different services online is comparatively new in India, the number of respondents in the Beginner category is seen to be the highest followed by Enhanced and Advanced users. However, in the beginner category, the number of Aware users being higher is a positive indication of the improving conditions.

Table 10. Frequencies of users in each level of adoption.

Category	Levels of adoption in the category	Frequency
		473 (56.5)
Beginner	Non-user	137 (16.4)
	Aware	234 (28.0)
	Contemplative	102 (12.1)
		264 (31.6)
Enhanced	Enlightened	45 (5.4)
	Hot prospects	66 (7.9)
	Newbies	80 (9.6)
	Adopters	73 (8.7)
		100 (11.9)
Advanced	Utilisers	38 (4.5)
	Restless	32 (3.8)
	User innovators	30 (3.6)

7.2. *Differences in the characteristics of the categories*

The questionnaire enquired about certain digital aspects of the respondents as well, and based on the differences spotted (*from the responses*) among the three categories of users made the grouping of the categories stronger. Here are some of the most relatable differences amongst the categories. The first variable is the internet experience of the users in terms of years. The Internet experience of the respondents has been divided into two groups — users with less than three years of internet experience and the ones with more than three years of experience. When the percentage variation in the three groups is considered, it is seen that the number of Beginners with more than three years of experience is at 73.8%, for Enhanced it increases to 75%, and for the Advanced, it further increases to 87%. The second variable is the awareness of the users about the frequent modifications in digital platforms. These are the modifications that result in incremental innovations. It is seen that the awareness does increase with each category of users like the Beginners stands at 71.2%, Enhanced users at 79.5%, and Advanced users at 88%. Chi-Squared tests are conducted to determine if there is a statistically significant association between the three adopter categories and these two variables. The results generated are Table 11.

7.2.1. *Interpretation*

The p-value for both the variables when measured is seen to be significant at 0.05 levels. This confirms that there is some kind of significant association between the adopter categories based on awareness about the innovations in digital platforms and the internet experience of the users. The post-hoc test results based on the Phi values signify that there is a moderate level of relationship between the two variables and the adopter categories.

The users were enquired about the type of online services they mostly prefer, the top picks from each adopter category revealed certain interesting insights about how it might affect the transition process across the levels. The Beginners mostly use digital platforms for searching for information (32.8%) followed by banking (27.1%) while the enhanced users prefer online shopping the most (32.6%) followed by information seeking (30.7%). The Beginners involve the section of users who are aware of non-users and are contemplating the idea of using such innovations. In such a circumstance, using the information gathered from digital platform might help them to decide to whether to use the incremental innovations or not Advanced users, on the other hand, they are already comfortable with the frequent innovations and continuously look for ways to improve their experience with the help of information sought from the digital platforms. The motives and outcomes from the commonly

Table 11. Chi-squared test results summary.

Variables	Value	Sig. p-value	Phi value
Pearson chi-square			
(a) Awareness about incremental innovations in digital platforms	15.504	0.000	0.136
(b) Internet experience (in number of years)	12.512	0.050	0.122

preferred service online by the beginners and advanced users are thus different. The Enhanced set of users are in the mid of the other two categories in terms of awareness about digital platforms and the internet experience of the users. Nevertheless, they do exhibit certain unique characteristics of their own. As such in the case of users preferring either the use of apps or websites for operating digital platforms, it is seen that Enhanced users prefer websites more compared to Beginners and Advanced users. Another difference that the Enhanced users show lies in the preference of a traditional mode of availing services over digital ways more than that of the beginners and advanced users.

8. Findings

The insights gained from the study provide different aspects to the theoretical and practical framework of innovations in digital platforms. The most commonly used categorization in the adoption of innovations—Roger's adopter categories is used to define the different stages of a user of digital platforms. Five distinct categories of adopters are outlined, namely—Innovators, Early Adopters, Early Majority, Laggards, and Unaffected. The numbers of Unaffected users are seen to dominate implying that maximum Indian consumers are not bothered about innovation carried out in digital platforms. The demographic representation of this group of users revealed certain interesting characteristics about them. It is seen that most of the Unaffected users are seen to be in the age group of 15–24 years and are mostly undergraduate-level users. As can be predicted from their age group and education level, these users are mainly those who do not have an earning source of their own (*as revealed statistically too*). The places of residence for these users are in the non-rural areas of the country. However, the male and female ratios for Unaffected users are seen to be almost equal. Thus, it can be assumed that the young digital users who have not entered into their phase of earning and spend most of their time online residing in urban and semi-urban areas are not likely to turn loyal towards any digital innovation that easily. As the number of users in this category is found to be the highest, the marketers have a high potential of converting them into loyal consumers. They could be moulded into avid users by the time they start earning on their own by offering services at a low cost with updated features. As majority are seen hailing from non-rural areas, the spectrum of offerings does increase and marketers can dwell further into this section of users to earn a colossal amount of revenue. Amongst the users adopting digital innovations, the number of Early Majority is the highest followed by Early Adopters. The results indicate that though most of the digital platform users in India are not that affected by the online transition of daily services, the ones that are using these transitions in the form of innovations prefer adopting them only after a certain period. The Innovators are the fastest adopters with a lower percentage. What is further interesting that the percentage of Laggards is even lower than that of the Innovators. Thus, most of the Indian users are quick enough to adopt a digital innovation before it wears out but are also skeptical enough to review the benefits before finally using it. The statistical analysis indicates the presence of a linear relationship between the adoption score of the user and the launch year of the innovation. In simpler words, the chances of a newer innovation with a closer launch date has better chances of getting adopted. Demographic associations with the adopter categories are found to be weak except for the education level, which is seen to have a significant influence on the classification of the adopter categories. In the second objective, we specifically address the case of frequent incremental innovations made in the digital platforms that often have been overlooked by academic researchers. Ten mutually exclusive stages showing each step from being unaware to actively seeking every benefit out of each change are presented. The results indicate certain differences between these ten levels of adoption based on digital factors like awareness about the incremental innovations, preference of traditional or online modes of services, internet experience, and the highest availing services online. To get an instant recognition about the stage of any user, three simple categories are created out of the ten levels – Beginner, Enhanced, and Advanced. As discussed in Sec. 7.3, the percentage of users in each category aptly represents the current situation in India. The number of Beginners of the adoption of incremental innovations in digital platforms is the highest, followed by Enhanced users and then the Advanced users. The adoption of digital innovation in an emerging economy like India is thus at a very early stage where users take time to learn and understand the advantages of online services. However, a lower number of Laggards in adopting innovations and non-aware users in case of incremental innovations is a positive indication. The graph estimating a rise in the rate of adoption with a newer innovation launch gives an expectation of a rise in the adoption of innovations shortly.

9. Conclusion and Scope for Further Research

The marketers/digital platform providers can use the segregation based on the adoption level for expanding their user base by employing relevant strategies for specific users. The Beginners lack proper awareness about the benefits of adopting from frequent innovations. This group needs certain initiatives from marketers to lure them to use and enjoy the dynamic state of the digital platforms. Directly reaching out to the users via electronic sources to offer special benefits, making special offers to use the reward points while availing other services online, etc. could be beneficial. The Enhanced users are content with the benefits arising out of the modifications and hence are assets for the marketers. The main aim of the digital platform providers would be to manage this section of users to maintain the status quo. The innovations that make this section of users happy must be identified and further modified. Advanced users are the ones who are difficult to retain and demand special attention from the marketers. They are in search of maximum benefits and would not think before switching to competitors. They must be updated with the offerings and benefits to refrain from switching. Thus, the study portrays the picture of the ongoing situation on adoption of digital innovations in an emerging economy like India. Although the adoption process is at its initial stage, there is an increase in the effort and interest of the internet users towards understanding the benefits and efficiency online innovations provide.

In the future, the association of the stages of adoption with different factors affecting the adoption behavior of users could be explored. It is also seen that there is a comparatively lower section of users in the innovators and laggards category than the rest. This suggests that the users prefer adopting an innovation only during a certain period from launch. The factors impacting this kind of cognition in the mind of the users could be an interesting area to deal with.

References

Akesson, M. and AkramA. (2011). Value network transformation by digital service innovation in the vehicle industry. *PACIS 2011 Proceedings*.

Alam, I. (2010). Does the service innovation process differ across cultures?*Asia Pacific Journal of Marketing and Logistics*, **22**, 4: 460–472, doi: 1108/13555851011090501.

Alam, I. (2012). New service development in India's business-to-business financial services sector. *Journal of Business and Industrial Marketing*, **27**, 3: 228–241, doi: 10.1108/08858621211207243.

Bharwani, S. and Mathews, D. (2016). Customer service innovations in the Indian hospitality industry. *Worldwide Hospitality and Tourism Themes*, **8**, 4: 416–431, doi: 10.1108/WHATT-04-2016-0020.

Belvalkar, M. and Iyengar, J. (2010). Case study of online banking in India: User behaviors and design guidelines. *Human Work Interaction Design: Usability in Social, Cultural, and Organizational Contexts*. Springer, Berlin, pp. 180–188.

Busagara, T., Mori, N., Mossberg, L., Jani, D. and Andersson, T. (2020). Customer information sharing and new service development: is there a link? *The Bottom Line*, **33**, 2: 133–147, doi: 10.1108/BL-09-2019-0112.

Calantone, R. and Rosanna, G. (2002). A critical look at technological innovation typology and innovativeness terminology: a literature review. *The Journal of Product Innovation Management*, **19**, 2: 110–132, doi: 10.1111/1540-5885.1920110.

Chichkanov, N. (2020). The role of client knowledge absorptive capacity for innovation in KIBS. *Journal of Knowledge Management*, doi: 1108/JKM-05-2020-0334.

CIOL Bureau (2006). *India's First E-Wallet Launched.* Available at https://www.ciol.com/indias-wallet-launched-2/[accessed October 2019].

Davis, F. D. (1989). Perceived usefulness, perceived ease of use, and user acceptance of information. *MIS Quarterly*, **13**, 3: 319–340. Available at https://www.jstor.org/stable/249008.

Deloitte (2015). *Digital Media: Rise of On-demand Content.* CISCO Mobile VNI report.

Diwanji, S. (n.d.). *Digital population in India as of January 2019 (in millions).* Available at https://www.statista.com/statistics/309866/india-digital-population/.

Financial Express (2018). Swiggy expands services in 8 new cities including Vijayawada, Nashik, Guwahati. *Financial Express.* Available at https://www.financialexpress.com/industry/swiggy-expands-services-in-8-new-cities-including-vijayawada-nashik-guwahati/1320303/.

Flipkart Stories (2017). 10 years of flipkart—A timeline of milestones. *Flipkart Stories.* Available at https://stories.flipkart.com/10-years-timeline-milestones/.

Gene, H. E., Loucks, S. F., Rutherford, W. L. and Newlove, B. W. (1975). Levels of use of the innovation: A framework for analyzing innovation adoption. *Journal of Teacher Education*, **26**, 1: 52–56, doi: 10.1177%2F002248717502600114.

Hale, D. and Thakur, R. (2013). Service innovation: A comparative study of U.S. and Indian service firms. *Journal of Business Research*, **66**, 1108–1123.

Hurmelinna-Laukkanen, P., Sainio, L.-M. and Jauhiainen, T. (2008). Appropriability regime for radical and incremental innovations. *R&D Management*, **38**, 3: 278–289, doi: 10.1111/j.1467-9310.2008.00512.x-i1.

Khandelwal, S. (2019). *Believe it or not, IRCTC made it easier to book railway tickets — and could now get to run trains.* Available at https://scroll.in/article/928933/believe-it-or-not-irctc-made-it-easier-to-book-railway-tickets-and-could-now-get-to-run-trains [accessed 23 October 2019].

Kochar, R. (2016). How big is the Indian bill payment market? *Entrepreneur India.* Available at https://www.entrepreneur.com/article/273148 [accessed October 2019].

Lopes, L. F. and Godinho, M. M. (2019). Innovation and productivity in services: a methodological approach. *International Journal of Innovation and Technology Management*, **16**, 5: doi: 1142/S0219877019500342.

Mehra, A. (n.d.). Evolution of social media in India. *Silicon India Blogs.* Available at https://blogs.siliconindia.com/a2anuragmehra/Evolution_of_Social_Media_in_India-bid-7PZ8vuDN20048653.html [accessed 23 October 2019].

Mrazek, R. and Orr, D. (2009). Developing the level of adoption survey to inform collaborative discussion regarding educational innovation. *Canadian Journal of Learning and Technology*, **35**, 2.

OKD Institute of Social Change and Development. (2014). *Assam Human Development Report.* Government of India, Guwahati.

Pappenheim, B. C. (2016). Incremental innovation effects on consumer perception. *Science Journal of Business Management*, doi: 10.7237/sjbm/272.

Rautela, S. and Mavale, S. (2016). Incremental innovation for sustainable growth in restaurant businesses: global practices for the growth of local business. *Annual Research Journal of SCMS*, **4**, 80–87.

Ringberg, T., Reihlen, M. and Rydén. P. (2019). The technology-mindset interactions: Leading to incremental, radical or revolutionary innovations. *Industrial Marketing Management*, **79**, 102–113, doi: 10.1016/j.indmarman.2018.06.009.

Rogers, E. M. (1983). *Diffusion of Innovations*, 3rd edn. The Free Press, New York.

Sahin, I. (2006). Detailed review of Rogers' diffusion of innovations theory and educational technology-related studies based on Rogers' theory. *Turkish Online Journal of Educational Technology*, **5**, 2: 14–23.

Steiber, A., Aleange, S., Ghosh, S. and Goncalves, D. (2020). Digital transformation of industrial firms: an innovation diffusion perspective. *European Journal of Innovation*, doi: 10.1108/EJIM-01-2020-0018.

Sundbo, J. (1997). Management of innovation in services. *The Service Industries Journal*, **17**, 3: 432–455.

Velayati, R., Shabani, E. and Nazarian, A. (2020). Hope for the best, prepare for the worst: Barriers to service innovation. *Qualitative Market Research*, **23**, 4: 843–863, doi: 1108/QMR-05-2020-0062.

Ven, A. H. (1986). Central problems in the management of innovation. *Management Science*, **32**, 5: 590–607. Available at https://www.jstor.org/stable/2631848.

Venkatesh, V. and Bala, H. (2008). Technology acceptance model 3and a research agenda on interventions. *Decision Sciences*, **39**, 2: 273–315.

Venkatesh, V. and Davis, F. D. (2000). A theoretical extension of the technology acceptance model: Four longitudinal field studies. *Management Science*, **46**, 2: 186–204. 0025-1909/00/4602/0186$05.00.

Youngjin, Y., Henfridsson, O. and Lyytinen, K. (2010). The new organizing logic of digital innovation: An agenda for information systems research. *Information Systems Research*, **21**, 4: 724–735, doi: 10.1287/isre.1100.0322.

Biography

Dorothy Dutta is a Research Scholar in the Department of Business Administration, Tezpur University, Assam, India

Mrinmoy K. Sarma, is a Professor in the Department of Business Administration, Tezpur University, Assam, India

The Composition of University Entrepreneurial Ecosystems and Academic Entrepreneurship: A UK Study*

Daniel Prokop

School of Geography and Planning, Cardiff University
King Edward VII Avenue, CF10 3WA, Cardiff, Wales, UK
prokopd@cardiff.ac.uk

This paper examines the link between the composition of university entrepreneurial ecosystems and performance of higher education institutions (HEIs) in academic entrepreneurship, specifically founding academic spinoff companies. The paper studies a sample of 160 UK HEIs and their university entrepreneurial ecosystems related to formation of 784 academic spinoffs. It employs social network analysis (SNA) to inspect the composition and connections between university entrepreneurial ecosystems. It finds that HEIs based in better developed university entrepreneurial ecosystems are associated with formation of greater numbers of academic spinoff companies. The best performing ecosystems are based in the Greater South East region. It is concluded that policymakers need to recognize the importance of the composition of the university entrepreneurial ecosystems and the role it plays in academic entrepreneurship.

Keywords: Academic spinoffs; entrepreneurial ecosystems; universities; university entrepreneurial ecosystems; networks; knowledge commercialization.

1. Introduction

As the demand for university knowledge commercialization has grown in significance [Etzkowitz *et al.* (2000); Compagnucci and Spigarelli (2020)], universities are more frequently engaging in Third Mission activities, in part through their own initiative to improve institutional budgets [Chiesa and Piccaluga (2000); Giuri *et al.* (2019)] and/or due to government initiatives to support the generation of wealth and competitiveness [DTI (1993); HM Government (2017)]. Across many university knowledge commercialization modes – e.g. licensing patents, consultancy, and collaborative research – a growing attention is being paid to the academic spinoff companies by both institutional investors [Chiesa and Piccaluga (2000); Bank of England (2001); Library House/UBS (2006); Lenzer and Kulczakowicz (2021)] and economic development policymakers [Lambert (2003); Shane (2004)], especially from a regional perspective [Huggins *et al.* (2008)].

*This chapter was originally published in International Journal of Innovation and Technology Management, Vol. 19, No. 6, March 2018, published by World Scientific Publishing, Singapore. Reprinted with permission.

The role played by universities in securing the success of academic spinoffs goes beyond considerations of IP protection, and involves the provision of access to business incubators [Library House/UBS (2006)] and science parks [Link and Scott (2005)], as well as networks of investors [Mosey and Wright (2007); Munari *et al.* (2018); Bonardo *et al.* (2011)] and experienced entrepreneurs [Lockett *et al.* (2003); Library House/BVCA (2005)] that can be considered as a university's network capital [Huggins (2010)]. These actors, inclusive of Technology Transfer Offices (TTOs), which play important roles in university knowledge commercialization through spinoff formation [Fini *et al.* (2017)] and contribute to their longer-term success [Prokop *et al.* (2019)], constitute the core components of the university entrepreneurship ecosystem (UEE) [Hayter *et al.* (2018)].

The current development of knowledge concerning the role of the UEE in the success of academic spinoffs is largely fragmented [Phan and Siegel (2006); Hayter *et al.* (2018)] and focused on internal institutional or spinoff characteristics [Jensen and Thursby (2001); Di Gregorio and Shane (2003); Lockett *et al.* (2003); Shane (2004); Debackere and Veugelers (2005); Clarysse *et al.* (2011)], with the recent qualitative evidence pointing to the importance of configurations of the UEEs [Prokop (2021)]. Furthermore, the literature concerning the critical perspectives and problems of academic spinoffs and spinoff company formation has been growing in strength [Lambert (2003); Siegel *et al.* (2007); Swamidass and Vulasa (2008); Harrison and Leitch (2010); Markman *et al.* (2008); Gianiodis *et al.* (2016); Lindholm Dahlstrand *et al.* (2016)], emphasizing the evident need for a more holistic approach to researching the topic. Specifically, little is known whether a more developed UEE composed of most of these actors, i.e. business incubators, science parks, investors, experienced entrepreneurs, TTOs, is linked to greater spinoff numbers.

The paper systematically reviews the importance of the university entrepreneurial ecosystem indicated above in the process of university spinoff creation by applying a network perspective. It has an exploratory character and attempts to shed light on the following question: Is the composition of the university entrepreneurial ecosystems associated with supporting spinoff company creation? The paper is based on an empirical study of 160 HEIs and their ecosystems in the UK. It leads to the consideration of structural disparities between spinoff company formation performance across the UEEs, and offers recommendations on reducing these disparities. The key contribution of the paper is in recognizing a link between the spinoff formation and the composition of the university entrepreneurial ecosystems, with those that are more developed generating a greater number of firms. Specifically, HEIs that intend to focus on the academic spinoff formation activity require an ecosystem composed of business incubators, science parks, investors, and external entrepreneurs.

2. Academic Entrepreneurship and University Entrepreneurial Ecosystems

2.1. *Academic spinoffs and economic development*

The "Third Mission" extension of the key roles (i.e. teaching and research) of the universities has drawn an increased and intensified interest from academia

[Goldstein (2010)] and government [e.g. Lambert [2003] to the now officially ascribed responsibility of universities for a significant part of economic development [Lawton Smith (2007); Wong *et al.* (2007); Etzkowitz and Dzisah (2008); Lopez *et al.* (2009); Goldstein (2010)]. The fact that the university contribution to the economic development has been formalized does not mean there was no such contribution before. The difference between the two is the recent focus on the university research commercialization as playing more important role in the economic development, rather than typical university inputs, e.g. employment, expenditure, quantity of students [Goldstein *et al.* (1995); Garrido-Yserte and Gallo-Rivera (2010)] which do not capture the full scale of economic contribution of the university [Thanki (1999)]. These effects could also be observed from the creation of academic spinoff companies [Berggren and Lindholm Dahlstrand (2009)], accredited with greater economic potential [Lambert (2003); Shane (2004); Phan and Siegel (2006); Siegel *et al.* (2007); Huggins *et al.* (2008)].

As the academic spinoff firms are based on specific innovation [Etzkowitz (1998); Shane (2004)], it is important to note that the size of those companies – predominantly small – [Harrison and Leitch (2010)] may not necessarily act against them in the competitive markets, as small firms have been reported to experience better rates of innovation than their larger counterparts [Gellman Research Associates (1976); The Futures Group (1984); Audretsch (1991); Chakrabarti (1991); Audretsch (1995)]. Furthermore, small innovative firms attracted by university R&D intensity are found to contribute positively to the local/regional economic development both directly and indirectly through related multiplier effects [Kirchhoff *et al.* (2007)]. However, these localized effects could migrate outside if the local/regional absorptive capacity and resources to support the innovative firms are not adequately developed [Christopherson and Clark (2010)].

The studies that focused on the contribution of the university through academic spinoffs have demonstrated positive effects on economic development [Chrisman *et al.* (1995); Lawton Smith (2000); Dahlstrand and Jacobsson (2003); Shane (2004); Clarysse *et al.* (2005); Vincett (2010)]. In the UK some of the economic contribution of the academic spinoffs could also be observed via exits, either through Initial Public Offerings (IPOs) [Wright *et al.* (2007)] or acquisitions, with over 80 having taken place thus far [Prokop *et al.* (2019)]. It is important to note that these contributions become more significant in scale over a longer time frame [Vincett (2010)]. However, not all evidence is large enough in scope to provide a clear and robust picture of the spinoffs' contribution to the economy. Thus, some doubt could be observed as to the economic value of the university spinoffs [Harrison and Leitch (2010)]. Lambert Review [2003] already highlighted a problem of quality versus quantity orientation in university strategies towards academic entrepreneurship, with the evidence suggesting the second to be dominant. This is in many instances a result of focusing support activities on creating rather than developing the spinoffs [Siegel and Wright (2007)]. However, this does not necessarily diminish the importance of spinoffs as an economic development mechanism, as the quantity-orientation follows the logic of intensification of economy-developing activities performed by the universities. Similarly, although based on Higher Education Funding Council for England

(HEFCE) and Higher Education-Business and Community Interaction (HE-BCI) survey data and their own research Harrison and Leitch [2010] argue that the spinoffs' contributions to the economic development are rather insignificant, it is important to note that their contributions require broader consideration in terms of the role played in the local ecosystem [Benneworth and Charles (2005)] and through their non-local links [Prokop (2021)].

2.2. *University entrepreneurial ecosystems*

The concern of many researchers in a recent decade was focused on the effectiveness of the academic spinoff company creation [Meoli and Vismara (2016); Neves and Franco (2018)], but also performance [Corsi *et al.* (2017); Fini *et al.* (2017); Prokop *et al.* (2019)]. However, recent developments in the field suggest that a wider university environment is critical to academic entrepreneurship [Boh *et al.* (2016)]. Specifically, the studies identified a number of key actors that play important roles in supporting academic entrepreneurship that constitute the university's entrepreneurial ecosystem: universities, TTOs, business incubators, science parks, investors, and external entrepreneurs [Hayter *et al.* (2018); Prokop (2021)]. Each of these actors is examined individually below.

2.2.1. *Technology transfer office*

The primary development in the university commercialization activities and the commitment to its increased economic role is expressed in the establishment of an internal unit/department concerned with the knowledge transfer –TTO [Etzkowitz *et al.* (2000); Siegel *et al.* (2007)]. The role of the TTO is principally concerned with administrative burden of technology/knowledge transfer with a focus on legal aspects (IP – Intellectual Property) and commercial exploitation [Huggins (2008); Goldstein (2010)] through, for example, creating a company or licensing the university IP. This administrative function is not definitive as can be found in Siegel *et al.* [2007] who discussed a much wider role of TTOs in relation to strategic decisions concerned with invention disclosure and commercialization, and institutional responsibility. Lockett *et al.* [2003] also stress the importance of TTOs in relation to identifying the commercial opportunities at the universities. In addition to that Shane [2004] also points at another role – providing the "network of stakeholders" (p.76), in particular the providers of "human and financial resources" (p. 78). In essence, the TTO needs to play a role of a boundary spanning actor [Alexander and Martin (2013)] between the university, the spinoff company, and the rest of the UEE.

2.2.2. *Business incubators and science parks*

Business incubators are in essence institutions created to aid new firms, particularly technology-based, by providing a range of business support services, for example office space, equipment and business advice [Grimaldi and Grandi (2005)] to increase their initial survival chances [Sun *et al.* (2007)]. As noted by Sun *et al.* [2007] there is little doubt in the effectiveness of business incubation, proving it to be a vital element of UEEs for academic spinoff companies. The concept of science parks is very close to that of business incubators [Tamasy (2007)], with the difference in scope of support and profile of tenant firms – typically being a mix of startups and subsidiaries of large firms. Thus, science parks still "facilitate commercialization of technologies, stimulate development of technology-based SMEs and promote regional development" [Malairaja and Zawdie (2008, p. 729); Zeng *et al.* (2010)] to as much a degree as business incubators do [Wynarczyk and Raine (2005)]. However, this may come at a different price point for the tenant firms [Tamasy (2007)]. Importantly, whilst these incubating components of the UEE clearly have an important role, there is only limited evidence of their use by academic spinoff companies [e.g. Hewitt-Dundas (2015)], which typically incubate within university departments. However, notably business incubators and science parks may contribute to the availability of entrepreneurial networks for spinoff companies [Prokop (2021)].

2.2.3. *Investors*

The investors in the format of public funds [Huggins (2008)], university venture funding [Munari *et al.* (2018)], business angels [Mosey and Wright (2007)] and venture capital [Bonardo *et al.* (2011)], endow spinoffs with critical start-up resources that typical new firms lack. In 2006 approximately 19% of the UK Venture Capital market's portfolios consisted of university spinoffs or start-ups, with average investment of £3.6 m per company, which was below the average for similar investments in independent start-ups (£4.1 m) and corporate spinoffs (£7.0 m) [Library House/UBS (2006)]. This could be related to the fact that academic ventures are often perceived as high-risk investments by venture capitalists [Harding (2000); Oakey (2003); Shane (2004)], due to their very early stage of technology development and the consequent long time of product-to-market delivery [Shane (2004)]. As a result, it is often hard for the inventors to fund their ventures due to inherent information asymmetry issues, especially considering the low availability of early-stage funding [Murray (1999); Lockett *et al.* (2002); Wright *et al.* (2006); Huggins (2008); Pinch and Sunley (2009)]. This, in particular, emphasizes the need for the university TTOs to develop links with investors which may often mean "life or death" for the new ventures [Shane (2004)]. Such cooperation is typified by very early engagement of specialist spinoff-focused investors that select the most prominent disclosures [Prokop (2021)].

2.2.4. *External entrepreneurs*

Another important part of the UEE is concerned with external entrepreneurs [Franklin *et al.* (2001); Lockett *et al.* (2003); Shane (2004); Library House/BVCA (2005); Wennberg *et al.* (2011)]. The Library House/BVCA [2005] report specifically stresses the importance of TTOs engaging with experienced entrepreneurs in order to develop academic spinoffs, as these contribute commercial [Wennberg *et al.* (2011)] and management [Grandi and Grimaldi (2003)] experience as well as their own networks [Franklin *et al.* (2001)]. As such, they play important roles in spinoff company formation, both passive – expressed in enhanced commercial credibility of the spinoffs [Wright *et al.* (2006)] – and proactive – reflected in fund-raising [Vohora *et al.* (2004)]. This is especially important, as venture capitalists assess a company's investment attractiveness by focusing strongly on its management team [Gompers *et al.* (2020)]. Hayter [2013] finds that spinoff formation is associated with the presence of the external entrepreneur in the management team. In fact, academic spinoffs that have a management team composed of academic and non-academic individuals achieve greater early-stage performance [Visintin and Pittino (2014)], highlighting the post-start-up role of external entrepreneurs. This mixed background is related to firm's innovative capability [Arvanitis and Stucki (2012)]. This is further evidenced in Lundqvist [2014], who found that spinoffs with external entrepreneurs performed better than those run by academic founders only. Additionally, having more external entrepreneurs in the management team is found to contribute to greater entrepreneurial orientation of the spinoff company [Diánez-González and Camelo-Ordaz (2016)].

2.2.5. *Networks*

The actors discussed above form networks [Hayter (2016)] which underpin the organization of entrepreneurial ecosystems [Spigel (2017)]. As such, it is important to refer to the concept of social capital which is concerned with the value of links between different social actors [Lin (1999)]. As the social capital concept originates from the focus on social actors, it may be over-stretched in the considerations of more institutionalized ones, i.e. organizations or firms. A more adapted to organizational character concept has been proposed in a form of network capital [Huggins (2010)]. Huggins [2010] argues that network capital can be managed, unlike social capital being based on individual actors difficult to control at an organizational level. This paper acknowledges the two concepts, as the UEEs involve both human and institutional actors.

Within the network considerations, there is a clear relationship between densely populated networks and better performance of firms or organizations [Fleming *et al.* (2007); Hochberg *et al.* (2007); Schilling and Phelps (2007)], as better connectedness increases the flows of knowledge. This paper explores whether academic entrepreneurship activity differs across UEEs of different composition (i.e. having more or less of the key actors/being more or less connected).

2.2.6. *The university entrepreneurial ecosystem model*

The university entrepreneurial ecosystem is composed of the following key actors: universities, TTOs, business incubators, science parks, external entrepreneurs, and investors. Whilst this is not a comprehensive list of actors (more detailed work is offered in Hayter *et al.* [2018]), they have been identified as critical in the functioning of the UEEs [Prokop (2021)]. We posit that the TTOs hold central ecosystem positions in the UEEs, as they make decisions whether the entrepreneurial activity,

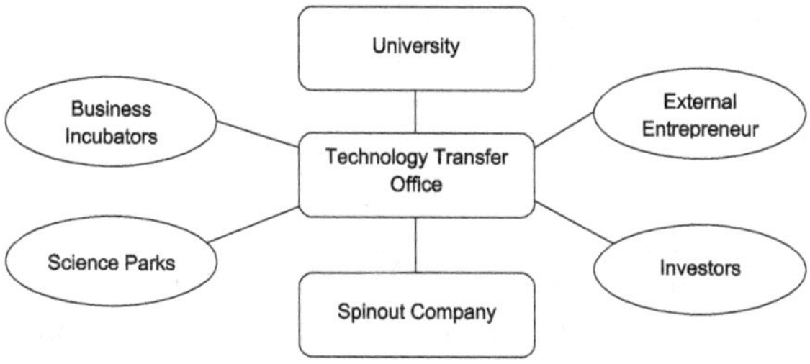

Fig. 1. University entrepreneurial ecosystem.

reflected through academic spinoffs, would take place or not. As such, they also employ their extensive networks and resource access to endow a spinoff company and enable its development. Figure 1 captures these actors diagrammatically.

3. Methodology

The data sources used to construct the sample are available in the public domain, specifically consisting of all UK HEIs' websites, research reports, and have been collected from sources published between 2005 and 2008 period of time. Many universities list spinoff companies for reputational reasons, showcasing their commercialization successes. This step identified 784 spinoff companies formed across 73 HEIs. The firm data was complemented using the MINT (Bureau van Dyke) database, which holds financial and other descriptive data on UK companies. Whilst it holds data on many incorporated companies, the financial and employment type data availability is inconsistent, largely due to UK Companies House regulations on filing, where small- and medium-sized firms enjoy different types of exemptions, allowing them to report very basic information (normally key items from balance sheet such as capital, liabilities, etc.). As most of the UK spinoffs are small [Hewitt-Dundas (2015); Prokop *et al.* (2019)], this limits greatly availability of such information. For the purpose of this paper data on the firms' incorporation date and status was mainly collected. The status of firms that were found to be in receivership, liquidation, dormant or ceased trading is referred to as "inactive."

The final sample focuses on 160 HEIs, inclusive of those that generated spinoffs (73) and those that did not (87). The dataset includes ecosystem information on the following elements: business incubators, science parks, and venture capital investors (i.e. institutional investors) identified in HE-BCI survey (HEFCE). Additionally, by using the data on venture capital investors, the external entrepreneurs' element was identified by classifying the links of universities with external venture capital firms as indicative of having links with the entrepreneurs. The data from HE-BCI survey relates to 2007–2008 academic year for the analysis of university entrepreneurial ecosystems, and refers back to 2002–2003 to present trends in technology transfer surrounding the spinoff activity.

The analysis presented in this paper focuses on the social network analysis (SNA), which is performed using open-source software Pajek. The SNA provides not only statistical but also graphical perspective that enhances the understanding of relations between the ecosystem actors. The links between the components of the UEE based on Figure 1 are constructed into a network. The graphical exploration of the network links between the components of the UESI allows to analyze the interactions from a range of perspectives. The paper first explores the networks graphically by presenting all UEEs and how they relate to each other, followed by extracting a *k-core* cohesive subgroup [Borgatti *et al.* (1990)]. Cohesive subgroups identify the core structures within networks, importantly so tied by similar structural properties expressed in the same number of connections to each other. The data is then explored with two additional network measures: betweenness centrality [Freeman (1977)] and structural holes [Burt (1992)]. The former relates to a specific property of an actor in a network, where it essentially plays a role of a network hub with its centrality calculated on the basis of ties having to pass through that actor. The latter assesses the redundancy of immediate contacts, with the redundancy present if actor i's ties are connected. When the immediate contacts are not linked to each other, the lack of a network tie signifies a structural hole, as actor i gains an advantage in mediating between them.

4. Findings

4.1. *HE-BCI survey*

The HE-BCI survey data provides an overview of UK HEIs' spinning out activity from 160 institutions. Figures 2–5 capture a 6-year period and paint an interesting picture of academic spinoff formation. From Figs. 2 and 3, it can be observed that the number of spinoffs established each consecutive year was growing since 2004/2005[1] period (Fig. 2), however this increase was not attributed to a greater participation of the UK HEIs in creating spinoffs (Fig. 3), but rather intensified activities of the HEIs already actively involved in academic entrepreneurship. It is quite known from the case study research [e.g. Braunerhjelm (2007); Harrison and Leitch (2010); Fogelberg and Lundqvist (2013)] that certain HEIs are more prominent in

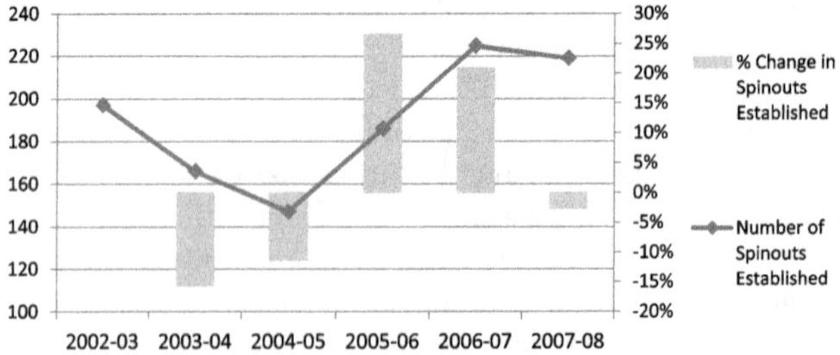

Fig. 2. Established spinoffs: 2002/2003–2007/2008.

[1] The annual spinoff company generation does not follow a linear path, annual variations are to be expected, as observed in Prokop [2021] who studied a longer time frame.

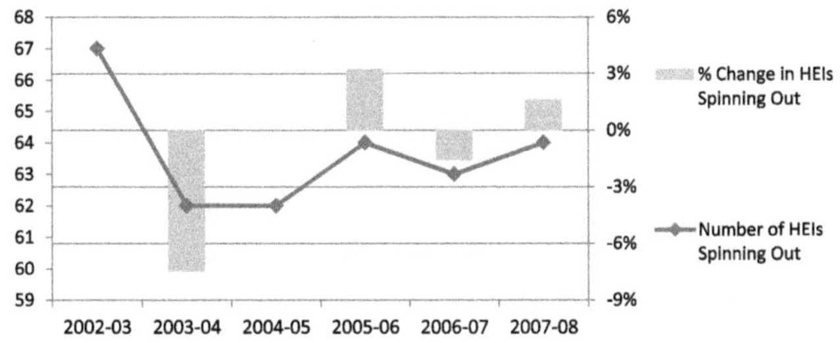

Fig. 3. HEIs that established spinoffs: 2002/2003–2007/2008.

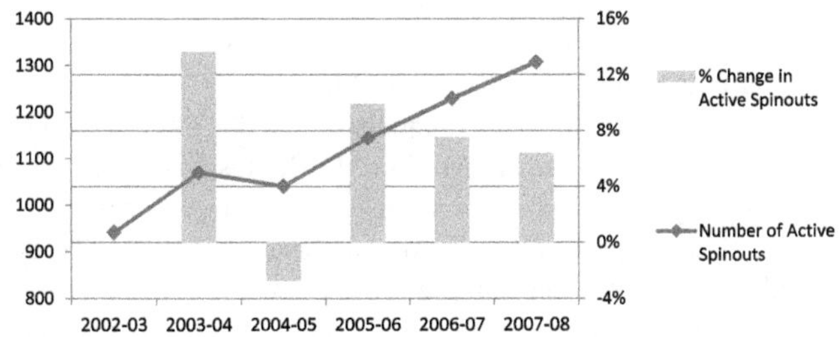

Fig. 4. Active spinoffs: 2002–2003 to 2007–2008.

spinoff formation than others, signifying a variable availability of resources and dissimilar commercialization capabilities of HEIs.

When considering the "survival" of academic spinoffs, it is observable that nearly each year consistently (excluding 2004/2005) the number of active spinoff firms was increasing (Fig. 4). This trend seems again unrelated to a greater participation of UK HEIs in "developing" firms [Siegel and Wright (2007)], and draws attention to only a certain (decreasing) amount of universities that appear to be successful in having created sustainable (i.e. surviving) firms (Fig. 5). This evidence compared with the average of 15 years ($n = 145$) that the UK TTOs have been established for could be indicating that the accumulated experience in technology transfer is not utilized by all HEIs that have such a unit or department. In fact, there may be a variable set of

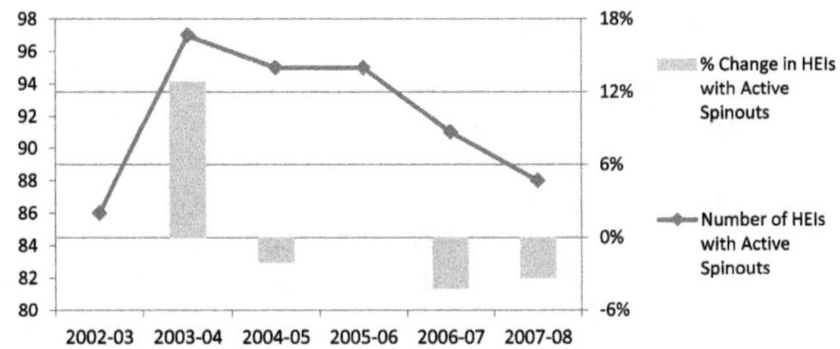

Fig. 5. HEIs with active spinoffs: 2002–2003 to 2007–2008.

Table 1. HEIs and infrastructure elements (HE-BCI survey 2007–2008).

Business incubators	80.6%
Science parks	41.9%
Institutional investors	60.6%
External entrepreneurs	58.8%

approaches adopted by TTOs to academic entrepreneurship [Prokop (2021)]. Furthermore, Figs. 2 and 3 suggest that the fact that new spinoff company creation started to fall in numbers whilst the experience of TTOs is theoretically growing (subject to staff rotation) suggests five explanations: (1) TTOs have reached a plateau in their productivity, (2) TTOs are shifting from quantity to quality orientation in spinoff formation (as noticeable in Fig. 4), or (3) there was significantly less research that could be commercially exploited in 2007–2008 than in the previous years, (4) there has been a change in recording the disclosures either driven through administrative changes (policies) or revision of resource endowments, (5) a shift away from academic entrepreneurship mode has been observed, with other knowledge commercialization routes becoming more prominent.

Table 1 depicts the percentage of HEIs with access to each particular element of the UEE. It suggests that many HEIs already operate within a more developed ecosystem for commercializing their knowledge through creating spinoff companies. Specifically, over 80% of UK HEIs have access to business incubators, either on campus or provided by a partner organization. This suggests that the majority of UK HEIs are capable of providing some sort of facilities for their new innovative firms. However, it remains unknown as to what composition of the UEE (which elements together) signifies that HEIs are well equipped for spinning out firms. This is especially important as academic entrepreneurship is a result of a combination of factors [e.g. Krabel and Mueller (2009); Hayter (2013); Fini *et al.* (2017)], not least related to the development of each UEE. As HE-BCI survey data captures only those spinoffs that are still active it does not give a clear picture of absolute spinoff rates (as it excludes firms that ceased trading). Thus, in the next section, the data collected on 784 academic spinoffs is utilized, complemented with HE-BCI survey data.

4.2. *The composition of UEEs*

Table 2 depicts the regional character of the sample, based on the region of the HEI a spinoff originated from. From the table, it is evident that the East of England is the most "productive" region in spinoff company formation, and when considering the average lifespan (both active and inactive) of the academic spinoffs from the region it appears the universities located in the East of England are characterized by more experience in academic entrepreneurship. The explanation for this could be sought in the presence of Cambridge University and the general entrepreneurial culture in the locality [Garnsey and Heffernan (2005)]. The typical prevalence of the Greater South East regions (in many economic activities) is disrupted by high performance of the

Table 2. Regional distribution of the spinoffs in the dataset.

$N = 785$*	Number of HEIs in the dataset	% Number of spinoffs	% Active spinoffs	% Inactive spinoffs	Average lifespan of active spinoffs	Average lifespan of non-active spinoffs
East of England	5	17.5	14.1	3.4	11.7	8.3
London	13	13.6	11.3	2.4	8.2	5.1
Scotland	12	14.6	12.4	2.3	10.6	5.5
South East	8	10.7	9.3	1.4	10.1	6.5
West Midlands	8	8.7	7.1	1.7	10.6	4.8
Yorkshire and the Humber	5	8.5	6.9	1.5	8.1	6.7
East Midlands	4	6.4	5.6	0.8	9.7	8.0
South West	6	6.4	5.4	1.0	10.0	6.5
North East	2	4.4	3.5	0.9	10.6	8.0
North West	3	4.6	4.1	0.5	9.2	5.3
Wales	7	4.5	3.6	0.9	7.9	2.4
Northern Ireland	1	0.1	0.1	0.0	11.0	n/a

Note: *The number of spinoffs used in this table includes John Innes Centre (JIC) and its 1 spinoff, however, as JIC is not listed in HE-BCI survey data, it is excluded from further analysis.

Table 3. Ecosystem completeness and spinoff rates.

Number of elements in the UEE	HEIs and TTOs ($n = 160$)		% of total number of spinoffs ($n = 784$)		Average of spinoff creation rates ($n = 784$)	
	TTO	No TTO	TTO	No TTO	TTO	No TTO
0	19	5	0.04	0.00	0.02	0.00
1	25	2	1.51	0.00	0.47	0.00
2	17	1	4.72	0.00	2.18	0.00
3	40	0	23.66	0.00	4.64	n/a
4	50	1	66.50	3.57	10.43	28.00

Scottish universities in the creation of academic spinoffs. This could be partly explained by the higher level of commitment from the Scottish Government to supporting spinoff companies, with over 60% of them being in receipt of public funding [Hewitt-Dundas (2015)]. Surprisingly, a similar proportion of Northern Irish spinoffs reported such support, however this is not reflected in the academic entrepreneurship outcome for the region. It is also interesting to observe that regions responsible for lower proportions of spinoff companies differ quite substantially on the average life-span measures. For example, HEIs from North East and Wales formed a similar number of spinoffs, yet spinoffs in North East tend to stay active for longer than those in Wales, even those that become inactive survive longer than Welsh firms.

From merging two datasets: the data on 784 academic spinoffs and the HE-BCI survey (2007–2008) a clearer picture is observed on the role played by the UEE components. As depicted in Table 3, it appears there is a strong link between the UEE's completeness and spinning out rates. The higher spinoff creation rates are observable among the HEIs that have a TTO and a more developed UEE, with the HEIs that have a complete 4-element UEE having created on average more than 10 spinoff firms. This is approximately 2.25 times more than those HEIs with the TTO that have a 3-element UEE, circa 4.79 times more than those HEIs with the TTO that have a 2-element UEE, and circa 22.03 times more than those HEIs with the TTO that have a 1-element UEE. Furthermore, it appears that 61 HEIs with TTOs and up to 2 elements in their UEEs are responsible for spinning out approximately 6.27% of firms, whilst a lower number of universities (50) with complete UEEs are responsible for nearly two thirds of all spinoffs. This finding provides two key interpretations: (1) TTOs need to be better connected with access to all elements of the UEE to increase their spinoff rates (importance of building networks), (2) it appears that the average experience of the TTOs of 15 years shows that fairly many TTOs did little academic entrepreneurship activity, suggesting either institutional struggles (e.g. top-down management of knowledge commercialization that may prove to be counterproductive [Philpott *et al.* (2011)] or other commercialization modes pursued.

4.3. *Social network analysis*

Figure 6 presents a macro perspective on the links of the components of UEE of 160 UK HEIs. The network was energized using Kamada–Kawai Separate

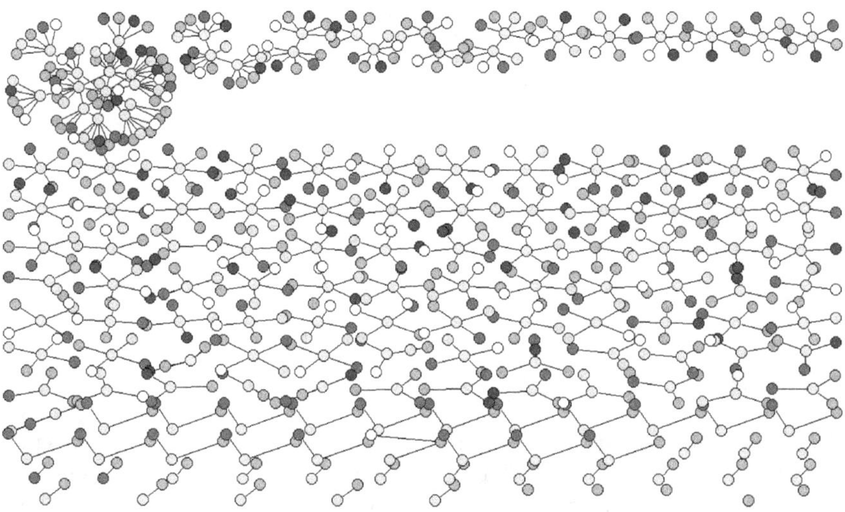

Fig. 6. Network of university entrepreneurial ecosystems.

Components algorithm. The light blue vertices represent HEIs, the yellow vertices TTOs, green vertices academic spinoffs, red vertices business incubators, dark blue vertices science parks, pink vertices investors, and the white vertices represent external entrepreneurs. In the dataset of 784 spinoffs some of the firms have originated from more than one HEI, thus this is also captured in the graph. Although the network appears to be densely populated, its actual density is very low – 0.00215 (Table 4), and resembles the isolation of most of the HEIs and their UEEs built into

Table 4. Average regional network results of ecosystems and network diagnostics.

	Average betweenness centrality	Average structural holes	Diagnostics
East of England	0.00034	0.32829	
London	0.00047	0.42391	
Scotland	0.00011	0.32178	
South East	0.00011	0.29562	
West Midlands	0.00015	0.33690	
Yorkshire and the Humber	0.00004	0.33182	
East Midlands	0.00019	0.26661	
South West	0.00003	0.36667	
North East	0.00032	0.19845	
North West	0.00002	0.48452	
Wales	0.00005	0.20909	
Northern Ireland	0.00003	0.45556	
Density			0.00215
Average degree			1.66537
Clustering coefficient (Watts-Strogatz)			0.00594
Betweenness centralization			0.00578
Average aggregate constraint			0.86280

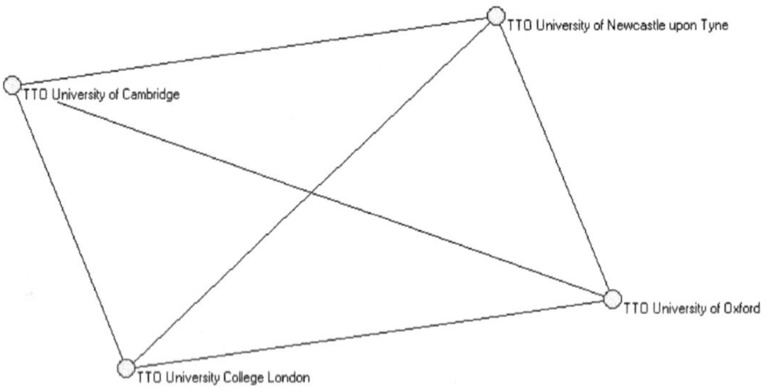

Fig. 7. 3-Core cohesive subgroup.

the network, further emphasized by the low average degree (1.66537) and clustering coefficient (0.00594). The UEEs linked together forming the largest component in the network are represented by the following HEIs: Royal Veterinary College, Universities of Birmingham, Nottingham, Newcastle, Cambridge, Oxford, School of Pharmacy, Imperial College London, University College London, King's College London, Queen Mary (University of London), Birkbeck College, and Institute of Cancer Research. Although many of them are located in relatively close proximity (e.g. London), their network originates from more than one collaboration in creating a spinoff company (e.g. University College London is found to have worked with nine other HEIs in the process of creating spinoff companies).

The network shows that on average each HEI has at least two elements in its infrastructure, with the most frequent being: business incubators (16.7% of the network elements), then institutional investors (12.6%), external entrepreneurs (12.2%), and finally science parks (8.7%). In order to depict the most interlinked element of the network a cohesive subgroup is extracted from the network (Fig. 7). This cohesive subgroup consists of a 3-core sub-network (each vertex has at least three links, or its degree is 3). The identified cohesive subgroup consists of those actors most highly involved in spinoff-creating interactions with at least three different other actors. The actors forming the 3-core cohesive subnetwork are TTOs of Universities of Cambridge, Newcastle upon Tyne, Oxford, and College London, with a clear Greater South East concentration. Such well-connected actors form a network of trust, where each of them has the same or similar access to opportunities [Burt (1992)], here considered as commercial exploitation of university knowledge.

After exploring the most interlinked component of the network it is essential to consider the concept of centralization of the network by looking at its betweenness [Freeman (1977)], which treats as central the vertices that are the main, in this particular consideration, technology transfer hubs. In this network, it appears that the three key "hubs" are University College London, Imperial College London and University of Cambridge TTOs (Table 5). This is consistent with the findings of Bagchi-Sen *et al.* [2020], who point out that the research-intensive HEIs are responsible for larger numbers of spinoff firms. Consequently, such institutions would

Table 5. Key technology transfer hubs (betweenness centrality).

Rank	Value	TTO*
1	0.0058	TTO University College London
2	0.0030	TTO Imperial College London
3	0.0029	TTO University of Cambridge
4	0.0026	TTO King's College London
5	0.0015	TTO University of Oxford
6	0.0015	TTO University of Nottingham
7	0.0015	TTO University of Newcastle upon Tyne
8	0.0012	TTO Queen Mary, University of London
9	0.0012	TTO University of Birmingham
10	0.0012	TTO Institute of Cancer Research

Note: All TTOs listed have at least one link with another TTO formed from creating a spinoff company.

tend to hold more central positions in their networks. It is also important to stress that those key "hubs" have at least three elements in their respective UEEs.

Since the technology transfer is very related to the commercial opportunities it is important to consider the structural holes [Burt (1992)] in the network. Structural holes could be best described as actors linked indirectly by another actor – the lack of direct link is regarded as a structural hole, and thus an opportunity for the linking actor to convey information between the two (or more actors). When considering the structural holes present in the network University College London appears as one that can benefit the most in the network (Table 6), suggesting it holds a superior structural network position. Given it is London-based its spinoffs have access to a network rich in connections with key businesses [Huggins and Prokop (2017)],

Table 6. HEIs with greatest commercial opportunities (structural holes).

Rank	Value*	TTO**
1	0.087	TTO University College London
2	0.105	TTO University of Cambridge
3	0.113	TTO Imperial College London
4	0.125	TTO University of Edinburgh
5	0.126	TTO University of Newcastle upon Tyne
5	0.126	TTO University of Oxford
7	0.130	TTO King's College London
8	0.133	TTO University of Nottingham
9	0.143	TTO Napier University
9	0.143	TTO University of Glasgow
9	0.143	TTO University of Aberdeen
9	0.143	TTO Keele University
13	0.157	TTO Institute of Cancer Research

Notes: *The values represent aggregate constraint; structural hole is an inverse of aggregate constraint. **All TTOs listed here have at least one link with another TTO formed from creating a spinoff company.

endowing them with greater levels of network capital [Huggins (2010)]. Furthermore, all of the HEIs in Table 6 have a UEE consisting of at least three components.

The SNA points at structural disparities between HEIs and their UEEs at a national level. Those TTOs that had a chance to work together to commercially exploit knowledge residing at their institutions created links, and thus networks. Being networked provides them with greater opportunities compared to isolation [Vonortas (2009)], as observed from the empirical evidence presented through SNA, where none of the isolated TTOs was ranked high on betweenness centrality or structural holes. These inequalities found in the presented network confirm the dominating individualistic approach of UK HEIs to academic entrepreneurship.

5. Conclusions

The evidence presented in this paper, although subject to certain limitations, outlines major differences in academic entrepreneurship activity related to a variable composition of university entrepreneurial ecosystems. It shows that HEIs with a well-developed ecosystem consisting of multiple actors: business incubators, science parks, investors, and external entrepreneurs, tend to display greater commercialization activity focused on academic entrepreneurship. This effect persists when controlling for the network characteristics.[2]

Furthermore, it is evident that although the dataset did not capture all the existing connections, being linked with other TTOs is associated with improved network characteristics of the TTOs, as opposed to being in isolation. In addition to that, as the analysis focused on the links with the UEE components, it is even more essential for the technology transfer professionals to work together forming cross-institutional alliances. The building of such alliances can be seen as accumulating the network capital [Huggins (2010)], and eventually expanding the support offered to academic spinoffs – through a stronger UEE. This should be especially important for the TTOs (representing HEIs) with less developed UEEs.

5.1. *Policy implications*

The findings presented here indicate a number of important policy implications. At the micro level of the university entrepreneurial ecosystem, those HEIs that do engage in academic entrepreneurship should evaluate the composition of their UEEs. Where weaker configurations are identified, the role of local policymakers needs to be in supporting development of UEEs either through devoting resources to create its components (e.g. business incubators and science parks) or contributing to stronger connectivity between the UEEs to improve access to better architectures. The challenge to achieve improved academic spinoff company generation through a particular UEE composition is in acknowledging that these cannot be short-term

[2] This has been examined with negative binomial regression of academic spinoff rates against university entrepreneurial ecosystem elements and controlled with betweenness centrality variable (both entering the equation at a 1% significance level).

one-off uncoordinated adjustments, but should ideally be aligned with wider cultural reconfigurations [Kirby (2006)].

At the meso level of the higher education sector, the attention should be drawn to the prominent HEI isolationism in technology transfer. Both HEI administrators and policymakers should consider the UEEs to have a greater spatial reach rather than being set-up predominantly around individual HEIs. This could enable a more supportive environment to a greater number of HEIs and their academic entrepreneurs. This can be especially important for those HEIs based in more peripheral places [Siegel *et al.* (2007)], where developing UEEs is more difficult due to limited access to a diverse set of actors. At the same time, higher education sector needs to be sensitive to the variable configurations of UEEs [Prokop (2021)], which may lead to different outcomes in terms of spinoff formation, supporting its growth, or later-stage success [Colombo *et al.* (2010)].

At the macro/national level, it is important to recognize that not all HEIs engage in academic entrepreneurship activity. This is merely one of the modes of commercialization, as such the central policymakers need to recognize that not all HEIs may have the necessary knowledge and skills essential for generating spinoff companies. However, they may be engaging in other Third Mission activities, for example focusing on a more extensive graduate start-up activity [Åstebro *et al.* (2012)]. Finally, it is important to recognize that policy lessons presented here are drawn from an example of a developed country. Whist many of the recommendations may appear sound within the UK's context, their application and subsequent effectiveness may differ across countries characterized by different development levels, but also and crucially so, varied institutional arrangements [Foss and Gibson (2015)].

5.2. *Directions for further research*

This study focused on a limited structural perspective, which encourages many questions. Therefore, further research is recommended to provide a more robust picture of the university spinning-out activity taking into consideration measures of spinoff success, university characteristics and the existing links formed by all elements of the presented UEE. Specifically, the scholarly attention could be devoted to functional compositions of UEEs, exploring a range of outcomes based on specific configurations, identifying blueprints for organizing and managing academic entrepreneurship activities. Furthermore, an interesting avenue of research would be to explain why spinoff numbers have not increased more drastically in line with accumulated experience of TTOs. Finally, future researchers could also investigate a range of cases of UEEs by employing qualitative methods to unpack the complexities of different configurations and their dynamics, especially focusing on the institutional and cultural dimensions.

Acknowledgment

The author is grateful to ESRC funding (Grant Award Reference RES-171-25-0023) that partly sponsored the data collection for this research.

References

Alexander, A. T. and Martin, D. P. (2013). Intermediaries for open innovation: A competence-based comparison of knowledge transfer offices practices. *Technological Forecasting and Social Change*, **80**, 1: 38–49.

Arvanitis, S. and Stucki, T. (2012). What determines the innovation capability of firm founders? *Industrial and Corporate Change*, **21**, 4: 1049–1084.

Åstebro, T., Bazzazian, N. and Braguinsky, S. (2012). Startups by recent university graduates and their faculty: Implications for university entrepreneurship policy. *Research Policy*, **41**, 4: 663–677.

Audretsch, D. B. (1991). New-firm survival and the technological regime. *Review of Economics and Statistics*, **73**, 3: 441–450.

Audretsch, D. B. (1995). Innovation, growth and survival. *International Journal of Industrial Organization*, **13**, 441–445.

Bagchi-Sen, S., Baines, N. and Lawton-Smith, H. (2020). Characteristics and outputs of university spin-offs in the United Kingdom. *International Regional Science Review*, doi: 10.1177/0160017620925129.

Bank of England. (2001). *Financing of Technology-Based Small Firms*. Bank of England Domestic Finance Division, London.

Benneworth, P. and Charles, D. (2005). University spin-off policies and economic development in less successful regions: Learning from two decades of policy practice. *European Planning Studies*, **13**, 4: 537–557.

Berggren, E. and Lindholm Dahlstrand, A. (2009). Creating an entrepreneurial region: Two waves of academic spin-offs from Halmstad University. *European Planning Studies*, **17**, 8: 1171–1189.

Boh, W. F., De-Haan, U. and Strom, R. (2016). University technology transfer through entrepreneurship: Faculty and students in spinoffs. *The Journal of Technology Transfer*, **41**, 661–669.

Bonardo, D., Paleari, S. and Vismara, S. (2011). Valuing university-based firms: The effects of academic affiliation on IPO performance. *Entrepreneurship Theory and Practice*, **35**, 4: 755–776.

Borgatti, S. P., Everett, M. G. and Shirey, P. R. (1990). LS sets, lambda sets and other cohesive subsets. *Social Networks*, **12**, 337–357.

Braunerhjelm, P. (2007). Academic entrepreneurship: Social norms, university culture and policies. *Science and Public Policy*, **34**, 9: 619–631.

Burt, R. S. (1992). *Structural Holes: The Social Structure of Competition*. Cambridge, MA, Harvard University Press.

Chakrabarti, A. K. (1991). Industry characteristics influencing the technical output: A case of small and medium-sized firms in the U.S. *R&D Management*, **21**, 2: 139–152.

Chiesa, V. and Piccaluga, A. (2000). Exploitation and diffusion of public research: the case of academic spin-off companies in Italy. *R&D Management*, **30**, 4: 329–340.

Chrisman, J. J., Hynes, T. and Fraser, S. (1995). Faculty entrepreneurship and economic development: The case of the University of Calgary. *Journal of Business Venturing*, **10**, 267–281.

Christopherson, S. and Clark, S. (2010). Limits to 'The Learning Region': What university-centered economic development can (and cannot) do to create knowledge-based regional economies. *Local Economy*, **25**, 2: 120–130.

Clarysse, B., Wright, M., Lockett, A., Van de Velde, E. and Vohora, A. (2005). Spinning out new ventures: A typology of incubation strategies from European research institutions. *Journal of Business Venturing*, **20**, 2: 183–216.

Clarysse, B., Wright, M. and Van de Velde E. (2011). Entrepreneurial origin, technological knowledge and the growth of spin-off companies. *Journal of Management Studies*, **48**, 6: 1420–1442.

Colombo, M., Mustar, P. and Wright, M. (2010). Dynamics of science-based entrepreneurship. *The Journal of Technology Transfer*, **35**, 1: 1–15.

Compagnucci, L. and Spigarelli, F. (2020). The Third Mission of the university: A systematic literature review on potentials and constraints. *Technological Forecasting and Social Change*, **161**, 1–30.

Corsi, C., Prencipe, A., Rodriguez-Gulias, M. J., Fernandez-Lopez, S. and Rodeiro-Pazos, D. (2017). The effect of parent university on firm growth: An analysis of the Spanish and Italian USOs. *Journal of Management Development* **36**, 2: 233–249.

DTI. (1993). *Realising Our Potential: A Strategy for Science, Technology and Engineering.* Department of Trade and Industry, London.

Dahlstrand, A. L. and Jacobsson, S. (2003). Universities and technology-based entrepreneurship in the Gothenburg region. *Local Economy*, **18**, 10: 80–90.

Debackere, K. and Veugelers, R. (2005). The role of academic technology transfer organizations in improving industry science links. *Research Policy*, **34**, 3: 321–342.

Di Gregorio, D. and Shane, S. (2003). Why do some universities generate more startups than others? *Research Policy*, **32**: 209–227.

Diánez-González, J. P. and Camelo-Ordaz, C. (2016). How management team composition affects academic spin-offs' entrepreneurial orientation: The mediating role of conflict. *Journal of Technology Transfer*, **41**: 530–557.

Etzkowitz, H. and Dzisah, J. (2008). Rethinking development: Circulation in the triple helix. *Technology Analysis & Strategic Management*, **20**, 6: 653–666.

Etzkowitz, H., Webster, A., Gebhardt, C. and Cantisano Terra, B. R. (2000). The future of the university and the university of the future. *Research Policy*, **29**, 313–330.

Etzkowitz, H. (1998). The norms of entrepreneurial science: Cognitive effects of the new university-industry linkages. *Research Policy*, **27**, 823–833.

Fini, R., Fu, K., Mathisen, M. T., Rasmussen, E. and Wright, M. (2017). Institutional determinants of university spin-off quantity and quality: A longitudinal, multilevel, cross-country study. *Small Business Economics*, **48**, 2: 361–391.

Fleming, L., King, III C. and Juda, A. I. (2007). Small worlds and regional innovation. *Organization Science*, **18**, 6: 938–954.

Fogelberg, H. and Lundqvist, M. A. (2013). Integration of academic and entrepreneurial roles: The case of nanotechnology research at Chalmers University of Technology. *Science and Public Policy*, **40**, 1: 127–139.

Foss, L. and Gibson, D. V. (2015). The entrepreneurial university: Context and institutional change, *The Entrepreneurial University: Context and Institutional Change*, eds. L. Foss and D. V. Gibson, Routledge, London, pp. 1–17.

Franklin, S., Wright, M. and Lockett, A. (2001). Academic and surrogate entrepreneurs in university spin-out companies. *Journal of Technology Transfer*, **26**, (1–2): 127–141.

Freeman, L. C. (1977). A set of measures of centrality based on betweenness. *Sociometry*, **40**, 135–141.

Garnsey, E. and Heffernan, P. (2005). High-technology clustering through spin-out and attraction: The Cambridge case. *Regional Studies*, **39**, 8: 1127–1144.

Garrido-Yserte, R. and Gallo-Rivera, M. T. (2010). The impact of the university upon local economy: Three methods to estimate demand-side effects. *Annals of Regional Science*, **44**, 39–67.

Gellman Research Associates. (1976). *Indicators of International Trends in Technological Innovation.* US Small Business Administration, Office of Advocacy, Washington, DC.

Gianiodis, P. T., Markman, G. D. and Panagopoulos, A. (2016). Entrepreneurial universities and overt opportunism. *Small Business Economics*, **47**, 609–631.

Giuri, P., Munari, F., Scandura, A. and Toschi, L. (2019). The strategic orientation of universities in knowledge transfer activities. *Technological Forecasting and Social Change*, **138**, 261–278.

Goldstein, H. A., Maier, G. and Luger, M. I. (1995). The university as an instrument for economic and business development: U.S. and European comparisons. *Emerging Patterns of Social Demand and University Reform: Through a Glass Darkly*, eds. D. Dill and B. Sporn, Oxford, Pergamon.

Goldstein, H. A. (2010). The 'entrepreneurial turn' and regional economic development mission of universities. *Annals of Regional Science*, **44**, 83–109.

Gompers, P. A., Gornall, W., Kaplan, S. N. and Strebulaev, I. A. (2020). How do venture capitalists make decisions? *Journal of Financial Economics*, **135**, 1: 169–190.

Grandi, A. and Grimaldi, R. (2003). Exploring the networking characteristics of new venture founding teams. *Small Business Economics*, **21**, 4: 329–341.

Grimaldi, R. and Grandi, A. (2005). Business incubators and new venture creation: An assessment of incubating models. *Technovation*, **25**, 111–121.

HM Government. (2017). *Industrial Strategy: Building a Britain Fit for the Future*. HM Government, London.

Harding, R. (2000). Venture capital and regional development: Towards a venture capital 'system'. *Venture Capital*, **2**, 4: 287–311.

Harrison, R. T. and Leitch, C. (2010). Voodoo Institution or Entrepreneurial University? Spin-off companies, the entrepreneurial system and regional development in the UK. *Regional Studies*, **44**, 9: 1241–1262.

Hayter, C. S., Nelson, A. J., Zayed, S. and O'Connor, A. C. (2018). Conceptualizing academic entrepreneurship ecosystems: A review, analysis and extension of the literature. *The Journal of Technology Transfer*, **43**, 1039–1082.

Hayter, C. S. (2013). Conceptualizing knowledge-based entrepreneurship networks: perspectives from the literature. *Small Business Economics*, **41**, 899–911.

Hayter, C. S. (2016). Constraining entrepreneurial development: A knowledge-based view of social networks among academic entrepreneurs. *Research Policy*, **45**, 475–490.

Hewitt-Dundas, N. (2015). *Profiling UK University Spin-Outs*. ERC Research Paper No. 35, Enterprise Research Centre, Birmingham, July.

Hochberg, Y. V., Ljungqvist, A. and Lu, Y. (2007). Whom you know matters: Venture capital networks and investment performance. *The Journal of Finance*, **62**, 1: 251–301.

Huggins, R. and Prokop, D. (2017). Network structure and regional innovation: A study of university-industry ties. *Urban Studies*, **54**, 4: 931–952.

Huggins, R., Johnston, A. and Steffenson, R. (2008). Universities, knowledge networks and regional policy. *Cambridge Journal of Regions, Economy and Society*, **1**, 321–340.

Huggins, R. (2008). Universities and knowledge-based venturing: Finance, management and networks in London. *Entrepreneurship and Regional Development*, **20**, 2: 185–206.

Huggins, R. (2010). Forms of network resource: Knowledge access and the role of inter-firm networks. *International Journal of Management Reviews*, **12**, 3: 335–352.

Jensen, R. and Thursby, M. (2001). Proofs and prototypes for sale: The licensing of university inventions. *American Economic Review*, **91**, 1: 240–259.

Kirby, A. D. (2006). Creating entrepreneurial universities in the UK: Applying entrepreneurship theory to practice. *The Journal of Technology Transfer*, **31**, 599–603.

Kirchhoff, B. A., Newbert, S. L., Hasan, I. and Armington, C. (2007). The influence of university R&D expenditures on new business formations and employment growth. *Entrepreneurship Theory and Practice*, **31**, 4: 543–559.

Krabel, S. and Mueller, P. (2009). What drives scientists to start their own company? *Research Policy*, **38**, 6: 947–956.

Lambert, R. (2003). *Lambert Review of Business-University Collaboration*. Norwich, HMSO.

Lawton Smith, H. (2000). *Technology Transfer and Industrial Change in Europe*. MacMillan, Basingstoke.

Lawton Smith, H. (2007). Universities, innovation, and territorial development: A review of the evidence. Environment and Planning C: *Government and Policy*, **25**, 98–114.

Lenzer, J. and Kulczakowicz, P. (2021). Fueling spin-offs: Case studies of university-based technology start-up funding. *Technology and Innovation*, **22**, 1–13.

Library House/BVCA. (2005). *Creating Success from University Spin-Outs*. UK.

Library House/UBS. (2006). *Beyond the Chasm: The Venture-Backed Report*. UK.

Lin, N. (1999). Building a network theory of social capital. *Connections*, **22**, 1: 28–51.

Lindholm Dahlstrand, Å. T., Lawton Smith, H. and Baines, N.2016. Academic entrepreneurship: Spinoffs in Sweden and the UK. *University Evolution, Entrepreneurial Activity and Regional Competitiveness, International Studies in Entrepreneurship*, eds. D. Audretsch, E. Lehman, M. Meoli and S. Vismara, Vol. 32, Springer, Cham, pp. 127–150.

Link, A. N. and Scott, J. T. (2005). Opening the ivory tower's door: An analysis of the determinants of the formation of the U.S. spin-off companies. *Research Policy*, **34**, 3: 1106–1112.

Lockett, A. and Wright, M. (2005). Resources, capabilities, risk capital and the creation of university spin-out companies. *Research Policy*, **34**, 7: 1043–1057.

Lockett, A., Murray, G. and Wright, M. (2002). Do UK venture capitalists still have a bias against investment in new technology firms. *Research Policy*, **31**, 6: 1009–1030.

Lockett, A., Wright, M. and Franklin, S. (2003). Technology transfer and universities' spin-out strategies. *Small Business Economics*, **20**, 2: 185–201.

Lopez, S. F., Otero, L., Rodeiro, D. and Rodriguez, A. (2009). Entrepreneurial university, transfer technology and funding: An empirical analysis. *Journal of Enterprising Culture*, **17**, 2: 147–179.

Lundqvist, M. A. (2014). The importance of surrogate entrepreneurship for incubated Swedish technology ventures. *Technovation*, **34**, 93–100.

Malairaja, C. and Zawdie, G. (2008). Science parks and university-industry collaboration in Malaysia. *Technology Analysis & Strategic Management*, **20**, 6: 727–739.

Markman, G. D., Gianiodis, P. T. and Phan, P. H. (2008). Full-time faculty or part-time entrepreneurs. *IEEE Transactions on Engineering Management*, **55**, 1: 29–36.

Meoli, M. and Vismara, S. (2016). University support and the creation of technology and non-technology academic spin-offs. *Small Business Economics*, **47**, 2: 345–362.

Mosey, S. and Wright, M. (2007). From human capital to social capital: A longitudinal study of technology-based academic entrepreneurs. *Entrepreneurship Theory and Practice*, **31**, 6: 909–935.

Munari, F., Sobrero, M. and Toschi, L. (2018). The university as a venture capitalist? Gap funding instruments for technology transfer. *Technological Forecasting & Social Change*, **127**, 70–84.

Murray, G. (1999). Early-stage venture capital funds, scale economies and public support. *Venture Capital*, **1**, 4: 351–384.

Neves, M. and Franco, M. (2018). Academic spin-off creation: barriers and how to overcome them. *R&D Management*, **48**, 5: 505–518.

Oakey, R. P. (2003). Funding innovation and growth in UK new technology-based firms: Some observations on contributions from the public and private sectors. *Venture Capital*, **5**, 2: 161–179.

Phan, P. H. and Siegel, D. S. (2006). *The Effectiveness of University Technology Transfer: Lessons Learned from Quantitative and Qualitative Research in the U.S. and the U.K.* Rensselaer Polytechnic Institute, Troy, NY.

Philpott, K., Dooley, L., O'Reilly, C. and Lupton, G. (2011). The entrepreneurial university: Examining the underlying academic tensions. *Technovation*, **31**, 4: 161–170.

Pinch, S. and Sunley, P. (2009). Understanding the role of venture capitalists in knowledge dissemination in high-technology agglomerations: A case study of the University of Southampton spin-off cluster. *Venture Capital*, **11**, 4: 311–333.

Prokop, D., Huggins, R. and Bristow, G. (2019). The survival of academic spinoff companies: An empirical study of key determinants. *International Small Business Journal*, **37**, 5: 502–535.

Prokop, D. (2021). University entrepreneurial ecosystems and spinoff companies: Configurations, developments and outcomes. *Technovation* 107, 102286.

Schilling, M. A. and Phelps, C. C. (2007). Interfirm collaboration networks: The impact of large-scale network structure on firm innovation. *Management Science*, **53**, 7: 1113–1126.

Shane, S. (2004). *Academic Entrepreneurship. University Spinoffs and Wealth Creation.* Edward Elgar, Cheltenham.

Siegel, D. S. and Wright, M. (2007). Intellectual property: The assessment. *Oxford Review of Economic Policy*, **23**, 4: 529–540.

Siegel, D. S., Veugelers, R. and Wright, M. (2007). Technology transfer offices and commercialization of university intellectual property: Performance and policy implications. *Oxford Review of Economic Policy*, **23**, 4: 640–660.

Spigel, B. (2017). The relational organization of entrepreneurial ecosystems. *Entrepreneurship Theory & Practice*, **41**, 1: 49–72.

Sun, H., Ni, W. and Leung, J. (2007). Critical success factors for technological incubation: Case study of Hong Kong Science and Technology Parks. *International Journal of Management*, **24**, 2: 346–363.

Swamidass, P. M. and Vulasa, V. (2008). Why university inventions rarely produce income? Bottlenecks in university technology transfer. *Journal of Technology Transfer*, **34**, 4: 343–363.

Tamasy, C. (2007). Rethinking technology-oriented business incubators: Developing a robust policy instrument for entrepreneurship, innovation, and regional development? *Growth and Change*, **38**, 3: 460–473.

Thanki, R. (1999). How do we know the value of higher education to regional development? *Regional Studies*, **33**, 84–89.

The Futures Group (1984). *Characterization of Innovations Introduced on the U.S. Markets in 1982.* US Small Business Administration, Office of Advocacy, Washington, DC.

Vincett, P. S. (2010). The economic impacts of academic spin-off companies, and their implications for public policy. *Research Policy*, **39**, 736–747.

Visintin, F. and Pittino, D. (2014). Founding team composition and early performance of university-based spin-off companies. *Technovation*, **34**, 31–43.

Vohora, A., Wright, M. and Lockett, A. (2004). Critical junctures in the development of university high-tech spinout companies. *Research Policy*, **33**, 1: 147–175.

Vonortas, N. S. (2009). Innovation networks in industry. *Innovation Networks in Industries*, eds. F. Malerba and N. S. Vonortas, Edward Elgar, Cheltenham, pp. 27–44.

Wennberg, K., Wiklund, J. and Wright, M. (2011). The effectiveness of university knowledge spillovers: Performance differences between university spinoffs and corporate spinoffs. *Research Policy*, **40**, 8: 1128–1143.

Wong, P. K., Ho, Y. O. and Singh, A. (2007). Towards an "Entrepreneurial University" model to support Knowledge-based economic development: the case of the National University of Singapore. *World Development*, **35**, 6: 941–958.

Wright, M., Lockett, A., Clarysse, B. and Binks, M. (2006). University spin-out companies and venture capital. *Research Policy*, **35**, 481–501.

Wright, M., Clarysse, B., Mustar, P. and Lockett, A. (2007). *Academic Entrepreneurship in Europe.* Edward Elgar, Cheltenham.

Wright, M., Hmieleski, K. M., Siegel, D. S. and Ensley, M. D. (2007). The role of human capital in technological entrepreneurship. *Entrepreneurship Theory and Practice*, **31**, 6: 791–806.

Wynarczyk, P. and Raine, A. (2005). The performance of business incubators and their potential development in the North East Region of England. *Local Economy*, **20**, 2: 205–220.

Zeng, S., Xie, X. and Tam, C. (2010). Evaluating innovation capabilities for science parks: A system model. *Baltic Journal on Sustainability*, **16**, 3: 397–413.

Biography

Daniel Prokop holds a PhD from Cardiff University. He is a lecturer in Economic Geography at the School of Geography and Planning, Cardiff University, previously holding positions as lecturer in International Business at Sheffield Business School, Sheffield Hallam University and research associate at Centre for International Competitiveness at Cardiff Metropolitan University.

Impact of Self-Regulated Learning on Entrepreneurial Opportunity Recognition and Academic Entrepreneurship Performance*

Noorlizawati Abd Rahim*, Zainai Mohamed, Astuty Amrin and Maslin Masrom

Razak Faculty of Technology and Informatics
Universiti Teknologi Malaysia
54100, Kuala Lumpur Malaysia
**noorlizawati@utm.my*

The ratio of academic scientists to the labor force in Malaysia has increased. However, the contribution of academic scientists to commercialize research discoveries remains limited. Successful research commercialization or university technology transfer requires entrepreneurial effort that may involve skills beyond the traditional roles of academics. The ability to identify the commercial opportunity of research, i.e. entrepreneurial opportunity recognition, has been proven to be a critical skill for an academic entrepreneur. Earlier findings in this area would have been far more useful if the antecedents of entrepreneurial opportunity recognition were recognized. Although self-regulated learning has been inferred to as informal entrepreneurship education for academic entrepreneurs, there has been a lack of evidence on how it influences their academic entrepreneurship performance. This paper examined the characteristics of academic entrepreneurs and the key success factors, whether academics' opportunity recognition ability is influenced by their self-regulated learning behavior. A quantitative research design was employed based on a case study of a technological university in Malaysia involving 115 academic entrepreneurs. Structural equation modeling analysis results revealed that academics' opportunity recognition and social capital are the most important determinants of their academic entrepreneurship performance. The efficiency of the Technology Transfer Office and the ease of securing funding play influential roles too, but to a smaller extent. Most importantly, opportunity recognition is strengthened by self-regulated learning, through frequent deliberate practices in information and knowledge seeking that enable scientists to be more creative and innovative in translating research into marketable products and technology.

Keywords: Academic entrepreneur; funding; opportunity recognition; self-regulated learning; research commercialization; technology transfer office; university technology transfer.

*Corresponding author.

*This chapter was originally published in International Journal of Innovation and Technology Management, Vol. 18, No. 4, March 2018, published by World Scientific Publishing, Singapore. Reprinted with permission.

1. Introduction

A competitive environment with a shrinking research budget has led the shift of higher education institutions from ivory towers to entrepreneurial universities [Audretsch *et al.* (2015); Etzkowitz (2016)]. This shift is also driven by the significant contribution of academic research to a nation's gross domestic product [Guerrero *et al.* (2015); Iacobucci and Micozzi (2015); Vincett (2010)]. Consequently, the traditional roles of higher education in teaching and research have now been extended to include academic entrepreneurship [Barth and Schlegelmilch (2013); Wood (2011)]. However, the 2014 Global Entrepreneurship Monitor (GEM) report highlighted a gap in entrepreneurial activity rates between Malaysia and other countries [Roland *et al.* (2011); Singer *et al.* (2015)], even though the total number of academic scientists in Malaysia increased four-fold over the six-year period since 2006 [MASTIC (2013)]. Recent data also showed that R&D transfer is highly insufficient under Malaysia's current entrepreneurial framework conditions [GEM (2020)]. These gaps exist partly due to academic scientists' limited contribution to commercialize research discoveries and their lack of involvement in academic entrepreneurship.

Academic entrepreneurs are academic scientists who are involved in research commercialization or university technology transfer activities. Academic scientists are deemed key factors whose research works lead to discoveries with commercial potential [Jain *et al.* (2009); Wood (2011)]. Nonetheless, such entrepreneurial pursuit is beyond their scientific expertise and traditional roles [Franklin *et al.* (2001); Wright *et al.* (2007)]. The endeavor to bring innovation from the lab to the market inherently demands a long gestation period and pits academic scientists against unknown challenges due to their lack of entrepreneurship skills and knowledge. Regardless of these pessimistic claims, there have been successful cases of academic entrepreneurs [Closs *et al.* (2013); Petkewich (2009); Rahim *et al.* (2015)].

An investigation of the relationship between scientists' entrepreneurial characteristics and their academic entrepreneurship performance is imperative to unfold the skills and behaviors that enable them to become more entrepreneurial than their colleagues. Opportunity recognition, or the ability to identify the commercial opportunity of research, has been proven as a critical skill of an academic entrepreneur [Clarysse *et al.* (2011)]. However, earlier findings in this area would have been far more useful if the antecedents of entrepreneurial opportunity recognition ability had been recognized. The answers to why and how some individuals are capable to identify opportunity have always been associated to prior knowledge and thinking process that contribute to their enhanced alertness to entrepreneurial opportunity [Hajizadeh and Zali (2016)]. Indeed, numerous studies have been focused on uncovering the cognitive functioning that contribute to individual's ability to recognize opportunity easily and successfully [Kuckertz *et al.* (2017); Mitchell *et al.* (2002); Santos *et al.* (2015)]. For instance, entrepreneurial learning is a dynamic and self-regulated process that contribute towards entrepreneurial success [Fust *et al.* (2017)]. Although self- regulated learning has been thought to act as an informal entrepreneurship education to academic entrepreneurs [Feldmann (2014)], there has been a lack of evidence on how it influences their academic entrepreneurship performance. The main aim of this study is thus to determine the relationship between academic entrepreneurs' self-regulated learning and their ability to identify the commercial opportunity of research discoveries.

Research pertaining the determinants of research commercialization success has been a continuing concern within the field of academic entrepreneurship. The literature would have been far more comprehensive if the under-researched effects of scientists' entrepreneurial characteristics and institutional culture [Kirchberger and Pohl (2016)] had been examined concurrently with institutional support. As policy implementation should be relevant to the university context [Wright *et al.* (2012)], an evaluation of the effectiveness of the infrastructure support system is another beneficial purpose of this study.

2. Literature Review

2.1. *Entrepreneurial activity in the university*

Academic entrepreneurship is a concept that embodies the idea of an entrepreneurial university [Barth and Schlegelmilch (2013); Gibb and Hannon (2006); Wood (2011)] and is often associated with the commercialization of new knowledge generated from academic research discoveries. Siegel and Wright [2015] defined academic entrepreneurship as the initiatives undertaken by a university to stimulate commercialization within academia. Similarly, Grimaldi *et al.* [2011] denoted it as technological entrepreneurship via a university's effort to commercialize academic scientists' research findings or innovations through activities like patenting, licensing, spin-off creation, and university-industry partnership. In addition, Wood [2011] described it as the efforts and activities undertaken by a university and its industry partners to commercialize discoveries from research. On the other hand, Yusof *et al.* [2010] perceive academic entrepreneurship as a value creation process that involves organizational innovation through patenting, licensing, and design rights as well as organizational creation through spin-offs and joint ventures. They further suggested that this process also involves organizational renewal through research groups, research centers, and technology transfer schemes. Altogether, this value creation process leads to the commercialization of research and technology originating from the university. Accordingly, entrepreneurial activities in university reinforce the bond between universities and industry that bring significant impact to the regional and social development [Pattnaik and Pandey (2016)].

Siegel and Wright [2015], in their work advocating the rethinking of academic entrepreneurship, claimed that the benchmarking of entrepreneurial activities based on the metrics of patenting, licensing, and start-up activity (as in the United States and Canada) may not represent the true outcomes of academic entrepreneurship. Furthermore, these traditional indicators often require a long gestation period to materialize [Reynolds *et al.* (2004)]. This presents challenges in gauging the progress of entrepreneurial activity, especially for universities that are novices in academic entrepreneurship. Therefore, this study examined the academic entrepreneurship

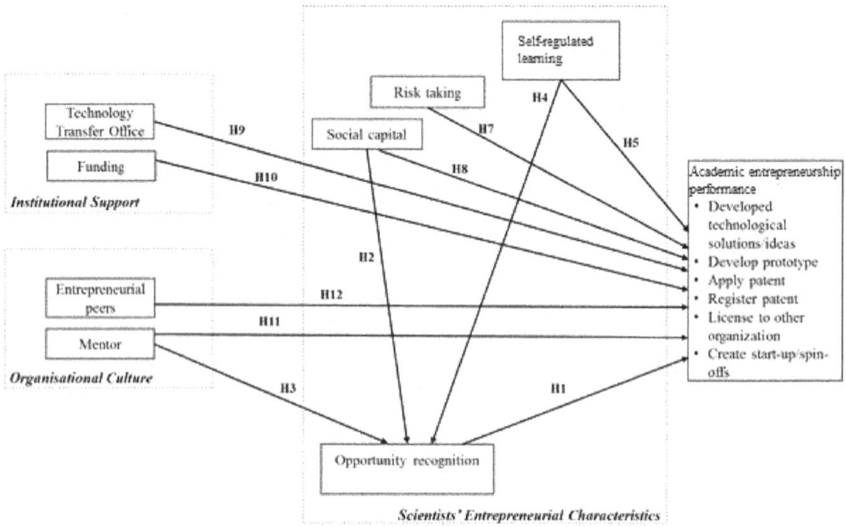

Fig. 1. Conceptual framework.

performance of academic entrepreneurs on a much wider spectrum by including the progress in developing commercial opportunities (e.g. technological solution ideas and potential prototypes) in addition to the other academic entrepreneurship performance indicators depicted in Fig. 1. Accordingly, the term "academic entrepreneurship performance" in this study refers to entrepreneurial activities undertaken by academic scientists in their quest to commercialize research or transfer technology-based innovation from academia to external organizations that utilize and apply the technology for marketable products [Kirchberger and Pohl (2016); Mom *et al.* (2012)].

2.2. *Opportunity recognition*

Opportunity recognition is one of the key foundational concepts in entrepreneurship research [Chell (2013)] that explains why some individuals become entrepreneurs and some do not [Shane and Venkataraman (2000)]. Although scholars have long debated opportunity recognition [George *et al.* (2014)], this concept has not been extensively examined from the academic entrepreneurship perspective. The few notable exceptions have acknowledged academic entrepreneurship as a process arising from opportunity recognition [d'Este *et al.* (2012); Prodan and Drnovsek (2010)]. Opportunity recognition refers to the ability of an academic entrepreneur to detect opportunities from research that can be converted into commercial market applications [Clarysse *et al.* (2011); Fernández-Pérez *et al.* (2015); Rasmussen and Rice (2011)]. Prior evidence suggests that academic scientists who have a stronger self-belief in their opportunity recognition ability have a higher entrepreneurial intention to create a start-up company by transferring technology related to research discoveries [Fernández-Pérez *et al.* (2015)]. Similarly, Clarysse *et al.* [2011] showed that academic scientists with a higher degree of opportunity recognition capability are more likely to create ventures themselves. Accordingly, this study proposed the following hypothesis:

H1: *Scientists' ability to identify the commercial opportunity of academic research relates positively to their academic entrepreneurship performance*

A common theme in most studies on the antecedents of opportunity recognition has been the crucial role of information in preceding this process. Generally, there are two main reasons why some individuals can recognize opportunity [Casson (2005)]. First, these individuals have better information. Second, they can put that information to better use towards value creation. The influence of information in the opportunity recognition process raises the question of how individuals can get better information. In this regard, connections with diverse people provides access to external knowledge [Ramos-Rodríguez *et al.* (2010)], whereby the strength of the social network between entrepreneurs, managers, and entrepreneurial associations influences the number of opportunities an individual can develop and exploit [Fuentes *et al.* (2010)]. In addition, Fernández-Pérez *et al.* [2015] adopted a broader perspective to investigate the indirect influence of academic scientists' distinct social networks (professional forums and business and personal networks) on entrepreneurial intention. Their analysis of 630 Spanish scientists provided evidence on the positive effect of perceived informational support from business and personal networks on scientists' higher self-belief in opportunity recognition. In the same manner, the presence of entrepreneurial mentors among senior academics may also bestow scientists with relevant information, which in turn facilitates opportunity recognition. Evidence in sustainable entrepreneurship revealed that entrepreneurs' opportunity recognition is influenced by their knowledge of natural and communal environments that provide them with the edge of having additional information [Hanohov and Baldacchino (2018)]. Hence, this study predicted as follows:

H2: *Scientists' social capital relates positively to their ability to identify the commercial opportunity of academic research*

H3: *Influence from mentors to provide informational support relates positively to scientists' ability to identify the commercial opportunity of academic research*

H13: *Scientists' social capital indirectly relates to academic entrepreneurship performance through their ability to identify the commercial opportunity of academic research*

2.3. *Self-regulated learning*

Theoretically, self-regulated learning is an independent learning approach that requires an individual to (i) take his/her own initiative in identifying learning needs to achieve a certain goal and (ii) acquire learning resources with or without the assistance of others [Brookfield (2009)].

The idea of self-regulated learning parallels with the entrepreneurial personality literature, which suggests that behavioral characteristic of entrepreneurs involves autonomous and strategic actions to identify and organize resources for the purpose of converting opportunities to marketable products [Chell *et al.* (1991); Cromie (2000)]. Furthermore, self-regulated learning behavior allows entrepreneurs to take accountability and to control both self-monitoring and self-management processes in achieving specific learning goals [Tseng (2013)].

Academic scientists generally lack business-related knowledge and are relatively unfit for entrepreneurial tasks [Franklin *et al.* (2001)]. In the pursuit of research commercialization and technology transfer, scientists encounter knowledge gaps due to their unfamiliarity with entrepreneurship, as being an entrepreneur goes beyond their traditional roles and scientific expertise. In facing the conditions of uncertainty, scientists must self-regulate their behavior, environment and cognition within the entrepreneurial context. Even though they may start as novices, their capability can be developed through self-regulated learning [Winkler *et al.* (2016)]. This study argues that scientists who step out of their comfort zones and attempt to accomplish self-regulated learning to bridge these knowledge gaps will potentially make the difference. Specific environmental features beyond comfort zone enable entrepreneur to build up diverse skills and network relations conducive to entrepreneurship that led to opportunities discovery [Schlepphorst *et al.* (2020)]. Besides, entrepreneurs also learn to develop opportunity recognition through market interaction and real-life process formed by prior knowledge, accumulated resources and industrial contexts [Sanz-Velasco (2006)]. Accordingly, this study defines scientists' entrepreneurial effort in self-regulated learning as determined attempts to acquire and organize resources related to academic entrepreneurship with the explicit goal of transferring technologies from academic research.

In their attempts to realize successful research commercialization, scientists may independently learn about research ideas and opportunities by attending conferences and university-run product exhibitions. The source of scientists' self-regulated learning may also come from discussions with industrial contacts about problems that can potentially be resolved through research [Thursby and Thursby (2001)]. Furthermore, Smilor [1997, p. 344] asserted that "*effective entrepreneurs are exceptional learners who learn by doing and learn from everything including customers, suppliers, and competitors*". Therefore, scientists' self-regulated learning may also be accomplished through their active seeking of information from potential customers, suppliers, competitors, investors, business partners, as well as other organizations. These autonomous efforts in entrepreneurial learning allow scientists to gather external information that exposes them to more ideas and opportunities, which may influence their opportunity recognition ability. Hence, this study conjectured as follows:

H4: *Scientists' self-regulated learning relates positively to their ability to identify the commercial opportunity of academic research*

H5: *Scientists' self-regulated learning relates positively to their academic entrepreneurship performance*

H6: *Scientists' self-regulated learning indirectly relates to academic entrepreneurship performance through their ability to identify the commercial opportunity of academic research*

2.4. *Risk-taking*

It has long been argued that entrepreneurs have a risk-taking trait [Brockhaus (1980); Nielsen (2015)], which is a measure of the degree to which individuals are willing to make huge and risky resource commitments to seize opportunities with high chances of costly failure [Kirkman (2013)]. Fear of failure influences one's decision to engage in entrepreneurial activity, given that venturing into a new business poses the risk of financial losses that may affect one's future and emotional state [Xavier *et al.* (2012)]. Scientists often encounter uncertainty regarding the usefulness of technology as well as its commercial application and replication in the industry since technology is usually transferred at the infancy stage [Jensen and Thursby (2003)]. Therefore, academic entrepreneurs are those who bold enough to embrace these risks [Fernández-Pérez *et al.* (2015); Guerrero *et al.* (2008)]. Accordingly, this study predicted the following hypothesis:

H7: *The risk-taking propensity of scientists positively relates to their academic entrepreneurship performance*

2.5. *Social capital*

Social capital is described as "*resources individuals obtain from knowing others, being part of a social network with them, or merely from being known to them*" [Baron and Markman (2000, p. 10)]. In the academic context, these social networks involve personal, professional, and business linkages between scientists and other individuals. A large body of literature has focused on the contribution of social capital to academic entrepreneurship, specifically to the formation of entrepreneurial intention [Aldridge and Audretsch (2011); Fernández-Pérez *et al.* (2015); Karlsson and Wigren (2012); Landry *et al.* (2006); Prodan and Drnovsek (2010); Sequeira *et al.* (2007)] to opportunity recognition and start-up survival [Pugalia *et al.* (2020)]. Scientists benefit from their social network in terms of both the tangible and intangible resources needed for technology transfer. For instance, apart from enhancing informational access to business markets, new opportunities [Prodan and Drnovsek (2010)] and consumer needs [Fernández-Pérez *et al.* (2015)], social capital also provides scientists with technical support [Karlsson and Wigren (2012); Ozgen and Baron (2007)], emotional support [Fernández-Pérez *et al.* (2015)], and financial resources [Baron and Markman (2000)]. In accordance with these considerations, this study hypothesized:

H8: *Scientists' social capital positively relates to their academic entrepreneurship performance*

2.6. *Institutional support*

2.6.1. *Technology transfer office*

The establishment of a Technology Transfer Office (TTO) is a major area of interest within the field of academic entrepreneurship [Grimaldi *et al.* (2011); Siegel and

Wright (2015)] as universities continue to play crucial role to develop and enhance their capabilities to support the growth of technology-based new ventures [Rao and Mulloth (2017)]. The term TTO in this study refers to assistance and support measures provided by a university entity to facilitate academic entrepreneurs in research commercialization and technology transfer. Some scholars attested that the establishment of TTO has impacted the performance of academic entrepreneurship [Clarysse *et al.* (2011); Muscio *et al.* (2016); Nosella and Grimaldi (2009); Phan *et al.* (2005); Rizzo and Ramaciotti (2014)]. However, there have been contradictory evidence to this [Clarysse *et al.* (2011)]. For instance, Nosella and Grimaldi [2009] revealed no direct linkage between a TTO's establishment and the number of start-ups. This inconsistent observation could be due to inhomogeneity of TTO across different universities [Markman *et al.* (2005)] that impact universities in a dissimilar manner [Aldridge and Audretsch (2011)].

Recent studies have instead attempted to explain the influences of a TTO's size [Aldridge and Audretsch (2011); Muscio *et al.* (2016)], resources [Osiri *et al.* (2013)] and efficiency [Aldridge and Audretsch (2011); Clarysse *et al.* (2011)] on the development of academic entrepreneurship. Institutional support from a TTO to academic entrepreneurs through its collective services is critical [Rasmussen and Wright (2015)], especially in the early stages of technology transfer [Rasmussen and Rice (2011); Wood (2011)]. However, the specific types of TTO services that are conducive to scientists' academic entrepreneurship performance remain unclear. For instance, an examination of 128 universities' TTOs showed that their mission statements prioritize licensing for royalties and intellectual property (IP) protection more than facilitating scientists in the disclosure process [Markman *et al.* (2005)]. This study argues that if a TTO is effective, its presence should have a positive impact on scientists' involvement in entrepreneurial activity and their consequent academic entrepreneurship performance. Accordingly, this study predicted the following:

H9: *The efficiency of a Technology Transfer Office positively relates to scientists' academic entrepreneurship performance*

2.6.2. *Funding*

A growing body of literature recognizes the importance of financial assistance in the early stages of a technology transfer pursuit [Kochenkova *et al.* (2015); Rasmussen and Sørheim (2012)]. Through the provision of proof-of-concept funds, translational funds, or pre-seeds funds, the financial gap between research and commercialization is bridged, freeing scientists from having to redistribute research and development (R&D) funds. Moreover, proper funding of research discoveries with commercial potential allows scientists to proceed with proofs-of- concept, enter the market, and seize opportunities at the right time without postponing a technology's potential [Gubitta *et al.* (2016)]. While there is evidence on the positive effect of funding amount on the entrepreneurial activity rate [Aldridge and Audretsch (2011); O'shea *et al.* (2005); Rasmussen *et al.* (2006); Rizzo and Ramaciotti (2014)], some studies have observed contrary findings [Di Gregorio and Shane (2003)]. For instance, Stanford University, with a sponsored research expenditure of USD 391 million, managed to generate 25 start-ups while Duke University, with a sponsored research expenditure of USD 361 million, did not generate any [Di Gregorio and Shane (2003)]. The inconsistency of these findings raises the question of whether it is the complexity of funding procedures that matters rather than the amount of funding. Therefore, this study hypothesized as follows:

H10: *The ease of getting financial assistance positively relates to scientists' academic entrepreneurship performance*

2.7. *Organizational culture*

2.7.1. *Mentor support*

Variations in entrepreneurial activity rates [Di Gregorio and Shane (2003)] may be attributed to differences in entrepreneurial cultures at organizational and faculty levels [Osiri *et al.* (2013); Tartari *et al.* (2014)]. Social norms influence scientists' entrepreneurial behavior [Ajzen (1991)] when most faculty members embrace attitudes, values, goals, and practices favoring entrepreneurship [Osiri *et al.* (2013)]. Indeed, organizational culture is the closest environmental factor that affects scientists' engagement in entrepreneurial activity [Bercovitz and Feldman (2008); Huyghe *et al.* (2015); Prodan and Drnovsek (2010); Tartari *et al.* (2014)].

Leadership direction [Bercovitz and Feldman (2008)] and interaction with other faculty members [Osiri *et al.* (2013)] are two elements that establish culture, which subsequently impels the attitude of a scientist towards academic entrepreneurship. Senior management support and culture that encourage cooperation across organizational boundaries have also been found to contribute towards a successful commercialization and technology transfer in the public-private cooperation [Geisler and Turchetti (2015)]. Furthermore, the presence of a mentor to confer knowledge and support relating to academic entrepreneurship may persuade scientists on the feasibility of an entrepreneurial pursuit. Indeed, a study on the learning development of novice entrepreneurs indicated positive learning outcomes from mentorship programs [St-Jean and Audet (2012)]. This is because formal mentoring program can effectively strengthen mentee's entrepreneurial self-efficacy through support from mentors [St-Jean *et al.* (2018)].

Accordingly, this study predicted the following:

H11 *Support from mentor positively relates to scientists' academic entrepreneurship performance*

2.8. *Entrepreneurial peers*

The entrepreneurial peer effect reflects scientists' interaction with other faculty members who have prior experience in technology transfer. This effect inspires scientists to become academic entrepreneurs [Tartari *et al.* (2014)], especially if they have low exposure to entrepreneurship [Nanda and Sørensen (2010)]. Similar to

Prodan and Drnovsek [2010], Huyghe *et al.* [2015] provided evidence that the presence of colleagues who have been involved in spin-off creation, patenting, licensing, contract research, or consulting positively affects scientists' propensity to engage in technology transfer activities. This is partly because entrepreneurial peers deliver the message that their dual roles as academics and entrepreneurs are socially accepted, which in turn enhances scientists' perceived desirability towards research commercialization and technology transfer pursuits [Ajzen (1991)]. Indeed, a recent study on the power of peers reveals that encouragement from peers strengthen the relationship between creativity and entrepreneurial intention [Bello *et al.* (2018)]. Besides, risk-averse scientists may be relieved of the stigma of failure after learning from their entrepreneurial peers' experiences [Nanda and Sørensen (2010)]. Therefore, this study predicted the following:

H12: *The presence of entrepreneurial peers among colleagues positively relates to scientists' academic entrepreneurship performance*

Figure 1 summarizes this study's conceptual framework, indicating the expected relationships between scientists' entrepreneurial characteristics (opportunity recognition, self-regulated learning, risk-taking, social capital), institutional support (TTO efficiency, ease of getting funding), organizational culture (mentors, entrepreneurial peers), and academic entrepreneurship performance.

3. Methodology

The study sample consisted of academic scientists from a public research university in Malaysia, i.e. Universiti Teknologi Malaysia (UTM). Statistics show that local commercial products and technologies originating from academic research are mostly contributed by the engineering sciences [MASTIC (2013b)], implying that academic entrepreneurs are more common among scientists from the engineering field [Reguera (2016); Philpott *et al.* (2011); Zhang *et al.* (2014)]. Therefore, the selection of UTM as a case study was justified given that its primary focus is the teaching and research of engineering [UTM Organisational Management Division (2016)]. However, despite its core establishment for engineering teaching and research, UTM lags behind Universiti Sains Malaysia (USM) and Universiti Malaya (UM) in its contribution to commercialize local products and technologies [MASTIC (2013b)]. The number of active scientists in UTM is almost comparable to USM and is higher than UM [MASTIC (2015b)], suggesting that UTM's low performance is due to the limited contribution of its engineering scientists to the commercialization of research discoveries. Based on these considerations, the population of engineering scientists investigated in this study was derived from UTM.

Pertaining to research relating to the determinants of scientists' opportunity recognition capacity and engagement in technology transfer, there has been a significant body of literature, known variables and existing theories to support the work undertaken in this area of interest. Hence, the positivism research paradigm was adopted as it focuses on the quantitative descriptors [Creswell (2003); Dawson

Table 1. Profile of respondents.

	Frequency	Percentage
Gender		
Male	83	72.2
Female	32	27.8
Research Experience		
Below 10 years	19	16.5
10 to 20 years	31	27
20 to 30 years	39	33.9
More than 30 years	26	22.6
Faculty		
Chemical Engineering	13	11.3
Civil Engineering	24	20.9
Electrical & Electronic Engineering	22	19.1
Mechanical Engineering	32	27.8
Biosciences & Medical Engineering	5	4.4
Chemistry	4	3.5
Computer Science	3	2.6
Physics	1	0.9
Geo-Information & Real Estate	9	7.8
Others	2	1.7

(2002)] for this study sought to confirm, support or challenge the findings of other scholars in a different research context. A cross-sectional survey study was employed in this study to develop generalizations to provide better prediction, explanation and understanding of the phenomena under study.

The size of the target population was 1453. A power analysis [Cohen (1988); Hair *et al.* (2014)] using the G*power software [Faul *et al.* (2009)] computed the minimum sample size to be 109, with the maximum number of predictors set at eight, the effect size set at medium (0.15), and the power level set at 0.80 [Gefen *et al.* (2011)]. A survey instrument was developed comprising measurement items for all the variables in this study (see Appendix A). A total of 115 valid responses were received. The demographic profile of the respondents is shown in Table 1. These respondents were a mixture of Professors, Associate Professors and Senior Lecturers. Most of them were from engineering faculties and had more than 10 years of experience.

4. Data Analysis and Results

Hair *et al.* [2014] guided the data analysis in selecting between partial least square (PLS-SEM) and a covariance-based approach (CB-SEM). CB-SEM is not suitable as the goal of this study is neither towards theory testing nor towards comparison of alternative theories. PLS-SEM is considered as the primary approach in this study since the hypothesized model incorporate both formative and reflective constructs. The research model was analyzed using PLS-SEM approach via the SmartPLS 3.0 software [Ringle *et al.* (2015)]. Following the recommended two-stage analytical procedure (Anderson and Gerbing, 1988), the measurement model (validity and reliability of the measures) was tested first, followed by the structural model which examined the hypothesized relationships. The bootstrapping method was used to test the significance of the path coefficients and loadings [Hair *et al.* (2014)].

4.1. *Measurement model evaluation*

The validity and reliability of reflective measures were evaluated in terms of convergent validity, internal consistency, and discriminant validity. Factor loadings, composite reliability (CR), and average variance extracted (AVE) were used to assess convergent validity. The loadings for all reflective items were higher than the acceptable value of 0.5 (see Table 2). The composite reliabilities and AVE values were all higher than 0.7 and 0.5 respectively, exceeding their threshold values. This demonstrated the satisfactory internal consistency reliability and convergent validity of the reflective measurement items.

The discriminant validity of the measures was examined through Fornell and Larcker's [1981] criterion of inter-correlation matrix. As shown in Table 3, the constructs' square root of the AVE (bold values in the diagonals) were higher than the correlations between constructs (values in corresponding rows and columns), indicating adequate discriminant validity. In sum, both convergent and discriminant validity of the reflective measures in this study were established.

The validity of formative measures was evaluated in terms of construct validity, indicator collinearity, and outer weights. For formative measures, a modified multitrait–multimethod (MTMM) matrix analysis [Loch *et al.* (2003)] was employed to assess construct validity [Andreev *et al.* (2009); Lowry and Gaskin (2014)]. Both formative measures established sufficient discriminant validity. The measurement of discriminant validity for these formative measures is discussed in Rahim *et al.* [2019].

The variance inflation factors (VIF) for formative measures were below 3.3 (see Table 2), indicating the absence of multicollinearity. The three indicators with insignificant outer weights were TTO4, SC3, and SC5. Indicator TTO4 was retained as deletion is deemed necessary only if its outer loading is neither significant nor below 0.5 [Hair *et al.* (2014)]. Indicators SC3 and SC5 were also retained as their corresponding outer loadings were above 0.5 and significant. As per the guidelines of Cenfetelli and Bassellier [2009], significant indicators with positive weights were compared based on their magnitudes whereas significant indicators with negative weights (TTO5: efficiency of TTO staff, SC1: professional forums) were interpreted as having negative effects when the effects of other indicators within the same construct were controlled. The results showed the relative effect of all indicators towards the TTO construct was the strongest from TTO2 (commercialization services), followed by TTO1 (awareness programs) and TTO3 (financial planning services). For the social capital construct, the indicator with the strongest effect was SC2 (personal network) followed by SC4 (new partners and potential investors).

4.2. *Structural model evaluation*

The structural model was assessed by evaluating the coefficients of determination (R^2), standardized regression weights (β), and corresponding t-values (see Table 4). The SmartPLS bootstrapping function with 500 resamples was applied to 115 cases.

Table 2. Convergent validity of measurement model.

Type of measures	Construct	Item	Loadings	AVE[a]/Weights[b]	CR	VIF
Reflective measures	Opportunity recognition (OR)	OR1	0.914	0.855	0.959	
		OR2	0.941			
		OR3	0.912			
		OR4	0.932			
	Academic entrepreneurship performance (AEP)	AEP1	0.843	0.551	0.878	
		AEP2	0.521			
		AEP3	0.86			
		AEP4	0.794			
		AEP5	0.712			
		AEP6	0.67			
	Risk taking	RT1	0.881	0.751	0.9	
		RT2	0.918			
		RT3	0.796			
	Mentor support	SM1	0.893	0.776	0.954	
		SM2	0.883			
		SM3	0.834			
		SM4	0.93			
		SM5	0.931			
		SM6	0.808			
	Self-regulated learning	SD2	0.744	0.734	0.951	
		SD3	0.799			
		SD4	0.863			
		SD5	0.912			
		SD6	0.908			
		SD7	0.906			
		SD8	0.854			
	Entrepreneurial peers	EP1	0.95	0.888	0.96	
		EP2	0.949			
		EP3	0.929			
	Funding	FG1	0.824	0.692	0.9	
		FG2	0.83			
		FG3	0.856			
		FG4	0.817			
F	TTO efficiency	TTO1	0.723**	0.449**		1.38
		TTO2	0.863**	0.730**		2.05
		TTO3	0.480**	0.292*		1.27
		TTO4	0.481**	0.056		1.81
		TTO5	0.358**	−0.337*		1.87
	Social capital	SC1	0.263**	−0.216*		1.30
		SC2	0.960**	0.897**		2.09
		SC3	0.625**	0.016		1.96
		SC4	0.731**	0.261*		1.92
		SC5	0.580**	−0.009		1.79

[a]Rows indicate AVE for reflective measures.
[b]Rows indicate weights for formative measures. Items SD1, EP4 and EP5 were deleted due to indicator's loading below the threshold values based on a consideration that the deletion led to an increase in composite reliability and average variance extracted [Hair *et al.* (2014)].
Notes: $^{*}p < 0.05$ ($t > 1.645$), $^{**}p < 0.01$ ($t > 2.33$).

The R^2 values were both above 0.35 indicating a substantial model [Cohen (1988)]. Six hypotheses (H1, H2, H4, H8, H9, and H10) were significant with β values ranging from 0.166 to 0.52 in expected directions. The six significant relationships also showed

Table 3. Discriminant validity of reflective measures.

Construct	SD	EP	FG	OR	RT	SM	AEP
SD	**0.857**						
EP	0.408	**0.943**					
FG	0.379	0.489	**0.832**				
OR	0.685	0.355	0.445	**0.925**			
RT	0.58	0.459	0.521	0.659	**0.866**		
SM	0.173	0.462	0.216	0.2	0.207	**0.881**	
AEP	0.668	0.453	0.568	0.671	0.58	0.174	**0.742**

Notes: SD: Self-regulated learning, EP: Entrepreneurial peers, FG: Funding, OR: Opportunity recognition, RT: Risk taking, SM: Mentor support, AEP: Academic entrepreneurship performance.

substantive effects with medium effect sizes (f^2). The predictive relevance (Q^2) of the model was estimated using the SmartPLS blindfolding function (omission distance setting, $D = 6$). The results showed that the Q^2 value was more than zero, suggesting that the exogenous constructs had a large predictive relevance for the endogenous constructs under consideration [Fornell and Cha (1994); Hair *et al.* (2014)].

The indirect hypothesized relationships were tested using the "boostrapping the indirect effect" method [Preacher and Hayes (2004, 2008)]. The results in Table 4 show that two indirect effects (H6 and H13) were significant. Their 95% bootstrapping confidence intervals, [LL = 0.052, UL = 0.226] and [LL = 0.014, UL = 0.134], did not straddle a "0", thus verifying that there was mediation. These results confirmed that scientists' self-regulated learning and social capital indirectly relate to academic entrepreneurship performance through their ability to identify the commercial opportunity of academic research.

Table 4. Results of structural model assessment.

No.	Relationship	β	Std.	t-value	R^2	f^2	Q^2	Hypothesis
H1	OR →AEP	0.293	0.088	3.338**		0.105		Supported
H2	SC → OR	0.219	0.096	2.289*		0.048		Supported
H3	SM → OR	0.064	0.053	1.197		0.008		Not supported
H4	SD →OR	0.52	0.097	5.363**	0.5	0.273	0.420	Supported
H5	SD → AEP	0.123	0.083	1.49		0.017		Not supported
H7	RT → AEP	−0.064	0.059	1.082		0.005		Not supported
H8	SC → AEP	0.308	0.077	3.993**		0.130		Supported
H9	TTO → AEP	0.202	0.084	2.397**	0.674	0.065	0.345	Supported
H10	FG → AEP	0.166	0.078	2.113*		0.048		Supported
H11	SM → AEP	−0.103	0.086	1.2		0.024		Not supported
H12	EP →AEP	0.071	0.065	1.091		0.009		Not supported
H6	[a]SD→OR→AEP	0.153	0.052	2.944*				Supported
H13	[b]SC→OR→AEP	0.064	0.038	1.699*				Supported

[a,b]indirect relationships.

Note: $^{*}p < 0.05$ ($t > 1.645$), $^{**}p < 0.01$ ($t > 2.33$).

SD: Self-regulated learning, EP: Entrepreneurial peers, SC: Social capital, FG: Funding, TTO: Technology Transfer Office, ORC: Opportunity recognition, RT: Risk taking, SM: Mentor support, AEP: Academic entrepreneurship performance.

Demographic characteristics such as gender [Koellinger (2008); Ramos-Rodriguez (2010); Tartari *et al.* (2014)] and academic post status [Kalar and Antoncic (2015); Tartari *et al.* (2014)] were tested as control variables. In SmartPLS, these control variables were treated as independent variables together with the other eight latent variables [Jabbour *et al.* (2015)]. The regression weights and their significances were then examined to test the effect of the control variables on the hypothesized relationships that were statistically significant before the post-hoc analysis (TTO → AEP, FG → AEP, SC → AEP, ORC → AEP). The results of the post-hoc analysis showed that these relationships remained statistically significant despite the inclusion of the control variables. Therefore, the effects of the control variables were ruled out.

5. Discussion

This study's main findings reveal that scientists' opportunity recognition ($\beta = 0.293$) and social capital ($\beta = 0.308$) are the strongest contributing factors to their academic entrepreneurship performance. TTO efficiency ($\beta = 0.202$) and ease of getting funding ($\beta = 0.166$) also play influential roles, albeit to a lesser extent. Contrary to expectations, this study did not find organisational culture to significantly improve scientists' engagement in academic entrepreneurship. Interestingly, the findings provide new evidence that scientists' self-regulated learning indirectly influences academic entrepreneurship performance by developing their opportunity recognition.

Consistent with Clarysse *et al.* [2011] and Ramos-Rodríguez *et al.* [2010], this study corroborates that scientists' academic entrepreneurship performance is strongly impacted by their opportunity recognition ability. Scientists with this ability can assume the role of academic entrepreneurs because they are good at perceiving unmet customer needs and unique value propositions offered by their research discoveries to the market [Chesbrough and Rosenbloom (2002)]. The measures of opportunity recognition in this study (see Appendix A) further suggest that a trait of academic entrepreneurs that differentiates them from their non entrepreneurial colleagues is the ability to identify the disruptive or sustaining technological potentials of their academic research. Scientists' higher opportunity recognition is reflected by their increased ability to identify research ideas and design new products or services that benefit other organizations, solve consumer problems, or improve existing products. The sustaining or disruptive characteristics of these technological discoveries [Kassicieh *et al.* (2002); Walsh *et al.* (2002)] raise the commercial value of academic research [Markman *et al.* (2008); Rasmussen *et al.* (2011)]. This study found weak support for the hypothesized positive relationship between scientists' self-regulated learning and their academic entrepreneurship performance, similar to Keith *et al.* [2016]. Nevertheless, this study empirically proves that scientists' self-regulated learning indirectly influences their academic entrepreneurship performance by developing their opportunity recognition. This finding is in line with the psychological perspective that asserts the influence of deliberate practice on reinforcing skills in a particular domain [Ericsson *et al.* (1993)]. Scientists' self-regulated learning is shown by their frequent deliberate activities in developing a commercialization plan; in attending seminars or conferences to gain more knowledge on other research ideas; in attending exhibitions to learn about commercialized products; in discussing problems that can potentially be resolved through research with contacts from the industry; in gathering market information about potential customers, suppliers, and competitors; in seeking potential investors; in sourcing business or industrial partners; and in consulting external agencies to refine and enhance their business plan. Through these self-regulated learning efforts, scientists are exposed to information and knowledge that allow them to become more creative and innovative in exploring opportunities to translate their research into marketable products or technology. Indeed, learning behavior plays a crucial role in developing entrepreneurial creativity [Rigolizzo and Amabile (2015)] and proactive learning efforts [Kickul and Walters (2002)] align well with Kuckertz *et al.* [2017] who found that entrepreneurs have higher chance to recognize opportunity as a result their active involvement in searching, being alert, gathering information, communicating, addressing customer needs and evaluating. These findings are consistent with those of Kaish and Gilad [1991], who attested that a characteristic of entrepreneurs is their frequent involvement in information seeking, through which entrepreneurial opportunities are discovered in a systematic search process. This is because scientists' frequent involvement in information seeking reinforces their cognitive resources, as conjectured in cognitive psychology and social cognition theory [Mitchell *et al.* (2002)], that enable them to assess, judge and decide the emerging opportunities [Neill *et al.* (2017)]. Scientist's self-regulated learning behavior introduced in this study could also be perceived as a form practical entrepreneurship education that has been proven to contribute to the academic entrepreneurship performance [Sansone *et al.* (2019)].

The results from the formative measurement model imply that scientists' personal network, consisting of their close family and friends, is the most important social resource for their academic entrepreneurship performance. The second most important social resource is their business partners and potential investors. These observations are consistent with earlier reports [Sequeira *et al.* (2007)] that a supportive and strong relationship with one's personal network engenders a stronger effect on entrepreneurial intention than non-affective contacts like business networks. A significant inverse relationship was found between scientists' professional network and their academic entrepreneurship performance, which is in accordance with Fernández-Pérez *et al.* [2015] but in contrast with Aldridge and Audretsch [2011]. Academic scientists are likely to gain many professional contacts through their attendance at conferences, workshops and seminars; however, these knowledge-sharing platforms often revolve around scientific knowledge rather than academic entrepreneurship.

Consistent with earlier studies [Fernández-Pérez *et al.* (2015); Ramos-Rodríguez *et al.* (2010)], the results support the indirect relationship between scientists' social capital and academic entrepreneurship performance by way of their opportunity recognition. Furthermore, this study discovers that the influence of scientists' self-regulated learning behavior in enhancing their opportunity recognition ability is far greater than the influence of social capital. Since scientists' social capital is mostly built on a personal network that provides emotional support, the role of scientists' self-regulated learning behavior exceeds that of social capital by enabling scientists to gain more access to external knowledge that helps them better recognize entrepreneurial opportunity.

In line with Clarysse *et al.* [2011], institutional support through TTO plays a weaker role than personal factors in improving scientists' academic entrepreneurship performance. The results from the formative measurement model, which are partly discussed in Rahim *et al.* [2019], grant new insights into TTO services by highlighting that facilitating patent application and technology licensing is its most important role. The second most important role of a TTO is to organize programs to increase scientists' understanding of the technology transfer process. In accordance with Slavtchev and Göktepe-Hultén [2015], the findings also suggest that the TTO's third most vital role is to aid scientists' financial planning. However, contrary to Aldridge and Audretsch (2011), it is intriguing to discover a significant inverse relationship between the efficiency of TTO employees and scientists' technology transfer pursuit. This observation is partly due to the relatively new establishment of the TTO in UTM (TTO age < 10 years) compared to the average age of those in developed countries (United States: 18.5 years; United Kingdom: 17.5 years; Spain: 18 years; Denmark: 13 years) [Rizzo and Ramaciotti (2014)].

The ease of getting funding shows the weakest influence on scientists' academic entrepreneurship performance. The Malaysian government steadily increased the amount of funding between the year 2000 and the year 2012 [MASTIC (2016)]. However, several qualitative studies suggest that the low entrepreneurial activity rate among Malaysian scientists is caused by a lack of financial support [Khademi *et al.* (2015)]. This study provides evidence from a new perspective, indicating that instead of the funding amount, the difficulty scientists face in the process of applying for and obtaining funds deters them from participating in technology transfer and research commercialization activities.

Unexpectedly, neither mentor support nor the presence of entrepreneurial peers among colleagues were found to significantly improve academic entrepreneurship performance. Contradictory to previous studies [Fernández-Pérez *et al.* (2015); St-Jean and Audet (2012); Tartari *et al.* (2014)], the reason for this insignificant result is because entrepreneurial culture in a university is a rather intangible element [Bradley *et al.* (2013)]. The hypothesized relationships, therefore, may only hold in a certain population of scientists under a particular context. The cultural revolution towards an entrepreneurial society in the United States took root in the early 1960s, when the entrepreneurial mindset to create new values, new products, and new industries was instilled and passed down through generations [Audretsch (2007)]. In contrast, the sample in this study was drawn from a population of scientists from UTM who relative novices in academic entrepreneurship.

Regarding scientists' risk-taking propensity, though the regression coefficient showed a negative value, there was insufficient evidence to verify the significance of its impact on scientists' academic entrepreneurship performance. The potential reason behind this finding's refutation of earlier studies [Fernández-Pérez *et al.* (2015); Guerrero *et al.* (2008); Kirkman (2013)] could be the cultural difference across countries. For instance, the relative lack of entrepreneurial activity in Japan [Fukao and Kwon (2011)] has been attributed to Japanese culture that accentuates conventionality and consistency in a way that discourages risk-taking behavior, which is the opposite of American culture [Kagami (2015)]. Accordingly, this study implies a mindset in UTM that ascribes a mixed level of appreciation towards academic entrepreneurship, which explains the insignificant influence of culture on scientists' academic entrepreneurship performance.

6. Implications, Limitations, and Future Research

Research on the antecedents of opportunity recognition has paid less attention to intentional systematic search or the discovery of an opportunity by deliberately searching for it [Fiet *et al.* (2005); George *et al.* (2014)]. This study expands the literature by building upon the concept of deliberate practice [Ericsson *et al.* (1993)] and the operationalization of this construct in the academic entrepreneurship context [Keith *et al.* (2016)]. Eight indicators were developed in this study to measure scientists' self-regulated entrepreneurial learning. The results augment the limited evidence on how autonomous deliberate effort in entrepreneurial learning positively influences opportunity recognition, which further explains improved academic entrepreneurship performance. The results provide a basis for aspiring academic entrepreneurs among scientists on how they could self-develop their entrepreneurial ability. Scientists should position themselves strategically in their environment and manage their knowledge acquisition through deliberate practice. This finding emphasizes the importance of entrepreneur's self-regulatory capability and the underlying mechanism that make some scientists increasingly better at recognizing opportunity while others unable to develop such capability.

The outcomes of this research provide practical implications for the authorities to spur academic entrepreneurship among scientists. Universities should inculcate science and engineering students with an entrepreneurial mindset and entrepreneurial abilities as they are the closest candidates to potentially be groomed into academic entrepreneurs [Morales-Alonso *et al.* (2016); Philpott *et al.* (2011); Reguera (2016); Zhang *et al.* (2014)]. Integrating an entrepreneurship training module that encourages students to assess unique value propositions of technology start-ups would expose them to how entrepreneurs align important problems with feasible technological solutions and viable businesses, which in turn would develop students' opportunity recognition. Moreover, the indicators of academic entrepreneurs' self-regulated learning efforts are useful to universities' engineering faculty to promote deliberate practices among scientists to advance their opportunity recognition. As seminars about intellectual property and patenting procedures are already widely held, universities' engineering faculty should focus more on raising awareness about opportunity creation and recognition from academic research. The findings of weak relationship between risk taking propensity and academic entrepreneurship performance imply that university should focus on developing a positive attitude and strengthen entrepreneurial skills among scientists to rethink about commercial challenge and be less risk averse. Entrepreneurial proactive behavior among scientists to gather external information that exposes them to more ideas and opportunities should be encouraged that will further enhance academic entrepreneurship performance.

The findings of this study are limited to the case study population of UTM; thus, they are not generalizable to other contexts. Future studies should extend the proposed research model to broader geographical scopes and populations. This study suggests two avenues for future research. First, future studies may explore the extent to which academic entrepreneurs discover opportunity by chance during R&D or by strategic plans to create opportunity from the onset of academic research. New findings that distinguish between opportunity discovery and opportunity creation would be valuable for theoretical advancement in the academic entrepreneurship literature. For instance, researchers may consider a longitudinal setting to investigate how tacit knowledge developed from experience and prior education allows academic scientists to discover or create entrepreneurial opportunities from academic research. Longitudinal research is also recommended to eliminate the possibility of reverse causality since this study is based on cross-sectional data. Second, future studies can build upon the operationalization of academic entrepreneurs' self- regulated learning behavior in this study to explore the possible moderating effect of entrepreneurial alertness [George *et al.* (2014); Kirzner (1979)] in strengthening opportunity recognition.

Appendix A

Table A.1. Survey instrument comprising measurement items for all the variables

Variable	Item	Source
Academic entrepreneurship performance (AEP)	AEP1—Applied patent (patent filing) for my research findings. AEP2—Registered patent (patent granted) for my research findings. AEP3—Licensed to other organization my research findings for them to develop and sell product. AEP4—Developed potential prototype, technology and process which can be commercialized to the industry. AEP5—Developed *solutions that can enhance the product of other industry. *technology or know-how(ideas) that could stand alone/used with other technologies AEP6—Created spin-off companies to commercialize research products	Adapted from Prodan and Drnovsek [2010], D'Este *et al.* [2012]
Self-regulated learning (SD)	SD1—Develop commercialization plan for my research findings. SD2—Attended seminar and onferences to gain more knowledge on other research ideas SD3—Attended exhibition to gain more knowledge on products that has been commercialized SD4—Discuss with contacts from the industry on their problems that potentially being resolved through research. SD5—Gather market information about potential customer, supplier or competitor	Adapted from Macnamara *et al.* [2014], Keith *et al.* [2016]

Table A.1. (*Continued*)

Variable	Item	Source
	SD6—Seek potential investor who is interested to fund the commercialization of my research findings.	
	SD7—Seek business or industrial partner who is interested to commercialize my research findings.	
	SD8—Consult external support such as TTO or external agencies to refine and enhance business plan.	
Opportunity recognition (OR)	OR1—Identify *research ideas* that can be converted into new product or services (even though I may not pursue them).	Adapted from Clarysse *et al.* [2011]
	OR2—Identify research ideas that can improve existing product or services (even though I may not pursue them)	
	OR3—Identify research ideas that can benefit other organizations (even though I may not pursue them)	
	OR4—Design product or services to improve consumer problems (even though I may not pursue them)	
Risk taking (RT)	RT1—I am capable to work productively under pressure and stressful condition.	Adapted from Fernández-Pérez *et al.* [2015]
	RT2—I am persistent in achieving my mission even though facing with adversity.	
	RT3—If I identified commercial application of my research, I would seriously consider putting more effort to commercialize the opportunity.	
Technology Transfer Office (TTO)	TTO1—I think that programs organized by TTO increase my understanding about the process of commercializing research findings.	
	TTO2—I think that the *commercialization services provided by TTO has assisted me to commercialize research findings. (*prototype development, patent application, technology licensing/assignment)	
	TTO3—I think that the services provided by TTO has assisted me to develop *financial planning to commercialize research findings. (*business plan, market validation)	
	TTO4—I think that the *services provided by TTO has assisted me to secure partners to commercialize research findings. (* marketing, promotion, exhibition)	
	TTO5—I think that the TTO personnel are efficient in assisting me to commercialize research findings.	
Social capital (SC)	SC1—My contacts from professional forums* have been facilitating me with information and support that encourage me to commercialize my research findings. *professional forums: Conferences/Workshop/Seminars	Adapted from Fernández-Pérez *et al.* [2015]
	SC2—My contacts from personal network have been facilitating me with information and support that encourage me to commercialize my research findings. *personal network: Friends/Close Family/Colleagues	
	SC3—My contacts or discussion with potential customers or potential suppliers has been facilitating me with information and support that encourage me to commercialize my research findings.	
	SC4—My contacts or discussion with new partners or potential investors has been facilitating me with	

Table A.1. (*Continued*)

Variable	Item	Source
	information and support that encourage me to commercialize my research findings.	
	SC5—My contacts or discussion with potential competitors has been facilitating me with information and support that encourage me to commercialize my research findings.	
Funding (FG)	FG1—I think that the grant offered for *research and development activities is easily obtainable. (*Value analysis, concept idea, basic R&D, applied R&D)	
	FG2—I think that the grant offered for *pre-commercialization activities is easily obtainable. (* Experimental Research Prototype, Incubation)	
	FG3—I think that the grant offered for *commercialization activities is easily obtainable. (* Pilot production, Early Growth, Mature Production, Value Realization)	
	FG4—Various grants that are easily obtained encourage me to pursue effort to commercialize research findings (*grants for R&D, pre-commercialization and commercialization)	
Entrepreneurial peers (EP)	EP1—A colleague who has been involved in *transfer of knowledge activities inspires me to get involved in the same activity too. (* book writing/consultation/contract research)	Adapted from Huyghe and Knockaert [2015]
	EP2—A colleague who has been involved in *transfer of technology activities inspires me to get involved in the same activity too. (* licensing/patenting)	
	EP3—A colleague who has been involved in *transfer of product activities inspires me to get involved in the same activity too. (* creation of spin-offs)	
	EP4—A colleague who has been involved in *pre-commercialization activities inspires me to get involved in the same activity too. (* Experimental Research Prototype/Incubation)	
	EP5—A colleague who has been involved in *commercialization activities inspires me to get involved in the same activity too. (* Pilot production/Early Growth, Mature Production/Value Realization)	
Mentor support (SM)	SM1—I have a mentor who has been facilitating me to identify ideas on how my research can be exploited for commercialization.	Adapted from Fernández-Pérez *et al.* [2015]
	SM2—I have a mentor who has been facilitating me with information and support to undertake *pre-commercialization activities. (*Experimental Research Prototype/Incubation)	
	SM3—I have a mentor a mentor who has been facilitating me with information and support to undertake *commercialization activities. (*Pilot production/Early Growth/Mature Production/Value Realization)	
	SM4—I have a mentor who has been facilitating me with information and support to get involved in book writing or consultation or contract research activities.	

Table A.1. (*Continued*)

Variable	Item	Source
	SM5—I have a mentor who has been facilitating me with information and support to get involved in licensing and patenting.	
	SM6—I have a mentor who has been facilitating me with information and support to get involved in creation of spin-offs	

Acknowledgments

This paper draws on support from Research University Grant Tier 2, awarded by Universiti Teknologi Malaysia for a research project entitled 'Connecting Academic Entrepreneurs' Self-Directed Learning to their Entrepreneurial Performance' (Q.K130000.2656.17J26).

References

Ajzen, I. (1991). The theory of planned behaviour. *Organizational Behavior and Human Decision Processes*, **50**, 2: 179–211.

Aldridge, T. T. and Audretsch, D. (2011). The Bayh-Dole Act and scientist entrepreneurship. *Research Policy*, **40**, 8: 1058–1067.

Alvarez, S. A. and Barney, J. B. (2007). Discovery and creation: alternative theories of entrepreneurial Action. *Strategic Entrepreneurship Journal*, **1**, 2: 11–26.

Andreev, P., Heart, T., Maoz, H. and Pliskin, N. (2009). Validating formative partial least squares (PLS) models: Methodological review and empirical illustration. In *ICIS 2009 Proceedings*, Phoenix, Arizona, USA, p. 193.

Anderson, J. C. and Gerbing, D. W. (1988). Structural equation modeling in practice: A review and recommended two-step approach. *Psychological Bulletin*, **103**, 3: 411.

Audretsch, D. B. (2007). *The Entrepreneurial Society*. Oxford University Press, Oxford.

Audretsch, D. B., Lehmann, E. E. and Paleari, S. (2015). Academic policy and entrepreneurship: A European perspective. *The Journal of Technology Transfer*, **40**, 3: 363–368.

Baron, R. A. and Markman, G. D. (2000). Beyond social capital: How social skills can enhance entrepreneurs' success. *The Academy of Management Executive*, **14**, 1: 106–116.

Barth, T. D. and Schlegelmilch, W. (2013). Academic entrepreneur, academic entrepreneurship. *Encyclopedia of Creativity, Invention, Innovation and Entrepreneurship*, ed. O. Torre. Springer, New York, pp. 1–8.

Bercovitz, J. and Feldman, M. (2008). Academic entrepreneurs: Organizational change at the individual level. *Organization Science*, **19**, 1: 69–89.

Bello, B., Mattana, V. and Loi, M. (2018). The power of peers: A new look at the impact of creativity, social context and self-efficacy on entrepreneurial intentions. *International Journal of Entrepreneurial Behavior & Research*, **24**, 1: 214– 233.

Bradley, S. R., Hayter, C. S. and Link, A. (2013). Models and methods of university technology transfer. *Foundations and Trends in Entrepreneurship*, **9**, 6.

Brockhaus, R. H. (1980). Risk taking propensity of entrepreneurs. *Academy of Management Journal*, **23**, 3: 509–520.

Brookfield, S. D. (2009). Self-directed learning. *International Handbook of Education for the Changing World of Work*, ed. R. Maclean and D. Wilson. Springer, Netherland, pp. 2615–2627.

Campbell, D. T. and Fiske, D. W. (1959). Convergent and discriminant validation by the multitrait-multimethod matrix. *Psychological Bulletin*, **56**, 2: 81.

Casson, M. (2005). The individual–opportunity nexus: A review of Scott Shane: A general theory of entrepreneurship. *Small Business Economics*, **24**, 5: 423–430.

Cenfetelli, R. T. and Bassellier, G. (2009). Interpretation of formative measurement in information systems research. *MIS Quarterly*, **33**: 689–707.

Chell, E. (2013). Review of skill and the entrepreneurial process. *International Journal of Entrepreneurial Behavior & Research*, **19**, 1: 6–31.

Chell, E., Haworth, J. M. and Brearley, S. A. (1991). *The Entrepreneurial Personality: Concepts, Cases and Categories*. Routledge, London.

Chesbrough, H. and Rosenbloom, R. S. (2002). The role of the business model in capturing value from innovation: Evidence from xerox corporation's technology spin-off companies. *Industrial and Corporate Change*, **11**, 3: 529–555.

Clarysse, B., Tartari, V. and Salter, A. (2011). The impact of entrepreneurial capacity, experience and organizational support on academic entrepreneurship. *Research Policy*, **40**, 8: 1084–1093.

Closs, L., Ferreira, G., Brasil, V., Sampaio, C. and Perin, M. (2013). What motivates brazilian academic researchers to transfer technology?*Journal of Technology Management and Innovation*, **8**, 4: 79–90.

Cohen, J. (1988). *Statistical Power Analysis for the Behavioral Sciences*. Lawrence Erlbaum Assoc, London.

Creswell, J. W. (2003). *Research Design: Qualitative, Quantitative and Mixed Method Approaches*, 2nd edn.. Sage Publications, California.

Cromie, S. (2000). Assessing entrepreneurial inclinations: Some approaches and empirical evidence. *European Journal of Work and Organizational Psychology*, **9**, 1: 7–30.

Dawson, C. (2002). *Practical Research Methods: A User-Friendly Guide to Mastering Research*. Cromwell Press, Oxford.

D'Este, P., Mahdi, S., Neely, A. and Rentocchini, F. (2012). Inventors and entrepreneurs in academia: What types of skills and experience matter?*Technovation*, **32**, 5: 293–303.

Di Gregorio, D. and Shane, S. (2003). Why do some universities generate more start-ups than others? *Research Policy*, **32**, 2: 209–227.

Ericsson, K. A., Krampe, R. T. and Tesch-Römer, C. (1993). The role of deliberate practice in the acquisition of expert performance. *Psychological Review*, **100**, 3: 363.

Etzkowitz, H. (2016). The entrepreneurial university: Vision and metrics. *Industry and Higher Education*, **30**, 2: 83–97.

Faul, F., Erdfelder, E., Buchner, A. and Lang, A. G. (2009). Statistical power analyses using G* Power 3.1: Tests for correlation and regression analyses. *Behavior Research Methods*, **41**, 4: 1149–1160.

Feldmann, B. (2014). Dissonance in the academy: The formation of the faculty entrepreneur. *International Journal of Entrepreneurial Behavior & Research*, **20**, 5: 453–477.

Fernández-Pérez, V., Alonso-Galicia, P. E., Rodríquez-Ariza, L. and del Mar Fuentes-Fuentes, M. (2015). Professional and personal social networks: A bridge to entrepreneurship for academics?*European Management Journal*, **3**, 1: 37–47.

Fiet, J. O., Piskounov, A. and Patel, P. C. (2005). Still searching (systematically) for entrepreneurial discoveries. *Small Business Economics*, **25**, 5: 489–504.

Fust, A. P., Jenert, T. and Winkler, C. (2017). Experiential or self-regulated learning: A critical reflection of entrepreneurial learning processes. *Entrepreneurship Research Journal*, **8**, 2: 20170098.

Fornell, C. and Cha, J. (1994). Partial least squares. *Advanced Methods in Marketing Research*. ed. R. P.Bagozzi. Blackwell, Cambridge, pp. 52–78.

Fornell, C. and Larcker, D. F. (1981). Structural equation models with unobservable variables and measurement error: Algebra and statistics. Graduate School of Business Administration, Univerisity of Michigan.

Franklin, S. J., Wright, M. and Lockett, A. (2001). Academic and surrogate entrepreneurs university spin-out companies. *The Journal of Technology Transfer*, **26**, 1–2: 127–141.

Fuentes, M. D. M. F., Arroyo, M. R., Bojica, A. M. and Pérez, V. F. (2010). Prior knowledge and social networks in the exploitation of entrepreneurial opportunities. *International Entrepreneurship and Management Journal*, **6**, 4: 481–501.

Fukao, K. and Kwon, H. U. (2011). Sources of future economic growth in japan: An empirical analysis based on micro- data. RIETI Discussion Paper Series, No. 11-J-045.

Gefen, D., Straub, D. W. and Rigdon, E. E. (2011). An update and extension to sem guidelines for administrative and social science research. *Management Information Systems Quarterly*, **35**, 2: 3–14.

Geisler, E. and Turchetti, G. (2015). Commercialization of technological innovations: The effects of internal entrepreneurs and managerial and cultural factors on public–private inter-organizational cooperation. *International Journal of Innovation and Technology Management*, **12**, 2.

George, N. M., Parida, V., Lahti, T. and Wincent, J. (2014). A systematic literature review of entrepreneurial opportunity recognition: Insights on influencing factors. *International Entrepreneurship and Management Journal*, **1**, 42.

Gibb, A. and Hannon, P. (2006). Towards the entrepreneurial university. *International Journal of Entrepreneurship Education*, **4**, 1: 73–110.

Global Entrepreneurship Monitor, GEM (2020). *Malaysia Entrepreneurial Framework Conditions*. https://www.gemconsortium.org/economy-profiles/malaysia-86 [accessed on 8 July 2020].

Goethner, M., Obschonka, M., Silbereisen, R. K. and Cantner, U. (2011). Foundations of academic entrepreneurship: A path model for the prediction of scientists' academic entrepreneurial intentions. In *DIME Final Conference*, 6–8 April, IEEE, Maastricht, the Netherlands.

Gregorio, D., D. and Shane, S. (2003). Why do some universities generate more start-ups than others? *Research Policy*, **32**, 2: 209–227.

Greve, A. (1995). Networks and entrepreneurship: An analysis of social relations, occupational background and use of contacts during the establishment process. *Scandinavian Journal of Management*, **11**, 1: 1–24.

Grimaldi, R., Kenney, M., Siegel, D. S. and Wright, M. (2011). 30 years after Bayh-Dole: Reassessing academic entrepreneurship. *Research Policy*, **40**, 8: 1045–1057.

Gubitta, P., Tognazzo, A. and Destro, F. (2016). Signaling in academic ventures: The role of technology transfer offices and university funds. *The Journal of Technology Transfer*, **41**, 2: 368–393.

Guerrero, M., Cunningham, J. A. and Urbano, D. (2015). Economic impact of entrepreneurial universities' activities: An exploratory study of the United Kingdom. *Research Policy*, **44**, 3: 748–764.

Guerrero, M., Rialp, J. and Urbano, D. (2008). The impact of desirability and feasibility on entrepreneurial intentions: A structural equation model. *International Entrepreneurship and Management Journal*, **4**, 1: 35–50.

Guerrero, M. and Urbano, D. (2012). The development of an entrepreneurial university. *The Journal of Technology Transfer*, **37**, 1: 43–74.

Guerrero, M. and Urbano, D. (2014). Academics' start-up intentions and knowledge filters: An individual perspective of the knowledge spillover theory of entrepreneurship. *Small Business Economics*, **43**, 1: 57–74.

Hair, J. F., Hult, G. T. M., Ringle, C. and Sarstedt, M. (2014). *A Primer on Partial Least Squares Structural Equation Modeling (PLS-SEM)*. Sage Publications, London.

Hajizadeh, A. and Zali, M. (2016). Prior knowledge, cognitive characteristics and opportunity recognition. *International Journal of Entrepreneurial Behavior & Research*, **22**, 1: 63–83.

Hanohov, R. and Baldacchino, L. (2018). Opportunity recognition in sustainable entrepreneurship: An exploratory study. *International Journal of Entrepreneurial Behavior & Research*, **24**, 2: 333–358.

Huyghe, A. and Knockaert, M. (2015). The influence of organizational culture and climate on entrepreneurial intentions among research scientists. *The Journal of Technology Transfer*, **40**, 1: 138–160.

Iacobucci, D. and Micozzi, A. (2015). How to evaluate the impact of academic spin-offs on local development: An empirical analysis of the Italian Case. *The Journal of Technology Transfer*, **40**, 3: 434–452.

Jabbour, C. J. C., Jugend, D., de Sousa Jabbour, A. B. L., Gunasekaran, A. and Latan, H. (2015). Green product development and performance of Brazilian firms: Measuring the role of human and technical aspects. *Journal of Cleaner Production*, **87**, 442–451.

Jain, S., George, G. and Maltarich, M. (2009). Academics or entrepreneurs? investigating role identity modification of university scientist involved in commercialization activity. *Research Policy*, **38**, 6: 922–935.

Jensen, R. and Thursby, M. (2003). The disclosure and licensing of university inventions: The best we can do with the s**t we get to work with. *International Journal of Industrial Economics*, **21**, 9: 1271–1300.

Kagami, S. (2015). Innovation and university entrepreneurship: Challenges facing Japan Today. ed. *Innovation, Technology Transfers, Finance, and Internationalization of SMEs' Trade and Investment*, eds. S. P. Oum, G. Intarakumnerd Abonyi and S. Kagami. ERIA Research Project Report (No.14), ERIA, Jakarta, pp. 97–121.

Kaish, S. and Gilad, B. (1991). Characteristics of Opportunities Search of Entrepreneurs versus Executives: Sources, Interests, General Alertness. *Journal of Business Venturing*, **6**, 1: 45–61.

Kalar, B. and Antoncic, B. (2015). Social capital of academics and their engagement in technology and knowledge transfer. *Science and Public Policy*, **42**, 6.

Karlsson, T. and Wigren, C. (2012). Start-ups among university employees: The influence of legitimacy, human capital and social capital. *The Journal of Technology Transfer*, **37**, 3: 297–312.

Kassicieh, S. K., Kirchhoff, B. A., Walsh, S. T. and McWhorter, P. J. (2002). The role of small firms in the transfer of disruptive technologies. *Technovation*, **22**, 11: 667–674.

Keith, N., Unger, J. M., Rauch, A. and Frese, M. (2016). Informal learning and entrepreneurial success: A longitudinal study of deliberate practice among small business owners. *Applied Psychology: An International Review*, **65**, 3: 515–540.

Khademi, T., Ismail, K., Lee, C. T. and Shafaghat, A. (2015). enhancing commercialization level of academic research outputs in research university. *Jurnal Teknologi*, **74**, 4.

Kickul, J. and Walters, J. (2002). Recognizing new opportunities and innovations: The role of strategic orientation and proactivity in internet firms. *International Journal of Entrepreneurial Behavior & Research*, **8**, 6: 292–308.

Kirchberger, M. A. and Pohl, L. (2016). Technology commercialization: A literature review of success factors and antecedents across different contexts. *The Journal of Technology Transfer*, **41**, 5: 1077–1112.

Kirkman, D. M. (2013). Survival and growth motivations as predictors of university-biotechnology technology transfer activities. *Journal of Entrepreneurship Education*, **16**, 33.

Kirzner, I. M. (Ed.) (1979). *Perception, Opportunity and Profit*. University of Chicago Press, Chicago.

Kochenkova, A., Grimaldi, R., & Munari, F. (2016). Public Policy measures in support of knowledge transfer activities: A review of academic literature. *The Journal of Technology Transfer*, **41**, 3: 407–429.

Koellinger, P. (2008). Why are some entrepreneurs more innovative than others? *Small Business Economics*, **31**, 1: 21.

Kuckertz, A., Kollmann, T., Krell, P. and Stöckmann, C. (2017). Understanding, differentiating and measuring opportunity recognition and opportunity exploitation. *International Journal of Entrepreneurial Behavior & Research*, **23**, 1: 78–97.

Landry, R., Amara, N. and Rherrad, I. (2006). Why are some university researchers more likely to create spin-offs than others? Evidence from Canadian Universities. *Research Policy*, **35**, 10: 1599–1615.

Loch, K. D., Straub, D. W. and Kamel, S. (2003). Diffusing the internet in the Arab world: The role of social norms and technological culturation. *IEEE Transactions on Engineering Management*, **50**, 1: 45–63.

Lowry, P. B. and Gaskin, J. (2014). Partial least squares (PLS) structural equation modeling (SEM) for building and testing behavioral causal theory: When to choose it and how to use it. *IEEE Transactions on Professional Communication*, **57**, 2: 123–146.

Macnamara, B. N., Hambrick, D. Z. and Oswald, F. L. (2014). Deliberate practice and performance in music, games, sports, education, and professions: A meta-analysis. *Psychological Science*, **25**, 8: 1608–1618.

Malaysian Science and Technology Information Centre MASTIC (2013). *National Research and Development Studies*. MOSTI, Putrajaya: http://www.mastic.gov.my/[accessed on 15 December 2015].

Malaysian Science and Technology Information Centre MASTIC (2013b). Science and Technology Inventory, TECHMart. Putrajaya: MOSTI. Retrieved January 10, 2016 from http://www.mastic.gov.my/.

Malaysian Science and Technology Information Centre MASTIC (2015b). STI Human Resources. Putrajaya: MOSTI. Retrieved Dec 15, 2015 from http://www.mastic.gov.my/.

Markman, G., Phan, P., Balkin, D. and Gianiodis, P. (2005). Entrepreneurship and university-based technology transfer. *Journal of Business Venturing*, **20**, 2: 241–263.

Markman, G. D., Siegel, D. S. and Wright, M. (2008). Research and technology commercialization. *Journal of Management Studies*, **45**, 8: 1401–1423.

Markuerkiaga, L., Igartua, J. I. and Errasti, N. (2014). Factors fostering entrepreneurial universities to develop academic entrepreneurship activities: An assessment of European universities. *International Journal of Technology Transfer and Commercialisation*, **13**, 1–2: 107–132.

Mitchell, R. K., Busenitz, L., Lant, T., McDougall, P. P., Morse, E. A. and Smith, J. B. (2002). Toward a theory of entrepreneurial cognition: Rethinking the people side of entrepreneurship research. *Entrepreneurship Theory and Practice*, **27**, 2: 93–104.

Mom, T. J., Oshri, I. and Volberda, H. W. (2012). The skills base of technology transfer professionals. *Technology Analysis & Strategic Management*, **24**, 9: 871–891.

Morales-Alonso, G., Pablo-Lerchundi, I. and Vargas-Perez, A. M. (2016). An empirical study on the antecedents of knowledge intensive entrepreneurship. *International Journal of Innovation and Technology Management*, **13**, 5: 1640011.

Muscio, A., Quaglione, D. and Ramaciotti, L. (2016). The effects of university rules on spinoff creation: The case of Academia in Italy. *Research Policy*, **45**, 7: 1386–1396.

Nanda, R. and Sørensen, J. B. (2010). Workplace peers and entrepreneurship. *Management Science*, **56**, 7: 1116–1126.

Neill, S., Metcalf, L. E. and York, J. L. (2017). Distinguishing entrepreneurial approaches to opportunity perception. *International Journal of Entrepreneurial Behavior & Research*, **23**, 2: 296–316.

Nielsen, K. (2015). Human capital and new venture performance: The industry choice and performance of academic entrepreneurs. *The Journal of Technology Transfer*, **40**, 3: 453–474.

Nosella, A. and Grimaldi, R. (2009). University–level mechanisms supporting the creation of new companies: An analysis of italian academic spin-offs. *Technology Analysis & Strategic Management*, **21**, 6: 679–698.

O'shea, R. P., Allen, T. J., Chevalier, A. and Roche, F. (2005). Entrepreneurial orientation, technology transfer and spinoff performance of US universities. *Research Policy*, **34**, 7: 994–1009.

Osiri, J. K., McCarty, M. M. and Jessup, L. (2013). Entrepreneurial culture in institutions of higher education: Impact on academic entrepreneurship. *Journal of Entrepreneurship Education*, **16**, 1.

Ozgen, E. and Baron, R. A. (2007). Social sources of information in opportunity recognition: Effects of mentors, industry networks, and professional forums. *Journal of Business Venturing*, **22**, 2: 174–192.

Pattnaik, P. N. and Pandey, S. C. (2016). Revisiting university spinoffs: Conceptual advancements and theoretical underpinnings. *International Journal of Innovation and Technology Management*, **13**, 1: 1650005.

Petkewich, R. (2009). Entrepreneurs in academic. *Chemical & Engineering News*, **87**, 16: 28–30.

Petter, S., Straub, D. and Rai, A. (2007). Specification and validation of formative constructs in IS research. *MIS Quarterly*, **31**, 4: 623–656.

Phan, P. H., Siegel, D. S. and Wright, M. (2005). Science parks and incubators: Observations, synthesis and future research. *Journal of Business Venturing*, **20**, 2: 165–182.

Philpott, K., Dooley, L., O'Reilly, C. and Lupton, G. (2011). The entrepreneurial university: Examining the underlying academic tensions. *Technovation*, **31**, 4: 161–170.

Pugalia, S., Sai, L. P. and Cetindamar, D. K. (2020). Personal networks' influence on student entrepreneurs: A qualitative study. *International Journal of Innovation and Technology Management*, **17**, 5: 1–23.

Podsakoff, P. M. and Organ, D. W. (1986). Self-reports in organizational research: Problems and prospects. *Journal of Management*, **12**, 4: 531–544.

Preacher, K. J. and Hayes, A. F. (2004). SPSS and SAS procedures for estimating indirect effects in simple mediation models. *Behavior Research Methods*, **36**, 4: 717–731.

Preacher, K. J. and Hayes, A. F. (2008). Asymptotic and resampling strategies for assessing and comparing indirect effects in multiple mediator models. *Behavior Research Methods*, **40**, 3: 879–891.

Prodan, I. and Drnovsek, M. (2010). Conceptualizing academic-entrepreneurial intentions: An empirical test. *Technovation*, **30**, 5–6: 332–347.

Rahim, N. A., Mohamed, Z. B. and Amrin, A. (2015). Commercialization of emerging technology: The role of academic entrepreneur. *Procedia — Social and Behavioral Sciences*, **169**, 53–60.

Rahim, N. A., Mohamed, Z. B., Amrin, A., Masrom, M. and Shariff, S. A. (2019). Conceptualization and measurement of university technology transfer office efficiency as a formative construct. *International Journal of Engineering and Advanced Technology*, **8**, 5c: 191–197.

Ramos-Rodriguez, A., Medina-Garrido, J., Lorenzo-Gómez, J. and Ruiz-Navarro, J. (2010). What you know or who you know? The role of intellectual and social capital in opportunity recognition. *International Small Business Journal*, **28**, 6: 566–582.

Rao, B. and Mulloth, B. (2017). The role of universities in encouraging growth of technology-based new ventures. *International Journal of Innovation and Technology Management*, **14**, 4: 1750014.

Rasmussen, E., Moen, Ø. and Gulbrandsen, M. (2006). Initiatives to promote commercialization of university knowledge. *Technovation*, **26**, 4: 518–533.

Rasmussen, E. and Rice, M. P. (2011). A framework for government support mechanisms aimed at enhancing university technology transfer: The norwegian case. *International Journal of Technology Transfer and Commercialisation*, **11**, 1–2: 1–25.

Rasmussen, E., Mosey, S. and Wright, M. (2011). The evolution of entrepreneurial competencies: A longitudinal study of university spin-off venture emergence. *Journal of Management Studies*, **48**, 6: 1314–1345.

Rasmussen, E. and Sørheim, R. (2012). How governments seek to bridge the financing gap for university spin-offs: Proof- of-concept, pre-seed and seed funding. *Technology Analysis & Strategic Management*, **24**, 7: 663–678.

Rasmussen, E. and Wright, M. (2015). How can universities facilitate academic spin-offs? An entrepreneurial competency perspective. *The Journal of Technology Transfer*, **40**, 5: 782–799.

Reguera, G. (2016). Leaving the comfort zone: The path to academic entrepreneurship. *2016 SIMB Annual Meeting and Exhibition.* Society for Industrial Microbiology and Biotechnology, Virginia.

Renzulli, L. A., Aldrich, H. and Moody, J. (2000). Family matters: Gender, networks and entrepreneurial outcomes. *Social Forces*, **79**, 2: 523–546.

Reynolds, P. D., Carter, N. M., Gartner, W. B. and Greene, P. G. (2004). The prevalence of nascent entrepreneurs in the United States: Evidence from the panel study of entrepreneurial dynamics. *Small Business Economics*, **23**, 4: 263–284.

Richter, N. F., Cepeda, G., Roldán, J. L. and Ringle, C. M. (2015). European management research using partial least squares structural equation modeling (PLS-SEM). *European Management Journal*, **33**, 1: 1–3.

Rigolizzo, M. and Amabile, T. (2015). Entrepreneurial creativity: The role of learning processes and work environment supports. *The Oxford Handbook of Creativity, Innovation and Entrepreneurship*, Oxford University Press, United States, pp. 61–78.

Ringle, C. M., Wende, S. and Becker, J.M. (2015). SmartPLS 3. Hamburg: SmartPLS. http://www.smartpls.com [accessed on 23 Jan 2015]

Rizzo, U. and Ramaciotti, L. (2014). The determinants of academic patenting by italian universities. *Technology Analysis & Strategic Management*, **26**, 4: 469–483.

Roland, X., Noorseha, A., Leilanie, M. N. and Mohar, Y. (2011). Entrepreneurship in Malaysia. *Global Entrepreneurship Monitor Malaysian Report.* Global Entrepreneurship Research Association, London.

Sansone, G., Battaglia, D., Landoni, P. and Paolucci, E. (2019). Academic spinoffs: The role of entrepreneurship education. *International Entrepreneurship and Management Journal*, **17**, 1:369–399.

Santos, S. C., Caetano, A., Baron, R. and Curral, L. (2015). Prototype models of opportunity recognition and the decision to launch a new venture. *International Journal of Entrepreneurial Behavior & Research*, **21**, 4: 510–538.

Sanz-Velasco, S. A. (2006). Opportunity development as a learning process for entrepreneurs. *International Journal of Entrepreneurial Behavior & Research*, **12**, 5: 251–271.

Sarstedt, M., Ringle, C. M., Smith, D., Reams, R. and Hair, J. F. (2014). Partial least squares structural equation modeling (PLS-SEM): A useful tool for family business researchers. *Journal of Family Business Strategy*, **5**, 1: 105–115.

Schlepphorst, S., Koetter, E. C., Werner, A., Soost, C. and Moog, P. (2020). International assignments of employees and entrepreneurial intentions: The mediating role of human capital, social capital and career prospects. *International Journal of Entrepreneurial Behavior & Research*, **26**, 6: 1259–1279.

Sequeira, J., Mueller, S. L. and McGee, J. E. (2007). The Influence of social ties and self-efficacy in forming entrepreneurial intentions and motivating nascent behavior. *Journal of Developmental Entrepreneurship*, **12**, 3: 275–293.

Shane, S. and Venkataraman, S. (2000). The promise of entrepreneurship as a field of research. *Academy of Management Review*, **25**, 217–226.

Siegel, D. and Wright, M. (2015). Academic entrepreneurship: Time for a rethink? *British Journal of Management*, **26**, 4: 582–595.

Singer, S., Amorós, J. E., Arreeola, D. M. (2015). 2014 global report. *Global Entrepreneurship Monitor.* Global Entrepreneurship Research Association, London.

Slavtchev, V. and Göktepe-Hultén, D. (2015). Support for public research spin-offs by the parent organizations and the speed of commercialization. *The Journal of Technology Transfer*, **41**, 6: 1507–1525.

Smilor, R. W. (1997). Entrepreneurship: Reflections on a subversive activity. *Journal of Business Venturing*, **12**, 5: 341–346.

St-Jean, E. and Audet, J. (2012). The role of mentoring in the learning development of the novice entrepreneur. *International Entrepreneurship and Management Journal*, **8**, 1: 119–140.

St-Jean, E., Radu-Lefebvre, M. and Mathieu, C. (2018). Can less be more? Mentoring functions, learning goal orientation, and novice entrepreneurs' self-efficacy. *International Journal of Entrepreneurial Behavior & Research*, **24**, 1: 2–21.

Tartari, V., Perkmann, M. and Salter, A. (2014). In good company: The influence of peers on industry engagement by academic scientists. *Research Policy*, **43**, 7: 1189–1203.

Thursby, J. G. and Thursby, M. C. (2001). Industry perspectives on licensing university technologies sources and problems. *Industry and Higher Education*, **15**, 4: 289–294.

Tseng, C. C. (2013). Connecting self-directed learning with entrepreneurial learning to entrepreneurial performance. *International Journal of Entrepreneurial Behavior & Research*, **19**, 4: 425–446.

UTM Organisational Management Division (2016). Sejarah Penubuhan UTM. Universiti Teknologi Malaysia. Retrieved January 10, 2017 from http://registrar.utm.my/bpo/publication/panduan-staf-utm/tujuan/.

Vincett, P. S. (2010). The economic impacts of academic spin-off companies and their implications for public policy. *Research Policy*, **39**, 6: 736–747.

Walsh, S. T., Kirchhoff, B. A. and Newbert, S. (2002). Differentiating market strategies for disruptive technologies. *IEEE Transactions on Engineering Management*, **49**, 4: 341–351.

Willaby, H. W., Costa, D. S., Burns, B. D., MacCann, C. and Roberts, R. D. (2015). Testing complex models with small sample sizes: A historical overview and empirical demonstration of what partial least squares (PLS) can offer differential psychology. *Personality and Individual Differences*, **84**, 73–78.

Winkler, C., Fust, A. and Jenert, T. (2016). Differentiating novice, non-expert and expert entrepreneurs: A self-regulated learning perspective. In *Academy of Management Proceedings*, Vol. 2016, No. 1. Academy of Management, Briarcliff Manor, NY, pp. 12056.

Wood, M. S. (2011). A process model of academic entrepreneurship. *Business Horizons*, **54**, 2: 153–161.

Wright, M., Hmieleski, K. M., Siegel, D. S. and Ensley, M. D. (2007). The role of human capital in technological entrepreneurship. *Entrepreneurship Theory and Practice*, **31**, 6: 791–806.

Wright, M., Mosey, S. and Noke, H. (2012). Academic entrepreneurship and economic competitiveness: Rethinking the role of the entrepreneur. *Economics of Innovation and New Technology*, **21**, 5–6: 429–444.

Xavier, S. R., Kelley, D., Kew, J., Herrington, M and Vorderwulbecke, A. (2012). 2012 global report. *Global Entrepreneurship Monitor Report.* Global Entrepreneurship Research Association.

Yusof, M., Abdul-Samad, Z., Hassan, F., Darus, Z. M., Mohammed, M. F. and Zaharim, A. (2010). Academic Entrepreneurship and Innovation in Higher Education: An Integrated Framework for Malaysian Universities. In *6th WSEAS/IASME International Conference on Educational Technologies*, Sousse, Tunisia.

Zhang, Y., Duysters, G. and Cloodt, M. (2014). The role of entrepreneurship education as a predictor of university students' entrepreneurial intention. *International Entrepreneurship and Management Journal*, **10**, 3: 623–641.

Biography

Noorlizawati Abd Rahim is a Senior Lecturer at Science, Management and Design Department, Razak Faculty of Technology and Informatics, Universiti Teknologi Malaysia. Her current research interests are in the areas of entrepreneurship, academic entrepreneurship, entrepreneurial leadership, and entrepreneurship education. She has a multidisciplinary background in electronic engineering, postgraduate qualification in nanotechnology, PhD in entrepreneurship, with industrial experiences in chipset design and development, semiconductor manufacturing and technology commercialization from Intel, Freescale Semiconductor and NanoMalaysia respectively. Her teaching focuses on entrepreneurship, creativity and innovation management, quantitative data analysis, electronic systems and semiconductor materials engineering. She received her BEng in Electrical & Electronic Engineering from Cardiff University, MSc in Nanotechnology from University College London and PhD in entrepreneurship from Universiti Teknologi Malaysia.

Zainai Mohamed is an Emeritus Professor, who was the founder Vice Chancellor (VC) of Universiti Malaysia Kelantan (UMK), the 19th public university in Malaysia. Upon his retirement as the VC of UMK, he has returned to serve Universiti Teknologi Malaysia (since February 2012) as a senior professor. He has a wide experience not only as a Professional Civil Engineer but also in engineering and entrepreneurship education, curriculum development across multidiscipline, management of higher education, and teaching/research. He obtained his PhD in Structural/Civil Engineering from the University of Cambridge, England, Master and Bachelor's degree in Civil Engineering from University of Strathclyde, Scotland.

Astuty Amrin is a Professor at the Department of Engineering, Razak Faculty of Technology and Informatics, Universiti Teknologi Malaysia (UTM). Currently, she is the Dean of Razak Faculty of Technology and Informatics UTM. She received her Bachelor in Materials Engineering from Universiti Sains Malaysia, MSc in Corrosion Sc. and Eng. from UMIST, UK and PhD in 2005. Her research interest is devoted to Materials Engineering. Her teaching focuses on research methodology, technology management, creativity and innovation management, maintenance management, innovation & new product development, materials science and technology.

Maslin Masrom is an Associate Professor at Science, Management and Design Department, Razak Faculty of Technology and Informatics, Universiti Teknologi Malaysia. She received her Bachelor in Computer Science from Universiti Teknologi Malaysia, Master of Science in Operations Research from Western Michigan University, USA, and PhD in Information Technology/Information System Management from Universiti Putra Malaysia. Her teaching focuses on operations research/operations management, IT/IS management, knowledge management, and ethics in computing. Her current research interest includes IT-adoption, e-government, technology management, information security management, women and technologies, cloud computing, structural equation modelling, and creativity and innovation management.

Part 2

Digital Technologies and Digital Innovation

Eight Building Blocks for Managing Digital Transformation*

Christoph Buck*,§, Clara Probst Marques† and Michael Rosemann‡

*Project Group Business and Information Systems Engineering of the Fraunhofer Institute for Applied Information Technology FIT
FIM Research Center, University of Bayreuth
Wittelsbacherring 10, 95444 Bayreuth, Germany

†FIM Research Center, University of Bayreuth
Wittelsbacherring 10, 95444 Bayreuth, Germany

‡Centre for Future Enterprise, QUT Business School
Queensland University of Technology
QUT Gardens Point Campus, 2 George St
Brisbane City QLD 4000, Australia
§christoph.buck@fim-rc.de

Organizations across all sectors and industries are facing the need for structural change towards a digital future. Rapid developments in digital technologies and their easy accessibility are changing organizations' competitive environment and require the design and implementation of a sustainable digital transformation. To master this organizational task in a targeted manner and align it strategically, organizations must carry out a comprehensive analysis of the digital transformation fields of action. The developed integrated framework for digital transformation is structured into eight building blocks and associated action items, and includes a systematic literature analysis. It serves as a valuable framework and guideline on digital change for organizations.

Keywords: Digital transformation; framework; guideline; incumbent organizations; structured literature review.

1. Introduction

With the current trend toward digitalization, organizations are in the midst of one of the most significant technological upturns since the invention of electric light and power grids. Individuals and companies are currently in a period of massive change, where the availability of digital technologies is radically transforming societies, industries, and companies. Environmental conditions for companies are changing rapidly: customers are demanding new (and digital) value propositions, and employees need an adequate skillset workplace. Competitors of decades are disappearing from the market and being displaced by young and rapidly growing digitally-based organizations. As a result, incumbent firms need to proactively drive and shape their digital transformation [Litvinenko (2020); Saarikko *et al.* (2020)].

§Corresponding author.

*This chapter was originally published in International Journal of Innovation and Technology Management, Vol. 18, No. 5, March 2018, published by World Scientific Publishing, Singapore. Reprinted with permission.

Due to the disruptive nature of innovations in information technology (IT), the profound digitalization of businesses, and their cross-organizational and systemic effects, information systems (IS) are considered a significant asset for leveraging organizational transformation [Besson and Rowe (2012); Lucas *et al.* (2013); Tekic and Koroteev (2019)]. As digital transformation is influencing firms' operations across different industries at a fast pace, it gives rise to radical changes and innovation and, thus, the opportunity to transform business practices at the organizational level [Gao *et al.* (2019)]. By changing processes, relationships, user experiences, markets, and customers, IT alters traditional ways of doing business [Kindermann *et al.* (2020)]. Following Hess *et al.* [2016], new digital technologies offer a tremendous market-changing potential as they enable the creation of innovative products and services [Belingheri and Neirotti (2019)]. They include new technological solutions, for example, Industry 4.0, artificial intelligence or blockchain, as well as more diffused technologies such as social media, mobile computing, advanced analytics, and cloud computing [Fitzgerald *et al.* (2013); Gimpel *et al.* (2018); Weking *et al.* (2020)]. Digital technologies can change the structure of an organization [Möller *et al.* (2011)]. While only a few years ago IT and ISs assumed a purely supportive function, they are now enabling numerous business chances and thus occupy an important place in developing competitive advantages [Kohli and Melville (2019)].

Since the digital transformation of an organization requires a long-term strategy [Kindermann *et al.* (2020); Kohli and Melville (2019)], a clear implementation plan, and the cooperation of all actors, it is a crucial strategic direction for incumbent firms to initiate and manage the transformation process in its entirety [Bharadwaj *et al.* (2013); Heavin and Power (2018); Nambisan *et al.* (2019); Vial (2019)]. Digital transformation is of particular relevance for incumbent organizations [Crittenden *et al.* (2019)], as these represent a significant part of most economies. However, incumbent organizations struggle with fundamental shifts threatening their established structures [Heavin and Power (2018); Siachou *et al.* (2021)]. This involves adjustments in strategy, structure, and power distribution domains, creating a qualitatively different organization, and is therefore characterized as transformational [Besson and Rowe (2012); Romanelli and Tushman (1994)].

Although research on digital transformation is increasing, comprehensive coverage of the field is scarce [Verhoef *et al.* (2021)]. The first frameworks for the digital transformation of organizations have been established in the literature [Heavin and Power (2018); Rueckel *et al.* (2020); Verhoef *et al.* (2021); Vial (2019)]. Nevertheless, to use these frameworks to support the strategic planning and implementation of organizations' digital transformation, existing frameworks come with only limited applicability in terms of providing guidelines for organizations. Thus, Kahre *et al.* [2017] ask for more "research on the 'how'" to guide and understand the transformational process of organizations, as Matt *et al.* [2015] call for more research, as "integrating digital transformation strategies into firms" is one of the most important strategic fields of organizations. Therefore, the chances and challenges of incumbent organizations are of great interest because of digital transformation. The challenges for incumbent organizations are reflected in particular in a structural and cultural change, which is reflected both in the involvement of the employees and in far-reaching organizational changes [Crittenden *et al.* (2019); Saarikko *et al.* (2020); Siachou *et al.* (2021)]. Thus, a framework is needed to achieve long term success by integrating important characteristics, ranging from technical foundations as one side of the continuum of digital transformation to culture and organizational change on the other side, to avoid the digitalization paradox and help organizations to create value with digital means [Gebauer *et al.* (2020)]. As various academic studies were published in the field, we contribute to science and practice by enhancing the six-factor framework of Gimpel *et al.* [2018]. We therefore pose the following research question:

How can the academic literature be structured as an integrative framework for digital transformation?

This paper's remainder is structured as follows: Section 2 provides a definition of digital transformation and gives an overview of the relevant approaches for mapping existing academic literature. Section 3, presents the systematic literature review. Section 4 presents the integrative framework for digital transformation. Besides the structure of the framework, the identified building blocks are derived from the literature. Subsequently, we provide a conclusion and theoretical and managerial implications before future research directions are presented.

2. Structuring Digital Transformation

2.1. *Defining digital transformation*

The term digital transformation itself is often a buzzword, and the existing literature offers somewhat ambiguous definitions [Fitzgerald *et al.* (2013); Vial (2019)]. While, for example, Bounfour [2016] defined it as "a new development in the use of digital artifacts, systems, and symbols within and around organizations", Hess *et al.* [2016] see "the changes digital technologies can bring about in a company's business model, which result in changed products or organizational structures or the automation of processes" in digital transformation. What these digital technologies and changes in products, organizational structures, and processes look like remains unclear.

Digitization is the underlying technical process providing the ground for digital transformation. It describes the conversion of analog to digital information, which can then be processed, transmitted, and stored in enormous quantities at a low cost. While digitization is a technical process that can be defined quite unambiguously, the literature lacks a clear differentiation between digital transformation and digitalization. In general, both are socio-technical phenomena that entail changes in the technological and social world — in people's lives, work, and interactions [Legner *et al.* (2017); Tilson *et al.* (2010)]. However, digitalization is more general and describes the increasing penetration of society and the economy through digital technologies. Digitalization, i.e. the adoption of digital technologies, challenges established patterns and brings about fundamental organizational changes. Three critical criteria can characterize the broad scope of digitalization. One crucial feature of digitalization mentioned in various studies is the "processes of adopting" [Legner *et al.* (2017)] or "use of" [Gartner Inc (2020)] digital technologies. Accordingly, digital technologies are employed to process digitized data. Second, digital technologies are applied in "broader social and institutional contexts" [Tilson *et al.* (2010)]. As a result, digitalization not only affects individual processes and products, but the entire private and professional environment of people changes [Yoo *et al.* (2010)]. Third, the emergence of an interconnected socio-technical world through digitalization triggers the modification of physical and organizational structures in societies and enterprises [Bharadwaj *et al.* (2013); Kompella (2019); Tilson *et al.* (2010); Urbach *et al.* (2017)]. Thus, today IT is no longer used exclusively in support activities but takes over core functions by contributing to an interconnected infrastructure across all business processes and boundaries.

As digitalization affects individuals, companies, and societies, several researchers call this development transformative [Porter and Heppelmann (2014)]. Transformation is a form of change that was already discussed in early literature on organizational growth. Watzlawick *et al.* [2011] distinguish between firstorder transition within an existing system and second-order change. The latter form of change involves adaptions in strategy, structure, and power distribution domains, creating a qualitatively different organization, and is therefore characterized as transformational [Besson and Rowe (2012); Romanelli and Tushman (1994)]. It is the answer to the change of environmental or resource conditions and ensures a company's further existence. Orlikowski [2000] argues technologies must change the organization's existing structure to be considered transformational. Due to the disruptive nature of IT innovations, the profound digitalization of businesses, and their cross-organizational and systemic effects, IS are considered a significant asset for leveraging organizational transformation [Besson and Rowe (2012); Lucas *et al.* (2013)]. By changing processes, relationships, user experiences, markets, and customers, IT alters traditional ways of doing business. Following Hess *et al.* [2016], digital technologies offer the most significant market-changing potential as they enable innovative products and services. They include emerging technologies, for example, internet of things or blockchain, as well as more diffused technologies such as social media, mobile computing, advanced analytics, and cloud computing known under the acronym SMAC [Fitzgerald *et al.* (2013); Gimpel *et al.* (2018); Liao *et al.* (2013)]. Embedded into a larger organizational system, these technologies can change an organization's structure and are seen as transformational [Möller *et al.* (2011); Orlikowski (2000)].

Consciously considering and merging the two concepts, digitalization and transformation, leads to the definition of digital transformation. Vial [2019] defines digital transformation as "a process that aims to improve an entity by triggering significant changes to its properties through combinations of information, computing, communication, and connectivity technologies". This is in line with the definition of Fitzgerald *et al.* [2013]. From a more practical perspective, they call digital transformation the use of new digital technologies to improve business by changing customer experience, operations, or business models. Matt *et al.* [2013] also refer to a change in value creation, which at the same time influences the structure of an organization. Based on the definitions above, we conclude that digital transformation refers to the measures taken by a company in response to advancing digitalization. To successfully transform and enable new business models, companies must break away from old structures [Bharadwaj *et al.* (2013); Hess *et al.* (2016); Matt *et al.* (2013); Trapp *et al.* (2018)]. Thus, digital transformation involves strategic and structural changes within organizations [Heavin and Power (2018); Lucas *et al.* (2013)].

2.2. *Structuring digital transformation*

The blurring of traditional sector boundaries disrupts business models across various industries. The disruption of industries forces companies to transform and change their routines digitally. While the digital transformation's urgent changes affect all sectors, industries, and organizations, academic literature has so far only cautiously dealt with an overview of the digital transformation. While, for example, Mani and Chouk [2018] examine consumer resistance to the innovation of services triggered by digital transformation, Martinelli and Tunisini [2018] highlight the opportunity of customer integration into supply chains. Hannola *et al.* [2018] observe efficiency improvements by applying digital technologies in the production environment, while Denner *et al.* [2018] criticize companies' uncertainties in the use of digital technologies.

A comprehensive framework and model for digital transformation can serve as an overview and provide considerable benefits. The diversity of chances and challenges is why researchers develop frameworks that guide and support companies' digital transformation [Gimpel *et al.* (2018); Hess *et al.* (2016)]. Lichtenthaler [2020] distinguishes between technology-related and market-related factors of digitalization initiatives. While these insights are essential for companies to better prepare for digital transformation, they take up only a limited view of the change and its implications. A first step was undertaken by Gimpel *et al.* [2018], who developed a generic framework for the digital transformation of companies, "because existing frameworks focus only on individual facets of digital transformation or build on case-based evidence ..." [Gimpel *et al.* (2018)]. Based on a review of academic literature, they conducted 21 expert interviews and seven cross-functional group interviews in more than 50 organizations in total [Gimpel *et al.* (2018)].

An extensive literature analysis provided by Vial [2019] examines the existing literature about the process of digital transformation. Vial [2019] analyzed 59 studies on digital transformation and has identified four clusters which are relevant for digital transformation on an organizational level: General organizational structure, organizational culture, leadership, and employee roles and skills. Based on the analysis, the author conceptualizes eight overarching building blocks that describe digital transformation as a process. While Vial [2019] takes a detailed look at the literature, his further analysis of the literature provides a very good meta-view on digital transformation. Heavin and Power [2018] also look at the different levels of tasks within digital transformation on a meta-level. In their decision support guide,

Heavin and Power [2018] show a relation between tactical tasks, operational tasks, and strategic tasks. They relate the increasing maturity of digital transformation with a growing value contribution. Verhoef *et al.* [2021] in their paper discuss digital transformation in the light of a flow model and distinguish three different fields: External drivers of digital transformation, phases of digital transformation, and strategic imperatives of digital transformation. Rueckel *et al.* [2020] in their work present a Digital Transformation Enabling Framework which consists of four layers (normative, strategic, tactical, operational) and nine enabling factors. They conceptualize digital transformation with a design science approach and come up with nine enabling factors: Innovative organizational culture, internal and external collaboration, strategic embeddedness, digital leadership, digital platform infrastructures, bimodal IT structures, institutionalized innovation processes, individual creativity and innovation capabilities, and ICT literacy.

While the observations of Vial [2019], Heavin and Power [2018], Verhoef *et al.* [2021], and Rueckel *et al.* [2020] provide valuable insights into the current state of research, the process of digital transformation, and the interrelation of decisions regarding different task levels, the framework of Gimpel *et al.* [2018] demonstrates a high degree of applicability and usability for both research and business practice. Particularly for the complex and long-term management task of organizations' digital transformation, both the required depth of detail and high applicability is of high relevance, by using different analogies and anchor points from the business model canvas [Osterwalder and Pigneur (2013)]. Gimpel *et al.* [2018] present six action fields to structure digital transformation in companies. To refine their framework, they provide four exemplary action items per action field. The authors state, "By considering these action fields, organizations will ensure they develop a holistic yet concrete perspective on digital transformation, which will reduce the risk that they will experience silo thinking with individual departments' striving for partial solutions." [Gimpel *et al.* (2018)]. Thus, we classify the framework of Gimpel *et al.* [2018] as a valuable element for structuring digital transformation for theory and practice. Its relevance and the applicability of the framework were emphasized by various practitioners and organizations [Gimpel *et al.* (2018); Rosemann and Vessey (2008)].

Nevertheless, the framework's development lacks academic support as the action fields and action items are not assessed by literature. Furthermore, while the authors identify exact action items, they do not state to what extent these action items describe opportunities or challenges for organizations' digital transformation. Beyond that, Gimpel *et al.* [2018] call for further research and additional development regarding their work. In this respect, the authors take up the call for research from Rosemann and Vessey [2008] towards improving relevance and rigor in IS research. This paper aims at analyzing the chances and challenges of digital transformation and assessing their impact. Therefore, a systematic literature review was conducted to gather and examine existing knowledge on the subject of digital transformation. Its rigorous documentation makes the procedure transparent, objective, and replicable [Vom Brocke *et al.* (2009)].

3. Literature on Digital Transformation

3.1. *Systematic literature review*

To develop an integrated framework for digital transformation, building on the existing work of Gimpel *et al.* [2018], we analyzed the current literature by conducting a systematic review. A systematic literature review provides a full overview of the research question's studies using an unbiased search strategy. It reveals gaps in existing research by creating a more precise picture [Vom Brocke *et al.* (2009)]. Our literature review followed a three-step approach inspired by the recommendations of Webster and Watson [2002], Kitchenham [2004], Levy and Ellis [2006], and Vom Brocke *et al.* [2009].

Step one involves the search for literature that addresses the research questions [Kitchenham (2004)]. Digital transformation is a dynamic field and continues to evolve with effects that can only be proven over the past decade. In addition, Brynjolfsson and Hitt [2000] state ITs effects combined with organizational changes must be measured with a certain distance since organizational adjustments take more time to unfold. To limit the analysis to high quality and current research, only peer-reviewed papers published in a ten-year period (2009 to 2018) were considered. Keywords were derived from existing literature. To avoid excluding relevant papers, the keywords were extended by synonyms for both digital transformation and its assumed impacts [Kitchenham (2004)]. Connecting them by the Boolean operators OR and AND, the search string was applied as follows: ("digital transformation" OR digitalization OR "digital technolog*") AND (impact OR effect* OR influence OR outcome* OR result* OR consequence* OR chance* OR opportunit* OR challenge* OR difficult* OR problem* OR barrier*).

Due to the large dispersion of IS literature, the literature search was extended over multiple online databases for IS and business journals, including AIS eLibrary, Business Source Premier, Emerald, IEEE Xplore Digital Library, JSTOR, science direct, and Wiley Online Library [Levy and Ellis (2006)]. Additionally, the top IS conferences ICIS and ECIS were included in the search to take account of their high standards of currency [Webster and Watson (2002)] and the senior basket journals of IS. The query was applied on title, abstract, keywords, or the closest that each database search engine allowed, since all of them differed.

Step two of the systematic literature review refers to the selection of literature as our database search yielded more than 3000 hits. The subsequent selection process required the definition of inclusion criteria that allowed studies for further review and exclusion criteria that eliminated studies without further review [Levy and Ellis (2006); Okoli and Schabram (2010)]. First, papers not published within the field of IS or management were excluded. Since the aim is to reflect the current state of research on digital transformation in leading journals, criteria for selecting high-quality literature were defined. Thus, only journals with impact factors greater than or equal to 1 were considered for further examination [Hufnagl *et al.* (2019); Zupanc (2014)]. For the remaining papers, a two-stage selection process was carried out: the abstract check and the paper check. First, all papers whose abstracts did not address digital transformation were excluded. Second, the remaining studies were retrieved, entirely read, and appraised critically. A paper was discarded if it was out of scope. If digital transformation was only referred to as background information without referring to its consequences for companies, the paper was excluded. After adding studies of the basket of eight and the two conferences ICIS and ECIS, a final set of 58 papers remained for in-depth analysis.

3.2. *Mapping academic research*

To structure the findings [Webster and Watson (2002)], we matched the identified body of knowledge with the elements of the six-factor framework for digital transformation from Gimpel *et al.* [2018] in step three. We codified the 58 papers against the original framework and matched them with the initial framework's action fields and action items. The analysis of the existing body of literature reveals that the provided action fields and action items are covered by literature. This makes it clear that an organization's digital transformation is a complex undertaking, affecting different areas and levels of the organization simultaneously. The identified literature strengthens the relevance of the action fields and items presented in the six-factor framework of Gimpel *et al.* [2018]. Following the initial publication and the limitations expressed therein, our literature analysis backs up the framework's areas with scientific findings. Also, several topics relevant to digital transformation could be identified that were not mentioned in the original six-factor framework, as shown in Table 1. We headline these topics as "Decentralization" [Bienhaus and Haddud (2018); Chou *et al.* (2012); Dremel *et al.* (2017); Gölzer and Fritzsche (2017); Herterich *et al.* (2016a); Holotiuk *et al.* (2018)], "Cross-functional collaboration" [Berghaus and Back (2017); Chou *et al.* (2012); Dremel *et al.* (2017); Fulgoni (2014); Herterich *et al.* (2016a); Holotiuk *et al.* (2018); Lyytinen *et al.* (2016); Nylén and Holmström (2015); Sebastian *et al.* (2017); Yoo *et al.* (2012)], "Blurring boundaries" [Berghaus and Back (2017); Caputo *et al.* (2019); Herterich *et al.* (2016a); Martinelli and Tunisini (2018); Piccinini *et al.* (2015); Rachinger *et al.* (2018)], and "Redefinition of organizational functions" [Bienhaus and Haddud (2018); Dremel *et al.* (2017); Jaw *et al.* (2016); Leonhardt *et al.* (2017); Piccinini *et al.* (2015)].

In the following section, we present our integrated framework for digital transformation, which builds on the six-factor framework of Gimpel *et al.* [2018]. Based on our coding of the identified literature, we develop eight building blocks of digital transformation.

4. Integrative Framework for Digital Transformation

As the literature analysis shows, the six-factor framework of Gimpel *et al.* [2018] represents a valuable first guidance for digitally tranformation an organization. Based on our analysis of the identified literature, we conceptually extend the digital transformation framework by splitting up the action fiedl "Organization" into the three building blocks "Human Resources", "Organizational structure", and "Culture". While we were able to confirm the fields "Value Proposition", "Customers", "Data", "Operations", and "Transformation Management" from the

Table 1. Concept matrix of identified literature.

Authors and publication year		Customer				Value Proposition				Operations				Data				Organization				Transformation Management				Additional Findings				Journal
		Customer experience management	Customer insights	Multi/omni channel management	Hybrid customer interaction	Smart products	Smart services	Individualization	Digital ecosystems	Integrated IT	Flexible operations	Digital supply network	Digital manufacturing	Data integration	Data analytics	Data ownership & privacy	Data security	Organizational agility	Workplace of the future	Digital skillset	Digital mindset	Digital strategy	Transformation management	Change management	Digital value assurance	Decentralization	Cross-functional collaboration	Blurring company boundaries	Redefinition of organizational functions	
Beier, Michael; Wagner, Kerstin	2016																							x	x					ECIS
Berghaus, Sabine; Back, Andrea	2017	x		x															x	x	x	x	x	x			x	x		ICIS
Bienhaus, Florian; Haddud, Abubaker	2018														x	x	x		x		x	x		x		x			x	BPMJ
Candi, Marina; Beltagui, Ahmad	2018									x																				Technovation
Caputo, Andrea; Fiorentino, Raffaele; Garze	2018											x																x		BPMJ
Chou, Tzu-Chuan; Liu, Day-Yang; Chen, Sh	2012							x	x			x		x												x	x			ManDec
Coreynen, Wim; Matthyssens, Paul; van Bo	2017				x															x	x									IMM
Denner, Marie-Sophie; Püschel, Louis; Rögli	2018									x																				BISE
Dremel, Christian; Wulf, Jochen; Herterich,	2017		x		x					x				x	x	x	x	x		x			x	x		x	x		x	MISQE
Endres, Herbert; Stoiber, Kristina; Wenzl, N	2020			x		x		x																						JBS
Ferreira, João J.M.; Fernandes, Cristina I.; F	2018					x	x											x												JBR
Fulgoni, Gian M.	2014		x	x																							x			JAR
Gerth, Anthony B.; Peppard, Joe	2016																						x	x						BusHoriz
Gölzer, Philipp; Fritzsche, Albrecht	2017													x	x											x				PPC
Hannola, Lea; Richter, Alexander; Richter, S	2018												x								x									IJPR
Hansen, Anne Mette; Kraemmergaard, Perni	2011																							x						MISQE
Herterich, Matthias M.; Eck, Alexander; Ue	2016					x	x																		x	x	x	x		ECIS
Herterich, Matthias M.; Uebernickel, Falk; B	2016							x	x			x		x									x		x					MISQE
Hess, Thomas; Matt, Christian; Benlian, Ale	2016										x									x		x	x	x	x					MISQE
Holotiuk, Friedrich; Beimborn, Daniel; Jents	2018																		x							x	x			ECIS
Isaksson, Alf J.; Harjunkoski, Iiro; Sand, Gu	2018									x	x	x	x		x	x									x					CCE
Jaw, Yi-Long; Chen, Ying-Yu Kerri; Wu, Bi	2016				x														x										x	InternetRes
Kane, Gerald C.; Palmer, Doug; Philipps, An	2015	x						x												x	x	x								MIT SMR
Kauffman, Robert J.; Li, Ting; van Heck, Er	2010								x		x																			IJEC
Kindermann, Bastian; Beutel, Sebastian; Ga	2020																			x		x	x						x	EMJ
Leonhardt, Daniel; Haffke, Ingmar; Kranz, J	2017																		x			x					x		x	ECIS
Leonhardt, Daniel; Hanelt, Andre	2018																													ICIS
Li, Chunqing; Guo, Shuojia; Cao, Li; Li, Jie	2018										x			x					x					x						IMM
Li, Liang; Su, Fang; Zhang, Wei; Mao, Ji-Ye	2018								x																					ISJ
Li, Weizi; Liu, Kecheng; Belitski, Maksim; G	2016		x						x	x	x				x			x		x										JIT
Liere-Netheler, Kirsten; Vogelsang, Kristin;	2018						x					x		x					x	x		x								ECIS
Lyytinen, Kalle; Yoo, Youngjin; Boland Jr.,	2016			x																										ISJ
Mani, Zied; Chouk, Inès	2018				x												x													JPIM
Martinelli, Elisa Martina; Tunisini, Annalisa	2018							x			x																	x		JBIM
Müller, Sune D.; Obwegeser, Nikolaus; Glud	2019																	x	x		x									SJIS
Nudurupati, Sai S.; Tebboune, Sofiane; Hard	2016								x			x			x		x								x					PPC
Nwankpa, Joseph K.; Roumani, Yaman	2016					x	x																		x					ICIS
Nylén, Daniel; Holmström, Jonny	2015		x			x	x													x	x									BusHoriz
Pagani, Margherita; Pardo, Catherine	2017				x				x		x																			IMM
Pflaum, Alexander A.; Gölzer, Philipp	2018						x		x													x		x						IEEE PerCom
Piccinini, Everlin; Hanelt, Andre; Gregory, R	2015								x		x						x	x		x	x							x	x	ICIS
Quinton, Sarah; Simkin, Lyndon	2017		x	x	x									x	x			x				x								IJMR
Rachinger, Michael; Rauter, Romana; Mülle	2018		x	x	x			x		x		x		x						x								x		JMTM
Rauch, Madeleine; Wenzel, Matthias; Wagn	2016					x	x																							ICIS
Remane, Gerrit; Hanelt, Andre; Wiesboeck,	2017																			x										ECIS
Saarikko, Ted; Westergren, Ulrika H.; Blom	2020									x						x					x		x			x	x			BusHoriz
Schaarschmidt, Mario; Bertram, Matthias	2020																					x	x							IJIM
Sebastian, Ina M.; Ross, Jeanne W.; Beath, C	2017	x	x	x	x	x	x			x					x			x				x			x					MISQE
Setia, Pankaj; Venkatesh, Viswanath; Joglek	2013																			x										MISQ
Solberg, Elizabeth; Traavik, Laura E. M.; W	2020																													CMR
Trabucchi, Daniel; Buganza, Tommaso; Dell	2018		x		x									x	x															CIM
Tumbas, Sanja; Berente, Nicholas; Vom Bro	2018																				x		x	x						JIT
Tumbas, Sanja; Berente, Nicholas; Vom Bro	2017		x		x										x					x			x							MISQE
Wu, Lynn; Hitt, Lorin	2015		x																	x										ICIS
Wunderlich, Nico; Beck, Roman	2017																	x		x										ECIS
Xie, Kang; Xiao, Jinghua; Wu, Yao; Hu, Qin	2014			x																										ICIS
Yoo, Youngjin; Boland Jr., Richard J.; Lyyti	2012			x								x				x														OrgSci
Zangiacomi, Andrea; Oesterle, Jonathan; Fo	2017												x																	PPC
Number of articles		3	10	9	10	7	8	6	9	8	8	8	3	9	10	5	5	8	8	16	10	11	10	10	8	7	8	6	6	

framework of Gimpel *et al.* [2018], we identified structural ambiguities with the action field "Organization".

The action field "Organization" in the six-factor framework of Gimpel *et al.* [2018] derives important organizational implications for a successful digital transformation with its action items, but does not give them a strategically high priority. We justify our conceptual extension of the framework with the buildings blocks

"Human Resources", "Organizational structure", and "Culture" with their strategic relevance for organizational change. We argue that a company's employees and the targeted development of their expertise and competencies are central resources and success factors. In organizational culture and organizational structure we identify two further building blocks that have a central influence on the successful implementation of an organization's strategy. In order to be able to take these elementary components of digital transformation into account as a strategically fundamental task, they represent separate building blocks in the derived integrative framework for digital transformation.

With the extension of the framework to eight building blocks and the associated restructuring of the underlying six-factor framework by Gimpel, we are creating a more comprehensive perspective on the field of digital transformation. The resulting integrative framework for digital transformation enables organizations to analyze the different areas and their implications for planning and implementing digital transformation. Figure 1 illustrates the integrative framework of digital transformation with the associated eight building blocks. The framework also proposes related fields of action, which serve as detailed sub-areas for organizations regarding their transformational change.

4.1. *Operations*

While customers increasingly expect individualized offers, companies no longer generate the value proposition in isolation [Isaksson *et al.* (2018); Kauffman *et al.* (2010)]. Digitalization leads to a closer integration of IT and operations [Isaksson *et al.* (2018)], as organizations need a uniform database, standardized common services, and seamless and transparent transactions [Sebastian *et al.* (2017)]. To effectively use digital technologies, organizations must integrate operations and IT

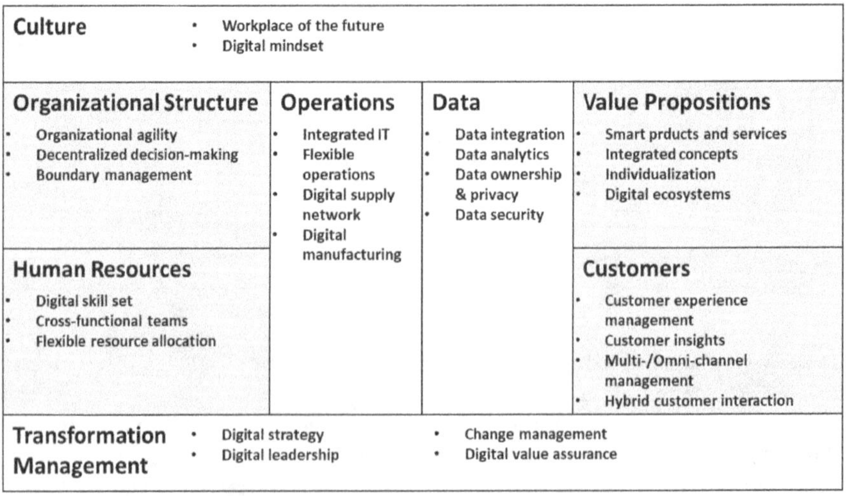

Fig. 1. Integrative framework on digital transformation based on Gimpel *et al.* [2018].

[Candi and Beltagui (2018)]. The integration of IT helps streamline processes leading to seamless operations, which is an essential competency to execute a digital strategy. Altogether, the controlled access to enterprise data and standardization of business processes provides companies with speed, accuracy, and cost savings [Saarikko *et al.* (2020); Sebastian *et al.* (2017)]. Dremel *et al.* [2017] warn that the structural adjustments in traditional organizations can result in a "two-speed IT organization" [Dremel *et al.* (2017, p. 98)] with centralized and harmonized IT systems on the one hand and rapid and agile digitization initiatives on the other hand. The IT infrastructure must support an organization's internal operations across the whole value chain [Sebastian *et al.* (2017)]. At the same time, the IT infrastructure must take an external perspective and provide access to the customers [Li *et al.* (2016)] and introduce new digital products and technologies [Sebastian *et al.* (2017)]. These new technologies must be selected to suit the company's processes [Denner *et al.* (2018)] and implemented at the right time [Rachinger *et al.* (2018)].

Transaction transparency, access to customer data, and participation in a digital ecosystem enable flexible operations [Isaksson *et al.* (2018); Kauffman *et al.* (2010)]. Organizations can better respond to the customer's needs [Martinelli and Tunisini (2018); Pagani and Pardo (2017)]. This is supported by Li *et al.* [2016], who argue that integrating IT into operational and administrative processes leads to standardization and efficiency, which increases flexibility and responsiveness to the business environment. This is essential since organizations must respond to changing customer behaviors and requirements [Kauffman *et al.* (2010)]. However, organizations face challenges in adapting their existing systems. Companies must decide whether to integrate new systems into their current operations or to establish new units [Hess *et al.* (2016); Piccinini *et al.* (2015)].

Digital transformation extends the operational activities of companies to large-scale platforms [Yoo *et al.* (2012)]. Firm value chains are connected to partners building a digital supply network [Caputo *et al.* (2019)]. Thus, digital transformation facilitates the collaboration with partners beyond industry sectors. It improves relationships with customers and suppliers [Rachinger *et al.* (2018)]. Being part of a business network allows companies with a smaller resource base to enter the market [Herterich *et al.* (2016b); Isaksson *et al.* (2018)]. The scope of operations is increased from devices and units to networks within the enterprises and among the enterprises where collaboration takes place [Isaksson *et al.* (2018); Liere-Netheler *et al.* (2018)]. Such ecosystems come along with increased complexity. Centralized management must be replaced with distributed control methods that are more flexible [Isaksson *et al.* (2018)]. In a successful network, all stakeholders share relevant skills and resources and engage jointly, which is why supply chain partners must be wisely selected [Chou *et al.* (2012)]. Nevertheless, organizations face the challenge of being bypassed or attacked by other actors [Caputo *et al.* (2019); Nudurupati *et al.* (2016)].

Regarding digital manufacturing, digital technologies such as the internet of things enhance connectivity between previously isolated functions and the distribution of information across operations [Isaksson *et al.* (2018)]. The exchange of information between processes and stakeholders enhances the overall transparency, which supports decision-making [Zangiacomi *et al.* (2017)]. The collection and analysis of data during production processes, such as problems and bottlenecks, can be identified and addressed. Thus, unplanned disruptions are reduced, leading to an efficiency enhancement, reduced production times, and increased product quality [Hannola *et al.* (2018)]. The higher the efficiency, the shorter are life-cycles of processes, which increase flexibility to better respond to the customer's demand [Zangiacomi *et al.* (2017)].

4.2. *Data*

Data support organizations in detecting opportunities and threats in their environment [Li *et al.* (2016)]. Through the vertical and horizontal integration across value networks and the increased interaction with customers among various touchpoints, organizations get access to an extended data repertoire. While some data is already being used, new data needs to be integrated [Gölzer and Fritzsche (2017); Trabucchi *et al.* (2018)]. To generate and further use valuable information, data sets must be linked together [Trabucchi *et al.* (2018)]. Data integration aims to organize data and provide access for employees across the company [Dremel *et al.* (2017); Quinton and Simkin (2017); Rachinger *et al.* (2018)]. Data stored in separate databases needs to be accessible via an individual information model [Gölzer and Fritzsche (2017)]. As a "single source of truth" [Sebastian *et al.* (2017), p. 205], the general database for the entire organization must provide correct, reliable, and high-quality data. In addition, the increasing amount of data requires higher storage capacities [Li *et al.* (2018a)]. Organizations face challenges in terms of transmitting large amounts of data. Thus, companies must invest in their existing corporate network architecture and infrastructure to be able to store and transmit the vast amount of data [Herterich *et al.* (2016b)]. By making data accessible across departmental boundaries, silo structures can be overcome. It not only improves collaboration between internal departments but across the entire value network [Chou *et al.* (2012); Li *et al.* (2018a); Liere-Netheler *et al.* (2018)].

In their interviews of 42 successful SME leaders, Li *et al.* [2016] identified data analytics as an essential technology capability to realize chances offered by digital transformation. The collection, processing, and analysis of data throughout a company's ecosystem is crucial to create competitive value [Li *et al.* (2016)]. To transform data into information, the further development of data analytics capabilities is a prerequisite [Tumbas *et al.* (2017)]. With its high volume, velocity, and variety, big data has specific characteristics and challenges the established data handling routines. Thus, the organization must consider the elaboration of new strategies for data treatment for further usage [Gölzer and Fritzsche (2017)]. Literature distinguishes between descriptive analytical tools that provide insight into the past and predictive forecasting techniques for understanding the future [Bienhaus and Haddud (2018); Dremel *et al.* (2017)]. The focus of digital transformation is on the latter, as it improves, automates, and accelerates business processes [Bienhaus and Haddud (2018)]. The most significant opportunity, however, is the generation of customer insight, which improves the value proposition [Quinton and Simkin (2017); Sebastian *et al.* (2017); Trabucchi *et al.* (2018)]. Thus, the application of data analytics can provide companies with a competitive advantage [Nudurupati *et al.* (2016)]. Organizations can not only optimize the value proposition towards the customers but also towards the partners in the ecosystem [Li *et al.* (2016); Trabucchi *et al.* (2018)]. Digital analytics creates transparent processes that allow problems to be identified at an early stage [Isaksson *et al.* (2018)]. The increase in transparency and traceability improves relationships and the level of trust within the digital ecosystem [Bienhaus and Haddud (2018)]. The analysis of data across company boundaries provides insights into the market and supports well-founded decisions such as the entry into new partnerships [Li *et al.* (2016)]. To ensure the company's responsiveness to the dynamic environment, it must happen in real-time [Gölzer and Fritzsche (2017)]. However, complex interrelations in the digital ecosystem hamper the drawing of concrete conclusions [Dremel *et al.* (2017)]. Rather than supporting decision-making, it can result in information overload [Gölzer and Fritzsche (2017); Nudurupati *et al.* (2016)].

Another significant impact on businesses is the shift from data ownership to data sharing, which can violate privacy [Saarikko *et al.* (2020)]. To harness the power of digital transformation, data must be exchanged across organizational boundaries, which challenges traditional data ownership standards [Yoo *et al.* (2012)]. Especially in digital ecosystems, the flow of information is critical as it creates transparency and traceability and strengthens the level of trust among participants [Bienhaus and Haddud (2018)]. However, for fear of a loss of power, organizations are reluctant to provide insight into data [Dremel *et al.* (2017)]. To realize the opportunities, organizations must create a data-sharing and datadriven culture [Isaksson *et al.* (2018)].

Data security is a key issue when implementing a data exchange culture and offering intelligent products and services. No matter what changes the digital transformation may bring, the customer and the organization must feel secure in providing its data [Mani and Chouk (2018)]. The availability of larger amounts of data and information exchange exposes the security system to higher risks [Piccinini *et al.* (2015)]. This is a challenge since customers want to retain control over their data [Dremel *et al.* (2017)]. As a result, companies must identify and optimize potential vulnerabilities regarding data security [Bienhaus and Haddud (2018)]. Trust, security, and responsibility constitute a basis for collaboration and co-creation and must be anchored in the organization [Nudurupati *et al.* (2016)].

4.3. *Value propositions*

By embedding digital technologies into products and services, digital transformation changes the value proposition of an organization [Endres *et al.* (2020); Piccinini *et al.* (2015); Yoo *et al.* (2012)]. Liere-Netheler *et al.* [2018] and Sebastian *et al.* [2017] observe a shift in the value proposition's focus from the sale of products to services. Services are increasingly used as a source to create competitive advantages [Liere-Netheler *et al.* (2018)]. The literature analysis proves this trend since smart products and smart services are mostly mentioned in combination and with a strong focus on services. Sensors allow smart products to collect additional data [Sebastian *et al.* (2017)], which, translated into information, enables new service offerings [Pflaum and Gölzer (2018)]. Various individuals can add such service in an ecosystem due to smart products' generative capacity [Herterich *et al.* (2016a)]. This opens up possibilities for integrated solutions and enhanced customer experiences since a single artifact can meet multiple demands [Piccinini *et al.* (2015)]. The recurring revenue from ongoing services increases organizations' turnover [Pflaum and Gölzer (2018); Sebastian *et al.* (2017)]. However, the reprogrammable and generative nature of digital technologies shortens technology cycles and accelerates new products and services. Thus, organizations face an increasing pace of change [Piccinini *et al.* (2015); Yoo *et al.* (2012)]. The pace of change forces organizations to continuously update their value proposition [Nwankpa and Roumani (2016); Nylén and Holmström (2015)]. The accelerated introduction of new products and services stands in contrast to the long formation of relationships and platforms [Ferreira *et al.* (2018); Yoo *et al.* (2012)]. Business models become more dynamic because companies must rapidly react to changes in their environment [Endres *et al.* (2020); Piccinini *et al.* (2015)]. Sebastian *et al.* [2017] found that especially incumbent organizations with traditional revenue sources face challenges on how to navigate digital transformation and reposition themselves in the digital economy. Furthermore, Rauch *et al.* [2016] revealed that incumbent organizations are more likely to renew the technological foundation of their existing products and services than to enter new markets. They aim to strengthen their established product concept instead of embarking on a strategic change [Rauch *et al.* (2016)].

The integration of the customer into supply chains enables customization and tailoring of products and services [Endres *et al.* (2020); Martinelli and Tunisini (2018)], which in the framework is referred to as individualization. Also, data collected by smart products can be used to personalize the offering by adapting the content to the customer [Endres *et al.* (2020); Rachinger *et al.* (2018)]. Based on customer insights, organizations develop services according to the customers' needs [Herterich *et al.* (2016b)]. Customer insights and segmentation support a company in creating individual products or services for different groups [Kane *et al.* (2015a)]. The fulfillment of the customer's requirements increases the company's reputation and the acquisition of new customers [Chou *et al.* (2012)].

Moreover, digital technologies generate links between activities, resources, and actors. The exchange of data across these couplings generates new interactions among processes and actors and thus blurs and extends organizational boundaries [Nudurupati *et al.* (2016); Pagani and Pardo (2017)]. Organizations become part of the so-called digital ecosystem in which diverse actors collaborate to create value [Pagani and Pardo (2017); Piccinini *et al.* (2015)]. As part of a digital ecosystem, organizations can avail themselves of new resources, especially in areas outside their core businesses [Li *et al.* (2016)]. According to Pagani and Pardo [2017], access to additional resources affects a company in two ways. Either it enables the rationalization of internal activities or unleashes innovation opportunities based on the resources offered by ecosystem actors [Pagani and Pardo (2017)]. This is especially beneficial if a firm cannot produce the offering more economically on its own.

In addition, the access to capabilities of multiple firms enhances flexibility in production [Kauffman *et al.* (2010)]. Organizations can optimize their production processes by quickly adopting smart products from the market [Pflaum and Gölzer (2018)]. As a consequence, digital transformation changes relationships of previously competing organizations to partners that co-create value [Chou *et al.* (2012); Herterich *et al.* (2016a); Kauffman *et al.* (2010); Li *et al.* (2016, 2018b); Nudurupati *et al.* (2016); Pagani and Pardo (2017); Piccinini *et al.* (2015)].

4.4. *Customer*

Digital transformation moves the customer into the center of attention [Berghaus and Back (2017)]. Accordingly, Berghaus and Back [2017] and Kane *et al.* [2015a], state that firms must create an integrated experience around the customer's needs. Organizations that are comparatively slow in digital transformation, but feel increasing pressure due to changing customer behavior, concentrate on customer experience initiatives [Berghaus and Back (2017)]. This includes, for example, a userfriendly application as well as offers tailored to the customer. Personalized and integrated customer experiences are the basis for customer loyalty and trust [Sebastian *et al.* (2017)]. Kane *et al.* [2015a] even claim that to predict the future it is more important to observe the customer experience than new technological trends. They recommend developing a future perspective of the customer experience as a method to prioritize relevant and profitable initiatives in the respective industry [Kane *et al.* (2015a)].

Digital technologies gather massive data among various touchpoints with the customer [Dremel *et al.* (2017); Sebastian *et al.* (2017); Trabucchi *et al.* (2018)]. Collected data can be transferred into useful information for the company, offering valuable customer insights [Quinton and Simkin (2017)]. By engaging with customers via several touchpoints and data collection through digital technologies, firms can generate a more detailed customer profile [Tumbas *et al.* (2017)]. Thus, firms can grasp their customers' demands and create matching offerings [Li *et al.* (2018a); Sebastian *et al.* (2017)]. In particular, organizations can assess customer behavior, enabling operational improvements [Wu and Hitt (2015)]. Rachinger *et al.* [2018] identify a specific value of customer insights for sales and distribution activities, as they have the closest contact. Customer segmentation is a means to analyze the customer base. With the information about consumer groups and their path-to-purchase, organizations can address their customers with a more needs-oriented approach [Fulgoni (2014); Nylén and Holmström (2015); Rachinger *et al.* (2018)].

Digital technologies increase touchpoints during the path-to-purchase. The expansion of digital channels is a frequent starting point for organizations' digital transformation [Berghaus and Back (2017)]. In contrast to limited access through physical channels, the customer is now available anytime, anywhere. To ensure a seamless customer experience, the organization must develop an omnichannel management [Endres *et al.* (2020); Sebastian *et al.* (2017)]. According to Fulgoni [2014], omnichannel management is defined as the linkage and homogenization of online and offline activities across all platforms. Thanks to digitization, the customer can assess the same media content from different devices [Lyytinen *et al.* (2016); Yoo *et al.* (2012)]. It provides customers with more flexibility, allowing them to purchase products regardless of time and space [Fulgoni (2014); Sebastian *et al.* (2017)]. The extended access increases the loyalty of existing customers and improves the visibility of the company on the market. Companies can thus better reach their customers [Rachinger *et al.* (2018); Sebastian *et al.* (2017)]. Also, the adoption of multiple online and offline channels decreases information asymmetry between customers and firms. However, incumbent firms, in particular, that have operated offline in the past risk channel conflicts when adding online channels [Xie *et al.* (2014)]. Xie *et al.* [2014] suggest that companies must pursue a strategic approach that integrates offline and online channels into an overall concept.

Regarding the challenges of digital transformation, [Fulgoni (2014); Quinton and Simkin (2017); Rachinger *et al.* (2018)] recognize that the increased flexibility in the purchasing process and the improved visibility of organizations make customers less dependent on specific suppliers of products. Customers can quickly assess relevant information for their purchase decision, such as product quality or service [Xie *et al.* (2014)]. Consequently, digital transformation leads to the empowerment of customers. They can research products on various channels and compare them with alternative offers [Fulgoni (2014)]. Better access to information allows them to exert pressure on companies, for example, on product prices through quickly finding a cheaper offer on the market [Fulgoni (2014); Rachinger *et al.* (2018)].

Finally, digital transformation changes customer interaction from unidirectional, i.e. from organization to customer, into bidirectional ones, i.e. in both directions. Thereby, digital channels and touchpoints offer new opportunities to communicate with customers. Besides traditional customer approaches, especially visits and calls, companies can add videos, text, and email [Rachinger *et al.* (2018); Sebastian *et al.* (2017)]. Due to their global and unlimited connectivity, interactive web portals improve customer access [Jaw *et al.* (2016)]. Also, information and communication technologies for continuous interaction and digital technologies such as customer relationship management intensify relationships [Coreynen *et al.* (2017); Pagani and Pardo (2017)]. This is supported by Sebastian *et al.* [2017] and Pagani and Pardo [2017], who revealed that customer interaction, when integrated into a seamless omnichannel experience, increases customer loyalty and trust. The consumer becomes the center of attention [Endres *et al.* (2020); Tumbas *et al.* (2017)]. The literature analysis reveals a shift from indirect influence on the customer to the customer's direct involvement. Whereas, before digitalization, organizations could guide consumers through their path-to-purchase, customers are now increasingly gaining control of their digital journey [Quinton and Simkin (2017)]. By adapting their product and service offerings to the customer's needs and preferences, these become active value co-creators [Dremel *et al.* (2017); Quinton and Simkin (2017); Trabucchi *et al.* (2018)]. The end-to-end interaction with customers enhances collaboration on new ideas [Quinton and Simkin (2017)]. As a result, a study conducted by Mani and Chouk [2018] revealed that the integration of customers and human interaction decreases resistance towards new services. Nevertheless, the same study also showed that resistance might increase when the interaction no longer involves a person but a machine [Mani and Chouk (2018)]. A challenge is the risk of losing control of the brand's image. Encouraging customer participation and providing platforms for interaction increases the amount of user-generated content. Customer contributions, however, can generate unwelcome consequences: a negative customer experience shared online can have an adverse impact on the organizations reputation [Quinton and Simkin (2017)].

4.5. *Transformation management*

As digital transformation affects a firm in various facets, it is not sufficient to just implement digital technologies [Kane *et al.* (2015a)]. Especially incumbent organizations face difficulties in breaking with established standards [Sebastian *et al.* (2017)]. The potential of failure is high and thus must be well managed [Hess *et al.* (2016); Pflaum and Gölzer (2018)].

Academic researchers are convinced that a clear digital strategy is crucial for success [Bienhaus and Haddud (2018); Kindermann *et al.* (2020); Sebastian *et al.* (2017)]. Digital strategy affects the operational level in terms of new business models based on changed products and processes and the functional level. IT functionality is shifting into the company's focus and increasingly merges with business strategy [Leonhardt *et al.* (2017); Liere-Netheler *et al.* (2018)]. Hess *et al.* [2016] recommend the development of a standalone digital strategy. In contrast to an IT strategy, which is primarily concerned with the stability and efficiency of existing business processes, a digital strategy encourages rethinking and challenges existing working methods. Digital strategies are based on individual business models and core competencies [Hess *et al.* (2016)]. From a digital strategy, companies can derive concrete actions [Bienhaus and Haddud (2018)]. Such clearly defined goals are the premises for making proactive investment decisions and identifying barriers [Pflaum and Gölzer (2018); Sebastian *et al.* (2017)]. Schaarschmidt and Bertram [2020], for example, research the relationship between digital business intensity and constructive process deviance. However, the digital strategy must comply with the organization's overall strategy [Berghaus and Back (2017); Kane *et al.* (2015a); Quinton and Simkin (2017)].

Apart from developing a digital strategy, an organization's success towards a digital future depends on the leadership of the transformation journey [Berghaus and Back (2017); Hess *et al.* (2016)]. The transformational leader must coordinate the ongoing digital initiatives and align the individual tasks [Berghaus and Back (2017); Tumbas *et al.* (2017)]. Also, she must detect valuable opportunities that provide a competitive advantage [Saarikko *et al.* (2020); Tumbas *et al.* (2018)]. One possibility is the redefinition of existing roles. For example, when the Chief Information Officer (CIO), or the business unit's senior manager most affected by digital transformation, becomes responsible for the organization's digital transformation [Hess *et al.* (2016)]. In this context, ambidexterity plays an important role [Gerth and Peppard (2016); Tumbas *et al.* (2017)]. However, a study on the role of CIOs conducted by Gerth and Peppard [2016] showed that IT is still strongly associated with stability rather than change. That is why several studies recommend that digital should not become part of the traditional IT executive's agenda as it would be deprioritized against the maintenance of running processes [Tumbas *et al.* (2017)]. Therefore, another possibility mentioned is to hire a Chief Digital Officer (CDO) who prioritizes digital transformation and drives change [Dremel *et al.* (2017); Tumbas *et al.* (2017, 2018)]. The advantage here is that the focus of an entire position is on digital transformation.

In contrast, already existing positions such as the CIO have additional responsibilities, e.g. maintaining the IT infrastructure. The CDO often acts as a buffer between the business and the IT unit, focusing on end customers and leading the digital strategy. Through the integration of data and detection of new opportunities, she links the external with the internal perspective. No matter which option the organization chooses, the role and responsibilities must be precisely defined [Dremel *et al.* (2017); Gerth and Peppard (2016)]. Regardless of how the role is anchored in the organization, raising awareness of digital technologies' opportunities at the entire management level is cited as the prerequisite for a successful digital transformation [Herterich *et al.* (2016b)].

Digital leaders must share their digital spirit across the whole organization [Tumbas *et al.* (2018)]. Since new structures usually accompany organizational change, resistance can arise at the employee level [Berghaus and Back (2017); Dremel *et al.* (2017)]. Change management becomes indispensable to gently free employees from existing habits and thought patterns [Dremel *et al.* (2017); Hess *et al.* (2016); Kindermann *et al.* (2020)]. To accept the integration of digital technologies, the employees must understand the technologies' usefulness and positive impact on the organization [Beier and Wagner (2016)]. The transition is made easier for employees by training them in digital technologies before these are implemented [Pflaum and Gölzer (2018)]. In addition to guidance, the employees must also be guaranteed space for experimentation and learning. A trust-building environment is the precondition for a smooth change process [Berghaus and Back (2017); Bienhaus and Haddud (2018)]. Managers need to build trust and reliability as a first step to create a safe environment where employees can free their fears and concerns regarding the change process [Bienhaus and Haddud (2018)]. In addition, participatory and interactive methods reinforce shared values and positive attitudes towards digital transformation [Li *et al.* (2018a)]. Communication problems, e.g. using different vocabulary, hampers cooperation across business units [Hansen *et al.* (2011)]. Thus, the use of a common language, for example, supports a participatory change process and the development of a shared understanding of the need for digital transformation across business units. Resistance must be accepted and used as an impetus for adjustments in the organizational change process [Hansen *et al.* (2011)]. Apart from resistance towards change, another challenge mentioned is the pace of change. Organizations offer finite capacities for change. Consequently, companies must find the right balance between creating change too slowly, leading to derailments, and promoting change too quickly, which can lead to mistakes [Gerth and Peppard (2016)]. Some organizations hire external experts to support the change process [Pflaum and Gölzer (2018)].

An organization must finance the transformation determined by its background and size [Hess *et al.* (2016)]. Studies have shown the positive relationship between digital transformation and business performance [Nwankpa and Roumani (2016)]. However, organizations must find a way to quantify digital technologies' added value, referred to as digital value assurance. It helps to reveal its chances [Beier and Wagner (2016); Isaksson *et al.* (2018)]. Digital transformation leads to higher complexity and interlinkage of functionalities as well as unlimited opportunities. Organizations have to decide which activities bring additional value and make sense regarding their circumstances and technical feasibility [Isaksson *et al.* (2018)]. Nudurupati *et al.* [2016] demand that performance measurement in the digital era must be modernized. As organizations become part of a digital ecosystem, both internal and external performance measurement within the network is essential. Besides incorporating various stakeholders, organizations must assess traditional financial indicators and behavioral metrics [Nudurupati *et al.* (2016, p. 232)]. Performance indicators such as learning and developing skills drive the change of organizational culture [Nudurupati *et al.* (2016)]. Also, organizations can monitor and quantify how digitized products contribute to value creation and bill them adequately [Herterich *et al.* (2016a)]. The quantification supports the reflection of the whole ecosystem's value proposition [Herterich *et al.* (2016b)]. New revenue sources can be uncovered, which are essential to remain competitive [Hess *et al.* (2016)].

4.6. *Human resources*

As employees are a central resource for digital transformation [Fenech *et al.* (2019)], we define human resources as an important building block for digital transformation and assign the fields of action "digital skillset", "cross-functional teams", and "flexible resource allocation" to it. Thus, we refer to the management of human resources as "the management of work and people towards desired ends" [Boxall *et al.* (2009)]. Thus, the success of digital transformation is influenced by the expertise and the appropriate competencies of its employees [Vieru *et al.* (2015)].

Changing customer expectations in digital transformation increases the need for cross-departmental exchange and collaboration to enhance the customer experience [Barann (2018); Kauffman *et al.* (2010)]. An often-mentioned silo structure enhances rivalry between departments in the organization. Due to the lack of cooperation, departments can develop conflicting goals that hampers a common digital transformation approach. Therefore, the framework must consider the reduction of conflicts through the support establishment of cross-functional teams. Instead of focusing on optimizing departmental processes, cross-functional teams can share their interests and develop a mutual understanding. Since the customer passes several touchpoints with the company during her purchase journey, the involvement of varying competencies across departmental boundaries in an organization becomes necessary [Barann (2018); Berghaus and Back (2017)].

Furthermore, the flexible allocation of resources responds to the unpredictability of environmental changes. Instead of long-term capacity planning, organizations must enable a short-term formation of interdisciplinary teams [Kindermann *et al.* (2020)]. Apart from daily routines, they must have the flexibility to work on innovative solutions. It allows companies to remain competitive, as organizations can release digital initiatives in the short run and react to changing circumstances. The digital business intensity of an organization, thus, has an effect on obligations felt by employees and subsequently to constructive process deviance [Schaarschmidt and Bertram (2020)]. Resources are limited and must be allocated according to the importance of the initiatives.

4.7. *Organizational structure*

The increasing use of information technologies and the far-reaching digitalisation of society and the economy and organizations is leading to a change in the structure of organizations [Doherty *et al.* (2010)]. As the organizational structure helps management to define and delineate responsibilities and communication channels [Jemison (1981); Simon (1997)], it is an important influencing factor on any the strategic task like digital transformation [Doherty *et al.* (2010); Fredrickson (1986)]. Organizational structure refers to internal model of an organization's authority, decision-making, and relationships [Thompson (2008)], and, thus, defines information processing and the environment of decision-making in an organization [Bower (1986); Fredrickson (1986)]. Organizational structure can be analyzed according to the three dimensions centralization, formalization, and complexity [Fredrickson (1986)].

The literature analysis strongly emphasizes that a decentralized organizational structure supports a collaborative company culture [Herterich *et al.* (2016b); Saarikko *et al.* (2020)]. On the one hand, employees are strongly affected by all these changes. The missing commitment of employees and resistance to change is a significant field for digital transformation in academic literature [Berghaus and Back (2017); Dremel *et al.* (2017); Müller *et al.* (2019)]. Anchored in the silo structure and due to underlying administrative regulations, employees have an isolated view and difficulties understanding the need for digital transformation. The missing insight into the outcome of digital transformation beyond their activities hampers acceptance of the need to change their routines [Müller *et al.* (2019)].

On the other hand, they have the closest contact with the organization's customers. Therefore, employees must be integrated into the transformation process by being given responsibility. In a decentralized organization, employees can make their own decisions [Holotiuk *et al.* (2018)]. Employee autonomy meets their demand to be actively involved in the transformation process. Data can not only serve as evidence [Dremel *et al.* (2017); Gölzer and Fritzsche (2017)], but increase the speed and accuracy of decisions [Chou *et al.* (2012)]. Thus, decentralized decision-making must be integrated parallel with transformation leadership, which is already included in the framework. Providing employees with responsible roles in the change process could be an appropriate solution [Bienhaus and Haddud (2018)].

The offer of integrated solutions and the need for external expertise blurs company boundaries, which is a much-discussed topic in research and practice.

The cooperation with ecosystem players becomes increasingly important [Piccinini *et al.* (2015); Rachinger *et al.* (2018)]. By providing resources, the ecosystem allows the rationalization of internal activities and greater flexibility in production. As previous competitors become partners, organizations are facing changing relationships. The increased interdependency is perceived as a challenge because they involve new processes among actors and processes. Organizations must adapt their administrative regulations and motivate employees to collaborate with people outside their organization. At the same time, the value proposition's uniqueness must be secured, which means that employees must find an adequate balance between cooperation and competition. The introduction of boundary management can be a means to handle the complexity of inter-and intra-organizational coordination across the supply chain [Caputo *et al.* (2019)]. Thus, organizational agility plays an important role in the digital transformation of organizations. Conboy referes to agility as the ability to "rapidly or inherently create change, proactively or reactively embrace change, and learn from change while contributing to perceived customer value" [Conboy (2009, p. 340)] which in fact refers to the organizational environment of decision-making and, thus, is nurtured by the structure of an organization and spans the boundary to its culture.

4.8. *Culture*

Based on the literature's in-depth analysis, we introduce an additional building block to the integrated framework of digital transformation with culture [Kane *et al.* (2015b); Saarikko *et al.* (2020)]. As the current and expected behavior within an organization is oriented towards its organizational culture, the culture of an organization is an essential influencing factor for a far-reaching organizational transformation [Schein (2010)]. Thus, "culture is viewed as an inescapable context" [Iivari and Iivari (2011, p. 511)] organizational life and change takes place [Geertz (1973a,b); Schein (2010)]. Thus, we follow the definiton of Schein [2010, p. 3] and see culture as a "dynamic phenomenon and a coercive background structure" that influences the digital tranformation of an organization as it is "constantly reenacted and created by our interactions with others and shaped by our own behavior". While none of the analyzed papers mention a digital culture explicitly as a prerequisite for a successful digital transformation, different contributions speak of cultural aspects accompanying organizational change [Berghaus and Back (2017); Bienhaus and Haddud (2018); Müller *et al.* (2019)]. A digital culture is described in many contributions as a subliminal momentum and a basis for change. Since all employees are directly or indirectly affected by digital transformation, Herterich *et al.* [2016b] argue that a decentralized organizational structure supports a collaborative organizational culture. Isaksson *et al.* [2018] even make use of a data-driven corporate culture to make data usable as corporate resources. Thus, a digital culture is seen as an essential prerequisite for a successful digital transformation.

To become agile and enhance creativity, organizations need to adapt to the workplace. Open workspaces, modern infrastructure, flexible work models, and social platforms are means which enhance a collaborative company culture [Berghaus and

Back (2017); Bienhaus and Haddud (2018); Müller *et al.* (2019)]. Participatory and interactive methods facilitate the production and diffusion of knowledge, improving a company's operational performance [Li *et al.* (2018a)]. To improve efficiency and simplicity in daily business activities, employees need platforms, remote access, and common user interfaces [Bienhaus and Haddud (2018)]. Integrating digital technologies into business operations enhances effectiveness and working conditions [Bienhaus and Haddud (2018); Liere-Netheler *et al.* (2018)]. As a barrier to agile organizations, Holotiuk *et al.* [2018] identified formalized structures that hinder the speed of response and execution of new ideas. Because employees at agile companies may perform several tasks due to limited resources, they may not be willing to invest time in learning and applying new digital technologies [Jaw *et al.* (2016)]. To develop creative solutions, employees need freedom and flexibility. Leonhardt *et al.* [2017] conclude that employees must be relieved of parts of their day-to-day tasks.

The new work practices go hand in hand with the company culture's adaption, which may require the establishment of a digital mindset before digital technologies can be leveraged effectively [Hannola *et al.* (2018); Kane *et al.* (2015a); Solberg *et al.* (2020)]. When the digital logic is confronted with the traditional reasoning in departments, tensions arise [Tumbas *et al.* (2018)]. Working practices that originated in the digital world find growing popularity in the physical world [Piccinini *et al.* (2015)]. However, companies often face initial resistance arising from established routines. Especially employees who have worked in the traditional business for several years must be persuaded to embrace digital technologies in daily business [Berghaus and Back (2017); Coreynen *et al.* (2017)]. Thus, employees' beliefs regarding their growth mindset as well as their their beliefs regarding the availability of resources can have an influence on to which extent of they perceive new technologies as valuable to implement for digital transformation [Solberg *et al.* (2020)]. Furthermore, Müller *et al.* [2019] identify an influence of control orientation of the culture of a company on its success in digital innovation.

Although most employees are aware of the necessity of digital transformation for the organizational future, they find it challenging to identify the relevant technologies [Bienhaus and Haddud (2018)]. Companies have to implement a "startup-like mentality" [Piccinini *et al.* (2015, p. 11)]. Permitting failures encourages employees to use digital technologies as they are more willing to experiment and take risks [Kane *et al.* (2015a); Nylén and Holmström (2015)].

5. Conclusion, Limitations, and Further Research

Due to the fundamental effects of digitization on society and the economy, organizations face a fundamental organizational transformation towards a digital future [Verhoef *et al.* (2021); Vial (2019)]. The digital transformation of organizations requires a long-lasting transformation process. As organizations struggle with fundamental transformations threatening their established structures [Heavin and Power (2018)], they need guidelines and points of orientation to make the change predictable and sustainable. While academic research investigates numerous aspects of digital transformation, work on an integrative framework is scarce. The models of

Vial [2019], Heavin and Power [2018], Rueckel *et al.* [2020], and Verhoef *et al.* [2021] provide insights into digital transformation, but their applicability in organizations seems complicated due to their high level of abstraction. The six-factor framework of Gimpel *et al.* [2018], on the other hand, represents an easily applied approach, which is, however, an initial framework based on an interview study and not broadly supported and evaluated by scientific results. The presented work is based on the framework for digital transformation of Gimpel *et al.* [2018]. Utilizing a systematic literature review, high-quality scientific publications on digital transformation are identified, codified, and analyzed in a structured way.

With our work, we contribute to the academic discourse and create a structured overview of the existing sub-themes in digital transformation. We confirm the action fields and action items of the six-factor framework of Gimpel *et al.* [2018]. Numerous scientific papers document the areas of the initial framework identified by the interview study. The analysis of the identified literature enables us to extend the framework of Gimpel *et al.* [2018] to an integrative framework for digital transformation. With eight building blocks, we present an integrative framework for digital transformation. Besides the action fields Operations, Data, Value Proposition, Customer, and Transformation Management, our integrative framework specifically addresses organizational areas such as Human Resources, Culture, and Organizational Structure. The integrative framework for digital transformation thus facilitates a more targeted organizational transformation into a digital future. The framework and the underlying structured literature search and systematic literature analysis allow researchers to classify their digital transformation work and establish existing thematic references. As we base our conceptually integrative framework on existing literature it does not come without limitations. Future research should build on our integratvie framework and evaluate it with a broader view on literature. Furthermore, due to the conceptual nature of our work, future research should validate the building blocks and action items identified in our integrative framework. Especially the added building blocks Human Resources, Organizational Structure, and Culture and their influence on a successful digital transformation of organizations should be investigated more indepth.

For organizations, the integrative framework for digital transformation represents a valuable model and a basis for implementing organizational change into a digital future. The framework shows the central fields of digital transformation and their dependencies and provides significant scientific findings in the individual subfields. The framework serves as a basis for developing a digital strategy and the derivation of a digital roadmap for organizations.

The developed integrative framework for digital transformation will contribute to further research in the digital change of organizations. While the literature analysis reveals numerous sub-fields of digital transformation, the identified publications mainly deal with the opportunities and chances for digital transformation organizations. More detailed insights into the options associated with digitization in different types of organizations and industries and the challenges related to digital transformation should be areas of future research in the field of digital transformation.

References

Barann, B. (2018). An IS-perspective on omni-channel management: Development of a conceptual framework to determine the impacts of touchpoint digitalization on retail business processes. In *European Conference Information Systems 2018 Proceedings*, https://aisel.aisnet.org/ecis2018_rip/18.

Beier, M. and Wagner, K. (2016). Social media adoption: Barriers to the strategic use of social media in SMEs. In *European Conference Information Systems 2016 Proceedings*, Istanbul, Paper No 100, https://aisel.aisnet.org/ecis2016_rp/100.

Belingheri, P. and Neirotti, P. (2019). Digitalising products: Towards an integrated view of challenges in development, design and user acceptance. *International Journal of Technology Management*, **80**, 1/2: 99773, doi: 10.1504/IJTM.2019.099773.

Berghaus, S. and Back, A. (2017). Disentangling the fuzzy front end of digital transformation: Activities and approaches. In *Int. Conference Information Systems Proceedings*, Seoul, 2017, pp. 1–17, https://aisel.aisnet.org/icis2017/PracticeOriented/Presentations/4.

Besson, P. and Rowe, F. (2012). Strategizing information systems-enabled organizational transformation: A transdisciplinary review and new directions. *The Journal of Strategic Information Systems*, **21**, 2: 103–124, doi: 10.1016/j.jsis.2012.05.001.

Bharadwaj, A., El Sawy, O. A., Pavlou, P. A. and Venkatraman, N. (2013). Digital business strategy: Toward a next generation of insights. *MIS Quarterly*, **37**, 2: 471–482.

Bienhaus, F. and Haddud, A. (2018). Procurement 4.0: Factors influencing the digitisation of procurement and supply chains. *Business Process Management Journal*, **24**, 4: 965–984, doi: 10.1108/BPMJ-06-2017-0139.

Bounfour, A. (2016). From IT to digital transformation: A long term perspective. *Progress in IS Digital Futures, Digital Transformation: From Lean Production to Acceluction*, ed. A. Bounfour. Springer, pp. 11–29, doi: 10.1007/978-3-319-23279-9_2.

Bower, J. L. (1986). *Managing the Resource Allocation Process: A Study of Corporate Planning and Investment* (Rev. ed.). Harvard Business School Classics, Vol. 3. Harvard Business School Press.

Boxall, P., Purcell, J. and Wright, P. M. (2009). *Human Resource Management: Scope, Analysis, and Significance*, Vol. 1. Oxford University Press, doi: 10.1093/oxfordhb/9780199547029.003.0001.

Brynjolfsson, E. and Hitt, L. M. (2000). Beyond computation: Information technology, organizational transformation and business performance. *Journal of Economic Perspectives*, **14**, 4: 23–48, doi: 10.1257/jep.14.4.23.

Candi, M. and Beltagui, A. (2018). Effective use of 3D printing in the innovation process. *Technovation*, **80-81**, 63–73, doi: 10.1016/j.technovation.2018.05.002.

Caputo, A., Fiorentino, R. and Garzella, S. (2019). From the boundaries of management to the management of boundaries: Business processes, capabilities and negotiations. *Business Process Management Journal*, **25**, 3: 391–413, doi: 10.1108/BPMJ-11-2017-0334.

Chou, T.-C., Liu, D.-Y. and Chen, S.-W. (2012). Resource fit in digital transformation: Lessons learned from the CBC Bank global e-banking project. *Management Decision*, **49**, 10: 1728–1742, doi: 10.1108/00251741111183852.

Conboy, K. (2009). Agility from first principles: Reconstructing the concept of agility in information systems development. *Information Systems Research*, **20**, 3: 329–354, doi: 10.1287/isre.1090.0236.

Coreynen, W., Matthyssens, P. and van Bockhaven, W. (2017). Boosting servitization through digitization: Pathways and dynamic resource configurations for manufacturers. *Industrial Marketing Management*, **60**, 42–53, doi: 10.1016/j.indmarman.2016.04.012.

Crittenden, A. B., Crittenden, V. L. and Crittenden, W. F. (2019). The digitalization triumvirate: How incumbents survive. *Business Horizons*, **62**, 2: 259–266, doi: 10.1016/j.bushor.2018.11.005.

Denner, M.-S., Püschel, L. and Röglinger, M. (2018). How to exploit the digitalization potential of business processes. *Business & Information Systems Engineering*, **60**, 4: 331–349.

Doherty, N. F., Champion, D. and Wang, L. (2010). An holistic approach to understanding the changing nature of organizational structure. *Information Technology & People*, **23**, 2: 116–135, doi: 10.1108/09593841011052138.

Dremel, C., Wulf, J., Herterich, M. M., Waizmann, J.-C. and Brenner, W. (2017). How AUDI AG established big data analytics in its digital transformation. *MIS Quarterly Executive*, **16**, 2: 81–100.

Endres, H., Stoiber, K. and Wenzl, N. M. (2020). Managing digital transformation through hybrid business models. *Journal of Business Strategy*, **41**, 6: 49–56, doi: 10.1108/JBS-07-20190142.

Fenech, R., Baguant, P. and Ivanov, D. (2019). The changing role of human resource management in an era of digital transformation. *Journal of Management Information and Decision Sciences*, **22**, 2: 1–10. https://search.proquest.com/openview/683dd7c5bc7a3658475b0fce99e160d9/1?pqorigsite=gscholar&cbl=38743&casa_token=nb7ky0ychg4aaaaa:qg1yaizlh5jutpjgcj7bmiyyarebcyivyiz7pqbj3m7pklqylw5_si41oxae9kvp8_skp65ujg.

Ferreira, J. J. M., Fernandes, C. I. and Ferreira, F. A. F. (2018). To be or not to be digital, that is the question: Firm innovation and performance. *Journal of Business Research*, **101**, 583–590, doi: 10.1016/j.jbusres.2018.11.013.

Fitzgerald, M., Kruschwitz, N., Bonnet, D. and Welch, M. (2013). Embracing digital technology: A new strategic imperative. *MIT Sloan Management Review*, **55**, 2: 1–12.

Fredrickson, J. W. (1986). The strategic decision process and organizational structure. *Academy of Management Review*, **11**, 2: 280–297, doi: 10.5465/amr.1986.4283101.

Fulgoni, G. M. (2014). "Omni-channel" retail insights and the consumer's path-to-purchase. *Journal of Advertising Research*, **54**, 4: 377–380, doi: 10.2501/JAR-54-4-377-380.

Gao, S., Hakanen, E., Töytäri, P. and Rajala, R. (2019). Digital transformation in asset-intensive businesses: Lessons learned from the metals and mining industry. In *Proceedings of the Annual Hawaii Int. Conference System Sciences, Proceedings 52nd Hawaii Int. Conference System Sciences, Hawaii Int. Conference System Sciences.* ed. T. Bui, Hawaii, pp. 4927–4936, doi:10.24251/HICSS.2019.593.

Gartner Inc. (2020). Digitalization, https://www.gartner.com/en/information-technology/glossary/digitalization.

Gebauer, H., Fleisch, E., Lamprecht, C. and Wortmann, F. (2020). Growth paths for overcoming the digitalization paradox. *Business Horizons*, **63**, 3: 313–323, doi: 10.1016/j.bushor.2020.01.005.

Geertz, C. (1973a). *Cultures.* https://naph.or.th/storage/app/uploads/public/601/91e/701/60191e701e50e768179418.pdf.

Geertz, C. (1973b). *The Interpretation of Cultures*, Vol. 50, 19th edn. Basic Books Inc. Publishers. https://scholar.google.com/citations?user=v4ppw_caaaaj&hl=de&oi=sra.

Gerth, A. B. and Peppard, J. (2016). The dynamics of CIO derailment: How CIOs come undone and how to avoid it. *Business Horizons*, **59**, 1: 61–70, doi: 10.1016/j.bushor.2015.09.001.

Gimpel, H., Hosseini, S., Huber, R., Probst, L., Röglinger, M. and Faisst, U. (2018). Structuring digital transformation: A framework of action fields and its application at ZEISS. *Journal of Information Technology Theory and Application*, **19**, 1: 31–54.

Gölzer, P. and Fritzsche, A. (2017). Data-driven operations management: Organizational implications of the digital transformation in industrial practice. *Production Planning & Control*, **28**, 16: 1332–1343, doi: 10.1080/09537287.2017.1375148.

Hannola, L., Richter, A., Richter, S. and Stocker, A. (2018). Empowering production workers with digitally facilitated knowledge processes — a conceptual framework. *International Journal of Production Research*, **56**, 14: 4729–4743, doi: 10.1080/00207543.2018.1445877.

Hansen, A. M., Kraemmergaard, P. and Mathiassen, L. (2011). Rapid adaptation in digital transformation: A participatory process for engaging IS and business leaders. *MIS Quarterly Executive*, **10**, 4: 175–185.

Heavin, C. and Power, D. J. (2018). Challenges for digital transformation — towards a conceptual decision support guide for managers. *Journal of Decision Systems*, **27**, Supp. 1: 38–45, doi: 10.1080/12460125.2018.1468697.

Herterich, M. M., Eck, A. and Uebernickel, F. (2016a). Exploring how digitized products enable industrial service innvovation — An affordance perpective. In *European Conference Information Systems 2016 Proceedings*, Istanbul, Paper No 156, https://aisel.aisnet.org/ecis2016_rp/156.

Herterich, M. M., Uebernickel, F. and Brenner, W. (2016b). Stepwise evolution of capabilities for harnessing digital data streams in data-driven industrial services. *MIS Quarterly Executive*, **15**, 4: 297–318.

Hess, T., Matt, C., Benlian, A. and Wiesböck, F. (2016). Options for formulating a digital transformation strategy. *MIS Quarterly Executive*, **15**, 2: 123–139.

Holotiuk, F., Beimborn, D. and Jentsch, C. (2018). The determinants and role of agility in digital organizations. In *European Conference Information Systems 2018 Proceedings*, Portsmouth, UK, pp. 1–17, Paper No. 182, https://aisel.aisnet.org/ecis2018_rp/182.

Hufnagl, C., Doctor, E., Behrens, L., Buck, C. and Eymann, T. (2019). Digitisation along the patient pathway in hospitals. In *Proceedings 27 European Conference Information Systems 2019*, Stockholm, Sweden, pp. 1–16.

Iivari, J. and Iivari, N. (2011). The relationship between organizational culture and the deployment of agile methods. *Information and Software Technology*, **53**, 5: 509–520, doi: 10.1016/j.infsof.2010.10.008.

Isaksson, A. J., Harjunkoski, I. and Sand, G. (2018). The impact of digitalization on the future of control and operations. *Computers & Chemical Engineering*, **114**, 9: 122–129, doi: 10.1016/j.compchemeng.2017.10.037.

Jaw, Y.-L., Chen, Y.-Y. K. and Wu, B.-L. (2016). Effect of digital transformation on organizational performance of SMEs: Evidence from the Taiwanese textile industry's web portal. *Internet Research*, **26**, 1: 186–212, doi: 10.1108/IntR-12-2013-0265.

Jemison, D. B. (1981). The contributions of administrative behavior to strategic management. *Academy of Management Review*, **6**, 4: 633–642, doi: 10.5465/amr.1981.4285714.

Kahre, C., Hoffmann, D. and Ahlemann, F. (2017). Beyond business-IT alignment — Digital business strategies as a paradigmatic shift: A review and research agenda. In *Proceedings Annual Hawaii Int. Conference System Sciences, Proceedings 50th Hawaii Int. Conference System Sciences (2017), Hawaii Int. Conference System Sciences.* Waikoloa, pp. 4706–4715, doi:10.24251/HICSS.2017.574.

Kane, G. C., Palmer, D., Philipps, A. N. and Kiron, D. (2015a). Is your business ready for a digital future?*MIT Sloan Management Review*, **56**, 4: 37–44.

Kane, G. C., Palmer, D., Phillips, A. N., Kiron, D. and Buckley, N. (2015b). Strategy, not technology, drives digital transformation. *MIT Sloan Management Review*, **14**, 1–25. https://sloanreview.mit.edu/projects/strategy-drives-digital-transformation/?switch_view=pdf.

Kauffman, R. J., Li, T. and van Heck, E. (2010). Business network-based value creation in electronic commerce. *International Journal of Electronic Commerce*, **15**, 1: 113–143.

Kindermann, B., Beutel, S., Garcia de Lomana, G., Strese, S., Bendig, D. and Brettel, M. (2020). Digital orientation: Conceptualization and operationalization of a new strategic orientation. *European Management Journal.* In press, doi: 10.1016/j.emj.2020.10.009.

Kitchenham, B. (2004). Procedures for performing systematic reviews. *Keele University*, **33**, 1–26.

Kohli, R. and Melville, N. P. (2019). Digital innovation: A review and synthesis. *Information Systems Journal*, **29**, 1: 200–223, doi: 10.1111/isj.12193.

Kompella, L. (2019). Digital innovation in the public sector: The role of embeddedness in socio technical transitions. *International Journal of Innovation and Technology Management*, **16**, 7: 1950059, doi: 10.1142/S0219877019500597.

Legner, C., Eymann, T., Hess, T., Matt, C., Böhmann, T., Drews, P., Mädche, A., Urbach, N. and Ahlemann, F. (2017). Digitalization: Opportunity and challenge for the business and information systems engineering community. *Business & Information Systems Engineering*, **59**, 4: 301–308, doi: 10.1007/s12599-017-0484-2.

Leonhardt, D., Haffke, I., Kranz, J. and Benlian, A. (2017). Reinventing the IT function: The role of IT agility and IT ambidexterity in supporting digital business transformation. In *European Conference Information Systems 2017 Proceedings*, Guimarães, Portugal, pp. 1–17, https://aisel.aisnet.org/ecis2017_rp/63.

Levy, Y. and Ellis, T. J. (2006). A systems approach to conduct an effective literature review in support of information systems research. *Informing Science*, **9**, 181–212.

Li, W., Liu, K., Belitski, M., Ghobadian, A. and O' Regan, N. (2016). e-Leadership through strategic alignment: An empirical study of small- and medium-sized enterprises in the digital age. *Journal of Information Technology*, **31**, 2: 185–206, doi: 10.1057/jit.2016.10.

Li, C., Guo, S., Cao, L. and Li, J. (2018a). Digital enablement and its role in internal branding: A case study of Huanyi travel agency. *Industrial Marketing Management*, **72**, 152–160, doi: 10.1016/j.indmarman.2018.04.010.

Li, L., Su, F., Zhang, W. and Mao, J.-Y. (2018b). Digital transformation by SME entrepreneurs: A capability perspective. *Information Systems Journal*, **28**, 6: 1129–1157, doi: 10.1111/isj.12153.

Liao, A., Hull, C. E. and Sriramachandramurthy, R. (2013). The six facets model of technology management: A study in the digital business industry. *International Journal of Innovation and Technology Management*, **10**, 4: 1350019, doi: 10.1142/S0219877013500193.

Lichtenthaler, U. (2020). Building blocks of successful digital transformation: Complementing technology and market issues. *International Journal of Innovation and Technology Management*, **17**, 1: 2050004.

Liere-Netheler, K., Vogelsang, K., Packmohr, S. and Hoppe, U. A. (2018). Towards a framework for digital tranformation success in manufacturing. *European Conference Information Systems 2018 Proceedings*, https://aisel.aisnet.org/ecis2018_rp/193.

Litvinenko, V. S. (2020). Digital economy as a factor in the technological development of the mineral sector. *Natural Resources Research*, **29**, 3: 1521–1541, doi: 10.1007/s11053-01909568-4.

Lucas, H., Agarwal, R., Clemons, E., El Sawy, O. A. and Weber, B. (2013). Impactful research on transformational information technology: An opportunity to inform new audiences. *MIS Quarterly*, **37**, 2: 371–382.

Lyytinen, K. J., Yoo, Y. and Boland, R. J. J. (2016). Digital product innovation within four classes of innovation networks. *Information Systems Journal*, **26**, 1: 47–75, doi: 10.1111/isj.12093.

Mani, Z. and Chouk, I. (2018). Consumer resistance to innovation in services: Challenges and barriers in the internet of things era. *Journal of Product Innovation Management*, **35**, 5: 780–807, doi: 10.1111/jpim.12463.

Martinelli, E. M. and Tunisini, A. (2018). Customer integration into supply chains: Literature review and research propositions. *Journal of Business & Industrial Marketing*, doi: 10.1108/JBIM-07-2017-0162.

Matt, C., Hess, T. and Weiß, C. (2013). The differences between recommender technologies in their impact on sales diversity. In *Int. Conference Information Systems 2013 Proceedings*, Milano, Italy, pp. 1–17, https://aisel.aisnet.org/icis2013/proceedings/EBusiness/15.

Matt, C., Hess, T. and Benlian, A. (2015). Digital transformation strategies. *Business & Information Systems Engineering*, **57**, 5: 339–343, doi: 10.1007/s12599-015-0401-5.

Möller, D., Legner, C. and Heck, A. (2011). Understanding it transformation – An explorative study. *European Conference Information Systems 2011 Proceedings.* Helsinki, Finland, Paper No 15.

Müller, S. D., Obwegeser, N., Glud, J. V. and Johildarson, G. (2019). Digital innovation and organizational culture. *Scandinavian Journal of Information Systems*, **31**, 2: 1. https://aisel.aisnet.org/cgi/viewcontent.cgi?article=1526&context=sjis.

Nambisan, S., Wright, M. and Feldman, M. (2019). The digital transformation of innovation and entrepreneurship: Progress, challenges and key themes. *Research Policy*, **48**, 8: 103773, doi: 10.1016/j.respol.2019.03.018.

Nudurupati, S. S., Tebboune, S. and Hardman, J. (2016). Contemporary performance measurement and management (PMM) in digital economies. *Production Planning & Control*, **27**, 3: 226–235, doi: 10.1080/09537287.2015.1092611.

Nwankpa, J. K. and Roumani, Y. (2016). IT capability and digital transformation: A firm performance perspective. In *Int. Conference Information Systems Proceedings, 2016.* Dublin, Ireland, pp. 1–16, https://aisel.aisnet.org/icis2016/ISStrategy/Presentations/4.

Nylén, D. and Holmström, J. (2015). Digital innovation strategy: A framework for diagnosing and improving digital product and service innovation. *Business Horizons*, **58**, 1: 57–67, doi: 10.1016/j.bushor.2014.09.001.

Okoli, C. and Schabram, K. (2010). A guide to conducting a systematic literature review of information systems research. *Sprouts: Working Papers on Information Systems*, **10**, 26. https://d1wqtxts1xzle7.cloudfront.net/3250666/OkoliSchabram2010SproutsLitReview-Guide.pdf?response-content-disposition=inline%3B+filename%3DA_Guide_to_Conducting_a_Systematic_Liter.pdf&Expires=1622717076&Signature=-JgLHIETr9hBqjlBU9c3jpZ2~~EgOVw0PlTKZJtIxLd~zhTxGIRYG5hcEG8VQlx4dESyoAXa5OC8zrb3~c992huEnZfOqwO8jAFqSxOmGHTtoXCVSFhvzLvvnpjh5N5QI~RBjLeBd5PNT3kQ53fq7YePl~ozznKGopXWZKrxCxcVaOt8c-hSJZEzgM5-wAFNDD2~tRUdzVjfRfgsEWWvQaCz2wEAFcwH5EPO0zAwTSvS4EsRsHJWyWfQegULPIjkEXiF2ND0rm3B4GbxRQ7Q6xYYDSvtzKDiRSt337QJ2u4tltaSVb6LPrjx~sCeThHXHiA1pgPMl8qFzeDvEd19HTPyL-YM2H0CA_&Key-Pair-Id=APKAJ-LOHF5GGSLRBV4ZA.

Orlikowski, W. J. (2000). Using technology and constituting structures: A practice lens for studying technology in organizations. *Organization Science*, **11**, 4: 404–428, doi: 10.1287/orsc.11.4.404.14600.

Osterwalder, A. and Pigneur, Y. (2013). *Business Model Generation: A Handbook for Visionaries, Game Changers, and Challengers.* Wiley & Sons.

Pagani, M. and Pardo, C. (2017). The impact of digital technology on relationships in a business network. *Industrial Marketing Management*, **67**, 185–192, doi: 10.1016/j.indmarman.2017.08.009.

Pflaum, A. A. and Gölzer, P. (2018). The IoT and digital transformation: Toward the data-driven enterprise. *IEEE Pervasive Computing*, **17**, 1: 87–91, doi: 10.1109/MPRV.2018.011591066.

Piccinini, E., Hanelt, A., Gregory, R. and Kolbe, L. (2015). Transforming industrial business: The impact of digital transformation on automotive organizations. In *Int. Conference Information Systems 2015 Proceedings*, Fort Worth, Texas, USA, https://aisel.aisnet.org/icis2015/proceedings/GeneralIS/5.

Porter, M. E. and Heppelmann, J. E. (2014). How smart, connected products are transforming competition. *Harvard Business Review*, **92**, 11: 64–88.

Quinton, S. and Simkin, L. (2017). The digital journey: Reflected learnings and emerging challenges. *International Journal of Management Reviews*, **19**, 4: 455–472, doi: 10.1111/ijmr.12104.

Rachinger, M., Rauter, R., Müller, C., Vorraber, W. and Schirgi, E. (2018). Digitalization and its influence on business model innovation. *Journal of Manufacturing Technology Management*, **30**, 8: 1143–1160, doi: 10.1108/JMTM-01-2018-0020.

Rauch, M., Wenzel, M. and Wagner, H.-T. (2016). The digital disruption of strategic paths: An experimental study. In *Int. Conference Information Systems Proceedings 2016*, Dublin, Ireland, pp. 1–19, https://aisel.aisnet.org/icis2016/HumanBehavior/Presentations/22.

Romanelli, E. and Tushman, M. L. (1994). Organizational transformation as punctuated equilibrium: An empirical test. *Academy of Management Journal*, **37**, 5: 1141–1166, doi: 10.5465/256669.

Rosemann, M. and Vessey, I. (2008). Toward improving the relevance of information systems research to practice: The role of applicability checks. *MIS Quarterly*, **32**, 1: 1–22.

Rueckel, D., Muehlburger, M. and Koch, S. (2020). An updated framework of factors enabling digital transformation. *Pacific Asia Journal of the Association for Information Systems*, **12**, 4: 1–26, doi: 10.17705/1pais.12401.

Saarikko, T., Westergren, U. H. and Blomquist, T. (2020). Digital transformation: Five recommendations for the digitally conscious firm. *Business Horizons*, **63**, 6: 825–839, doi: 10.1016/j.bushor.2020.07.005.

Schaarschmidt, M. and Bertram, M. (2020). Digital business intensity and constructive process deviance: A study of reactions to digitisation-focused process innovation. *International Journal of Innovation Management*, **24**, 7: 2050065, doi: 10.1142/S1363919620500656.

Schein, E. H. (2010). *Organizational Culture and Leadership* (4., Auflage), The Jossey-Bass Business and Management Series (US). John Wiley & Sons.

Sebastian, I. M., Ross, J. W., Beath, C., Mocker, M., Moloney, K. G. and Fonstad, N. O. (2017). How big old companies navigate digital transformation. *MIS Quarterly Executive*, **16**, 3: 197–213.

Siachou, E., Vrontis, D. and Trichina, E. (2021). Can traditional organizations be digitally transformed by themselves? The moderating role of absorptive capacity and strategic interdependence. *Journal of Business Research*, **124**, 408–421, doi: 10.1016/j.jbusres.2020.11.011.

Simon, H. A. (1997). *Administrative Behavior*, 4th edn. Free Press.

Solberg, E., Traavik, L. E. M. and Wong, S. I. (2020). Digital mindsets: Recognizing and leveraging individual beliefs for digital transformation. *California Management Review*, **62**, 4: 105–124, doi: 10.1177/0008125620931839.

Tekic, Z. and Koroteev, D. (2019). From disruptively digital to proudly analog: A holistic typology of digital transformation strategies. *Business Horizons*, **62**, 6: 683–693, doi: 10.1016/j.bushor.2019.07.002.

Thompson, J. D. (2008). *Organizations in Action: Social Science Bases of Administrative Theory*, 6th edn., Classics in Organization and Management. Transaction Publishers.

Tilson, D., Lyytinen, K. J. and Sørensen, C. (2010). Research commentary — Digital infrastructures: The missing IS research agenda. *Information Systems Research*, **21**, 4: 748–759, doi: 10.1287/isre.1100.0318.

Trabucchi, D., Buganza, T., Dell'Era, C. and Pellizzoni, E. (2018). Exploring the inbound and outbound strategies enabled by user generated big data: Evidence from leading smartphone applications. *Creativity & Innovation Management*, **27**, 1: 42–55, doi: 10.1111/caim.12241.

Trapp, M., Voigt, K.-I. and Brem, A. (2018). Business models for corporate innovation management: Introduction of a business model innovation tool for established firms. *International Journal of Innovation Management*, **22**, 1: 1850007, doi: 10.1142/S136391961850007X.

Tumbas, S., Berente, N. and Vom Brocke, J. (2017). Three types of chief digital officers and the reasons organizations adopt the role. *MIS Quarterly Executive*, **16**, 2: 292–308.

Tumbas, S., Berente, N. and Vom Brocke, J. (2018). Digital innovation and institutional entrepreneurship: Chief digital Officer perspectives of their emerging role. *Journal of Information Technology*, **33**, 3: 188–202, doi: 10.1057/s41265-018-0055-0.

Urbach, N., Drews, P. and Ross, J. W. (2017). Digital business transformation and the changing role of the IT function. *MIS Quarterly Executive*, **16**, 2: 2–4.

Verhoef, P. C., Broekhuizen, T., Bart, Y., Bhattacharya, A., Qi Dong, J., Fabian, N. and Haenlein, M. (2021). Digital transformation: A multidisciplinary reflection and research agenda. *Journal of Business Research*, **122**, 889–901, doi: 10.1016/j.jbusres.2019.09.022.

Vial, G. (2019). Understanding digital transformation: A review and a research agenda. *The Journal of Strategic Information Systems*, **28**, 2: 118–144, doi: 10.1016/j.jsis.2019.01.003.

Vieru, D., Bourdeau, S., Bernier, A. and Yapo, S. (2015). Digital competence: A multi-dimensional conceptualization and a typology in an SME context. *48th Hawaii Int. Conference System Sciences (HICSS 2015)*, Kauai, Hawaii, USA, 5–8 January 2015, eds. T. X. Bui and R. H. Sprague, IEEE, pp. 4681–4690. doi: 10.1109/HICSS.2015.557.

Vom Brocke, J., Simons, A., Niehaves, B., Reimer, K., Plattfaut, R. and Cleven, A. (2009). Reconstructing the giant: On the importance of rigour in documenting the literature search process. *European Conference Information Systems 2009 Proceedings*. Verona, Italy, pp. 2206–2217.

Watzlawick, P., Weakland, J. H. and Fisch, R. (2011). *Change: Principles of Problem Formulation and Problem Resolution*. W.W. Norton & Co.

Webster, J. and Watson, R. T. (2002). Analyzing the past to prepare for the future: Writing a literature review. *MIS Quarterly*, **26**, 2: xiii–xxiii.

Weking, J., Stöcker, M., Kowalkiewicz, M., Böhm, M. and Krcmar, H. (2020). Leveraging industry 4.0 – A business model pattern framework. *International Journal of Production Economics*, **225**, 107588, doi: 10.1016/j.ijpe.2019.107588.

Wu, L. and Hitt, L. (2015). How do data skills affect firm productivity: Evidence from process driven versus innovation-driven practices. In *Int. Conference Information Systems 2015 Proceedings*, Fort Worth, Texas, USA, pp. 1–19, https://aisel.aisnet.org/icis2015/proceedings/EconofIS/14.

Xie, K., Xiao, J., Wu, Y. and Hu, Q. (2014). Ecommerce: Channel or strategy? Insights from a comparative case study. In *Int. Conference Information Systems 2014 Proceedings*, Auckland, New Zealand, pp. 1–19, https://aisel.aisnet.org/icis2014/proceedings/EBusiness/35.

Yoo, Y., Boland, R. J. J., Lyytinen, K. J. and Majchrzak, A. (2012). Organizing for innovation in the digitized world. *Organization Science*, **23**, 5: 1398–1408, doi: 10.1287/orsc.1120.0771.

Yoo, Y., Henfridsson, O. and Lyytinen, K. J. (2010). Research commentary — The new organizing logic of digital innovation: An agenda for information systems research. *Information Systems Research*, **21**, 4: 724–735, doi: 10.1287/isre.1100.0322.

Zangiacomi, A., Oesterle, J., Fornasiero, R., Sacco, M. and Azevedo, A. (2017). The implementation of digital technologies for operations management: A case study for manufacturing apps. *Production Planning & Control*, **28**, 16: 1318–1331, doi: 10.1080/09537287.2017.1375142.

Zupanc, G. K. H. (2014). Impact beyond the impact factor. *Journal of Comparative Physiology A*, **200**, 2: 113–116, doi: 10.1007/s00359-013-0863-1.

Biography

Christoph Buck is a department head of the Fraunhofer Project Group Business and Information Systems Engineering (Germany) and an adjunct associate professor at the Queensland University of Technology (Australia). After graduating in business administration at the University of Bayreuth, he completed his Doctorate at the university's Faculty of Law and Economics. Christoph has led numerous transformation projects with asset-intensive incumbents in the areas of digitalization and innovation. His research interests include digital transformation, innovation systems, digital ecosystems, and information privacy. ORCID: 0000-0003-1636-1874

Clara Probst Marques studied International Business Studies at the Friedrich-Alexander University Erlangen-Nuremberg and Business Administration at the University of Bayreuth with a strong focus on information systems management. At the FIM Research Center, she researched how digitalization affects companies. From a management perspective Clara is still involved with digital transformation.

Michael Rosemann is the Director of the Centre for Future Enterprise and Professor at the Business School, Queensland University of Technology. His main areas of research are the management of innovation, business processes and trust. Dr Rosemann published more than 350 refereed papers and his eight books are available in five languages. He is on the editorial board of 10 international journals and has globally conducted invited keynote presentations at academic and professional conferences. Dr Rosemann is also the Honorary Consul for the Federal Republic of Germany in Southern Queensland. ORCID: 0000-0003-3303-2896

Digital Innovation in Incumbent Firms: An Exploratory Analysis of Value Creation*

Micha Bosler*, Wolfgang Burr and Leonie Ihring

Chair of General Business Administration
esp. Innovation & Service Management
University of Stuttgart, Germany
**micha.bosler@bwi.uni-stuttgart.de*

Incumbent firms' competitiveness largely depends on the ability to develop digital innovation as novel combination of digital and physical components. This paper provides a better understanding of value creation through digital innovation, focussing on market offerings from incumbent firms. Based on the insights of an exploratory multiple case study with seven cases from the automotive, machine engineering, and consumer goods industries in Germany, we explain the multi-sided changes required for the development and management of digital innovations. Afterwards, we contribute to the further theorization of digital innovation. According to our empirical findings, we decided to discuss the applicability of the resource-based and competence-based approach.

Keywords: Digital innovation; digital innovation management; digital transformation; value creation; resource-based view; competence-based view.

1. Introduction

Digital innovation results from the increasing pressure on organizations to apply digital technologies in their products and transform existing business models [Kohli and Melville (2019)]. As one of the most important innovation drivers, digitization affects nearly all industries with disrupting effects [Echterfeld and Gausmeier (2018)]. In response, incumbent firms expand their industrial-age products through embedded digital capability. Those enhancements enable digital innovations like novel digital functions and services [Yoo (2010)]. From a product-related perspective, digital innovation is a new combination of digital resources and physical components [Yoo (2010); Henfridsson *et al.* (2018)]. This type of innovation is characterized through the immanence of digital technologies [Nambisan *et al.* (2017)] relating to all artifacts with signal and information processing based on a binary

*Corresponding author.

*This chapter was originally published in International Journal of Innovation and Technology Management, Vol. 18, No. 2, March 2018, published by World Scientific Publishing, Singapore. Reprinted with permission.

computer language [Hinings *et al.* (2018)]. Examples are sensors, technologies for information and communication, the Global Positioning System (GPS), cloud and mobile computing, artificial intelligence, or machine learning [Abrell *et al.* (2016); Lyytinen *et al.* (2016); Teece (2018a); Yoo (2010)].

Given their ubiquity, the competitiveness of incumbent firms depends on using digital technologies during the development of innovations [Abrell *et al.* (2016)]. Therefore, digital product functions are a crucial factor for market differentiation [Echterfeld and Gausmeier (2018)]. In conclusion, digital innovation is accompanied by profound changes in value creation [Teece (2018a)], especially for incumbent firms [Svahn *et al.* (2017)]. Thus, the phenomenon of digital innovation has gained interest in science in recent years [Holmström (2018)]. However, this research domain is not yet fully developed, but rather an aggregation of heterogeneous research efforts [Holmström (2018)]. Current works about digital innovation — and the belonging transformations in value creation — handle preferentially with conceptual explanations and frameworks, e.g. Teece [2018a], Henfridsson *et al.* [2018], Helfat and Raubitschek [2018], or Lyytinen *et al.* [2016]. In contrast, there are only few publications with an empirical methodology [for example, Abrell *et al.* (2016) or Svahn *et al.* (2017)]. Consequently, we see a significant lack of empirical research about digital innovation in general as well as about the specific changes of incumbent firms' value creation in particular.

Apart from that, Holmström [2018] asserts a need for deeper theorization and criticizes the far-reaching absence of theories in previous research on digital innovation. Regarding the approach to theorizing, there are controversial opinions. Some authors like Nambisan [2017] or Yoo [2013] argue that digitization causes such profound changes and challenges for companies, for which reason existing theories are no longer contemporary. Instead, the understanding of digital innovation would require the development of new theories and, if necessary, even the use of new research methods [Nambisan (2017)]. In contrast, Holmström [2018] opines that it is illusory to exclude established theories from the outset. This contrary view calls to adjust and expand existing theories for the specifics of digital innovation.

This paper addresses the explained need for further empirical and theoretical research about digital innovation in incumbent firms. Before a conclusion about the applicability of a specific established theory is possible, we argue that it first needs a deeper understanding of the occurred changes in incumbent firms triggered by digital innovation, resting upon empirical findings. The exploratory research objective is to comprehend how value creation through digital innovation management takes place, how incumbent firms developed the capability to provide digital innovation, and which central challenges they are faced during digital transformation. Intending a precise focus, the research proposal is restricted to market offerings in terms of product or service innovations enabled through digital technologies. In our understanding of value creation, we refer to Chesbrough *et al.* [2018] who define "*value creation as an actor's attempt to increase value. In other words, an actor is engaging in a resource-deployment process and the perceived benefits of that process outweigh the perceived sacrifices.*"

To answer the research questions presented, we conducted a multiple case study. Our research includes seven different digital innovations from five companies. More detailed explanations about the methodology are presented in the third section of this paper. Beforehand, the second section deals with the object of investigation and already known insights into changes of value creation caused by the digital business. Based on the findings of our case study, we then aim for a discussion below from a theoretical perspective. In summary, this paper follows a double-sided research proposal. First, we provide general empirical insights into digital innovation in incumbent firms, and then we contribute to the progress of theory development.

2. Digital Innovation

Following Nambisan *et al.* [2017], digital innovation describes "*the creation of (and consequent change in) market offerings, business processes, or models that result from the use of digital technology.*" According to this, digital innovation management includes "*practices, processes, and principles that underlie the effective orchestration of digital innovation*" [Nambisan *et al.* (2017)]. The origin of this new type of innovation is the digitization, which refers to the embedding of digital technologies into physical products [Holmström (2018)]. This evolution has fundamental consequences on incumbent firms in the sense that their competitiveness largely depends on the effective use of digital technologies in innovation [Abrell *et al.* (2016)]. In line with our research question, the following explanations about digital innovation are focussed on market offerings.

The digitization of products, based on the integration of digital technologies, leads to novel functionalities. In addition, the use of digital technologies leaves an unprecedented extent of digital traces, known as big data [Yoo *et al.* (2012)]. The systematic analysis of the generated data enables smart services, e.g. predictive maintenance of production machines through the automatic transfer of status data to the original equipment manufacturer [Echterfeld and Gausmeier (2018)]. The development of digital products or services changes the logic of value creation, which implies the formation of digital business models [Echterfeld and Gausmeier (2018)]. Such digital product functions or services make a crucial contribution to differentiation on markets [Echterfeld and Gausmeier (2018)]. In this context, there is a close relationship with platforms [Nambisan (2018)]. Digital technologies make it possible to design a digitized product as a platform [Yoo (2010)]. Digital platforms may be only software-based or composed of a combination of hardware and software [Teece (2018a)]. They provide a set of digital resources, interfaces, and common standards for the extensible offering of digital products and services developed by the platform owner or suppliers of complementary assets [Helfat and Raubitschek (2018); Teece (2018a); Constantinides *et al.* (2018); Tiwana *et al.* (2010)].

2.1. *Value creation from an architectural perspective*

A first architectural-driven understanding of the underlying mechanism of value creation in the context of digital innovation is provided by Henfridsson *et al.* [2018]

and Nambisan [2018]. They characterize digital innovation as the result of the recombination of digital resources. A digital resource is a building block in the creation of value and belongs to a specific value space, which is defined as an evolving network of interlinked digital resources [Henfridsson *et al.* (2018)]. The value spaces are associated with the layered architecture of digital technologies including content, service, network, and device layers [Yoo (2010)]. Each layer represents a possible value space. The content layer typically contains digital data such as text, image, video, or sounds which are used for the functions of a digital offering on the service layer. Display as well as use of content and services requires appropriate hardware with storing and processing capabilities on the device layer. Furthermore, the network layer enables the transmission of data through network standards and physical transport resources [Henfridsson *et al.* (2018); Yoo (2010)]. To give an example, we refer to the vehicle infotainment system *MBUX* by Mercedes-Benz, launched in 2018 for the A-Class. In literature, vehicle infotainment systems are a widely acknowledged type of digital innovation [Lyytinen *et al.* (2016); Maniak *et al.* (2014); Svahn *et al.* (2017)]. Monitor and CPU represent the device layer while a communication module enables the internet connection (network layer). MBUX offers the driver many digital services, for instance, information about dangerous spots on the route (service layer), based on data which is registered by sensors of other vehicles (content layer) [Daimler (2018a)].

In summary, digital innovation offered to consumers is the result of generating a value path by connecting resources among different value spaces through multiple layers. The value scope of a digital innovation will be greater, the wider the range of functions enabled through value connections between the dedicated resources will grow [Henfridsson *et al.* (2018)]. The solution provided by the value creator does not necessarily have to consist solely of digital resources, but might do so (e.g. a smartphone application). However, due to the device and network layers, at least the use requires physical resources. Therefore, in our view, digital innovation refers to a complex heterogeneous resource bundle including digital and non-digital resources, which causes differences in manageability, protectability, and the economic character (e.g. cost structure or replaceability) compared with traditional physical products. Besides this, the mentioned recombination of resources does not necessarily take place in a single firm. Rather, in the case of digital innovation, the importance of value co-creation in innovation ecosystems is increasing [Lyytinen *et al.* (2016)]. This goes along with the mutual exchange of resources [Lusch and Nambisan (2015)].

In addition to the primary value creation, Henfridsson *et al.* [2018] highlight the so-called path channeling as another important activity in digital business. The path channeling describes a competitive strategy to steer value connections provided by other actors through their own value offering [Henfridsson *et al.* (2018)]. For example, Amazon Echo (respectively, the cloud-based voice control Alexa) integrates numerous third-party devices and services such as connected cars, smart home products, or music streaming like Spotify. Consequently, path channeling bundles several value paths from different providers in an offering to increase its value from the user's perspective [Henfridsson *et al.* (2018)].

2.2. *Implications for incumbent firms*

There is a consensus in the literature that digital innovation comes along with radical changes for incumbent firms [Teece (2018a); Lyytinen *et al.* (2016)]. It is well known that incumbent firms often struggle to adopt disruptive technologies [Tushman and Anderson (1986); Christensen (1997)]. The cross-industry diffusion of digital technologies is likely to trigger such far-reaching effects [Abrell *et al.* (2016)]. Examples for the disrupting force of digitization can be found in the retail sector (Amazon), in the entertainment business (Netflix and Spotify), or in the travel industry (Airbnb) [Echterfeld and Gausmeier (2018)]. Companies which formerly offered industrial-age goods extend those products by digital functions and services [Yoo (2010)]. However, this close connection with the core business leads to specific challenges for incumbent firms. While expanding physical products through digital functions, they are responsible for the service layer as well as the device layer. Famous disruptors from the digital economy like Spotify, Netflix, Uber, or Airbnb neither provide nor operate the necessary physical assets. Their "hardware-free business models" deliver new services for third-party devices.

When embedding digital technology, incumbent firms must handle the different life cycles of physical and digital technologies [Huang *et al.* (2017)]. For example, in the automotive context, the specification of a new car model is planned several years before the start of production. After the start of production, a car model is manufactured over 6 to 10 years. Such long planning and life cycles do not fit to the fast pace of digital business. However, the performance of digital services in connected vehicles (e.g. real-time traffic, music streaming, or augmented reality navigation) depends on the early specified computing capacity of the infotainment system. Consequently, while applying digital technologies, incumbent firms need to turn away from established innovation paths and develop new innovation capabilities [Svahn *et al.* (2017)]. Moreover, digital innovation in incumbent firms implies a fundamental turning away from the ingrained understanding of the own product [Svahn *et al.* (2017)]. When leaving the production plant, a car without connectivity was completed. In contrast, a connected vehicle is able to receive software updates (over the air) with new digital services or functionalities. Therefore, a modern car is not finished after production: Updates during the whole life cycle lead to totally new opportunities in the aftermarket business [Svahn *et al.* (2017)]. In addition, incumbent firms are faced with historically grown legacy burdens. In the chosen example, automotive carmakers have to integrate their digital services into an existing vehicle architecture which has not originally been designed for this case of application. In contrast, the newcomer Tesla was able to design a completely new architecture.

Furthermore, digital technologies affect the business environment. One result is the phenomenon of digital business convergence: Industry boundaries become blurred and organizations from different industries are competing with different resources [Lyytinen *et al.* (2016); Seo (2017)]. For instance, Skype is a competing solution against incumbent telecommunication providers [Yoo *et al.* (2012)]. On the contrary, digital companies are potential partners, among others for the aim of path channeling. Giving a concrete example, the pay TV provider Sky integrated the sport streaming service of rival DAZN in its receiver *Sky Q Box* (for German customers). Therefore, besides the new formation of incumbent firms' internal skills, the importance of value co-creation demands the engagement of new external partners [Svahn *et al.* (2017)]. However, partnerships between an incumbent firm and an organization from the digital business are challenging. Svahn *et al.* [2017] describe the problems Volvo had while engaging digital partners. Such external actors like TuneIn or Spotify engage on radically different premises than traditional automotive suppliers. They see the car as another device providing their service to consumers. Unlike established suppliers, partnerships with digital companies are not necessarily based on monetary transactions. Instead, such new partners formulate demands regarding the stability of the services in the car. Incumbent firms must learn to bargain and work together with digital partners. This, for instance, requires completely new contract designs [Svahn *et al.* (2017)].

3. Exploratory Multiple Case Study

The radical changes for established companies presented above require further research leading to a deeper understanding of the phenomenon of digital innovation. We especially see an urgent research need based on empirical findings concerning incumbent firms' digital innovation management for value creation. An exploratory study is the first approach to capture the transformations and challenges in detail.

3.1. *Methodology*

The mentioned lack of empirical work causes an unexplored character of the research domain, which implies the use of a qualitative methodology. Therefore, current research about digital innovation is often based upon a qualitative approach [e.g. Abrell *et al.* (2016); Svahn *et al.* (2017); or Echterfeld and Gausmeier (2018)]. For this paper, a multiple case study approach was selected. This research strategy is commonly suitable for "how" questions [Yin (2018)], also in the specific domain of digital innovation [Abrell *et al.* (2016)]. It focusses on understanding the dynamics present within the chosen cases [Eisenhardt (1989)]. In general, case study research investigates a contemporary phenomenon in-depth and within its real-life context, thereby assuming that the insights gained are necessary to receive important findings about contextual conditions [Yin (2018)]. Compared to a single case, the multiple case approach allows a cross-case analysis, which leads to more robust results due to the varied empirical evidence [Yin (2018); Eisenhardt and Graebner (2007)].

Due to the exploratory nature of the research design, no explicit research propositions or hypotheses are formulated in advance, because they are not necessarily constructive in this context [McCutcheon and Meredith (1993); Yin (2018)]. Instead, a research purpose is sufficient [Yin (2018)]. To put it in a nutshell, this paper's purpose is to generate exploratory insights in incumbent firms' value creation through digital innovation. Based on Sec. 2.2, our study follows the central assumption that digital innovation management in industrial-age organizations is associated with multi-sided transformations. In response to the research need explained, our study's research questions seek for detailed answers on how incumbent firms shape digital innovation capabilities, how their value creation takes place, and what concrete challenges they face.

The data presented within case studies rely on different sources [Yin (2018)]. In this regard, it can be distinguished between primary sources (interviews of people involved or own observations) and secondary sources (e.g. analysis of existing documents or records) [McCutcheon and Meredith (1993)]. Due to the unexplored character of the research field, expert interviews have the highest importance for data collection. Additionally, other available sources are used in order to ensure data triangulation. In particular, information about the investigated innovations presented in press releases, annual reports, and public documents is relevant. The need for expert interviews has a significant impact on the sampling of the cases. Based on our prior experiences in qualitative research, we prefer personal face-to-face-interviews to gain better results. For geographical reasons, we put our research focus on Germany to increase the probability of face-to-face conversations. In order to generate cross-sectoral findings, we decided to investigate organizations from different industries.

Regarding the selection of industries, we refer to the Annual German Innovation Survey, a representative study on innovation activity within the German Economy [ZEW (2018)]. According to this study, the automotive industry and the machine engineering industry were the sectors with the highest innovation intensity in 2017. In addition, we seek a more differentiated analysis including the consumer goods industry, which is characterized through the strongest growth in innovation intensity. Regarding this superior innovation performance data, we investigated companies which belong to one out of the three industries. Within these industries, appropriate digital innovations limited to market offerings were sought. The criterion of an incumbent firm was that it was found more than 30 years ago, so the firm already offered industrial-age products. Additionally, in order to reduce the population and to increase the comparability, we limited our focus on companies which generate at least two billion euros in sales and have at least 10,000 employees. Another important aspect was the firms' willingness to participate in interviews. We used personal contacts as well as social business networks to inquire potential experts. Finally, our study comprises seven different innovative digital market offerings from five companies which meet the definition presented earlier. For reasons of confidentiality, we refer to them as Companies A, B, C, D, and E.

Beforehand, an expert was defined as an employee with digital innovation responsibilities. The experts' positions depend on the organizational structure. While collecting data for Companies B and E, for example, we spoke with the respective product managers, because they were in authority for the innovation management. Companies A and D organized the development of the analyzed innovations as a temporary project. In these cases, we contacted project leaders as well as team members. Company C decided one year ago to bundle the activities for digital offerings in an own division. Therefore, we interviewed employees with leading functions responsible in the digital business division for strategy, business models, and sales. Due to the agreed anonymization, more detailed explanations about the experts and the firms are not possible. All conversations were held as semi-structured interviews and followed a guideline with open-ended questions specifying the research questions (length: 45–90 min; average: 69 min). The questions were about the (1) necessary internal or external activities, (2) resources, and (3) competencies for value creation of digital innovation. The guideline also addressed (4) central challenges of the digital transformation, (5) significant changes in value creation with digital innovation compared with traditional business, (6) potential sources of competitive advantages for digital innovation in incumbent firms, and (7) mission critical factors.

Besides the interviews, we searched in existing documents for additional information about the investigated innovations and the companies. If possible, we enhanced the case databases through our own observations. All data collected were structured pursuant a qualitative content analysis. To analyze the single cases, in a first step, we used a coding scheme deduced from the questions in the guideline. Due to the exploratory approach, the second step was an iteration of the coding scheme including emergent issues which were extracted directly out of the case data through an inductive strategy. Based on the coded information, we wrote a detailed report for each case. Finally, we conducted a cross-case analysis focussing on matching patterns across the cases [Yin (2018)].

3.2. *Cases*

The following section gives an overview about the case studies. At this point, we desist from a more detailed presentation of individual cases because the research interest is dedicated to the cross-case analysis and the generalized results in Sec. 4.

Case 1 deals with an intelligent sensor device offered by Company A, an automotive supplier. It is an adapter for the cigarette lighter in the car, which is connected via Bluetooth with a smartphone application. Based on the device as a tangible resource including acceleration sensors, this digital innovation enables different services. The application provides insights about the individual driving characteristics and triggers an automatic emergency call (eCall) in the event of a serious accident. The data on driving behavior are transferred via interfaces to third-party players, e.g. vehicle insurance companies for so-called "pay-how-you-drive" tariffs. *Cases* 2 and 3 are two different location-based services for the connected cars of Company B. One of them shows the vehicle owner the current position of his connected car in a mobile application or in a browser-based web portal. The second service of the automotive manufacturer is called speed fence and informs the owner via push notifications, if other drivers exceed a defined speed limit. The next two case studies are both part of a supplier from the machine engineering industry. Company C developed a digitized valve whose functionalities can be flexibly modified by software applications (*Case* 4). As a result, this component can be used instead of many different valves. In addition, the intelligent product collects data that support predictive maintenance. Whereas this digital innovation consists of hardware and software, *Case* 5 addresses a solely software-based novelty released by Company C. The manufacturer-independent software for the machine maintenance management includes an app-based mobile calendar for the operators and a browser interface used by production managers for maintenance planning. This allows the digitization of maintenance management and replaces physical documentation folders stored on the machine. Thereby, we also considered the case in which a hardware manufacturer acts as a software provider. In *Case* 6, we analyzed Company D's smart irrigation control. The WLAN-enabled device is connected to the irrigation system. A smartphone application allows the user to remotely regulate the irrigation, adapted to current weather and humidity data. In addition, the mobile application contains plug-ins for social networks, which can be assigned to path channeling. *Case* 7 contains a connected robot vacuum cleaner, which can be controlled via smartphone or tablet application. The belonging Company E is a manufacturer operating in the cleaning technology business.

The research design contains deliberately different cases aiming for more robust results. Beside the various industries, there are more differences between the investigated digital innovations. Cases 2, 3, 6, and 7 are B2C market offerings. In contrast, Cases 4 and 5 deal with B2B offerings. The first case is special, because adapter as well as services address consumers, but the sale is realized by the mentioned third-party players. The automotive cases differ to the extent that Company B offers its connected car services linked to vehicle sales, whereas Company A's digital innovation is a retrofit solution independent of the car manufacturer. With the exception of Case 5, all analyzed digital innovations are based — at least partially — on a device layer developed by the related incumbent firm, for instance, the connected vehicles in Cases 2 and 3. Besides this, the analyzed companies are in different stages of the open-ended process of digital transformation. Some are more at the beginning, developing initial digitization strategies driven by competition, whereas others are already pursuing clear visions regarding the shift to a software and service provider.

3.3. *Cross-case analysis: Value creation and digital innovation management*

Below, we briefly present insights in incumbent firms' value creation through digital innovation applying a cross-case synthesis of the collected data about digital innovation management. Afterwards, in the fourth section, we take up key aspects for a more detailed discussion leading to generalized results, which, in turn, provide implications for theory development.

In general, digital innovation in incumbent firms sustains on novel recombination of digital and physical resources as well as on the ability to use existing data or to generate new data. Although we have chosen different cases, digital innovation management and the belonging value creation encompass several predominant phases. First, in most cases, the market and customer analysis leads to new product ideas. Sometimes, digital innovation arises at random. For instance, the digitized valve (Case 4) is the result of an accidental discovery of valve design when working together with a customer. In this initial phase of digital innovation management, it is crucial to evaluate each idea systematically with a strong focus on customer expectations. Incumbent firms often make the mistake that digital innovations are driven initially by the hardware-oriented R&D division. However, their engineers are not necessarily familiar with users' demands for digital solutions. The second step in digital innovation management addresses the conceptual planning of the digital offering. This often takes place internally. The planning as well as the following development (third phase) of a digital innovation not only requires the original hardware-related competence profile but also the know-how with digital technologies and software engineering. Therefore, a renewal of incumbent firms' resources and competencies is necessary in order to close gaps compared to the state of the art in digital business.

In addition, all investigated organizations practice an intensive integration of partnerships. Among them are specialized companies commissioned with software or application development (Cases 1, 2, 3, 6), mobile network providers (Cases 2 and 3), cloud infrastructure providers (Cases 2, 3, 6, 7), agencies for user interface and user experience design (Cases 1, 2, 3, 5), professionals for legal issues (Case 6), and consulting firms with expertise in digital business models or in commercialization of digital services (Cases 4 and 5). "*Formerly it was unimaginable to rely on external resources in such a large scale during the development of an innovative product,*" a Company E expert said. Consequently, during the planning phase, digital innovation management has to decide for each innovation what they can realize in-house and which parts should be provided by partners. If necessary, certain digital resources must also be purchased, such as digital maps in Cases 2 and 3 or weather data in Case 6. Four out of five companies emphasize that internal developments are often based on new agile methods to shorten product development cycles and realize a solution-focussed orientation convincing the customer, e.g. Design thinking (A, C, D), Scrum (A, C, D, E), or Lean startup (A). An expert in Case 1 formulates it as follows: "*The conventional product management has had its day* [...] *An agile mindset is a basic requirement.*"

All obligatory digital and physical components that are developed internally or provided externally have to be combined into an overall solution. Digital innovation management must ensure the necessary processes to effectively orchestrate the different value creation activities leading to the final solution. This step sometimes includes the integration of the digital innovation into an existing platform-based infrastructure. For example, Company B operates the investigated digital services through a connected car platform. In general, the underlying architecture of those platforms is divided into frontend and backend areas. The frontend enables the use of the digital service (e.g. via the smartphone application), whereas the backend refers to a complex, customer-hidden IT infrastructure for the communication between vehicle and platform, process management, and data storage. Furthermore, the backend needs interfaces to cooperating partners, if digital resources like content are provided by third parties [Bosler *et al.* (2017)]. After finishing the development, digital innovation management also contains an intensive testing to prevent errors and adequate measures to ensure data privacy as well as cybersecurity. Regarding the emergence of cybertheft problems, being secure to market may take precedence over a fast market access in digital business [Teece (2018a)]. The process of innovation management ends with the commercialization, which requires appropriate marketing activities as well as an offering concept.

4. General Results

Our multiple case study confirms that value creation on digital innovation in incumbent firms leads to miscellaneous changes and new challenges. Condensed, it is necessary to renew resources and competencies, revise internal organizational structures, and manage the development of hybrid market offerings in value co-creation networks. The general results presented below provide implications for theorizing the phenomenon of digital innovation.

4.1. *Digital innovation capability*

The formation of a digital innovation capability requires the renewal of an incumbent firm's resources and the evolution of new competencies. It is obvious that the examined companies identified demand of new resources and skills in digital technologies, software development, cloud-based infrastructures, or user experience. In this context, it is important to regularly scrutinize previous decisions made in the course of the digital transformation in order to reduce legacy burdens resulting by refactoring the architectures. By turning away from the previous "hardware-selling-only" business model, incumbent firms have to evolve new competencies in the digital aftermarket business for the successful rollout of a digital innovation. This commercialization phase of digital innovation management is challenging, because industrial-age companies have no experience with the market launch of digital solutions. Consequently, they need a deep comprehension of digital markets and related business models.

Compared to the multi-annual lead time of a machine or a vehicle, digital businesses are characterized by significantly shorter development cycles and higher uncertainty. For example, it is hard to predict if a particular social network will still be equally popular in two years. In contrast, as already mentioned, developing on new car series in the automotive industry is several years ahead. Also, the life cycle of a vehicle (up to more than 20 years) is not comparable to the life cycle of a digital offering. This demands suitable structures enabling agility to deal with the fast pace of digital products and to facilitate a quick time to market without jeopardizing existing hardware development processes [see also Svahn *et al.* (2017)]. It can be stated that these divergent cycles require a synchronized competence management. Appropriate organizational structures have to ensure an intensive and effective collaboration between hardware engineers and software developers. Given the technological heterogeneity, incumbent firms need a technical ambidexterity including abilities to use and to develop both digital resources and physical resources. As an implication of digital transformation, it becomes a crucial challenge for established companies to unite two formerly separated business areas, each with completely different conditions. Furthermore, the heterogeneity of the markets in which incumbent firms operate also increases. For example, Company C offers digitized products (like the valve in Case 4), provides software solutions (Case 5), and additionally continues to sell products without digital components. Consequently, the whole innovation management of incumbent firms becomes more complex because more markets are addressed.

Therefore, a multi-sided and fundamental alteration is necessary before a firm is able to develop and rollout digital innovation. Incumbent firms have to fulfill a transformation of their organizational structures. But sometimes, in particular, existing structures can restrict the ability of companies to act. A successful digital transformation takes time and is implemented more quickly in some business areas, whereas other divisions first react reluctant necessitating persuasion. Besides the creation of new divisions for digital products and the reorganization of internal processes to enhance interdivisional collaboration, the investigated companies also responded to the identified need for change by acquiring specialized firms in areas such as software development, artificial intelligence, or cloud computing.

The commitment of the top management and clear objectives are essential for the digital transformation in incumbent firms. Otherwise, digitization initiatives in the company will be carried out decentralized and uncoordinated without any common conception. In addition, incumbent firms have to form a business culture characterized by openness to digital technologies and allowing mistakes. This goes along with an attitude shift, ranging from the advancement of the original core business to, in extreme cases, a change in the vision from a former hardware manufacturer to a software company. In summary, digital transformation can be described as a balancing act between traditional values and ensuring future competitiveness through the exploration of digital technologies.

4.2. *Development of digital innovation in value co-creation networks*

However, the essential resources and competencies for digital innovation development do not necessarily have to be exclusively internally available. In the cases, we observed a shift of value creation into value networks, confirming existing literature about digital innovation (see Sec. 2). Almost all companies practiced an intensive value co-creation with new partnerships. Of course, exceptions are possible: The development of Company C's digital innovations occurred predominantly internally. Nonetheless, compared with the traditional business, in the majority of cases value creation depends to a great extent on collaborations and the selection of partners is more complex. Most of the partners are still integrated with classic contracts. Sometimes, collaborative project partners participate in revenues or generated data are shared. We suppose that such collaborative models will become more important in incumbent firms' digital innovation management.

The conducted case studies suggest that a firm's opening toward a value creation network depends on the progress of digital transformation. Initially, the established firm has to recognize the importance of new partnerships in the digital business. At an early stage, these partners are also a strategic option for the short time closing of existing resource and skill gaps. The more advanced the digital transformation, the more intensively integration of partners is practiced. In such a value creation network, incumbent firms act as an orchestrator coordinating all activities of value creation and combining the different building blocks developed internally or externally to an overall solution. The control of the partners typically takes place via specifications sheets. Nonetheless, orchestrating activities presupposes an understanding of digital technologies and thus appropriate internal human resources. However, the recruiting of software developers is challenging, given the high demand on the job market. As a result, incumbent firms, traditionally from the hardware business, compete with software companies in the war for talents.

The increasing importance of value creation networks in the context of digital innovation has significant implications. First, value creation becomes more dependent on partnerships. To reduce this dependency, especially on core components of the product which are relevant for competition, it becomes apparent that firms with a high degree of digital transformation are making parallel efforts to strengthen their in-house development by building up their own resources and competencies. Thus, our case study suggests that the expansion in value creation networks is not an open-ended movement: At some point with a highly advanced digital transformation, we see a slightly declining trend. But, of course, partner integration in value creation stays a high priority. This in turn means that different companies for certain components rely on the identical external digital resources of the same partners, for example, providers of map data or cloud infrastructures. Therefore, this implies a common pool of resources and digital innovation goes along with resource convergence. For the sake of completeness, this does not necessarily have to be a disadvantage: If several firms address similar demands to a specific provider, the implementation of these requests becomes more likely.

4.3. *Digital innovation and competitive advantage*

Due to the resource convergence and easier ways of copying software-based functions, competitive advantages are less anchored in single resources, but rather in the orchestrating capabilities of the overall solution. It is mission critical to better understand customer needs and orchestrate internal and external resources faster than competitors resulting in an overall solution which is predominant regarding usability, user interface, user experience, stable operation without errors, and support concepts. However, competitive advantages are not permanent by reason of the difficult protection of digital innovation and the resulting uncomplicated imitation. As an outcome, in digital business incumbent firms are faced with a high pressure to innovate. To sustain a competitive advantage, digital innovation management has to respond quickly to customer needs and release novelties in short intervals.

Besides that, the experts in our research highlighted the importance of data as superior resource. An interviewee of Company A summarized concisely: "*Data are the assets of the future.*" It is crucial to secure an exclusive access to data, for example, about the usage behavior of customers, despite the intensive integration of partners. Incumbent firms must carefully consider whether and which data they share with third parties. One possible way of generating data is to operate a digitized product as a platform. However, the mere possession of data does not automatically lead to a competitive advantage. Firms must be able to exploit the data by intelligent analysis, which may be the basis for new innovative digital services. In addition, data analysis supports the improvement of existing products. Summing up it can be stated that competitive advantages arise from the right treatment and handling of data, but not solely from the ownership.

4.4. *Diversifying into digital hybrid resource bundles*

Furthermore, it is important to point out the close linkage between the incumbent firms' core business and the released digital innovation. On the one hand, the essential financial resources to invest in the development of digital innovation are based on the revenues generated by the core business. On the other hand, established resources, competencies, and know-how are often the source of the investigated digital innovations. For instance, the development of the eCall-adapter (Case 1) required deep capacity in the crash analysis to detect an emergency based on sensor data, the release of a digital car service (Cases 2 and 3) would not be possible without access to the connected vehicle, and engineering a digitized valve (Case 4) needs experience in the construction of a conventional valve. That demonstrates the complex design of the overall solution in form of a hybrid resource bundle, which requires knowledge from both the digital world and the conventional business.

Consequently, incumbent firms must use their treasure trove of experience for value creation in digital innovation systematically. In this case, they have an advantage in creating interconnected asset stocks. This implies the emergence of complementary digital business models in addition to the traditional core business. However, it should be considered that the complexity of the products increases due to the embedded digital technologies. Thus, the component variety caused through digital innovation forces up the risk of errors, which would displease the customer. Therefore, incumbent firms need architectural competencies to design digital hybrid resource bundles which ensure a stable operation.

5. Theoretical Discussion: Resource- and Competence-Based View of the Firm

Based on the exploratory findings presented about digital innovation and value creation in incumbent firms, we aim for a discussion from a theoretical perspective to provide a first answer, whether and to what extend established theories are applicable for digital innovation. Our results presented in the fourth section are strongly related to an organization's resources and competencies. Besides the required renewal of the resource endowment (Sec. 4.1), digital innovation in incumbent firms is often linked to existing resources and competencies of the core business (Sec. 4.4). Following this implication, the available resources of a firm determine the markets, the performance, and the innovation success. In addition, the observed value co-creation goes along with the integration of resources from partners (Sec. 4.2) and leads to digital resource convergence, which affects the formation of competitive advantages in digital business (Sec. 4.3). Therefore, we decided to choose the *resource-based and competence-based view of the firm* as a starting point for further theory development.

In general, a central question of theories in the field of strategic management concerns the formation of a competitive advantage [Barney (1991)]. Belonging to the dominant paradigm in strategic management [Hitt *et al.* (2016)], the research-based approach explains the emergence of a sustained competitive advantage and the capture of economic rents with the firm's superior resources [Barney (1991); Wernerfelt (1984)]. Firm-specific resource endowment as well as competencies in the use of these resources are the crucial determinants of firm performance [Teece *et al.* (1997); Sanchez and Heene (1997)]. Since the original resource-based theory was criticized for its static view [Priem and Butler (2001)], the dynamic capabilities approach [Teece *et al.* (1997)] as an important extension emerged [Burr *et al.* (2016)]. In consideration of the results of our multiple case study, a resource- and competence-based approach of theorizing seems possible. However, regarding the insights in incumbent firms' value creation, there is at least a need for theory refinements. In the following sections, we provide first implications for the underlying question, where the existing theory approach is still suitable and where its significance for digital innovation is restricted.

5.1. *Platform-based and data-based extensions*

A basic element of the resource-based theory stream is to classify resource categories [Barney (1991); Grant (1996)] or to identify attractive resources [Wernerfelt (1984)], which are defined as valuable, rare, imperfectly imitable, and non-substitutable [Barney (1991)]. In this context, a theory refinement with respect to digital resources is necessary. According to the explanations in Sec. 4.3, data and platforms are superior resource categories in digital business. Platforms have an enabling character in that they are essential for the operation of some digital innovation. Additionally, platforms create an interface for customer data. The possession and intelligent analysis of data are sources for competitive advantage in digital business. Consequently, data can be valuable, inimitable, not substitutable, and rare resources, if firms secure an exclusive access.

In this context, sustainable competitive advantages may arise under three conditions. First, incumbent firms must be able to create interconnected asset stocks by combining their core business with platform-based digital services. Secondly, digital innovation must meet customer needs to a great extent. Under this condition, a high intensity in the use of the digital innovation through the customer occurs, which, in turn, leads to more valuable data. Thirdly, these data ensure competitive advantages — if the organization has the capabilities to exploit the data in order to develop new value-added services.

5.2. *Dynamic digital business*

Besides the platform-based and data-based approach, value creation in digital innovation requires a refinement and renewal of well-known resource categories such as human capital, top management, technology, organizational capital, or business culture (see Sec. 4.1). This perfectly fits into the existing dynamic capabilities approach. Teece *et al.* [1997] define "*dynamic capabilities as the firm's ability to integrate, build, and reconfigure internal and external competences to address rapidly changing environments.*" The alignment of a firm's resources with identified customer needs depends on the strength of the dynamic capabilities [Teece (2018a)]. For example, the mentioned emergence of new digital business models besides the traditional core business can be seen as an indicator of a firm's dynamic capabilities [Teece (2018b)].

As explained in Sec. 4.3, competitive advantages are anchored in the ability to understand customer needs and orchestrate internal as well as external resources leading to a superior overall solution. Following Helfat and Raubitschek [2018], such integrative capabilities for ecosystem orchestration are one type of dynamic capabilities having an outstanding importance in digital business. Our research confirms that integrative capabilities are fundamental for competitive success: They enable firms to better orchestrate activities with and among partners [Helfat and Raubitschek (2018)]. Moreover, an incumbent firm's ability to develop digital innovation, which, in general, inheres on the organizational level within teams or groups and are underpinned by routines, can also be assigned to the dynamic capabilities [Helfat and Raubitschek (2018)].

To sum up, the dynamic capabilities approach has a high relevance as theoretical foundation for digital innovation management in incumbent firms. In contrast, a static approach as in resource-based view's origin of Wernerfelt [1984] or Barney [1991] may be able to represent value creation in digital innovation only in a very limited way. Given short development cycles, the easy copying of digital functions, the world-wide availability of digital resources and the intensive integration as well as the replacement of partners, digital business is characterized through high dynamics. Consequently, the former resource- and competence-based concept of sustainable competitive advantage must be questioned and reformulated. With exception of data, compared with the industrial-age business, the exclusive control of rare resources becomes less important for incumbent firms. Instead, competitive advantages are primarily based on pace advantages in orchestrating value creating activities and building up digital platforms faster than competitors. This assumes that companies are able to handle the increased resource complexity: Resources and competencies of the core business remain important while new digital resources as well as novel partners are added (see Sec. 4.4). Therefore, competencies in the simultaneous handling of the hardware and the digital business are essential for digital innovation management (managing technical ambidexterity).

5.3. *Digital standard resources and digital gap closing resources*

In addition, theory development has to consider the phenomena of co-creation and resource convergence explained in Sec. 4.2. The resource-based view presupposes that each firm is represented by a unique heterogeneous bundle of resources [Barney (1991)]. Although a single firm's resource complexity increases (micro-perspective: resources of the core business are expanded through digital resources), the assumed resource heterogeneity is weakened from a macro-perspective due to the digital resource convergence between firms. The use of identical digital resources from the same digital partners in different companies leads to a partial harmonization of their resource endowment. In some cases, the openness for a flexible integration of external resources in a value creation network may take precedence over the possession of own internal resources. This is reminiscent of streams within the resource-based theory domain which considers the firm as an open system of asset stocks and flows [Dierickx and Cool (1989)] distinguishing between *firm-specific resources* and *firm-addressable resources* [Sanchez and Heene (1997)]. Firm-specific resources reside within the firm, whereas firm-addressable resources belong to other organizations. A company uses both firm-specific and firm-addressable resources [Sanchez and Heene (1997)]. Based on our insights, we propose two new types of firm-addressable resources with a dominant role for digital innovation management. We call them *digital standard resources* and *digital gap closing resources.*

Digital gap closing resources are essential for the near-term development of a digital innovation, but it is not possible for the firm to build them up as firm-specific resources on short notice. Accordingly, the digital gap closing resources comprise those specific assets an incumbent firm integrates through partnerships during the expansion in value creation networks. As mentioned in Sec. 3.3, in four cases, third parties were commissioned with software development due to missing internal capabilities or capacities. However, due to the use of digital gap closing resources, incumbent firms limit their build-up of internal know-how. Consequently, digital innovation management need to recognize which used firm-addressable resources have a superior impact on the offered digital solutions. To reduce dependency, strengthen their competitive advantage, and improve profitability, companies have to initiate efforts to establish them as firm-specific resources. This explains why the observed expansion in value creation networks decreases at some point (see Sec. 4.2). Therefore, the progress of digital transformation determines the necessary development of firm-specific resources. Sustainable competitive advantages are favored, if an organization is able to balance value creation in an open system and the growth of the own digital resource endowment. At the beginning, companies primarily require know-how about digital technologies in order to orchestrate the integration of digital gap closing resources. Later, internal digital resources and competencies are needed for the own development of digital offering's core functionalities.

Digital standard resources refer to offerings from one or more providers for a particular scope of applications that are used by the majority of the other actors. Examples are providers for cloud infrastructure, map data, mobile network services, music streaming, live traffic information, or natural voice control. Usually, those generic resources are essential for the development of a digital innovation, but they don't provide a competitive advantage. One of the most popular digital standard resources is Google Maps, coupled with heterogeneous devices or services and used in varied ways [Yoo (2013); Henfridsson *et al.* (2018)]. In most cases, it would not make sense to build up own resources instead of using those digital standard resources because their providers are very specialized, deliver a predominant level of quality, and realize economies of scale. Exceptions exist if the available digital standard resources clearly do not meet the requirements and are insufficient to gain differentiation on market. An example can be found outside our case study in the already mentioned infotainment system MBUX by Mercedes-Benz. As one of the strengths, MBUX contains a newly developed voice control with natural language comprehension at the service layer. Previously, conventional voice control of Mercedes-Benz vehicles only worked with certain direct commands. In contrast, natural language speech recognition allows the driver to speak to the system in full sentences. Therefore, a central digital service in the value proposition of MBUX is to provide a more intuitive operating concept in order to convince the customers and gain differentiation. However, available standard digital resources offered for natural voice control such as Google, Amazon Alexa, or Apple's Siri require an online connection. These solutions do not perfectly fit the requirements of a car manufacturer, as connected vehicles often lose access to the internet, e.g. on the highway or in rural areas. Due to the high importance, Mercedes-Benz as original equipment manufacturer decided to develop a new operating system, of course with the aid of specialized partners, instead of using digital standard resources. They designed the voice control service as a hybrid system combining cloud-based modules as well as on-board software. By using the cloud, the system provides a far greater recognition accuracy, but in case of no internet connection, the voice control answers are based on on-board functionalities [Daimler (2018b,c,d)].

6. Conclusion

Focussing on incumbent firms, this paper provides insights about value creation in digital innovation. Our research confirms the profound changes in firms' strategy and structure caused through digital transformation. We empirically demonstrated which necessary multi-sided alterations an incumbent firm has to fulfill during the formation of digital innovation capabilities. Besides the renewal of internal resources and competencies, an opening toward a value creation network with the intensive integration of new partners is required. Competitive advantages of incumbent firms' digital innovation management are based on (1) orchestrating capabilities to coordinate internal and external value creation activities regarding customer needs, (2) the use of platforms and valuable data, and (3) the fast offering of digital hybrid resource bundles (4) combining digital innovation with the core business. Regarding further research, the conducted multiple case study provides a better understanding of value creation in the context of digital innovation.

Our discussion in the fifth section showed that established theories should not be excluded *a priori* while theorizing the phenomenon of digital innovation. Existing theory approaches may provide explanations, as shown with the dynamic capabilities approach [Teece *et al.* (1997)] and the concept of the open system of asset stocks and flows from Dierickx and Cool [1989] for the resource-based and competence-based approach. In this context, we introduced *digital gap closing resources* and *digital standard resources*. Consequently, the use of an established theory for digital innovation management requires adequate adjustments and extensions. If there are any future efforts to develop a *digital resource-based view*, the former concept of sustainable competitive advantage must be questioned and reformulated, based on the dynamic capabilities approach.

In the beginning, we justified the applied qualitative methodology referring to the lack of empirical research in the object of investigation. However, this inevitably leads to limitations we recognize in our research design. A critical disadvantage of qualitative research compared with quantitative methods is statistical representativeness. Despite the cross-case analysis enabling more robust insights, we cannot claim that our findings apply to the whole population of all incumbent firms. Counteracting this limiting factor, we have deliberately chosen different cases from several industries. Another basic limitation is the focus on incumbent firms. Needless to say, other companies like software providers or startups are faced with varied circumstances. Such limitations lead to further research, starting from our results. Even though our research provides an overview about value creation in digital innovation, selected aspects need to be further considered in more detail. For instance, the management of digital partners in value co-creation networks is significantly different from collaborations of traditional businesses. Furthermore, there is a need for further theorization of digital innovation. For example, decisions between in-house development and external procurement are the heart of several theories (e.g. transactional cost theory), calling for an extension with regard to digital business. Giving an outlook, not only value creation is changing for incumbent firms, but also value capture [Teece (2018a)]. This requires further research about the potential to return profits from digital innovation.

References

Abrell, T., Pihlajamaa, M., Kanto, L., Vom Brocke, J. and Uebernickel, F. (2016). The role of users and customers in digital innovation: Insights from B2B manufacturing firms. *Information and Management*, **53**, 3: 324–335.

Barney, J. B. (1991). Firms resources and sustained competitive advantage. *Journal of Management*, **17**, 1: 99–120.

Bosler, M., Jud, C. and Herzwurm, G. (2017). Platforms and ecosystems for connected car services. In *Proceedings of the 9th International Workshop on Software Ecosystems.*

Burr, W., Valentowitsch, J. and Carpentieri, R. (2016). The resource-based theory: On the eve of a paradigm change?*International Journal of Business Environment*, **8**, 3: 265–283.

Chesbrough, H., Lettl, C. and Ritter, T. (2018). Value creation and value capture in open innovation. *Journal of Product Innovation Management*, **35**, 6: 930–938.

Christensen, C. M. (1997). *The Innovator's Dilemma: When New Technologies Cause Great Firms to Fail.* Boston: Harvard Business School Press.

Constantinides, P., Henfridsson, O. and Parker, G. (2018). Platforms and infrastructures in the digital age. *Information Systems Research*, **29**, 2: 381–400.

Daimler (2018a). Under the microscope: Mercedes me connect: New services, easy operation. Available at https://media.daimler.com/marsMediaSite/ko/en/32997897 [accessed on 17 May 2019].

Daimler (2018b). Under the microscope: LINGUATRONIC voice control: "Hey Mercedes". Available at https://media.daimler.com/marsMediaSite/ko/en/32997867 [accessed on 13 May 2019].

Daimler (2018c). Annual Report 2018. Available at https://www.daimler.com/investors/reports-news/annual-reports/2018/ [accessed 13 May 2019].

Daimler (2018d). Supplier Magazine. Hey! Available at https://supplier-magazine.daimler.com/en/hey-harman-2/ [published on 4 May 2018, accessed 13 May 2019].

Dierickx, I. and Cool, K. (1989). Asset stock accumulation and sustainability of competitive advantage. *Management Science*, **35**, 12: 1504–1511.

Echterfeld, J. and Gausmeier, J. (2018). Digitising product portfolios. *International Journal of Innovation Management*, **22**, 5: 1–27.

Eisenhardt, K. (1989). Building theories from case study research. *Academy of Management Review*, **14**, 4: 532–550.

Eisenhardt, K. and Graebner, M. (2007). Theory building from cases: Opportunities and challenges. *Academy of Management Journal*, **50**, 1: 25–32.

Grant, R. (1996). Toward a knowledge-based theory of competitive advantage. *Strategic Management Journal*, **17**, 2: 109–122.

Helfat, C. E. and Raubitschek, R. S. (2018). Dynamic and integrative capabilities for profiting from innovation in digital platform-based ecosystems. *Research Policy*, **47**, 8: 1391–1399.

Henfridsson, O., Nandhakumar, J., Scarbrough, H. and Panourgias, N. (2018). Recombination in the open-ended value landscape of digital innovation. *Information and Organization*, **28**, 2: 89–100.

Hinings, B., Gegenhuber, T. and Greenwood, R. (2018). Digital innovation and transformation: An institutional perspective. *Information and Organization*, **28**, 1: 52–61.

Hitt, M. A., Xu, K. and Carnes, C. M. (2016). Resource based theory in operations management research. *Journal of Operations Management*, **41**, 1: 77–94.

Holmström, J. (2018). Recombination in digital innovation: Challenges, opportunities, and the importance of a theoretical framework. *Information and Organization*, **28**, 2: 107–110.

Huang, J., Henfridsson, O., Liu, M. and Newell, S. (2017). Growing on steroids: Rapidly scaling the user base of digital ventures through digital innovation. *MIS Quarterly*, **41**, 1: 301–314.

Kohli, R. and Melville, N. (2019). Digital innovation: A review and synthesis. *Information Systems Journal*, **29**, 1: 200–223.

Lusch, R. and Nambisan, S. (2015). Service innovation: A service-dominant logic perspective. *MIS Quarterly*, **39**, 1: 155–175.

Lyytinen, K., Yoo, Y. and Boland, R. J. Jr (2016). Digital product innovation within four classes of innovation networks. *Information Systems Journal*, **26**, 1: 47–75.

Maniak, R., Midler, C., Beaume, R. and von Pechmann, F. (2014). Featuring capability: How carmakers organize to deploy innovative features across products. *Journal of Product Innovation Management*, **31**, 1: 114–127.

McCutcheon, D. M. and Meredith, J. R. (1993). Conducting case study research in operations management. *Journal of Operations Management*, **11**, 3: 239–256.

Nambisan, S. (2018). Architecture vs. ecosystem perspectives: Reflections on digital innovation. *Information and Organization*, **28**, 2: 104–106.

Nambisan, S. (2017). Digital entrepreneurship: Toward a digital technology perspective of entrepreneurship. *Entrepreneurship Theory and Practice*, **41**, 6: 1029–1055.

Nambisan, S., Lyytinen, K., Majchrzak, A. and Song, M. (2017). Digital innovation management: Reinventing innovation management research in a digital world. *MIS Quarterly*, **41**, 1: 223–238.

Priem, R. L. and Butler, J. E. (2001). Is the resource based "view" a useful perspective for strategic management research? *The Academy of Management Review*, **26**, 1: 22–40.

Sanchez, R. and Heene, A. (1997). Reinventing strategic management: New theory and practice for competence-based competition. *European Management Journal*, **15**, 3: 303–317.

Seo, D. (2017). Digital business convergence and emerging contested fields: A conceptual framework. *Journal of the Association for Information Systems*, **18**, 10: 687–702.

Svahn, F., Mathiassen, L. and Lindgren, R. (2017). Embracing digital innovation in incumbent firms: How Volvo cars managed competing concerns. *MIS Quarterly*, **41**, 1: 239–253.

Teece, D. J. (2018a). Profiting from innovation in the digital economy: Enabling technologies, standards, and licensing models in the wireless world. *Research Policy*, **47**, 8: 1367–1387.

Teece, D. J. (2018b). Business models and dynamic capabilities. *Long Range Planning*, **51**, 1: 40–49.

Teece, D. J., Pisano, G. and Shuen, A. (1997). Dynamic capabilities and strategic management. *Strategic Management Journal*, **18**, 7: 509–533.

Tiwana, A., Konsynski, B. and Bush, A. A. (2010). Research commentary — Platform evolution: Coevolution of platform architecture, governance, and environmental dynamics. *Information Systems Research*, **21**, 4: 675–687.

Tushman, M. L. and Anderson, P. (1986). Technological discontinuities and organizational environments. *Administrative Science Quarterly*, **31**, 3: 439–465.

Yin, R. (2018). *Case Study Research and Applications: Design and Methods*, 6th edition. Los Angeles: Sage Publications Ltd.

Yoo, Y. (2010). Computing in everyday life: A call for research on experiential computing. *MIS Quarterly*, **34**, 2: 213–231.

Yoo, Y. (2013). The tables have turned: How can the information systems field contribute to technology and innovation management research? *Journal of the Association for Information Systems*, **14**, 5: 227–236.

Yoo, Y., Boland, R. J., Lyytinen, K. and Majchrzak, A. (2012). Organizing for innovation in the digitized world. *Organization Science*, **23**, 5: 1398–1408.

Wernerfelt, B. (1984). A resource-based view of the firm. *Strategic Management Journal*, **5**, 2: 171–180.

ZEW (2018). Annual German Innovation Survey, 2018. Leibniz Centre for European Economic Research. Available at https://www.zew.de/en/publikationen/zew-gutachten-und-forschungsberichte/forschungsberichte/innovationen/innovationserhebung/.

Biography

Micha Bosler is a doctoral researcher at the Chair of Business Administration, esp. Innovation & Service Management at the University of Stuttgart. He holds a Master Degree with distinction in technically oriented Business Administration. In his research, he focuses on digital innovation in incumbent firms, particularly in the context of connected cars.

Wolfgang Burr is a professor at the University of Stuttgart in Germany. He holds the Chair of Business Administration, esp. Innovation & Service Management. His research focuses on innovation management in several industries (e.g. pharmaceutical industry or watch industry), service engineering and digitization of services.

Leonie Ihring holds a Master Degree with distinction in technically oriented Business Administration from the University of Stuttgart. She has been researching the digitization of vehicles for several years and has practical experience in the management of connected car services at a leading German automotive carmaker.

How to Organize Digital Innovation? The Role of Involvement, Structure, and Technology*

Lena Franziska Kaiser, Charlotte Wehking and Jan vom Brocke

University of Liechtenstein, Fürst-Franz-Josef-Strasse, 9490 Vaduz, Liechtenstein

Innovation, especially digital innovation, is indispensable for organizations that want to remain competitive. Employees play a crucial role in developing innovations, but the use of digital technologies for innovation methods that foster employee-driven innovation has rarely been researched. Using a sample of 215 participants and two innovation methods (i.e. digital, non-digital), we show that employees value a digital innovation more if they are involved in the digital innovation, the involvement follows a structured process, and the digital innovation process uses digital technologies. These results have implications for both practice and the innovation and information systems literatures.

Keywords: Digital innovation; design thinking; enterprise crowdfunding.

1. Introduction

Innovation has become indispensable in enabling organizations to survive and thrive [Bäckström and Lindberg (2019)]. The importance of innovation has made it a sought-after topic among researchers and practitioners for years. Many methods have been developed that companies can use to be innovative and to involve multiple actors in innovation processes. One well-known and widely used approach to fostering creativity in human-centric innovation is the design thinking (DT) method [Brown (2008)]. DT is defined as "methodology that imbues the full spectrum of innovation activities" [Brown (2008, p. 1)] and is structured along five steps: empathize, define, ideate, prototype, and test [Stanford d.school (2018)]. Many organizations, including Apple, IBM, and SAP, apply DT with a cross-disciplinary team of employees to identify problems and develop solutions, often in offline settings without the use of digital technologies [e.g. Brown (2008)]. The participation in innovation processes of employees who are not part of management or the innovation team is a strong driver of innovation [Kesting and Ulhøi (2010)]. With employee-driven innovations (EDIs), all employees are regarded as sources of idea creation, idea execution, and the co-creation of innovations [Smith *et al.* (2012)].

*This chapter was originally published in International Journal of Innovation and Technology Management, Vol. 18, No. 3, March 2018, published by World Scientific Publishing, Singapore. Reprinted with permission.

However, the influence of digital technologies has completely changed the means of innovating [Fichman *et al.* (2014)].

In companies' efforts to remain competitive, digital innovations are more important than innovations are, and not only for the technology companies [Grossman (2016); Yoo *et al.* (2010)]. Digital innovations are either the direct outcome of an innovation (i.e. a "product, process, or business model that is perceived as new, requires some significant changes on the part of adopters, and is embodied in or enabled by information technology (IT)" [Fichman *et al.* (2014, p. 330)]), or they refer to the process of innovating (i.e. "use of digital technology during the process of innovating" [Nambisan *et al.* (2017, p. 223)]). The digitalization of innovation processes diminish boundaries between innovation phases, and innovation actors become more widely distributed [Nambisan *et al.* (2017)]. A loosely connected set of actors in an organization can now be identified and mobilized by digital technology to orchestrate the crowd [Huesig and Endress (2019); Nambisan *et al.* (2017)]. Enterprise crowdfunding (ECF) is an innovation method that relies entirely on digital technologies to facilitate the development of innovations and orchestrate multiple actors in the innovation process [Simons *et al.* (2019)]. In ECF, actors follow two main steps: propose the project and evaluate the project [Simons *et al.* (2019)]. Companies like IBM and BMW have used ECF for such purposes as engaging their employees in their innovation processes [e.g. Jovanović *et al.* (2017)].

Not only does the transformation from innovation to digital innovation challenge EDI, so does innovation's tendency to happen in unstructured and spontaneous ways [Reibenspiess *et al.* (2019)]. As a result, a digital innovation's value may not be fully exploited, which has a negative impact on the organization's competitive performance. Structured processes are needed to increase employees' innovation capacity, enable them to bond with the innovation, and facilitate organizations' ability to execute the innovation process [Ciriello *et al.* (2018); Reibenspiess *et al.* (2019)]. In addition, digital technologies fundamentally change the nature and the development of innovations [Fichman *et al.* (2014); Nambisan *et al.* (2017)], enabling new forms of innovation by involving many parts of the value chain in innovation processes. Assumptions about traditional innovation need to be reconsidered in terms of digital innovation [Nambisan *et al.* (2017)], especially since the digitalized innovation process has gained importance [Agostini *et al.* (2020); Brem and Viardot (2017); Huesig and Endress (2019)].

Non-digital innovation methods (i.e. DT) are executed offline without digital technologies, whereas the digital innovation methods (i.e. ECF) are executed online and rely on digital technologies. For the purposes of this paper, we define traditional innovation management in accordance with [Nambisan and Sawhney (2011)] as that which is realized without digital technologies in a centralized manner, and we define the management of digital innovations in accordance with [Nambisan *et al.* (2017)] as being supported by digital technologies and using a decentralized method (e.g. through EDI). Therefore, we refer to the process definition of a digital innovation according Nambisan *et al.* [2017]. The aim of this study, then, is to determine whether employees value a digital innovation more when they are involved in a structured development process through digital technologies or not. Against this background, the following research question arises: *How does the use of digital innovation methods influence employees' attitude toward new digital innovations?*

Accordingly, the study is positioned at the intersection of digital innovation and EDI and identifies how EDI can be used in the field of digital innovations so employees value the innovation. To answer the research question, we conduct a hypothetical-choice experiment with 215 participants that tests whether employees value a digital innovation more if (1) they are involved in the digital innovation (as opposed to only being informed), (2) the involvement follows a structured process, and (3) the digital innovation process uses digital technology (as opposed to an offline process). We also derive drivers of and barriers to EDI based on a qualitative analysis of the answers to follow-up questions in the experiment.

This study contributes to the research on EDI innovation methods, shares insights regarding the digital innovations process, and responds to research calls to connect the research streams of EDI and digital innovation. Our results show that employees value a digital innovation more when they are part of a structured development process than they do when they are not involved. Our results also suggest that employees attach more value to their own digital innovations when they are engaged through a digital (online) innovation method (i.e. ECF), as opposed to a non-digital (offline) innovation method (i.e. DT). Furthermore, we help to explain why employees like or do not like being involved in the digital innovation process.

The paper is structured as follows: First, we explain the influence of digital technologies on innovation, introduce employees as drivers of innovation, and outline the IKEA effect as our analytical lens. Then, after deriving our hypotheses, we present our experimental research design. Next, we report our results, followed by a discussion, including implications for research and practice, limitations, and recommendations for future research. Finally, we draw conclusions.

2. Related Work

2.1. *The influence of digital technologies on innovations*

Today's business innovations have gradually given way to digital innovations. An innovation is "an idea, practice or object that is perceived as new by an individual or other unit of adoption" [Rogers (2003, p. 11)]. This definition is still valid, but digital innovations also include a digital technology component. Therefore, a digital innovation is defined as a "product, process or business model that is perceived as new, requires significant changes on the part of adopters, and is embodied in or enabled by IT" [Fichman *et al.* (2014, p. 333)]. The research stream of digital innovation management is younger than the research traditional innovation management stream [Nambisan *et al.* (2017); Yoo *et al.* (2010)]. According to Fichman *et al.* [2014], the process steps of a digital innovation process — discovery, development, diffusion, and impact — are general enough to reflect all types of innovations (i.e. product, service, business model, process). Except for the use of digital technologies, these process steps do not necessarily differ from those of a traditional innovation process

[Fichman *et al.* (2014); Rogers (2003)], which results in the aspects of what distinguishes an innovation from a digital innovation.

Many assumptions about innovation management, including the nature, the context, and the boundaries of innovations, have changed with regard to digital innovations [e.g. Fichman *et al.* (2014); Nambisan *et al.* (2017)]. The nature of innovations has changed in that the features or value of a digital innovation can unfold even after the innovation has been implemented, frequently resulting in disrupted business models, products, or services (e.g. Airbnb, Netflix, Uber) [Skog *et al.* (2018)]. The context of innovations has changed, as stakeholders other than the primary innovator, who can have different motivations, can participate in the process of developing a digital innovation, such as through the crowd approach that allows suppliers, customers, or employees to take part in the process [Chesbrough and Crowther (2006)]. At the same time, the boundaries of an innovation and its development process have become fluid as the use of digital technologies has broken down the boundaries of each development step and sped up the process, making it difficult to determine when a development-process step starts and ends [Agostini *et al.* (2020); Nambisan (2017)]. Correspondingly, innovation methods have evolved (e.g. ECF) and other little-used methods are now considered as suitable because of their case-study-like structure [Fichman *et al.* (2014); Nambisan *et al.* (2017)].

The methods of developing digital innovations have also changed [cf. Nambisan *et al.* (2017)]. In general, methods are a "collection of problem-solving approaches," where users are guided in a systematic and structured way to achieve a particular goal — in this case, a digital innovation [Dumas *et al.* (2018, p. 305)]. We use two innovation methods as examples to represent the traditional innovation management approach, where the innovation method is performed offline (i.e. DT), and the digital innovation management approach, where the innovation method is performed digitally (i.e. ECF). We chose these methods because of their popularity with and numerous executions by organizations worldwide like SAP, IBM, and BMW [Micheli *et al.* (2018); Simons *et al.* (2019)]. Like DT, ECF can be used for all types of innovation, as it is not just a simple method, but a holistic mindset. As ECF and DT can enable an organizational culture in which entrepreneurial spirit, intrinsic motivation, and appreciation have top priority [van Delden and Chia (2020)]. While many organizations use these methods in their daily business, there are just as many (e.g. IDEO, innosabi) that support these organizations in an advisory capacity to reduce complexity and to teach them to extract the maximum benefit of applying these innovation methods [Jeltsch (2019)]. Nevertheless, these two examples, DT and ECF, act as representatives of digital and non-digital innovation methods, respectively, in this research study. Other innovation methods can be considered in the future, such as the LEGO serious-play method and virtual (immersive) brainstorming [Frick *et al.* (2014); Hidalgo and Albors (2008)].

DT is a problem–solution approach [Buchanan (1992)] to generating human-centered innovations that match customers' needs, that are technologically feasible, and that are viable for an organization's business strategy [Brown (2008)]. Such innovations are designed based on the creative ideas of a small cross-disciplinary team that focuses on users' problems and needs. Five interrelated steps —

empathize, define, ideate, prototype, and test — guide the team through the innovation process [Stanford d.school (2018)]. The team performs the steps mainly in offline settings because factors like user involvement, visualization, creativity, and experimentation heavily influence the outcome of DT. These factors function best with conventional face-to-face DT [Micheli *et al.* (2018)], which is why designers prefer to work offline to obtain good results. Previous work has already started to translate DT to the digital world and has developed digital solutions for single steps or activities of the DT process [e.g. [Schoormann *et al.* (2020); von Thienen *et al.* (2016)]. Despite these first attempts to digitalize DT, there is no fully functional software or digital approach to practicing DT entirely in a digital world. Designers must still switch to offline activities or perform process steps without digital technologies, so we categorize DT as a non-digital innovation method for the purposes of this paper.

Contrary to DT, ECF is representative of a digital innovation method that leverages the power of the crowd through an online platform for purposes such as marketing, open innovation, and prototyping [Simons *et al.* (2019)]. ECF can be divided into internal and external crowdfunding [Simons *et al.* (2019)]. Internal crowdfunding takes place within the sphere of an organization in which employees are involved in the organization's innovation management and collaboration among employees is fostered [e.g. Muller *et al.* (2013)], so we refer to internal crowdfunding [Simons *et al.* (2019)] as EDI that happens within the organization's realms. With external crowdfunding, no direct promotion of creativity takes place, and no particular creativity-enhancing methods are used, although participants may be inspired by ideas that others have uploaded on the platform, thus promoting creativity indirectly [Elerud-Tryde and Hooge (2014)].

Table 1 shows the main differences between the two innovation methods. Employees play a crucial role in both methods, as they are an active part of the method, contribute to the problem with their knowledge, and follow the various steps to develop an innovation [Brown (2008); Simons *et al.* (2019)].

Table 1. Comparison of innovation methods.

Characteristic	Design thinking	Enterprise crowdfunding
Use of digital technologies	None; participants meet offline	Yes, participants meet online
Number of participants	Small	Large
Promotion of creativity	Direct	Indirect
Role of employees	High	High

2.2. *Employees drive innovations*

As an organization's carriers of its knowledge and creativity, its employees have great potential to drive innovation [Mollick (2014); Muller *et al.* (2013)]. In contrast to traditional innovation management, which focuses on a centered approach and only on employees who work in R&D or in innovation departments for innovation development, EDI encourages employees (on an individual or group level) to engage in innovation processes, no matter what their backgrounds or roles in the organization [Laviolette *et al.* (2016)]. With EDI, all employees are regarded as sources of idea creation, idea execution, and of the co-creation of innovations [Parjanen *et al.* (2020); Smith *et al.* (2012)]. Employees have in-depth and contextual knowledge that can be critical in identifying new business opportunities [Henderson and McAdam (2001)]. In addition, they are creative and, being deeply involved in the business, are likely to spot new opportunities [Kirzner (1997)]. They also have personal networks that can be sources of new knowledge and ideas [Galbreath (2002)].

According to Høyrup [2012] and Høyrup *et al.* [2018], the three levels of EDI are (1) EDI as a bottom-up process in which innovation is the outcome but is not purposefully initiated; (2) EDI as a mixture of a bottom-up and a top-down process in which employees intend to be involved in an innovation process and know that the management supports their involvement; and (3) EDI as a top-down process in which the management calls the employees to come up with ideas for innovation.

The concept of EDI is still fresh, but it has a solid ancestry. Scholars have long recognized the importance of entrepreneurship in organizations and have conceptualized it as intrapreneurship, corporate entrepreneurship, and corporate venturing [e.g. Pinchot (1985)]. However, research on intrapreneurship has focused on the individual level, whereas research on EDI has focused on the group level [Soderquist *et al.* (2016)]. Research from an information systems (IS) perspective is rare and has large gaps [Erickson *et al.* (2012)], as it has focused on EDI work models, drivers, and barriers only for public organizations [Reibenspiess *et al.* (2019)] or on how employees use technology (e.g. enterprise social-media platforms, intranets, PowerPoint) to engage in EDI [Ciriello *et al.* (2015)] or how they leverage digital communication and communication tools in an open innovation context [Tirabeni and Soderquist (2019)].

Although EDI is a promising approach to fostering innovation, it lacks research with regard to digital innovation. For example, little is known about employees' participation in EDI concerning, for instance, what drives and/or impedes their EDI participation on an individual level [Høyrup (2012); Høyrup *et al.* (2018)]. In addition, management's use of digital technologies to monitor, evaluate, and select employees' ideas needs further investigation and requires coordination among the actors (e.g. managers and employees) in the innovation process [Gressgård *et al.* (2014)]. What's more, little is known about the implications of applying digital technologies to involve employees in creating EDIs without neglecting their day-to-day business [Bäckström and Lindberg (2019)].

2.3. *The IKEA effect as an analytical lens to determine the value employees place on a digital innovation*

The IKEA effect refers to individuals' valuing their own creations, the development process, and the corresponding implementations more than is likely to be accurate, even if their creations are not unique or not as customized as other objectively similar products [Norton *et al.* (2012); Thomas and Alluru (2016)]. The IKEA effect's positive side occurs when individuals build products themselves, thus gaining a feeling of control over their environment and a sense of ownership [Sarstedt *et al.* (2017)] by demonstrating their own competencies to themselves and others [Mochon *et al.* (2012)].

The IKEA effect has been researched in various areas. Steve Jobs experienced the IKEA effect when one of the first Apple computers failed, as he changed from a neutral observer to one who held strong emotional attachment to the computer and would not admit that the computer was not a success [Thomas and Alluru (2016)]. The IKEA effect has been analyzed in such areas as food production [Dohle *et al.* (2014)], handicrafts [Marsh *et al.* (2018)], hand-based labor [Fuchs *et al.* (2015)], and mass customization [Ling *et al.* (2020)]. Most of the research on the IKEA effect focuses on individual settings, as each individual develops a solution on his or her own [Norton *et al.* (2012)]. A few researchers have also started to consider the role of the IKEA effect in group settings, proposing a positive impact on the jointly developed solution [e.g. Vuculescu *et al.* (2018)].

The role of the IKEA effect has become increasingly important in the age of customization and co-creation, of which digital technologies are often part [cf. Marsh *et al.* (2018); Norton *et al.* (2012)]. Consumers who are involved in an innovation process value a product more than do consumers who simply receive a product [Norton *et al.* (2012)], as they want to justify their effort [Marsh *et al.* (2018)]. The Becker–DeGroot–Marschak (BDM) method can be used to measure the subjective value that individuals place on goods and assets and the effort that has been put into making them [Thomas and Alluru (2016)]. This method is commonly used to test the IKEA effect based on individuals' willingness to pay for an innovation [e.g. Norton *et al.* (2012); Sarstedt *et al.* (2017)]. The basic idea behind the BDM is to increase the accuracy of individuals' stated value of a good. In a first step, participants are asked to state the maximum amount they would be willing to pay for a particular good within a given price range. When the actual price of this good is assigned (i.e. the price offer), those who stated a higher amount than the randomized price are willing to pay the assigned price, while those who stated a lower price are not [Becker *et al.* (1964)].

3. Hypothesis Development

The management of digital innovations refers to "the practices, processes, and principles that underlie the effective orchestration of digital innovation" [Nambisan *et al.* (2017, p. 224)]. Employee support is critical for innovation success, as employees have hidden abilities for innovation [Ford and Randolph (1992)] that can be used for the benefit of the organization [Gressgård *et al.* (2014)]. In traditional innovation management, employees value an innovation more when they are involved in the innovation process [Norton *et al.* (2012)]. However, digital technology enables new forms of innovating by, for instance, facilitating innovation collectives [Fichman *et al.* (2014); Nambisan *et al.* (2017)] and increasing employees' involvement in the innovation process through, for example, the use of innovation platforms [Reibenspiess *et al.* (2019)].

As such involvement is now possible, employees must understand digital technologies to know how to create and manage them. We consider whether employees value a digital innovation more when they are involved in the development process using the IKEA effect as an analytical lens. Against this background, we expect that:

H1: *Employees value digital innovations more when they are involved in the development digital innovation process than when they are not.*

The problem of unstructured and spontaneous involvement in the digital innovation process must be addressed, particularly when employees enjoy and value such involvement [Reibenspiess *et al.* (2019)]. Research has identified the importance of structured innovation processes, which can be used to guide employees through the digital innovation process using a step-by-step method that can be either non-digital or digital. Since individuals consume digital technologies (e.g. smartphones) in their private lives and work with digital technologies (e.g. cloud computing services) that enhance their professional lives [Westerman and Bonnet (2015)], it is likely that innovations that emerge from a structured digital innovation method will provide more value than would non-digital structured innovation methods that are performed offline. Therefore, we hypothesize that:

H2: *Employees value digital innovations more when they apply a digital innovation method during the digital innovation process than they do when they apply a non-digital innovation method.*

This study extends existing research by including structured innovation methods that are either non-digital and executed in an offline environment (i.e. DT) or digital and supported by a digital technology (i.e. ECF) to generate a digital innovation [Bäckström and Lindberg (2019)]. We focus on the claim that the use of digital technologies is beneficial in involving employees in the digital innovation process and use DT and ECF as examples of these kinds of innovation methods.

Our study's research setting considers the IKEA effect in the field of EDI and digital innovations. Until now, research has not focused on this combination, despite its elements fitting together well, as employees are an important source of (digital) innovation and should value their innovations. To the best of our knowledge, this study is the first to consider the IKEA effect in the fields of EDI and digital innovations.

4. Research Design

4.1. *Experiment design*

We conducted an online hypothetical-choice experiment in which participants thought through a scenario but did not experience it themselves. Despite this limitation, it is an appropriate strategy of inquiry because it is a common and valid procedure in experimental design [Kühberger *et al.* (2002)] that has been used in a number of research studies [e.g. Tietz *et al.* (2016)]. It also allows us to create a particular, controlled environment for our research. Before the experiment was carried out, we conducted a pre-test with 10% of the calculated sample size (21 participants) and discussed the experiment in detail with fellow researchers to ensure the experiment had a clear and comprehensive set-up. The pre-test did not show any conspicuous issues.

Materials and procedure. We created a hypothetical scenario in which participants selected the options they believed they would choose in real life. In the scenario, participants imagined that they were employees of an international organization with offices around the world. The organization was facing a serious problem with communications between its offices, so management asked the participants either to develop a digital innovation that solved the communication issue or to read through written material about a digital innovation that solved the issue. This scenario represents the third level of EDI [Høyrup (2012)], where the management asks the employees to provide innovation ideas.

We focused on an internal organizational digital innovation so employees could recognize the benefits of the digital innovation for themselves. Research has shown that employees play a critical role in successful digital innovation implementations, as they use digital innovations in their work [Fichman *et al.* (2014); Klein and Knight (2005)]. We prepared the scenario so participants in the treatment conditions would feel that they personally needed to solve a challenge (i.e. "How might we improve the communication to foster efficient communication?") by developing a digital innovation (i.e. virtual reality technology, chatbot, telephone/video communication tool).

The experimental procedure consisted of eight steps (Fig. 1). First, the participants were given written instructions that illustrated the organization's current situation. The participants were made familiar with the organization's communication problems, especially the problem related to communication between employees in different locations, which was diagnosed as the major challenge. We introduced the particular innovation method and provided the participants instructions how the method works. For instance, we explained the purpose and which steps are part of the method.

In the second step, an attention check was conducted to ensure that the participants had read the instructions properly. Third, we used Qualtric's Randomizer to assign the participants randomly to one of three conditions, which are described in depth in the subsection *treatment and measures*, below. The fourth step consisted of the participants' estimating how much they were willing to pay to own the digital innovation using a scale between USD 1000 and 5000 (i.e. the communication solution). Participants whose bids were above the randomly generated price of the management board indicated a high willingness to pay, which meant that the participant value the innovation so much that they would like to have the innovation implemented [cf. Horowitz (2006)]. In the fifth step, the participants in both treatment conditions were asked if they liked being involved in the digital innovation process, and the participants in the baseline condition were asked if they would have preferred to have been involved and to explain their answers. Then the participants completed the sixth step by answering some check questions to ensure that they had

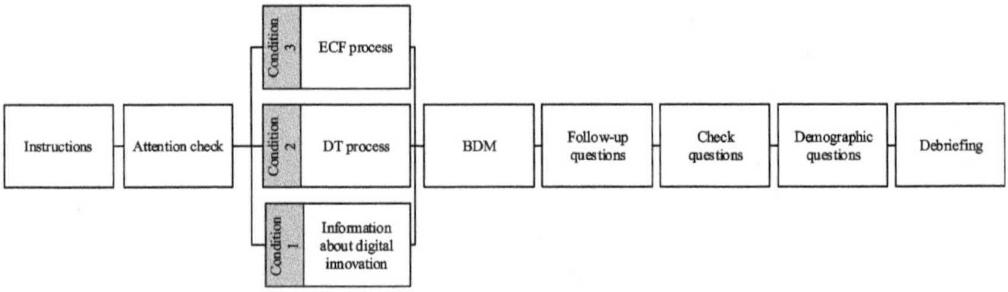

Fig. 1. Experiment procedure.

read through the scenarios, along with some demographic questions in the seventh step. Finally, the participants were debriefed about the purpose of the study.

Treatment and measures. The experiment had three conditions: a baseline condition in which the management presented the participants with a digital innovation that would soon be implemented (the baseline condition, $n = 73$); a treatment condition in which the participants used DT as a non-digital structured innovation method in the digital innovation process (i.e. the DT condition, $n = 70$); and a treatment condition in which the participants used ECF as a digital structured innovation method in the digital innovation process (i.e. the ECF condition, $n = 72$). In the baseline condition, the participants did not actively participate in the digital innovation process but only read through detailed information management provided about a new digital innovation, such as the type of innovation, its functions and application scenarios, that would be implemented soon to solve the communication issue between employees. In the DT condition, the participants went through the five phases (i.e. empathize, define, ideate, prototype, test) of the DT process and developed a digital innovation for the communication problem. In the ECF condition, the participants developed a digital innovation for the communication problem in the form of a crowdfunding project, including a project title, project description, and the funding volume to convince their fellow employees of their solution's value. Subsequently, we applied the BDM method to measure the participants' willingness to pay [Becker *et al.* (1964)], as the BDM method is commonly used to test the IKEA effect [e.g. Mochon *et al.* (2012); Norton *et al.* (2012)]. After the participants stated their willingness to pay for the communication tool, they rated how much they liked the digital innovation on a 7-point Likert scale (ranging from 1 = not at all to 7 = very much) [Norton *et al.* (2012)].

Participants. We calculated the required sample size ($n = 207$) for this experiment using G*Power [Faul *et al.* (2009)]. We used the online recruitment platform prolific.co for data collection in August 2019 and recruited more participants than necessary so we could exclude participants who did not participate conscientiously. Using prolific.co, we recruited 231 native English speakers who were at least 18 years of age, had not participated in previous experiments, and were employed at the time of the experiment. We excluded 16 participants who did not answer the attention check or control questions correctly. The resulting sample consisted of 215 participants, 64.2% of whom were women. The participants' ages averaged 36.3 years. All participants were employed, with 39.1% working in small organizations, such as start-ups, and 60.9% working in medium-sized or large organizations.

4.2. *Qualitative design*

We used an open coding approach for the qualitative analysis of the open questions [Corbin and Strauss (1990)] to identify concepts that were related to the use of EDI. As part of the open coding, we broke down the collected data analytically with the purpose of providing us with further insights we did not receive from the quantitive data [Yin (2015)]. Two coders coded the open questions independently before aligning their results and coming up with 23 codes. The 23 codes were merged into nine broad concept codes, which were split up into two broader areas: drivers and barriers.

5. Results

The results of our experiment show that the participants in the baseline condition liked the digital innovation the least of the three groups. Participants in the DT condition ($M = 2.605$; $SD = 1.085$) and those in the ECF condition ($M = 3.060$; $SD = 1.286$) valued the digital innovation more than participants in the baseline condition did ($M = 2.578$; $SD = 1.382$). We conducted a one-way between-group analysis of variance (ANOVA) to determine whether there was a significant difference between the groups' means ($F(2, 212) = 3.29$; $p = 0.038$) using Fisher's least significant difference (LSD) test to determine the differences between the means. The test is widely discussed in literature, but it is not as conservative as other post hoc tests are, and it does not protect the data from inflated type 1 error rates in some cases [Field (2009)]. However, it works well when one is dealing with three means, which is the case in this study [e.g. Hayter (1986)]. The test showed statistically significant differences between the baseline condition and the ECF condition ($p = 0.022$) and between the DT condition and the ECF condition ($p = 0.032$), so the participants in the ECF condition valued the digital innovation more than the participants in the DT condition or those in the baseline condition did. Two key findings result.

First, employees are likely to value a digital innovation more when they are involved in the development of the digital innovation, which supports our first hypothesis (H1). One explanation for this result could be that they liked being part of the digital innovation process because they felt that management supported, recognized, and valued their work — that is, they felt appreciated. Our results led us to identify six drivers of EDI, as shown in Table 2. Employees like to be involved in digital innovation processes because they like sharing their knowledge, are often intrinsically motivated to contribute, enjoy work activities other than their daily work, and want to understand the upcoming innovation before it is implemented. Another explanation for this result could be that the difference in the kind of management that is required for a traditional innovation and a digital innovation is not as significant as anticipated. With reference to the structure of the involvement, we used two innovation methods that rely on a step-by-step approach to guide the employees through the digital innovation process. As no participants complained about the structured approach, we assume that the structured approach, as identified by prior research, was favorable.

The second key finding from the results of the experiment is that employees value the digital innovation even more when the innovation method used to develop the digital innovation is an online method (e.g. ECF). Thus, our data also support the second hypothesis (H2). In this study, the online innovation method is represented by ECF, so participants in our experiment used an ECF platform to pitch ideas for the digital innovation. Participants in the second treatment group, the DT condition, valued their digital innovation less than those in the ECF group did, perhaps because using digital technology fascinates and/or motivates employees more than using working in an offline setting with no digital technologies does. In addition, using ECF was more convenient, as individuals use digital technologies daily and often so intuitively that it enriches innovation processes. The use of digital technologies makes the involvement in the innovation process more attractive, as employees can use their time efficiently. A simple example is typing ideas on a keyboard instead of noting ideas on a small post-it and digitizing it afterward to share them with other team members. In addition, the participants in the ECF treatment group might feel more ownership of their digital innovation idea because it was their own idea. In DT, a single person does not solve the challenge, as a team with multiple members finds the solution, so the degree of ownership for one particular solution is not as distinct as it is in ECF.

To gain a richer contextual basis and deeper insights for interpretation and to validate the results, we conducted a qualitative analysis based on the participants' answers to the open-ended question [Kaplan and Duchon (1988)]. Overall, 87.9% of the participants answered that they liked being involved in the digital innovation process. The qualitative data analysis identified six major drivers of EDI: involvement, knowledge-sharing, understanding, appreciation, fun, and personal motivation.

Participants in all three conditions valued *involvement* in the digital innovation process, a condition that results in the rapid adoption of digital innovations. They enjoyed being part of (or would like to have been part of) something great and innovative. As one participant put it, "You are part of the change rather than the change happening to you." *Knowledge-sharing* refers to sharing with others insights and knowledge from personal experience to develop a solution that is tailored to employees' needs. The baseline group, which did not participate in the digital innovation process, expressed that they felt left behind, that their voices were not heard, and that their skillsets and ideas would have been valuable inputs. For example, a participant in the baseline group commented, "I may have ideas others won't think of." The last four drivers originate mainly from the treatment groups. The *understanding* driver refers to employees' opportunity to understand a digital technology and become familiar with its functions before it is implemented, that is, "to understand the technology, to get the best out of it." The *appreciation* driver reflects employees' feelings of being valued by colleagues and top management, including knowing that their personal opinions matter and that they play a worthwhile role in the organization. As one participant said, "I felt useful and wanted." The *fun* driver refers to making work easier, more enjoyable, and more interesting, as "Being part of the future of an innovative organization excites me." Finally, *personal motivation* was a reason that participants gave for preferring EDI over receiving the digital innovation as a *fait accompli*. They were proud to have played a part in the process while championing their own ideas and developing themselves, as "It empowered me to challenge myself."

However, 12.1% of the participants did not want to be part of the digital innovation process because they felt they lacked qualifications in terms of (technical) expertise, skills, or experience, as "there are other people who would be far more qualified to help"; they lacked a sense of responsibility, as "I prefer other people to make decisions"); or they lacked motivation to support the digital innovation process, as they saw it only as "additional effort on top of my job." All of these reasons can hinder an employee's willingness to engage in EDI. Table 2 summarizes the six drivers of and three barriers to EDI.

Table 2. Drivers of and barriers to EDI.

Driver		Barrier	
Involvement	Employees want to strengthen their feeling of belonging to the organization and to identify with the final (implemented) innovation in the end.	*Lack of qualifications*	Employees are concerned they have too little (technical) expertise, too few skills, or lack experience to master the tasks required in joining the innovation process.
Knowledge-sharing	Employees want to share their personal knowledge, information, or experience to push forward the innovation and find a suitable solution for users' needs and problems.	*Lack of responsibility*	Employees are worried about making wrong decisions and do not want to take responsibility for wrong actions and decisions.
Understanding	Employees want to be aware of something new that others might not know about yet. They want to learn about and understand the innovation before it is implemented.	*Lack of motivation*	Employees are not interested in taking on additional tasks besides their daily work.
Appreciation	Employees want to be recognized by their colleagues and management and to feel valued during and after the innovation process.		
Fun	Employees want to do something besides the normal, daily tasks of the job and enjoy getting to know other colleagues quickly.		
Personal Motivation	Employees want to experience new situations, feel intrinsically motivated to learn something new, and be part of a greater collective task.		

6. Discussion

6.1. *Contributions and implications*

The present study is one of the first to test whether employees value a digital innovation more when they are involved in the development process, and to test which type of innovation method increases employees' valuation more. The study makes several *contributions to research.*

Our findings align with previous research that has suggest that management should clearly communicate to employees its support for innovation [e.g. [Micheli *et al.* (2018)]], as well as information about digital innovations and the resulting organizational changes [Jarvenpaa and Ives (1991)].

We also find that the barriers to EDI include — missing qualifications, a missing sense of responsibility, and lack of motivation. These barriers align with those that Reibenspiess *et al.* [2019] identified for public organizations: technology-enabled drivers (e.g. an efficient way to document ideas) and organizational-enabled drivers (e.g. time of innovation). We extend these barriers to include individual-enabled drivers, as we find that employees' personal attitudes about their involvement in EDI is a central success factor, particularly the need to be empowered and taken seriously. This finding aligns with Kerpedzhiev *et al.* [2020], who identified employee-centricity as an important future capability of organizations, and with Parjanen *et al.* [2020], who found that the understanding of employees for an innovation increased when they are involved in the innovation process. Employees should have sufficient freedom to make decisions on their own.

EDI has received attention from various disciplines (e.g. entrepreneurship, management, innovation) [Bäckström and Lindberg (2019)]. However, innovation methods that provide guidance for projectable EDI have not been considered. Our findings show that employees must be integrated into innovation processes to reduce their resistance to change by engaging them in the change. This finding concretizes Meissner and Schuchert's [2017] findings using a DT workshop that provides new insights for research in the innovation and entrepreneurship stream.

We also build on the findings of the innovation and entrepreneurship literature by developing the ECF approach further in terms of a digital innovation process. Since communication is a key driver of successful innovation management [Kivimäki *et al.* (2000)], we proposed that digital technologies could make EDI easier and more intuitive. Our study focuses on innovation methods for employees and serves as a starting point for further discussion in the IS community about using digital innovation methods like ECF and integrating these methods into organizational innovation processes. We apply the digital innovation methods that accompany the digital innovation process, thus focusing on the process as well as the outcome. We share new insights into digital technologies' involvement in the innovation process, which involvement enables changes in the digital innovation process, thus, changing the outcome — and vice versa. In this specific example, digital technologies changed the digital innovation process, so the outcome (e.g. a new communication solution) influences employees' work processes. Therefore, our work contributes to the emergent body of EDI in IS, as the IS literature has rarely researched EDI in combination with digital technologies and currently focuses on how employees use IT programs to engage in EDI (e.g. enterprise social-media platforms, intranets, PowerPoint) [Ciriello *et al.* (2015)].

Our results also have important *implications for practice.* Our findings highlight the importance of incorporating digital technologies in innovation processes to increase innovation success. Internal innovation management is as important as external innovation management [Ortt and van der Duin (2008)], so managers should include innovation methods like DT in their strategic management approaches to their daily business [Knight *et al.* (2020)]. Practitioners can use our results to organize or adjust their innovation management processes by directly involving employees from the outset when developing a digital innovation, by providing time for employees to participate in the digital innovation process in a creative environment, by using an innovation method that structures EDI, and by using digital innovation methods like ECF. This approach allows employees to value a digital innovation from the outset, before it is implemented in the organization, which helps to ensure faster adoption of the innovation. Employees often fear that an internal digital innovation will challenge their existing skills and job security [Wolfe *et al.* (2006)], so if they can become familiar with the digital innovation before it is implemented, they are less likely to resist the change. Enabling employees to participate in the digital innovation process using digital technologies has the advantage of making the entire process more transparent in such a way that employees notice what others are doing and are influenced through social effects to participate in EDI.

Our results also have implications for external stakeholders. Our insights help policy makers to develop suitable guidelines and policies to support organizations that seek to pursue digital innovation. The results can also increase customers' awareness of other organizations' efforts to bias them by involving them in the digital innovation process to gain their emotional attachment.

6.2. *Limitations*

Our study has several limitations regarding our data collection and data analysis processes. The study is a hypothetical-choice experiment, so the participants did not develop a solution for a real organization and did not participate in a real DT workshop or on an ECF platform. Although the participants were guided step-by-step through the ECF or DT procedure, they may not have perceived DT as a holistic methodology and mindset but as a way to understand problems and generate innovative solutions. However, hypothetical-choice experiments are a common procedure in an experimental design to study decision-making [Kühberger *et al.* (2002)] and have been used in a number of studies [e.g. Tietz *et al.* (2016); Weitzman (2014)]. In addition, the participants had to evaluate their digital innovation, but it is difficult to value something that is not real. Furthermore, we did not explicitly ask the participants whether they had experience with either of the two innovation methods. Participants who had such experience may have had an advantage in imagining themselves in the hypothetical-choice experiment. However, we instructed and explained the major steps of each innovation method and what the methods are used for, as part of the introduction of the experiment.

Another limitation is that our qualitative analysis is based on the participants' short answers from the experiment, as we did not follow up on the participants' ideas or concerns. This approach may have limited our understanding of the participants' answers and the generalizability of the qualitative analysis. However, the participants' answers often overlapped, so a relatively clear picture emerged.

Given the EDI approach, we assumed that anyone who is working for an organization is suitable for involvement in the innovation process and, therefore, for being part of this experiment. However, information about participants' experience regarding, for instance, digital innovation is missing.

The study is also limited in its having tested only two innovation methods — one offline method (DT) and one online method (ECF) — as guidance for future EDI. Our findings refer to this setting and not to all existing offline and online innovation methods. We equated ECF with DT as an innovation method because, with ECF, employees are encouraged to take responsibility for the future of the company, to develop an entrepreneurial spirit, and to drive cultural change [Jeltsch (2019)]. However, by using only DT and ECF as examples in this study, our intention is not to demonstrate that ECF represents a "mindset, process, and toolbox," as DT does [Brenner *et al.* (2016, p. 3)]. We considered DT as a solely non-digital innovation method, even though first solutions have been proposed for practicing DT partially digitally. However, as important factors of DT like creativity and user involvement are best practiced in a face-to-face, conventional setting [Micheli *et al.* (2018)], and research has not yet provided a way to practice DT entirely digitally, we considered DT a non-digital innovation method.

Finally, we considered the IKEA effect as our analytical lens and measured the results based on the BDM method. The IKEA effect and the BDM method have usually been applied for product innovation, rather than for digital innovations [e.g. Norton *et al.* (2012)]. Further, the IKEA effect itself can have negative consequences, as falling in love with one's own creation could lead one to overestimate its value [Thomas and Alluru (2016)]. In addition, the role of the IKEA effect in group settings has been researched only to a limited extent, which could limit our results, as DT assumes collaboration by a team [Brown (2008)]. The limited amount of research that focuses on such settings has shown that the IKEA effect is positive in groups as it relates to the jointly developed solution. Membership on a team that seeks to build a particular solution together encourages individual members to share ideas with others and get to know each other [Wolf and McQuitty (2011)]. Vuculescu *et al.* [2018] even found that the IKEA effect increases the performance of collective problem-solving compared to groups that do no experience the IKEA effect, and their conclusion that feelings of togetherness and collective problem-solving support our results. However, as research is scant, we acknowledge that the analytical foundation for the IKEA effect in groups like a DT team might not be as strong as we would have liked.

6.3. *Future research*

We position our work as a starting point for future discussions in the field of IS, especially EDI in digital innovation.

This study is a first experiment in the area of digital innovations and EDI. Future research could explore, analyze, and interpret the findings of this study across a *broader scope*. Researchers could collect primary data from participants who actually experience the scenario by means of field experiments in multiple organizations and carry out personal interviews to clarify issues and employees' decisions. Thus, valuable insights into how digital technologies support EDI and how such ecosystems can be designed can be gained.

Another suggestion involves experimentally testing *additional innovation methods* (e.g. LEGO serious play method, virtual immersive brainstorming) instead of using DT as an offline innovation method and ECF as an online innovation method, which would increase the generalizability of the results. Future research could also consider DT a "hybrid solution," where some parts of the method are executed digitally and others are executed in face-to-face settings. The comparison of a non-digital, a hybrid, and a digital innovation method in an experiment might reveal new insights involving how employees can push digital innovations.

Future research could also consider *additional theoretical perspectives*, such as that on how creativity or the number of participants involved per (digital) innovation method influences the results. For instance, Amabile's [1988] and Amabile and Pratt's [2016] well-known concept of creativity can be considered a theoretical lens for real-world ECF projects or DT workshops. We recommend taking the concept of digital creativity into account in research on creative support systems [e.g. Müller-Wienbergen *et al.* (2011); Shneiderman (2007)] to deliver valuable insights on how to involve employees in digital innovation processes.

Since our case focused on an internal digital innovation (i.e. process), future research can not only focus on internal digital innovations with reference to online innovation methods in the field of EDI but also consider *external digital innovations* or *other types of innovation* (e.g. business models).

Another suggestion has to do with our study's having analyzed how digital innovation can be developed through an employee-driven approach, such as through DT or ECF, as the focus was not on the resulting solution. Future research could shift the focus to the *innovativeness of the resulting solution* and analyze, for instance, which approaches lead to the most innovative solutions.

Finally, researchers could *combine this research stream with the stream of digital nudging* [Weinmann *et al.* (2016)] to explore how employees who do not want to be part of such processes can be encouraged to do so. The socio-technical relationship of these processes could be considered, as such a system is useful only if it is used continuously. The outcome of this study, especially in combination with digital nudging, could also be of interest to IS developers, who could collaborate with designers to address the psychological effects that can occur on such platforms.

7. Conclusion

EDI has received increasing attention from research disciplines like entrepreneurship and management [Bäckström and Lindberg (2019); Laviolette *et al.* (2016)], but research on digital innovation and EDI in the IS literature is lacking [Bäckström and Lindberg (2019)]. This paper contributes to the IS field by providing insights into the relationship between employees and the use of digital and non-digital innovation methods in the digital-innovation process. Employees value a digital innovation more when they are involved through a digital innovation method like ECF as the innovation method, but only a fraction of our experiment's participants preferred not to be involved in the digital innovation process at all. We identified six major drivers of EDI — involvement, knowledge-sharing, understanding, appreciation, fun, and personal motivation — and three barriers — lack of a sense of responsibility, lack of expertise, and lack of motivation.

References

Agostini, L., Galati, F. and Gastaldi, L. (2020). The digitalization of the innovation process: Challenges and opportunities from a management perspective. *European Journal of Innovation Management*, **23**: 1–12.

Amabile, T. M. (1988). A model of creativity and innovation in organizations. *Research in Organizational Behavior*, **10**: 123–167.

Amabile, T. M. and Pratt, M. G. (2016). The dynamic componential model of creativity and innovation in organizations: Making progress, making meaning. *Research in Organizational Behavior*, **36**: 157–183.

Bäckström, I. and Lindberg, M. (2019). Varying involvement in digitally enhanced employee-driven innovation. *European Journal of Innovation Management*, **22**: 524–540.

Becker, G. M., DeGroot, M. H. and Marschak, J. (1964). Measuring utility by a single-response sequential method. *Behavioral Sciences*, **9**: 226–232.

Brem, A. and Viardot, E. (2017). Revolution of innovation management: Internationalization and business models. *Revolution of Innovation Management*, eds. A. Brem and E. Viardot. Palgrave Macmillan, London, pp. 1–14.

Brenner, W., Uebernickel, F. and Abrell, T. (2016). Design thinking as mindset, process, and toolbox. *Design Thinking for Innovation*, eds. W. Brenner and F. Uebernickel. Springer-Verlag, Cham, Switzerland, pp. 3–21.

Brown, T. (2008). Design thinking. *Harvard Business Review*, **86**: 84–92.

Buchanan, R. (1992). Wicked problems in design thinking. *Design Issues*, **8**: 5–21.

Chesbrough, H. and Crowther, A. K. (2006). Beyond high tech: Early adopters of open innovation in other industries. *R&D Management*, **36**: 229–236.

Ciriello, R. F., Richter, A. and Schwabe, G. (2015). PowerPoint use and misuse in digital innovation. In *Proceedings of the 23rd European Conference on Information Systems, ECIS*, Münster, Germany, pp. 1–15.

Ciriello, R. F., Richter, A. and Schwabe, G. (2018). Digital innovation. *BISE*, **60**: 563–569.

Corbin, A. and Strauss, A. (1990). Grounded theory research: Procedures, canons, and evaluative criteria. *Qualitative Sociology*, **13**: 3–21.

Dohle, S., Rall, S. and Siegrist, M. (2014). I cooked it myself: Preparing food increases liking and consumption. *Food Quality and Preference*, **33**: 14–16.

Dumas, M. *et al.* (2018). *Fundamentals of Business Process Management*, Springer, Berlin.

Elerud-Tryde, A. and Hooge, S. (2014). Beyond the generation of ideas: Virtual idea campaigns to spur creativity and innovation. *Creativity and Innovation Management*, **23**: 290–302.

Erickson, L. B., Trauth, E. M. and Petrick, I. (2012). Getting inside your employees' heads: Navigating barriers to internal-crowdsourcing for product and service innovation. In *Proceedings of the 33rd International Conference on Information Systems, ICIS*, Orlando, FL, USA, pp. 1–11.

Faul, F. *et al.* (2009). Statistical power analyses using G* Power 3.1: Tests for correlation and regression analysis. *Behavior Research Methods*, **41**: 1149–1160.

Fichman, R. G., Dos Santos, B. L. and Zheng, Z. E. (2014). Digital innovation as a fundamental and powerful concept in the information systems curriculum. *MIS Quarterly*, **38**: 329–353.

Field, A. (2009). *Discovering Statistics Using IBM SPSS Statistics*. Sage, London.

Ford, R. C. and Randolph, A. (1992). Cross-functional structures: A review and integration of matrix organization and project management. *Journal of Management*, **18**: 267–294.

Frick, E., Tardini, S. and Cantoni, L. (2014). LEGO serious play applications to enhance creativity in participatory design. *Creativity in Business*, **2**: 200–210.

Fuchs, C., Schreier, M. and van Osselaer, S. M. J. (2015). The handmade effect: What's love got to do with it? *Journal of Marketing*, **79**: 98–11.

Galbreath, J. (2002). Twenty-first century management rules: The management of relationships as intangible assets. *Management Decision*, **40**: 116–126.

Gressgård, L. J. *et al.* (2014). Use of information and communication technology to support employee-driven innovation in organizations: A knowledge management perspective. *Journal of Knowledge Management*, **18**: 633–650.

Grossman, R. (2016). The industries that are being disrupted the most by digital. *Harvard Business Review*, **94**: 2–5.

Høyrup, S. (2012). Employee-driven innovation: A new phenomenon, concept and mode of innovation. *Employee-Driven Innovation: A New Approach*, eds. S. Høyrup, M. Bonnafous-Boucher, C. Hasse, M. Lotz and K. Møller. Palgrave Macmillan, London, pp. 3–33.

Høyrup, S., Redien-Collot, R. and Teglborg, A.-C. (2018). Introduction to special issue on employee-driven innovation. *International Journal of Entrepreneurship and Innovation Management*, **22**: 317–322.

Hayter, A. J. (1986). The maximum familywise error rate of Fisher's Least Significant Difference test. *Journal of the American Statistical Association*, **81**: 1000–1004.

Henderson, J. and McAdam, R. (2001). Decision making in the fragmented organisation: A utility perspective. *Management Decision*, **39**: 461–469.

Hidalgo, A. and Albors, J. (2008). Innovation management techniques and tools: A review from theory and practice. *R&D Management*, **38**: 113–127.

Horowitz, J. K. (2006). The Becker-DeGroot-Marschak mechanism is not necessarily incentive compatible even for non-random goods. *Economics Letters*, **93**: 6–11.

Huesig, S. and Endres, H. (2019). Exploring the digital innovation process: The role of functionality for the adoption of innovation management software by innovation managers. *European Journal of Innovation Management*, **22**: 302–314.

Jarvenpaa, S. L. and Ives, B. (1991). Executive involvement and participation in the management of information technology. *MIS Quarterly*, **15**: 205–227.

Jeltsch, P. (2019). Crowdfunding with employees. Available at https://blog.innosabi.com/en/crowdfunding-with-employees [accessed on 20 January 2021].

Jovanović, T. *et al.* (2017). The crowdfunding idea contest of BMW. In *Proceedings of the 26th International Association for Management of Technology Conference*, Vienna, Austria, pp. 1–15.

Kühberger, A., Schulte-Mecklenbeck, M. and Perner, J. (2002). Framing decisions: Hypothetical and real. *Organizational Behavior and Human Decision Processes*, **89**: 1162–1175.

Kaplan, B. and Duchon, D. (1988). Combining qualitative and quantitative methods in information systems research: A case study. *MIS Quarterly*, **12**: 571–586.

Kerpedzhiev, G. D. *et al.* (2020). An exploration into future business process management capabilities in view of digitalization. *Business & Information Systems Engineering*, **63**: 83–96.

Kesting, P. and Ulhøi, J. P. (2010). Employee-driven innovation: Extending the license to foster innovation. *Management Decision*, **48**: 65–84.

Kirzner, I. M. (1997). Entrepreneurial discovery and the competitive market process: An Austrian approach. *Journal of Economic Literature*, **35**: 60–85.

Kivimäki, M, *et al.* (2000). Communication as a determinant of organizational innovation. *R&D Management*, **30**: 33–42.

Klein, K. J. and Knight, A. P. (2005). Innovation implementation: Overcoming the challenge. *Current Directions in Psychological Science*, **14**: 243–246.

Knight, E., Daymond, J. and Paroutis, S. (2020). Design-led strategy: How to bring design thinking into the art of strategic management. *California Management Review*, **62**: 30–52.

Laviolette, E. M., Redien-Collot, R. and Teglborg, A. C. (2016). Open innovation from the inside: Employee-driven innovation in support of absorptive capacity for inbound open innovation. *International Journal of Entrepreneurship and Innovation*, **17**: 228–239.

Ling, I. L. *et al.* (2020). Exploring IKEA effect in self-expressive mass customization: Underlying mechanism and boundary conditions. *Journal of Consumer Marketing*, **37**: 365–374.

Müller-Wienbergen, F. *et al.* (2011). Leaving the beaten tracks in creative work: A design theory for systems that support convergent and divergent thinking. *Journal of the Association for Information Systems*, **12**: 714–740.

Marsh, L. E., Kanngiesser, P. and Hood, B. (2018). When and how does labor lead to love? The ontogeny and mechanisms of the IKEA effect. *Cognition*, **170**: 245–253.

Meissner, T. and Schuchert, S. (2017). Addressing employee barriers to BMI through workshops. In *Proceedings of the 28th ISMIM Innovation Conference, ISMIM*, Vienna, Austria.

Micheli, P. *et al.* (2018). Doing design thinking: Conceptual review, synthesis, and research agenda. *Journal of Product Innovation Management*, **36**: 124–148.

Mochon, D., Norton, M. I. and Ariely, D. (2012). Bolstering and restoring feelings of competence via the IKEA effect. *International Journal of Research in Marketing*, **29**: 363–369.

Mollick, E. (2014). The dynamics of crowdfunding: An exploratory study. *Journal of Business Venturing*, **29**: 1–16.

Muller, M. *et al.* (2013). Crowdfunding inside the enterprise: Employee-initiatives for innovation and collaboration. In *Proceedings of the Conference on Human Factors in Computing Systems, SIGCHI*, Paris, France, pp. 1–10.

Nambisan, S. and Sawhney, M. (2011). Orchestration processes in network-centric innovation: Evidence from the field. *Academy of Management Perspectives*, **25**: 40–57.

Nambisan, S. *et al.* (2017). Digital innovation management: Reinventing innovation management research in a digital world. *MIS Quarterly*, **41**: 223–238.

Nambisan, S. (2017). Digital entrepreneurship: Toward a digital technology perspective of entrepreneurship. *Entrepreneurship Theory and Practice*, **41**: 1029–1055.

Norton, M. I., Mochon, D. and Ariely, D. (2012). The IKEA effect: When labor leads to love. *Journal of Consumer Psychology*, **22**: 453–460.

Ortt, J. R. and van der Duin, R. P. (2008). The evolution of innovation management towards contextual innovation. *European Journal of Innovation Management*, **11**: 522–538.

Parjanen, S. M., Saunila, M., Kallio, A. and Harmaakorpi, V. (2020). An effective employee-driven innovation (EDI) manual process supporting innovativeness. *European Journal of Innovation Management*, in press.

Pinchot, G. (1985). Introducing the "Intrapreneur". *IEEE Spectrum*, **22**: 74–79.

Reibenspiess, V. A., Drechsler, K. and Eckhardt, K. A. (2019). A work model for employee-driven innovation in public organizations. In *Proceedings of the 27th European Conference on Information Systems, ECIS*, Stockholm, Sweden, pp. 1–15.

Rogers, E. M. (2003). *Diffusion of Innovations*. The Free Press, New York, NY.

Sarstedt, M., Neubert, D. and Barth, K. (2017). The IKEA effect: A conceptual replication. *Journal of Marketing Behavior*, **2**: 307–312.

Schoormann, T., Hofer, J. and Knackstedt, R. (2020). Software tools for supporting reflection in design thinking projects. In *Proceedings of the 53rd Hawaii International Conference on System Sciences, HICSS*, Maui, HI, USA, pp. 407–416.

Shneiderman, B. (2007). Creativity support tools: Accelerating discovery and innovation. *Communications of the ACM*, **50**: 20–32.

Simons, A., Kaiser, L. F. and vom Brocke, J. (2019). Enterprise crowdfunding: Foundations, applications, and research findings. *Business & Information Systems Engineering*, **61**: 113–121.

Skog, D. A., Wimelius, H. and Sandberg, J. (2018). Digital disruption. *Business & Information Systems Engineering*, **60**: 431–437.

Smith, P., Ulhøi, J. P. and Kesting, P. (2012). Mapping key antecedents of employee-driven innovations. *International Journal of Human Resources Development and Management*, **12**: 224–236.

Soderquist, K. E., Tirabeni, L. and Pisano, P. (2016). Exploring business model innovation's missing part: Employee-driven innovation in Cisco. In *Proceedings of the R&D Management Conference*, Cambridge, UK, pp. 1–11.

Stanford d.school (2018). Available at http://dschool.stanford.edu/resources/design-thinking-bootleg/[accessed 20 January 2021].

Thomas, M. and Alluru, J.-R. (2016). The disastrous consequences of the IKEA effect: Apple, Intel and Wang Labs learning the cost of true love. *Strategic Direct*, **32**: 8–11.

Tietz, M. *et al.* (2016). The decoy effect in reward-based crowdfunding: Preliminary results from an online experiment. In *Proceedings of the 37th International Conference on Information Systems*, Dublin, Ireland, pp. 1–11.

Tirabeni, L. and Soderquist, K. E. (2019). Connecting the dots: Framing employee-driven innovation in open innovation contexts. *International Journal of Innovation Technology and Management*, **16**: 1950031-1–1950031-27.

van Delden, C. and Chia, D. (2020). *Connect the Dots — Agile Innovation and Collaborative Ecosystems*, innosabi Publishing, München.

von Thienen, J. P. A. *et al.* (2016). Smart documentation with tele-board med. *Design Thinking Research: Making Design Thinking Foundational*, eds. H. Plattner, C. Meinel and L. Leifer. Springer-Verlag, Cham, Switzerland, pp. 203–234.

Vuculescu, O., Bergenholtz, C. and Beretta, M. (2018). The IKEA effect in collective problem solving. In *Proceedings of the Academy of Management Proceedings*, Briarcliff Manor, NY, USA.

Weinmann, M., Schneider, C. and vom Brocke, J. (2016). Digital nudging. *Business & Information Systems Engineering*, **58**: 433–436.

Weitzman, M. L. (2014). Can negotiating a uniform carbon price help to internalize the global warming externality? *Journal of the Association of Environmental and Resource Economy*, **1**: 29–49.

Westerman, G. and Bonnet, D. (2015). Revamping your business through digital transformation. *MIT Sloan Management Review*, **56**: 10–13.

Wolf, M. and McQuitty, S. (2011). Understanding the do-it-yourself consumer: DIY motivations and outcomes. *AMS Review*, **1**: 154–170.

Wolfe, R., Wright, P. M. and Smart, D. L. (2006). Radical HRM innovation and competitive advantage: The Moneyball story. *Human Resource Management*, **45**: 111–145.

Yin, R. K. (2015). *Qualitative Research from Start to Finish*. Guilford Publications, New York, NY.

Yoo, Y., Henfridsson, O. and Lyytinen, K. (2010). Research commentary: The new organizing logic of digital innovation: An agenda for information systems research. *Information Systems Research*, **21**: 724–735.

Biography

Lena Franziska Kaiser holds a PhD in Business Economics from the University of Liechtenstein. In her research she focused on digital innovation with a special focus on the involvement of different innovation actors. As a Project Manager at etventure Switzerland she drives digital innovation and transformation in business and society.

Charlotte Wehking holds a PhD in business economics from the University of Liechtenstein. In her studies she focused on business process management in the digital age especially with regard to context awareness and methods. As IT Strategy Manager at Gebrüder Weiss GmbH she works at the intersection of business and IT to drive strategic projects in the corporate IT.

Jan vom Brocke is the Hilti Endowed Chair of Business Process Management and Director of the Institute of Information Systems at the University of Liechtenstein. His research focuses on various aspects of digital innovation and transformation and is characterized by a distinct process- and design-oriented perspective. Jan has published in many of the Financial Times Top 50 journals, such as Management Science, MIS Quarterly, Journal of Management Information Systems and MIT Sloan Management Review, and he is the author and editor of best selling books such as "Business Process Management Cases. Digital Innovation and Business Transformation in Practice". He has received several international awards and held important leadership positions in Information Systems research and education. Also, Jan serves as an invited speaker and trusted advisor for many organizations around the world.

The Digital Platform as Digital Innovation: A Study from the Perspective of Dynamic Capabilities*

Marcelo Tsuguio Okano*,‡, Henry de Castro Lobo dos Santos†,§ and Edson Luiz Ursini†,¶

*Paula Souza Center and University of Campinas
Rua dos Bandeirantes 169, São Paulo, SP 01124-010 Brazil

†College of Technology, University of Campinas
Rua Paschoal Marmo 1888, Limeira, SP 13484-332, Brazil
‡marcelo.okano@cps.sp.gov.br
§h190839@dac.unicamp.br
¶ursini@ft.unicamp.br

The objective of this study is to examine how digital platforms digitally innovate companies and organizations, using the business model for dynamic capacity in three Brazilian companies. To achieve the proposed objective, a case study research method was used, with theoretical models of digital platforms, digital innovation and dynamic capabilities. The empirical research results proved that the three companies have a digital platform for business transactions as their main component, and that this model connects customers and suppliers through services.

Keywords: Digital innovation; digital transformation; digital platform; dynamic capabilities.

1. Introduction

Digital technologies present new capabilities and functionalities when launching new versions and updates of their products and services, such as the benefit of integrating different types of tests (immunoassays, chemistry, coagulation and other emerging tests such as molecular tests) in a single platform [Sista *et al.* (2008)]. The outperformance of digital platforms compared to non-digital platforms for the T790M mutation is identified in advanced non-small cell lung cancer (NSCLC) patients [Thress *et al.* (2015)]. In turn, digital media platforms have revolutionized marketing, offering new ways to reach, inform, engage, sell to, learn about and provide service to customers [Lamberton and Stephen (2016)]. While these cannot always be considered a type of innovation, in the vast majority, they represent digital innovation.

For Hinings *et al.* [2018], digital innovation is about creating and implementing new products and services; by digital transformation, we understand the combined

‡ Corresponding author.

*This chapter was originally published in International Journal of Innovation and Technology Management, Vol. 19, No. 3, March 2018, published by World Scientific Publishing, Singapore. Reprinted with permission.

effects of various digital innovations bringing new actors (and constellations of actors), structures, practices, values, and beliefs that change, threaten, replace, or complement the existing rules of the game within organizations and fields. According to Behne *et al.* [2021], growing competitive pressure as well as more mature and increasingly advanced products are making successful innovation and digitalization process of a company, one of the most important competitive factors. Digital innovation is indispensable for organizations that want to remain competitive [Kaiser *et al.* (2021)].

One of the main digital innovations is the digital platform, which is a business model that allows producers and consumers to exchange value [Mancha *et al.* (2018)], such as the identification of the change in the tourism digital behavior, which pointed to a need for rethinking the tourism and hospitality firms' digital presence [Tiago *et al.* (2021)]. In addition to transforming business models, digital innovation also leads to a change in corporate culture: digital ventures can grow at a massive rate and scale [Huang *et al.* (2017); Ciriello *et al.* (2018)].

In addition to generating dynamism in companies, digital innovation innovates all aspects and scenarios of companies and organizations quickly and efficiently through digital technologies.

To answer the research question, "How do digital platforms digitally innovate in companies and organizations", we will use a business model for dynamic capacity.

The dynamic capability method highlights the importance of incorporating the role of environmental dynamics in determining competitive advantage, especially in the way the company responds to such dynamics over time [Helfat and Peteraf (2003)].

The concept of dynamic capacity is defined as the ability to reconfigure, redirect, transform, model and adequately integrate the existing essential competencies with external resources and strategic and complementary assets, to face the challenges of a competitive and imitation world, pressed by time, and rapidly change, as defined in the seminal paper by Teece *et al.* [2007].

The objective of this paper is to verify how digital platforms innovate digitally in companies and organizations under the theoretical lens of dynamic capabilities.

To achieve this objective, the following theoretical models were used:

- Digital platform: Elements of the Platform Business Model [Mancha *et al.* (2018)],
- Characteristics of digital platforms [Mancha *et al.* (2018)], Platform business models [Morvan *et al.* (2016)] and Platforms according to their main objective [Gawer (2014); Evans and Gawer (2016)].
- Digital innovation: Framework with the company's products, its digital environment, and organizational properties [Nylén and Holmström (2015)].
- Dynamic capabilities: Business model for dynamic capabilities [Teece (2018)].

This paper presents the importance of the digital platform as a digital innovation to carry out digital transformation, which qualifies as companies and associations creating new business models and providing new value propositions such as social and sustainable, in addition to economic, thus allowing new areas of activity, types of business and organizational scenarios. For example, data are increasing in importance for firms trying to create and maintain a competitive advantage. As value creation is highly dependent on this key resource, data, the necessity of redesigning firms' business models arises [Mosig *et al.* (2021)].

These transformations are creating unprecedented forms of business, which would be impossible to implement without digital platforms, or would take a long time to be made possible, such as the digital inclusion of segments of society that were excluded or marginalized, as reported by the company Alpha, while Beta's platform combines technology and information to optimize the research, evaluation, and management of companies' social investment to help civil society organizations (CSOs). This is similar to Gamma's proposal to make the urban passenger transport system more flexible and versatile, integrating different cities, systems and modals through technology.

2. Theoretical Reference

2.1. *Digital innovation*

Innovating digitally means to innovate products, processes, or business models using digital technology platforms as a means or an end within and between organizations [Ciriello *et al.* (2018)]. According Ballestar *et al.* [2020], digitization, innovation and robotization bring productivity-augmenting effects.

According to Ciriello *et al.* [2018], digital technology has three main characteristics that change the nature of innovations. First, once digitalized, information can be stored, transformed, transmitted and tracked by any digital device, regardless of its content [Yoo *et al.* (2010)]. Second, digital information is editable through reprogramming, making digital solutions liable to change after implementation through interaction with external systems [Kallinikos *et al.* (2013)]. Third, inherently self-referential, digital technology is necessary to create digital technology [de Reuver *et al.* (2018); Yoo *et al.* (2010)].

Nambisan *et al.* [2017] considered that the definition of digital innovation is intended to capture three important and simultaneous phenomena. First, digital innovation includes a range of innovation results, such as new products, platforms and services, as well as new customer experiences and other value paths; as long as these results are possible through the use of digital technologies and digitized processes, the results themselves need not be digital. Second, digital innovation includes a wide range of tools and digital infrastructure (for example, 3D printing, data analysis, mobile computing, etc.) to make innovation possible. Third, digital innovation includes the possibility that the results can be disseminated, assimilated, or adapted to specific contexts of use such as those typically experienced with digital platforms.

Nylén and Holmström [2015] proposed a framework that identifies the following five key areas to be measured and evaluated in the search for managing the innovation of digital products and services:

- First, digital products and services must not only be efficient and easy to learn, but also provide a rich user experience. This user experience can be measured in terms of usability, aesthetics and involvement.

- Second, companies need to clearly articulate the value proposition of each digital product and service. The quality of such value propositions is assessed in the dynamics of customer segmentation, product and service packages and commissions to channel owners.
- Third, scanning the digital evolution involves collecting intelligence on new devices, digital channels such as web services, mobile operating systems, social media and app stores, as well as standards and application programming interfaces (APIs), to identify and explore opportunities for innovation in emerging usage contexts and new user behaviors.
- Fourth, as digital innovation requires new skills, companies need to assess their mechanisms to support the continuous learning of the unique properties of digital technologies in order to establish dynamic innovation teams.
- Fifth, and finally, how digital innovation processes are often initiated when members of the organization improvise with digital technology in the form of learning by doing, assessing the space and time available for improvisation, and the mechanisms for coordinating these efforts, are critical.

Table 1 presents the framework of the company's products, digital environment and organizational properties.

Nylén and Holmström [2015] developed a diagnostic tool that helps companies take the first step in implementing the structure (see Appendix A). Based on the structure, the tool consists of 15 Likert-type questions. Here, members of the organization are asked to score the company's current operations, assigning a value on a scale of 1–3 for three questions in each key area. For each area, the participants were asked to calculate and complete the composite score.

2.2. *Digital platform*

According to Mishra and Tripathi [2020], a digital platform is a web-centric platform for delivering content (such as, Facebook, Twitter, blogs, websites and, sometimes, SMS)and a significant portion of the world's population spends time online every day using these digital platforms [Yee *et al.* (2007)]. The paper by Vardarlier and Ozsahin [2021] demonstrates the digital transformation of human resource management by digital platforms, through the use of modern communication tools (LinkedIn, Workplace, Microsoft teams and so on), digitally connecting employers and candidates in the recruiting process. Further, digital platforms also help diffusing innovation [Claussen and Halbinger (2020)].

This contrasts with an analog platform, including billboards, direct mail, telemarketing, events and word of mouth. A promotion is the message you would use on platforms to communicate. This could sponsor manufactured goods or facilities, and interconnect them on digital and analog platforms.

On the other hand, a digital technology platform is "a building block, providing an essential function for a technological system — which acts as a basis on which other companies can develop complementary products, technologies or services" [Gawer (2014); Yoo *et al.* (2012)]. Digital business platforms are being developed

Table 1. Framework with the company's products, its digital environment and organizational properties [Nylén and Holmström (2015)].

Dimension	Area	Scope	Element
Product	User experience	Digital products and services must offer high levels of usability, possess carefully designed aesthetic properties and evoke engagement.	Usability Aesthetics Engagement
	Value proposition	Digital innovation involves an articulated value proposition, i.e. a customer segmentation including strategic pricing and positioning of the product portfolio, dynamic bundling of product units and carefully negotiated commissions to channel owners.	Segmentation Bundling Commissions
Environment	Digital evolution scanning	In order to identify opportunities for innovation, firms need to scan their digital environment. This involves gathering information on new digital devices, channels and associated user behaviors.	Devices Channels Behaviors
Organization	Skills	In order to reap the benefits of digital innovation, firms need to acquire new skills both internally and externally while establishing new digital roles. In doing so, firms should promote continuous learning of the unique properties of digital technologies in order to secure dynamic innovation teams.	Learning Roles Teams
	Improvisation	The malleability and low cost of digital technologies affords a higher degree of improvisation. As a consequence, managers need to ensure that they provide organizational members with an improvisational space where structure and flexibility is balanced in such a way that the constraints maximize creativity, dedicated time is given, and improvisational efforts are coordinated to deal with overlaps and waste.	Space Time Coordination

with the aim of pleasing and satisfying users, and being user friendly [Gomes and Okano (2019)].

For Mancha *et al.* [2018], a digital platform is a business model with enabled technology allowing producers and consumers to exchange value. In a platform business (Fig. 1), producers and consumers create and exchange value through the platform in the form of information (for example, reviews, behavioral data) and products or services (e.g. use of a good transportation service).

The main characteristics of digital platforms are as follows:

(1) They are external platforms based on software and hardware.
(2) Applications offer services or systems to end users.
(3) Through the Internet, they allow the interaction of different groups of people, companies and organizations.
(4) They innovate with new business models that are intrinsically based on information and technology features.
(5) They create value by allowing direct communication and interaction between groups.

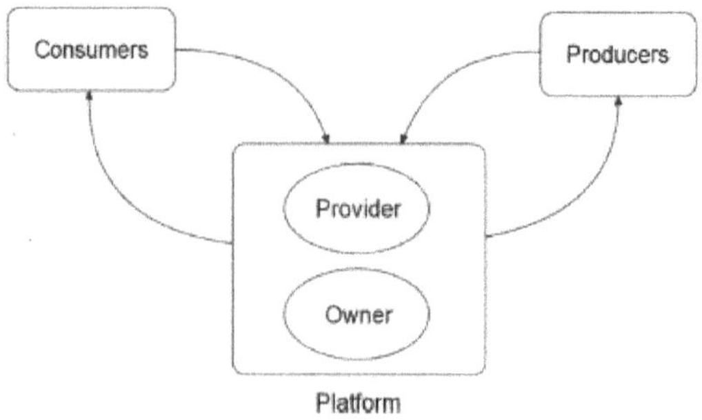

Fig. 1. Elements of the platform business model [Mancha *et al.* (2018)].

Morvan *et al.* [2016] classified digital platforms according to the platform business models, that is, according to collaboration, orchestration, creation and correspondence:

- Collaboration is a type of platform business model that allows internal and/or external partners in the business ecosystem to work together in new ways. For example, FirstBuild allows instructors to share inventions with a community, and obtain feedback. Collaboration can also take place within the same ecosystem (such as the government), or between different ecosystems (such as the government and financial services).
- Orchestration is a business model that allows business processes in a business ecosystem. Orchestration platforms can also integrate with the platforms of other partners in the business ecosystem, such as supply chain partners and suppliers. For example, PokitDok allows seamless transactions to take place between healthcare providers, producers and consumers. It orchestrates and connects activities such as scheduling, identity management, connectivity and payments to the business ecosystem.
- Creation is a type of platform business model that allows partners in the business ecosystem to create new applications, products/services, resources and business models. For example, Apple HealthKit provides APIs for developers who can take advantage of the health and activity data from iPhones and Apple Watches. Developers can create mobile apps for iOS and watchOS. YouTube allows providers to create and share content with consumers. In this way, consumers can become suppliers.
- Match is a business model that allows providers to find consumers. For example, Uber connects users with drivers. Airbnb connects owners with people who need a place to stay.

Regarding the classification of digital platforms, Evans and Gawer [2016] and Gawer [2014] classify them according to their main objectives, identifying three different types of platforms:

(1) Transaction platform, sometimes called multi-sided markets or trading platforms. Its main objective is to facilitate transactions between different

organizations, entities and individuals such as connecting buyers with sellers, drivers with passengers, composers with music companies, etc.

(2) Innovation platform. Innovation platforms are formed by technological blocks that provide a basis for the development of services and products. A typical example of an innovation platform is the Android mobile operating system, which allows third-party developers to build applications on top of the operating system. Innovation platforms provide third-party developers with their own set of tools and resources that developers combine and use to enable new applications for commercial or other uses [Evans and Gawer (2016)].

(3) Integration platform. Integration platforms combine aspects of the two main types of platforms: transaction and innovation platforms [Evans and Gawer (2016)].

2.3. *Business model for dynamic capacity*

Teece's definition [2010] emphasizes the value creation function of a business model:

- A business model describes the design or architecture of the mechanisms for creating, delivering and capturing the values employed. The essence of a business model is that it crystallizes customer needs and ability to pay, defines the way in which the company responds and offers value to customers, attracts customers to pay the value, and converts those payments into profits through the project and operation of the various elements of the value chain [Teece (2010, p. 179)].

Identifying customers' unmet needs, specifying the technology and organization that will serve them, and finally, capturing the value of activities are important functions of the business model. Without the right balance between creation, delivery and capture, the model will not be in operation for long, at least not by for-profit companies. While the model is similar to that of Osterwalder and Pigneur [2020], it is later compiled into three main categories [Teece (2018)]. Slightly adapted, the list is as follows:

- Value proposition: Product and service; Customer needs; Geography.
- Revenue model: Pricing logic; Channels; Customer interaction.
- Cost model: Essential assets and capabilities; Main activities; Partner Network.

Teece [2018] considered that dynamic capabilities include the detection, apprehension and transformation necessary to design and implement a business model. They can allow a company to update its common resources and direct them, as well as partner resources, to high-return ventures. This requires developing and coordinating, or "orchestrating" the resources of the company (and partner companies) to address and shape changes in the market or in the business environment in general.

The strength of a company's dynamic capabilities determines the speed and degree (and associated cost) of aligning the company's resources, including its business model (s) with the customer's needs and aspirations. To achieve this alignment, organizations must be able to seize opportunities continuously, by periodically transforming organizational and cultural aspects to proactively encounter threats and opportunities Teece [2018].

According to Teece [2018], "strong dynamic capabilities" generally mean strong (in relation to competitors) in all relevant areas of detection, seizure and transformation. A company with strong dynamic capabilities will be able to profitably build and renew common resources, assets and capabilities, reconfiguring them as needed to innovate and respond to (or bring about) changes in the market. The company's resources must be smartly orchestrated and coordinated with the activities of partner companies to deliver value to customers. Dynamic capabilities are supported in part by organizational routines and processes, the gradual evolution of which is punctuated by non-routine management interventions.

The dynamic capabilities structure is a multidisciplinary model of a company with dynamic capabilities at its core, reflecting this interdependence. A simplified version of the structure, omitting feedback channels, such as that between the organization's design and dynamic capabilities, is shown in Fig. 2. Dynamic capabilities and strategies combine to create and refine a defensible business model, which guides organizational transformation. Ideally, this leads to an adequate profit level to allow the company to sustain and improve its capabilities and resources [Teece (2018)].

Business models are enabled by dynamic features in the sense that an organization with dynamic capabilities will be able to quickly implement, test and refine new and revised business models. Successful implementation is based on architectural management design, asset orchestration and learning functions, which are essential dynamic resources. At the same time, dynamic capabilities depend in part on the

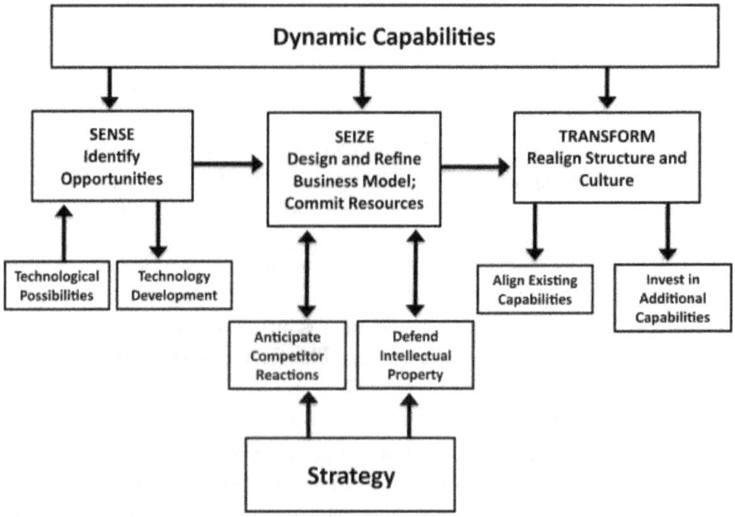

Fig. 2. Simplified scheme of dynamic capabilities, business models and strategy [Teece (2018)].

organizational flexibility allowed or denied by business model choices, such as outsourcing the manufacturing of a new product, or building a factory [Teece (2018)].

Management's ability to develop and refine business models is a central microfoundation of dynamic capabilities for both the original model, and to replace and recombine elements of the model over time [Teece (2007), (2018)].

An initial step for the innovative company is to note the existence of customers with unmet needs who are willing and able to pay for a product or service that can correct their situation. A successful business model provides a solution to the customer, which can afford a price high enough to cover all costs and leave a satisfactory profit [Teece (2018)].

3. Methodology

The research method chosen was the case study, because it has increased chances of addressing the proposed research question, meeting the research objectives and the study can be conducted with the necessary methodological rigor [Dresch *et al.* (2015)]. As noted by [Yin (2018)], the case study is suitable for research scenarios that aim to answer questions such as "how" and "why", with a low possibility of controlling the event observed by the researcher. Furthermore, according to Miguel [2007], the case study is an empirical study that investigates a certain phenomenon, usually contemporary, within a real life context, when the boundaries between the phenomenon and the context are not clearly defined.

Mainly, all types of case studies try to clarify why certain decisions were made, how they were implemented, and what results were achieved [Yin (2018)].

The research evidence points were documents provided by companies and organizations, websites and Internet documents, and interviews with a semi-structured script with open questions extracted from the theoretical models of the literature review.

Data collection was carried out from July 2019 to June 2020, with six respondents from three companies. The details of the interviewees are listed in Table 2.

3.1. *Companies and organizations*

(1) Alpha

Alpha was born out of the need to provide peripheral neighborhoods in the Brasilândia region with a transport service (São Paulo neighborhood with an HDI of

Table 2. Characteristics of the interviewees.

Interviewee	Company	Role
E1	Alpha	CIO (founder)
E2	Alpha	CFO
E3	Beta	CFO (founder)
E4	Beta	Project manager
E5	Gamma	CIO
E6	Gamma	Developer

0.762, according to the Municipality of São Paulo [Prefeitura de São Paulo (2017)]. When the popular transport apps decided to block these regions for lack of security due to robberies and thefts, the founder saw an opportunity and created an app for this region about two years ago. The service started simply through a landline and a WhatsApp mobile phone, with drivers awaiting calls in a waiting room. The service accepts credit and debit cards as well as cash as payment.

The calculation system is much more rudimentary than that of Uber. The price of the drive is determined only by the distance measured between the start and finish points on Google Maps. The prices charged by Alpha at the beginning were similar to those charged by Uber. Each kilometer traveled was charged R $2.00, against R $1.80 for Uber, which also charges a municipal fee.

According to Alpha's founder, the driving requirements are similar to those of other transport applications: A 2010 or newer car model, with four doors and five seats, clean and with air conditioning. However, even when it comes to cleaning, it is necessary to consider the particularity of Alpha, whose cars are required to travel through streets usually without asphalt.

Alpha currently has 400 registered drivers and a fleet of approximately 60 cars. Of these, about 20 work only for Alpha, while the rest are also divided into other transportation apps.

(2) Beta
Beta was born from the feelings of uneasiness and frustration of its founding partners, who saw relevant social proposals being shelved by the lack of resources. Through the Access to Information Law, they analyzed investment data via incentive laws, especially the Rouanet Law, from 1991 to the present day. They found that in practice, 71% of the 182 000 projects that requested incentive funds in Brazil remained on paper, and 50% of the resources that could be made available by companies were not directed.

Beta provides a platform that combines technology and information to optimize the research, evaluation and management of a company's social investment. With an intelligent data management system related to more than 30 000 social initiatives, it is possible to have a complete view of the ecosystem of cultural, sports and health projects approved in incentive laws in Brazil since 1992. Thus, the company contributes to the strategic decisions of sponsors and social projects, connecting the ends efficiently, and generating a positive impact on society.

The startup's clients include companies such as Bayer, Kroton, Facebook, Heineken and Via Varejo, among others. Entrepreneurs generate the potential to target $ 250 million for projects. With a team of 17 employees, Beta currently has 33 corporate clients, and more than 80 social organizations have received resources via the platform, including the Choir of Small Singers of Camaçari, Virada Sustentável and UNAS — Union of Nuclei, Associations of Residents of Heliópolis and Region.

(3) Gamma
In 2015, one of Gamma's founders read a story that showed eight types of industries that could disappear by 2020. Two of them were credit cards and wallets. This initiated the idea of a payment means capable of integrating the urban

transport system as a whole, allowing the user to access various modes and services through a single device, the smartphone. With this platform, people can buy credits and manage them using cell phones in a simple and fast way. The idea turned into a final course work at college, and became a real project.

"*I looked at my wallet and only the bus pass card was left. Why is this not yet on my phone?(E6)*"

Gamma is a startup that provides exclusive means of payment for public transport, and can integrate the urban passenger transport system on a global scale. The proposal is to make the urban passenger transport system more flexible and versatile, integrating different cities, systems and modes through technology.

The company's project aims to replace money, cards, tickets and passes through the mobile application. By creating an account within the system, the user purchases and manages credits and uses the smartphone itself in the transport validator. All public means of transportation will be available in the program, such as buses, subways, trains, bicycles, ferries and trams, in any city that operates with it, including in other countries.

The application eliminates the need for the population to go to a ticket window, terminal, or machinery to purchase or load credit cards for tickets. This also reduces public expense. In addition, it promises to be a safer system than the current one, since the chances of fraud decrease.

4. Results and Analysis

4.1. *Digital platform*

To characterize the technological products of the companies surveyed as a digital platform, the following theoretical models were used, as presented in Table 3.

The results of the interviews indicated that the three companies use digital platforms, connecting customers to suppliers to obtain a value proposition. While Alpha's platform is developed by another company, the others are self-developed; the platform owners are the companies themselves.

The three platforms are composed of hardware and software, offer services to end users and organizations, creating value for customers and suppliers, and the business model works under the platform.

What all three companies have in common are being transaction platforms and a business model of platform as correspondence (match); that is, they connect customers and suppliers. The business models innovate in their respective areas, the products offered are services and companies have clearly mapped the values and segments of customers.

4.2. *Digital innovation*

The framework of Nylén and Holmström [2015] allowed the diagnosis of the companies surveyed in five key areas: user experience, value proposition, scanning digital evolution, skills and improvisation. The answers are provided in Appendix B.

Table 3. Digital platform.

	Alpha	Beta	Gamma
(a) Elements of the platform's business model [Mancha *et al.* (2018)]			
(a.1) Consumers	Residents of Vila Brasilândia	Are the companies (sponsors) that want, or that usually donate part of the resources for payment of taxes.	Public transport users
(a.2) Producers	Drivers	Organizations (proponents) that struggle to raise money with projects	Public transport concessionaires
(a.3) Supplier	Outsourced companies	Beta	Gamma
(a.4) Owner	Alpha	Beta	Gamma
(b) Characteristics of digital platforms [Mancha *et al.* (2018)]			
(b.1) Are they external platforms based on software and hardware?	The company uses business platforms based on software and hardware	The company uses business platforms based on software and hardware	The company uses its own digital platform for one of the applications and also has a chatbot on Facebook
(b.2) Do the applications offer services or systems to end users?	The company offers a transport service through an application for residents of the Brasilândia village	A system that manages to connect the need for social projects from all over the country to the capital of large companies and searches for projects that are relevant to their investment through the platform that collects and analyzes data through robots allocated in different public bases involved with the incentive laws, at the federal, state and municipal levels	"We use social networks and artificial intelligence so that users can purchase credits for their transport cards without having to download applications or spend a data plan. (E6)"

Table 3. (*Continued*)

	Alpha	Beta	Gamma
(b.3) Does it allow the interaction, through the Internet, of different groups of people, companies and organizations?	Yes	Yes	Yes
(b.4) Do you innovate with new business models that are intrinsically based on information and technology features?	Yes	Yes	Yes
(b.5) Creates value by allowing direct communication and interactions between groups.	Yes	Yes	Yes
(c) Platform business models [Morvan *et al.* (2016)]	Match	Match	Match
(d) Platforms according to their main objective [Gawer (2014); Evans and Gawer (2016)]	Transaction platform	Transaction platform	Transaction platform

In relation to the user experience, companies are concerned with offering customers a pleasant and friendly experience with an application design that has the ability to adjust and optimize, that considers the characteristics and format of each device, speed of use, ease of use and attractive and captivating look. The three companies agreed to use user experience in their products, as can be seen from the experience and role of the interviewees, see Table 2.

As for the value proposition, customer segments are well defined and digital profits are obtained according to the value proposition of the three companies described below. Alpha offers decent transport to Vila Brasilândia residents, as other applications avoid the area, which is considered a risk area. Beta strengthens the connection between the first, second and third sectors by developing a new way of thinking and directing resources through incentive laws. Gamma is bringing competitiveness to the country's public transport, adding value and facilities to customers. The value propositions are clear, and aligned with the goals of digital platforms.

The digital evolution scan is used in its entirety by two companies, and partially by the third to identify and explore opportunities for innovation in emerging contexts of usage and new user behaviors. At Alpha, in the beginning, the technology used by customers was the free multi-platform instant messaging application WhatsApp. Currently, WhatsApp continues to be used, but the platform and application are being used for customer relationships and social networks such as Facebook, Twitter and Instagram. At Beta, the digital platform collects data through robots distributed in different public places related to incentive laws at the federal, state and municipal levels. For this, the team of developers is looking for new technologies and solutions for AI, deep learning, etc., and Gamma is always looking for new payment methods to be introduced on its own or third-party platforms.

Digital innovation requires new skills; the three companies considered it important to continue looking for new technologies and stated that they are always evaluating their mechanisms to support the continuous learning of the unique properties of digital technologies, in order to establish dynamic innovation teams.

Regarding improvisation, respondents from the three companies agreed that the first technological products started in the form of learning by doing, where the available resources had to be managed and improvised.

The companies Alpha, Beta and Gamma demonstrated a high commitment to digital innovation, and it was possible to diagnose that the companies are investing in the five areas surveyed.

4.3. *Dynamic capabilities*

To analyze the dynamic capabilities, Teece's [2018] business model for dynamic capabilities was used, as a successful business model provides a solution to the client that can support a price high enough to cover all costs and leave a satisfactory profit [Teece (2018)]. Business models are enabled by dynamic features in the sense that an organization with dynamic capabilities will be able to quickly implement, test and refine new and revised business models.

4.3.1. *Simplified scheme of dynamic capabilities, business models and strategy*

(1) Sense

(i) Identifying opportunities

The three companies reported in the interviews that the companies were born from opportunities identified in the community or from the owners' perceptions. Alpha was born from the need to supply peripheral neighborhoods in the Brasilândia region with an application-based transport service. When the most popular apps decided to block these regions, the founder saw an opportunity to create an app. Beta was born from the discomfort and frustration of its founding partners, who saw relevant social proposals being shelved due to a lack of resources. Thus, they saw the opportunity to offer notices of social projects to organizations that could carry them out. The CEO of Gamma (E5) read a report that showed eight types of industries that could disappear by 2020. Two of them were credit cards and wallets. "I looked at my wallet and all that was left was the bus card. Why is it not yet on my cell phone?" he asked. This question led to the idea of a means of payment capable of integrating the urban transport system as a whole, allowing the user to access various modes and services through a single device, the smartphone. With this platform, people can buy credits and manage them using cell phones in a simple and agile way.

(ii) Technological possibilities

According to Teece [2018], it takes time for business model innovation to reach technological possibilities, perhaps because business models are more context-dependent than technology-dependent. According to the interviews, the companies did not use all technological possibilities from the beginning. At Alpha, service started simply: orders were received through a landline and a WhatsApp cell phone, while drivers waited for a call in a waiting room. Beta started with Internet searches for the notices of social projects across the country, and later evolved into a digital platform. At Gamma, the company's project aims to replace cash, cards, tickets and passes through the mobile application. When creating an account within the system, the user buys and manages credits, and uses the smartphone itself in the transport validator. These accounts of company beginnings reveal that companies did not start with digital platforms, but rather, evolved to reach this point.

(iii) Technology development

The companies surveyed reported that they developed the technologies needed for business models. Alpha initially developed a digital platform app for transportation, and then complemented it with an app for food delivery and payments. Beta created a platform that combines technology and information to optimize the research, evaluation and management of a company's social investment. Gamma's technological value proposition is to develop solutions for the online recharge of public transport cards through the application or through Facebook.

(2) Seize

(i) Design and refine BM

According to Teece [2018], dynamic resources and strategies combine to create and refine a defensible business model that guides organizational transformation. Ideally, this leads to an adequate level of profits, allowing the company to sustain and enhance its capabilities and resources. Alpha's business model could be the same as that of other transportation app companies, but the characteristics of the region, such as no streetsigns, uneducated and humble residents who may not know how to use smartphones, led the founders to adapt their operations, such as having a phone number to serve customers, and having resident drivers who know all the streets to drive them. Beta's business model has as its main value proposition to strengthen the connection between the first, second and third sectors by developing a new way of thinking to direct resources through incentive laws. Companies that hire the social impact startup start a process of managing taxes intelligently and quickly; organizations, in turn, now have the resources to take important projects off the ground. Gamma is a startup that provides exclusive means of payment for public transport, and is able to integrate the urban passenger transport system on a global scale. The proposal is to make the urban passenger transport system more flexible and versatile, integrating different cities, systems and modes through technology.

(ii) Commit resources

The three companies responded that they were committing resources to new projects. Committed to the Brasilândia region, Alpha is creating two more delivery services for the area. Beta and Gamma are investing in their respective digital platforms and human resources to scale and improve services.

(iii) Anticipating competitors' reactions

- Alpha — Yes
- Beta — Yes
- Gamma — Yes

(iv) Defending intellectual property

- Alpha — Yes
- Beta — Yes
- Gamma — Yes

(3) Transform

(i) Realigning structure and culture

The changes caused by the new business models forced companies to realign the structures and cultures of the new scenarios. Alpha focuses on serving Brasilândia and maintains an alternative for people with reading difficulties through the

WhatsApp service and the call center, in addition to investing in two new delivery services for the region. Beta started as consulting and advisory services for investments in social projects. With the launch of the platform, Beta focused on offering correspondence services (match) between companies that wish to invest in projects and companies that have social projects, effectively collaborating with the socio-environmental responsibility strategies of the private sector, offering investment auditing and adding more reliability to the entire process. Gamma emerged with the objective of digitizing public transport systems, improving the passenger experience through payment methods, and with the experience gained in the market, began to develop solutions for online recharge of public transport cards via the app or chatbots on social networks.

(ii) Investing in additional resources

All three companies are investing in new resources to enable new business models. Alpha intends to take its project to other peripheral regions with mobility difficulties similar to those in Brasilândia, and has launched an application for food delivery. Beta intends to launch an index that works as a national ranking of project scores, considering the social impact generated and the investments made by the companies. Based on APIs to enable and facilitate integration, the Gamma ticket is integrated with telemetry, applications and chatbots. Digital Ticketing is based on the Account-Based Ticketing concept, where each customer has an account in the system that allows integration with any other agreed modal. That is, the true billing of Cloud Mobility as a Service (MaaS).

The theoretical model of Teece [2018] made it possible to understand the business models of companies based on dynamic capabilities, and thus prove that dynamic capabilities include the detection, apprehension and transformation necessary to design and implement a business model, thus allowing a company to update its common resources and direct them, as well as the resources of partners, to high-return ventures.

5. Conclusion

The results of the empirical research showed that Alpha, Beta and Gamma have a digital platform as their main component, use the digital platform for business transactions, and connect customers and suppliers through their services. The companies' business models are based on current technologies, and these technologies contribute to their digital profit.

The case studies showed that digital platforms help companies and organizations to offer social value propositions, such as in the case of Alpha, which offered its users a service not provided by other applications due to security. Similarly, Beta's platform allows CSOs to find companies that want to sponsor social projects, while Gamma makes the urban passenger transport system more flexible, versatile and democratic digitally.

The concern and focus of companies on digital innovation is justified by the continuity of business, which has been proven by investments in new projects, new technologies and technological solutions.

The theory of dynamic capabilities made it possible to understand how processes such as the ability to reconfigure resources and organizational skills, a quick and flexible response and providing a competitive advantage, resulting from digital innovation applied on a digital platform, create value for the company, and thus achieve the objective of this paper.

The academic contribution of this paper is to encourage the discussion that digital platforms are innovating companies and associations with new business models, and creating new value propositions that cause social innovation. The study further provides an analysis of the effects and capabilities of digital platforms to innovate through the theoretical lens of dynamic capacity, which can help companies and associations in future endeavors.

As a suggestion for future research, it is suggested to analyze how other technological products innovate digitally. For instance, a Digital Twin, in literal translation, is a virtual version of a physical object or even an organizational process. The Digital Twin solution is designed to optimize inspection and optimization activities.

Acknowledgment

This study was financed in part by the Coordenação de Aperfeiçoamento de Pessoal de Nível Superior — Brasil (CAPES) — Finance Code 001.

Appendix A. Diagnostic Tool [Nylén and Holmström (2015)]

Table A.1.

		I do not agree	Partially agree	Accept	Score	Diagnosis (low score) with point 0 or 1
User experience						
Usability	Our digital products and services are easy to learn and interact with.	1	2	3	0	The user experience of products and services included in the company's current product portfolio needs to be redesigned.
Aesthetics	They have articulated aesthetic properties that evoke a positive emotional response.	1	2	3	0	
Engagement	They are created to offer our customers meaningful experiences.	1	2	3	0	
		Composite measure: 0				
Value offer						
Segmentation	We analyzed our customer base and divided it into several segments.	1	2	3	0	The company's digital profits can be increased by reconfiguring the value proposal inscribed on the company's products and services.
Package	The components of our digital portfolio of products and services are differentiated and the limits and relationships among them are clearly specified.	1	2	3	0	
Commissions	We continuously evaluate and negotiate our relationships with channel owners.	1	2	3	0	
		Composite measure: 0				
Digital evolution scanning						
Devices	We carefully follow which new hardware components and devices are under development.	1	2	3	0	The company needs to develop evolving digital scanning mechanisms.
Channels	We follow the evolution of digital distribution channels (for example, software platforms, operating systems and web services).	1	2	3	0	

Table A.1. (*Continued*)

		I do not agree	Partially agree	Accept	Score	Diagnosis (low score) with point 0 or 1
Behaviors	We pay attention to emerging user behaviors in contexts and markets.	1	2	3	0	
		Composite measure: 0				
Skills						
Learning	We promote continuous learning of the unique properties of digital technologies.	1	2	3	0	The company needs to acquire new skills internally and externally while promoting continuous learning.
Functions	The balance between general digital skills and specialized digital functions is adequate.	1	2	3	0	

Appendix B. Responses to the Nylén and Holmström [2015] Framework

Table B.1.

		Alpha	Beta	Gamma
User experience				
Usability	Our digital products and services are easy to learn and interact with.	3	3	3
Aesthetics	They articulated aesthetic properties that evoke a positive emotional response.	3	3	3
Engagement	They are created to offer our customers meaningful experiences.	3	3	3
Value offer				
Segmentation	We analyzed our customer base and divided it into several segments.	2	3	3
Package	The components of our digital portfolio of products and services are differentiated and the limits and relationships between them are clearly specified.	3	3	3
Commissions	We continuously evaluate and negotiate our relationships with channel owners.	2	2	2
Digital evolution scanning				
Device	We carefully follow which new hardware components and devices are in development.	3	3	3
Channels	We follow the evolution of digital distribution channels (for example, software platforms, operating systems and web services).	3	3	3
Behaviors	We pay attention to emerging user behaviors in different contexts and markets	3	3	3
Skills				
Learning	We promote continuous learning of the unique properties of digital technologies.	3	3	3
Functions	The balance between general digital skills and specialized digital functions is adequate.	3	3	3
Times	We can bring teams together with the right combination of skills for each digital project.	3	3	3
Improvisation				
Space	We try to organize the work so that structure and flexibility are balanced.	3	3	3
Time	We dedicate time to improvisation efforts in each profession.	3	3	3
Coordination	We have mechanisms to coordinate improvisation efforts.	3	3	3

References

Ballestar, M. T., Camiña, E., Díaz-Chao, Á. and Torrent-Sellens, J. (2020). Productivity and employment effects of digital complementarities. *Journal of Innovation & Knowledge*, **6**, 3: 177–190, Available at https://doi.org/10.1016/j.jik.2020.10.006.

Behne, A., Beinke, J. H. and Teuteberg, F. (2021). A framework for cross-industry innovation: Transferring technologies between industries. *International Journal of Innovation and Technology Management (IJITM)*, **18**, 3: 1–27.

Ciriello, R. F., Richter, A. and Schwabe, G. (2018). Digital innovation. *Business & Information Systems Engineering*, **60**, 6: 563–569.

Claussen, J. and Halbinger, M. A. (2021). The role of pre-innovation platform activity for diffusion success: Evidence from consumer innovations on a 3D printing platform. *Research Policy*, **50**, 8: 103943.

de Reuver, M., Sørensen, C. and Basole, R. C. (2018). The digital platform: A research agenda. *Journal of Information Technology*, **33**, 2: 124–135.

Dresch, A., Lacerda, D. P. and Miguel, P. A. C. (2015). Uma análise distintiva entre o estudo de caso, a pesquisa-ação e a design science research. *Revista Brasileira de Gestão de Negócios*, **17**, 56: 1116–1133.

Evans, P. and Gawer, A. (2016). *The Rise of the Platform Enterprise: A Global Survey*, The Emerging Platform Economy Series, No. 1.The Center for Global Enterprise. New York, NY, USA

Gawer, A. (2014). Bridging differing perspectives on technological platforms: Toward an integrative framework. *Research Policy*, **43**, 7: 1239–1249.

Gomes, J. G. C. and Okano, M. T. (2019). Plataformas digitais como modelos de negócio: Uma pesquisa exploratória. *South American Development Society Journal*, **5**, 13: 232.

Helfat, C. E. and Peteraf, M. A. (2003). The dynamic resource-based view: Capability lifecycles. *Strategic Management Journal*, **24**, 10: 997–1010, doi: 10.1002/smj.332.

Hinings, B., Gegenhuber, T. and Greenwood, R. (2018). Digital innovation and transformation: An institutional perspective. *Information and Organization*, **28**, 1: 52–61.

Huang J., Henfridsson O., Liu M. J. and Newell S. (2017) Growing on steroids: rapidly scaling the user base of digital ventures through digital innovation. MIS Q **41**, 1: 301–314.

Kaiser, L. F., Wehking, C. and vom Brocke, J. (2021). How to organize digital innovation? The role of involvement, structure, and technology. *International Journal of Innovation and Technology Management (IJITM)*, **18**, 3: 1–22.

Kallinikos, J., Aaltonen, A. and Marton, A. (2013). The ambivalent ontology of digital artifacts. *MIS Quarterly*, **37**, 2: 357–370.

Lamberton, C. and Stephen, A. T. (2016). A thematic exploration of digital, social media, and mobile marketing: Research evolution from 2000 to 2015 and an agenda for future inquiry. *Journal of Marketing*, **80**, 6: 146–172.

Mancha, R., Gordon, S. and Iyer, B. (2018). Figayou pursues a platform strategy: A case study of digital platform entrepreneurship. *Journal of Information Technology Case and Application Research*, **20**, 2: 55–70.

Miguel, P. A. C. (2007). Estudo de caso na engenharia de produção: Estruturação e recomendações para sua condução. *Production*, **17**, 1: 216–229.

Mishra, S. and Tripathi, A. R. (2020). Literature review on business prototypes for digital platform. *Journal of Innovation and Entrepreneurship*, **9**, 1: 1–19.

Morvan, L., Hintermann, F. and Vazirani, M. (2016). Five ways to win with digital platforms. G-20 Young Entrepreneur Alliance.

Mosig, T., Lehmann, C. and Neyer, A. K. (2021). Data-driven business model innovation: About barriers and new perspectives. *International Journal of Innovation and Technology Management (IJITM)*, **18**, 2: 1–32.

Nambisan, S.*et al.*. (2017). Digital Innovation Management: Reinventing innovation management research in a digital world. *MIS Quarterly*, **41**, 1: 223–238.

Nylén, D. and Holmström, J. (2015). Digital innovation strategy: A framework for diagnosing and improving digital product and service innovation. *Business Horizons*, **58**, 1: 57–67.

Osterwalder, A. and Pigneur, Y. (2020). *Business Model Generation: Inovação Em Modelos De Negócios.* Alta Books (in Portuguese). Rio de Janeiro, RJ, Brazil

Prefeitura de São Paulo. (2017). A dinâmica do IDH-M e suas dimensões entre 2000 e 2010 no município de São Paulo, p. 29. Informes Urbanos (in Portuguese).

Sista, R., Hua, Z., Thwar, P., Sudarsan, A., Srinivasan, V., Eckhardt, A., ... and Pamula, V. (2008). Development of a digital microfluidic platform for point of care testing. *Lab on a Chip*, **8**, 12: 2091–2104.

Teece, D. J. (2010). Business models, business strategy and innovation. *Long Range Planning*, **43**, 2–3: 172–194.

Teece, D. J. (2018). Business models and dynamic capabilities. *Long Range Planning*, **51**, 1: 40–49.

Teece, D. J. (2007). Explicating dynamic capabilities: The nature and micro-foundations of (sustainable) enterprise performance. *Strategic Management Journal*, **28**, 13: 1319–1350.

Teece, D. J., Pisano, G. and Shuen, A. (1997). Dynamic capabilities and strategic management. *Strategic Management Journal*, **18**, 7: 509–533.

Thress, K. S., Brant, R., Carr, T. H., Dearden, S., Jenkins, S., Brown, H., ... and Barrett, J. C. (2015). EGFR mutation detection in ctDNA from NSCLC patient plasma: A cross-platform comparison of leading technologies to support the clinical development of AZD9291. *Lung Cancer*, **90**, 3: 509–515.

Tiago, F., Gil, A., Stemberger, S. and Borges-Tiago, T. (2021). Digital sustainability communication in tourism. *Journal of Innovation & Knowledge*, **6**, 1: 27–34.

Vardarlier, P. and Ozsahin, M. (2021). Digital transformation of human resource management: Social media's performance effect. *International Journal of Innovation and Technology Management*, **18**, 3: 2150005.

Yee, N., Bailenson, J. N., Urbanek, M., Chang, F. and Merget, D. (2007). The unbearable likeness of being digital: The persistence of nonverbal social norms in online virtual environments. *CyberPsychology & Behavior*, **10**, 1: 115–121.

Yin, R. K. (2018). *Estudo De Caso: Planejamento E Métodos*. Bookman, Porto Alegre.

Yoo, Y. *et al.* (2012). Organizing for innovation in the digitized world. *Organ Science*, **23**, 5: 1398–1408.

Yoo, Y., Henfridsson, O. and Lyytinen, K. (2010). Research commentary: The new organizing logic of digital innovation: An agenda for information systems research. *Information Systems Research*, **21**, 4: 724–735.

Biography

Marcelo T. Okano is Permanent Professor of Professional Master in Productive Systems, holds PhD degree in Production Engineering from UNIP and PhD Degree in Business Administration from EAESP/FGV. Research areas are innovation, ICT and business.

Henry de Castro Lobo Dos Santos is a Doctorate Student at School of Technology - Unicamp with a Master degree in Technology from Campinas State University. He works with data networks and information security. His research area are innovation, ICT, business, queuing models, data traffic, discrete event simulation, continuous simulation and performance analysis.

Edson L. Ursini is an Associate Professor at School of Technology, Unicamp with a doctoral degree in Electrical Engineering(electronics and communications) from Campinas State University. He works with data networks, stochastic processes, queuing models, teletraffic and data traffic, discrete event simulation, continuous simulation, fuzzy logic systems, performance analysis, innovation, ICT and business.

Global Diffusion of Innovation during the Fourth Industrial Revolution: The Case of Additive Manufacturing or 3D Printing*

Harm-Jan Steenhuis*, Xin Fang† and Tolga Ulusemre‡

Hawaii Pacific University
College of Business 900 Fort St. Mall
Suite 600, Honolulu, HI 96813, USA
**hsteenhuis@hpu.edu*
†xfang@hpu.edu
‡tulusemre@hpu.edu

Additive manufacturing can be considered an innovative and high-technology and one of its characteristics is that it has limited dependency on the location. The purpose of this study is to examine this aspect by investigation how additive manufacturing is spreading globally. The focus is on established manufacturers of industrial additive manufacturing machines. It was found that the early-stage diffusion of this technology is primarily in advanced economies. Furthermore, many of the currently established companies that manufacture industrial 3D printers come from already existing companies that expanded into AM or that led to spin-off companies. The complexity of AM which requires expert knowledge across a range of fields may be the key reason for this finding. Recommendations for further research are provided.

Keywords: Additive manufacturing; 3D printing; industrialization; technological development; innovation.

1. Introduction

After the first industrial revolution based on steam power from roughly 1790 until 1840, a second industrial revolution based on electricity from roughly 1890 to 1930, and a third industrial revolution based on informatics which started around 1970 [von Tunzelmann (1997)], the world is currently experiencing a fourth industrial revolution that started at the turn of the century [Schwab (2016)]. This fourth revolution is fundamentally different from the previous three as it is based not on a technology but on the fusion of technologies and their interactions across the physical, digital and biological domains [Schwab (2016)]. One of the drivers of this revolution is additive manufacturing (AM), also known as 3D printing [Schwab (2016)].

Although AM is not just one technology, i.e. there are seven process categories [Redwood *et al.* (2017)], these seven categories share a commonality namely that

*Corresponding author.

*This chapter was originally published in International Journal of Innovation and Technology Management, Vol. 17, No. 1, March 2018, published by World Scientific Publishing, Singapore. Reprinted with permission.

AM involves a process of additively building up a part one layer at a time [Redwood *et al.* (2017)]. The AM industry in 2016 had a size of roughly $6 billion [Wohlers Associates (2017)] and it is expected to grow to almost $24 billion by 2025 [Grand View Research (2018)]. Manufacturing with AM provides several advantages such as cost benefits and simpler processes to produce complex products [Atzeni *et al.* (2010)] and these characteristics have a range of implications across many industries [Steenhuis and Pretorius (2017); Caviggioli and Ughetto (2019)].

AM has been the topic of academic studies related to business, for instance, through special issues of Technological Forecasting and Social Change [Ford *et al.* (2016)] and the Journal of Manufacturing Technology Management [Ortt (2016)] in 2016, the International Journal of Physical Distribution & Logistics Management [Rogers *et al.* (2017)] and the Journal of Manufacturing Technology Management [Ortt (2017)] in 2017, and the International Journal of Manufacturing Technology and Management in 2018 [Rayna and Striukova (2018)]. Since AM is not just one technology but a bundle, and because it has a variety of aspects, studies have looked at AM from many different perspectives. Some studies have looked at the economics of AM, e.g. Atzeni and Salmi [2012] and Niaki *et al.* [2019], improvements in production [Marzi *et al.* (2018)] and many studies have looked at AM in the context of the supply chain, e.g. Oettmeier and Hofmann [2016], Chan *et al.* [2018], Martinsuo and Luomaranta [2018] and Fratocchi [2018] and related to the business models, e.g. Öberg *et al.* [2018], Woodson *et al.* [2019], as well as how AM can be disruptive, e.g. Rayna and Striukova [2016] and Beltagui *et al.* [2020]. Other areas that have received attention are the consumer or prosumer side of things, e.g. de Jong and de Bruijn [2013], Fox [2014], Matias and Rao [2015], Steenhuis and Pretorius [2016], Halbinger [2018], Kleer and Piller [2019] and law and intellectual property [Ballardini *et al.* (2018); Kannattukunnel (2016)] or society related issues, e.g. Smith [2017], Matos and Jacinto [2019]. What has received less attention is the geography of the AM innovation, i.e. how it has spread. This geography aspect is the topic of this paper. Next, in Sec. 2 the literature on innovation will be covered and the research questions are developed. This is followed by an explanation of the methodology used in Sec. 3, the findings in Sec. 4 are followed by a discussion in Sec. 5. The conclusion is provided in Sec. 6.

2. Innovation

Innovation is important for society and is often considered a key factor in economic development [Porter (2003); Artz *et al.* (2010)]. As such, policies on innovation, e.g. Wydra [2015], Morgan and Nauwelaers [2003] as well as the processes of innovation diffusion, e.g. Ortt and Schoormans [2004] and Rogers [1995] and innovation adoption, e.g. Hossain *et al.* [2016], Adams *et al.* [2017]; Ebrahimi Sarcheshmeh *et al.* [2018] and Baiyegunhi *et al.* [2019], have received significant academic attention. High technology has received specialized attention as the adoption of high technology adds several complications to the adoption process, see e.g. Chiesa and Frattini [2011], Moore [2014] and Aarikka-Stenroos and Lehtimäki [2014]. Although the definition of high technology is far from straight forward [Hooton (2018)], AM can be considered high technology due to the newness, novelty and complexity.

Additive manufacturing provides a fairly unique (high) technology situation to study in the context of innovation and geography. This is because 3D printers are used in the production process, that is, can be considered machine tools. The machine tool industry is often considered an important industry for industrial and economic development [Kaplan (1987); Saxena and Sharma (2014)]. This explains why locations with less developed machine tool industries are less economically developed. However, AM has a very low dependency on location [Gress and Kalafsky (2015); Hannibal and Knight (2018)] and can be applied in virtually any location. For instance, AM has been used in a rural location in Nepal that was struck by an earthquake [Scott and Simple (2015)], it has been used in the Sahara desert [Nikolov (2017)], and even in space [Goldstein (2018)]. Furthermore, regions that are challenged by a limited spread of manufacturing can benefit from do-it-yourself (DIY) [Fox (2014)] which is enhanced by AM. For instance, in the US AM has led to maker societies [Anderson (2012)]. Another peculiarity of AM is that it can replicate itself, i.e. a 3D printer can be used to print additional 3D printers [Jones *et al.* (2011)].

With a goal to examine the spread of the AM innovation, this study, therefore, deals with elements of innovation and diffusion. Academic research on innovation and its diffusion can be separated in a few main research streams that have been developed historically. One research stream is that of the origin of innovation. This can be seen as the supply side of innovation. Main theoretical views on the origin or the process of innovation include the linear model, see Fig. 1, with its origins traced back to the first half of the 20th century [Godin (2006)] and the chain-linked model [Kline and Rosenberg (1986)]. Subsequent studies have reassessed the validity of these theoretical models, e.g. Balconi *et al.* [2010] or suggested modifications such as the cyclic innovation model [Berkhout *et al.* (2006)] and the multi-channel interactive learning model [Caraça *et al.* (2009)]. Studies have also focused on specific actors in the innovation process such as the importance of lead users [Von Hippel (1986)] and the role of universities [Jaffe (1989)]. Research continues in each of these aspects of the innovation process which have led to refinements in understanding, see for example on the lead user aspect [Von Hippel (2005); Hienerth *et al.* (2014); Kankanhalli *et al.* (2015); Brem *et al.* (2018)] and on the role of universities [Cowan and Zinovyeva (2013); Chen *et al.* (2019)].

Another important research stream is that of the diffusion of innovation. This can be viewed as the demand side of innovation. A comprehensive view is provided by Rogers [1995], see Fig. 2. This stream of research examines the process by which users adopt an innovation. Some studies relate to narrower models compared to Rogers [1995] such as the Technology Acceptance Model which is specific to the acceptance by users of information technology [Davis (1989)]. Research on innovation diffusion is extensive and has many different angles. Recent studies cover for

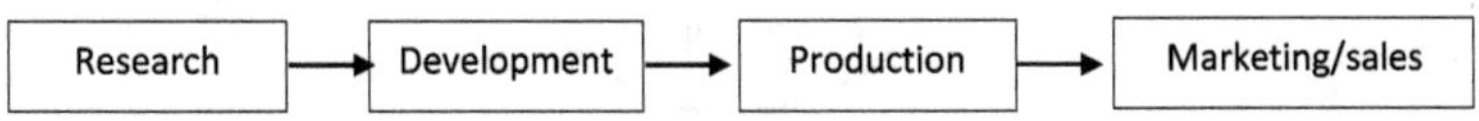

Fig. 1. Linear model of innovation.

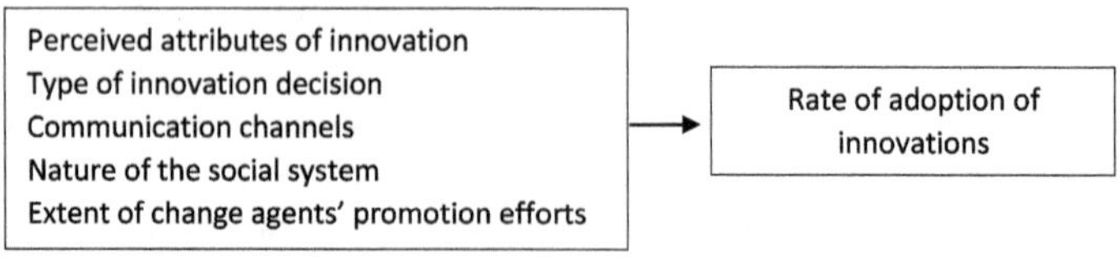

Fig. 2. Innovation diffusion variables, adopted from Rogers [1995].

instance diffusion of innovations with specific characteristics such as frugal innovation [Hossain *et al.* (2016)] or energy technologies [Hyysalo *et al.* (2017)], diffusion in a particular industry such as automotive [Schulze *et al.* (2015)], and decision maker characteristics for example relating to the not-invented-here syndrome [Hannen *et al.* (2019)]. Research into the diffusion of innovation related to technology platforms [Fichman (2004); Cenamor *et al.* (2013)] provides an overlap with studies on the origin of innovation as in particular open-source platforms provide insight into both the creation as well as the diffusion of technology [Foster and Heeks (2013); Kwak *et al.* (2018); Oh and Hong (2018)].

A third related stream of research into innovation and its diffusion is that of commercialization of the innovation in the context of business which relates to entrepreneurship and intrapreneurship. Examples of topics that are investigated in this research area are academic entrepreneurs and what makes them start companies [Krabel and Mueller (2009)], how universities can help [Fini *et al.* (2011)] and the type of companies created [Pirnay *et al.* (2003); Minshall and Wicksteed (2005); O'Shea *et al.* (2005)]. Similar studies exist for other types of research organization [Clarysse *et al.* (2005); Khanagha *et al.* (2018)] as well as for corporate spin-off companies [Yeganegi *et al.* (2016)].

The purpose of this study is to look at a recent high-technology innovation, i.e. additive manufacturing, and examine its global spread in the context of business situations. Based on the three identified research streams related to the diffusion of innovations, the current study relates to the overlap of these three areas as illustrated in Fig. 3.

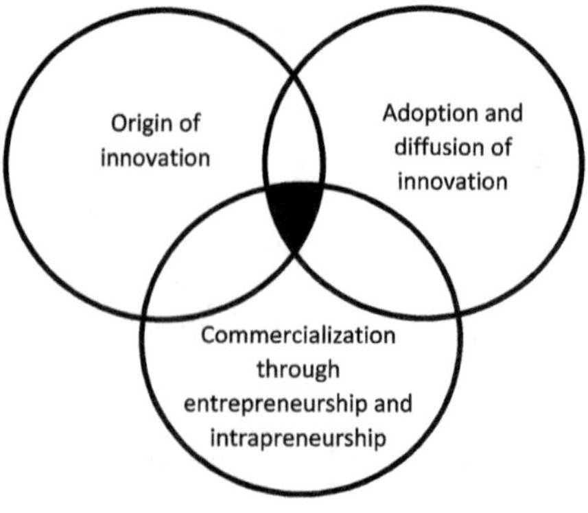

Fig. 3. Identification of the research area.

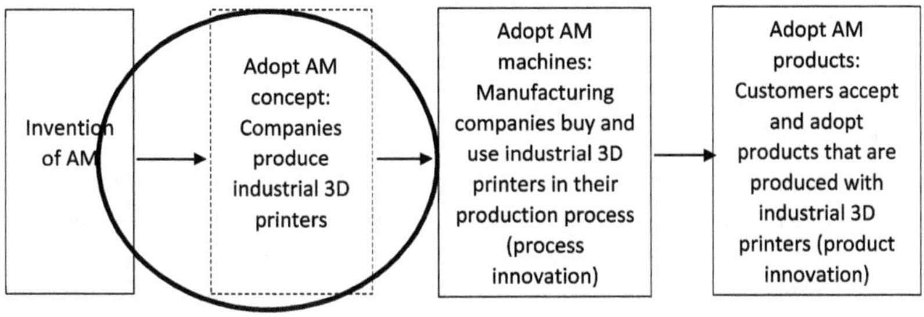

Fig. 4. Focus of the research.

The focus is on the location of innovative companies that produce and sell these new, industrial type, AM machines. Specifically, the central research question is: where are the successful companies that develop and sell industrial AM machines located? The emphasis is on exploring where and how these companies were formed. This is illustrated in Fig. 4.

Figure 4 illustrates that there are different stages of adoption of AM. After the invention of AM, the first stage of adoption is that of companies that adopt the idea or concept of AM and use it to produce industrial 3D printers. This is indicated with a dotted line box in Fig. 4 to emphasize the unusual nature of this step. This is because AM machines are created which are then used to produce products rather than immediately creating final products. The next stage is where companies accept and adopt AM by acquiring an industrial 3D printer for their production process, see e.g. Schniederjans [2017], Candi and Beltagui [2019], Marak *et al.* [2019]. This adoption of AM is going slowly and can be viewed as dealing with the chasm that occurs with diffusion of high technology [Moore (2014)]. The communication efforts of the companies that produce industrial 3D printers typically relate to explaining how AM can be (financially) beneficial for manufacturing companies. The last stage of adoption is that of customers who adopt or accept a 3D printed product [Norman *et al.* (2017); Lyu *et al.* (2018); Anastasiadou and Vettese (2019)]. This adoption also faces difficulties, for instance, the acceptance of 3D printed houses is faced with challenges because of uncertainties related to the safety, durability, etc. of 3D printed construction.

It is important to stress that the study is not focused on the adoption of 3D printed products, nor on the adoption of industrial 3D printers. The connection between Figs. 3 and 4 is that typical studies that focus on the "creation" of an innovation are on the left side of Fig. 4. Studies that focus on the diffusion of innovation are typically dealing with the right two blocks of Fig. 4. Studies that focus on commercialization through entrepreneurship or intrapreneurship typically focus on the first and third blocks in Fig. 4. The goal of the study is to determine the location of the production of industrial 3D printers and to subsequently investigate the reason behind this location which relates to the second and partially the first block in Fig. 4. In the following sub-sections, the four research questions and related theories are covered: innovative locations (covered in Sec. 2.1), innovation and entrepreneurship (Sec. 2.2), spin-off companies (Sec. 2.3) and academic spin-off companies (Sec. 2.4).

2.1. *Innovative locations*

It has long been recognized that different locations have different innovative outputs [Feldman and Florida (1994)]. For instance, a typical example of a location that is considered very innovative is Silicon Valley. It has also been established that higher innovation rates, in terms of patents, are linked to higher productivity levels that support higher wages [Porter (2003)]. What has been a focus in academic studies is to find out why these differences occur which has led to numerous studies in the field, see e.g. de la Mothe and Paquet [1998], Feldman [1994], Audretsch and Feldman [1996], Audretsch [1998], Kuchiki and Tsuji [2010] and Zanello *et al.* [2016]. Porter and Stern [2001] sum up the main conclusion: "the vitality of innovation in a location is shaped by national innovative capacity". This national innovative capacity relates to three broad elements: the common innovation infrastructure, the cluster-specific environment for innovation and the quality of linkages [Porter and Stern (2001)]. What this means is that for example the presence of research universities [Mowery and Ziedonis (2014)] but also the agglomeration and proximity of companies, see Kuchiki and Tsuji [2010] and Balland *et al.* [2015], and people, see Orlando and Verba [2005], play a role in creating innovations and related to this economic development for instance through higher income levels. Note that for instance Varga [1998] found for the US that there are four tiers of Metropolitan Statistical Areas (MSA) and that while a $ 0.5 million university research spending can be expected to yield 20 innovations in an average top MSA, this value is only 2 in the fourth tier MSA. Based on the above, when looking at the national level it can be expected that most innovations take place in already developed nations and/or nations that have well-developed technologies. Consequently, it can be expected that innovative companies that operate in the AM industries are located in those countries. However, developed nations may, due to for example outsourcing of certain activities have eroded their industrial commons and consequently may have lost the critical mass of work, skills and scientific knowledge [Pisano and Shih (2009)]. Also, AM may have less dependency on location. Thus, AM may not fit the general pattern. The first research question deals with this issue and is formulated as follows: in what type of countries are AM companies located?

2.2. *Age of companies*

Aside from the issue of the type of country where innovation occurs or is diffused/adopted, another issue is the type of firm that exhibits innovative behavior. This relates to the size or age of the firm. These two variables are connected, i.e. companies less than 10 years old tend to be smaller while companies over 10 years old tend to be larger [Breitzman and Hicks (2008)]. Entrepreneurs, in the sense of new firms, are often viewed as a main source for innovation, see e.g. Miller and Garnsey [2000], and young firms rather than small firms make the largest contribution to job creation [Coad *et al.* (2016)]. However, data for instance for the US reveals that roughly 60% of private-sector innovations originate in large businesses, i.e. more than 500 employees, and only 16% in firms with fewer than 25 employees [Breitzman and Hicks (2008); Information Technology & Innovation Foundation (2016)]. Also, young firms are less persistent in their innovative behavior [García-Quevedo *et al.* (2014)]. However, younger [Balasubramanian and Lee (2008)] and smaller [Breitzman and Hicks (2008); Shane (2016)] firms tend to be more productive in terms of innovations. This leads to the second research question: what types of companies are active in the industrial AM industry, in particular in terms of age?

2.3. *Origin of companies*

As discussed in Sec. 2.2, while some industrial AM companies may have already been established, i.e. larger and older, some companies in this new and innovative field may be new, i.e. a start-up situation. Establishment of new firms is an important mechanism through which entrepreneurs use technology to bring new products into existence [Shane (2001)]. There are different types of start-up companies such as university- and company spinoffs, see e.g. Lindhold Dahlstrand [1997] and Wennberg *et al.* [2011]. Schramm [2018] identified three types of start-up companies and provides the following rough estimation in terms of percentages of start-up firms: 5% of entrepreneurs are what many people think of as start-ups, that is, companies created by young high-tech wizards such as Bill Gates (Microsoft), Steve Jobs (Apple) and Mark Zukerberg (Facebook). 15% of the entrepreneurs are company employees in spin-out situations either because the existing company decides to dispose that line of business or because the employees decide to strike out on their own due to lack of support in the company for a new idea, product or service. 80% of startups are replicative, i.e. copy an already existing idea. Half of those are created as franchises, the other half are unaffiliated retail businesses. While this last category of firms is unlikely to occur in the AM industry, the first two categories, i.e. high tech entrepreneurs and spin-out situations are more likely to occur [Goehrke (2019)]. Entrepreneurs seem to particularly have a role in the formation of entirely new industries around technological innovation [Miller and Garnsey (2000)]. This could apply to the AM industry. In terms of spin-off start-ups, previous research from Sweden on technology-based firms concluded that as many as two-thirds of the spin-offs had originated in private firms, and only one-sixth from universities [Lindhold Dahlstrand (1997)]. However, another study indicated that about 55% of new technology-based firms were academic spin-offs while 45% were corporate spin-offs [Löfsten and Lindelöf (2005)]. This leads to the third research question: for those AM companies that were start-ups, what type of startup situation do they represent?

2.4. *Academic spin-off companies*

A specific type of start-up situation is the academic spin-off company. With the basic idea of knowledge economies, universities are considered an important source of innovative activity [Miyata (2000)] and component of regional economic development [Steenhuis and Gray (2006); Trani and Holsworth (2010)]. Universities play a role in firm creation, e.g. through academic spin-off companies [Steffensen *et al.* (1999); Fini *et al.* (2011); Ferretti *et al.* (2019)] but also in other forms of knowledge spillovers [Khanagha *et al.* (2018); Mowery and Ziedonis (2014); Hsu and Yuan (2013)]. For instance, one study found that the number of graduates of a university is the main source of university spillovers that explains new business location near universities [Acosta *et al.* (2011)]. Another study found that local pools of graduates in biophysical sciences did not have a significant impact on the location choice of academic entrepreneurs [Kolympiris *et al.* (2015)]. Also, new knowledge and technology-based firms in general, i.e. not necessarily academic spin-off companies, have a high propensity to locate close to universities [Audretsch *et al.* (2005)]. There are different definitions for academic spin-off companies, mostly relating to whether technology and/or people related to a university are at the core of the new company [Carayannis *et al.* (1998); Pirnay *et al.* (2003)]. In this study, the people connection is used and therefore academic spin-offs are those where people connected to a university start a new company.

It has previously been established that universities with higher quality research tend to be more innovative [Miyata (2000); Zahringer *et al.* (2017)]. Similarly, academic spin-offs are more likely to occur for more eminent universities [Di Gregorio and Shane (2003)]. Research has also shown that many academic entrepreneurs locate spin-off companies close to the university but that academic entrepreneurs at later stages of their career are considerably more likely to start their firm away from their academic homes. This leads to the fourth research question: from what type (level) of university did the academic spin-off companies originate? And, related to this, is the spin-off located in the university's vicinity?

3. Methodology

The research questions posed, and thus the study in general, are exploratory in nature. The purpose is to look at a recent high technology innovation, i.e. additive manufacturing, and look at its global spread in the context of established innovative companies that develop, produce and sell industrial type AM machines. In this regard, four research questions were formulated related to: in what types of countries the companies are located, their age, for new companies the type of start-up, and for academic start-ups the type of university it relates to and whether it is located in the vicinity of the university.

There are five main research strategies, i.e. survey, experiment, case study, grounded theory approach and desk research [Verschuren and Doorewaard (2005)]. Since the data that is sought is mostly secondary data, the desk research strategy was selected.

The focus in the study is on established companies that produce industrial AM machines. This means, there has to be some recognition of their established position. To determine the sample for the study, a main industry source [Wohlers Associates (2017)] was used which identifies the important globally established companies. A total of 33 companies are recognized in Wohlers Associates [2017]; however, three of these have become subsidiaries of other companies. Arcam and Concept Laser

Table 1. Sample of established industrial AM companies.

North American companies	European companies	Other
Carbon	Additive Industries	Aspect
Cincinnatti	AddUp	Carima
Envision TEC	DWS Systems	Farsoon
ExONE	EOS	Stratasys
Formlabs	Lithoz	Tiertime
GE Additive	Mcor	Xery
HP	Prodways	
Markforged	ReaLizer	
Optomec	Renishaw	
Skiaky	Sisma	
3D Systems	SLM Solutions	
	Trumpf	
	Voxeljet	

were both acquired by GE Additive [Anderson Goehrke (2016)] while Solidscape was acquired by Stratasys [Andorka (2011)]. Therefore, the sample for the study contains 30 companies, as shown in Table 1.

Data were mainly collected from company websites. Most of the established companies that produce industrial 3D printers have websites that include a section on their location, start-up history, etc. Where necessary, additional information was sought by searching online. Stories, for example interviews with company founders, frequently appeared in industry newsletters such as: 3dprint (https://3dprint.com), 3dprintingindustry (www.3dprintingindustry.com/), All3DP (https://all3dp.com), Fabbaloo (www.fabbaloo.com) and Sculpteo (www.sculpteo.com/en/).

To determine the type of country, three sources were used. The World Bank provides a classification of economies based on the income level, i.e. Gross National Income (GNI) per capita. Four types of economies are distinguished in terms of GNI/capita: Low-income countries ($1025 or less), lower middle income ($1026–$4035), upper middle income ($4036–$12 475), and high income ($12 476 or more) [World Bank (2017)]. Therefore, the World Bank's World Development Indicators [World Bank (2017)] is used as one source to classify countries. Another type of classification is provided by Porter [1990] who classifies economies based on the sources in an economy that cause its industries to be internationally competitive. The World Economic Forum (WEF) applies this distinction of factor-driven, efficiency-driven and innovation-driven economies and, therefore, the WEF's Global Competitiveness Report [World Economic Forum (2017)] is used for determining this classification. Since the topic, AM, can be considered high-technology, another source used for country classification is the high-technology indicators [Porter *et al.* (2008)]. This source provides country rankings in terms of high technology.

For the universities, two world rankings were used: the QS World University Ranking 2018[a] and the Times Higher Education World University Rankings 2018.[b]

[a] https://www.topuniversities.com/university-rankings/world-university-rankings/2018.
[b] https://www.timeshighereducation.com/world-university-rankings/2018/world-ranking#!/page/0/length/25/sort_by/rank/sort_order/asc/cols/stats.

Both of these are established rankings that provide insight into the (perceived) quality and eminence of the universities. Additional variables such as age, and the type of start-up were determined from the available data, i.e. company websites, and thus these were not related to one main source. Based on the above description and data presented below, there is a high reliability of the study, i.e. the findings can easily be checked and the study repeated with the same result.

4. Findings

The four research questions are answered below, i.e. country of companies (Sec. 4.1), age of companies (Sec. 4.2), type of start-up (Sec. 4.3), universities for academic start-ups (Sec. 4.4). In each of these sections, the findings are presented and discussed in the context of the literature.

4.1. *Location of the companies*

The location of the main industrial 3D printer companies is shown in Fig. 5. This illustrates that there is a concentration in Europe and in the US. Additionally, there are some companies located in Asia. In the analysis, one company, i.e. Stratasys, was determined to be located in Israel. This is somewhat debatable. Stratasys was initially founded in the US. In 2012, Stratasys merged with Israel-based Object and the new headquarters were determined to be in Israel. That is why, in Table 1 and Fig. 5, Stratasys was classified as a company that is located in Israel. There is no prominent 3D printer company in Latin America, Africa or Australia. Companies in the US are mostly on the east side of the country.

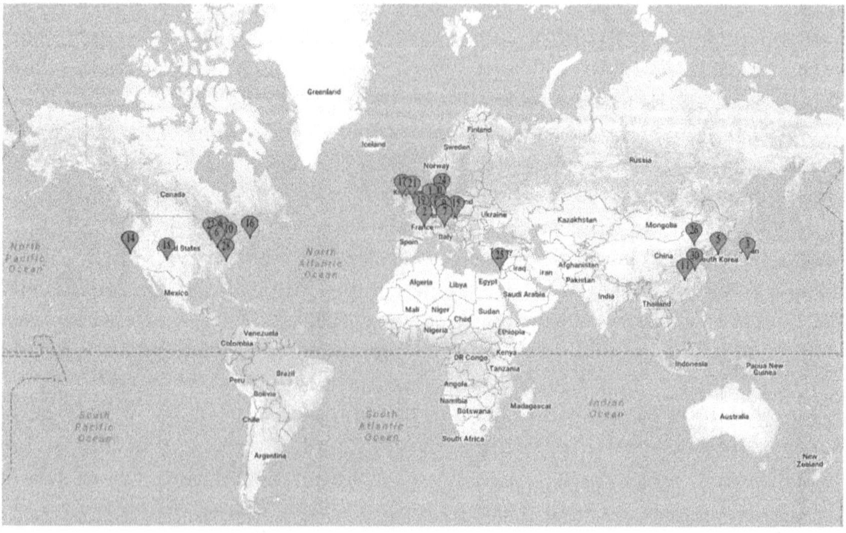

Fig. 5. Location of established industrial AM companies.

Table 2. Countries in which established industrial AM companies are located.

Country	Number of companies	Stage of development based on GNI	Stage of development based on source	High technology ranking
USA	11	High income	Innovation-driven	2
Germany	5	High income	Innovation-driven	3
China	3	Upper-middle income	Efficiency-driven	1
Italy	2	High income	Innovation-driven	17
France	2	High income	Innovation-driven	5
Ireland	1	High income	Innovation-driven	14
Israel	1	High income	Innovation-driven	18
Austria	1	High income	Innovation-driven	n.a.
Netherlands	1	High income	Innovation-driven	9
South Korea	1	High income	Innovation-driven	6
UK	1	High income	Innovation-driven	7
Japan	1	High income	Innovation-driven	4

Table 2 shows the number of companies per country and the classification of the country. This shows that in terms of country location, established AM companies are mostly in advanced countries. The one exception is China which has a lower income level, and is also at the efficiency-driven stage instead of the innovation-driven stage. There is some linkage of the Chinese companies and other countries, see also Fig. 6. For instance, Farsoon is a company that operates in the field of powder bed fusion, more specifically selective laser sintering. Farsoon's founder Xu Xiaoshu is a Chinese American who worked as technology director for several American leading laser sintering manufacturing companies before founding Farsoon.[3]

The comparison with the high-tech indicators ranking in Table 2 shows that many of the companies are based in countries that have top high-technology standing ranking.

These findings show that although AM has less dependence on location [Gress and Kalafsky (2015); Hannibal and Knight (2018), the established companies are still confirming theories that explain that advanced economies are more likely to have innovations [Zanello *et al.* (2016)]. However, this does not mean that AM does not exist in developing countries. For instance, Brahma3 is an Indian 3D printer company (www.brahma3.com). Perhaps what it explains more is that companies that produce 3D printers need advanced knowledge that is more likely to be available in innovation-driven economies. It may also relate to the challenges of companies in countries other than innovation-driven economies with becoming an established global company. This relates to the source of the competitive advantage of industries [Porter (1990)] and with a high technology such as AM, it is more likely that the most innovative and economically established countries are able to develop companies that are main competitors in the global marketplace. The exception to this is China, which is not considered an innovation-driven economy. However, China ranked first in the high-tech indicators, and it has a large population which may explain why China is the exception to the rule.

Also noteworthy are countries that are missing from Table 2. Note that while Austria is represented in Table 2, it was not part of the high-tech indicators. Notable countries that are missing from Table 2 are: Singapore (ranked 8th), Taiwan (10),

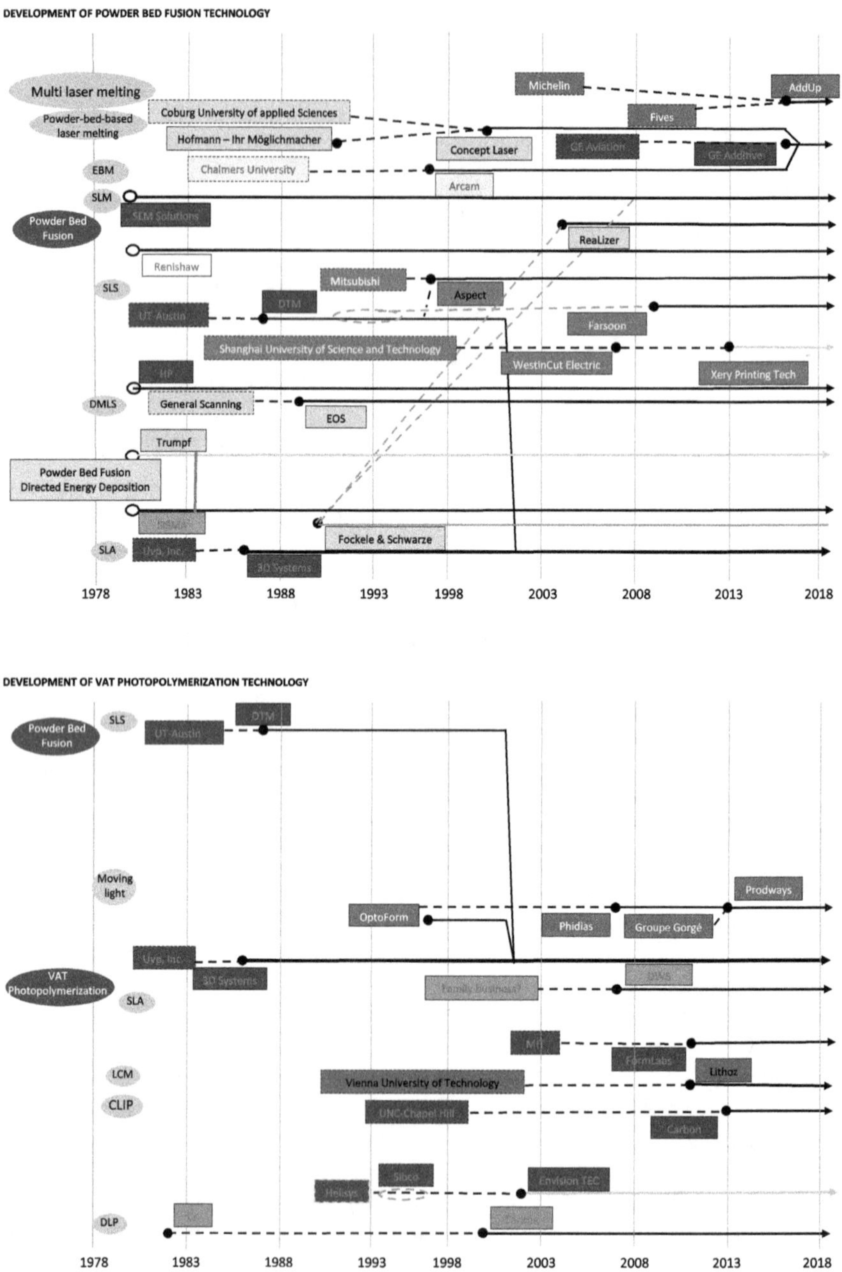

Fig. 6. Historical development of industrial 3D printer companies in different AM technologies.

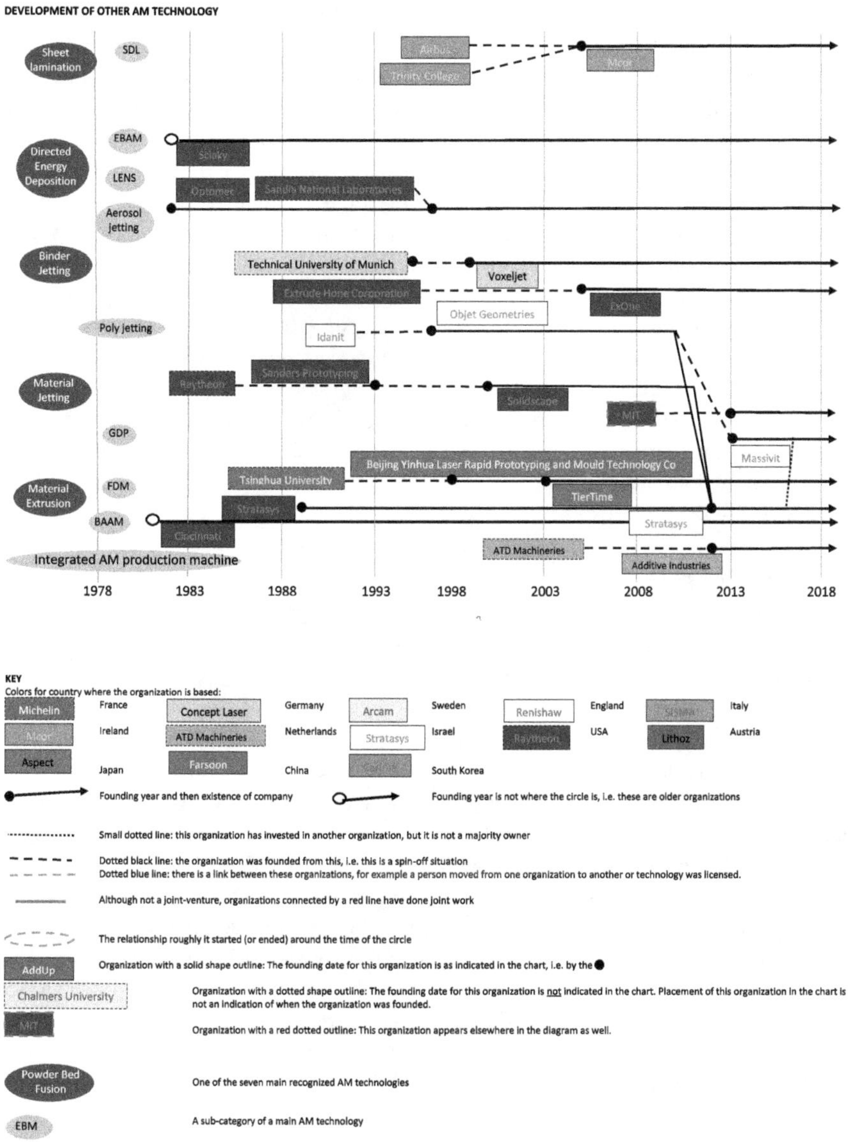

Fig. 6. (*Continued*)

Malaysia (11), Switzerland (12), Canada (15) and Mexico (16). These countries, with the exception of Malaysia and Mexico, are high-income economies and are in the innovation-driven stage. These countries seem to have missed the development of this new industry. Part of the explanation for this might be the sample selection, i.e. the main companies that produce industrial 3D printers. There are additional companies that are in an early life stage and/or have not yet established themselves. Some of these companies are located in Singapore, Taiwan and Switzerland [Wohlers Associates (2017)]. Nevertheless, Malaysia, Canada and Mexico are among the countries that are underrepresented in terms of companies that produce industrial 3D printers. Another part of the explanation may be the reasoning behind the high-technology indicators ranking. This high technology ranking is that of technological standing which is defined as an indicator of a country's recent overall success in exporting high technology products [Porter *et al.* (2008)]. This measure has an emphasis on electronics as this is assumed to be a vital contributor to much of the high-technology development in recent years [Porter *et al.* (2008)]. However, it is not clear whether there is a correlation between success in electronics and success in additive manufacturing equipment. Hence, the ranking of high-technology countries may not be that applicable to the design, development and production of industrial 3D printers.

It is also noteworthy that within the US, the companies are mostly oriented in the north-east region and the number of companies in for example the Silicon Valley area is limited.

4.2. *Age of the companies*

The second research question focuses on the age of companies. It is important to provide a little context about "the age" of additive manufacturing. There is some controversy over the initial AM invention. For example, the laser curing approach actually originated in Japan in 1980 by Dr. Kodama from the Nagoya Municipal Industrial Research Institute who initially applied for a patent in 1980 but the full application was not submitted on time and there were also French inventors who had earlier ideas but did not accomplish a patent [Fabbaloo (2018)]. The result is that the initial three main patents that were granted in the area of additive manufacturing were established about 30–35 years ago. Vat Photopolymerization technology, US Patent 4575330 for Chuck Hill founder of 3D systems, is from 1984. The initial material extrusion technology, US Patent 5121329 for Scott Crump co-founder of Stratasys, is from 1989. And, the initial powder bed fusion technology, US Patent 4863538, is from 1989 for Carl Deckard who was at the University of Texas at Austin. In this context, Table 3 shows the age of established AM companies. This table shows for companies that were 20 years or younger age groups based on five-year intervals. An additional category was added for the companies that were 20–30

Table 3. Age of established industrial AM companies.

Age group	Companies
Founded 2013 or later	5
Founded 2008–2012	4
Founded 2003–2007	6
Founded 1998–2002	3
Founded 1988–1997	3
Founded 1987 or earlier	9

years old. Companies that were older than that were grouped together. In addition to Table 3, Fig. 6 provides an overview of the history of the companies by the AM process in which they are active.

Table 3 shows that 70% of the companies are 10 or more years old, 40% of the companies are 20 or more years old, while 30% of the companies are 30 or more years old. Only 17% of the companies are five or less years old. This confirms the innovative behavior of older firms [García-Quevedo *et al.* (2014)]. Since the sample is based on established companies, this is not necessarily surprising. However, what is noteworthy is that there are several companies that are relatively old but that are active in this innovative and high technology industry. The nine companies that were established before 1987 are: Cincinnatti (established 1890), HP (1939), Optomec (1982), Renishaw (1973), Skiaky (1939), Sisma (1961), SLM Solutions (1863), Trumpf (1923) and 3D Systems (1986). As discussed above, 3D Systems was an initial patent holder and started by Chuck Hill. The other eight companies all existed before the first AM patent was granted. They were operating in different industries and all demonstrate innovative behavior that led them to enter the new AM industry.

4.3. *Origin of the companies*

As discussed in Sec. 2.3, five types of origins of companies can be distinguished: existing companies that expanded into AM, the traditional start-up company, a start-up company that is the result of a corporate spin-off, and a start-up company that is the result of an academic spin-off company. Companies can also be founded as the result of a merger or acquisition. It should be noted that in a few instances, it is challenging to classify a company because it could be categorized in different ways. For example, GE Additive was categorized under corporate spin-off because it was founded in 2007 as a new business which resulted from a spin-off from GE Aviation. However, it could be argued that this is an existing business because GE has existed for a considerable time. It could also be argued that this can be categorized under the merger and acquisition category because GE Additive more or less immediately acquired two existing 3D printer companies. The reason that it was classified as a corporate spin-off and not an existing business is because it was established as a separate entity. The reason that it was not classified as a merger/acquisition is because the acquisitions were done by GE Additive and did not lead to a new entity. Another example is Stratasys. This company was categorized as a "traditional" start-up company. This is because the founder of Stratasys was basically working from his garage when he invented one of the key 3D printing technologies and as a result founded the company in 1989. In 2012, Stratasys and Objet merged. However, since the merged company continued under the same name and since it was essentially the combination of two existing businesses and not the creation of an entirely new business, it was decided not to include Stratasys in the merger/acquisition category. The resulting classification is illustrated in Table 4.

First, as was mentioned in Sec. 4.2, eight of the companies already existed before the invention of 3D printing, i.e. the patents. These companies had expertise in a

Table 4. Origin of the established industrial AM companies.

Company origin source	Number of companies
Existing company that expanded into AM	8
Merger/acquisition	2
"Traditional" start-up	1
Corporate spin-off company	13
Academic spin-off company	6

related area, for example operating in the machine tool or printing industry, and 3D printing was a logical extension of their business. An example is US-based HP. Second, two companies were founded as the result of a merger or acquisition of existing businesses which were operating in related fields and where knowledge or awareness of 3D printing existed. The merger or acquisition led to a new company that was dedicated to 3D printing. An example is France-based AddUp which is a new joint venture company created by Michelin and Fives. Third, one company, Stratasys, was started as a traditional entrepreneurial start-up. That means, it is not a corporate or academic spin-off company. Fourth, 13 of the companies can be considered as corporate spin-offs. That means, the founder(s) of these companies were already working in industry and due to this work experience had become exposed to 3D printing or the idea of 3D printing which led to the founding of the 3D printer company. An example of this is Japanese-based Aspect, the founder worked at Mitsubishi before founding the company. Fifth, six of the companies can be considered as academic spin-offs. That means, the founder(s) of these companies were studying or working at a university during or immediately prior to founding the company. An example is US-based Carbon which was founded by professors who were working at the University of North-Carolina in Chapel Hill.

For virtually all of these main industrial 3D printer companies, the founding was based on a product orientation, i.e. development of 3D printers, and for virtually all of these companies, this was related to specific knowledge and expertise in 3D printing processes. More specifically, the founders had a process innovation, which had intellectual property such as a trademark or patent connected to it, which was utilized to develop (a range of) 3D printers. In some situations, this related to expertise in printing specific materials such as ceramics or carbon or a mix of materials.

Overall, 20 of the companies are based on a start-up situation with a break-down as shown in Table 5.

This confirms Schramm [2018] in the sense that the percentage of pure start-ups is low and that many more start-ups originate from spin-off situations. These figures

Table 5. Break-down of start-up situation of established industrial AM companies.

Type of start-up	Percentage of companies
Traditional start-up	5%
Corporate spin-off	65%
Academic spin-off	30%

also provide insight to other studies discussed in Sec. 2.3. First, not all studies use the same breakdown of start-up situations. For example, most do not include the replicative option. This may be because in high technology situations, such as AM, this option is not (yet) available. The traditional start-up is also not always separately considered. Second, similar to the AM data, some studies find that the percentage of technology-based spin-offs from corporations is higher than from academic institutions, e.g. Lindhold Dahlstrand [1997], while others find the reverse, e.g. Löfsten and Lindelöf [2005].

4.4. *Academic spin-offs*

In this section, the academic spin-offs and their related universities will be analyzed. In Sec. 4.3, it was shown that 6 of the 30 established industrial 3D printer companies were founded as academic spin-offs. The list of six has been expanded by three companies for the improvement of the analysis: Arcam, Concept Laser and Mcor. Arcam and Concept Laser were added to the list because these were academic spin-off companies, and prior to 2016, when they were acquired by GE Additive, these were considered established companies in their own right [Wohlers Associates (2017)]. Mcor was added because even though in the analysis in Sec. 4.3 it was listed as a corporate spin-off in Table 4, this is an example of a company where the founding can be considered as a mix of a corporate spin-off and an academic spin-off. The issue is how the spin-off is defined. Often a company is considered an academic spin-off if a core technology is transferred but it might also be considered as a spin-off if it involves personnel transfer but not technology transfer [Pirnay *et al.* (2003)].

These resulting nine academic spin-off companies were started out of eight universities as two of them originated from the same university, that is, MIT. Table 6 illustrates the ranking of the eight universities based on the QS World University Ranking 2018, this includes 959 ranked universities, as well as the Times Higher Education World University Rankings 2018 which includes 1000 universities. As 3D

Table 6. Academic spin-offs and university rankings.

Academic spin-off	University	QS world university ranking 2018 (out of 959)	Times higher education world university rankings 2018 (out of 1000)
Formlabs & Markforged	MIT	1 (1)	5 (4)
Tiertime	Tsinghua University	25 (10)	30 (22)
Voxeljet	Technical University of Munich	64 (24)	41 (20)
Carbon	University of North Carolina-Chapel Hill	80 (196)	56 (not ranked)
Mcor	Trinity College	88 (155)	117 (101–135)
Arcam	Chalmers University of Technology	133 (98)	201–250 (79)
Lithoz	Vienna University of Technology	182 (115)	301–350 (126–150)
Concept Laser	Coburg University of Applied Sciences	Not ranked	Not ranked

printing is a technical area, the rankings of these eight universities in the field of engineering and technology are also stated (between brackets). Both rankings include 501 universities in this category.

The following provides additional background on some of the academic spin-off companies as well as some of the complexities in categorizing the founding of these companies.

- Mcor: In the early 2000s, Conor McCormack, one of the founders of the family firm Mcor was working with Airbus as an engineer on the A380 and was exposed to a lot of 3D CAD packages and 3D printing. While working on his PhD at Trinity College, he realized that, due to the high cost of the materials, only one of the students had an opportunity to print a model at the end of the year — just one – defeating the whole purpose of a 3D printer. Conor and his brother Fintan saw that while machine prices were coming down, the price of consumables kept going in the opposite direction. That was the seed of an idea that started with, "Could we make a super low cost machine that is also very eco-friendly for everyone to use?" Mcor was set up in 2005 and Conor and Fintan worked on developing the technology and from this the Mcor Matrix was born [3D Printing Industry (2013)].
- Concept Laser: Frank and Kerstin Herzog met at Coburg University. During the mid-1990s, Frank joined a nearby prototyping shop owned by Kerstin's uncle. The machines in the shop included one of Germany's first stereolithography machines, which "printed" 3D models from successive layers of resin and solidified them with ultraviolet light. Frank wondered if the same could be done with metals. He registered the idea as his master's thesis at Coburg University and built a small prototype. This was improved with a laser that Kerstin had purchased for her master's project and eventually led to the incorporation of the company in 2000 [GE reports (2018)].
- Lithoz: Many years of research at the Vienna University of Technology equipped Dr. Johannes Homa and Dr. Johannes Benedikt with extensive technical knowledge of additive manufacturing of high-performance ceramics. In 2011 they founded Lithoz GmbH as a spin-off from the TU Vienna [Lithoz (2019)].
- Voxeljet: Voxeljet's roots reach back to the year 1995 with the first successful dosing of UV-resins. In the context of a "hidden" project, initial 3D-printing tests are performed at the Technical University of Munich. In 1996, the project participates in the 1st Munich Business plan contest and in 1998 the first patent is granted. The first sand molds are printed at the University in 1998. The company was established in 1999 with the goal of developing new generative processes for the production of casting and plastics components using 3D printing. In the beginning, operations were launched with four employees at the Technical University of Munich. Shortly afterwards the headquarters in Augsburg were established [Voxeljet (2019)].

Seven of the eight universities are ranked amongst the top universities in the world. The exception is the Coburg University of Applied Sciences. Since this is a

University of Applied Sciences, with less emphasis on research, it is not surprising that this university is not ranked.

The performance of universities in terms of start-ups, commercialization of technology and for instance income generated from developed technology has previously been identified as being very much skewed [Di Gregorio and Shane (2003); Scherer and Harhoff (2000); Pressman *et al.* (1995)], so it is to be expected that not all of the 501 universities have spin-off companies in the field of AM. However, it is noteworthy that out of the main industrial 3D printer companies that were formed as academic spin-offs, only two universities from the top-10 of the universities in technology and engineering were involved, see Table 7.

As previously noted, there are additional AM companies that are in an early life stage and/or have not yet established themselves and therefore these companies may also include academic spin-off companies. Nevertheless, notable top-10 technology-oriented universities in the world that are not represented in Table 7 include for example Stanford University and the University of Cambridge, both of these are known for having relatively successful academic spin-off experiences.

It should be noted, however, that these types of descriptive quantitative data do not always cover the "full story". For instance, the University of Texas — Austin is neither mentioned in Table 6, nor in Table 7. Yet, it seems to have played an important role in AM development, in particular for selective laser sintering. Carl Deckard, initially an undergraduate student at the UT-Austin and later graduate and PhD student played an important role. By the end of his senior year in 1984, Deckard had come up with the idea of using a directed energy beam (such as a laser or electron beam) to melt particles of powder together to make a part. This turned into a graduate school project and led to the formation of a company Nova Automation which became DTM [University of Texas at Austin (2012)]. Dr. Xu, the founder of the Chinese company Farsoon is one of the people who worked at DTM in the mid-1990s and when Farsoon established a US subsidiary in 2017, it did so in the Austin area [University of Texas at Austin (2012)]. Thus, Farsoon can be linked to the University of Texas — Austin. Another company that can be linked is the Japanese company Aspect. Seiji Hayano worked at the Mitsubishi Corporation where he learned about stereolithography. He left Mitsubishi in 1996 to start Aspect and soon acquired exclusive rights to distribute equipment and materials

Table 7. University rankings in engineering and technology.

Rank	QS world university ranking	Times higher education world university rankings
1	Massachusetts Institute of Technology	Stanford University
2	Stanford University	California Institute of Technology
3	University of Cambridge	University of Oxford
4	ETH — Zurich	Massachusetts Institute of Technology
5	Nanyang Technological University	University of Cambridge
6	Imperial College London	Princeton University
7	National University of Singapore	Peking University
8	University of Tokyo University of Oxford	National University of Singapore
9		ETH Zurich
10	Tsinghua University	Imperial College London

Table 8. Academic spin-offs and distance from academic institution.

Academic spin-off	Headquarter location	University	Main campus location	Approximate distance in miles
Formlabs	Somerville, MA	MIT	Cambridge, MA	2
Markforged	Watertown, MA	MIT	Cambridge, MA	7
Tiertime	Near Beijing	Tsinghua University	Near Beijing	37
Voxeljet	Friedberg	Technical University of Munich	Munich	37
Carbon	Redwood, CA	University of North Carolina-Chapel Hill	Chapel Hill, NC	2827
Mcor	Dunleer	Trinity College	Dublin	37
Arcam	Mölndal	Chalmers University of Technology	Gothenburg	4
Lithoz	Vienna	Vienna University of Technology	Vienna	2
Concept Laser	Lichtenfeld	Coburg University of Applied Sciences	Coburg	11

developed by DTM [Farsoon Technologies (2017)]. DTM merged with 3D systems in 2001.

Table 8 shows the current headquarters of the academic spin-off companies and the distance to the academic institution to which it is linked. Determining whether an academic spin-off locates near a university is a bit fuzzy because not all geographical areas are comparable. For instance, in terms of size of a region, Tiertime is in the Beijing area and thus in the same geographic area as Tsinghua University which is also Beijing but nevertheless they are 37 miles apart. While Mcor and Trinity College are also 37 miles apart but in this situation they seem to be in different parts of the country.

Table 8 shows that most of the academic start-ups are relatively close to the academic institution. The one exception is Carbon. Carbon's CLIP technology was invented at UNC-Chapel-Hill in North Carolina. A main founder of Carbon is Joe DeSimone, a serial entrepreneur and professor at UNC. The reason for the founding of the company in California rather than in North Carolina, may well have to do with DeSimone's experience as entrepreneur and the ability to raise money. Venture Capital is highly concentrated in a few areas in the US which does not include North Carolina but does include California. In particular, the San Francisco area is the top location in the US [Aspect (2019)]. This is exactly where Carbon is located. Furthermore, the series A round of financing for Carbon was led by Sequoia Capital in Menlo Park [Citylab (2017)] which is approximately four miles from Redwood City where Carbon is located. A series B round of financing for Carbon was led by Silver Lake Krafwerk which is also located in Menlo Park [Recode (2015)].

5. Discussion

In this study, the focus was on looking at how a high technology, i.e. additive manufacturing, is spreading globally. A choice was made to look at the established companies in AM that produce industrial 3D printers and determine where they are located and how they were formed. The result is that the technology that was considered for this study has very specific characteristics:

(1) The technology can be considered high-technology in terms of its newness, novelty and complexity.
(2) The diffusion that is examined is in a way the idea or concept of AM. In the current study, the companies have adopted the idea behind AM and based on this they have used and further developed this to produce machines (3D printers). This focus differs from many previous studies that distinguish between product, process, organization and positioning innovation [Boer and During (2001); Francis and Bessant (2005)] and generally focus on the customer, e.g. consumer adoption of electric vehicles [Egbue and Long (2012)] or on the process improvement, e.g. adoption of a new healthcare process [Cho *et al.* (2009)]. In the context of AM, these latter studies are more comparable to next stages of adoption of AM such as the adoption of industrial 3D printers by companies for use in the production process or the subsequent adoption by customers of the 3D printed products.
(3) The technology is a break-through technology. Although the AM technology already exists for 34 years, this technology is expected to have a huge impact on society in general and is considered a key part of the fourth industrial revolution technologies. In a broader sense, it is comparable to the development of the home computer. There are many parts of the development of AM, such as different technologies, developments in materials, aspects such as recycling machines, etc.

The overall pattern for the diffusion of the concept of AM, which is closely related to the creation of AM technologies for the development of the industrial 3D printers, leads to several conclusions:

First, the diffusion is mostly taking place in advanced, i.e. innovation-driven nations. Although in theory AM has less connection to a location, the established companies are almost all located in high-income and innovation-driven countries. What this indicates is that while adoption of 3D printers by companies for use in their production process or the adoption by customers of 3D printed products (the two blocks on the right in Fig. 4) may be less dependent upon location, the creation and the diffusion of the concept of AM seems very much dependent upon the location. The reason for this is in line with what was discussed in Sec. 2.1, that is, the vitality of innovation relates to national innovative capacity. What this also indicates is that while advanced nations such as the US may have been faced with erosion of its industrial commons due to outsourcing [Pisano and Shih (2009)], it still has considerable capabilities that are more upstream in the supply chain.

Second, the creation and subsequent initial diffusion of AM is overwhelmingly (77%) through existing companies that show a history that involved development of AM knowledge. For 57% of these (43% of the total group of companies), it led to a new company via a corporate spin-off. This type of start-up situation already often receives attention in the literature. However, for another 43% of these already existing companies (33% of the total number of companies) the companies expanded their business into the AM field. This highlights the importance of existing businesses as a source for innovation, see for example Breitzman and Hicks [2008] and Information Technology & Information Technology & Innovation Foundation [2016]. Among the companies studied, traditional start-ups are rare. The reason for this is that AM is a complex technology that goes beyond the simple idea of producing in layers. The capability to produce 3D printers requires expert knowledge of several other fields such as material science, machine coding, and also expert knowledge of processes such as photopolymerization or binder jetting. Companies that are already operating in related fields and that already possess expert knowledge have the potential to expand into AM. A traditional start-up by a young high-tech wizard is unlikely because of the level of expertise in a variety of fields that is required to make this successful.

Third, an additional 20% of the companies were formed through an academic spin-off situation. This confirms the previous conclusion in terms of the requirement of expert knowledge to start a company to manufacture industrial 3D printers. It also confirms previous studies such as Lindhold Dahlstrand [1997] about the importance of corporate spin-offs compared to academic spin-offs, that is, in this study there were roughly twice as many corporate spin-offs than academic spin-offs. The reason for this may be similar to the previously drawn conclusion: expert knowledge is required across several areas. While companies that are already competing in related areas may already possess expertise in a variety of areas, academics are typically narrow in their focus. Therefore, unless very specific expertise is developed at a university that provides exceptional value and where additional expertise can somehow be acquired it seems more likely that an existing company is able to capitalize on the situation. Note for example that for the academic spin-offs Carbon founders already had experience with start-up companies which helped commercialization, Mcor founders already possessed design and 3D printing knowledge due to industry experience, and Concept Laser already possessed expertise with stereolithography. It was also found that academic spin-off companies generally located fairly close to the university, i.e. within 40 miles, confirming Audretsch *et al.* [2005].

The findings discussed above are summarized in Table 9.

Table 9. Overall findings.

Topic	Finding
Location of company that produces industrial 3D printers	90%: Innovation-driven, high-income country 10%: Efficiency-driven, upper-middle income country
Origin of the company	77% existing companies – 43% via corporate spin-off – 33% via expansion into AM – 20% academic spin-off companies
Academic spin-offs	88% from a worldwide top-20% ranked university Only 20% of worldwide top-10 universities 89% of academic spin-offs locate within 40 miles of the university

6. Conclusion

This study focused on the geography of the diffusion of AM technology through established companies that manufacture industrial 3D printers. This focus deviates from most diffusion studies as it deals with the early-stage adoption of the AM concept into the production of machines. Most diffusion studies are more focused on the diffusion and adoption of process innovation (which would be equivalent to the adoption of 3D printers in a manufacturing company) or the adoption of a product innovation (which would be equivalent to the adoption of 3D printed products). The study combines elements of the creation of innovation, the diffusion of innovation and the commercialization of innovation.

It was found that in this situation of early-stage adoption the majority of companies are located in innovation-driven economies and that most of the companies were existing companies that expanded into AM as a related area or that were corporate spin-offs. The reason for this is probably that AM technology for industrial 3D printers requires expert knowledge in a variety of fields and existing companies that operate in related fields have the best opportunity to capitalize on this, this is illustrated in Fig. 7.

6.1. *Theoretical implications*

This study, while acknowledging its very specific scope as illustrated in Fig. 3, created some important insights that have theoretical implications.

Technology/innovation: It seems that the creation and diffusion of technology has something to do with the particular technology characteristics. The study focused on AM which can be considered high technology although the definition of high technology is unclear [Hooton (2018)]. There are many studies on the nature of technology or innovation such as for instance the distinction of island or integrated technologies based on the dependence upon the environment [Steenhuis and de Bruijn (2004)] and another distinction is the classification by Berkhout *et al.* [2006]. They distinguish five classes of innovation from class 1, i.e. innovation as a result of

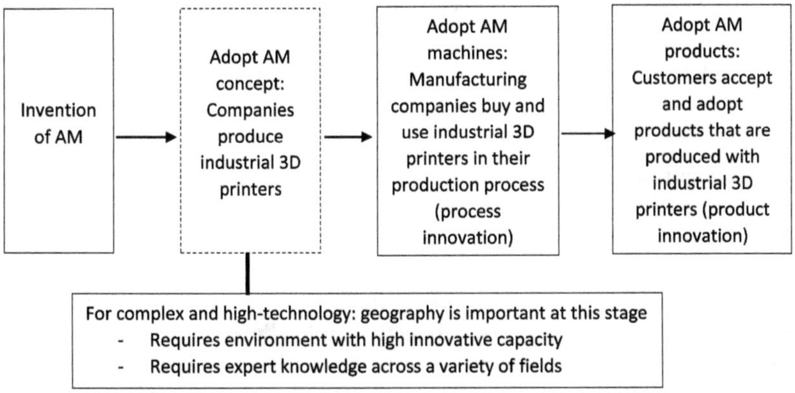

Fig. 7. Link of early-stage adoption of complex and high technology and location.

new developments in a single node in their cyclic innovation model, to class 5 where all cycles of change are linked. Based on the study, it is proposed:

- The higher the number of advanced technological areas that are integrated into an innovation, the higher the likelihood that the initial creation and diffusion of the innovation will be in advanced nations.

This is because these nations present a higher likelihood of possessing the knowledge in the variety of advanced technological areas which allows for the integration to take place.

Start-up: Related to the above, it is proposed:

- The higher the number of advanced technological areas that are integrated into an innovation, the higher the likelihood that the initial creation and diffusion of the innovation will come from the expansion or spin-off from existing corporations that already compete in related fields rather than universities.

This is because these corporations present a higher likelihood of possessing the knowledge in the variety of advanced technological areas which increases the probability that the integration takes place. Researchers at universities have a higher likelihood of operating in more narrowly defined areas which decreases the likelihood of the initial creation and diffusion of the innovation to come from the academic side.

Entrepreneurial: It should be noted that there is considerable vagueness in terminology. For instance, when employees of an existing company work on an academic degree and subsequently start their own company it could potentially be classified as a corporate spin-off, an academic spin-off or even a traditional start-up. This type of complexity or overlap is usually reasoned away for the sake of simplicity but to benefit the development of theory it may be more beneficial to leave some of this in place. Based on the study, it is proposed:

- The higher the number of advanced technological areas that are integrated into an innovation, the higher the likelihood that there may not be a clear distinction and that the entrepreneur possesses a varied background that includes (a variety of) industrial as well as academic experience and knowledge.

6.2. *Practical implications*

Due to the narrow focus of the study, it is not possible to develop strong practical implications that have generalizability. Nevertheless, a few thoughts are presented on implications for companies, universities as well as for governments or public administrators.

Companies: There are two important implication for companies. First, while many companies have outsourced production to low labor-cost countries because advanced economies have become too expensive, the results indicate that companies can still benefit from locating in advanced nations as these locations provide innovation potential. Second, existing companies in related fields have the highest probability to capitalize on AM. Companies should therefore continuously scan the environment and be aware of technological developments that may create new markets. In particular, technologies that require expertise across a variety of fields may present great opportunities as the number of competitors with sufficient expertise across these various areas may be limited. Engagement in university-industry cooperative research such as through NSF's IUCRC program (https://www.nsf.gov/eng/iip/iucrc/home.jsp) is a concrete example of how companies can increase their awareness of technological progress.

Universities are often considered a key part of the knowledge economy and as a source of innovative activity. Nevertheless, this study found that corporations play a more important role. This may be due to the need to have expertise in a variety of fields. Successful universities often already provide an infrastructure that guides the commercialization of university research. This in itself may not be enough and it is recommended to set-up mechanisms that focus on bringing together expertise across a variety of fields and with a focus on the market. Two concrete examples of such mechanisms are the already mentioned university-industry cooperative research and also faculty internships inside corporations. These types of engagements can allow faculty to broaden their perspective and in particular to learn about implications of their research, potential market applications and with this the insight into what kind of changes are necessary in technology to increase the potential.

Public administrators: A few recommendations can be made for countries or governments. First, while advanced nations may have been faced with an erosion of industrial commons, the study illustrates that advanced nations may very well have a competitive edge in the creation and early-stage diffusion of complex (high) technology that requires extensive R&D and innovation capacity. For long-term competitiveness and prosperity, this should remain a focus. Furthermore, while universities play a role in knowledge development, the importance of the expertise of existing companies and the opportunities to capitalize on this expertise should not be underestimated. Policies that encourage companies to continue to do (fundamental) research can lead to opportunities in new fields. Additionally, policies that encourage corporate spin-offs may be beneficial. For countries that are not yet in the innovation-driven stage, it may be most beneficial to build up general innovative capabilities in order to enter the innovation-driven stage.

6.3. *Limitations and suggestions for further research*

A main limitation of this study is that it took place in a narrowly defined area. Due to this context, the study provides limited insight into more general diffusion patterns.

Related to this, some recommendations can be made for further research. First, not all of the innovation-driven economies have established companies that manufacture industrial 3D printers. It would be interesting to find out why some countries do while others do not, as at least in theory they are in a similar stage of innovation. Perhaps, some countries due to their industry portfolio are more likely to be successful in AM. Another area for potential research is to study AM in countries that are not in the innovation-stage. The adoption and diffusion of AM may still occur in these countries but may be related more to the adoption of industrial 3D printers or the products that are made with these 3D printers. It might also be worthwhile to study differences between consumer and industrial 3D printer adoption and whether the stage of economic development of a nation has any influence as the cost of these 3D printers is quite different. A last area for future research is that for academic start-ups. Many of the prominent universities do not have academic spin-offs related to industrial 3D printing while Concept Laser related to Coburg University of Applied Sciences is successful. Studies with a focus on academic spin-off related to applied universities can help to improve understanding under which conditions these universities can play a bigger role in company formation in high technology. Delving deeper into other prominent research universities and what they do in terms of AM can help clarify why not all of the best engineering and technology-oriented universities have been able to spin-off AM-oriented companies.

References

3D Printing Industry (2013). Executive interview – Conor MacCormack. https://3dprintingindustry.com/news/executive-interview-series-conor-maccormick-5490/, February 12, 2013 [accessed 12 February 2019].

Aarikka-Stenroos, L. and Lehtimäki, T. (2014). Commercializing a radical innovation: Probing the way to the market. *Industrial Marketing Management*, **43**: 1372–1384.

Acosta, M., Coronado, D. and Flores, E. (2011). University spillovers and new business location in high-technology sectors: Spanish evidence. *Small Business Economics*, **36**: 365–376.

Adams, P., Farrell, M., Dalgarno, B. and Oczkowski, E. (2017). Household adoption of technology: The case of high-speed broadband adoption in Australia. *Technology in Society*, **49**: 37–47.

Anastasiadou, C. and Vettese, S. (2019). "From souvenirs to 3D printed souvenirs". Exploring the capabilities of additive manufacturing technologies in (re)-framing tourist souvenirs. *Tourism Management*, **71**: 428–442.

Anderson, C. (2012). *Makers, The New Industrial Revolution*. Crown Business, New York.

Anderson Goehrke, S. (2016). GE Announces $1.4 Billion Investment: Acquisition of Arcam AB and SLM Solutions. 3DPrint.com. https://3dprint.com/148290/ge-acquires-arcam-slm-solutions/, September 6, 2016 [accessed 12 March 2019].

Andorka, F. (2011). Stratasys Acquires 3-D Printer Solidscape For $38 Million. Industry Week. https://www.industryweek.com/information-technology/stratasys-acquires-3-d-printer-solidscape-38-million, May 4, 2011 [accessed 12 March 2019].

Artz, K. W., Norman, P. M., Hatfield, D. E. and Cardinal, L. B. (2010). A longitudinal study on the impact of R&D, patents, and product innovation on firm performance. *Journal of Product Innovation Management*, **27**: 725–740.

Aspect (2019). Opening up a new future with AM (3D printing). http://aspect.jpn.com/english/company/index.html. n.d. [accessed 12 February 2019].

Atzeni, E., Iuliano, L., Minetola, P. and Salmi, A. (2010). Redesign and cost estimation of rapid manufactured plastic parts. *Rapid Prototyping Journal*, **16**, 5: 308–317.

Atzeni, E. and Salmi, A. (2012) Economics of additive manufacturing for end-usable metal parts. *International Journal of Advanced Manufacturing Technology*, **62**: 1147–1155.

Audretsch, D. B. (1998). Agglomeration and the location of innovative activity. *Oxford Review of Economic Policy*, **14**, 2: 18–29.

Audretsch, D. B. and Feldman, M. P. (1996). R&D spillovers and the geography of innovation and production. *The American Economic Review*, **86**, 3: 630–640.

Audretsch, D. B., Lehmann, E. E. and Warning, S. (2005). University spillovers and new firm location, *Research Policy* **34**: 1113–1122.

Baiyegunhi, L. J. S., Hassan, M. B., Danso-Abbeam, G. and Ortmann, G. F. (2019). Diffusion and adoption of integrated Striga management (ISM) technologies among smalholder maize farmers in rural northern Nigeria. *Technology in Society*, **56**: 109–115.

Balasubramanian, N. and Lee, J. (2008). Firm age and innovation. *Industrial and Corporate Change*, **17**, 5: 1019–1047.

Balconi, M., Brusoni, S. and Orsenigo, L. (2010). In defence of the linear model: An essay. *Research Policy*, **39**: 1–13.

Balland, P. A., Boschma, R. and Frenken, K. (2015). Proximity and innovation: From statistics to dynamics. *Regional Studies*, **49**, 6: 907–920.

Ballardini, R. M., Flores Ituarte, I. and Pei, E. (2018). Printing spare parts through additive manufacturing: Legal and digital business challenges. *Journal of Manufacturing Technology Management*, **29**, 6: 958–982.

Beltagui, A., Rosli, A. and Candi, M. (2020). Exaptation in a digital innovation ecosystem: The disruptive impacts of 3D printing. *Research Policy*, **49**, https://www.sciencedirect.com/science/article/pii/S0048733319301532.

Berkhout, A. J., Hartmann, D., van der Duin, P. and Ortt, R. (2006). Innovating the innovation process. *International Journal of Technology Management*, **34**, 3/4: 390–404.

Boer, H. and During, W. E. (2001). Innovation, what innovation? A comparison between product, process and organizational innovation. *International Journal of Technology Management*, **22**, 1/2/3: 83–107.

Breitzman, A. and Hicks, D. (2008), An analysis of small business patents by industry and firm size, Small Business Administration, Office of Advocacy.

Brem, A., Bilgram, V. and Gutstein, A. (2018). Involving lead users in innovation: A structured summary of research on the lead user method. *International Journal of Innovation and Technology Management*, **15**, 3, https://www.worldscientific.com/doi/abs/10.1142/S0219877018500220.

Candi, M. and Beltagui, A. (2019). Effective use of 3D printing in the innovation process. *Technovation*, **80-81**: 63–73.

Caraça, J., Lundvall, B. A. and Mendonça, S. (2009). The changing role of science in the innovation process: From queen to Cinderella? *Technological Forecasting & Social Change*, **76**: 861–867.

Carayannis, E. G., Rogers, E. M., Kurihara, K. and Allbritton, M. M. (1998). High-technology spin-offs from government R&D laboratories and research universities, *Technovation*, **18**, 1: 1–11.

Caviggioli, F. and Ughetto, E. (2019). A bibliometric analysis of the research dealing with the impact of additive manufacturing on industry, business and society. *International Journal of Production Economics*, **208**: 254–268.

Cenamor, J., Usero, B. and Fernández, Z. (2013). The role of complementary products on platform adoption: Evidence from the video console market. *Technovation*, **33**: 405–416.

Chan, H. K., Griffin, J., Lim, J. J., Zeng, F. and Chiu, A. S. F. (2018). The impact of 3D printing technology on the supply chain: Manufacturing and legal perspectives. *International Journal of Production Economics*, **205**: 156–162.

Chen, G. Yang, G., He, F. and Chen, K. (2019). Exploring the effect of political borders on university-industry collaborative research performance: Evidence from China's Guangdong province. *Technovation*, **82-83**: 58–69.

Chiesa, V. and Frattini, F. (2011). Commercializing technological innovation: Learning from failures in high-tech markets. *Journal of Product Innovation Management*, **28**: 437–454.

Cho, S., Mathiassen, L. and Gallivan, M. (2009). Crossing the diffusion chasm: From invention to penetration of a telehealth innovation. *Innovation Technology & People*, **22**, 4: 351–366.

Citylab (2017). Venture capital remains highly concentrated in just a few cities. https://www.citylab.com/life/2017/10/venture-capital-concentration/539775/, October 3 2017 [accessed 12 February 2019].

Clarysse, B., Wright, M., Lockett, A., van de Velde, E. and Vohora, A. (2005). Spinning out new ventures: A typology of incubation strategies from European research institutions. *Journal of Business Venturing*, **20**: 183–216.

Coad, A., Segarra, A. and Teruel, M. (2016). Innovation and firm growth: Does firm age play a role?*Research Policy*, **45**: 387–400.

Cowan, R. and Zinovyeva, N. (2013) University effects on regional innovation. *Research Policy*, **42**: 788–800.

Davis, F. D. (1989). Perceived usefulness, perceived ease of use, and user acceptance of information technology. *MIS Quarterly*, **13**, 3: 319–340.

de la Mothe, J. and Paquet, G. (eds.) (1998). *Local and Regional Systems of Innovation.* Kluwer Academic Publishers, Boston.

De Jong, J. P. J. and de Bruijn, E. (2013). Innovation lessons from 3-D printing. *MIS Sloan Management Review*, **54**, 2: 43–52.

Di Gregorio, D. and Shane, S. (2003). Why do some universities generate more start-ups than others? *Research Policy*, **32**: 209–227.

Ebrahimi Sarcheshmeh, E., Bijani, M. and Sadighi, H. (2018). Adoption behavior towards the use of nuclear technology in agriculture: A causal analysis. *Technology in Society*, **55**: 175–182.

Egbue, O. and Long, S. (2012). Barriers to widespread adoption of electric vehicles: An analysis of consumer attitudes and perceptions. *Energy Policy*, **48**: 717–729.

Fabbaloo (2018). The final word: the first 3D printer. https://www.fabbaloo.com/blog/2018/10/25/final-word-the-first-3d-printer? 25 October 2018 [accessed 30 January 2019].

Farsoon Technologies (2017). Farsoon Technologies Expands Global Strategy with Establishment of Americas Subsidiary. http://en.farsoon.com/news_detail/newsId=34.html. September 21 2017 [accessed 12 February 2019].

Feldman, M. P. (1994). *The Geography of Innovation.* Kluwer Academic Publishers, Dordrecht.

Feldman, M. P. and Florida, R. (1994). The geographic sources of innovation: Technological infrastructure and product innovation in the United States. *Annals of the Association of American Geographers*, **84**, 2: 210–229.

Ferretti, M., Ferri, S., Fiorentino, R., Parmentola, A. and Sapio, A. (2019). Neither absent nor too present: The effects of the engagement of parent universities on the performance of academic spin-offs. *Small Business Economics*, **52**: 153–173.

Fichman, R. G. (2004). Real options and IT platform adoption: Implications for theory and practice. *Information Systems Research*, **15**, 2: 132–154.

Fini, R., Grimaldi, R., Santoni, S. and Sobrero, M. (2011). Complements or substitutes? The role of universities and local context in supporting the creation of academic spin-offs. *Research Policy*, **40**: 1113–1127.

Ford, S., Mortara, L. and Minshall, T. (2016). The emergence of additive manufacturing: Introduction to the special issue. *Technological Forecasting & Social Change*, **102**: 156–159.

Foster, C. and Heeks, R. (2013). Conceptualising inclusive innovation: Modifying systems of innovation frameworks to understand diffusion of new technology to low-income consumers. *European Journal of Development Research*, **25**, 3: 333–355.

Fox, S. (2014). Third wave do-it-yourself (DIY): Potential for presumption, innovation, and entrepreneurship by local populations in regions without industrial manufacturing infrastructure. *Technology in Society*, **39**: 18–30.

Francis, D. and Bessant, J. (2005). Targeting innovation and implications for capability development. *Technovation*, **25**: 171–183.

Fratocchi, L. (2018). Additive manufacturing technologies as a reshoring enabler: A why, where and how approach. *World Review of Intermodal Transportation Research*, **7**, 3: 264–293.

García-Quevedo, J., Pellegrino, G. and Vivarelli, M. (2014). R&D drivers and age: Are young firms different? *Research Policy*, **43**: 1544–1556.

GE reports (2018), The Metal Head: How A High School Dropout Built A Pioneering 3D Printing Business. https://www.ge.com/reports/metal-head-high-school-dropout-built-pioneering-3d-printing-business/, April 30, 2018 [accessed 12 February 2019].

Godin, B. (2006). The liner model of innovation, the historical construction of an analytical framework. *Science, Technology & Human Values*, **31**, 6: 639–667.

Goehrke, S. (2019). The 3D printing startup within a major company. https://www.fabbaloo.com/blog/2019/1/15/the-3d-printing-startup-within-a-major-company, January 15, 2019 [accessed 29 January 2019].

Goldstein, P. (2018). NASA Turns to 3D Printing to Help Astronauts Aboard the International Space Station. https://fedtechmagazine.com/article/2018/10/nasa-turns-3d-printing-help-astronauts-aboard-international-space-station, October 24, 2018 [accessed 11 January 2019].

Grand View Research (2018). 3D Printing (3DP) Market Worth $23.79 Billion By 2025 — CAGR: 16.5%. https://www.grandviewresearch.com/press-release/global-3d-printing-market, October 2018 [accessed 11 January 2019].

Gress, D. R. and Kalafsky, R. V. (2015). Geographies of production in 3D: Theoretical and research implications stemming from additive manufacturing. *Geoforum*, **60**: 43–52.

Halbinger, M. A. (2018). The role of makerspaces in supporting consumer innovation and diffusion: An empirical analysis. *Research Policy*, **47**: 2028–2036.

Hannen, J., Antons, D. Pillar, F., Salge, T. O., Coltman, T. and Devinney, T. M. (2019). Containing the not-invented-here syndrome in external knowledge absorption and open innovation: The role of indirect countermeasures. *Research Policy*, **48**, https://www.sciencedirect.com/science/article/pii/S0048733319301428?via%3Dihub.

Hannibal, M. and Knight, G. (2018). Additive manufacturing and the global factory: Disruptive technologies and the location of international business. *International Business Review*, **27**: 1116–1127.

Hienerth, C., von Hippel, E. and Jensen, M. B. (2014). User community vs. producer innovation development efficiency: A first empirical study. *Research Policy*, **43**: 190–201.

Hooton, C. A. (2018). Defining tech: An examination of how the 'technology' economy is measured. *Journal of NBICT*, **1**: 101–120.

Hossain, M., Simula, H. and Halme, M. (2016). Can frugal go global? Diffusion patterns of frugal innovations. *Technology in Society*, **46**: 132–139.

Hsu, D. W. L. and Yuan, B. J.C. (2013). Knowledge creation and diffusion of Taiwan's universities: Knowledge trajectory from patent data. *Technology in Society*, **35**: 172–181.

Hyysalo, S., Johnson, M. and Juntunen, J. K. (2017). The diffusion of consumer innovation in sustainable energy technologies. *Journal of Cleaner Production*, **162**: S70–S82.

Information Technology & Innovation Foundation (2016). https://itif.org/publications/2016/02/24/demographics-innovation-united-states, February 24, 2016 [accessed 25 January 2019].

Jaffe, A. B. (1989). Real effects of academic research. *The American Economic Review*, **79**, 5: 957–970.

Jones, R., Haufe, P., Sells, E., Iravani, P., Olliver, V., Palmer, C. and Bowyer, A. (2011). RepRap – The replicating rapid prototype. *Robotica*, **29**: 177–191.

Kankanhalli, A., Ye, H. and Teo, H. H. (2015). Comparing potential and actual innovators: An empirical study of mobile data services innovation. *MIS Quarterly* **39**, 3: 667–682.

Kannattukunnel, R. S. (2016). Global patents on 3D printing: Revelations based on vector autoregression analysis for three decades. *International Journal of Innovation Technology Management*, **13**, 6, https://www.worldscientific.com/doi/10.1142/S0219877017500043.

Kaplan, D. (1987). Machinery and industry: The causes and consequences of constrained development of the South African machine tool industry. *Social Dynamics, A Journal of African Studies*, **13**, 1: 60–67.

Khanagha, A., Mobnini Dehkordi, A., Zali, M. R. and Reza Hejazi, S. (2018). Measuring the entrepreneurial orientation of public research centers. *International Journal of Innovation and Technology Management*, **15**, 3, https://www.worldscientific.com/doi/10.1142/S0219877018500281.

Kleer, R. and Piller, F. T. (2019). Local manufacturing and structural shifts in competition: Market dynamics of additive manufacturing. *International Journal of Production Economics*, **216**: 23–34.

Kline, S. J. and Rosenberg, N. (1986). An overview of innovation. *The Positive Sum Strategy: Harnessing Technology for Economic Growth*, eds. R. Landau and N. Rosenberg. National Academy Press, Washington DC, pp. 275–305.

Kolympiris, C., Kalaitzandonakes, N. and Miller, D. (2015). Location choice of academic entrepreneurs: Evidence from the US biotechnology industry. *Journal of Business Venturing*, **30**: 227–254.

Krabel, S. and Mueller, P. (2009). What drives scientists to start their own company? An empirical investigation of Max Planck Society scientists. *Research Policy*, **38**: 947–956.

Kuchiki, A. and Tsuji, M. (eds.) (2010). *From Agglomeration to Innovation*. Palgrave Macmillan, Houndmills.

Kwak, K., Kim, W. and Park, K. (2018). Complementary multiplatforms in the growing innovation ecosystem: Evidence from 3D printing technology. *Technological Forecasting & Social Change*, **136**: 192–207.

Lindhold Dahlstrand, A. (1997). Growth and inventiveness in technology-based spin-off firms. *Research Policy*, **26**: 331–344.

Lithoz (2019), Company overview. http://www.lithoz.com/en/company/company-overview [accessed 12 February 2019].

Löfsten, H. and Lindelöf, P. (2005). R&D networks and product innovation patterns — academic and non-academic new technology-based firms in Science Parks. *Technovation*, **25**: 1025–1037.

Lyu, J., Hahn, K. and Sadachar, A. (2018). Understanding millennial consumer's adoption of 3D printed fashion products by exploring personal values and innovativeness. *Fashion and Textiles*, **5**: 11–35.

Marak, Z. R., Tiwari, A. and Tiwari, S. (2019). Adoption of 3D printing technology: An innovation diffusion theory perspective. *International Journal of Innovation*, **7**, 1: 87–103.

Martinsuo, M. and Luomaranta, T. (2018). Adopting additive manufacturing in SMEs: Exploring the challenges and solutions. *Journal of Manufacturing Technology Management*, **29**, 6: 937–957.

Marzi, G., Zollo, L., Boccardi, A. and Ciappei, C. (2018). Additive manufacturing in SMEs: Empirical evidences from Italy. *International Journal of Innovation and Technology Management*, **15**, 1, https://www.worldscientific.com/doi/10.1142/S0219877018500074.

Matias, E. and Rao, B. (2015). 3D printing: On its historical evolution and the implications for business. In *2015 Proceedings of PICMET '15: Management of the Technology Age*, pp. 551–558.

Matos, F. and Jacinto, C. (2019). Additive manufacturing technology: Mapping social impacts. *Journal of Manufacturing Technology Management*, **30**, 1: 70–97.

Minshall, T. and Wicksteed, B. (2005). *University Spin-out Companies: Starting to Fill the Evidence Gap, A Report on a Pilot Research Project Commissioned by the Gatsby Charitable Foundation.* St. John's Innovation Centre Ltd., Cambridge.

Miller, D. and Garnsey, E. (2000). Entrepreneurs and technology diffusion, How diffusion research can benefit from a greater understanding of entrepreneurship. *Technology in Society*, **22**: 445–465.

Miyata, Y. (2000). An empirical analysis of innovative activity of universities in the United States. *Technovation*, **20**: 413–425.

Moore, G. A. (2014). *Crossing the Chasm*, 3rd edn., HarperCollins Publishers, New York.

Morgan, K. and Nauwelaers, C. (2003). *Regional Innovation Strategies, The Challenge for Less-favoured Regions.* Routledge, London.

Mowery, D. C. and Ziedonis, A. A. (2014). Markets versus spillovers in outflows of university research. *Research Policy*, **44**: 50–66.

Niaki, M. K., Nonino, F., Palombi, G. and Torabi. S. A. (2019). Economic sustainability of additive manufacturing. *Journal of Manufacturing Technology Management*, **30**, 2: 353–365.

Nikolov, N. (2017). Solar-powered 3D printer uses light and sand to sculpt glass objects. https://mashable.com/2017/03/29/solar-powered-3d-printer-sahara-desert/#kfbq6y-PytmqH, March 29, 2017 [accessed 11 January 2019].

Norman, J., Madurawe, R. D., Moore, C. M. V., Khan, M. A. and Khairuzzaman, A. (2017). A new chapter in pharmaceutical manufacturing: 3D-printed drug products. *Advanced Drug Delivery Reviews*, **108**: 39–50.

O'Shea, R. P., Allen, T. J., Chevalier, A. and Roche, F. (2005). Entrepreneurial orientation, technology transfer and spinoff performance of U. S. universities. *Research Policy*, **34**: 994–1009.

Öberg, C., Shams, T. and Asnafi, N. (2018). Additive manufacturing and business models: Current knowledge and missing perspectives. *Technology Innovation Management Review*, **8**, 6: 15–33.

Oettmeier, K. and Hofmann, E. (2016). Impact of additive manufacturing technology adoption on supply chain management processes and components. *Journal of Manufacturing Technology Management*, **27**, 7: 944–968.

Oh, G. and Hong, Y. S. (2018). The impact of platform update interval on platform diffusion in a cooperative mobile ecosystem. *Journal of Intelligent Manufacturing*, **29**: 549–558.

Orlando, M. J. and Verba, M. (2005). Do only big cities innovate? Technological maturity and the location of innovation. *Economic Review – Federal Reserve Bank of Kansas City*, Second Quarter 2005, pp. 31–57.

Ortt, R. (2016). Guest editorial. *Journal of Manufacturing Technology Management*, **27**, 7: 890–897.

Ortt, R. (2017). Guest editorial. *Journal of Manufacturing Technology Management*, **28**, 1: 2–9.

Ortt, J. R. and Schoormans, J. P. L. (2004). The pattern of development and diffusion of breakthrough communication technologies. *European Journal of Innovation Management*, **7**, 4: 292–302.

Pirnay, F., Surlemont, B. and Nlemvo, F. (2003). Toward a typology of university spin-offs. *Small Business Economics*, **21**: 355–369.

Pisano, G. P. and Shih, W. C. (2009). Restoring American competitiveness. *Harvard Business Review*, **87**, 7/8: 114–125.

Porter, A. L., Newman, N. C., Jin, X. Y., Johnson, D. M. and Roessner, J. D. (2008). High tech indicators, technology-based competitiveness based on 33 countries, 2007 report. Report to the Science Indicators Unit, Division of Science Resources Statistics, National Science Foundation under Contract # NSFDACS07P1121. Atlanta, GA: Georgia Institute of Technology, Technology Policy and Assessment Center, January 22, 2008.

Porter, M. E. (1990). *The Competitive Advantage of Nations.* The Free Press, New York.

Porter, M. E. (2003). The economic performance of regions. *Regional Studies*, **36**, 6/7: 549–578.

Porter, M. E. and Stern, S. (2001). Innovation: location matters. *MIT Sloan Management Review*, **42**, 4: 28–36.

Pressman, L., Guterman, S., Abrams, I., Geist, D. E. and Nelsen, L. L. (1995). Pre-production investment and jobs induced by MIT exclusive patent licenses: A preliminary model to measure the economic impact of licensing. *Journal of the Association of University Technology Managers*, **7**: 49–82.

Rayna, T. and Striukova, L. (2016). From rapid prototyping to home fabrication: How 3D printing is changing business model innovation. *Technological Forecasting & Social Change*, **102**: 214–224.

Rayna, T. and Striukova, L. (2018). Editorial. *International Journal of Manufacturing Technology and Management*, **32**, 1: 1–4.

Recode (2015). Startup says new 3-D printing technique could shift use from prototype to production. https://www.recode.net/2015/3/16/11560306/startup-says-new-3-d-printing-technique-could-shift-use-from, March 16, 2015 [accessed 12 February 2019].

Redwood, B., Schöffer, F. and Garret, B. (2017). *The 3D Printing Handbook*. 3D Hubs B. V., Amsterdam.

Rogers, E. M. (1995). *Diffusion of Innovations*. 4th edn., The Free Press, New York.

Rogers, H., Braziotis, C. and Pawar, K. S. (2017). Guest editorial. *International Journal of Physical Distribution & Logistics Management*, **47**, 10: 950–953.

Saxena, P. K. and Sharma, A. (2014). Role of machine tools industry in economic development. *International Journal of Enhanced Research in Science Technology & Engineering*, **3**, 5: 188–193.

Scherer, F. M. and Harhoff, D. (2000). Technology policy for a world of skew-distributed outcomes. *Research Policy*, **29**: 559–566.

Schniederjans, D. G. (2017). Adoption of 3D-printing technologies in manufacturing: A survey analysis. *International Journal of Production Economics*, **183**: 287–298.

Schramm, C. J. (2018). *Burn the Business Plan, What Great Entrepreneurs Really Do*. Simon & Schuster, New York.

Schulze, A., MacDuffie, J. P. and Täube, F. A. (2015). Introduction: Knowledge generation and innovation diffusion in the global automotive industry – change and stability during turbulent times. *Industrial and Corporate Change*, **24**, 3: 603–611.

Schwab, K. (2016). *The Fourth Industrial Revolution*. World Economic Forum, Geneva.

Scott. C. and Simple, A. (2015), 3D Printed Pipe Fitting Has Huge Implications for Disaster Relief. https://3dprint.com/113155/field-ready-nepal-earthquake/, December 30, 2015 [accessed 11 January 2019].

Shane, S. (2001). Technological opportunities and firm creation. *Management Science*, **47**, 2: 205–220.

Shane, S. (2016). Patents Granted to Small Entities in Decline, Small Business Trends. https://smallbiztrends.com/2010/07/how-smart-is-the-average-entrepreneur.html, January 20, 2016 [accessed 29 January 2019].

Smith, A. (2017). From IP goals to 3D holes: Does intellectual property law provide a map or gap in the era of 3D printing? *Journal of Intellectual Property Law*, **25**, 1: 85–107.

Steenhuis, H. J. and de Bruijn, E. J. (2004). Assessing manufacturing location. *Production Planning & Control*, **15**, 8: 786–795.

Steenhuis, H. J. and Gray, D. O. (2006), The university as the engine of growth: An analysis of how universities can contribute to the economy. *International Journal of Technology Transfer and Commercialization*, **5**, 4: 421–432.

Steenhuis, H. J. and Pretorius, L. (2016). Consumer additive manufacturing or 3D printing adoption: An exploratory study. *Journal of Manufacturing Technology Management*, **27**, 7: 990–1012.

Steenhuis, H. J. and Pretorius, L. (2017). The additive manufacturing innovation: A range of implications. *Journal of Manufacturing Technology Management*, **28**, 1: 122–143.

Steffensen, M., Rogers, E. M. and Speakman, K. (1999). Spin-offs from research centers at a research university. *Journal of Business Venturing*, **15**: 93–111.

Trani, E. P. and Holsworth, R. D. (2010). *The Indispensible University, Higher Education, Economic Development, and the Knowledge Economy.* Rowman & Littlefield Publishers, Lanham.

University of Texas at Austin (2012). Selective Laser Sintering, Birth of an Industry. http://www.me.utexas.edu/news/news/selective-laser-sintering-birth-of-an-industry, December 6, 2012 [accessed 12 February 2019].

Varga, A. (1998). *University Research and Regional Innovation, A Spatial Econometric Analysis of Academic Technology Transfer.* Kluwer Academic Publishers, Boston.

Verschuren, P. and Doorewaard, H. (2005). *Designing a Research Project.* Lemma, Utrecht.

Von Hippel, E. (1986). Lead users: A source of novel product concepts. *Management Science*, **32**, 7: 791–805.

Von Hippel, E. (2005). Democratizing innovation: The evolving phenomenon of user innovation. *Journal für Betriebswirtschaft*, **55**, 1: 63–78.

von Tunzelmann, G. N. (1997). Innovation and industrialization: A long-term comparison. *Technological Forecasting and Social Change*, **56**: 1–23.

Voxeljet (2019), The Voxeljet company history. https://www.voxeljet.com/unternehmen/unternehmensgeschichte/ [accessed 12 February 2019].

Wennberg, K., Wiklund, J. and Wright, M. (2011). The effectiveness of university knowledge spillovers: Performance differences between university spinoffs and corporate spinoffs. *Research Policy*, **40**: 1128–1143.

Wohlers Associates (2017). *Wohlers Report 2017, 3D Printing and Additive Manufacturing State of the Industry*, Annual worldwide progress report, Wohlers Associates Inc., Fort Collins.

Woodson, T., Torres Alcantara, J. and Silva do Nascimento, M. (2019). Is 3D printing an inclusive innovation? An examination of 3D printing in Brazil. *Technovation*, **80-81**: 54–62.

World Bank (2017). *World Development Indicators 2017.* Washington, DC. https://openknowledge.worldbank.org/handle/10986/26447, 2017 [accessed 30 January 2019].

World Economic Forum (2017). *The Global Competitiveness Report 2017-2018.* https://www.weforum.org/reports/the-global-competitiveness-report-2017-2018, 2017 [accessed 30 January 2019].

Wydra, S. (2015). Challenges for technology diffusion policy to achieve socio-economic goals. *Technology in Society*, **41**: 76–90.

Yeganegi, S., Laplume, A. O., Dass, P. and Huynh, C.-L. (2016). Where do spinouts come from? The role of technology relatedness and institutional context. *Research Policy*, **45**: 1103–1112.

Zahringer, K., Kolympiris, C. and Kalaitzandonakes, N. (2017). Academic knowledge quality differentials and the quality of firm innovation. *Industrial and Corporate Change*, **26**, 5: 821–844.

Zanello, G., Fu, X., Mohnen, P. and Ventresca, M. (2016). The creation and diffusion of innovation in developing countries: A systematic literature review. *Journal of Economic Surveys*, **30**, 5: 884–912.

Biography

Harm-Jan Steenhuis is Associate Dean and Professor of Management, International Business in the College of Business at Hawai'i Pacific University. He previously worked at Eastern Washington University, North Carolina State University, and the University of Twente in Enschede, the Netherlands. He received his MSc in Industrial Engineering and Management and his PhD in International Technology Transfer from the University of Twente. His research areas relate to technological development and economic development related issues such as clusters, technology transfer and diffusion, and innovative technologies.

Xin Fang joined Hawai'i Pacific University in Fall 2011. Prior to that, she was a visiting assistant professor of economics at the University of Illinois at Chicago. She holds a M.A. in economics from Tufts University and a Ph.D. in Economics from University of Illinois at Chicago. Her major research fields are industrial organization, applied microeconomics and applied econometrics.

Tolga Ulusemre is an Assistant Professor at the College of Business, Hawaii Pacific University, where he teaches and researches in the areas of international business and strategy. Before joining Hawaii Pacific University, he was a Visiting Instructor at the Parker College of Business, Georgia Southern University. He holds a PhD in International Business from the University of South Carolina, and a Master of Science in Marketing from the University of Bath, UK.

The Digital Platform Experience of a Leading Country in Wine Tourism: From COVID-19 to the New Era*

Alfonso Marino* and Paolo Pariso†

Engineering Dept. - University of Campania Luigi Vanvitelli
Via Roma Aversa (CE), Italy
**alfonso.marino@unicampania.it*
†paolo.pariso@unicampania.it

The paper's goals are to comprehend strategies for tourism destinations after the coronavirus. The research question (RQ) is if the digital platform experience of a leading country in wine tourism can help to overcome COVID-19 and to turn the sector. The general topics related to destinations, specifically Italian wine tourism destinations, have been elaborated on in the introduction. Starting with a literature review relating to the destination tourism crisis in the tourism sector, the paper highlights the potential and basic lessons for coping with the current crisis. The method, which is connected to a wine tourism destination in Italy, emphasizes both qualitative and quantitative approaches. The results demonstrate the best practices as well as the bottlenecks. The discussions would result in the creation of strategic alternatives specific to the sector and its destinations. The study limits, considering bottlenecks that might arise in the future. The findings emphasize that the sector requires substantial funding from information and communication technology (ICT) to build smart destinations.

Keywords: Wine; technology; tourism; COVID-19; destinations; Italy.

1. Introduction

According to the new World Tourism Organization [UNWTO (2020)], Organization for Economic Cooperation and Development [OECD (2020)], and European Travel Commission (ETC) [(2020)] forecasts, scenarios with projections to July 2021, September 2021, and December 2021 have negative values in terms of tourism [Santos *et al.* (2021); Pelet *et al.* (2019)] spending globally. The spending values indicate a loss for the business of 1170 billion dollars, projected for December 2020, and sadly, this pattern is confirmed by sector forecasts for the first half of 2021. COVID-19 has exposed the vulnerability of the global tourism infrastructure [Qiu *et al.* (2020)], especially of local and regional destinations. The fragility is due to both

† Corresponding author.

*This chapter was originally published in International Journal of Innovation and Technology Management, Vol. 19, No. 7, March 2018, published by World Scientific Publishing, Singapore. Reprinted with permission.

the low organizational structure of the destinations and the inadequate participation of Information and Communication Technologies (ICT). In fact, many destinations have on one hand, a deep digital divide [Dutta and Sarma (2020); Marino and Pariso (2020a); Morrar *et al.* (2019)] and, on the other, peculiar characteristics of natural heritage which can only be used by a restricted number of tourists or small groups, as well as the reaction of individual national governments on which the sector relies. Many of these vulnerabilities appeared after the pandemic, although they existed before COVID-19. However, these flaws were aided by the natural and almost instantaneous arrival of massive tourist flows, which eliminated the need for destinations to play a constructive role. Many European countries, including Italy, Greece, Spain, and Portugal, as well as those in the Organisation for Economic Co-operation and Development (OECD) region, including Brazil, Korea, and Japan, had an over-tourism issue that affected all destinations while ignoring environmental sustainability [Dodds and Butler (2019); Koens *et al.* (2018)]. This phenomenon of spontaneous filling of tourist destinations by destination promotion alone was not a good ally during the pandemic period, when it was appropriate to react with a management-oriented culture, and thus with the marketing mix levers commodity, operation, price, and communication [Capone *et al.* (2020)]. COVID-19 aided in the closing of the promotion tout court, necessitating dramatic shifts in supply and demand [Portela *et al.* (2020)]. For example, the need for a nice vacation contributes to the health protection crisis in terms of trust in those who offer tourist facilities in tourist destinations [Canovi and Pucciarelli (2019)]. These elements, which contribute to making the concept of the tourism sector's supply chain much more complicated, in particular, the theme of health protection, in the post-COVID-19, will be viewed by the tourist as a required, lucrative aspect of his holiday expenditure, not only economic but also of time spent without problems in the destination. In the established tourist service, health protection is a global variable, not relating to specific states where vaccination is needed [Sigala and Haller (2019); Campos *et al.* (2018)]. Destination rivalry [Xu *et al.* (2020)] must incorporate this new factor, which is mainly due to choices taken within the destination. According to this logic, the spread of intelligent travel technology (ITT) [Phaosathianphan and Leelasantitham (2021)] such as intelligent personal assistants (IPAs) [Phaosathianphan and Leelasantitham (2019, 2020)] for travel and tourism, and social networks are even more in according to visitors' behaviors. With the pandemic, this prerogative becomes one of the basic factors in terms of health protection, in the commodity of the sector [Huerta-Álvarez *et al.* (2020)]. The pandemic represents a point of no return and foreshadows a situation in which pre-COVID-19 turnovers are conceivable in the long run, but only by acting on the composition of the tourist offer, as well as the activity and management of the network that contributes to the development of the overall bid. In this case, wine tourism, a part of the tourist supply, has a different pattern in some Italian destination areas. Following the very high levels reported with the 2018 harvest, when more than 50 million hectoliters were produced on the Peninsula, Italy recorded a small contraction of wine production in 2019, 47 million hectoliters, still significant figures in any case. The Italian harvest of 2019 establishes Italy as the world's leading manufacturer, ahead of France and Spain [OIV (2020)]. There are significant figures who, in terms of selling the commodity, represent both a potential for exceptional effect and a significant contribution constraint. The two major trajectories of wine tourism [ISTAT (2021)], presences in 2019 and the economic importance of the total wine tourism supply chain in 2020 are as follows:

(a) 14 million wine tourism presences in 2019, taking into account all overnight stays and daily returns in wine tourism resorts;
(b) 2.5 billion euros of the economic value of the entire wine tourism supply chain in 2019, taking into account the only revenue provided by wineries from wine tourism: direct sales, tastings, and lodging.

As a result, wine tourism has become a true economic, social, and cultural heritage of the entire region. In addition to the areas designated as UNESCO World Heritage Sites, for the wine-growing landscape, in addition to the regions that are now a UNESCO World Heritage Site for the landscape and a wine landscape, the whole country of Italy is a single remarkable wine-growing "theater" in the sky. The consequences of COVID-19 are profound in 2020–2021, affecting the tourism industry as a whole. The Italian government assists the sector through both micro and macro actions. The following activities have been described at the micro-level: new internet services, marketing linked to the content of the territories, cultural, food, and wine itineraries. At the macro-stage, a new public–private partnership is being planned to increase the incisiveness of tourism spending opportunities. Furthermore, the need for new funding in conjunction with the strategic presence of local agencies. Wine tourism is a significant and consolidated destination for tourists and turnover in Italy, but it has some shortcomings outlined in the pandemic period by COVID-19. The following study questions are proposed in this paper: Can Italy, despite being a major player in wine tourism, remains a destination in the post-pandemic phase? The study aims at evaluating if the digital development of some touristic wine destination is correlated with return on assets (ROAs) performance, present in the same areas and how is when it exists this correlation the study elaborates a statistical model with a correlation analysis between values that includes both digital and financial aspects. The model also seeks to detect the most influential digital levers on destinations' profitability. The research question (RQ) is: Can the digital platform experience of a leading country in wine tourism help to overcome COVID-19 and to turn the sector?

2. Theorethical Overview

Tourist destinations Destination Management Organization (DMO) [Morrison (2018)] are one of the sector's strategic nodes and are named, in this current pandemic scenario, to the rehabilitation of destinations in terms of reception in health welfare. The required innovation is also a joint target for DMOs who have historically carried out marketing and promotion operations since their field of operation has expanded significantly and requires the critical task of collaboration of the various stakeholders working in the destination. Since health safety is provided by interactions between people and interactions between people and systems, any touch, outside the dimension known to sector stakeholders, must provide for health safety. In recent years, the literature on destination management has centered on the success of DMOs about different issues relating to strategic leadership, organizational management, and governance [UNWTO (2020)]. Furthermore, the problems and opportunities associated with ICT [Hall and Williams (2019)] and the advancement of intelligent technologies in the context of smart destinations are highlighted. It is interesting to note how destinations can benefit economically, as well as knowledge about the solutions provided by emerging digital technologies: destination intelligence, tourist information, visitor management, and marketing can provide the DMO with valuable resources for strategic-relational and organizational decisions, by feeding destination information systems with up-to-date data [Ivars-Baidal *et al.* (2019)]. The pandemic forces people to "stay at home," while removing the noble proposal of a lived relationship between the destination and the tourist. In this respect, it should be noted that the success of responses is connected to the implementation of a mindset capable of identifying recovery actions, both technological, social, and governance related [McKercher (2020)]. The indications given by governments and destination organizations are dependent on reports of treatment and patient care received in the health sector. These indicators are not as consistent as the pandemic in all parts of the world; consider the various positions of individual governments on the ability to wear the mask as the first defensive behavior. These signs come at a time when the various players engaged in destination device management around the world should have taken a more proactive approach. Some destinations have taken constructive measures, such as implementing a communicative brand security policy, and have quickly enabled, establishing contact with their audience, displaying their existence, and being concerned about the well-being of their prospective visitors. On the contrary, and especially during the first phase of the pandemic, tourist destinations such as Italy and Greece have remained quiet, failing to establish constructive, confident actions with their reference markets. Some governments in the OECD region have initiated proactive communication-based actions, as Europe has had involved governments such as the Portuguese, "Cannot Miss Hope" or Spanish #visitbarcelona#. This method of communication occurs using a network and interactive media, i.e. a set of tools that do not solve, but rather aid in #stare contact# rather than #stare isolation#. This communication is essential to remember that the destination considers the tourist, modifies its behavior to welcome safely, and therefore, invites the reopening. Reduce the difference by entertaining remotely. This revitalization of the destination must be balanced with the management of the endured crisis, employment, and economic crisis, so we must not overlook the quest for funds to help operators and, most importantly, sustain communication with the institutions. In this sense, tour operators and destinations have seen 2021 as a survival year [Eurostat Tourism Dataset (2021)] and should concentrate in the next years on three goals: cost savings, health protection growth, and tourist trust recovery. In light of the shift in market trends caused by the pandemic, these three goals must be pursued in a different way of doing and consuming tourism. Regenerate to re-balance supply and improve health protection of tourism goods and services that are in demand. The competition to draw visitors must be accompanied by ads focusing on territory connectivity related to restoration, generations of goods and services based on the customer. For example, a customer who, in addition to the need to have fun and enjoy, carries with his worries, distrust, and fears. This is the new consumer; a single operator cannot handle the new consumer; the vaccination is the initiative of the state and private citizens, and the destination's effort would be to certify its COVID-free status. The system wins, not the particular destination; in this context, tourism requires a period of the reconstruction as an industry. The scheme benefits if the European funds, next generation plan, planned for European states, with Italy receiving the most money in Europe, are spent on investments that boost the country's competitiveness. The global tourism industry will need new ways of cooperation across destinations to effectively relaunch in 2021. The current post-COVID-19 normal will not be the same as the previous one, and tourism will need to find a new equilibrium that is only partially dependent on the past, in which you handled attendance and marketing, assured convenience, and the information gathered and processed was adequate to foresee the demand. It is important to adapt to an unknown time reinvent oneself, seek new sources of funding, reposition the destination, and diversify markets, goods, and services. Regulations are the starting point, not the result. Joint concrete actions between the public and private sectors are needed, for example, addressing the environmental issue, economic exploitation of places, or overcrowding [Niewiadomski (2020)]. It is true that in the initial stage, domestic demand is the destination of choice, but the world economy, of which the domestic market is just a small portion, should not be overlooked. The crisis in tourist destinations due to COVID-19 is still ongoing and there are no elements of significant recovery. This trend also includes Italian wine tourist destinations, which show elements of digital weakness, as evidenced by the application of the OECD classification to Italian wine tourist destinations.

3. Method

The method implemented analyzes the main Italian destinations of wine tourism to verify what emerged from the introduction and the conceptual background. The main destinations are 80 and represent the areas of the north (57 destinations), the center (13 destinations) and the south (10 destinations) Italy. The geographical areas, destinations and comparison ROA are shown in Table 1. Table 1 is displayed in the method because it is the elaboration of our database

The 80 destinations were evaluated by the research group through the participating observation method [Spradley (2016)] and classified, assigning a score from 0 to 1 about the degree of interaction, following the OECD method. For each

Table 1. Geographical areas and destinations of wine tourism in Italy.

Geographic area	Destination	ROA (%)
Agrigento Sicilia South	1	10
Ancona Marche Central	1	7
Aosta Valle d'Aosta North	2	3
Asti Piemonte North	5	3
Avellino Campania South	1	12
Biella Piemonte North	2	4
Benevento Campania South	3	9
Bologna Emilia North	2	5
Caserta Campania South	1	10
Chieti Abruzzo Central	2	6
Cuneo Piemonte North	3	3
Firenze Toscana North	1	4
Frosinone Lazio Centro	1	7
Gorizia Friuli North	1	6
Grosseto Toscana Central	2	4
Livorno Toscana Central	2	5
Modena Emilia North	1	6
Novara Piemonte North	5	4
Piacenza Emilia Nord	1	4
Padova Veneto Nord	1	5
Pescara Abruzzo Central	3	6
Perugia Umbria Central	1	4
Pisa Toscana Central	1	6
Pordenone Friuli North	1	3
Roma Lazio Centro	2	4
Salerno Campania Sud	1	11
Siena Toscana Central	2	3
Siracusa Sicilia South	2	11
Sassari Sardegna South	1	11
Savana Liguria North	1	3
Isernia Molise South	1	12
Trento Trentino North	5	3
Torino Piemonte North	1	3
Terni Umbria Central	1	4
Treviso Veneto North	12	4
Udine Friuli North	2	4
Vercelli Piemonte North	1	4
Venezia Veneto North	1	4
Vicenza Veneto North	1	3
Verona Veneto North	1	3
Vibo Calabria South	1	3
Total	80	

Source: Our elaboration on ISTAT [2015–2019].

destination, referring to the geographical area, it has been verified, following the OECD classification of web services within the destination and its degree of interaction with visitors, to classify the destination as a smart destination concerning both the sale of wine and the reception. The OECD classification has five levels, as explained in Box 1 (Results) below. A smart destination is a destination where companies, tourists, and local administrations, constantly interact to carry out four main activities: collect destination data from all possible sources. Analyze the collected data by elaborating specific algorithms to determine the tourist behavior and the operations. Implement useful ideas to improve the use of the destination from the management side and from that of tourist satisfaction. Implementing measures through economic, financial, and territorial interventions, aimed at improving the destination, making it more sustainable and adaptable to the needs and tastes of tourists who can, in this way, further customize their experience. After classification, the balance sheets of individual destinations were verified, using data from the National Institute of Statistics (ISTAT) 2015–2019, to check whether the destinations with the highest score in terms of web users are also those that have lost the least turnover. The database is characterized by Italian Economic Activity code 11.02.10, 11.02.20, 55.20.52. From the results of the first analysis, the study detected a meaningful statistical sample on which to apply a regression analysis. Analyzing digital performances of the meaningful statistical sample the study evaluated the eventual presence of a statistical correlation with their economic performance. Digital performances linked to tourism destinations have been detected Osservatorio.net dataset [2021] that analyzes Italian digital trends, also in tourism destinations, applying European digital economy society index (DESI) methodology. Starting from these data the study elaborated a data normalization using the min-max method ranging the results on a scale between 0 and 1. The hypothesis leads us to verify the existence of a linear relationship between DESI and destinations' ROA, which we can describe with a linear regression model in which x is DESI and y is ROA. ROA is calculated as the ratio between profit for the year and total assets of the reclassified balance sheet. To be satisfactory, the value obtained must be at least higher than the interest rate paid on the debt capital, that is: % ROA >% bank interest: management is generating value; % ROA <% bank interest: management is destroying value. This indicator suggests how a company can act based on what it owns, regardless of the form of financing implemented. It is very useful for comparing competing companies that are part of the same market sector. In order to identify the correlation level the analysis used Pearson $(-1 > r > 1)$ and Determination coefficient $(r_2 > 0,4)$. The assessment of the regression model's consistency with the data was performed by using a Student T-test and a Fischer F-test. The collected data were statistically analyzed using the statistical package for the social sciences (SPSSs) version 26.0. The following paragraph will be present the results.

4. Results

Starting from OECD classification, Web measure model, the destinations, 80, have been classified from Stage I to Stage V. In the box below is shown the classification and its content.

Box 1. Web measure model: Stages of smart destination evolution

Emerging Presence is **Stage I** representing information, which is limited and basic. The destination online presence comprises a web page and/or an official website; links to other public links, as police/departments, health, welfare, accommodations', regional/local opportunities; some archived information may be available online, most information remains static with the fewest options for visitors.

Enhanced presence is **Stage II** in which the online services of the destination enter the interactive mode with services to enhance the convenience of the visitors such as downloadable forms for tax payment, to buy, to book. Audio and video capability is provided for relevant public information. The destination officials can be contacted via email, fax, telephone, and post. The site is updated with greater regularity to keep the information current and up to date for the visitors.

Interactive presence is **Stage III** in which the online services of the destination enter the interactive mode with services to enhance the convenience of the visitors such as downloadable forms for tax payment, to buy, to booking. Audio and video capability is provided for relevant public information. The destination officials can be contacted via email, fax, telephone and post. The site is updated with greater regularity to keep the information current and up to date for the visitors.

Transactional presence is **Stage IV** that allows two-way interaction between the visitors and his/her destination. It includes options for paying and booking; applying for credit cards, and other similar interactions by allowing him/her to submit these online. The visitors can pay for services, such as other transactions through their credit, bank, or credit card. Providers of goods and services can bid online for public contacts via secure links.

Networked presence is **Stage V** which represents the most sophisticated level in the destination marketing strategy. This stage includes III and IV but is characterized by an integration of technology and reverse interactions. The destination encourages participatory deliberative decision-making and is willing and able to involve the area in a two-way open dialogue. Through interactive features such as the web comment form and innovative online consultation mechanisms, the destination actively solicits visitors' views on decisions and participatory decision-making. Implicit in this stage of the model is the integration of the destination with full co-operation and understanding of the concept of collective decision-making, participatory idea, and visitors' empowerment as a smart destination.

Source: Our elaboration on OECD [2017].

The destinations in Northern Italy represent the nucleus of wine tourism in Italy. Of the 57 destinations, more than 70% rank between level IV and V with a score between 0.7 and 0.9. In this target area, the best practices refer to the geographical areas of Asti, Novara, Siena, Trento, Turin, Treviso, Vercelli, and Verona with 0.9 all in Northern Italy. They follow with 0.8, Aosta, Biella, Bologna, Cuneo, Modena, Padua, Udine, Venice, and Vicenza, again all of Northern Italy. With the score of 0.7 for Northern Italy, we have Savona, Piacenza, Pisa, while in central Italy with the same score we have Rome and Florence. Destinations in central Italy are between level III and IV, totaling a score between 0.5 and 0.7. All southern destinations rank between Level I and III with a score of between 0.3 and 0.5. The destinations of the center, except Rome and Florence and all destinations in southern Italy, cannot be classified as the strong nucleus of wine tourism. Concerning the result it is classified in terms of web offer of the ranking product, 17 geographical areas emerge. In these 17 geographical areas and their destinations, it has been verified what are the consolidated turnover losses. In these 17 areas, the use of the Web, the high level of interaction with visitors, guarantee lower turnover losses to other destinations even in the presence of a negative number of visitors referring to the pre-COVID-19 periods. These 17 destinations can be considered smart and are all TED in Northern Italy. The trend of these 17 destinations was deepened with the DESI and destinations' ROA. To evaluate the smart destinations, context linear regression has been implemented (Table 2).

The results of the regression analysis show all positive correlations, so the statistical model reveals that both variables (ROA and digital variables) move in the

Table 2. DESI and destinations' ROA.

	ROA versus Conn	ROA versus HC	ROA versus UoI	ROA versus IoDT
Correlation	0,83142024	0,805681823	0,717604206	0,728363493
Determination	0,69125961	0,6491232	0,514955797	0,530513379
Observations	17			

		F	p-value
ROA versus Conn		33,5845085	3,53165E-05
ROA versus HC		27,7500478	9,46685E-05
ROA versus UoI		15,9250165	0,00118166
ROA versus IoDT		16,9497922	0,000914189

	b Coefficient	lower 95,0%	upper 95,0%
ROA versus Conn	0,74382107	0,470247562	1,017394569
ROA versus HC	0,59132154	0,352063309	0,830579773
ROA versus UoI	0,67369299	0,313863182	1,033522807
ROA versus IoDT	0,7585227	0,365822202	1,15122319

Notes: Legenda: ROAs = Return on assets; Conn = Connectivity; HC = Human capital; UoI = Use of internet services; IoDT = Integration of digital technology.

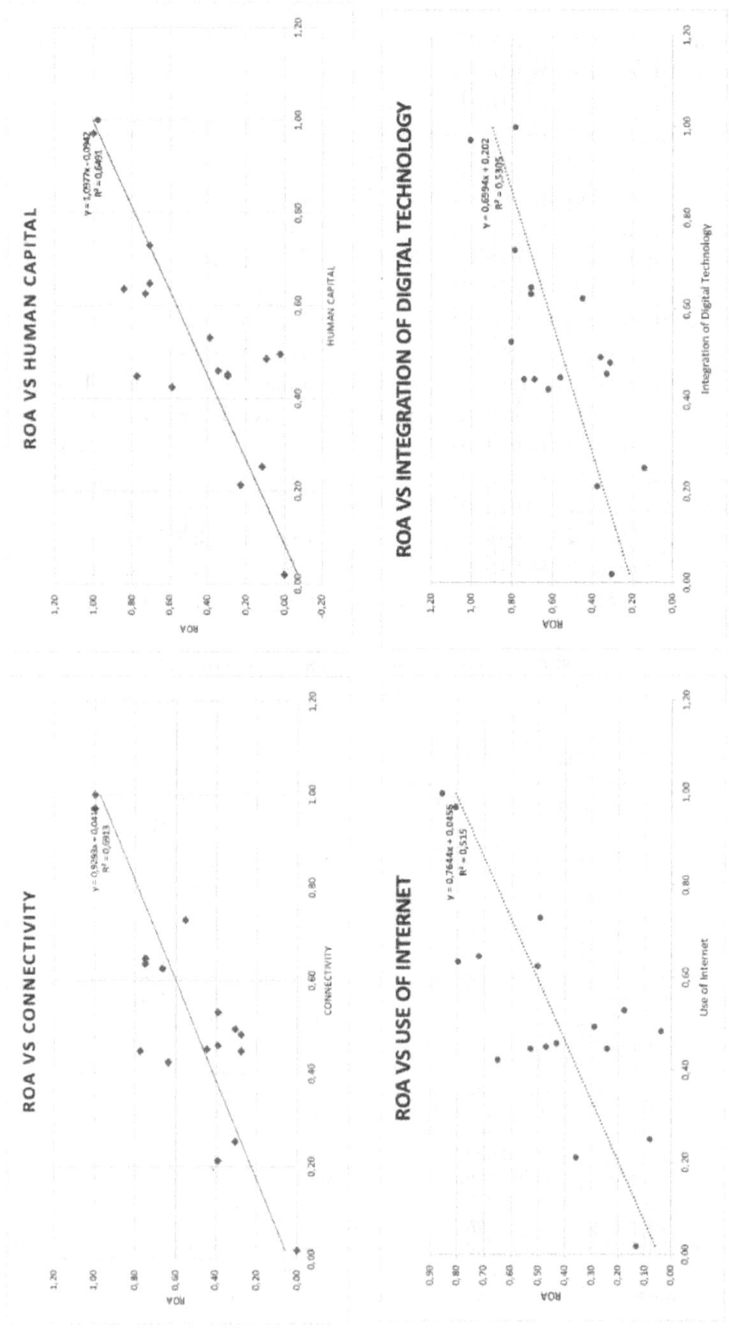
ROA VS CONNECTIVITY
y = 0,9293x + 0,0414
R² = 0,6913
CONNECTIVITY
ROA
ROA VS HUMAN CAPITAL
y = 1,0977x - 0,0942
R² = 0,6491
HUMAN CAPITAL
ROA
ROA VS USE OF INTERNET
y = 0,7644x + 0,0455
R² = 0,515
Use of Internet
ROA
ROA VS INTEGRATION OF DIGITAL TECHNOLOGY
y = 0,6994x + 0,202
R² = 0,5305
Integration of Digital Technology
ROA

same direction. In particular, Table 2 shows the measure of the correlation of the ROA with Connectivity ($r = 0.831$; $R_2 = 0.691$), Human Capital ($r = 0.717$; $R_2 = 0.514$), and Digital Technology ($r = 0.728$; $R_2 = 0.530$). In addition, the p-value and F values for all digital variables (Fig. 2) verified the regression and model's suitability. In this context, the results outlined that all digital dimensions express a leverage effect on ROA. According to the statistical model, this may imply that the digital dimensions could be the key factors on which touristic destinations should focus their efforts to enhance their profitability condition. As a consequence, the enhancement in the development of citizens' digital skills, the construction of new digital-advanced infrastructures, the digital upgrade of existing infrastructures, and in particular, a high level of digitization of the enterprises could minimize any digital divide of the touristic destination analyzed about these results.

5. Discussion

Wine destinations are characterized by a high level of interaction with the places of production, tasting, and purchase. In particular, to experience the culture, the atmosphere, the scents, the cellars, the vineyards, the villages, is fundamental the presence in the places and a sharing between people of the experiences lived. This is the context of the direct sale, on-site, of the product, with a minimum percentage of online sales. It is clear that there are contingent measures such as the distancing rules, the prohibition of gathering in small places (i.e. cellars and villages) and also structural bottlenecks since the villages of wine tourism are in Italy among the last for digital services to customers. On the other hand, Italy in the European ranking of the digital economic social index (DESI) and its key performance indicators (KPIs) is in third last place [Marino and Pariso (2019, 2020a,b, 2021)]. At the same time, it is interesting to note that the use of the web may mitigate the crisis from COVID-19 in this tourism sector. It is possible to state that the first question: "Will Italy, despite being a big player in wine tourism, still be in the post-pandemic phase, a destination?" Yes, is possible how to demonstrate by 17 geographic areas and related destinations. Furthermore, it is possible to state that the second question: "How the factors are organized based on their importance that influences the effectiveness of the destinations in COVID-19 times?" In the case of Italian wine tourism, it can be said that the use of information technology [Chouki *et al.* (2020)], and in particular, the web has caused fewer economic losses for those destinations classified at stage five.

5.1. *The proposal*

The examination of the literature and the results of Italian wine tourism also the recent one that studies the pandemic phase concerning the tourism sector shows that the regeneration of the sector must go through some strategic phases, supported by information and communication technologies (ICTs) and DESIs KPI. The first phase that ICT may support is the reopening. The phases of the proposal are presented in time order, although stakeholders in the sector must work at the same time as the different phases.

5.2. *The reopening and ICT: Connectivity*

This phase must reshape the target. The destination is an integrated, modular, reshaping service, product means structural investments in connectivity related to overcoming the digital divide and different tasks and roles of the stakeholders that are present in the supply chain. Connectivity can be a strategic enabling factor, supporting the post-pandemic phase for strong activity in terms of control, coordination of the entire supply chain, the goal is to make visitors, workers, and resident population bring in health safety. The adequate investments display in the last ICT Government Plan (2021–2023) can support the flows in the destination: health and quality of life of the local population; support local activities; organize the itineraries. The reopening should be oriented to integrate tourism destination and ICT investments, not only health, safety, sustainability, and local community well-being, but also ensure adequate economic returns. The reopening of the destination highlights the need for a change of vision: ICT and the tourism sector [Higgins-Desbiolles (2020)] should create integration, coordination, and control or ensure that visitors have a different experience from the mass experience [Paulauskaite *et al.* (2017); Pookhao Sonjai *et al.* (2018)] in line with the new post-pandemic dimension. The reopening and connectivity should promote the tourist competitiveness of the destination supported by ICT and its management. [Gretzel *et al.* (2016)].

5.3. *Regeneration and ICT: Human capital*

Regenerating means creating the conditions to generate a confident human capital linked to the destination towards the market and demand, but also towards the local system and the operators of the destination. In the regeneration phase, in addition to the economic theme, it is strategic to increase training and trust between the parties. The training and trust highlight the need for basic and advantage skills linked to ICT, e.g. web usage, within the destination, but also information about the zero contagion capacity that the visitor can bring inside the destination. ICT and its management may create a relational trust is at this stage, a good practice, a common good, for the entire supply chain of the sector present in that destination. In this logic, it is strategic to understand the needs, motivations, and concerns of the targets delivering products and services adapted to demand. This compliance is possible developing regeneration and human capital skills. In the regeneration phase, data collection is processed regarding visitor profiling as a strategic tool.

5.4. *Product development and ICT: Use of internet services*

This phase is the consequence of the work carried out in the connectivity and human capital phases. The two previous phases show the destination's ability to collect and process data to share with all the stakeholders of the system, a new, innovative activity to which destination, must arrive prepared in terms of skills and shared strategies. ICT and its management, at this level, may support product development service. Sharing is an action that must support to realize technological tools and applications, use of internet services (UoI), such as to provide the entire destination with key indicators related to the safety and economic sustainability of the service and product provided. The data, the information, become essential, and therefore, the supply of the destination and the effects of COVID-19 must be evaluated, monitoring the demand and its patterns of behavior, as well as the flows and behavior of the tourist within the destination. UoI, can play a key role, so the need to invest in the digital development model [Marino and Pariso (2020b); Femenia-Serra *et al.* (2019); Lee *et al.* (2020)].

5.5. *Trajectories for business models and ICT: Integration of Digital Technology*

Previous crises, not health, but economic, financial, terrorist, although very serious, have led to changes and the introduction of new trajectories for business models [Cook *et al.* (2018)] based on ICT. It is still too early to understand the extent and depth of this crisis in the post-pandemic phase, however, some trajectories are clear and to be developed. The first trajectory concerns the change of mass tourism and its need to regenerate about the phenomenon of overbooking and over-tourism: hotel chains, low-cost companies, and tour operators will have to review their volume-focused business. The second trajectory is that of protected tourist demand, therefore, destinations and tourist proposals not crowded personalized will be a trajectory that in the post-pandemic will play a central role. The demand for tourism for low-popular destinations will increase, but also a demand for higher quality in the service. Furthermore, the long period of isolation indoors accelerates the demand for open spaces and meaningful relationships between people. The third trajectory can be identified in digital tourism that presents one of the key characteristics of tourists' desire to remain continuously in contact with other people's activities and from the fear of being excluded from events, experiences, or rewarding social contexts, this need for integrating connection. The fourth trajectory is that of the holiday for personal well-being understood as health, therefore, also of micro-holidays, also to the stress caused by the pandemic and the relative loss of income or work. These trajectories, over-tourism, slow tourism, digital tourism, micro-holidays, also if different between them, highlight the need to accelerate in the same area: the integration of digital technologies (IoDTs), with particular attention to connectivity as strategic support to reopening phase, human capital, and digital skills, as strategic support to regeneration and UoI as support to product development. With this perspective, sustainability, and safety, become priority values and a transversal axis for the tourist development of the destination. The destination must be empathetic with its tourists. Based on these results and discussion if the Italian wine destinations will be able to improve these four bottlenecks, come back to be a major player in the wine tourism destination.

6. Limitations of the Research

The web affects the performance of destinations, but it is not the only variable. The other key factors investigated in the study highlight not always comparable outputs. Despite this limit, the appropriate use of technologies and digital innovations represent the strategic resources to develop the destinations. Regarding methodological remarks, the research was designed and managed in the COVID-19 phases and since the destinations and the stakeholders are still engaged in the reorganization of services, the evaluation of the websites and related key factors was carried out by the research group through participating observation and processing consolidated balance sheet data of the destinations, registered with the ISTAT.

The web affects the performance of destinations, but it is not the only variable, the possible others are not investigated in the search. This limit is due to the period in which the research was designed and managed: in the Covid 19 phases, the destinations, the stakeholders are engaged in the reorganization of services, action more than a reflection. In fact, the evaluation of the websites was carried out by the research group with the participating observation and processing consolidated balance sheet data of the destinations, registered with the ISTAT.

7. Conclusions

This contribution has provided a timely and articulated analysis of the possible development path for tourist destinations, with specific attention to Italian wine tourism, after the COVID-19 emergency. The strategic importance to reducing and overcoming the digital bottlenecks that affect the Italian wine destinations has been valued about ICT by DESI application and its KPI. The reopening phase is closely linked to the connectivity, not only in an economic asset but also in, cultural one. The issue of health safety at the reopening stage (Sec. 5.2) is central. This path needs to abandon some comfort zones such as the trajectory of fast and compulsive over-tourism with slow tourism. The regeneration of human capital (Sec. 5.3) with strong investments in soft and hard digital skills are connected to the development of the service, product, and the identification of business models (Sec. 5.4) highlighting the need for a profound cultural change and ICT within the destinations. Destinations should focus completely on all activities related to destination management, not only marketing but involving stakeholders in a strategic development path aimed at regenerating the destination. The role of inland areas that, while presenting significant environmental, cultural, and landscape resources, have not been the subject of attention by operators and organizers can be a resource in terms of sustainability and health safety. Digital platforms can promote, in the absence of the digital divide, inland areas by enhancing territorial resources and expertise through their system. Business trajectories can accelerate the development of the sector in the post-pandemic knowing that all stakeholders must review the sector as a system that must provide health security and digital services among the first products.

References

Campos, A. C., Mendes, J., Valle, P. O. D. and Scott, N. (2018). Co-creation of tourist experiences: A literature review. *Current Issues in Tourism*, **21**, 4: 369–400, https://doi.org/10.1080/13683500.2015.1081158.

Canovi, M. and Pucciarelli, F. (2019). Social media marketing in wine tourism: winery owners' perceptions. *Journal of Travel and Tourism Marketing*, **36**, 6: 653–664.

Capone, V., Marino, L. and Donizzetti, A. R. (2020). The english version of the health profession communication collective efficacy scale (HPCCE scale) by Capone and Petrillo, 2012, *European Journal of Investigation in Health, Psychology and Education*, **10**, 4: 1065–1079.

Chouki, M., Talea, M., Okar, C. and Chroqui, R. (2020). Barriers to information technology adoption within small and medium enterprises: A systematic literature review. *International Journal of Innovation and Technology Management*, **17**, 1: 2050007, https://doi.org/10.1142/S0219877020500078.

Cook, R. A., Hsu, C. H. and Taylor, L. L. (2018). *Tourism: The Business of Hospitality and Travel,* Vol. 6. Pearson, New York.

Dodds, R. and Butler, R. (2019).*Overtourism: Issues, Realities and Solutions*, Vol. 1. De Gruyter Oldenbourg, Oldenbourg.

Dutta, D. and Sarma, M. K. (2020). Service innovation typologies and applications in India: A literature review. *International Journal of Business Innovation and Research*, **22**, 3: 359–373, https://doi.org/10.1504/IJBIR.2020.107963.

European Travel Commission (ETC) (2020). https://etc-corporate.org/.

Eurostat Tourism Dataset (2021). Retrieved from https://ec.europa.eu/eurostat/web/products-datasets/-/tour_dem_totot [accessed on December 2021].

Femenia-Serra, F., Neuhofer, B. and Ivars-Baidal, J. A. (2019). Towards a conceptualisation of smart tourists and their role within the smart destination scenario. *The Service Industries Journal*, **39**, 2: 109–133, https://doi.org/10.1080/02642069.2018.1508458.

Hall, C. M. and Williams, A. M. (2019). *Tourism and Innovation.* Routledge, London.

Higgins-Desbiolles, F. (2020). Socialising tourism for social and ecological justice after COVID-19. *Tourism Geographies*, **22**, 3: 610–623, https://doi.org/10.1080/14616688.2020.1757748.

Huerta-Álvarez, R., Cambra-Fierro, J. J. and Fuentes-Blasco, M. (2020). The interplay between social media communication, brand equity and brand engagement in tourist destinations: An analysis in an emerging economy. *Journal of Destination Marketing and Management*, **16**: 100413, https://doi.org/10.1016/j.jdmm.2020.100413.

ISTAT (2015–2019). Retrieved from https://www.istat.it/it/archivio/vino [accessed on January 2021].

Ivars-Baidal, J. A., Celdrán-Bernabeu, M. A., Mazón, J. N. and Perles-Ivars, Á. F. (2019). Smart destinations and the evolution of ICTs: A new scenario for destination management? *Current Issues in Tourism*, **22**, 13: 1581–1600, https://doi.org/10.1080/13683500.2017.1388771.

Koens, K., Postma, A. and Papp, B. (2018). Is overtourism overused? Understanding the impact of tourism in a city context. *Sustainability*, **10**, 1–15, https://doi.org/10.3390/su10124384.

Lee, P., Hunter, W. C. and Chung, N. (2020). Smart tourism city: Developments and transformations. *Sustainability*, **12**, https://doi.org/10.3390/su12103958.

Marino, A. and Pariso, P. (2019). Italian cloud tourism as tool to develop local tourist districts economic vitality and reformulate public policies. In *International Conference on P2P, Parallel, Grid, Cloud and Internet Computing.* Springer, Cham, pp. 609–615.

Marino, A. and Pariso, P. (2020a). From digital divide to e-government: Re-engineering process and bureaucracy in public service delivery. *Electronic Government, An International Journal*, **16**, 3: 314–325, https://doi.org/10.1504/EG.2020.108495.

Marino, A. and Pariso, P. (2020b). Value governance, digital divided and economic inequality in Italy during the Covid 19 emergency. In *The 4th International Conference on E-commerce, E-Business and E-Government*, Paris, France, pp. 45–53.

Marino, A. and Pariso, P. (2021). E-tourism: How ICTs help the local tourist district drive economic vitality — The case of Campania, Italy. *International Journal of Innovation and Technology Management*, https://doi.org/10.1142/S0219877021500097.

McKercher, B. (2020). Cultural tourism market: A perspective paper. *Tourism Review*, **75**, 1: 126–129, https://doi.org/10.1108/TR-03-2019-0096.

Morrar, R., Abdeljawad, I., Jabr, S., Kisa, A. and Younis, M. Z. (2019). The role of information and communications technology (ICT) in enhancing service sector productivity in Palestine: An international perspective. *Journal of Global Information Management*, **27**, 1: 47–65, doi: 10.4018/JGIM.2019010103.

Morrison, A. M. (2018). *Marketing and Managing Tourism Destinations*. Routledge, London.

Niewiadomski, P. (2020). COVID-19: From temporary de-globalisation to a re-discovery of tourism? *Tourism Geographies*, **22**, 3: 651–656, https://doi.org/10.1080/14616688.2020.1757749.

Paulauskaite, D., Powell, R., Coca-Stefaniak, J. A. and Morrison, A. M. (2017). Living like a local: Authentic tourism experiences and the sharing economy. *International Journal of Tourism Research*, **19**, 6: 619–628, https://doi.org/10.1002/jtr.2134.

Pelet, J. É., Barton, M. and Chapuis, C. (2019). Towards the implementation of digital through Wifi and IoT in wine tourism: Perspectives from professionals of wine and tourism. Management and marketing of wine tourism business, Phaosathianphan, N. and Leelasantitham, A. (2021). An intelligent travel technology assessment model for destination impacts of tourist adoption. *Tourism Management Perspectives*, **40**: 100882, doi:10.1016/j.tmp.2021.100882.

Phaosathianphan, N. and Leelasantitham, A. (2020). A plenary free individual traveler life cycle for assessment of adoption intelligent travel assistant. *Heliyon*, **6**, 7: e04428, doi: 10.1016/j.heliyon.2020.e04428.

Phaosathianphan, N. and Leelasantitham, A. (2019). Understanding the adoption factors influence to the use of intelligent travel assistant (ITA) for eco-tourists: An extension of the UTAUT. *International Journal of Innovation and Technology Management (IJITM)*, **16**, 8: 1950060, doi: 10.1142/s0219877019500603.236.

Pookhao Sonjai, N., Bushell, R., Hawkins, M. and Staiff, R. (2018). Community-based ecotourism: Beyond authenticity and the commodification of local people. *Journal of Ecotourism*, **17**, 3: 252–267, https://doi.org/10.1080/14724049.2018.1503502.

Portela, J. F. and Abad, C. J. P. (2020). Digital platforms in the development of wine tourism in castilla *y* león: Websites and social networks. *Cuadernos de Turismo*, **46**: 577–579.

Qiu, R. T., Park, J., Li, S. and Song, H. (2020). Social costs of tourism during the COVID-19 pandemic. *Annals of Tourism Research*, **84**: 102994, https://doi.org/10.1016/j.annals.2020.102994.

Santos, V., Ramos, P., Sousa, B. and Valeri, M. (2021). Towards a framework for the global wine tourism system. *Journal of Organizational Change Management*, https://doi.org/10.1108/JOCM-11-2020-0362.

Sigala, M. and Haller, C. (2019). The impact of social media on the behavior of wine tourists: A typology of power sources. *Management and Marketing of Wine Tourism Business*. Palgrave Macmillan, Cham, pp. 139–154.

Spradley, J. P. (2016). *Participant Observation*. Waveland Press, Illinois.

World Tourism Organization (UNWTO) (2020). https://www.unwto.org/statistics.

Xu, Y., Li, J., Belyi, A. and Park, S. (2020). Characterizing destination networks through mobility traces of international tourists — A case study using a nationwide mobile positioning dataset. *Tourism Management*, 82: 104195, https://doi.org/10.1016/j.tourman.2020.104195.

Biography

Alfonso Marino is a Professor Business Economics and Organization at the Engineering Department - University of Campania "Luigi Vanvitelli". His teaching and research interests are in technology and organizational innovation in the local public sector and enterprise start-up. He has published in a variety of international journals and has been a member of the Advisory Board of Sheffield Hallam University, Board of International Journal of Enterprise Studies and DPM - Doctoral Program in Management. He is mentioned by the Accademia della Crusca for his studies in the field of public services. Actually, he is a member of Editorial Board of JOTS - International Journal on Tourism and Sustainability.

Paolo Pariso is a PHD in Industrial Engineering, nominated Subject Expert and Teaching Assistant at the Engineering Department - University of Campania "Luigi Vanvitelli". His research interests are in technology and organizational innovation in the local public sector and enterprise start-up. He is involved in research regarding economic development of the tourism sector in some areas of northern and southern Italy and development of business models linked to the circular economy for enterprise startups. He has published in a variety of international journals concerning the issues of economy and organization of the public sector and circular economy.

Part 3

Exogenous Shocks and Responses to Pandemics

Influential Aspects of Knowledge Sharing in the Context of a Marketplace Platform During the COVID-19 Pandemic: A Brazilian Case Study*

Carlos Francisco Bitencourt Jorge*,†,||, João Guilherme de Camargo Ferraz Machado‡, Cláudia Herrero Martins Menegassi¶, Rodrigo da Silva Stecca‡ and Michael J. D. Sutton*,§

*Department of Business and Management Marília University (UNIMAR) Marília, São Paulo, Brazil

†Department of Information Science São Paulo State University (UNESP) School of Philosophy and Sciences, Marília, São Paulo, Brazil

‡Department of Agribusiness and Development São Paulo State University (UNESP) School of Sciences and Engineering, Tupã, São Paulo, Brazil

§Department of Business and Sustainable Management Anaheim University Anaheim, California, USA

¶Department of Knowledge Management in Organizations Cesumar University (Unicesumar), Brazil

||bitencourt@gmail.com

The COVID-19 pandemic and social distancing entangled physical trading of products and services worldwide. As a result, the Commercial and Industrial Association of Marília (ACIM) developed and provided businesses with a marketplace platform called "Marília.Dakki." In this context, knowledge emerged as a resource, and knowledge sharing became a fundamental activity for the marketplace implementation. Thus, the objective of the research was to identify and analyze the influential aspects of knowledge sharing (IAKS) in "Marília.Dakki." The research is characterized as qualitative and exploratory and used the case study method. Questionnaires were used to acquire data from the 19 subjects involved in the "Marília.Dakki" operations, as well as an interview with the Director of IT and Innovation. As a result of the research, people, processes, and culture were identified as IAKS, and these aspects, when related, generated nine other IAKS. The researchers concluded that these IAKS found in the research impacted the marketplace adoption, in addition to its maintenance as a collaborative environment, and are of great importance for the survival and development of companies, both during the pandemic and after it.

Keywords: Knowledge Sharing; Commercial and Industrial Association of Marilia; Online Sales; COVID-19; Marketplace.

|| Corresponding author.

*This chapter was originally published in International Journal of Innovation and Technology Management, Vol. 19, No. 7, March 2018, published by World Scientific Publishing, Singapore. Reprinted with permission.

1. Introduction

As a result of the COVID-19 pandemic, the need for social distancing — especially in the period of more restrictive isolation measures, such as the lockdown — suspended the activities of most commercial establishments. The only exceptions were those enterprises classified as essential services, represented in the retail sector by supermarkets, pharmacies, building material stores, and pet shops. In this context, many companies sought an alternative approach to remaining open to mitigate the negative effects on sales, especially during festivities such as Easter, Mother's Day, and Valentine's Day. One of these alternatives was the use of digital channels, a novelty for countless small and medium businesses.

The Brazilian Retail and Consumption Society (SBVC) carried out a survey with thousands of consumers from all over the country in partnership with Toluna, a research company focused on consumer insights [SBVC (2020a)]. The survey addressed "New digital habits in times of COVID-19" and discovered that the coronavirus crisis accelerated the digital transformation (DT) of the retail sector, especially with respect to maintaining business operations. Due to social distancing, the survey results reported an increase of up to 50% in the volume of online purchases during the lockdown (covering 61% of our sample businesses). The increase appeared to be mainly driven by purchases of food/drinks for immediate consumption through delivery, demonstrating a 79% growth among those interviewed [SBVC (2020a)]. According to Guissoni and Farinha [2019], the current retail scenario required radical changes within traditional companies and exploited the need to integrate physical and digital channels, while manufacturers began to serve and relate to consumers directly.

Consumers have been migrating their purchases to digital channels in several product categories, mainly using their smartphones. In addition, during the lockdown, consumers reduced purchases from foreign retailers by 11%. Consumers appear to be adopting digital habits and intentions to maintain their purchase choices after the end of the pandemic in 70% of the cases, i.e., retail will not continue as it was before this crisis. Because of this trend, better structured, more agile, and flexible companies should take advantage of this moment to intensify their DT, because DT tends to generate superior performance and greater competitive advantage [SBVC (2020a)].

Guissoni and Farinha [2019] highlighted the accelerated changes in consumer behavior. In order to obtain better results, they emphasized that companies needed to understand these transformations, including electronic commerce (e-commerce) operations. The investment and growth of a successful e-commerce business depend on actions to avoid operating with a negative margin, on understanding the events that cause changes in consumer behavior, and on transforming traditional business models to respond to DT. Digitalization is becoming even more important strategically, and the COVID-19 pandemic has become an accelerator for DT progress. In line with this statement, Pinkwart *et al.* [2021] mentioned that "Digitization offers several opportunities for an improvement of innovation management processes."

Organizations that founded a significant percentage of their businesses on the web appear to be in a more comfortable and competitive position to face the pandemic. Those organizations have developed digital resilience — a critical success factor that encompasses balance and collaboration [Islam *et al.* (2021)]. When new opportunities are commandeered and digital risks are appropriately managed, the organization can claim a balanced approach to their people, processes, and technology that integrate their most treasured resources: information and knowledge. Collaboration encompasses the working relationship and communications between the leadership team, internal entrepreneurs (intrapreneurs), and the key business departmental stakeholders (customer relationship management; marketing and advertising; human resources; logistics and supply chain; strategic, tactical, and operational planning; manufacturing, etc.). Digital resilience leads to increase success during tumultuous times, such as the pandemic period [Casalino *et al.* (2019)].

At the beginning of the pandemic, the Commercial and Industrial Association of Marília (ACIM) created a virtualization program with the objective of trading the products and services of its associated companies. The program, responsible for providing a marketplace platform to ACIM members, reached 367 companies by the end of July 2020, allowing entrepreneurs at no cost to digitize their businesses and enabling online trade of their products and services.

Although the program proposal appeared to be a promising solution, several issues related to knowledge sharing between the Association and the companies emerged. Many factors that provided for knowledge-sharing processes surfaced that were fundamental for the program to be successful. Notably, some of these knowledge sharing processes were critical failure factors that hindered the performance of the activities necessary for its successful implementation.

Given the present context and the need for a fluidic knowledge-sharing process between ACIM and companies, the researchers identified a research project to analyze the influential factors of knowledge sharing (IAKS) between ACIM and associated companies. The study focused on the implementation of a marketplace platform and its impact on the associated businesses.

The paper was structured into five sections, starting with this Introduction. In Sec. 2, the virtualization process in society is described, addressing information, technology, and communications as economic drivers and the foundation of digital platforms, along with a discussion of the influential aspects of knowledge sharing (IAKS) in the marketplace. In Sec. 3, the methodological procedures and the research universe. In Sec. 4, the data analysis is outlined and described in detail. Finally, Sec. 5 consists of the Conclusion.

2. Literature Overview

2.1. *Information, technology, and society: Virtualization process of enterprises*

Periodically, society is transformed by trends responsible for changing and supporting basic activities. Castells [2003] mentioned that changes were smooth, slow, and steady and modify the history of society's life. The transformations consist of a series of stable situations interrupted by important events that reshape the facts and help to re-establish the stable era that follows. The virtualization of society is one such significant change we will discuss.

Major social changes, for the most part, have taken place within this iterative and drawn-out process. However, the information revolution supported by Information and Communications Technologies (ICT) transformed this paradigm. Mattelart [2002] corroborated this idea by stating that ICT has led to inequality in the speed of communications and, as a consequence, society constitutes informational monopolies, transforming information into an important economic and social asset. The result is our so-called "information society." The information society is a new economically based suite of activities that rely upon information, technology, and communication. As a result, information is understood as a basic input for ICT-supported communication processes. The resulting new economy relates directly to the integration of knowledge and innovation processes that originated from the information. Thus, paths for development were created that required new attitudes towards social changes [Valentim (2002)].

When information is considered an asset, its access, use, and dissemination become guiding activities for society. Technologies have played a facilitating role in these activities and within the countless advances provided by ICT. The Internet provided a support media and channel for society, offering greater speed of access and information sharing, enabling society to access the underlying asset. These changes, according to Davis [2008], were in the fourth stage of the Internet evolution, since its constitution:

- Web 1.0: in this phase, the dynamics of the Internet was focused on information connection and acquisition on the network (Internet).
- Web 2.0: this phase of the Internet was also known as the Social Web, which was characterized by collaboration via social networks.
- Web 3.0: at this stage, also known as the Semantic Web, processes were centralized to provide context and meaning to information.
- Ubiquitous Web: this is the current stage of the Internet, whose foundation is the Internet of Things (IoT), mainly characterized by connectivity and interaction among people, processes, and objects linked to information. All of these relationships are dependent on the technologies that allow access to the network by individuals, regardless of their location and time.

Parallel to this emergent Internet process, the virtualization phenomenon can be observed. The "real" yields to the "non-real" world, especially in terms of the construction of a virtual world — a reflection of the physical world. "Virtual citizens' appear in society who are capable of carrying out any activities in the so-called cyberspace. In this way, society started to virtualize its data, characterizing its behaviors virtually, as these data were located in different places on the Internet, updated in real time, and enabled the construction of countless scenarios [Martin (2017); Becla (2012)]. These scenarios were built with technologies that are multi-format devices, including intelligent sensors. The devices (IoTs) are found in appliances, automobiles, clothing, etc., significantly changing the demands of the individuals who use them. The current stage of the Internet is distinguished by the recording of all information resulting from the users' interactions with the devices they use. Normally this interaction is intermediated by applications (or apps) that reinforce the virtualization of life in society, generating an unlimited range of data and recorded information [Otre *et al.* (2019)].

According to Chen [2020], the digital economy encompasses all economic activities that use or are facilitated by digitized data. Concomitantly, digital technology and the Internet introduced changes that reduced the costs of research, entry, transportation, and reproduction. Nonetheless, digital technology brought new challenges to the markets, especially in terms of the impacts from a wide range of application and technology platforms, in the value and protection of innovation, innovative products, and services, and in trade-offs between business data usage and consumer privacy.

As a result, day-to-day actions have also become virtualized, including personal and professional relationships, whether through social networks, email exchanges, and business transactions carried out on the Internet, which are increasingly present as boundaries disappear with the type of the object traded. A characteristic of the digital economy, according to Chen [2020], is the growing importance of application and technology platforms (e.g., digital platforms), which basically function as intermediaries for transactions. With these platforms, the research costs associated with the consumer are reduced, while the number of companies that a consumer can access increases dramatically. Whereas for the company, the market entry costs and time to identify consumers are reduced and the size of the markets is increased. Consequently, platforms are also especially valuable as information intermediaries and justify the need to understand their basic concepts and their multiple applications in depth. Now that we have established how society became virtualized, we will move to the section describing the marketplace in terms of digital platforms.

2.2. *Digital platforms: The emergence of e-commerce*

The history of e-commerce can be summarized in some important dates, according to Turban *et al.* [2015]:

- 1969, with the emergence of the Internet as an American government experiment, accessed in a restricted way by academic researchers and scientists;
- the early 1990s, with the emergence of the World Wide Web, an important milestone in the development of e-commerce, which enabled companies to be on the Internet with texts and photos;
- 2005, when attention was turned to social networks and m-commerce (mobile-based business and applications); and
- 2009, the start of operations in the social commerce channels, which expanded commercial activities.

This digital revolution created comparative advantages for organizations, in the long run, increasing the speed of e-commerce implementation and, consequently, increasing innovation and creativity in organizations [Hamidreza *et al.* (2017)]. With the introduction of digital technologies in business activities, e-commerce has been changing transaction patterns between sellers and buyers. On the one hand, e-commerce offers sellers greater revenue streams, reduced costs, easier access to new markets, greater customer loyalty, and streamlined supply chains. On the other hand, it offers buyers new and convenient shopping experiences, innovative products and services, and entertainment [Song *et al.* (2019)].

The use of the Internet to buy, sell, and streamline the process of transporting or trading goods and services has boosted electronic commerce, turning it into an ecosystem where buyers and sellers carry out an infinite number of business transactions, enabling the participation of any person or company, as a customer or supplier. Turban *et al.* [2015] reported the emergence of new businesses based on concepts such as the digital economy, founded on online transactions, such as businesses focused on the sharing of goods and services among people, for the new businesses have facilitated social impacts resulting from the improvement of communication and collaboration tools enabled by social media. Nevertheless, the authors point out that the most important change is reflected in people and the way they work and live, transforming daily activities such as work, leisure, shopping, entertainment, travel, health care, education, and others through digital platform engagement.

Currently, the evolution of e-commerce is displacing important issues that favored the physical shopping experience, i.e., the use of real-time information to predict future trends [Song *et al.* (2019)], the use of cyber-physical systems (CPS) to expand the service offerings and applications, integrating these systems into the IoT [Yaacoub *et al.* (2020)], and including the use of augmented reality to preview the product and its variations, such as color, size, style, and differences [Garg *et al.* (2021)]. All these changes are increasingly empowering the customer (understood as an integral element in the digital society) to share opinions about products, services, and suppliers on social networks, make social media online purchases, and use social communities wisely for their benefit [Turban *et al.* (2015)]. Since the beginning of 2020, the coronavirus pandemic (COVID-19) and the associated preventive measures (such as "staying at home") introduced in most countries have affected the economy and society. The result was a rapid increase in digitalization with reduced face-to-face contact, intensifying the use of digital media in the economy and society [Dannenberg *et al.* (2020)].

Brem *et al.* [2021] reinforced this idea and mentioned that the social distancing caused by the COVID-19 pandemic caused people to adopt new behaviors. The authors also claimed that these new behaviors have enabled six digital technologies to be leveraged. E-learning, e-gaming, video conferencing, internet streaming, cashless payment, e-commerce, and home delivery are identified as important digital technologies that provide greater comfort to society during the pandemic. These technologies have been virtualized in platform-based servitization and, with that, supply issues of teaching, social relationships, entertainment, and commercial transactions, especially purchases performed on e-commerce platforms [Brem *et al.* (2021); Tian *et al.* (2021)].

According to Saphores and Xu [2020], e-commerce is changing the way people shop, from expanding product offerings available to consumers, stimulating competition, and increasing the convenience of shopping. Several authors, such as Burt and Sparks [2013], Bressoles *et al.* [2014], Faqih and Jaradat [2015], Nilashi *et al.* [2015] and Towers and Xu [2016], described the worldwide evolution of technological agents as expressive drivers of the use of the Internet and e-commerce in general. These tech agents have facilitated access to products and brands through online retail. The newfound access represented a practically unlimited choice of products and services, enabling product and service customization in several cases, in addition to interactive and real-time communication between companies and customers. Globally, e-commerce is assuming an increasing share in total retail sales, although it is still far from being homogeneous from a geographical perspective [Saphores and Xu (2020)]. This finding can be extended to include different sectors of the economy and the size and structure of the organizations involved.

E-commerce has emerged as a facility for consulting data about products, with the possibility of comparing prices, making payments, and tracking orders [Turban *et al.* (2015)]. These traits are in addition to storing a multi-dimensional array of information that make transactions more efficient, displaying large amounts of data and information to customers and suppliers, and influencing business management as a whole. While this environment allows customers to exchange goods and services for cash or even for other goods, depending on the policy of the used platform, Jiang *et al.* [2013], Vissotto and Boniati [2013] and Rezaei *et al.* [2016] highlighted that this opportunity is available to people at any place and time. The simple common denominator is a reliable connection to the Internet and related devices, thus reinforcing the convenience of the process.

2.3. *Digital platforms: SMEs and e-commerce advantages and disadvantages*

SMEs represent a large portion of companies in all economies, and, therefore, when an external crisis affects the market, as in the case of the COVID-19 pandemic, they suffer the negative consequences the most. However, Egger [2020] highlighted that SMEs exhibit certain characteristics that can help them in times of crisis: flexibility to implement strategies in the face of opportunities or threats that arise and access to important market information that can be useful to react to crises. These are critical advantages regardless of the fact that SMEs are more vulnerable to internal and external events — the more recent the SME has established a business presence, the greater the risk of failure. The business value proposition is the smaller size of SMEs and the greater proximity between decision-makers and their customers and other stakeholders.

With the restrictions imposed by the lockdown and social distancing policies in the pandemic period, companies sought alternatives to minimize the impacts of the stifling drop in sales. According to Perrin [2020], the words e-commerce and marketplace became part of the vocabulary of many companies, pressured by the need to create online sales channels. Thus, the migration from physical commerce to the virtual marketplace became an accelerated trend and SMEs were taking advantage of this moment to intensify their DT in search of better results.

In this sense, Senarathna *et al.* [2014] reported that SMEs benefited from e-commerce by removing time and space barriers that resulted from the adoption of an Internet-based platform. The resulting implication was a fundamental benefit to the bottom line, such as cost reduction in office maintenance and operating costs for personnel and equipment. According to Shemi and Procter [2018], the adoption of e-commerce was a growth strategy, especially for SMEs, allowing them to compete with larger companies and take over new customers in global markets. However, although the benefits were realized in several countries, they were not reached by most companies.

This situation challenged the concept of diminishing benefits as the barriers to the adoption of e-commerce. According to Al-Tit [2020], the barriers ranged among an expansive domain of obstacles, including the manager's and employee's degree of knowledge in relation to technology; telecommunications infrastructure; cost of connectivity; technical knowledge; cost of technology; internet security, and legal barriers. Senarathna *et al.* [2014] also reported that several studies pointed to the influence of organizational culture in the adoption of e-commerce, which is often a barrier to innovation and the use of new technologies. As new trends in ICT were being developed, the application of e-commerce in SMEs needed to be transformed to adapt to new business standards and operational systems [Shemi and Procter (2018)]. Organizational factors that impacted the success and failure of e-commerce for SMEs included organizational structure, size and culture, leadership skills, management attitudes, education and skills of employees, technical readiness of IT infrastructure, financial readiness of the enterprise, and products and services offered by the company [Hamidreza *et al.* (2017)]. On the other hand, Al-Tit [2020] suggested that the adoption of e-commerce was motivated by factors such as customer preferences, the perceived value and cost of e-commerce, the readiness of the partner, technical knowledge, customer trust, employees' knowledge and experience, top management support, perceived ease of use, and organizational culture.

A survey coordinated by the E-commerce Brasil website in 2019 showed a turnover of R$ 75.1 billion (178.5 million orders placed on national websites) in Brazilian e-commerce, representing a 23% growth compared to 2018. The number of consumers shopping on the Internet also accounted for an increase of 41%, totaling 31.4 million Brazilians who made at least one online purchase in 2019 [E-CommerceBrasil (2020)]. In the first half of 2020, as a result of the pandemic, approximately 7 million new users purchased on e-commerce for the first time in Brazil, increasing the revenue of this type of purchase by 47%, when compared to the previous 12 months [ABCOMM (2021)]. Such a growth established the relevance of a marketplace for offering goods and services.

Among the range of e-commerce possibilities, platforms named marketplace or e-marketplace have been showing significant growth. The business model functions as a virtual shopping center, where several companies are known worldwide to participate by making products and brands available in one single platform, facilitating the purchase process by the consumer and contributing to the expansion of this modality [Zacho (2017)]. According to data from the survey conducted by Ebit/Nielsen, marketplaces had a 78% share in the total revenue of Brazilian e-commerce, which was crucial to preventing many companies from closing their doors [ABCOMM (2021)].

According to Tadelis [2016], in this online market modality, the advantage of the enterprises using the platforms was the generated savings (since maintaining a sales website had a higher cost than the commission paid to the companies that maintained these marketplace platforms), a channel for selling excess inventory, increased brand visibility and sales flow, as the environment has heavier traffic of online consumers. When defining marketplace, Simões [2016] pointed out that virtual marketplaces put together several online sellers who can continue to operate in the physical market in isolation, if they wish. In these online sales channels, companies can sell their products on renowned sites such as Amazon, Walmart, AliExpress, and Alibaba, among others. These platforms charge commission percentages that vary between 10% and 30% for each sale made, offering, in return, investments in credit analysis, anti-fraud actions, and digital marketing.

Trading through marketplace platforms generates advantages for the involved stakeholders: consumers, shopkeepers, and operators. For the small businesses, which probably would not reach significant access by consumers on an individual digital platform, the marketplace provides visibility, saves marketing and advertising efforts, and allows the monitoring of metrics to visualize best practices, in addition to providing trends and solutions for any problems that may arise and affect the business. For marketplace operators, the perceived advantages refer to the commission received by the sales, boosting their revenues, in addition to offering a greater variety of products, which stimulates purchase and raises the average ticket price for consumers, generating greater customer loyalty [SEBRAE (2021)]. However, for Sun *et al.* [2020], this model–considered traditional–already has a replacement called Taobao, owned by the Alibaba group, which does not charge fees or percentages on transactions, constituting a different billing model, based on website advertising. This business model attracts a large number of participants to the platform, increasing the traffic of users and companies interested in promoting their products and brands since it offers few entry barriers for these companies.

2.4. *Digital platforms: Pros and Cons of digital transformation initiatives*

Pimenta [2018] highlighted some issues to be handled with caution so that they are not seen as disadvantages for those using the platforms. An important concern for the marketplace maintainers of the digital platforms is the need to present a robust Web structure to keep the site up, considering higher traffic generated during days of special sales. Additionally, investments in transaction security increase, an important element due to the increased number of users and hacker attacks, which can cause problems for both retailers and customers.

A lack of control over the users' experience and legal issues has emerged, which diminishes the assurance that all hosted stores provide excellent service and fulfill the promises of their products. Additionally, a critical issue can emerge associated with the potential challenge presented by customer service omissions that results in limited or no problem resolution with customers, due to the volume of contact with thousands of customers [Pimenta (2018)]. The volume of transactions carried out through these digital platforms has been so significant as to arouse the attention of the Brazilian government, which instituted the National System for Digital Transformation (TD), through Decree n° 9.319, on March 21, 2018. The objective was to implement a broad strategy for DT of Brazilian companies. This strategy included the promotion of DT, the creation of logistics programs and services, and access to specific financing funds. The aim was to encourage SMEs to focus on e-commerce, seeking internationalization and expansion of cost reduction opportunities with the insertion of technological platforms, in addition to increasing customer prospecting, increasing product visibility, and multiplying direct sales channels [Luz (2018)].

DT goes beyond the use of technologies to "solve specific problems," since it is associated with a digital mindset, which incorporates a complete change in the understanding and strategic application of technology. According to Rogers [2017], organizations need to update their strategic mindset beyond the information technology infrastructure. Rogers [2017] highlighted five domains currently redefined by digital technologies and that reflect ways companies operate in the markets:

(1) customers, who are changing their relations with each other and with companies;
(2) competition, which witnesses a major change in the locus of competition, making the sector's borders more fluid;
(3) data, including how companies produce, manage, and use information;
(4) innovation, in which the process of developing new ideas involves continuous learning and rapid experimentation; and
(5) value, which is no longer immutable when considering all technologies that can extend and improve the value proposition to the customer.

Rabelo [2018] suggested that technologies need to be used to improve performance and achieve better results, based on a structural change in organizations. To Rabelo [2018], society is part of the technology evolution and is strongly affected by it, which leads companies to change the way they do business. This can be attributed to the growth in digital reach and the transition from physical to digital and highlights seven challenges along the DT process: (i) lack of initiative; (ii) technical difficulties; (iii) reputation and security; (iv) data silos; (v) guarantee of return; (vii) company culture; and (vii) IT problems.

Despite technological innovations and the availability of free tools on the Internet, Turchi [2019] stated that many SMEs do not take advantage of these available resources and are not familiar with the terminologies of the digital world. Among the reasons for the low participation of these companies is that 40% of them do not even have a website and a more consolidated digital presence, often labeled as an e-commerce gateway. The justification, according to the author, included aspects of the scarcity of time, resources, and ignorance, which keep SMEs away from investments in technological updating. These characteristics lead them to concentrate their efforts on the primary business channel, leaving behind the online presence.

When an opportunity arises for something that aggregates and helps them in this process (such as marketplace programs in which they can be inserted), other issues related to knowledge sharing between promoting organizations and SMEs emerge, with influencing factors (from this sharing) that promote or inhibit these companies' adherence to innovative trade practices. The IAKS, fundamental to the success of these interorganizational marketplace relationships, are presented in the next section.

2.5. *Influential aspects of knowledge sharing*

The implementation of a new competitive strategy is based on knowledge sharing between individuals or institutions. This sharing is based upon the alignment of the agents and stakeholders involved in formulating the strategy [Shih *et al.* (2006)]. Knowledge sharing is one of the Knowledge Management (KM) cycle processes, which aims to improve the organization's ability to carry out its activities, increasing its value and its competitive advantage. This sharing:

> involves two actions: transmission (sending or transmitting knowledge to a potential recipient) and absorption by that person or group. If knowledge is not absorbed, it will not have been transferred. The mere availability of knowledge is not transferred. Access is necessary, but it is by no means sufficient to guarantee that knowledge will be used [Davenport and Prusak (1999, p. 123)].

Additionally, the interaction between recipients and receivers is not a singular and isolated action between recipients and receptors, but rather a combination of one or more interactions that can lead to broad understandings [Dorow (2017)]. However, this process does not always take place organically, it is influenced by motivators and inhibitors of different natures, according to Davenport and Prusak [1999], Riege [2005], Freire [2010] and Dorow [2017]. Studies on knowledge-sharing influencers usually address this process at the intraorganizational level. The elements brought up by the authors above (more focused on intraorganizational sharing) have been adapted to the interorganizational context to meet the objectives of this study.

Multiple aspects influence KM implementation and applications and its processes in the context of organizations. Davenport and Prusak [1999] named them "frictions," Dorow [2017] mentioned "motivators and inhibitors." Considering that the same factor can be positive or negative for knowledge sharing, depending on how it manifests itself in organizations, this research paper defined all these aspects as influential in KM, a term coined by Jorge [2017]. The author also stated that identifying and considering the influential aspects of KM interfered with the successful implementation and application of KM processes, including knowledge sharing.

Knowledge sharing depends on several aspects related to the organization and its agents and also influences innovation in relation to marketing and new forms of business:

> Knowledge sharing relies on several fundamental aspects such as organizational internal commitment, business perception, employee

> engagement, and synergy integrated decision-making management. Innovation in the business world has several important aspects such as the application of the latest marketing ideas in the modern business world, the development of new designs, knowledge of business and integrated management governance, and the ability of Research and Development (R&D) to the effort of sharing and involving employees (Share of employee) as a form of maximizing the application of innovation ideas [Lestari *et al.* (2020, p. 56)].

These factors could be considered for both intra- and interorganizational knowledge sharing, requiring the existence of a common language (the basis for understanding and trust between the parties), so that an effective and efficient knowledge sharing takes place. In a study by Sinaga *et al.* [2017] about the use of e-marketplace to support users in selling their product, the role of knowledge sharing in the online community was identified as one of the fundamental elements to minimize the difficulties inherent in this type of commercial activity. When studying the motivations for knowledge sharing in this online community, the results were that "self-efficacy, personal outcome expectation, community-related outcome expectation from social cognitive theory are the motivations in knowledge sharing. In addition, of self-worth, enjoying helping, reciprocity and social support [...] are the motivations for sharing knowledge" [Sinaga *et al.* (2017, p. 143)].

This suggests that the relationship between those involved in the e-marketplace activity is one of the fundamental factors for knowledge sharing, which is so necessary for accomplishing and maintaining this activity. To reach this level of relationship and trust, in addition to language, there is also a need for proximity or affinity of knowledge culture between the parties. Davenport and Prusak [1999] noted that the closer people were to the culture of the knowledge being transferred, the easier it was to share and exchange. Hickey and Kozlovski [2020] proposed a trusted knowledge-sharing environment as an important element to create a collaborative environment in the e-marketplace context. In fact, trust is one of the bases for knowledge sharing and also for an environment conducive for it to occur and, thus, become a collaborative environment.

The authors also reported the importance of face-to-face meetings so that knowledge sharing could indeed be effective. We should consider that the relevance of the meeting still remains, as many managers are from generations who consider face-to-face meetings to be irreplaceable and an important part of the confidence-building process. Another issue that directly impacts confidence is the status of the knowledge holder, as to a large extent, people judge the information and knowledge they obtain based on who transmits it [Davenport and Prusak (1999)]. Thus, a "reputation judgment," which influences the attention and credit given to the knowledge shared by the transmitter. Another influential factor in knowledge sharing presented by Davenport and Prusak [1999] was the instinctive resistance to change, which is understandable as changes require reflections or breaking paradigms adopted by the organization — perhaps for decades.

When comparing and analyzing the elements KM pointed out by Wong [2005, p. 266–267], eleven critical factors were found and focused on the implementation of KM activities in SMEs:

- management leadership and support;
- culture;
- information technology;
- strategy and purpose;
- measurement;
- organizational infrastructure;
- processes and activities;
- motivational aids;
- resources;
- training and education; and
- human resources management (HRM).

The identification of these aspects and their relationship with KM activities are fundamental for the successful KM implementation in SMEs. Jorge [2017] related the influential aspects to the context of the KM cycle processes (knowledge generation, sharing, and application) and highlighted the processes that directly influenced the knowledge-sharing process, the focus of this research, described in Table 1.

When knowledge sharing takes place between different organizations, the positive or negative influences for knowledge sharing in organizations and between them are more intensified, since knowledge about organizational practices and culture is often an "uncertain" field that affects trust and control over all processes. Thus, understanding these knowledge-sharing relationships and their influencers is fundamental to analyze the effectiveness of the actions involving the process between different organizations, which is the case of the present study. The next section presents the methodological procedures used in this research.

3. Research Methodology

The present research is characterized as qualitative and exploratory. The chosen research strategy was the case study, which contributes to the understanding of the individual, organizational, social, and political phenomena [Yin (2003)]. The data collection techniques were the questionnaire with closed- and open-ended questions and semistructured interviews. The questionnaires were carried out with the subjects of the Commercial and Industrial Association of Marília (ACIM) who were acting directly in the marketplace implementation, maintenance, or clarification of questions with the companies. In this sense, the purpose of the questions was to identify the factors influencing knowledge sharing that impacted the decision of the entrepreneurs to join the ACIM marketplace, especially in the time of the pandemic, when they were unable to carry out the transactions of products and services physically, in their stores. It is noteworthy that the application of the closed-ended questionnaire enabled a greater speed in the data collection on the researched universe.

Table 1. KM influential aspects.

Critical aspects	Description of critical aspects
Management Leadership and Support	It consists of two main points: the top management support in the KM implementation and the role of leadership in the development of activities necessary for KM. The need to identify the real support of top management and formal and informal leadership in all organizational levels is highlighted, as these actions and influences will lead to successful KM.
Culture	Considered to be a critical aspect and one of the main KM guidelines, it consists of its impact on valuing information and knowledge in the organizational context. Culture, in this sense, is essential for KM implementation, and identifying it is fundamental for the development of strategies that aim to maintain (information and knowledge valorization in the organizational context), increase (partial valorization), and develop (does not valorize) it.
Information Technology	In isolation, it is not capable of performing KM; however, when used in a cohesive manner, it speeds up numerous processes of KM activities. Therefore, knowledge about existing IT in the organization is important to develop KM strategies, allowing to make the most of available technology or, when not available, to develop strategies that do not count on these resources. Without identifying the available IT resources, the assertiveness of proposed strategies and activities are jeopardized.
Strategy and Purpose	Aligning organizational strategy and purpose with KM is essential, as its results are not always used by the organization. They must make sense for the organizational subjects to use and see meaning in KM implementation and use, otherwise it could be discontinued and become a pro forma, as it starts to be seen as a bureaucratic process that does not bring value.
Organizational Infrastructure	The layout, physical structure, and devices should favor knowledge construction and sharing so that activities and processes responsible for knowledge construction and sharing between organizational subjects from different areas and departments are considered. This includes lowering barriers and encouraging knowledge exchange in spaces such as the coffee room, games room, work stations without walls, departments without walls, and with technologies that encourage and enable knowledge construction and sharing.
Processes and activities	Processes and activities must be built; however, it is highlighted that they should be discreetly inserted in the daily lives of organizational subjects to break resistance to their implementation. It is necessary to identify the processes and activities that favor knowledge construction and exchange in the organizational environment and structure them aiming at their best use.
Motivational Aids	People develop processes and activities aimed at building knowledge, but they need motivational stimuli to better carry out these activities. The development of motivational strategies that provide a greater engagement from the organizational subjects in KM activities and processes becomes necessary to develop favorable conditions for the subjects, who are often removed from the comfort zone and start to develop activities they had never performed before.
Resources	Analyzing the resources available in organizations is necessary for KM development, considering the alignment between the proposed strategies and the available resources. These resources are not limited to financial resources and, therefore, recognizing and analyzing them contributes to their best allocation during KM implementation and use.
Human Resources Management	Related to organizational culture, it impacts knowledge construction and uses in the organization. To understand it in order to identify positive and negative points is important to develop new strategies and take advantage of existing ones for KM aligned with culture, human resources, and its management process.

Source: Adapted from Jorge [2017].

Subsequently, a semistructured interview was conducted with the entity's Director of Technology and Innovation in order to validate the collected information and enrich the analysis. This type of interview consisted of a series of open-ended questions, asked verbally in a pre-established order, in which the interviewer can add clarification questions [Laville and Dionne (1999)]. The data were analyzed through content analysis, which is a set of communication analysis techniques that uses systematic and objective procedures to describe the content of messages [Bardin (2009)]. Thus, categories of analysis were used according to the basic theoretical framework, as well as those emerging from the collected data. As a result, it was possible to develop perspectives and parameters for intensifying the marketplace tool by entrepreneurs during and after the pandemic.

3.1. *Research universe*

The research was carried out at ACIM, a private and nonprofit organization, whose main pillar is the association of entrepreneurs in the city of Marília, state of São Paulo, Brazil, where companies have different sizes and operate in different economic segments. The entity, which directly represents 1800 members, has been in operation for 85 years, with the objective of participating in the development of the city and defending the interests of its members. ACIM's mission, as described on its website, is to stimulate, promote, support, and sustain the economic development of companies, generating jobs and income, contributing to a fairer Brazil [ACIM Marília-SP (2021)].

ACIM's history has shown leadership among the other commercial and industrial associations in the region it operates, thus indirectly representing the members of another 19 trade associations, providing continuous improvement to the associates' businesses. To this end, the organization has a body of collaborators responsible for supporting its activities and, among these, the universe of the present research chose a total of 19 subjects, only those collaborators who were directly related to the entrepreneurs in the offer, implementation, maintenance, and assistance with any question about the Marília.Dakki marketplace [Marília Dakki (2020)].

3.2. *Aspects related to the COVID-19 pandemic: Social distancing and lockdown*

The first case of COVID-19 in Brazil came out on February 26, 2020, and shortly after, in March 2020, the state of São Paulo became the epicenter of the pandemic in Brazil. On March 21, 2020, 26 days after the first case in São Paulo, the status of calamity was decreed throughout the state, with the beginning of the quarantine linked to social distancing by the 24th of March. Activities considered nonessential had their face-to-face activities suspended, with a penalty of warning or a fine to force companies to comply. The process lasts until the present day, with moments of restriction and flexibility for the nonessential activities. However, the flexibilization condition allows companies to operate only 24 h a week, that is, 4 h a day, excluding Sundays.

Right at the beginning of all this reported process, ACIM and some technology companies in the city built, in partnership, a marketplace environment called Marilia.Dakki for companies in the city of Marília, SP, in an attempt to virtualize stores and service provision for associated companies. This urgency forced the entity to direct all its efforts towards this process, offering the tool to its members, at no cost, for six months.

As a result of social distancing and, especially, for integrating the so-called risk groups, 21% of the subjects that compose the staff of ACIM's employees were removed, another 16% started to focus on financial support with the associates, 13% worked in the administrative operations of the marketplace, while the remaining 50% acted on the front line of the new tool, in direct contact with the entity's associated entrepreneurs. As a result, the subjects from the various departments were redirected to activities involving the Marilia.Dakki marketplace, since these subjects' regular activities could not be carried out due to social distancing. These employees were responsible for the initial contact, offering and implementing the tool, assisting with questions and tool support to the entrepreneurs, and collecting opinions, perceptions, and difficulties that influenced their adhesion or not to the platform. In this way, these subjects became strategic to analyze the factors that influence knowledge sharing between ACIM and associated companies in relation to the implementation of a marketplace platform.

4. Result and Discussion

The evaluation of the entrepreneurs' perceptions impacted by the marketplace offer and support was collected from the ACIM's employees' perspectives, who were responsible for directly contacting the entrepreneurs. These subjects responded to the statements related to the IAKS on the platform. The sample can be characterized as formed by a young team, in age and in the function, under 30 years old (42.1%) and having up to two years of working experience with the entity (50%). These subjects answered 25 statements divided into 10 groups to facilitate the identification of barriers reported to them by the entrepreneurs when joining the marketplace and inserting their products and services onto the platform. The subjects' statements sought to identify the level of barriers associated with the influential aspects in knowledge sharing, as seen in Table 2.

Almost all companies (or their managers) were interested in participating in the project when they first heard about it. This response deserves further reflection, since 21% of the association's employees agreed with this statement, while 73.7% partially agreed. Although about two-thirds of the entrepreneurs supported the insertion of their companies in the digital world, less than half of them were immediately interested in participating without further inquiry. However, entrepreneurs acknowledged minimal resistance or challenge to assuming an innovative leadership attitude for their businesses.

4.1. *Management leadership and support*

The results attributed to the statements presented to the ACIM's managers facilitated an understanding of each influential aspect in knowledge sharing in the context of the Marília.Dakki marketplace platform. We will navigate sequentially through

Table 2. Analysis of the barriers faced by the entrepreneurs who placed their products and services on the Marília.Dakki marketplace from the perception of ACIM.

Group	Questions	Scale									
		Totally disagree		Partially disagree		Indifferent		Partially agree		Totally agree	
		N	%	*N*	%	*N*	%	*N*	%	*N*	%
Management Leadership and Support*	There was support from senior management and leaders (formal and informal) at the intermediate level (Managers, Coordinators, and Supervisors) of the contacted companies so that there was the use (sharing) of the marketplace by the companies and ACIM.	—	—	—	—	—	—	6	31.6	13	68.4
	The companies (or their managers) were interested in participating in the project when they heard about it.	—	—	—	—	1	5.3	14	73.7	4	21
Culture	There was positive receptivity and valuation of the information and knowledge provided by ACIM from the contacted companies.	—	—	—	—	1	5.3	11	57.9	7	36.8
	The companies realized the importance of the information and knowledge offered by ACIM in the form of training and instructional videos.	—	—	—	—	2	10.5	10	52.6	7	36.8
	The culture presented by the associated companies was favorable towards the use of information and knowledge about the marketplace offered by ACIM.	—	—	2	10.5	2	10.5	6	31.6	9	47.4
	Entrepreneurs were particularly involved in requests for improvements to the platform.	—	—	1	5.3	5	23.6	9	47.4	4	21
	Information and knowledge about the awareness of the importance of the platform at the time of the pandemic were perceived by the companies.	—	—	—	—	1	5.3	7	36.8	11	57.9
	The companies perceived the benefits offered by the platform at this time of the pandemic.	—	—	—	—	3	15.8	8	42.1	8	42.1

Table 2. (*Continued*)

Group	Questions	Scale									
		Totally disagree		Partially disagree		Indifferent		Partially agree		Totally agree	
		N	%	*N*	%	*N*	%	*N*	%	*N*	%
Information Technology	The companies were aware of Information and Communication Technologies.	—	—	4	21	2	10.5	8	42.1	5	23.6
	The companies and their members were resistant to using technology.	—	—	2	10.5	3	15.8	10	52.6	4	21
	Business members (regardless of the level) knew how to use (or were competent to use) information technologies.	—	—	1	5.3	2	10.5	13	68.4	3	15.8
	Entrepreneurs are resistant to the marketplace because they prefer face-to-face trading.	—	—	2	10.5	3	15.8	9	47.4	5	23.6
	There was a common and easily understood language between ACIM and the companies, that is, there was a simplification of the technological language so that the companies could understand the project.	—	—	—	—	—	—	5	26.3	14	73.7
	ACIM offered training on the marketplace for companies.	—	—	—	—	2	10.5	7	36.8	12	63.1
	There was instinctive resistance to change (changing paradigms, that is, the entry of the company into the digital world) by the people who work in the companies.	1	5.3	1	5.3	2	10.5	11	57.9	4	21
Strategy and Purpose	There was an alignment between the ACIM's strategy and the purpose and the companies'.	—	—	—	—	—	—	6	31.6	13	68.4
	Entrepreneurs were aware of the actions taken by ACIM to implement tools to digitalize business and provide services.	—	—	—	—	2	10.5	8	42.1	9	47.4
Organizational Infrastructure	The companies have a structure that favors and facilitates information and knowledge sharing between them and ACIM.	—	—	1	5.3	2	10.5	9	47.4	7	36.8

Table 2. (*Continued*)

Group	Questions	Scale									
		Totally disagree		Partially disagree		Indifferent		Partially agree		Totally agree	
		N	%	*N*	%	*N*	%	*N*	%	*N*	%
	The companies had technological tools to use the marketplace offered by ACIM.	1	5.3	—	—	1	5.3	11	57.9	6	31.6
Processes and Activities	Companies are making changes and adaptations in their processes and activities to adapt to the use of the marketplace as a marketing tool for their products.	—	—	2	10.5	2	10.5	10	52.6	5	23.6
Motivational Aids	The companies promoted an adequate motivational environment to promote employees' commitment and engagement or stimulated the predisposition so that they could learn new ways of working and even act in different activities related to the marketplace.	1	5.3	3	15.8	5	23.6	5	23.6	6	31.6
Resources	The companies clearly had to identify the resources that should be allocated for the ACIM marketplace implementation.	—	—	2	10.5	4	21	6	31.6	7	36.8
	Companies were already considering, within their limitations (available resources), digitalization strategies for their businesses.	2	10.5	3	15.8	3	15.8	7	36.8	4	21
Human Resources Management	The companies evaluated their workforce and identified positive and negative aspects regarding the necessary adaptations for joining the ACIM marketplace.	2	10.5	3	15.8	4	21	5	23.6	5	23.6
Reliability	From the companies' perception, ACIM has a good reputation in terms of competence, reliability, and expression in the region, especially in relation to technological innovations.	—	—	—	—	1	5.3	3	15.8	15	78.9

Note: *Understanding information. Use and importance of information in the activities developed by these individuals.
Source: By the authors.

the *Critical Aspects* (*Groups*) outlined in Tables 1 and 2, discussing each one separately and then synthesizing our findings. The study identified that the group "Management Leadership and Support" presented a result considered as a positive influential aspect of knowledge sharing. A significant 68.4% of the subjects totally agreed that senior management and leaders (formal and informal) supported the use of the marketplace. Additionally, employees at the intermediate level (managers, coordinators, and supervisors) of the contacted companies also supported the use of the marketplace and sharing between the companies and ACIM.

4.2. *Culture*

The influence of "Culture" and its impacts on this business digitalization process showed a positive receptivity and the positive valuation of the information and knowledge provided by ACIM, according to 36.8% of the employees in contact with the businessmen. The fact that almost two-thirds of the respondents (57.9%) partially agreed with this aspect suggests fear/resistance from the entrepreneurs regarding the information and knowledge resulting from the online sales process, and the organizational culture was widely accepted by the entrepreneurs.

Only 36.8% of the subjects from the companies recognized the importance of the information and knowledge offered by ACIM through training and instructional videos. This result suggested to ACIM that the ability of the materials, their format and support to instill confidence, as well as other aspects involving the information and knowledge offered by ACIM needed to be analyzed. Once ACIM reviewed these tools for educating the stakeholders in the companies, new videos with greater devotion to the DT process and more self-assurance were created to help change these companies' culture towards digitalization.

Almost half of the research subjects (entrepreneurs) (47.4%) totally agreed with the statement that the culture presented by the associated companies was favorable to the use of information and knowledge about the marketplace offered by ACIM. This indicator reinforced the importance of building more consistent content aimed at raising awareness and meeting a social and legal need, and the importance of digitizing companies as a new market to be explored beyond this pandemic moment. This transformation of a new post-pandemic business model is a critical "carry forward" from this study for future marketplace development.

To meet this need, the entity produced a wide range of content to convey information and knowledge to the companies about the importance of the platform at the time of the pandemic and 57.9% of the entrepreneurs were aware of these actions. Few requests for improvements in the platform (21.0%) were made by the companies, demonstrating the platform's importance for pandemic and post-pandemic times. The identifiable benefits offered by the platform at the time of pandemic were mentioned by 42.1% of the subjects, reinforcing the need to intensify the availability of information and knowledge through the materials constructed by ACIM.

4.3. *Information technology*

In a similar manner as "Culture," the adoption and implementation of Information Technology (ICT) was crucial to establishing a viable marketplace. The entrepreneurs totally agreed (23.6%) that they were knowledgeable about ICT and 42.1% of them partially agreed with this statement, demonstrating a significant insight into ICT by the entrepreneurs in the marketplace. In parallel, 73.6% of ACIM's agents totally or partially agreed that resistance existed from businesses regarding the use of these technologies in their companies and by their members.

The resistance to using available technologies could be considered an important barrier to knowledge sharing since the feasibility of the marketplace operation demands a significant number of technologies. The ICTs include everything from the Internet platform itself, the use of digital cameras (e.g. those embedded in cell phones), as well as image processing. Thus, this type of resistance could permanently limit the feasibility of digitization of companies. Despite this resistance, members of the companies (regardless of the level of their positions — strategic, tactical, or operational) exhibited knowledge in using (or competence to use) these technologies. The resistance noted above was not related to the lack of knowledge or competence to use ICT (as indicated by 84.2% of the research subjects, who totally or partially agreed with this statement). This analysis is reinforced by the result of 71% of the entrepreneurs who appeared to be resistant to the marketplace because they preferred face-to-face trading.

An instinctive resistance to change by the people who work in the companies was confirmed by 78.9% of the research subjects. This situation could strongly suggest the need for structural changes in these organizations' business models and perceptions about being enabled in new market dynamics provided by the digital universe.

ACIM sought to simplify the entire process of implementing the marketplace by using different actions so that companies could adopt commercial digitalization in a short time period. Thus, ACIM used a simple and easy-to-understand language (simplification of technological language) so that companies could comprehend the project. Within the pool of interviewed subjects, a large majority totally (73.7%) or partially agreed (23.6%) with this statement. The simplest language was externalized through training offered to entrepreneurs, reaching 89.5% of the total or partial agreement of ACIM's companies in the marketplace.

Even though companies with ICT and knowledge (even if partially) capable of virtualizing their products have been identified, the resistance related to breaking paradigms needs to be addressed in the future. Despite ACIM providing important information and knowledge about the marketplace tool, companies were at differing levels of DT development, which revealed the importance of classifying them by their degree of maturity so that information and knowledge could be offered in a more effective manner.

4.4. *Strategy and purpose*

ACIM's effort to align strategies directed to the needs of companies, as well as their preparation for implementing the platform was positively perceived by entrepreneurs who aimed to implement tools for digitizing sales and services in the opinion of 89.5% of questioned subjects (47.4% totally agreed and 42.1% partially). All agents totally (68.4%) or partially (31.6%) agreed with the perception of the entrepreneurs that the association's strategy aligned with the company's explicit or implicit strategies. ACIM formulated the platform together with local technology companies, enabling the digitalization of the associates' commercial process at the time social distancing was imposed and the consequent decree closing businesses considered as nonessential in the municipality.

4.5. *Organizational infrastructure*

The perception of the existence of infrastructure in companies in favor of the marketplace and information and knowledge sharing was mentioned by 84.2% of the subjects, who totally or partially agreed that ACIM facilitated assistance and support. Additionally, the researchers observed that the companies had the infrastructure and technological tools to support the marketplace in sharing their information and knowledge with ACIM, in the search of specific aids for using the platform, with 89.5% of the research subjects who totally (31.6%) or partially agreed (57.9%). This finding suggested the companies' abilities to provide channels for sharing information and knowledge with ACIM through tools that supported the implementation of the offered platform.

4.6. *Processes and activities*

The perception that companies needed to make changes and adaptations in their processes and activities to adapt to the use of the platform as a tool for trading products was totally or partially verified by 76.2% of entrepreneurs. These results suggested that these companies are predisposed to change their processes and activities to enable the digital trading of their products or services.

4.7. *Motivational aids*

Achieving DT was facilitated when companies provided an appropriate motivational environment that promoted employee engagement and commitment or when they encouraged the adoption of new ways of working, learning, and acting, as in the case of different activities related to the marketplace. These conditions existed, totally and partially, in 55.2% of the cases, according to the interviewees. ACIM discovered the importance of looking for methods to foster these conditions among the associates. It is worth noting that these two aspects must be addressed by companies, as employees need encouragement to perceive their importance and the opportunities to engage in a new work perspective.

4.8. *Resources*

When considering the marketplace as a new business model, companies had already clearly identified the resources that should be allocated for such implementation, according to over two-thirds (68.4%) of the research subjects. However, this perspective from the companies references the lack of available resources beyond their limitations and digitization strategies, as a smaller number of subjects (57.8%) mentioned total or partial agreement about the statement regarding these internal resources. This result suggested a dilemma. Some companies identified the necessary resources, but presented minimal resources to advance the platform's implementation, creating an internal demotivational environment. On the other hand, for some companies when the necessary and minimum resources coincided, the predisposition to digitize the business increased. ACIM's role, (in that critical moment of offering the platform to its members), was to enable the associates of ACIM to identify their potential and limited resources for adopting online trading processes for their products and services.

4.9. *Human resources management*

The companies' evaluation of their employees indicated positive and negative aspects for 47.2% of the businesses in relation to the adaptations necessary for adopting the marketplace as their new digital business platform. Thus, the human factor needs to be considered as a critical resource in this new business model, especially in terms of quantity (possibility of the emergence of different processes and activities inherent to the newly implemented model) and quality (qualification to act and interact in the digital universe).

4.10. *Reliability*

An important aspect identified in this DT process was the high level of confidence the companies relied upon ACIM, with a 94.7% positive perception of ACIM's reputation (in terms of competence, reliability, and expression) in the region. This is especially apparent in the adoption of technological innovations, critical for the success of the marketplace platform project.

4.11. *Synthesis of critical IAKSs*

The IAKS validated the structural basis changing the culture of organizations in order to adopt the marketplace as a tool for trading products and services. This change involved management and support from the leadership, support from the principal managers of these companies, as well as an interest in participating in the platform. In this sense, the culture needed particular attention. Although there was support and positive perception, this aspect provided the basis for the others, such as better use of ICT and the alignment of purpose and strategy when using the platform.

In this context, culture also impacted the entire organizational infrastructure, processes, and activities, and when associated with motivational aids directed at human resources, culture can quickly reinforce positive behavior in the face of the challenge of adopting the marketplace. As a ripple effect, all the other resources could be reviewed and soon gain the guardianship of a new culture.

5. Conclusion

According to Anscombe [2020], the rapid adaptation of expanded or implemented new systems to allow remote customer service during the COVID-19 pandemic means that companies may return to the original scenario when the pandemic has subsided. However, decisions were made during COVID-19 to move towards the DT of businesses worldwide and, instead of returning to the previous status quo, perhaps companies should adopt these promoted changes beyond the pandemic period in providing services to customers.

Although the crisis forced adaptation in the short term, the positive aspect of this should be seen as a step towards DT, offering more flexibility to customers and opening new revenue opportunities for companies. According to KPMG [2020], although it is tempting to put the efforts of enterprises to improve and digitize their business to a second plan, companies should not slow down the actions to move strategically in the direction of DT. The events and incidents experienced during the COVID-19 pandemic will extend over a long time period, especially in terms of customer–company interaction and the purchase of products and services. Before the COVID-19, customers had already increased their knowledge of DT-based businesses, had previously become better connected, and learned to be more demanding. The context caused by the pandemic has evidenced this transformation.

The impacts of the "new normal" on DT can optimize processes and replace and/or redefine obsolete operations, providing better experiences for the consumer. In fact, DT can transform structures and relationship channels and form an organization with greater transparency, more open, sustainable, and socially engaged, based on digital responsive adaptations of the business (changes in the layout to adjust the site to different media, for example) [SBVC (2020b)].

The digitization proposal for companies based on the ACIM marketplace project is one of the critical examples of radical changes that tend to be established in the market during a crisis. In this case, knowledge sharing between the association and its members proved to be fundamental for the successful implementation and development process of the ACIM marketplace program. Some factors directly influenced the loyalty and continuity of the digitization of these companies' businesses in relation to the offered proposal. For example, a significant range of IAKMs became apparent, such as management leadership and support, culture, ICT, strategy and purpose, organizational infrastructure, processes and activities, motivational aids, resources, and human resources management.

In view of the presented results, the researchers suggest that companies focus their efforts on three essential components: people, processes, and culture. These components are responsible for understanding and processing the IAKS and, consequently, the acceptance of the online marketing environment by the companies for their products or services. Figure 1 shows the intersection of these components, enabling a regrouping of the influential factors, facilitating the construction of parameters for the construction of strategies aimed at the influential aspects in the context of the marketplace platform. Culture is noteworthy in this process since it acts far beyond an influential aspect, being considered as a fundamental organizational component for any change in the organizational paradigm, in addition to people and processes. If the culture is negative or not progressive, then the impact on the business could be detrimental to survival. If the culture is positive in the attitudes of management and employees and agile in orientation, then the enterprise is presented with an opportunity that creates the potential to expand the business and increase profits.

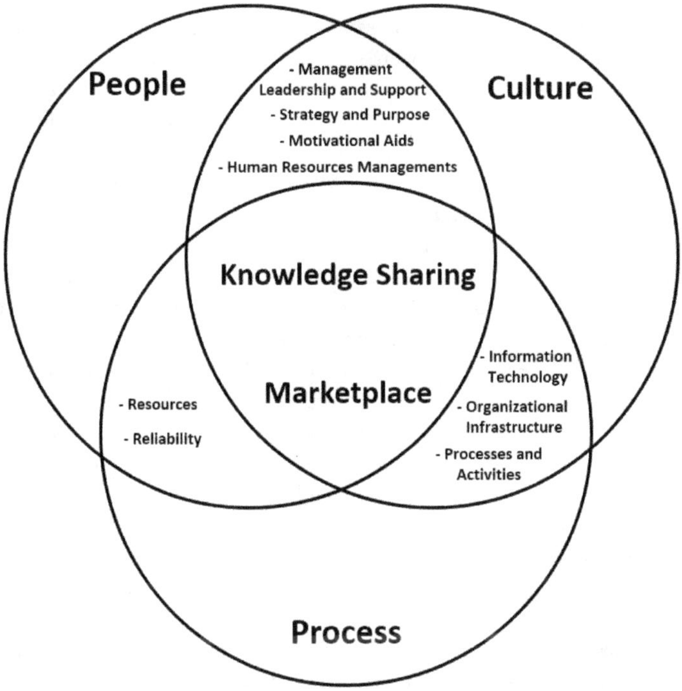

Source: Adapted from Jorge [2017].

Fig. 1. Pillars of organizational changes and influencing aspects.

The influential aspects resulting from these intersections suggest the need for specific parameters to achieve knowledge sharing in favor of virtualizing the associates' businesses on the marketplace platform developed and offered by ACIM. Management leadership and support were identified as a result of the intersection of the focus on people and culture. Each business is responsible through its directors and managers to clarify the importance of the platform for their employees, generating support and changes for comprehending new tools and knowledge sharing.

In this sense, knowledge sharing associated with the marketplace must be made explicit and recorded to support accessibility to entrepreneurs and their collaborators in terms of strategies and purposes when the company digitally inserts its products and services into the marketplace. With this, management leadership and support could act in an integrated manner in the construction of strategies and purposes, involving employees, and, thus, building a more solid organizational structure and architecture adhering more closely to the companies' context. This action should facilitate human resources management, with additional confidence in chosen actions during the construction of strategies and purposes with employees. In parallel, motivational aids for employees need to be built and considered integral to success, capitalizing on financial resources and the use of creativity.

These motivators may be, for instance, the public recognition of good practices/ actions carried out by employees for knowledge sharing, financial or nonfinancial bonuses, and the offer of small rewards. Such actions can reinforce the culture of proactive behavior expected from people during the innovative process of adopting and using the marketplace platform. Modifying people's behavior should enable a transformation in the culture of ICT use, increasing their involvement in the adoption, use, and/or suggestion of new technologies. This same behavior can be obtained for the organizational infrastructure and for processes and activities, making knowledge construction and sharing an important activating form of capital in companies. This positive behavior could improve the use of company resources and instill more confidence in employees to interact in the marketplace platform.

Until June 31st of 2020, the ACIM marketplace, named Marília.Dakki, registered 367 companies, with 7852 products available and a reach of 170374 views. The marketplace has notably been a disruption for shoppers, who need to adapt to this new way of purchasing products and services, which increases the number of views monthly. The marketplace requires continuous monitoring, regarding knowledge construction and sharing, even after the end of the pandemic. The flexibility of businesses in Marília, SP, and in other municipalities, will go through still unpredictable restriction phases related to reduced working hours and capacity for face-to-face service. Customers' fear of being exposed to the virus may significantly strengthen online marketing tools.

This increased momentum by the pandemic will be important for the consolidation of the platform as a new sales channel for these companies that had to abruptly adapt to overcome the difficulties triggered by the crisis resulting from the pandemic.

It is noteworthy that the present investigation did not bring together the perspective of the technological limitations, especially the lack of the Internet in some regions of Brazil, a condition that can be extended to other countries with similar contexts. The lack of the Internet in a territorial context hinders the application of technologies such as the marketplace. Additionally, the consumption relationship is limited during this time of previously outlined restrictions. Therefore, further studies focusing on the consumption relationship in the context of the lack of technologies are suggested in addition to the development of alternative strategies to allow products and services to be offered in times of restrictions.

References

ABCOMM (2021). Marketplaces: crescimento exponencial ao longo da pandemia. *Associacão Brasileira de Comércio Eletrônico*, 23 March 2021.

ACIM Marília-SP (2021). *Sobre Nós.* Retrieved from https://acim.org.br/quem-somos/.

Al-Tit, A. A. (2020). E-commerce drivers and barriers and their impact on e-customer loyalty in small and medium-sized enterprises (SMES). *Business: Theory and Practice*, **21**, 1: 146–157.

Anscombe, T. (2020). Digital transformation could be accelerated by COVID-19. *Welivesecurity.* Available at: https://www.welivesecurity.com/2020/05/07/digital-transformation-could-be-accelerated-covid-19/ Accessed 18 November 2020.

Bardin, L. (2009). *Análise de Conteúdo.* Lisboa, Edições Setenta, Portugal.

Becla, A. (2012). Information society and knowledge-based economy—development level and the main barriers—some remarks. *Economics & Sociology*, **5**, 1: 125–132.

Brem, A., Viardot, E. and Nylund, P. A. (2021). Implications of the coronavirus (COVID-19) outbreak for innovation: Which technologies will improve our lives?. *Technological Forecasting and Social Change*, **163**, 120451.

Bressoles, G., Durrieu, F. and Senecal, S. (2014). A consumer typology based on e-service quality and e-satisfaction. *Journal of Retailing and Consumer Services*, **21**, 6: 889–896.

Burt, S. and Sparks, L. (2013). E-commerce and the retail process: A review. *Journal of Retailing and Consumer Services*, **10**, 5: 275–286.

Casalino, N., Żuchowski, I., Labrinos, N., Munoz Nieto, Á. L. and Martín, J. A. (2019). Digital strategies and organizational performances of SMEs in the age of Coronavirus: Balancing digital transformation with an effective business resilience. *Law and Economics Yearly Review*, **8**, Part 2: 347–380.

Castells, M. A. (2003). *Galáxia da Internet: reflexões sobre a Internet, os negócios e a sociedade.* Zahar Editora, Rio de Janeiro.

Chen, Y. (2020). Improving market performance in the digital economy, *China Economic Review*, **62**, 101482. Available at: https://doi.org/10.1016/j.chieco.2020.101482. Accessed: 01 November. 2020.

Dannenberg, P., Fuchs, M., Riedler, T. and Wiedemann, C. (2020). Digital transition by COVID-19 pandemic? The German food online retail. *Tijdschrift voor Economische en Sociale Geografie*, **111**, 2: 543–560.

Davenport, T. and Prusak, L. (1999). *Conhecimento empresarial.* Traducão de LenkePerses. Rio de Janeiro: Campus; São Paulo: Publifolha.

Davis, M. (2008). Semantic Wave 2008 Report: Industry Roadmap to Web 3.0 &Multibillion Dollar Market Opportunities. *Executive Summary*, Available at: http://www.eurolibnet.eu/files/REPOSITORY/20090507165103_SemanticWaveReport2008.pdf. Accessed: 03 November. 2020.

Dorow, P. F. (2017). *Compreensão do compartilhamento do conhecimento em atividades intensivas em conhecimento nas organizacões de diagnóstico por imagem.* Dissertation Ph. D. in Engineering and Knowledge Management. Santa Catarina Federal University. Available at: https://repositorio.ufsc.br/xmlui/handle/123456789/180883 . Accessed: 13 November. 2020.

E-CommerceBrasil. (2020). Neotrust Report. 3. ed. Movimento Compre & Confie: *E-commerce Brasil.* Available at: https://www.compreconfie.com.br/relatorio-neotrust. Accessed: 11 November. 2020.

Egger, F. (2020) Masters of disasters? Challenges and opportunities for SMEs in times of crisis. *Journal of Business Research*, **116**, 199–208.

Faqih, M. and Jaradat, I. R. M. (2015). Assessing the moderating effect of gender differences and individualism-collectivism at individual-level on the adoption of mobile commerce technology: tam3 perspective. *Journal of Retailing and Consumer Services*, **22**, 37–52.

Freire, P. de S. (2010). *Compartilhamento do Conhecimento Interorganizacional: Causas Essenciais dos Problemas de Integracão em Fusões e Aquisicões (F&A). Florianópolis.* Master Thesis in Engineering and Knowledge Management. Santa Catarina Federal University. Available at: https://repositorio.ufsc.br/xmlui/handle/123456789/93449Accessed: 2 November 2020.

Garg, N., Pareek, A., Lale, A. and Charya, S. K. J. (2021). Evolution in E-Commerce with Augmented Reality. *IOP Conference Series: Materials Science and Engineering*, 1012 012041. Available at: https://doi.org/10.1088/1757-899X/1012/1/012041. Accessed 05 April 2021.

Guissoni, L. A. and Farinha, R. L. (2019). E-commerce com resultado. *GV Executivo*, **18**(1). Available at: http://bibliotecadigital.fgv.br/ojs/index.php/gvexecutivo/article/download/78193/74905. Accessed: 12 November 2020.

Hamidreza, S., Dehghani, H. and Khounsari, N. (2017). Analysis of organizational factors effect on performing electronic commerce strategy: a case study of the Namakin food industry. *International Journal of Economics and Management Engineering*, **11**, 6: 1593–1600.

Hasanali, F. (2002). *Critical success factors of knowledge management.* Available at: http://www.providersedge.com/docs/km_articles/Critical_Success_Factors_of_KM.pdf. Accessed: 24 November 2020.

Hickey, P. and Kozlovski, E. (2020). E-strategies for aftermarket facilitation in the global semiconductor manufacturing industry. *Journal of Enterprise Information Management*, **33**, 3: 457–481.

Islam, A., Jerin, I., Hafiz, N., Nimfa, D. T. and Wahab, S. A. (2021). Configuring a blueprint for Malaysian SMEs to survive through the COVID-19 crisis: The reinforcement of Quadruple Helix Innovation Model. *Journal of Entrepreneurship, Business and Economics*, **9**, 1: 32–81.

KPMG (2020). *COVID-19: A time for transformation and thinking for the future.* KPMG. Available at: https://home.kpmg/au/en/home/insights/2020/04/covid-19-coronavirus-digital-transformation-for-sme.html. Accessed: 18 November 2020.

Jiang, L. A., Yang, Z. and Jun, M. (2013). Measuring consumer perceptions of online shopping convenience. *Journal of Service Management*, **24**, 2: 191–214.

Jorge, C. F. B. (2017). *Análise de fatores críticos na gestão do conhecimento e no processo de Inteligência em organizacões complexas: uma análise teórico prática em múltiplas organizacões.* Dissertation Ph.D. in Information Science. São Paulo State University EstadualPaulista. Available at: https://repositorio.unesp.br/bitstream/handle/11449/152376/jorge_cfb_dr_mar.pdf?sequence=3. Accessed: 22 December 2020.

Laville, C. and Dionne, J. (1999). *A construção do saber: manual de metodologia da pesquisa em ciências humanas.* Porto Alegre: Artmed.; Belo Horizonte: Editora UFMG.

Lestari, S. D., Muhdaliha, E. and Putra, A. H. P. K. (2020). E-commerce performance based on knowledge management and organizational innovativeness. *The Journal of Distribution Science*, **18**, 2: 49–58.

Luz, C. (2018). A transformacão digital, o e-digital e o e-commerce. *E-commerce Brasil* [online]. Available at:https://www.ecommercebrasil.com.br/artigos/transformacao-digital-e-digital-e-commerce/. Accessed: 29 November 2020.

Marília Dakki (2020). *Access a Loja.* Retrieved from https://marilia.dakki.com.br/.

Martin, W. J. (2017). *The Global Information Society.* Taylor & Francis.

Mattelart, A. (2002). *História da sociedade da informação.* São Paulo: Loyola.

Nilashi, M., Ibrahim, O., Reza Mirabi, V., Ebrahimi, L. and Zare, M. (2015). The hole of security, design and content factors on customer trust in mobile commerce. *Journal of Retailing and Consumer Services*, **26**, 57–69.

Otre, M. A. C., Jorge, C. F. B. and Ferreira, T. G. (2019). Informação e moda na era do Big Data: como a informação digital inovou a moda e tornou a mais competitiva. *Revista Inteligência Competitiva*, **9**, 3: 123–139.

Perrin, F. (2020). Pandemia obriga migracao para comércio virtual. *Folha de São Paulo* [online]. Available at: https://www1.folha.uol.com.br/mpme/2020/05/pandemia-obriga-migracao-para-comercio-virtual-veja-pros-e-contras-de-cada-modelo.shtml. Accessed: 1 December 2020.

Pimenta, M. (2018). Marketplace: o que é, suas vantagens e desvantagens. *E-commerce Brasil — muito mais que e-commerce* [online]. Available at: https://www.ecommercebrasil.com.br/artigos/marketplace-vantagens-desvantagens/. Accessed: 12 November 2020.

Pinkwart, A., Block, J., Proksch, D. and Fisch, C. (2021). Editorial comments for the special issue on digital innovation management. *International Journal of Innovation and Technology Management*, 2002001.

Rabelo, A. (2018). Transformacão digital: o que é e quais os seus impactos na sociedade. *Rockcontent*[online]. Available at: https://rockcontent.com/blog/transformacao-digital/. Accessed: 18 November 2020.

Rezaei, S., Shahijan, M. K., Amin, M. and Ismail, W. K. W. (2016). Determinants of app sotores continuance behavior: A PLS path modelling approach. *Journal of Internet Commerce*15, 4: 408–440.

Riege, A. (2005). Three-dozen knowledge-sharing barriers managers must consider. *Journal of Knowledge Management*, **9**, 3: 18–35.

Rogers, D. L. (2017). *Transformacão digital:* repensando o seu negócio pra a era digital. São Paulo: Autêntica Business.

Saphores, J. D. and Xu, L. (2020). E-shopping changes and the state of E-grocery shopping in the US — Evidence from national travel and time use surveys. *Research in Transportation Economics May 12*, 100864.

SBVC (2020a). Novos hábitos digitais em tempos de Covid-19. *Estudos Especiais SBVC*. São Paulo: Sociedade Brasileira de Varejo e Consumo [online]. Available at: http://sbvc.com.br/novos-habitos-digitais-em-tempos-de-covid-19/. Accessed: 18 November 2020.

SBVC (2020b). 2° Estudo Transformacão Digital no Varejo Brasileiro. *Estudos Especiais SBVC*. São Paulo: Sociedade Brasileira de Varejo e Consumo[online]. Available at: http://sbvc.com.br/2a-edicao-estudo-transformacao-digital-no-varejo-brasileiro-sbvc-2020/. Accessed: 18 November 2020.

SEBRAE, (Feb. 13, 2021). Conheca as vantagens de vender seus produtos em um e-marketplace [website page]. Available at: https://m.sebrae.com.br/sites/PortalSebrae/artigos/conheca-as-vantagens-do-e-marketplace-para-os-pequenos-negocios,3f6402b5b-0d36410VgnVCM1000003b74010aRCRD. Accessed: 12 November, 2020.

Senarathna, I., Warren, M., Yeoh, W. and Salzman, S. (2014). The influence of organisation culture on E-commerce adoption. *Industrial Management & Data Systems*, **114**, 7: 1007–1021.

Shemi, A. P. and Procter, C. (2018). E-commerce and entrepreneurship in SMEs: Case of myBot. *Journal of Small Business and Enterprise Development*, **25**(3) 501–520.

Shih, M. H., Tsai, H. T., Wu, C. C. and Lu, C. H. (2006). A holistic knowledge sharing framework in high-tech firms: Game and co-opetition perspectives. *International Journal of Technology Management*, **36**, 4: 354–367.

Simões, N. (2016). Por que é importante conhecer cada marketplace? *E-commerce Brasil* — excelência em e-commerce. Available at: https://www.ecommercebrasil.com.br/artigos/por-que-e-importante-conhecer-cadamarketplace/. Accessed: 18 December 2020.

Sinaga, S. A., Handayani, P. W. and Pinem, A. A. (2017). Knowledge sharing motivation in e-commerce online community. *2017 International Conference on Advanced Computer Science and Information Systems (ICACSIS)*, Bali, Indonesia, pp. 143–148.

Song, Z., Sun, Y., Wan, J., Huang, L. and Zhu, J. (2019). Smart e-commerce systems: Current status and research challenges. *Electron Markets*, **29**, 221–238.

Sun, H., Fan, M. and Tan, Y. (2020). An empirical analysis of seller advertising strategies in an online marketplace. *Information Systems Research*, **31**, 1: 37–56.

Tadelis, S. (2016). Reputation and feedback systems in online platform markets. *Annual Review of Economics*, **8**, 321–340.

Tian, J., Coreynen, W., Matthyssens, P. and Shen, L. (2021). Platform-based servitization and business model adaptation by established manufacturers. *Technovation*, 102222.

Towers, N. and Xu, K. (2016). The influence of guanxi on physical distribution service quality availability in e-commerce sourcing fashion garments from China. *Journal of Retailing and Consumer Services*, **28**, 126–136.

Turban, E. *et al.*, (2015). *Electronic Commerce: A Managerial and Social Networks Perspective.* 8th ed. Springer.

Turchi, S. R. (2019). *Estratégias de marketing digital e e-commerce.* 2ª ed. São Paulo, Atlas.

Valentim. M. L. P. (2002). Inteligência competitiva em organizações: dado, informação e conhecimento. *DataGramaZero, Rio de Janeiro*, **3**, 4: 1–13.

Vissotto, E. M. and Boniati, B. B. (2013). Comércio eletrônico. Frederico Westphalen. *Rede E-tec Brasil* [online]. Available at: https://docplayer.com.br/2775893-Comercio-eletronico-elisa-maria-vissotto-bruno-batista-boniati.html. Accessed: 12 November 2020.

Wong, K. Y. (2005). Critical success factors for implementing knowledge management in small and medium enterprises. *Industrial Management & Data Systems*, **105**, 3: 261–279.

Yaacoub, J. P. A. *et al.* (2020). Cyber-physical systems security: Limitations, issues and future trends. *Microprocessors and Microsystems*, **77**, 103201.

Yin, R. K. (2003). *Case Study Research: Design and Methods.* Thousand Oaks: SAGE Publications.

Zacho, R. (2017). O que é Marketplace? — veja as vantagens e desvantagens. *E-commerce Brasil* — muito mais que e-commerce [online]. Availableat: https://www.ecommercebrasil.com.br/artigos/marketplace-vantagens-e-desvantagens/. Accessed: 3 November 2020.

Biography

Carlos Francisco Bitencourt Jorge is Associate Professor and Research in Management, Business & Innovation at Marília University (Unimar)/São Paulo-Brazil, also is Collaborate Professor in PhD program and Master Degree Information Science at São Paulo State University (Unesp)/São Paulo-Brazil. With a sound interest in innovation, knowledge management and digital transformation, has more than 40 articles published in many journals worldwide. Has Post-Doctor in Information Science (Information, Technology and Knowledge) at the Unesp (2019). PhD in Information Science with a focus on Knowledge Management and Competitive Intelligence in Complex Organizations from Unesp (2017). He is post-doctoral researcher in FGV - São Paulo School of Business Administration (EAESP)/São Paulo-Brazil with a focus on Knowledge Management and Digital Transformation. He is CEO of Connect Innovation Environment, CSO of Metafuter and Innovation Vice-President of chamber of commerce and Innovation of Marília (ACIM) - São Paulo/Brazil.

João Guilherme de Camargo Ferraz Machado is associate professor at São Paulo State University (Unesp), Faculty of Science and Engineering (FCE), Tupã Campus/São Paulo-Brazil, working in the Administration course and in the Graduate Program in Agribusiness and Development (PGAD). He holds a PhD (2007) in Production Engineering from the Federal University of São Carlos - UFSCar, postdoctoral degree at the Unesp (2019). As researcher he develops research in the following areas: management of rural organizations, management of agro-industrial systems, information management, strategic marketing and innovation in services.

Cláudia Herrero Martins Menegassi is a professor of the Master in Knowledge Management in Organizations at Unicesumar. She is post-doctoral researcher in Economics and Management at Sophia University Institute (Firenze/Italy) and PhD in Business Administration at Positivo University/Paraná-Brazil. As a researcher, she develops research focused mainly on the following topics: Knowledge Management, Organizational Intelligence, Economy of Communion and alternative management approaches, Organizational Studies.

Rodrigo da Silva Stecca is a PhD Candidate in Agribusiness and Development at Universidade Estadual Paulista Júlio de Mesquita Filho (Unesp) /São Paulo-Brazil, campus de Tupã/SP Brazil. He is technician school teacher at the Paula Souza State Technological Education Center-Amim Jundi State Technical School/São Paulo-Brazil. As researcher, he works in the context of Administration, with a focus on Business Management.

Michael J. D. Sutton is Professor and researcher at Anaheim University/California-USA and Marília University (Unimar). He holds a PhD in Information School from McGill University (2007). As researcher has experience in Management, Business, Innovation and Education. He has extensive experience in educating, teaching, managing, technically architecting and leading strategic business and educational initiatives. He has been Practice Director for over fifteen years, focusing his analysis, management and systems thinking talent on this emerging field of Knowledge Management practice. At academic business schools, he motivated his students to adopt an "entrepreneurial spirit" necessary to succeed in our complex world of volatility, uncertainty, complexity and ambiguity (VUCA). He has trained and mentored start-up founders, SMEs, as well as executives and managers at Fortune 500 companies.

How Social Networks Influence Organizational Innovation Adoption*

Axel Jacob*,‡ and Frank Teuteberg†

*Faculty of Business Management and Social Sciences
Osnabrück University of Applied Sciences, Osnabrück, Germany

†Department of Accounting and Information Systems
Osnabrück University, Osnabrück, Germany
‡a.jacob@hs-osnabrueck.de

The purpose of this paper is to provide a framework that explains the interdependency of organizations and different social networks in the process of organizational innovation adoption (OIA). We first develop a taxonomy of social networks relevant to OIA and then a conceptual framework based on a review of existing frameworks. Furthermore, a case study was conducted with two cases and six embedded units of analysis. The review of existing frameworks for OIA shows that the importance of social networks has not yet been fully addressed. The analysis of the cases reveals four types of influence (comparison, argumentation, reciprocal learning, and alignment) through which social networks influence the OIA on micro, meso and macro levels. Our results help to better understand how the adoption of innovations proceeds in organizations against the background of the increasing importance of social networks and concepts such as open innovation.

Keywords: Organizational innovation adoption; social networks; framework; case study.

1. Introduction

Technical and social advances force organizations to innovate in order to keep pace with the ever more demanding requirements of their stakeholders on the one hand; on the other hand, the ensuing innovations open up outstanding possibilities for organizations to develop further their products or services as well as themselves as a social structure [Damanpour *et al.* (1989)]. With networks and organizations becoming increasingly integrated in a collaborative value creation, the influence of networks on organizational innovation adoption (OIA) is also increasing [Di Gangi and Wasko (2009); Yan *et al.* (2017); Scuotto *et al.* (2017); Granstrand and Holgersson (2020)]. Concepts that involve external people or networks in the innovation process, e.g. suppliers and customers, have become increasingly important in recent years. Web 2.0 technologies have become a powerful tool for open innovation [Chesbrough (2017); Mount and Martinez (2014)] and collaborative innovation [Greer and Lei (2012)] because they have opened up possibilities for organizations to make use of the resources,

‡ Corresponding author.

*This chapter was originally published in International Journal of Innovation and Technology Management, Vol. 19, No. 8, March 2018, published by World Scientific Publishing, Singapore. Reprinted with permission.

knowledge and the creativity of external individuals and their social networks, in order to solve existing problems or to develop new processes, products or business models [Sawhney *et al.* (2005); Chesbrough (2017)]. Concepts such as crowdsourcing [Saxton *et al.* (2013)] or co-creation [Zhang *et al.* (2015)] are good examples for this development.

However, despite the increasing importance of networks in the process of OIA, their complexity is not yet sufficiently acknowledged in the literature. To the best of our knowledge, there is still no framework for OIA that takes into account the diversity of networks in an organization's environment and how these networks influence an organization in terms of innovation adoption. Rich literature exists which sheds light on OIA [e.g. DePietro *et al.* (1990); Frambach and Schillewaert (2002); van Oorschot *et al.* (2018)]. In most of the studies, organizations are regarded as socio-technical systems that are to a certain extent affected by the organization's environment, including the existing networks. In this context, networks primarily refer to connections to the suppliers (of an innovation) or to competitors. But with the rise of social media, the importance of networks has grown and the boundaries of organizations seem to be blurring [Leonardi and Vaast (2017)]. According to Castells [1996] and his profound theory of a network society, "networks have become the predominant organizational form of every domain of human activity." Therefore, a closer systematic examination of the growing variety of networks in an organization's ecosystem (for example, employees' private social networks, intra- and inter-organizational networks) and how these networks influence OIA seems necessary.

In consequence, the aim of this paper is to provide a systematic overview that explains the interdependency of organizations and networks in the process of OIA. By doing so, we seek to answer the following research question: How do networks influence the adoption of innovation in organizations? To address this research question, we develop a conceptual framework based on various data sources, i.e. a review of well-established OIA frameworks and a multiple-case embedded design case study research. While such a systematic overview of the influence of networks in an organization's ecosystem effectively closes a research gap, its weightier functions are to help to organize the complex subject of networks in OIA, to identify the relationships between different actors and to reveal areas in which further research is required. By developing such a framework, we respond to calls from Awa [2019], Zahra *et al.* [2020] and Jeyaraj *et al.* [2006] to bridge the concepts for organizational and individual innovation adoption; from Alves *et al.* [2018] to characterize organizational innovation at the inter-organizational level; from Eckhardt *et al.* [2009] to develop a theoretical perspective on adoption or non-adoption considering the social embeddedness of individuals; and, finally, from Leonardi and Vaast [2017] to research how social communities and other networks intersect with organizations.

This paper is organized as follows. Basic frameworks and theories are reviewed in Sec. 2 of the paper in order to establish the theoretical foundation. Following this, the research methodology and empirical setting are explained in Sec. 3. The development of the taxonomy and framework, based on the theoretical insights and things learned from case studies, takes place in Sec. 4. Implications for the theory and practice of OIA, limitations of this paper and further research are addressed in Sec. 5. Finally, the contributions of this paper are summarized.

2. Literature Survey

2.1. *Organizational innovation adoption*

Organizational innovation is a rather complex and multifaceted phenomenon. There is no consensus on a definition of the term "organizational innovation" and, therefore, it remains ambiguous [Lam (2006)]. To reach a deeper understanding of organizational innovation, it is beneficial to consider the different categories of research streams that focus on distinct aspects of organizational innovation. A first category of research focuses on the consequences of organizational innovation. Such research includes studies of the results of OIA in terms of performance improvement, economic success, and behavioral change in specific regional settings or industries [Sapprasert and Clausen (2012); Lichtenthaler (2016); Donbesuur *et al.* (2020)].

A second category of research refers to the elements of organizational innovation. This includes different types of innovation, its quality of impact, and the process of innovation. From the customary perspective, the types of innovation entail technological and administrative innovations [Kimberly and Evanisko (1981)]. Views that are more recent go beyond the classical perspective. According to Damanpour [1991], an innovation can be a new product, service, process, technology, policy, structure, or administrative system. Armbruster *et al.* [2008] provide an explicit classification of innovation types and distinguish between technical product innovations, non-technical service innovations, technical process innovations, and non-technical process innovations that "comprise changes in the structure and processes of an organization due to implementing new managerial and working concepts and practices." These types of innovations can affect organizations at different intensities and, therefore, lead to incremental or radical changes in the structure and functioning of an organization [Damanpour (1991)]. With regards to the process of organizational innovation, a frequently applied foundation for research on the innovation adoption process is the phase model of Rogers [1995]. According to him, innovation adoption is a sub-process of diffusion. He divides the innovation adoption process into five different stages: (a) knowledge; (b) persuasion; (c) decision; (d) implementation; and (e) confirmation. Because innovation adoption takes place on different levels, such as individual, organizational, industrial, and societal levels [Williams *et al.* (2009)], many studies apply the technology acceptance model (TAM) [Davis *et al.* (1989)] or the theory of planned behavior (TPB) [Ajzen (1991)] in order to describe the individual level of innovation adoption.

The final strand of literature focuses on the antecedents of innovation (adoption) and moderators that strengthen or weaken the effects of the antecedents. Several frameworks shed light on the determinants that influence OIA. A very prominent framework for OIA is the technology-organization-environment (TOE) framework [Baker (2012); DePietro *et al.* (1990)]. According to the TOE framework, the three contexts, technology, organization, and environment influence the innovation adoption behavior of an organization in the sense of "constraints and opportunities for technological innovation" [DePietro *et al.* (1990, p. 154)]. As the characteristics of the contexts are not exclusively defined and contain various factors in different studies [Baker (2012); Zhu and Kramer (2004, p. 63)] call the TOE framework "generic." There are also frameworks that aim to merge the organizational level of innovation adoption with the individual innovation adoption process by combining the TOE framework with the TAM [Davis *et al.* (1989)]. Some confine their approaches to using TOE in its original version and adapting TAM [Gangwar *et al.* (2015)]. Awa *et al.* [2015] proceed in the same way, but they also integrate the TPB [Ajzen (1991)]. Liu and Wang [2010] adapt TAM as well, but also TOE, by introducing the context of third-party consultation. Frambach and Schillewaert [2002] do not explicitly name the TOE framework but use perceived innovation characteristics (on the organizational level), adopter characteristics (on the organizational level), and environmental influences as "determinants" analogously to TOE [Frambach and Schillewaert (2002, p. 164)].

In the context of the present paper, the organizational environment is of high importance. As illustrated in Fig. 1, the environment comprises numerous different actors and institutions, giving it a high degree of complexity [Armbruster *et al.* (2008); Poutanen *et al.* (2016)].

The literature distinguishes between the environment as a source of innovation and as a moderator for the adoption of innovation. The industry structure, governmental regulation, technological intensity, supplier power, and customer demand [Roberts and Amit (2003); Cohen and Levin (1989); Chouki *et al.* (2020)] as well as collaboration with external partners or stakeholders and socio-economic factors [Lee *et al.* (2020); Vries *et al.* (2018)] represent characteristics of the environment that can constitute organizational innovation. Actors in an organization's environment can have resources or knowledge in technologies or concepts that are in an

Fig. 1. Elements of the environment of organizations [Damanpour (2020)].

organization's interest but are not part of its capabilities. An example is provided by Ucar [2018] who describes the impact of local creative culture on corporate innovation. The absorptive capacity theory [Cohen and Levinthal (1990)] helps to understand how organizations absorb new knowledge from external sources and incorporate such knowledge into the process of organizational innovation. The extent to which organizations involve external sources in the process of innovation can be regarded as a continuum of openness [Damanpour *et al.* (2018)], with open innovation [Chesbrough (2003); Oumlil *et al.* (2020)] as its most pronounced mode.

In addition to the nature of the environment as a source for innovation, the environment of an organization can also be the source for moderators that facilitate or impede OIA [Oliveira *et al.* (2019); Dedrick *et al.* (2015)]. For example, Bharati and Chaudhury [2019] prove that trustful relationships with customers and suppliers positively influence OIA.

In this paper, we do not focus on the consequences of organizational innovation. Our approach originates from an institutional and behavioral perspective [Lam (2006); Damanpour (2014); Birkinshaw *et al.* (2008)] and involves the process of organizational innovation [Rogers (1995)]. We refer to innovations in a holistic sense and do not differentiate between incremental and radical as well as technical innovations and non-technical innovations [Armbruster *et al.* (2008); Damanpour (1991)]. Consequently, we understand OIA as a change process in an organization related to the decision-making process and the implementation of a new product, service, process, technology, policy, structure, or administrative system [Lam (2006)]. We focus on approaches that describe determinants for innovation adoption on an organizational level, ones that are not primarily constituted in the individual person and their behavior [Laumer *et al.* (2016)]. However, we also seek to develop a framework that is compatible with current knowledge on innovation adoption on an individual as well as industrial and societal level. For this purpose, we do not consider the full range of antecedents of OIA, but rather confine ourselves to the organizational environment and to the different networks in the environment of organizations, for example.

2.2. *On the role of networks in the innovation adoption process*

External networks are attributed to influence OIA [Rothwell (1994); Pittaway *et al.* (2004); van Heck and Vervest (2007); Möller and Halinen (2017); Priyono *et al.* (2020)]. For example, Katz and Shapiro [1985] use the term "network externalities" to refer to the influence that interrelated partners within the environment of an organization with respect to an innovation have. Rothwell [1991] describes how small and medium enterprises overcome a lack of resources by creating technical, marketing, and manufacturing relationships as well as involving infrastructural institutions, such as universities and private sector research institutes. Networks can involve organizations as a whole but also specific users [Majchrzak *et al.* (2000); Pittaway *et al.* (2004); Lee *et al.* (2010); Ernst and Brem (2017)]. Therefore, different types of external networks are of importance for OIA, such as inter-organizational networks [Thorgren *et al.* (2009); Jenssen and Nybakk (2013)], but also private social networks that gain more influence in the research on OIA, especially against the background of emergent topics such as sustainability [Demirel and Payne (2018)] and open innovation [Tirabeni and Soderquist (2019)].

An overview of different types of networks is provided, for example, by van Heck and Vervest [2007] who differentiate networks among the categories network outcomes, network execution, network governance, network design, and enabling technologies. Another overview can be found in Huggins *et al.* [2012] who cluster different characteristics within the dimensions source, mechanisms, object, and impact. Besides the aforementioned distinguishing features, the literature attributes a variety of characteristics to networks. For example, Rank [2008] distinguishes between formal and informal as well as vertical and horizontal networks. Dagnino *et al.* [2016] introduce emergent and orchestrated inter-organizational networks. They describe emergent networks as long lasting and unintentional. In contrast, orchestrated networks are intentionally directed by a leader and exist basically for a short time period. In this regard, Ricciardi *et al.* [2018] emphasize the importance of the fragility of network commons in self-organizing networks and its consequences for the configuration and management of networks. Furthermore, Pel *et al.* [2020] name local embeddedness, translocal connectivity, and discursive resonance as essential constellations in the context of networks for social innovation. According to Bruque *et al.* [2014], networks can also be informational or supportive in the innovation adoption process. Informational networks provide concrete, task-related assistance, and guidance [Sparrowe *et al.* (2001)]. This kind of network is central to innovation because it enables knowledge transfer within and between organizations and provides access to resources that are necessary for the development of new ideas [Clegg *et al.* (2016)]. Supportive networks benefit the individual psychological well-being of the members in allowing the sharing of sentiments, a search for understanding, the venting of frustration, and bolstering of self-esteem [Lin *et al.* (1999)].

An explanation for the influence of networks on the innovation adoption process of a decision-making unit can be found in the perception of relative advantages, compatibility, and ease of use associated with an innovation adopted by network members [Kapoor *et al.* (2014b); Vagnani and Volpe (2017)]. Another explanation can be derived from the concept of proximity [Singh and Phelps (2013); Clegg *et al.* (2016)]. Two different models for the explanation of proximity can be identified in the literature: social cohesion and structural equivalence models [van Oorschot *et al.* (2018); Burt (1987); Singh and Phelps (2013)]. Social cohesion models focus on the intensity of the social ties and the agency between members in a network in order to explain the likelihood that a member of the network influence the decision-making unit [Singh and Phelps (2013)]. Against this background, Kapoor *et al.* use the term "social approval" to describe a "status gained in one's reference group [...] as a function of adopting a particular innovation" [Kapoor *et al.* (2014a, p. 338)]. In structural equivalence models, members of a network adopt an innovation because others in the same network who have comparable or desirable characteristics also adopted the innovation [Burt (1987)].

The theories of social capital [Coleman (1988)] and relational capital [Kale *et al.* (2000); Yli-Renko *et al.* (2001)] provide theoretical frameworks for how networks contribute to organizational innovation. As elements of the organizational environment, they can be both a source and a moderator of innovation [Ndou *et al.* (2011); Apostolov and Coco (2020)]. Nevertheless, networks involving organizations as a single entity are primarily described as sources of innovation [Meissner and Kotsemir (2016); Cap *et al.* (2019); Apostolov and Coco (2020)], while networks involving members of an organization are primarily described as moderators of innovation adoption [Barrot *et al.* (2013); Boland (2020); Heinze and Heinze (2020)].

Herein, we understand networks as social structures and, therefore, as social networks. Contractor *et al.* [2006] define a social network as "a set of actors and one or more relations between the actors," where "actors" may be "any kind of meaningful social unit, including individuals, collective entities, firms, organizations, and divisions within organizations." We adopt such a broad conception of social networks in the present paper because it more readily allows an organization itself to be conceived of as a social network with a social behavior comparable to that of individuals [Nohria (1992)]. Furthermore, the broader conception covers a wide spectrum, from privately used social networks to professional (inter-) organizational networks, all of which we consider to be relevant for OIA (cf. Fig. 2).

2.3. *Literature gap and research approach*

The reviewed literature reveals reasons to deepen the research on the role of networks on OIA. First, the nature of networks has changed. Today, many organizations are part of dynamic and distributed value creation systems, including customers and other stakeholders, that collaboratively develop and manufacture products [Co and Barro (2009); Alfalla-Luque *et al.* (2018)]. Networks are of great importance for such value creation. Simultaneously, this type of value creation also involves the use of Web 2.0 technologies [Aral *et al.* (2013)] and thus the integration of new networks, such as changing social networks [Fehrer and Nenonen (2020)].

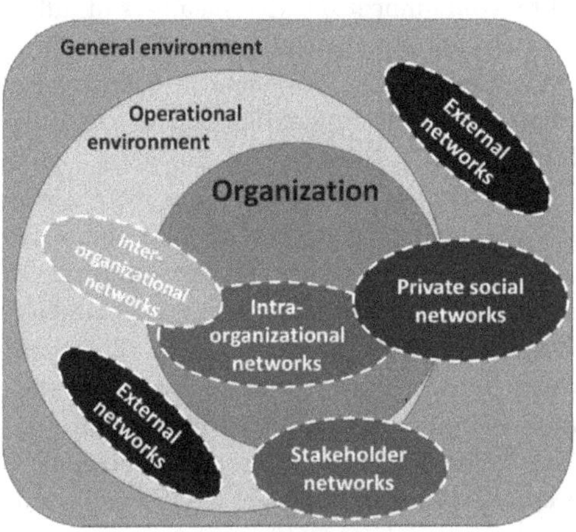

Fig. 2. Networks in the ecosystem of an organization in the context of this study.

However, the research on networks in the process of innovation adoption has so far focused mainly on static organizational networks rather than on dynamic (social) networks [Clegg *et al.* (2016)]. But especially highly responsive social networks foster the rate of diffusion and thereby contribute to the adoption of an innovation [Rogers *et al.* (2005); Wejnert (2010)].

Second, the influence of non-intra-organizational networks is increasing. For example, [Eckhardt *et al.* (2009)] researched the role of social influence within various intra-organizational workplace referent groups and concluded that a wider consideration of the social embeddedness of individuals is necessary. Leonardi and Vaast [2017] explicate how social media shift the boundaries of organizations and how they bring in communities that exist outside of the organization. Chesbrough [2017] likewise points to the importance of heterogeneous networks in open innovation when concluding that open innovation "will be more extensive, more collaborative, and more engaged with a wider variety of participants." In this paper we take a broader view of networks with the help of Castells' theory of a network society [Castells (1996, 2000)]. Castells examined the effects and implications of technological change on mass media culture, on urban life, and global politics. He postulates a "culture of real virtuality," in which dynamic social networks of individuals predominate but do not eliminate other social structures or institutions [Castells (1996)]. Organizations and companies especially are members in cooperative and flexible networks based not only on the sharing of capital and labor, but most fundamentally on the sharing of information and knowledge [Contractor *et al.* (2006)]. According to Castells, information processing and knowledge generation reinforce each other in a virtuous circle of interaction in social and organizational networks [Castells (1996)]. This procedure empowers autonomization and enables the network to preside to some degree over the institutions in which the networks are embedded [Castells (2000)].

In consequence, we argue that networks represent a variety of social systems that have not been sufficiently considered in the OIA literature. OIA is frequently initiated and shaped by communication with members of different social systems, i.e. an organization as the adopting social system or social systems that transfer further social influence [Burt (1973); Wejnert (2010)]. Members of both kinds of social systems influence the decision-making unit in the different stages of the adoption process [Rogers (1995); Burt (1973)]. However, the various sub-units of the decision-making unit do not necessarily constitute social units exclusively within the adopting social system; for, they are also embedded in social systems outside of the adopting social system and thus not subject to the authority of the adopting social system. In the literature, customers [Frambach and Schillewaert (2002)] or consultants [Awa (2019)] are mentioned in this regard. Awa *et al.* [2015] mention in this context the social influence of networks on the adoption decision. However, there is no systematic approach that incorporates the existing diversity of networks and their types of influence into the process of OIA. We therefore advocate a stronger consideration of networks in OIA and a multi-level framework that includes a network perspective.

3. Methodology

3.1. *Framework design*

The framework development process follows the guidelines of Eisenhart [1991]. A framework is used by researchers to structure their perspective on the research problem and to support their investigations [Eisenhart (1991)]. It helps to organize a complex subject, identify the relationships between the parts and reveal areas in which further developments are required [Sprague (1980)]. Eisenhart [1991] distinguishes three different kinds of frameworks: (a) theoretical, (b) practical, and (c) conceptual. Theoretical frameworks rely on a theory. The researcher derives hypotheses or questions based on the theory and chooses "to conform to the accepted conventions of argumentation and experimentation associated with the theory" [Eisenhart (1991, p. 205)]. Disadvantages of theoretical frameworks might arise when researchers follow the theory too rigorously while not considering other important information, or when the framework has no practical implications. Because of these shortcomings, practical frameworks focus on key features of the practical experience and its circumstances, based on accumulated practical knowledge [Scriven (1995)]. Limited generalizability is often a drawback of practical frameworks. "A conceptual framework is an argument including different points of view and culminating in a series of reasons for adopting some points — i.e. some ideas or concepts — and not others" [Eisenhart (1991, p. 209)]. Therefore, developing a conceptual framework is reasonable in the present case, inasmuch as there exist different approaches that include numerous and complex determinants of OIA with indistinct interdependencies which have not been investigated to this point.

3.2. *Empirical foundation*

3.2.1. *Case study research*

Case studies are well established in innovation adoption research, and they are important also for the development of frameworks [Eisenhardt (1989)]. According to Cavaye [1996], the nature of case study research is defined by the four characteristics, namely, epistemology, research objective, research method and research design. Epistemology refers in this context to how knowledge is created, which can be in the sense of positivism (i.e. the existence of a pre-defined theoretical construct), interpretivism (i.e. the absence of a pre-defined theoretical construct) or a combination of the two. The research objective can be to test an existing theory deductively [Bitektine (2007)], to build new theory [Eisenhardt and Graebner (2007)] or to combine deductive and inductive approaches. In doing so, case study research builds on qualitative methods, but in some cases, there may be a combination of qualitative and quantitative methods. Case study research can also be designed as single- or multi-case studies. Yin [2018] refines these characteristics by explaining that single- and multi-case designs can each cover unitary (holistic designs) or multiple (embedded) units of analysis. In consequence, Yin advocates four types of case study research designs: (a) single-case holistic designs; (b) single-case embedded designs; (c) multi-case holistic designs; and (d) multi-case embedded designs [Yin (2018)].

The intention of this paper is to propose a new theory based on existing theory and empirical findings. Thus, we chose a combined deductive and inductive approach in the sense of Dubois and Gadde [2002], with a multiple-case embedded design [Eisenhardt and Graebner (2007); Yin (2018)]. This approach is reasonable for our intention because deduction allows for a theoretical framing while inductive case studies allow for the development of a framework of the underlying structure of experiences or processes [Thomas (2016)]. Likewise, a multi-case embedded design is appropriate because it increases the likelihood that our results do not apply to a single setting only, thus making them more robust.

3.2.2. *Case selection, data collection and analysis*

Two different cases with embedded units of analysis were used for our case study. The first setting included four units of analysis in the field of logistics service providers (LSP), and the second setting included two units of analysis in the field of ethical fashion (EF) (cf. Fig. 3).

We applied a combination of information-based case selection and random case selection [Eisenhardt and Graebner (2007)]. First, we chose the two cases based on information. We decided for LSP as they are involved in a high number of organizational as well as social networks [Lemoine and Dagnæs (2003)] and surrounded by an environment that forces them to be innovative [Busse and Marcus Wallenburg (2011)]. Furthermore, we chose the field of EF because fashion is a good example for the influence of networks on the decision-making process [Cherrier (2007)]. Moreover, EF includes mainly small and micro enterprises that are characterized by a lack of sophisticated resources and thus are forced to be innovative [Roper and Hewitt-Dundas (2017)]. Second, we applied random case selection for the identification of the units of analysis. In the case of LSP, we contacted 17 companies that were relevant to us for reasons of practicability from a ranking of German LSP [Kille and Schwemmer (2014)]. We received positive feedback from four companies, which

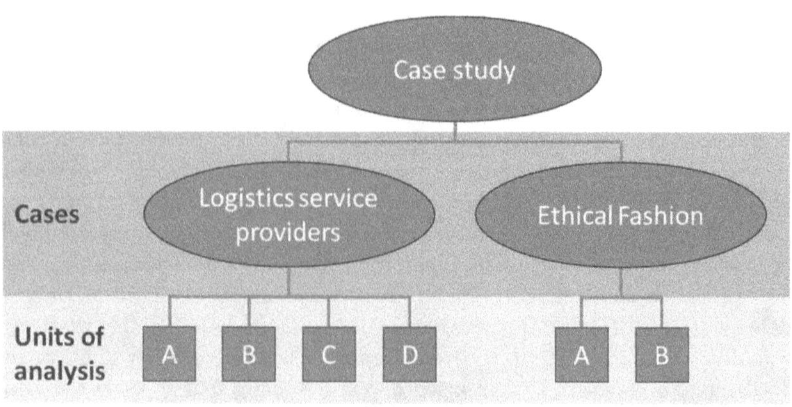

Fig. 3. Framework for OIA from a network perspective.

operate a large number of sites worldwide (from 12 to 244) with between 680 and 16,000 employees and offer logistics services for various industries such as pharmaceuticals, tires, consumer goods and fashion.

In the case of EF, we identified relevant participants through a call for participation among exhibitors of the Ethical Fashion Show Berlin, which is one of the leading exhibitions for EF. In the end, two out of 31 micro-enterprises joined our research. Both companies qualify as micro-enterprises in the sense of the definition of the European Commission [2003]. They sell sustainably produced accessories like bags, jewelry, and woolen fabrics, which are sourced from small communities in developing countries. All suppliers have to comply with labor standards and pay fair wages.

To enhance data triangulation [Eisenhardt and Graebner (2007)], we gathered data in different ways. The main source of data was qualitative, semi-structured interviews. We interviewed the managers at the LSP in July 2017 and the chief executives of the EF companies in September and October 2017. All interviews were recorded and later transcribed. In qualitative content analyses, the statements of the respondents were manually paraphrased and coded [Salda na (2009)]. In the case of EF, we also conducted a workshop in January 2018 with the two micro-enterprises and experts in the fields of marketing, logistics and production in order to discuss directions for the development of their businesses. Further sources of data were public and internal company-specific documents as well as on-site observations. In the various phases of data collection, we tried to adopt a neutral position as researchers who are as uninvolved as possible. Since we left this position during the organization and moderation of the workshop and took an active role, we only used that information from this phase of data collection, in which the participants presented the previous role of different networks on their organizations. The jointly elaborated findings on future directions for development of the businesses were not included in the development of the framework.

Within-case analysis showed how networks affect OIA in each unit of analysis [Bitektine (2007)]. Cross-case analysis was applied on two levels: first, to compare the different units of analysis within the two cases, and second, to reveal similarities and differences between the two cases [Eisenhardt (1989)]. Three different researchers evaluated the data independently. In the case of disagreements, the results were analyzed again and discussed until an agreement was reached. The final results of the case study were compared with the findings of the reviewed literature and used for developing the framework.

4. Framework Development

4.1. *Comparison of the reviewed organizational innovation adoption frameworks*

The reviewed OIA frameworks are compared in two steps. First, we illustrate the structural characteristics of the reviewed frameworks. This includes the academic discipline, the theoretical background, the field of application and the type of

Table 1. Structural characteristics of the reviewed frameworks.

Authors of the framework	Academic discipline				Theoretical origin				Scope		Frame-work type	
	Business administration	Information technology	Psychology	Sociology	Innovation diffusion theory	TAM	TOE[a]	TPB	Universal	Specific for companies	Conceptual	Theoretical
Awa *et al.* [2015]	x		x		x	x	x	x		x		x
DePietro *et al.* [1990]	x				x		x			x		x
Frambach and Schillewaert [2002]	x				x	x	x			x		x
Gangwar *et al.* [2015]		x			x	x	x			x	x	
Liu and Wang [2010]		x	x		x	x	x			x	x	
Rogers [1995]				x	x				x			x
Wejnert [2002]				x	x				x			x

Note: [a]Following Baker [2012], TOE is a framework but likewise a theory.

framework in accordance with Eisenhart [1991]. Table 1 gives an overview of the structural characteristics.

In the second step of the analysis, we analyze the content-related characteristics of the frameworks:

Technology. The technological context is most prominent in the TOE-framework and the referring sub-frameworks. In the TOE-framework, the characteristics are the kind of technology (equipment or process), the kind of integration (incorporated or available but not yet incorporated) and IT capabilities of the employees [Baker (2012); Collins *et al.* (1988)]. The sub-frameworks also use the characteristics, IT-knowledge [Awa *et al.* (2015)], IT-strategy [Liu and Wang (2010)], compatibility and complexity [Gangwar *et al.* (2015)].

Organization. In the TOE-framework and its sub-frameworks, the organizational context includes resources like technological, financial, and human resources, but it also includes characteristics of the organization that refer in the same way to the social system, such as size, degree of centralization, degree of formalization, the management structure and the linkages among employees [DePietro *et al.* (1990)]. The authors of the sub-frameworks [Awa *et al.* (2015); Liu and Wang (2010); Frambach and Schillewaert (2002)] add the characteristics, strategy, and change competence [Gangwar *et al.* (2015); Liu and Wang (2010)]. Rogers points out that organizations consist of specific structures and characteristics like those already mentioned, which may foster or limit the innovation adoption [Rogers (1995)]. Wejnert does not focus on organization: In her opinion, organizations can be part of the social system or of the environment [Wejnert (2002)].

Environment. The environmental context is rather indistinct. In the TOE-framework, it contains the wide fields of the industry (size and structure), the direct competitors, the macroeconomic, and the regulatory environment [DePietro *et al.* (1990)]. In Rogers' framework and, to an even greater extent, in Wejnert's framework, the environment is broader than in the TOE-framework, as she includes geographical settings, societal culture, political conditions and global uniformity in the sense of common practices and understandings [Wejnert (2002); Rogers (1995)].

Characteristics of the innovation. Wejnert [2002] uses the variables, "public versus private consequences" and "benefits versus costs" for describing the characteristics of innovations. Rogers points out the importance of the characteristics of an innovation for the individuals, but also for the social system, which are the relative advantage, the perceived compatibility, complexity, observability and trialability [Rogers (1995)]. The same characteristics are addressed in some sub-frameworks of TOE [Gangwar *et al.* (2015); Frambach and Schillewaert (2002)], but not in the general TOE-framework.

Individuals. The TOE-framework does not consider the innovation adoption on an individual level. The individual innovation adoption process is explained with TAM in its sub-frameworks [Frambach and Schillewaert (2002); Gangwar *et al.* (2015); Liu and Wang (2010)] and, in the case of Awa *et al.* [2015], also with TPB. Rogers [1995] and Wejnert [2002] use the term "actor" to describe an individual who is embedded in a social system (including other individuals, groups, or organizations), and they point out, as does Jeyaraj *et al.* [2006], that the innovation adoption process of an individual is different from the innovation adoption process in an organization.

Social systems. Social systems are very important because they can transmit information about an innovation and social influence [Burt (1973)]. Rogers [1995] and Wejnert [2010] argue for the importance of social systems and analyze them in more general terms. According to these authors, a social system reflects a society and its own culture, shared values, and beliefs instead of a group of individuals [Wejnert (2005); Rogers (1995)]. In the context of OIA, the social system of an organization is of central importance. On the organizational level, it is shaped by organizational culture [Mirvis *et al.* (1991)] social norms [Frambach and Schillewaert (2002)] as well as the aforementioned characteristics of a social system, i.e. degree of centralization, degree of formalization, the management structure, and the linkages among employees [DePietro *et al.* (1990)]. The latter includes the social influence of different workplace reference groups, e.g. superiors, colleagues, suppliers, and customers, on the individual employee [Frambach and Schillewaert (2002); Eckhardt *et al.* (2009); Makkonen *et al.* (2016)]. The diversity of reference groups indicates that there may be overlapping between different social systems that influence OIA, whereby some of these social systems may exist outside the company [Wejnert (2010)].

Organizational networks. As already mentioned, the TOE-framework is rather vague regarding the environment. Therefore, the authors of the sub-frameworks separate and thereby underline the importance of external partners like customers [Awa *et al.* (2015)], trading partners [Awa *et al.* (2015)], suppliers [Frambach and Schillewaert (2002); Liu and Wang (2010); Gangwar *et al.* (2015)] and competitors [Gangwar *et al.* (2015); Liu and Wang (2010)] in the value chain of the organization. Wejnert also points to the importance of organizational networks: "Networks composed of organizations similar in terms of structure, content, and goals [...] have effects similar to interpersonal networks, but they also provide means of diffusion of innovations that are independent of direct interpersonal interactions." [Wejnert (2002, p. 307)]. Rogers does not use the term "organizational networks." Instead, he uses the terms "centralization" and "virtual organizations" in a narrow sense to describe organizations in which power, control and employees are distributed in a social and geographical way [Rogers (1995)].

Communication channels. In the original TOE-framework, communication is understood as a characteristic of the organizational context [Oliveira and Martins (2011)]. Frambach and Schillewaert [2002] explicitly name the communication with external partners in their framework. In the concepts of Rogers [1995] and Wejnert [2002], communication channels and the influences among network members are the main drivers for the diffusion of innovations on an individual and organizational level. Furthermore, Rogers distinguishes between (a) localite and cosmopolite communication channels, and (b) interpersonal and mass media communication, which have changing roles in the innovation adoption process [Rogers (1995)].

Table 2 gives an overview of the content-related characteristics of the frameworks and the corresponding references.

Table 2. Content-related characteristics of the frameworks.

Characteristics	Frameworks/References
Technology	[Awa *et al.* (2015); DePietro *et al.* (1990); Liu and Wang (2010); Gangwar *et al.* (2015)]
Organization	[Awa *et al.* (2015); DePietro *et al.* (1990); Frambach and Schillewaert (2002); Gangwar *et al.* (2015); Liu and Wang (2010); Rogers (1995); Wejnert (2002)]
Environment	[DePietro *et al.* (1990); Rogers (1995); Wejnert (2002)]
Characteristics of the innovation	[Frambach and Schillewaert (2002); Gangwar *et al.* (2015); Rogers (1995); Wejnert (2002)]
Individuals	[Awa *et al.* (2015); Frambach and Schillewaert (2002); Gangwar *et al.* (2015); Liu and Wang (2010); Rogers (1995); Wejnert (2002)]
Social systems	[DePietro *et al.* (1990); Frambach and Schillewaert (2002); Rogers (1995); Wejnert (2002)]
Organizational networks	[Awa *et al.* (2015); Frambach and Schillewaert (2002); Gangwar *et al.* (2015); Liu and Wang (2010); Rogers (1995); Wejnert (2002)]
Communication channels	[Frambach and Schillewaert (2002); Rogers (1995); Wejnert (2002)]

4.2. *Case study results*

Our analysis of the existing OIA frameworks shows that networks influence OIA. In addition to our analysis of the existing literature, we use our case study as we attempt to shed light on what kinds of networks influence OIA and how they do so. The aforementioned characteristics of OIA frameworks serve as a structure for the analysis. Thus, we can identify 30 different networks in total that influenced OIA. These networks exist within the organizations, between the organizations and outside of the organizations. Some are formal networks organized by the organizations while others are informal.

For example, in the case of the LSP, we find in three units of analysis, intra- and inter-organizational formal networks of groups that are orchestrated in order develop innovative solutions for the usage of data from different sensors and social media in the tracking and tracing processes (network type numbers 5 and 6). A common characteristic of these networks is that their composition can change because requirements vary during the development process, making further participants or partners necessary.

In one unit of analysis we can also identify an inter-organizational network that is not orchestrated but has emerged during the adoption of an innovation (network type number 11). In this unit of analysis, several employees at the cross-dock terminals communicate with the customers of the LSP via social media in order to provide them with information about their transportation order. The reason for this innovative solution for improving the customer experience [Daugherty *et al.* (2019)] is that the drivers of the cooperating carter previously used to communicate with customers. Based on the interaction with the drivers, the employees at the cross-dock terminals felt some kind of pressure to join this behavior. Before they finally adopted this innovative procedure, they interestingly sought guidance in their own private social networks and perceived the response as some kind of approval for their intended behavior (network type number 14). In turn, the LSP, having recognized the behavior of the employees at the cross-dock terminals, initiated a new inter-organizational network (network type number 12) with other partners to advance this approach and make use of social media in the sense of a "lightweight IT" [Bygstad (2017)].

In addition to the aforementioned networks, there are also networks, e.g. federations or alliances, in all units of analysis that consist of value chain partners, competitors and stakeholders. The different units of analysis basically use these networks as a source of information, an advocacy group, a point of reference and occasionally as a basis for joint projects (network type numbers 1 and 2). The different members of these networks have different resources, practices, demands and other general characteristics which can appeal to the units of analysis and lead them to adopt or not to adopt an innovation because of structural equivalence considerations [Burt (1987)]. For example, we also discussed with the units of analysis the blockchain technology and its estimated benefits for the logistics industry [Korpela *et al.* (2017)]. Every unit of analysis stated that its organization will not use blockchain technology until either the customers demand blockchain-based solutions, most competitors use it successfully, or the partners within their network agree on the use of the technology.

In the case of EF, we can identify recurring patterns in the networks despite existing differences. Both units of analysis are likewise members in networks that comprise value chain partners, competitors, and stakeholders. One of the units of analysis states that it is only loosely integrated into the network. For this unit of analysis it is of paramount importance to be a member in a network with forerunners in the field of EF as the membership increases the brand awareness (network type number 3). However, the unit of analysis admits that such membership can also provide guidance for the development of the organization to a certain extent (network type numbers 8). The other unit of analysis is also strongly involved with the various members of its networks. Even if they do not cooperate in a narrow sense, they share information intensively and have a common understanding of what EF means to them and how to develop their business models consensually (network type numbers 4 and 7).

One unit of analysis involves an inter-organizational network that developed an innovative approach to improve the information exchange based on a learning process (network type number 13). This network includes the procurement department in one unit of analysis and some suppliers. The procurement department has realized that the existing IT infrastructure does not sufficiently support the procurement process because the suppliers in developing countries normally do not possess sophisticated IT infrastructures. Instead of using expansive and sometimes laborious IT systems, the suppliers use social media as a tool for order-related information exchange. Against this background, the procurement department has started to integrate social media into their work routines as an enhancement of the existing IT system in order to execute procurement orders more efficiently.

In both units of analysis, we can also identify informal networks that exist outside of the organizations and influence their innovation adoption behavior. Both units of analysis apply social media as a tool to source information and ideas from social networks in order to discuss and develop their business models (network type number 9). Moreover, most of the employees are members in external, mostly online networks that consist of friends, adherents, and experts in EF but also representatives of organizations that deal with EF (network type number 15). The employees use these networks to gather information about other perceptions of EF [Cherrier (2007)] and to discuss the approaches of their organizations. This kind of knowledge-sharing has become an important source for the discussion of intra-organizational networks (network type number 16) with respect to the development potentialities for the organization [Zahra *et al.* (2020)]. In one unit of analysis, this procedure has also led to the formation of a new inter-organizational network that comprises members of the formerly external networks with the goal to realize the discussed ideas (network type number 10).

4.3. *Classification of network types*

The reviewed literature and the findings of our case study allow us to set up a taxonomy of networks that are supposed to influence OIA (cf. Table 3).

The characteristics of our taxonomy are described in what follows. As we do not want to enlarge our taxonomy with combined characteristics, we do not strictly follow the well-reasoned guidelines for the development of taxonomies [Nickerson *et al.* (2013)] and allow for non-exclusive characteristics in the different dimensions.

Scope. This dimension explains the general focus of the network. We distinguish between formal networks that serve professional purposes and informal networks that are rather private and not (primarily) work-related [Eckhardt *et al.* (2009); Rank (2008)].

Setting. Networks can exist in different settings. These can be inside an organization (intra-organizational) or between different organizations (inter-organizational) [Frambach and Schillewaert (2002)]. With regards to our case study, we also introduce networks that exist completely outside of an organization (extra-organizational) and which are mainly interpersonal [Bouty (2000)] and cannot be influenced by an organization.

Table 3. Taxonomy of networks that influence OIA.

Dimension (D_i)	Characteristics ($C_{i,j}$)		
Scope (D_1)	Formal ($C_{1,1}$)		Informal ($C_{1,2}$)
Setting (D_2)	Intra-organizational ($C_{2,1}$)	Inter-organizational ($C_{2,2}$)	Extra-organizational ($C_{2,3}$)
Participants[a] (D_3)	Individuals ($C_{3,1}$)	Groups ($C_{3,2}$)	Organizations ($C_{3,3}$)
Relationship (D_4)	Cohesion ($C_{4,1}$)		Structural equivalence ($C_{4,2}$)
Purpose (D_5)	Membership ($C_{5,1}$)	Information-sharing ($C_{5,2}$)	Cooperation ($C_{5,3}$)
Functions[a] (D_6)	Approval ($C_{6,1}$)	Appeal($C_{6,2}$)	Pressure ($C_{6,3}$)
Communication[a] (D_7)	Personal ($C_{7,1}$)	ICT-based ($C_{7,2}$)	Social media-based ($C_{7,3}$)
Formation (D_8)	Emergent ($C_{8,1}$)		Orchestrated ($C_{8,2}$)
State (D_9)	Static ($C_{9,1}$)		Dynamic ($C_{9,2}$)

Note: [a]Dimensions with non-exclusive characteristics.

Participants. The participants of a network who influence the decision-making unit are in the narrower sense always individuals [Contractor *et al.* (2006); Nohria (1992)]. However, they can represent different institutions in a network. Based on our findings, we distinguish between individuals who represent themselves (individuals), groups or organizations. Because a network can consist of different participants with different roles, this dimension is a non-exclusive dimension.

Relationship. This dimension is based on Burt [1987] and describes the relationship between the participants of a network. According to Contractor *et al.* [2006] and Nohria [1992], the dimension helps to understand if the participants are likely to adopt innovation because of social cohesion or because of structural equivalence.

Purpose. Networks are established for different reasons [van Heck and Vervest (2007)]. Based on our findings, we use the characteristics, membership, information sharing or cooperation. Membership describes a rather loose affiliation with the purpose of allowing participants to show that they belong to a specific group. Information sharing refers to the purpose to exchange knowledge among the participants. Cooperation stands for a tight affiliation between the various participants, which can be exemplified by the sharing of resources or economic collaboration.

Functions. This non-exclusive dimension characterizes the kind of influence a network can have on the innovation adoption process [Bruque *et al.* (2014)]. As described by Kapoor *et al.* [2014a], we also found evidence in our cases of participants using networks to gain approval for their innovation adoption behavior. Likewise, we found evidence suggesting that networks can stimulate or exert pressure on participants to adopt an innovation.

Communication. This dimension represents the technical aspect of how communication takes place. Based on our findings, the communication can be personal, based on classical information and communication technologies, such as telephones and emails, or based on social media, which we distinguish from the aforementioned classical information and communication technologies [Kane *et al.* (2014)]. Because communication is not confined to only one communication technology, this dimension is also non-exclusive.

Formation. Following Dagnino *et al.* [2016], we distinguish between emergent networks that are rather long-lasting and develop independently of any authority on the one hand and orchestrated networks that are intentionally directed on the other hand.

State. The dimension "state" refers to changes in the network composition. Static networks include a stable composition of participants while dynamic networks have a variable composition of participants [Clegg *et al.* (2016)].

Applying this taxonomy to our case study, we can identify the following types of networks, presented in Table 4.

As depicted in Table 4, the identified networks can be clustered by their type of influence on OIA. However, the distinctive feature "type of influence" does not represent an enhancement of our taxonomy. It is much more a description for specific sets of characteristics. A detailed description of the four types of influence is given in the following section.

Table 4. Overview of networks identified during the case study.

Network type	Type of influence	Case	Units of analysis	Characteristics																						
				D_1		D_2			D_3			D_4		D_5			D_6			D_7			D_8		D_9	
				$C_{1,1}$	$C_{1,2}$	$C_{2,1}$	$C_{2,2}$	$C_{2,3}$	$C_{3,1}$	$C_{3,2}$	$C_{3,3}$	$C_{4,1}$	$C_{4,2}$	$C_{5,1}$	$C_{5,2}$	$C_{5,3}$	$C_{6,1}$	$C_{6,2}$	$C_{6,3}$	$C_{7,1}$	$C_{7,2}$	$C_{7,3}$	$C_{8,1}$	$C_{8,2}$	$C_{9,1}$	$C_{9,2}$
1	Comparison net-	LSP	A, B, C, D	x			x				x		x		x			x	x		x			x		x
2	works	LSP	A, B, C, D	x			x				x		x			x		x	x		x			x		x
3		EF	B	x			x				x		x	x				x		x	x		x		x	
4		EF	A	x			x				x	x			x			x		x	x	x	x		x	
5	Argumentation net-	LSP	A, C, D	x		x				x			x			x		x	x	x	x			x		x
6	works	LSP	A, C, D	x			x			x			x			x		x	x	x	x			x		x
7		EF	A	x			x				x	x				x		x	x	x	x	x	x			x
8		EF	A, B	x			x				x		x			x		x	x	x	x	x	x			x
9		EF	A, B		x			x	x			x			x		x					x	x			x
10		EF	A		x		x		x			x				x		x	x	x		x	x			x
11	Reciprocal learning	LSP	C	x			x		x	x			x		x				x	x	x	x	x			x
12	networks	LSP	C	x			x			x			x			x		x		x	x	x		x	x	
13		EF	A	x			x			x			x			x		x			x	x	x		x	
14	Alignment networks	LSP	C		x			x	x			x			x		x			x		x	x			x
15		EF	A, B		x			x	x		x	x			x		x			x	x	x	x			x
16		EF	A, B		x	x			x			x			x		x			x			x		x	
	Σ		**30**	**11**	**5**	**2**	**11**	**3**	**6**	**5**	**7**	**7**	**9**	**1**	**7**	**8**	**4**	**11**	**8**	**12**	**12**	**10**	**11**	**5**	**5**	**11**

4.4. *A Framework for organizational innovation adoption in the context of networks*

4.4.1. *Overview*

Based on the findings of the reviewed frameworks, the results of our inductive case study and the developed taxonomy, we developed a conceptual framework [Eisenhart (1991)]. Figure 4 depicts our framework for OIA from a network

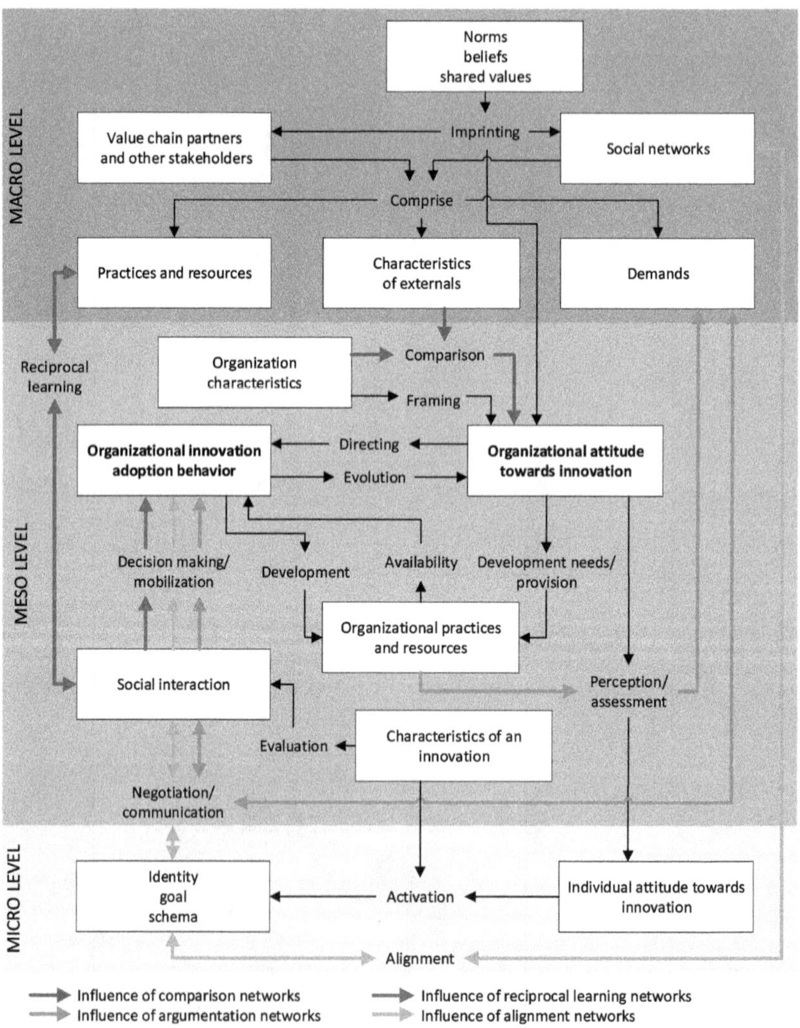

Fig. 4. Framework for OIA from a network perspective.

perspective. The four types of influence of networks on OIA are depicted with different colors.

The basic idea of our framework is derived from the institutional logics perspective of Thornton *et al.* [2012]. Institutional logics provide a beneficial lens on OIA and have already been discussed in the context of OIA [Oliveira and Martins (2011); Johnson (2018)]. As in the original framework, our framework allows direct and indirect relationships between the various elements.

4.4.2. *Meso level of OIA*

In our framework, we depict OIA as an organizational procedure on a meso level that is informed by individual behavior on a micro level and extra-organizational factors on a macro level. OIA consists of the general organizational attitude toward innovation, which entails normative and regulative elements, such as the attitude toward change [Rogers (1995); Liu and Wang (2010); Gangwar *et al.* (2015)] and the strategical importance of innovation [Awa *et al.* (2015); Frambach and Schillewaert (2002); Liu and Wang (2010); Rogers (1995)]. It also consists of OIA behavior that represents the final decision either to adopt or not to adopt an innovation and the implementation and confirmation stage of innovation adoption [Rogers (1995)]. Both influence each other, whereby the organizational attitude toward innovation permanently shapes the OIA behavior, but the OIA behavior only gradually changes the organizational attitude toward innovation. The organizational attitude toward innovation is further framed by the characteristics of the adopting organization, e.g. size, strategy, and risk-taking propensity [Frambach and Schillewaert (2002); Unsworth *et al.* (2012)]; and the comparison of these characteristics with the characteristics of externals, e.g. value chain partners and other stakeholders. The organizational attitude toward innovation also gives (a) an orientation for the development of existing organizational practices, e.g. process design, use of technology and work routines [Thornton *et al.* (2012); Rogers (1995); Awa *et al.* (2015); DePietro *et al.* (1990); Frambach and Schillewaert (2002); Gangwar *et al.* (2015); Liu and Wang (2010)] and resources, such as personnel, technology and finance [Rogers (1995); Oliveira and Martins (2011)], and (b) the provision of required resources for the innovation adoption process. Consequently, OIA behavior is influenced by the availability of organizational resources [Baker (2012); DePietro *et al.* (1990); Rogers (1995)] but also contributes to the development of the existing organizational practices and resources. Another important driver within the meso-level of our framework is social interaction, which includes the social interaction of individuals in their intra-organizational networks, e.g. with superiors and colleagues from the same or other departments [Eckhardt *et al.* (2009)], and the social interaction of members of an organization within inter-organizational networks. During social interaction, the different actors deepen their knowledge of the innovation, evaluate the characteristics of an innovation and form an opinion about the innovation. Thus, social interaction induces both mobilization and decision-making and, as a consequence, enables the final decision concerning the adoption of an innovation, its implementation, and its confirmation within the OIA behavior [Rogers

(1995)]. In the opposite direction, the experience gained during the different stages of the OIA behavior leads to further social interaction, especially with respect to the confirmation stage [Rogers (1995)]. Negotiation and communication among individuals within an organization and with extra-organizational participants are an important antecedent of social interaction.

4.4.3. *Micro level of OIA*

Individuals involved in OIA are considered on the micro level of our framework. The micro level consists of the individual attitude toward innovation, an attitude influenced by the organizational attitude toward innovation, assuming it is available and accessible for the individuals [Tumbas *et al.* (2015)], and the individual perception and assessment of the existing organizational practices and resources. The individual attitude toward innovation and the perceived characteristics of a specific innovation activate individual goals and helps the individual to develop a schema concerning the innovation and to determine their identity in the innovation adoption process. These three constructs (goal, schema, and identity) are aligned with the attitude in the individual's private social networks and then guide the individual behavior during the negotiation and communication on the meso level. Oppositely, the social interaction on the meso level shapes — via negotiation and communication — the goal, schema, and identity of the individual with respect to the OIA. This does not necessarily mean that the individuals involved adopt the innovation themselves. Although it is possible to combine the knowledge about individual innovation adoption behavior [Awa *et al.* (2015); Frambach and Schillewaert (2002); Gangwar *et al.* (2015); Liu and Wang (2010)] with our framework at this point, our framework in its present form is not designed to fully explain the innovation adoption of single individuals.

4.4.4. *Macro level of OIA*

The macro level of our framework comprises extra-organizational institutions that influence OIA, such as, above all, norms, values, and beliefs [Rogers (1995); Wejnert (2002)] and then networks, in which organizations and its members are embedded [Kooijman *et al.* (2017); Castells (2000)]. On the one hand, there are networks in which an organization is embedded in its entirety, i.e. value chains that include competitors, suppliers and customers, but also even broader institutions like society, macroeconomics, politics, as well as cultural beliefs [Awa *et al.* (2015); DePietro *et al.* (1990); Frambach and Schillewaert (2002); Gangwar *et al.* (2015); Liu and Wang (2010); Rogers (1995); Wejnert (2002)]. Referring to Contractor [2006] and Nohria [1992], we also consider these types of networks as social networks, regardless of whether the focus is on the interaction of individuals, departments or entire organizations within the networks. The participants of these networks (i.e. individuals, departments, or entire organizations) have a direct influence on OIA of the focal organization. They are equipped with practices and resources (e.g. innovative technologies) that affect the work practices of the focal organization; they serve as role models thanks to specific characteristics (e.g. high reputation in the network); and they postulate demands (e.g. customer expectations) that represent reference points for the OIA.

On the other hand, there are private social networks in which individuals are embedded, e.g. family and communities [Kooijman *et al.* (2017)]. Especially in these private social networks, the superordinate values and norms are not necessarily interpreted and evaluated in the same way as in the focal organization. Nevertheless, they influence the goals, schemes, and identities of the individuals with respect to an innovation and thus influence OIA behavior indirectly. In comparison to the aforementioned networks, the impact on OIA of this kind of networks can be assumed to be lower. However, these types of networks are also more complex [Acemoğlu *et al.* (2013)] and less likely to be influenced by organizations than those mentioned above.

4.4.5. *Influencing types of networks on OIA*

The aforementioned different networks exert influence on the OIA in various ways. Based on our case study analysis, we identify four major types of network influence on OIA: (a) comparison networks, (b) argumentation networks, (c) reciprocal learning networks, and (d) alignment networks (cf. Fig. 5).

Comparison networks describe formal, inter-organizational networks in which organizations as a whole are involved and which essentially serve as positive points of reference [Cofré-Bravo *et al.* (2019)]. In our framework, this influence type is presented as a comparison of the characteristics of the focal organization with those of external network participants. The assessment of the comparison by the focal

	Comparison networks	Argumentation networks	Reciprocal learning networks	Alignment networks
Scope	formal	mainly formal	formal	informal
Setting	inter-organizational	mainly inter-organizational	inter-organizational	mainly extra-organizational
Participants	organizations	diverse	groups	individuals
Relationship	mainly structural equivalence	diverse	structural equivalence	cohesion
Purpose	diverse	mainly cooperation	mainly cooperation	information-sharing
Functions	mainly appeal	mainly appeal or pressure	mainly appeal	approval
Communication	mainly ICT-based	diverse	diverse	personal or social media-based
Formation	diverse	mainly emergent	diverse	emergent
State	diverse	dynamic	mainly static	mainly dynamic

Fig. 5. Influencing types of networks on OIA.

organization influences the (longer-term) general attitude of the focal organization toward innovation. We see in our EF case how the comparison with network partners can lead to a generally more positive attitude toward innovation for reasons of cohesion or structural equivalence. In the LSP case, the discussion on block chain technology suggests that comparison networks can also lead to a rather reluctant attitude toward innovation. However, since this is the attitude toward a specific innovation, the statements cannot necessarily be assigned to the general attitude toward innovations.

Argumentation networks represent a group of emergent networks that stimulate as well as exert pressure on an organization and contribute in a cooperative way to the innovation of specific processes but also business models. We illustrate this type of network influence in our framework as demands of value chain partners or other stakeholders of an organization on the macro level based on the perception and assessment of organizational practices and resources. Through reciprocal negotiation and communication, the demands become the subject of social interaction on the meso level, possibly resulting in concrete OIA behavior via decision-making and mobilization. Especially customers and the society can postulate demands in the context of a customer-dominant logic [Heinonen *et al.* (2010)]. This is true in the case of EF when customers and interested persons formulate their expectations regarding the ethical production of clothing.

Networks that we cluster with the term "reciprocal learning networks" include formal, inter-organizational networks of groups of different organizations that are involved in conjoint business processes [Cofré-Bravo *et al.* (2019)]. These networks seek to adjust their processes and technologies in order to smoothen and improve intra-organizational processes. This type of network influence is a reciprocal connection between external practices and resources on the macro level and social interaction on the meso level. As a consequence, it may also generate a concrete OIA behavior via decision-making and mobilization. External network participants can be equipped with practices and resources that are beneficial for OIA in different ways. First, the external practices and resources can be attractive to the focal organization in terms of anticipated quantitative or qualitative performance improvements. This can be seen in our case study in the LSP case when first value chain partners use an already known technology such as social media in an innovative way to improve the tracking and tracing process, and, later on, this procedure leads to OIA in the focal LSP. Second, interconnected processes can entail the implementation of new work routines and also technologies. The joint further development of sensor-supported tracking and tracing demonstrates this in the LSP case, and so does the use of social media in the execution of order processes in the EF case.

Finally, alignment networks refer to informal, emergent, and private social networks of individuals within and outside of an organization. The individuals use these kinds of networks as a source of information for the evaluation of their attitude toward an innovation and an approval for their decision with regards to the adoption of the innovation [Buskens (2020)]. In our framework, alignment networks are portrayed as reciprocal connections of the elements of private social networks on the macro level, social interaction on the meso level and identity, goal, and schema on the micro level [Cofré-Bravo *et al.* (2019)]. Thus, the attitude of private social networks indirectly influences social interaction on the meso-level and can therefore also influence to a certain degree the elements, decision-making and mobilization as well as OIA behavior. This procedure becomes apparent in the LSP case, in which employees in their private social networks seek confirmation for an innovative process that is not driven by their company, but rather diffuses into the company through the practice of external network partners.

5. Discussion, Implications, and Future Research

5.1. *Key findings*

The importance of networks in the process of OIA is widely acknowledged [Rothwell (1994); Pittaway *et al.* (2004); van Heck and Vervest (2007); Möller and Halinen (2017)]. For example, Damanpour and Schneider [2006] highlight the importance of external environmental antecedents, e.g. external communication in OIA. Likewise, Tirabeni and Soderquist [2019] describe the importance of networks in open innovation. However, the reviewed existing frameworks of OIA struggle to provide sophisticated answers concerning what kinds of networks influence OIA and how they do so. The framework of Frambach and Schillewaert [2002] is the most enlightening. While employing the determinants "network externalities" and "social networks" to point out that organizations and individuals are both involved in different networks that are relevant for OIA, they remain rather hesitant to explain how these determinants act on OIA.

We argue that the existing literature conveys the view that organizations tend to be monolithic socio-technical systems and that networks exist in the environment distinctive from the organizations. In our opinion, this view no longer reflects the reality of most organizations and leads to the fact that important determinants for OIA have not been considered so far. Our framework contributes to the knowledge on how innovations can become relevant for an organization and how different networks can influence the process of OIA. Therefore, it provides an appropriate answer to our research question "How do networks influence the adoption of innovation in organizations?" and, in consequence, we believe our work is valuable for researchers and practitioners.

5.2. *Academic implications*

Our research contributes to the literature on OIA in different ways. First, we introduced two new theories into the discussion of networks in OIA, i.e. Castells' theory of a network society [Castells (2000)] and the institutional logics perspective [Thornton *et al.* (2012)]. The theory of the network society offers a new perspective on networks and makes it clear that network participants are members of multiple networks that mutually influence each other. Private networks based on social media are particularly important in this respect. According to Etter *et al.* [2019, p. 5], "social media enable the co-existence of multiple evaluations — often critical, at times subversive — that are actively co-produced by heterogeneous sources on an ongoing basis and largely outside of the control of organizations." Thus, social media enlarge the embeddedness of an organization into broader social structures [Kooijman *et al.* (2017); Castells (2000)]. This aspect of interaction has been given too little attention so far. The consideration of this aspect could represent a new approach to better understand the complexity of innovation adoption processes. For example, it could help to better understand the formation of trust within innovation networks [Giudici *et al.* (2018); Oumlil *et al.* (2020); Mitcheltree (2021)]. In the context of the current COVID-19 pandemic, it could likewise help to better understand why certain technologies (e.g. videoconferencing systems and cashless payment) are adopted more quickly than others [Brem *et al.* (2021); Pan and Zhang (2020); Akpan *et al.* (2020); Cobelli *et al.* (2021)].

The adaptation of the institutional logics perspective of Thornton *et al.* [2012] helps us to incorporate Castells' theory and allows us to provide a more comprehensive, multi-level framework of OIA, which can be an alternative or enhancement of the framework of Frambach and Schillewaert [2002]. In our framework, the process of OIA traverses different elements on the macro, meso, and micro level, which exist in part outside of an organization, resulting in a complex and reciprocal OIA system. External networks represent macro-level constructs that act on OIA on the meso-level directly and also indirectly by influencing individuals on the micro-level. Therefore, our framework can be beneficial to improve the knowledge on how networks influence the process of OIA. We offer a new conceptual perspective on OIA considering the social environments of organizations, involved individuals, and existing interrelationships [Jeyaraj *et al.* (2006); Eckhardt *et al.* (2009)]. Likewise, the micro-level of our framework offers the possibility of combining the knowledge of individual adoption with OIA. For example, it could help to better understand how individuals develop beliefs about information technology in the context of organizational behavior [Laumer *et al.* (2016)].

Second, we extend the knowledge with respect to the characteristics of networks that are relevant to OIA and how networks influence OIA [Rothwell (1994); Pittaway *et al.* (2004); van Heck and Vervest (2007); Möller and Halinen (2017)]. In addition to the previously known characteristics of networks [Huggins *et al.* (2012); Rank (2008); Dagnino *et al.* (2016)], we were able to identify further characteristics with respect to the setting, participants, purpose, and functions of networks. Furthermore, our research shows that networks related to OIA are not confined to classical communication channels, such as telephones and emails. Social media in particular frequently act as communication channels in different kinds of networks, particularly in dynamic social networks [Clegg *et al.* (2016)]. In this way, we contribute to a more comprehensive delineation of networks relevant to OIA and lay the ground for a better understanding of how networks act as moderators in the OIA process. Previous studies on the environment of an organization emphasize the pressure that institutions outside of an organization can exert [Teo *et al.* (2003); Liang *et al.* (2007); Oliveira *et al.* (2019)]. We identified four different types of networks that enable the processes of comparison, argumentation, reciprocal learning, and alignment. In doing so, we also shed light on the reciprocal action of networks and individuals in the context of OIA [Fernandes Rodrigues Alves *et al.* (2018); Leonardi and Vaast (2017)]. Our results show that institutions in the environment of organizations not only exert pressure on an organization, but can also possess characteristics that, with the support of networks as mediators, are considered attractive and desirable and thus trigger an adjustment process. Likewise, networks can be mediators of values, norms, and beliefs and thereby trigger cohesion processes. This implication is beneficial to the theory of OIA because it shows that the spectrum of different types of networks in the context of OIA is wider than hitherto described in the literature. The developed taxonomy allows you to characterize different kinds of networks that are relevant for OIA. Consequently, it can help researchers to identify further networks relevant to OIA beyond interorganizational networks.

Third, our findings have implications for the theories of open innovation, social capital as well as absorptive capacity. The research on open innovation has so far given too little consideration to the cross-level nature of open innovation [Bogers *et al.* (2017)]. For example, Chesbrough [2017, pp. 37–38] uses the term "innovation communities" to describe "large numbers of players across multiple phases of the innovation process," which exist within and outside of organizations and are "orchestrated." Likewise, Castells uses the term "network enterprises" [Castells (2000, p. 10)] to describe enterprises that comprise small, decentralized networks that temporarily form larger enterprises. However, a foundation is lacking for the analysis of open innovation in terms of structure, boundaries, and dynamics [Enkel *et al.* (2018)]. Our framework helps to fill this gap and can be a step toward a better understanding of the complex interaction between different levels at which open innovation develops. Our taxonomy and framework provide analytical tools to better conceptualize that kind of innovation communities.

With respect to social capital theory, our findings imply that, due to their involvement in a wide range of networks, organizations have far more social capital than the literature suggests, particularly because they are embedded in a multitude of private social networks and a plurality of values, norms, and beliefs that are present in the environment of organizations. These values, norms, and beliefs can be assessed as both beneficial and conflicting with respect to general value systems as well as the organization's value system. However, organizations are not only surrounded by these values, norms, and beliefs, but can also become an actor that absorbs and reproduces them. Both the aspect of the negative influence of social capital and the reproduction of values, norms, and beliefs of networks by organizations have received little attention in the literature on OIA and should be considered in more detail in the future. The same is true in the context of absorptive capacity theory. Therefore, our framework could be useful as a multilevel perspective on absorptive capacity that allows you to examine how recognition, assimilation, transformation, and exploitation of new knowledge are interactively produced [Marabelli and Newell (2014)].

5.3. *Managerial implications*

This study has important implications for practitioners and managers. First, our findings show that the organizational boundaries in OIA become indistinct and the process of OIA becomes more decentralized. The increasing importance of decentralization represents a challenge to organizations, for such networks may not be under the control of an organization and thus not be governable. Social media and other kinds of social software, e.g. gamification [Parjanen and Hyypiä (2019)], can foster this kind of uncontrollable decentralization in OIA. Due to the embeddedness in a large number of private social networks, it will be of great importance for organizations in the future to recognize types of influence through the networks in order to use positive influences and filter negative influences in the best possible way. Particularly in view of the changing nature of social networks, this represents a tremendous challenge for organizations. This fact necessitates forms of regulatory systems and coordination that meet the requirements of interorganizational und extra-organizational networks that are in part not under control of an organization. One solution could be to use other kinds of decentralized technologies that allow for decentralized governance, such as the blockchain technology [Matulevičius *et al.* (2015)]. A consolidation of the different technologies could be very fruitful for open innovation and OIA. It would unite different decentralized approaches in order to exploit crowd resources and to create trust.

Second, the involvement of networks into OIA facilitates the emergence of lightweight IT [Bygstad (2017)] in organizations. Social media and other social technologies can become a part of the IT infrastructure of organizations in the sense of a lightweight IT. Such IT is inexpensive, easy to use, supports the immediate needs of the users, and provides process support. Because of these characteristics, it is very useful in the process of OIA. Nevertheless, this progressive kind of IT infrastructure comes at the price of some challenges. For example, data storage and analysis, data security, and privacy present greater challenges than in conventional IT infrastructures.

Finally, organizational innovation will be an important aspect for organizations in recovering from the aftermath of the COVID-19 pandemic. Recent studies show that already during the COVID-19 pandemic, the adoption of innovations accelerated [Brem *et al.* (2021)]. At the same time, voices are emerging that see the COVID-19 pandemic as an excellent opportunity to act in solidarity and turn the crisis into an impetus for innovations to make the economy and society more sustainable [Pan and Zhang (2020)]. Networks will play a central role in these developments [Chesbrough (2020)]. As a consequence, managers need to develop their capabilities to build, coordinate, and utilize social networks inside and outside of their organization in a purposeful way. Of high importance is an alignment with the strategy and the existing resources of the organization [Chung *et al.* (2017); Valos *et al.* (2017)]. Likewise, the ability to interact with different networks without being an active participant in every network will be crucial. Möller and Halinen [2017] as well as Fehrer and Nenonen [2020] provide detailed frameworks for network management that can act as guidelines in this regard. Our taxonomy of OIA networks and our framework can be additional practical tools that will help practitioners to better manage organizational innovation.

5.4. *Limitations and future research*

Our research has certain limitations that justify additional research. Several issues are related to the nature of our case study. Although it was our aim to choose cases that provided interesting insights into the importance of networks in OIA, the cases of our case study in all likelihood do not cover the whole range of characteristics of networks in OIA and their influences. Especially, the investigation of microenterprises could be critically assessed, since they differ from conventional enterprises in terms of their organizational structure [Roper and Hewitt-Dundas (2017)]. Therefore, our study may have over-represented the specific characteristics of microenterprises while giving insufficient attention to the diversity of other organizations' networks. Moreover, only German companies were the subject of the study. Although most of these companies operate internationally, it would still be useful to investigate further organizations from other regions with different political, social, cultural, and legal backgrounds [Ngai *et al.* (2015)]. Therefore, future research could apply our framework in different settings in order to identify other influencing types of networks on OIA.

Likewise, the design of our study as an exploratory case study does not allow us to prove hypotheses with statistical data. In light of the well-established prevalence of quantitative research with respect to structural and process factors [Damanpour (2020)], additional quantitative research is indicated. This could better expose the occurrence of the processes that we introduced, the importance of the identified influencing factors, and the effectiveness of the outcome.

Furthermore, in our framework, the element, social interaction, is still quite broad and covers a wide range of different inter-organizational workplace referents, e.g. superiors and colleagues. These networks also influence innovation adoption in different ways [Eckhardt *et al.* (2009)]. Therefore, a more detailed description of the various actors inside an organization and their interrelationships is necessary for the improvement of our framework.

Further future research could build on our findings in various ways. First, our work can be the foundation for future work on the relationships between organizations, networks, and individuals involved in OIA. Such research could encompass investigations on the intensity and quality of the relationships. For example, Tasselli *et al.* [2014] argue that individual actions and the structure of organizational social networks coevolve in a dynamic process of reciprocal influence. It would be beneficial for OIA researchers to know whether the concept of co-evolution also applies to organizations and their inter- and extra-organizational networks during the different stages of the innovation adoption process [Rogers (1995)], whether organizations are shaped by their inter- and extra-organizational networks, or whether organizations shape their inter- and extra-organizational networks.

Second, future research could further explore the nature of networks that influence OIA, including the dark side of social capital [Kwon and Adler (2014)]. For example, it would be helpful to better understand which attributes of networks are instrumental or impedimental in influencing OIA. For example, trustworthiness or expertise are reported in the literature as attributes of networks that have a positive impact on OIA. In the same vein, other attributes such as the extent of diversity and inclusion in networks or multiple network membership could have an impact on OIA. In this context, it would also be interesting to understand whether attributes need to exceed thresholds for networks to exert a certain type of influence. In addition, it seems useful to examine whether there are structural relationships between certain types of networks and the quality of influence of the innovations. For example, reciprocal learning networks might be more likely to correlate with continuous innovation and thus trigger incremental change, while argumentation networks might be more likely to be associated with disruptive innovation, which involves radical changes in an organization's structure and functioning [Damanpour (1991)]. Such research would particularly help managers to identify innovation-specific relevant networks and to integrate relevant networks more effectively into the OIA process.

Third, future research could seize on the arising question of how to coordinate networks in OIA. Research in this field could seek to put the concept of network-influenced OIA in other theoretical contexts. We used the institutional logics perspective in this paper to provide a theoretical framework for our findings. However, other theories such as game theory [Ozkan-Canbolat and Beraha (2016)] could be applied in order to explain the behavior of different actors and to develop solutions for regulatory systems in network-influenced OIA. Further research on the coordination of networks in OIA could also focus on how to employ lightweight IT [Bygstad and Iden (2017)] in network-influenced OIA.

6. Conclusion

Networks influence OIA in different ways. We reviewed the most prevalent frameworks of OIA and analyzed a case study. This approach allowed us to develop a taxonomy and framework that help to characterize networks in OIA, bridge organizational and individual innovation adoption and explain how networks influence OIA through comparison, argumentation, reciprocal learning and alignment. Despite its limitations, our research contributes to the field of OIA and helps researchers as well as practitioners as it provides insight into how social communities and other networks intersect with organizations and which challenges may be on the horizon.

References

Acemoğlu, D., Como, G., Fagnani, F. and Ozdaglar, A. (2013). Opinion fluctuations and disagreement in social networks. *Mathematics of Operations Research*, **38**, 1: 1–27.

Ajzen, I. (1991). The theory of planned behavior. *Organizational Behavior and Human Decision Processes*, **50**, 2: 179–211.

Akpan, I. J., Soopramanien, D. and Kwak, D.-H. (2020). Cutting-edge technologies for small business and innovation in the era of COVID-19 global health pandemic. *Journal of Small Business and Entrepreneurship*, **84**, 4: 1–11.

Alfalla-Luque, R., Machuca, J. A. D. and Marin-Garcia, J. A. (2018). Triple-A and competitive advantage in supply chains: Empirical research in developed countries. *International Journal of Production Economics*, **203**: 48–61.

Apostolov, M. and Coco, N. (2020). Digitalization-based innovation: A case study framework. *International Journal of Innovation and Technology Management*, **19**, 1: 1–25.

Aral, S., Dellarocas, C. and Godes, D. (2013). Introduction to the special issue: Social media and business transformation: A framework for research. *Information Systems Research*, **24**, 1: 3–13.

Armbruster, H., Bikfalvi, A., Kinkel, S. and Lay, G. (2008). Organizational innovation. The challenge of measuring non-technical innovation in large-scale surveys. *Technovation*, **28**, 10: 644–657.

Awa, H. O. (2019). Some antecedent factors that shape actors' adoption of enterprise systems. *Enterprise Information Systems*, **13**, 5: 576–600.

Awa, H. O., Ojiabo, O. U. and Emecheta, B. C. (2015). Integrating TAM, TPB and TOE frameworks and expanding their characteristic constructs for e-commerce adoption by SMEs. *Journal of Science and Technology Policy Management*, **6**, 1: 76–94.

Baker, J. (2012). The technology–organization–environment framework. *Information Systems Theory, Integrated Series in Information Systems*, eds. Y. K. Dwivedi, M. R. Wade and S. L. Schneberger, Vol. 28. Springer, New York, pp. 231–245.

Barrot, C., Kuhlmann, J. A. N. and Popa, A. (2013). Influence of personal communication networks on innovation adoption: Using multi-agent simulations to project the launch of an innovative medical device. *International Journal of Innovation and Technology Management*, **10**, 5: 1340021.

Bharati, P. and Chaudhury, A. (2019). Assimilation of big data innovation: Investigating the roles of IT, social media, and relational capital. *Information Systems Frontiers*, **21**, 6: 1357–1368.

Birkinshaw, J., Hamel, G. and Mol, M. J. (2008). Management innovation. *Academy of Management Review*, **33**, 4: 825–845.

Bitektine, A. (2007). Prospective case study design. *Organizational Research Methods*, **11**, 1: 160–180.

Bogers, M., Zobel, A.-K., Afuah, A., Almirall, E., Brunswicker, S., Dahlander, L., Frederiksen, L., Gawer, A., Gruber, M., Haefliger, S., Hagedoorn, J., Hilgers, D., Laursen, K., Magnusson, M. G., Majchrzak, A., McCarthy, I. P., Moeslein, K. M., Nambisan, S., Piller, F. T., Radziwon, A., Rossi-Lamastra, C., Sims, J. and Ter Wal, A. L. J. (2017). The open innovation research landscape: Established perspectives and emerging themes across different levels of analysis. *Industry and Innovation*, **24**, 1: 8–40.

Boland, B. (2020). Social capital and the diffusion of learning management systems: A case study. *Journal of Innovation and Entrepreneurship*, **9**, 1: 27.

Bouty, I. (2000). Interpersonal and interaction influences on informal resource exchanges between R&D researchers across organizational boundaries. *Academy of Management Journal*, **43**, 1: 50–65.

Brem, A., Viardot, E. and Nylund, P. A. (2021). Implications of the coronavirus (COVID-19) outbreak for innovation: Which technologies will improve our lives? *Technological Forecasting and Social Change*, **163**, 120451.

Bruque, S., Moyano, J. and Eisenberg, J. (2014). Individual adaptation to IT-induced change: The role of social networks. *Journal of Management Information Systems*, **25**, 3: 177–206.

Burt, R. S. (1973). The differential impact of social integration on participation in the diffusion of innovations. *Social Science Research*, **2**, 2: 125–144.

Burt, R. S. (1987). Social contagion and innovation: Cohesion versus structural equivalence. *American Journal of Sociology*, **92**, 6: 1287–1335.

Buskens, V. (2020). Spreading information and developing trust in social networks to accelerate diffusion of innovations. *Trends in Food Science and Technology*, **106**: 485–488.

Busse, C. and Marcus Wallenburg, C. (2011). Innovation management of logistics service providers. *International Journal of Physical Distribution and Logistics Management*, **41**, 2: 187–218.

Bygstad, B. (2017). Generative innovation: A comparison of lightweight and heavyweight IT. *Journal of Information Technology*, **32**, 2: 180–193.

Bygstad, B. and Iden, J. (2017). A governance model for managing lightweight IT. *Recent Advances in Information Systems and Technologies, Advances in Intelligent Systems and Computing*, Rocha, Á., Correia, A. M., Adeli, H., Reis, L. P. and Costanzo, S. (Eds.), Vol. 569, Springer International Publishing, Cham, pp. 384–393.

Cap, J.-P., Blaich, E., Kohl, H., Raesfeld, A. von, Harms, R. and Will, M. (2019). Multi level network management: A method for managing inter-organizational innovation networks. *Journal of Engineering and Technology Management*, **51**, 3: 21–32.

Castells, M. (1996). *The Rise of the Network Society: The Information Age, Economy, Society and Culture/Manuel Castells*, 1st edn. Blackwell, Cambridge, MA.

Castells, M. (2000). Materials for an exploratory theory of the network society. *The British Journal of Sociology*, **51**, 1: 5–24.

Cavaye, A. L. M. (1996). Case study research: A multi-faceted research approach for IS. *Information Systems Journal*, **6**, 3: 227–242.

Cherrier, H. (2007). Ethical consumption practices: Co-production of self-expression and social recognition. *Journal of Consumer Behaviour*, **6**, 5: 321–335.

Chesbrough, H. W. (2003). *Open Innovation: The New Imperative for Creating and Profiting from Technology*. Harvard Business School Press, Boston, MA.

Chesbrough, H. W. (2017). The future of open innovation. *Research-Technology Management*, **60**, 1: 35–38.

Chesbrough, H. W. (2020). To recover faster from Covid-19, open up: Managerial implications from an open innovation perspective. *Industrial Marketing Management*, **88**, 6: 410–413.

Chouki, M., Talea, M., Okar, C. and Chroqui, R. (2020). Barriers to information technology adoption within small and medium enterprises: A systematic literature review. *International Journal of Innovation and Technology Management*, **17**, 1: 2050007.

Chung, A. Q. H., Andreev, P., Benyoucef, M., Duane, A. and O'Reilly, P. (2017). Managing an organisation's social media presence: An empirical stages of growth model. *International Journal of Information Management*, **37**, 1: 1405–1417.

Clegg, S., Josserand, E., Mehra, A. and Pitsis, T. S. (2016). The transformative power of network dynamics: A research agenda. *Organization Studies*, **37**, 3: 277–291.

Co, H. C. and Barro, F. (2009). Stakeholder theory and dynamics in supply chain collaboration. *International Journal of Operations and Production Management*, **29**, 6: 591–611.

Cobelli, N., Cassia, F. and Burro, R. (2021). Factors affecting the choices of adoption/non-adoption of future technologies during coronavirus pandemic. *Technological Forecasting and Social Change*, **169**, 3: 120814.

Cofré-Bravo, G., Klerkx, L. and Engler, A. (2019). Combinations of bonding, bridging, and linking social capital for farm innovation: How farmers configure different support networks. *Journal of Rural Studies*, **69**: 53–64.

Cohen, W. M. and Levin, R. C. (1989). Empirical studies of innovation and market structure, *Handbook of Industrial Organization*, eds. R.Schmalensee and R.Willig, Vol. 2. Elsever, Amsterdam, pp. 1059–1107.

Cohen, W. M. and Levinthal, D. A. (1990). Absorptive capacity: A new perspective on learning and innovation. *Administrative Science Quarterly*, **35**, 1: 128.

Coleman, J. S. (1988). Social capital in the creation of human capital. *American Journal of Sociology*, **94**, S95–S120.

Collins, P. D., Hage, J. and Hull, F. M. (1988). Organizational and technological predictors of change in automaticity. *Academy of Management Journal*, **31**, 3: 512–543.

Contractor, N. S., Wasserman, S. and Faust, K. (2006). Testing multitheoretical, multilevel hypotheses about organizational networks: An analytic framework and empirical example. *Academy of Management Review*, **31**, 3: 681–703.

Dagnino, G. B., Levanti, G. and Mocciaro Li Destri, A. (2016). Structural dynamics and intentional governance in strategic interorganizational network evolution: A multilevel approach. *Organization Studies*, **37**, 3: 349–373.

Damanpour, F. (1991). Organizational innovation: A meta-analysis of effects of determinants and moderators. *Academy of Management Journal*, **34**, 3: 555–590.

Damanpour, F. (2014). Footnotes to research on management innovation. *Organization Studies*, **35**, 9: 1265–1285.

Damanpour, F. (2020). *Organizational Innovation*. Edward Elgar Publishing, Cheltenham, UK.

Damanpour, F. and Schneider, M. (2006). Phases of the adoption of innovation in organizations: Effects of environment, organization and top managers. *British Journal of Management*, **17**, 3: 215–236.

Damanpour, F., Sanchez-Henriquez, F. and Chiu, H. H. (2018). Internal and external sources and the adoption of innovations in organizations. *British Journal of Management*, **29**, 4: 712–730.

Damanpour, F., Szabat, K. A. and Evan, W. M. (1989). The relationship between types of innovation and organizational performance. *Journal of Management Studies*, **26**, 6: 587–602.

Daugherty, P. J., Bolumole, Y. and Grawe, S. J. (2019). The new age of customer impatience. *International Journal of Physical Distribution and Logistics Management*, **49**, 1: 4–32.

Davis, F. D., Bagozzi, R. P. and Warshaw, P. R. (1989). User acceptance of computer technology: A comparison of two theoretical models. *Management Science*, **35**, 8: 982–1003.

Dedrick, J., Venkatesh, M., Stanton, J. M., Zheng, Y. and Ramnarine-Rieks, A. (2015). Adoption of smart grid technologies by electric utilities: Factors influencing organizational innovation in a regulated environment. *Electronic Markets*, **25**, 1: 17–29.

DePietro, R., Wiarda, E. and Fleischer, M. (1990). The context for change: Organization, technology and environment, *The Processes of Technological Innovation, Issues in Organization and Management Series*, L. G.Tornatzky and M.Fleischer. Lexington Books, Lexington, MA, pp. 151–175.

Demirel, B. and Payne, A. K. H. (2018). Social innovation adoption behavior: The case of Zumbara. *International Journal of Innovation and Technology Management*, **15**, 2: 1850016.

Di Gangi, P. M. and Wasko, M. (2009). Steal my idea! Organizational adoption of user innovations from a user innovation community: A case study of Dell IdeaStorm. *Decision Support Systems*, **48**, 1: 303–312.

Donbesuur, F., Ampong, G. O. A., Owusu-Yirenkyi, D. and Chu, I. (2020). Technological innovation, organizational innovation and international performance of SMEs: The moderating role of domestic institutional environment. *Technological Forecasting and Social Change*, **161**, 5: 120252.

Dubois, A. and Gadde, L.-E. (2002). Systematic combining: An abductive approach to case research. *Journal of Business Research*, **55**, 7: 553–560.

Eckhardt, A., Laumer, S. and Weitzel, T. (2009). Who influences whom? Analyzing workplace referents' social influence on IT adoption and non-adoption. *Journal of Information Technology*, **24**, 1: 11–24.

Eisenhardt, K. M. (1989). Building theories from case study research. *The Academy of Management Review*, **14**, 4: 532.

Eisenhardt, K. M. and Graebner, M. E. (2007). Theory building from cases: Opportunities and challenges. *Academy of Management Journal*, **50**, 1: 25–32.

Eisenhart, M. (1991). Conceptual frameworks for research Circa 1991: Ideas from a cultural anthropologist; implications for mathematics education researchers. *Proceedings of the 13th Annual Meeting of Psychology of Mathematics Education*, 1: 202–219.

Enkel, E., Bogers, M. and Chesbrough, H. (2018). Exploring open innovation in the digital age: A maturity model and future research directions. *R&D Management*, **50**, 1: 161–168.

Ernst, M. and Brem, A. (2017). Social media for identifying lead users? Insights into lead users' social media habits. *International Journal of Innovation and Technology Management*, **14**, 4: 1750022.

Etter, M., Ravasi, D. and Colleoni, E. (2019). Social media and the formation of organizational reputation. *Academy of Management Review*, **44**, 1: 28–52.

European Commission (2003). Commission recommendation of 6 May 2003 concerning the definition of micro, small and medium-sized enterprises (notified under document number C(2003) 1422), (text with EEA relevance), (2003/361/EG). *Official Journal of the European Union*, **L124**, 36–41.

Fehrer, J. A. and Nenonen, S. (2020). Crowdfunding networks: Structure, dynamics and critical capabilities. *Industrial Marketing Management*, **88**, 8: 449–464.

Fernandes Rodrigues Alves, M., Vasconcelos Ribeiro Galina, S. and Dobelin, S. (2018). Literature on organizational innovation: Past and future. *Innovation and Management Review*, **15**, 1: 2–19.

Frambach, R. T. and Schillewaert, N. (2002). Organizational innovation adoption: A multi-level framework of determinants and opportunities for future research. *Journal of Business Research*, **55**, 2: 163–176.

Gangwar, H., Date, H. and Ramaswamy, R. (2015). Understanding determinants of cloud computing adoption using an integrated TAM-TOE model. *Journal of Enterprise Information Management*, **28**, 1: 107–130.

Giudici, A., Reinmoeller, P. and Ravasi, D. (2018). Open-system orchestration as a relational source of sensing capabilities: Evidence from a venture association. *Academy of Management Journal*, **61**, 4: 1369–1402.

Granstrand, O. and Holgersson, M. (2020). Innovation ecosystems: A conceptual review and a new definition. *Technovation*, **90–91**, 102098.

Greer, C. R. and Lei, D. (2012). Collaborative innovation with customers. A review of the literature and suggestions for future research. *International Journal of Management Reviews*, **14**, 1: 63–84.

Heinonen, K., Strandvik, T., Mickelsson, K.-J., Edvardsson, B., Sundström, E. and Andersson, P. (2010). A customer-dominant logic of service. *Journal of Service Management*, **21**, 4: 531–548.

Heinze, K. L. and Heinze, J. E. (2020). Individual innovation adoption and the role of organizational culture. *Review of Managerial Science*, **14**, 3: 561–586.

Huggins, R., Johnston, A. and Thompson, P. (2012). Network capital, social capital and knowledge flow: How the nature of inter-organizational networks impacts on innovation. *Industry and Innovation*, **19**, 3: 203–232.

Jenssen, J. I. N. and Nybakk, E. (2013). Inter-organizational networks and innovation in small, knowledge-intensive firms: A literature review. *International Journal of Innovation Management*, **17**, 2: 1350008.

Jeyaraj, A., Rottman, J. W. and Lacity, M. C. (2006). A review of the predictors, linkages, and biases in IT innovation adoption research. *Journal of Information Technology*, **21**, 1: 1–23.

Johnson, J. D. (2018). Symbolic innovations: Consequences of convergence of adoption and of implementation. *International Journal of Innovation and Technology Management*, **15**, 6: 1830001.

Kale, P., Singh, H. and Perlmutter, H. (2000). Learning and protection of proprietary assets in strategic alliances: Building relational capital. *Strategic Management Journal*, **21**, 3: 217–237.

Kane, G. C., Alavi, M., Labianca, G. and Borgatti, S. P. (2014). What's different about social media networks? A framework and research agenda. *MIS Quarterly*, **38**, 1: 274–304.

Kapoor, K. K., Dwivedi, Y. K. and Williams, M. D. (2014a). Innovation adoption attributes: A review and synthesis of research findings. *European Journal of Innovation Management*, **17**, 3: 327–348.

Kapoor, K. K., Dwivedi, Y. K. and Williams, M. D. (2014b). Rogers' innovation adoption attributes: A systematic review and synthesis of existing research. *Information Systems Management*, **31**, 1: 74–91.

Katz, M. and Shapiro, C. (1985). Network externalities, competition, and compatibility. *American Economic Review*, **75**, 3: 424–440.

Kille, C. and Schwemmer, M. (2014). *Die Top 100 der Logistik: Marktgrößen, Marktsegmente und Marktführer; eine Studie der Fraunhofer Arbeitsgruppe für Supply Chain Services SCS*. DVV Media Group, Hamburg.

Kimberly, J. R. and Evanisko, M. J. (1981). Organizational innovation: The influence of individual, organizational, and contextual factors on hospital adoption of technological and administrative innovations. *Academy of Management Journal*, **24**, 4: 689–713.

Kooijman, M., Hekkert, M. P., van Meer, P. J. K., Moors, E. H. M. and Schellekens, H. (2017). How institutional logics hamper innovation: The case of animal testing. *Technological Forecasting and Social Change*, **118**: 70–79.

Korpela, K., Hallikas, J. and Dahlberg, T. (2017). Digital supply chain transformation toward blockchain integration. In *Proceedings of the 50th Hawaii International Conference on System Sciences (2017)*. Hawaii International Conference on System Sciences, pp. 1–10.

Kwon, S.-W. and Adler, P. S. (2014). Social capital: Maturation of a field of research. *Academy of Management Review*, **39**, 4: 412–422.

Lam, A. (2006). Organizational innovation. *The Oxford Handbook of Innovation*, eds. J. Fagerberg, D. C. Mowery and R. R. Nelson. Oxford University Press, Oxford, pp. 115–147.

Laumer, S., Maier, C., Eckhardt, A. and Weitzel, T. (2016). Work routines as an object of resistance during information systems implementations: Theoretical foundation and empirical evidence. *European Journal of Information Systems*, **25**, 4: 317–343.

Lee, B. C., Moorman, C., Moreau, C. P., Stephen, A. T. and Lehmann, D. R. (2020). The past, present, and future of innovation research. *Marketing Letters*, **31**, 2–3: 187–198.

Lee, S., Park, G., Yoon, B. and Park, J. (2010). Open innovation in SMEs: An intermediated network model. *Research Policy*, **39**, 2: 290–300.

Lemoine, W. and Dagnæs, L. (2003). Globalisation strategies and business organisation of a network of logistics service providers. *International Journal of Physical Distribution and Logistics Management*, **33**, 3: 209–228.

Leonardi, P. M. and Vaast, E. (2017). Social media and their affordances for organizing: A review and agenda for research. *Academy of Management Annals*, **11**, 1: 150–188.

Liang, Saraf, Hu and Xue (2007). Assimilation of enterprise systems: The effect of institutional pressures and the mediating role of top management. *MIS Quarterly*, **31**, 1: 59.

Lichtenthaler, U. (2016). Toward an innovation-based perspective on company performance. *Management Decision*, **54**, 1: 66–87.

Lin, N., Ye, X. and Ensel, W. M. (1999). Social support and depressed mood: A structural analysis. *Journal of Health and Social Behavior*, **40**, 4: 344–359.

Liu, H. and Wang, X. (2010). *Strategy Research of Enterprise Information Planning Based on TOE-TAM Model: Case Study for ERP Implementation of a Discrete Manufacturing*. Wuhan, China.

Makkonen, H., Johnston, W. J. and Javalgi, R. G. (2016). A behavioral approach to organizational innovation adoption. *Journal of Business Research*, **69**, 7: 2480–2489.

Majchrzak, A., Rice, R. E., Malhotra, A., King, N. and Ba, S. (2000). Technology adaptation: The case of a computer-supported inter-organizational virtual team. *MIS Quarterly*, **24**, 4: 569.

Marabelli, M. and Newell, S. (2014). Knowing, power and materiality: A critical review and reconceptualization of absorptive capacity. *International Journal of Management Reviews*, **16**, 4: 479–499.

Matulevičius, R., Dumas, M. and Norta, A. (Eds.) (2015). *Creation of Smart-Contracting Collaborations for Decentralized Autonomous Organizations: Perspectives in Business Informatics Research.* Springer, New York.

Meissner, D. and Kotsemir, M. (2016). Conceptualizing the innovation process towards the 'active innovation paradigm': Trends and outlook. *Journal of Innovation and Entrepreneurship*, **5**, 1: 63.

Mirvis, P. H., Sales, A. L. and Hackett, E. J. (1991). The implementation and adoption of new technology in organizations: The impact on work, people, and culture. *Human Resource Management*, **30**, 1: 113–139.

Mitcheltree, C. M. (2021). Enhancing innovation speed through trust: A case study on reframing employee defensive routines. *Journal of Innovation and Entrepreneurship*, **10**, 1: 4.

Möller, K. and Halinen, A. (2017). Managing business and innovation networks: From strategic nets to business fields and ecosystems. *Industrial Marketing Management*, **67**, 7: 5–22.

Mount, M. and Martinez, M. G. (2014). Social media: A tool for open innovation. *California Management Review*, **56**, 4: 124–143.

Ndou, V., Vecchio, P. D. and Schina, L. (2011). Open innovation networks: The role of innovative marketplaces for small and medium enterprises' value creation. *International Journal of Innovation and Technology Management*, **8**, 3: 437–453.

Ngai, E. W. T., Tao, S. S. C. and Moon, K. K. L. (2015). Social media research: Theories, constructs, and conceptual frameworks. *International Journal of Information Management*, **35**, 1: 33–44.

Nickerson, R. C., Varshney, U. and Muntermann, J. (2013). A method for taxonomy development and its application in information systems. *European Journal of Information Systems*, **22**, 3: 336–359.

Nohria, N. (1992). Is a network perspective a useful way of studying organizations, *Networks and Organizations: Structure, Form, and Action*, eds. N. Nohria and R. G. Eccles. Harvard Business School Press, Boston, MA, pp. 1–22.

Oliveira, T. and Martins, M. F. (2011). Literature review of information technology adoption models at firm level. *The Electronic Journal Information Systems Evaluation*, **14**, 1: 110–121.

Oliveira, T., Martins, R., Sarker, S., Thomas, M. and Popovič, A. (2019). Understanding SAAS adoption: The moderating impact of the environment context. *International Journal of Information Management*, **49**, 2: 1–12.

Oumlil, R., Faouzi, H. and Juiz, C. (2020). Uncovering two decades of open innovation benefits: A qualitative meta-analysis. *International Journal of Innovation and Technology Management*, **17**, 8: 2030006.

Ozkan-Canbolat, E. and Beraha, A. (2016). Evolutionary knowledge games in social networks. *Journal of Business Research*, **69**, 5: 1807–1811.

Pan, S. L. and Zhang, S. (2020). From fighting COVID-19 pandemic to tackling sustainable development goals: An opportunity for responsible information systems research. *International Journal of Information Management*, **55**: 102196.

Parjanen, S. and Hyypiä, M. (2019). Innotin game supporting collective creativity in innovation activities. *Journal of Business Research*, **96**: 26–34.

Pel, B., Wittmayer, J., Dorland, J. and Søgaard Jørgensen, M. (2020). Unpacking the social innovation ecosystem: An empirically grounded typology of empowering network constellations. *Innovation: The European Journal of Social Science Research*, **33**, 3: 311–336.

Pittaway, L., Robertson, M., Munir, K., Denyer, D. and Neely, A. (2004). Networking and innovation: A systematic review of the evidence. *International Journal of Management Reviews*, **5–6**, 3–4: 137–168.

Poutanen, P., Soliman, W. and Ståhle, P. (2016). The complexity of innovation: An assessment and review of the complexity perspective. *European Journal of Innovation Management*, **19**, 2: 189–213.

Priyono, A., Moin, A. and Putri, V. N. A. O. (2020). Identifying digital transformation paths in the business model of SMEs during the COVID-19 pandemic. *Journal of Open Innovation: Technology, Market, and Complexity*, **6**, 4: 104.

Rank, O. N. (2008). Formal structures and informal networks: Structural analysis in organizations. *Scandinavian Journal of Management*, **24**, 2: 145–161.

Ricciardi, F., Zardini, A. and Rossignoli, C. (2018). Business network commons and their fragilities: Emerging configurations of local organizational fields. *Journal of Business Research*, **89**, 4: 328–335.

Roberts, P. W. and Amit, R. (2003). The dynamics of innovative activity and competitive advantage: The case of Australian retail banking, 1981 to 1995. *Organization Science*, **14**, 2: 107–122.

Rogers, E. M. (1995). *Diffusion of Innovations.* Free Press, New York.

Rogers, E. M., Medina, U. E., Rivera, M. A. and Wiley, C. J. (2005). Complex adaptive systems and the diffusion of innovations. *The Innovation Journal: The Public Sector Innovation Journal*, **10**, 3: 1–26.

Roper, S. and Hewitt-Dundas, N. (2017). Investigating a neglected part of Schumpeter's creative army. What drives new-to-the-market innovation in micro-enterprises? *Small Business Economics*, **49**, 3: 559–577.

Rothwell, R. (1991). External networking and innovation in small and medium-sized manufacturing firms in Europe. *Technovation*, **11**, 2: 93–112.

Rothwell, R. (1994). Towards the fifth-generation innovation process. *International Marketing Review*, **11**, 1: 7–31.

Saldaña, J. (2009). *The Coding Manual for Qualitative Researchers.* Sage, London.

Sapprasert, K. and Clausen, T. H. (2012). Organizational innovation and its effects. *Industrial and Corporate Change*, **21**, 5: 1283–1305.

Sawhney, M., Verona, G. and Prandelli, E. (2005). Collaborating to create: The Internet as a platform for customer engagement in product innovation. *Journal of Interactive Marketing*, **19**, 4: 4–17.

Saxton, G. D., Oh, O. and Kishore, R. (2013). Rules of crowdsourcing: Models, issues, and systems of control. *Information Systems Management*, **30**, 1: 2–20.

Scriven, M. (1995). The logic of evaluation and evaluation practice. *New Directions for Evaluation*, **1995**, 68: 49–70.

Scuotto, V., Santoro, G., Bresciani, S. and Del Giudice, M. (2017). Shifting intra- and inter-organizational innovation processes towards digital business: An empirical analysis of SMEs. *Creativity and Innovation Management*, **26**, 3: 247–255.

Singh, P. V. and Phelps, C. (2013). Networks, social influence, and the choice among competing innovations. insights from open source software licenses. *Information Systems Research*, **24**, 3: 539–560.

Sparrowe, R. T., Liden, R. C., Wayne, S. J. and Kraimer, M. L. (2001). Social networks and the performance of individuals and groups. *Academy of Management Journal*, **44**, 2: 316–325.

Sprague, R. H. (1980). A framework for the development of decision support systems. *MIS Quarterly*, **4**, 4: 1–26.

Tasselli, S., Kilduff, M. and Menges, J. I. (2014). The microfoundations of organizational social networks. *Journal of Management*, **41**, 5: 1361–1387.

Teo, H. H., Wei, K. K. and Benbasat, I. (2003). Predicting intention to adopt interorganizational linkages: An institutional perspective. *MIS Quarterly*, **27**, 1: 19.

Thomas, D. R. (2016). A general inductive approach for analyzing qualitative evaluation data. *American Journal of Evaluation*, **27**, 2: 237–246.

Thorgren, S., Wincent, J. and Örtqvist, D. (2009). Designing interorganizational networks for innovation: An empirical examination of network configuration, formation and governance. *Journal of Engineering and Technology Management*, **26**, 3: 148–166.

Thornton, P. H., Ocasio, W. and Lounsbury, M. (2012). *The Institutional Logics Perspective: A New Approach to Culture, Structure, and Process.*Oxford University Press, New York.

Tirabeni, L. and Soderquist, K. E. (2019). Connecting the dots: Framing employee-driven innovation in open innovation contexts. *International Journal of Innovation and Technology Management*, **16**, 4: 1950031.

Tumbas, S., Schmiedel, T. and Vom Brocke, J. (2015). Characterizing multiple institutional logics for innovation with digital technologies. In *2015 48th Hawaii International Conference on System Sciences*, 5 January 2015 to 8 January 2015. IEEE, HI, USA, pp. 4151–4160.

Ucar, E. (2018). Local creative culture and corporate innovation. *Journal of Business Research*, **91**, 2: 60–70.

Unsworth, K., Sawang, S., Murray, J., Norman, P. and Sorbello, T. (2012). Understanding Innovation adoption: Effects of orientation, pressure and control on adoption intentions. *International Journal of Innovation Management*, **16**, 1: 1250004.

Vagnani, G. and Volpe, L. (2017). Innovation attributes and managers' decisions about the adoption of innovations in organizations: A meta-analytical review. *International Journal of Innovation Studies*, **1**, 2: 107–133.

Valos, M. J., Maplestone, V. L., Polonsky, M. J. and Ewing, M. (2017). Integrating social media within an integrated marketing communication decision-making framework. *Journal of Marketing Management*, **33**, 17–18: 1522–1558.

van Heck, E. and Vervest, P. (2007). Smart business networks. *Communications of the ACM*, **50**, 6: 28–37.

van Oorschot, J. A. W. H., Hofman, E. and Halman, J. I. M. (2018). A bibliometric review of the innovation adoption literature. *Technological Forecasting and Social Change*, **134**: 1–21.

Vries, H. de, Tummers, L. and Bekkers, V. (2018). The diffusion and adoption of public sector innovations: A meta-synthesis of the literature. *Perspectives on Public Management and Governance*, **1**, 3: 159–176.

Wejnert, B. (2002). Integrating models of diffusion of innovations: A conceptual framework. *Annual Review of Sociology*, **28**, 1: 297–326.

Wejnert, B. (2005). Diffusion, development, and democracy, 1800–1999. *American Sociological Review*, **70**, 1: 53–81.

Wejnert, B. (2010). A conceptual threshold model of adoption of innovations as a function of innovation's value and actor's characteristics. *Journal of Asia-Pacific Business*, **11**, 3: 197–217.

Williams, M. D., Dwivedi, Y. K., Lal, B. and Schwarz, A. (2009). Contemporary trends and issues in it adoption and diffusion research. *Journal of Information Technology*, **24**, 1: 1–10.

Yan, T., Yang, S. and Dooley, K. (2017). A theory of supplier network-based innovation value. *Journal of Purchasing and Supply Management*, **23**, 3: 153–162.

Yin, R. K. (2018). *Case Study Research and Applications: Design and Methods*, 6th edn. Sage, London.

Yli-Renko, H., Autio, E. and Sapienza, H. J. (2001). Social capital, knowledge acquisition, and knowledge exploitation in young technology-based firms. *Strategic Management Journal*, **22**, 6–7: 587–613.

Zahra, S. A., Neubaum, D. O. and Hayton, J. (2020). What do we know about knowledge integration: Fusing micro- and macro-organizational perspectives. *Academy of Management Annals*, **14**, 1: 160–194.

Zhang, H., Lu, Y., Wang, B. and Wu, S. (2015). The impacts of technological environments and co-creation experiences on customer participation. *Information and Management*, **52**, 4: 468–482.

Zhu, K., Kraemer, K. L., Xu, S. and Dedrick, J. (2004). Information technology payoff in E-business environments: An international perspective on value creation of e-business in the financial services industry. *Journal of Management Information Systems*, **21**, 1: 17–54.

Biography

Axel Jacob is an adjunct professor in the Department of Econmics and Social Sciences at Osnabrück University of Applied Sciences. The focus of his research is on the use of social media, gamification and blockchains in the areas of supply chain management, logistics and production.

Frank Teuteberg is professor and head of the Department of Accounting and Information Systems and speaker of the research center "Digital Society - Innovation - Regulation" at Osnabrück University. He is author of more than 400 publications in the research areas of blockchain, human-technology interaction, ehealth, and artificial intelligence.

Innovation Environment's Role in Supporting Industry 4.0 Technology Adoption to Address Effects of COVID-19*

Sean Kruger* and Adriana A. Steyn

Department of Informatics, University of Pretoria
Pretoria, 0083, South Africa
**sean.kruger@up.ac.za*

Health systems were severely strained at the start of the COVID-19 pandemic, where the demand for personal protection equipment (PPE) could not be met. The challenge faced by many countries was how to innovate quickly to create PPE and other needed solutions. The subsequent research gap identified was a lack of practical insights on how to support such novel technology adoption, particularly those that stem from Industry 4.0 (I4.0) within a developing world context. To address this previous literature on I4.0 technology, the role of innovation environments and theoretical principles of technology adoption was reviewed. A practical case from an academic makerspace based in a South African university was then assessed. It was selected due to its direct role in rapid solutions development of PPE using additive manufacturing (AM) until such a time that manufacturers could set up production on a larger scale. It was found that AM and other novel technologies have facilitated innovative solutions to address the significant impacts of the pandemic. Key to which were practices identified of an innovation environment that supported early-stage adoption of AM to achieve this even in a developing country context. The findings imply that innovation environments offer an agile platform to leverage innovation by streamlining certain critical success factors of I4.0 technology adoption, which is presented in a model. However, individual skills developed by such environments to enhance innovation capabilities within this paradigm require further research.

Keywords: 3D printing; additive manufacturing; COVID-19; fourth industrial revolution; innovation environment; makerspace; rapid prototyping; Industry 4.0.

1. Introduction

The pandemic attributable to SARS-CoV-2 (COVID-19) shocked existing paradigms on a global scale, where several countries were left scrambling to manage numerous adverse effects, including the loss of human life [Armijo *et al.* (2020)]. South Africa (SA), a developing world country, was no exception [World Health Organization (2021a)]. In an attempt to mitigate impending impacts, the country went into lockdown on March 26th, 2020, after the first cases were identified.

*Corresponding author.

*This chapter was originally published in International Journal of Innovation and Technology Management, Vol. 1, No. 6, March 2018, published by World Scientific Publishing, Singapore. Reprinted with permission.

This was to facilitate disaster planning and prepare for the anticipated wave of infections [NICD (2020)]. In addition, hospitals were pivotal centers to test and treat patients with COVID-19, causing healthcare workers to be exposed to the virus at much higher levels than the average person [Belhouideg (2020)]. Therefore, it was deemed vital that they were provided with personal protection equipment (PPE) and other resources to prevent further transmission and continue the delivery of their vital services [Armani *et al.* (2020); Singh *et al.* (2020)].

However, with the pandemic situation, supply chains were under severe strain [Tino *et al.* (2020)] despite advances in technologies [Ferrás-Hernández *et al.* (2019)]. This was because supplier capacities could not meet demands quickly enough [Mueller *et al.* (2020)]. This, alongside other cascading effects, caused concerns across the globe regarding the provision of needed medical equipment and PPE [Manero *et al.* (2020)]. Hence, a call for innovation went out to address this. A technology that has been strongly associated with Industry 4.0 (I4.0) came to light, additive manufacturing (AM) or three-dimensional (3D) printing [Lee *et al.* (2018)]. Existing literature has noted various forms of AM within a global context [Singh *et al.* (2020)], its applications [Lu (2017)] but also how it integrates with other I4.0 technologies [Xu *et al.* (2018)]. Reasons for its adoption include rapid prototyping of solutions for production or testing activities, to advance methods for superior industrialization [Prince (2017); Wesemann *et al.* (2020)].

Within the context of the pandemic, the adoption of AM was shown to facilitate rapid innovation by addressing supply chain shortages of PPE. This was achieved by producing face masks, straps, valves, ear savers, and other items until mass production systems could meet demand [Choong *et al.* (2020); Singh *et al.* (2020)]. The rapid production of these items was supported by a group of stakeholders including research and development (R&D) divisions of companies, universities, makerspaces, laboratories, and private hobbyists [Mueller *et al.* (2020)]. Notwithstanding, these stakeholders form part of larger innovation ecosystems, which have been shown to act as value creation mechanisms between actors in both academia and industry [Asplund *et al.* (2021)]. In more developed regions such as Europe, specific mechanisms such as digital innovation hubs (DIHs) [European Commission (2018)] have been implemented, where, even prior to COVID-19, have acted as catalysts to stimulate innovation through the adoption of digital technologies [Macedo *et al.* (2021)]. This is achieved by offering key functions such as testing viability, identifying investors, and developing needed skills, to name a few [Sassanelli *et al.* (2021)]. Moreover, they support small- and medium-sized enterprises (SMEs), as they are critical in economic development, to leverage digital innovation by offering platforms to foster networks and build key partnerships [European Commission (2020)]. As a result, the region continues to lead in the I4.0 context [Crupi *et al.* (2020)].

These mechanisms offer symbiotic collaboration and functions that enable novel technology adoption [Lu (2017)]. However, despite the several advancements, research has primarily focused on developed regions that have strong capabilities in driving automation with emerging technologies, as well as benchmarks in terms of support structures such as DIHs. As such, a gap in literature was identified, not concerning the importance of such technologies, rather insights into supporting the adoption of such novel technology to increase innovation performance and knowledge capabilities towards sustainable competitive advantage [Moeuf *et al.* (2020)] within developing countries A question raised in this regard is: "*How can innovation environments in developing countries enable novel technology adoption to develop relevant solutions?*".

To answer this question, two approaches are used from a methodological perspective. Firstly, previous literature on the pandemic in which technology adoption facilitated innovation is reviewed. This includes constructs of technology adoption models and critical success factors (CSFs) needed for I4.0. For this study, the technology acceptance model (TAM) and the unified theory of acceptance and use of technology (UTAUT) [Verma and Prakash (2021)] are primarily used due to their usage within I4.0 literature [Rüßmann *et al.* (2015)] and, by extension, the fourth industrial revolution (4IR) [Chang (2017); Gangwar *et al.* (2015); Luthra *et al.* (2020); Rahman *et al.* (2017)].

Secondly, a case study from an academic makerspace based within a South African university is presented. This was selected as the country is channeling efforts to innovate through the use of novel technologies, including AM [Ayentimi and Burgess (2019)], where academic institutions are noted as pivotal stakeholders in facilitating adoption [Chang (2017)]. The environment was also a direct stakeholder in developing rapid solutions of PPE using AM until such a time that manufacturers could set up production on a larger scale.

The objective of this study is to provide insights by developing a model on how to enable novel technology adoption of I4.0 such as AM [Xu *et al.* (2018)] using innovation environments [Sharma (2021)]. According to Hajoary [2021], Moeuf *et al.* [2020], Pozzi *et al.* [2021], and Sony and Naik [2020], several CSFs need to be considered. This study adds to this and existing technology management literature on innovation environment's ability to streamline novel technology adoption that stems from I4.0, which was accelerated by the pandemic, even in a developing world context.

This document is organized into three broad themes to address the research question. The first section reviews previous literature on the pandemic, innovating with technology, enhancing innovation with technology, forms of existing innovation infrastructure, and theoretical perspectives on technology adoption. The second section reviews the methodology and notes why a case is used to determine if innovation environments can be one of several societal movements to address real-world problems. Findings are then reviewed, noting the issues of innovating with novel technologies such as AM and the limitations identified. Finally, concluding remarks and reflections on future initiatives on the role technology plays and how they can be further integrated through innovation environments is presented.

2. Background

The severe acute respiratory syndrome, referred to as COVID-19, has been extensively analyzed in recent months due to its impact and consequential pandemic

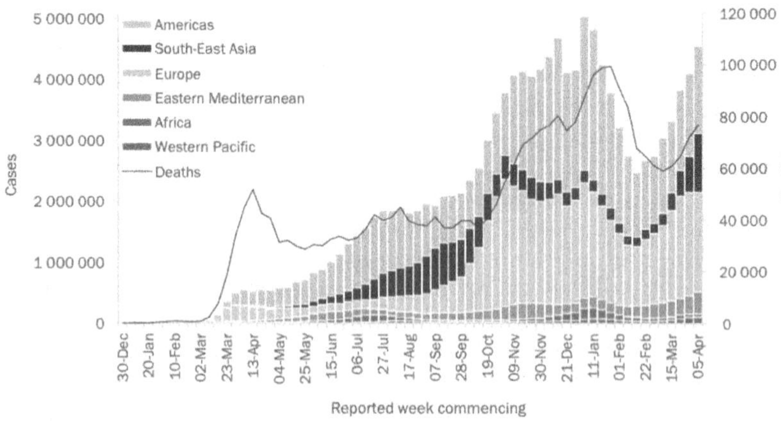

Fig. 1. Confirmed COVID-19 cases and deaths globally as of April 11th, 2021 [World Health Organisation (2021b)].

[Armijo *et al.* (2020); Tino *et al.* (2020); Verma and Prakash (2021)]. Research shows that this novel virus can sustain itself for up to 3 hours in the air and 72 hours on various materials, including plastics and metals [World Health Organization (2021a)]. This, alongside high viral loads in the upper respiratory tract with asymptomatic transmission modes, facilitated the virus's ability to rapidly spread across the globe [Wesemann *et al.* (2020)]. Sample rates for the world obtained from the World Health Organisation [2021b] show that, as of April 11th, 2021, there were severe impacts on human life: 135,057,587 confirmed cases globally and 2,919,932 deaths, as shown in Fig. 1. As of April 11th, 2021, SA had 1,557,527 confirmed cases with 53,256 deaths.

In an attempt to mitigate exposure, social distancing and PPE usage were claimed to prevent the virus spread and reduce deaths as far as possible [Koven (2020)]. A study conducted by Lindsley *et al.* [2014] tested the effectiveness of PPE through several experiments. Based on parameters, the findings suggest that a face shield reduces COVID-19, which carries similar airborne properties such as influenza by approximately 96%, supporting that such PPE is vital to protect frontline workers.

2.1. *Innovating with technology*

Even during a pandemic, literature shows that innovation was able to ensure a large-scale adoption of technology across economies to address challenges through the global community movement [Brem *et al.* (2021)], which leveraged rapid advances in I4.0 technology towards the next generation of manufacturing [Younes *et al.* (2020)]. Innovation then was not stagnant in this context [Corsini *et al.* (2021)] as various drives to rapidly prototype solutions were occurring across the globe [Coronado-Medina *et al.* (2020)]. This was facilitated by adopting I4.0 technologies that form part of the 4IR, which, as a premise, is the integration between the physical, digital, and biological spheres of human existence with technology [Schwab (2017)].

A key technology within this paradigm that supports rapid prototyping is AM [Rüßmann *et al.* (2015)]. Steenhuis *et al.* [2020] stated that this technology is novel as it has various applications but remains complex in terms of its usage and application. However, despite the complexities, it has several advantages from an innovation perspective when adopted, including testing of concepts, costing benefits, and being distributed across various geographical areas quickly [Matos and Jacinto (2019)].

Several examples were identified that support this. In Italy, a hospital ran out of valves required for respirators vital for COVID-19 patients who needed help breathing. The leading supplier could not meet the increased demand, so an engineering firm in Brescia used AM to address the high demand for respiratory valves and created printable versions quickly [Tarfaoui *et al.* (2020)]. Whilst this was occurring, mass production of these valves could be developed. In the United States of America (USA), a Boston based company developed testing swabs for COVID-19 and could print up to 75,000 swabs per day. This mass production allowed hospitals to access large quantities for testing noted as essential [World Health Organisation (2021b)]. A Saudi Arabian team was printing wrist clasps for surgeons to hold a bottle of sanitizer, which acted as a constant reminder to sanitize. These are only some of the examples occurring across the globe using AM [Wesemann *et al.* (2020)]. Hobbyists and the maker community also aided in developing PPE utilizing many devices with open-source design files. Within the community, the focus was on the users' level of protection, including the ability to wear an N95 mask underneath the face shield [Seo-Zindy and Heeks (2014)].

2.2. *Enhancing innovation through technology and infrastructure*

From a strategic perspective, innovation has been a vital construct to remain relevant [Verma and Prakash (2021)], where businesses have channeled resources and efforts into R&D to maximize economic value [Asplund *et al.* (2021)]. This sentiment remained true even during times of crisis, as was experienced at the start of the pandemic [George *et al.* (2020)].

However, several variables, including infrastructure, collaborative mechanisms, individual competencies, and collaboration between task forces, impact organizations' effectiveness to innovate [Walsh *et al.* (2017)]. These variables place a vast amount of pressure on actors such as academia and business to be agile in adopting relevant technologies [Hooton (2018)], which depends on their knowledge base [Guinan *et al.* (2019)]. In several instances, academic institutions that perform R&D can be considered vital in this scope to drive interdisciplinary research, where facets of knowledge can be created and combined to address pertinent issues [Antonites and Van Vuuren (2014); Van Der Schaaf and Daim (2020)]. Developed regions have used DIHs to not only share knowledge [Crupi *et al.* (2020)], but also generate it for SMEs by channeling digital technologies with initiatives such as the digital innovation HUBs and collaborative platforms for cyber-physical systems (HUBCAPs) [Asplund *et al.* (2021); Moeuf *et al.* (2020)]. Within these hubs, technology, including those of I4.0, have been shown to create value, even in times of crisis [Wegmann and Schärrer (2020)]. By increasing the adoption of such technologies to drive innovation and address needs quickly, the purpose of an innovation environment is brought to light [Masood and Sonntag (2020)], as it can facilitate the rapid response to challenges and opportunities [Kruger and Steyn (2020)]. If done well, these environments can enhance the innovation capacity [Das (2020)] that is required by an organizational strategy to address ever-changing needs and expectations [Coronado-Medina *et al.* (2020); Seo-Zindy and Heeks (2014)].

Part of this infrastructure includes innovation environments such as a makerspace. For this study, a makerspace is referred to as an environment that focuses on creating and prototyping through a do-it-yourself (DIY) philosophy [Sharma (2021)]. In some cases, reverse engineering commercial objects and redesigning them for a specific need [Seo-Zindy and Heeks (2014)]. They have been embedded in various scopes, including schools, universities, libraries, and museums [Adams *et al.* (2018)]. Research also notes that these spaces are supporters of innovative activities across science, technology, and art [Armani *et al.* (2020)]. Their role has been seen to enhance research through the exchange of ideas and collaboration, supporting entrepreneurial development and even design enhancement towards technology transfer. Technology transfer can be described as the process of transferring and disseminating technology from its creator to someone else, including corporate entities, to realize value from innovation activities [Kruger and Steyn (2019)]. As a result, makerspaces have received scholarly interest and stand to evolve critical aspects of technology adoption, including those of I4.0, through intellectual structures towards knowledge creation and innovation. This includes the support of business spin-offs [Steenhuis *et al.* (2020)]. Importantly though, to effectively implement such infrastructure, institutions' readiness to leverage such advanced technology needs to be assessed. Fortunately, theoretical maturity models alongside CSF exist within the I4.0 construct to establish this [Sassanelli *et al.* (2021)].

2.3. *Theoretical perspectives to ensure effective technology adoption*

I4.0 technology adoption is vital for stakeholders to improve their "triple-bottom line" through sustainable competitive supremacy [de Sousa Jabbour *et al.* (2018)]. However, it requires certain CSF to be realized [Sony and Naik (2020)]. By considering established CSF and contextual factors per Pozzi *et al.* [2021], strategies and associated activities, which have been noted as vital [Verma and Prakash (2021)], can be identified to support an effective implementation of I4.0 technologies [Santos *et al.* (2017)].

From a theoretical perspective, by leveraging symbiotic collaboration between teams and resources within a specific project, an innovation environment can directly address several CSFs towards the effective adoption of I4.0 technology [de Sousa Jabbour *et al.* (2018); Pozzi *et al.* (2021)]. Notwithstanding, this study considers how the innovation environment under investigation channeled activities to leverage rapid advances in industrialization using AM to address the challenges of the pandemic [Steenhuis *et al.* (2020)]. A key aspect was how this technology was adopted to support innovation to ensure a large-scale diffusion across geographical economies [Seo-Zindy and Heeks (2014)]. This supports earlier findings where

European regions have already realized the role innovation environments have in addressing CSF using I4.0 technologies [Schumacher *et al.* (2016)].

With regards to technology adoption, various arguments surround the models and theories in place that address the phenomenon. Tornatzky and Fleischer [1990] proposed the technology, organization, and environment (TOE) framework for technology adoption, while Davis [1985], who proposed the TAM model [Gangwar *et al.* (2015)], saw significant uptake as it was easy to understand and included perceived usefulness (PU) and perceived ease of use of technology (PEoU).

A more comprehensive model was later proposed by Venkatesh *et al.* [2003] called the UTAUT model. The UTAUT model proposes a critical aspect of information systems and technology management research to explain technology's acceptance and subsequent usage. This model is based on eight other models and theories. The purpose is to define CSF to predict behavioral intention to use and adopt the technology. The four primary constructs of UTAUT consist of (1) performance expectancy, the provided benefits to the user. (2) Effort expectancy, referring to the technologies' ease of use. (3) Social influence, noting how other users influence the users' perceived usefulness. (4) Facilitating conditions that consider the support and integration into existing systems.

For this study, we consider constructs of the TAM and UTAUT models as seen in Fig. 2. The primary purpose is to align from a theoretical standpoint on the CSFs that have been used and confirmed to affect I4.0 technology adoption [Venkatesh *et al.* (2012)]. For example, teamwork and collaboration, as it has been linked to organizational performance to develop trust and effectively integrate I4.0 technologies across business units demonstrating the usefulness and positively impacting their ease of use [de Sousa Jabbour *et al.* (2018)]. Subject areas of I4.0 that these models have been applied to include autonomous cars [Rahman *et al.* (2017)], cloud computing [Gangwar *et al.* (2015)], smart home technologies such as IoT [Nikou (2019); Shin *et al.* (2018)], and supply chain management with IoT [Luthra *et al.* (2020)]. A vital construct stemming from the UTAUT model, facilitating conditions, demonstrates a gap for further research. These conditions look to the organizational strategy and technical infrastructure as CSFs, noting how this will impact the overall system during technology adoption [de Sousa Jabbour *et al.* (2018)]. This aligns with the study's objective that seeks to identify innovation environments' role as infrastructure in streamlining adoption.

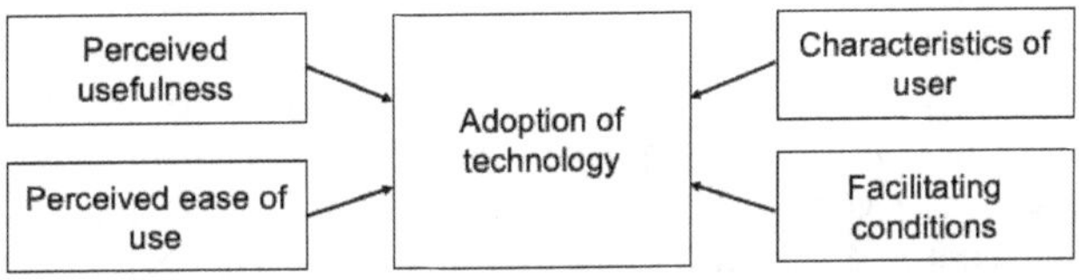

Fig. 2. Technology adoption based on the TAM Model and UTAUT Mode within I4.0 [Davis (1985); Luthra *et al.* (2020); Nikou (2019); Venkatesh *et al.* (2003)].

2.4. *Summary*

The COVID-19 pandemic caused several evident impacts on human society, where effective solutions were required immediately. The tools to do so have improved due to novel technologies of the I4.0, such as AM, and improved innovation ecosystems. It is argued that technology is a CSF of strategy and innovation, where responses now and into the future could be improved if well implemented [Sony and Naik (2020)]. The focus was on the adoption of such technologies to innovate in various spheres of I4.0, with the TAM and UTUAT models identified as relevant in this regard alongside certain CSF. The purpose of this study is to look at how to enable technology adoption such as AM through innovation environments [Steenhuis *et al.* (2020)]. The emphasis of this research is to help in understanding the role innovation environments have towards enhancing technology adoption to address real and pertinent issues.

3. Methodology

Previous literature reviewed demonstrated how AM as disruptive technology was used to facilitate innovative solutions to address the impacts of the pandemic across the globe. Theoretical fundamentals of technology adoption were also reviewed, noting usages of technologies associated with I4.0 that form part of the 4IR. The second method used for this study is the assessment of a practical case relating to the rapid adoption of smart technologies, mainly AM, at the start of the pandemic.

A case study was selected because the research called for an in-depth review of a specific phenomenon. The phenomenon itself was investigating how to streamline novel technology adoption. This pertained to an organization within the developing world of SA. As such, a case study was deemed appropriate, as this research called for an in-depth investigation into activities, methods, and practices used by an innovation environment to quickly address problems through effective adoption of I4.0 technologies [Dalmarco *et al.* (2019)]. The reason for only one case assessment was that the researchers were directly part of the development of the solutions within the environment during the time of adoption, allowing in-depth analysis of how it was streamlined on a practical level. Moreover, the environment offered insights into strategic collaboration activities as other innovation environments were sourced to deliver the solutions. With these insights, the case can be argued to have provided time-relevant insights into the activities of the study [Yin (2017)].

To achieve this, the academic makerspace activities that enabled rapid response and possible reasons for its innovation capabilities were directly observed. The coding used to log this was reports, documented achievements, news items, processes from observations, field notes, and publications. This state of coding was used until categories emerged to present findings that could be used to create the model. As per Fram [2013], inductive coding was used based on the constant comparative method to identify patterns and organize them into logical sections. This constant comparison allowed the researchers to reach a point where theoretical saturation for this case was obtained, and no additional coding within the studies' parameters was

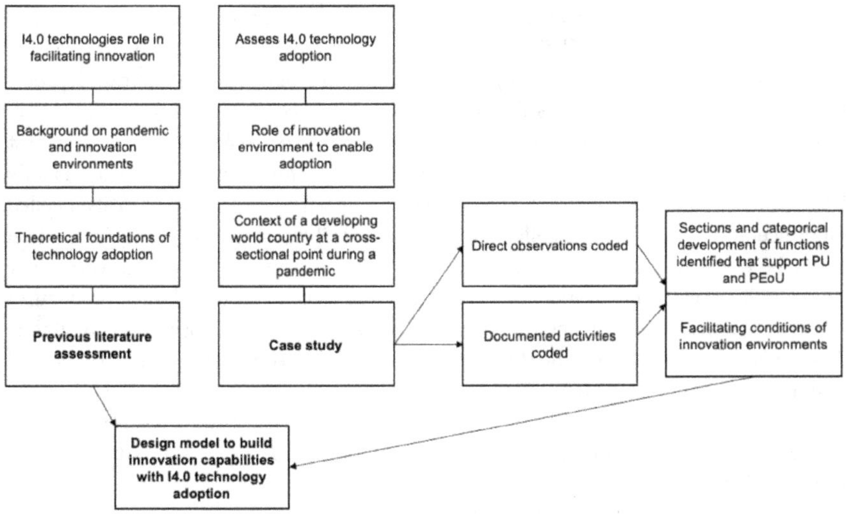

Fig. 3. Research methodology overview.

noted. In other words, the categories were developed with properties and dimensions identified during the start of the pandemic. Using this method, essential practices that supported PU and PEoU could be identified. Moreover, how an innovation environment can enhance facilitating conditions towards improved adoption if at all could be determined. This was a cross-sectional study due to the rapid nature of the response. Figure 3 presents an overview of the methodology.

4. Findings from the Case Study

4.1. *Academic makerspace as an innovation environment*

The Makerspace Centre under investigation was founded in April 2015. It is one of the first academic makerspaces in Southern Africa. Since then, it has developed a series of past successes to demonstrate how innovation can be integrated into the academic and business community. This ranges from the enhancement of research outputs across disciplines to develop new teaching and learning methods. One of which is the introduction and adoption of novel technologies brought on by the 4IR. From a business perspective, the usage of the space has seen training towards skills development to improve ideation and design thinking. These practices aim to ensure the usage and integration of technologies towards new business development and technology transfer. Through the effective diffusion of technology, there appears to be a drive to realize the full potential of technology and the associated potential it unlocks, from improved productivity to societal transformations. The current crisis showed significant pressures placed on ICT by emphasizing working remotely and communicating through different mediums. This is said to continually impact efficient tools for long-distance communications and professions that impact society, such as information systems, where consumers are becoming sources of innovation as well [Rayna *et al.* (2015); Peffers *et al.* (2018)]. One of which is rapid prototyping using the internet of things (IoT) development and 3D printing for rapid prototyping [Chong *et al.* (2018)]. This was done in the space. For example, over several months, with a doctor specializing in health physiology, the team developed best methods and practices using AM to enhance the learning experience of a visually impaired student. This was achieved by engaging with the user to identify needed guidance and then, through collaboration, develop iterations until a viable solution could be created [Punchoo *et al.* (2018)]. In other instances, within the veterinary sciences, lion teeth prototypes using plastics were developed to enhance procedures towards teaching and learning by providing access to resources not readily available. There also continues to be the development of testing equipment in the bovine and malaria fields [Kruger (2019)]. Teaching and experimentation with IoT while mentoring on cybersecurity risks have also been conducted to inspire interdisciplinary solutions through technology leadership and innovation [Kruger (2018); Turpin *et al.* (2020)].

By using document analysis and established literature guidelines, essential practices and associated outputs were investigated. This included sources through media outputs, academic engagements, and consultations with stakeholders of the environment. Table 1 below notes practices that facilitate rapid innovation established before the pandemic used to address the above findings.

4.2. *Community systems*

One of the above practices is collaborative engagements, predominantly within ecosystems of innovation. This is to form part of a larger community to share skills [George *et al.* (2020)]. Prior to the pandemic, there was a focus on academic

Table 1. Identified practices and outputs.

Practices that affect adoption	Support area outputs
Investigate new digital services	Support new business models
Provide access to novel I4.0 technologies	Facilitate an explorative mindset and ability to fail
	Facilitate safe interactions
	Support lifelong learning
Create projects that demonstrate 4IR technology	Rapid prototyping
	Interdisciplinary skill development
	Ideation
Aid in new methods of digitization	Increased access to knowledge
Provide advisory services on technology applications and advancement	Support innovation and creativity
	Research and development (R&D)
Mentorship	Facilitate relevant skill development
Industry and community collaboration	Technology validation and testing relevant concepts
	Access to needed skills
	Create effective partnerships
	Commercialization

Source: Adapted from [Chong *et al.* (2018); Kruger and Steyn (2020); Manero *et al.* (2020); Sony and Naik (2020); Turpin *et al.* (2020); Walsh *et al.* (2017)].

partnerships as well as a business [Rayna *et al.* (2015)]. However, the maker community is said to be a focal point. The systems used within these communities were developed for expertise to be shared, best practices brought, and open knowledge sharing. These efforts aided in each makerspace being more capable of addressing the unique contexts in which they operate, including the pandemic aligning with international efforts [Manero *et al.* (2020)]. As such, initiatives can be incorporated or channeled through such spaces, making them a key part of the strategy as a CSF [Sony and Naik (2020)].

4.3. *Addressing the pandemic problems through an innovative environment*

Manufacturers were struggling to address the demands for PPE. To address this, the Makerspace was a central space to develop solutions for the PPE shortages by channeling expertise and resources. One of the primary solutions was creating visor frames for facial shields for healthcare workers in the greater Tshwane metropolitan. The creation of these was done using open-source files provided by the international community and optimizing them where required using Computer-Aided Design (CAD). AM technologies use a layering approach to create objects from CAD and, as a result, are slower than mass production techniques such as injection molding [Manero *et al.* (2020)]. For this project, the challenge to create PPE quickly though was the focus point. To respond, several phases of implementation were noted, as reviewed in Fig. 4. Nevertheless, these lower-level technology solutions could be rapidly developed until such a time mass production occurred. This was because, despite the supply chain not being prepared as a whole, the innovation environment could capitalize on new production methods and innovation to rapidly shift production towards supply needs [Armani *et al.* (2020)]. From a CSF standpoint, the innovation environment aligned with existing literature by integrating smart technologies to create flexible and efficient production. Moreover, there was also effective project management to ensure effective implementation [Sony and Naik (2020)].

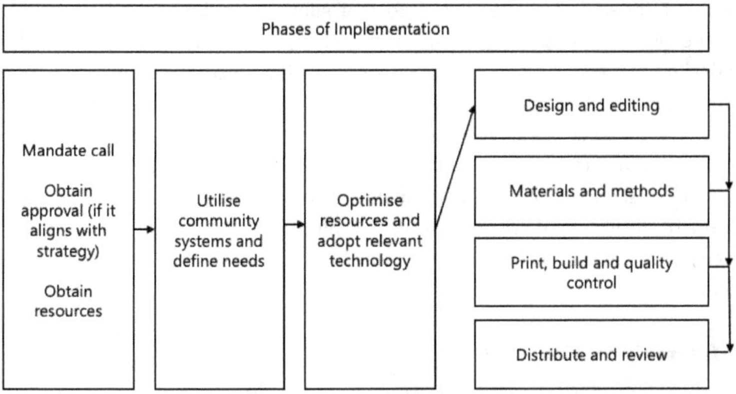

Fig. 4. Phases of implementation to address relevant problems such as PPE shortage.

4.4. *Processes to address relevant needs*

The call for innovation went out in early April 2020, stating that help was required to produce PPE quickly and create sustainable solutions that could aid frontline workers in the pandemic. Before embarking on the call, approval and scope are vital aspects for consideration. This includes the specific environments prioritized, quantities that can be produced as well as associated resources required. Once approved, internal networks were leveraged to pool expertise, materials, and access to the environment during the stringent lockdown, including updated operational procedures. The expert labor was noted, despite limited, and distribution would occur to local clinics as well as the universities' health sciences' faculty, who partnered with the metropolitan's academic hospital.

4.5. *Design methods and editing*

When designing how to make objects, there are various techniques at the disposal of makers today. From physically built prototypes to Computer Numerical Control (CNC), machines produce material through subtraction. However, for this movement, 3D printing was selected as it was said to be well suited to the task, with minimal modification to switch between product creation as and when needs changed. AM technologies facilitate an inherently agile ability to change input files created through CAD, with the advantage that complex geometric structures can be designed and created instead of having individual parts manufactured. These defined characteristics are impacted by the material used, the pattern assigned, and the infill density as specified in the G-code. As a result, fused filament fabrication (FFF) based on fused deposition modeling (FDM), which is a category of AM, was used [Steenhuis *et al.* (2020)]. FDM was used as it is quickly set up for manufacturing. In order to create objects, a file is required, which is created using CAD and then converted primarily to the G-code for a 3D printer to understand [Clifton *et al.* (2020)]. The G-code, also referred to as RS-274, has several variants and is a language used by people to inform computerized machine tools on how to make something. The machines use these instructions to move the motors and assign paths for a set outcome. Due to the lower cost of such technologies and associated filaments, the barriers to entry and support initiatives became more viable. For the actual design, there was a focus on open-source software and associated platforms to allow for the sharing of updated models [Chong *et al.* (2018)]. This made it possible for various stakeholders to create complex objects, even those with limited CAD skills. The primary designs used in the space are noted in Table 2. It also summarizes some of the design aspects and linkages to the standard open source files. It is important to note that 3D print volumes do have an impact; however, if the objects are placed and altered on the build plate for each machine, print volumes, times, and materials differ.

4.6. *Materials and methods*

The primary material used to create this was polylactic acid (PLA) and Super PLA plastic. This plastic is nontoxic, versatile, and affordable when compared to other

Table 2. Review of devices open to editing and reproduction.

Schedule	Capacity
NanoHack protective mask	Basic protection mask that is fitted directly to the face
PRUSA RC 1 face shield	RC1 face shield. A partially circumferential headframe that has a clamp to hold a visor in place. Originates from Prusa Research, Holešovice, Czech Republic
PRUSA RC 2 face shield	An updated face shield is known as RC2. The headframe provides similar structural rigidity without the need for a clamp. Both units provide large surface protection.
Easy 3D face shield	This is a face shield that does not require a clamp. Originates from Hanoch Hemmerich, La Laguna, Tenerife, Spain.
Budmen V3, face shield	Stiffened face shield holder with no clamps required. Budmen Industries, Philadelphia, PA.
H connector ventilators	Expand usage of a single ventilator to ventilate up to four adults.
Hand-free door opener	Attaches to handles to prevent contact

Source: Adapted from [Belhouideg (2020); Tarfaoui *et al.* (2020)].

materials. The filament made use of the FDM. Acrylonitrile butadiene styrene (ABS) was another option, but the focus remained on PLA as it required lower printing temperatures, ranging from 200°C to 225°C, with less warping and extrusion issues. On the other hand, the ABS materials print at a higher range — 230–255°C — and generate toxic fumes while printing. Although other durable materials and thermoplastics such as Nylon are available, the need for higher speeds and lower costs channeled the widespread adoption of PLA [Armijo *et al.* (2020)]. Another reason is that a small amount of this material is used for support structures and rafts, which needs to be removed for post-processing. The raft is used for printers that struggle with adhesion as they do not have a heated bed, which can be seen in Fig. 5, with small layers being placed for easy adhesion of print materials. Standard settings included using a 0.2 mm layer thickness, extruding at 215°C on a heated bed of 50°C, which is standard for such renders [Oth *et al.* (2019)].

Fig. 5. Creating a raft for 3D printed headband adhesion.

Several 3D printers were used to create these visor frames, where the number produced depends on the capabilities of the machine. In some instances, only one print could be handled at a time. On others, they were configured to print multiple versions stacked upon one another. Overall, this allowed for an average production time of one visor frame per hour and was also attributable to printer configurations as well as modifications to the files available. During the initial phases, the machines were tested and pushed to the limits, and failures did occur. However, after several iterations, quicker and durable versions could be created. The material also facilitates that the centre's staff could optimize printer settings for each printer to ensure optimal results. The capacity at the time allowed for the production of around 20 units per day. As additional resources and optimization took place, this increased accordingly. It is worth noting that the call for printing went out to anyone in the metropolitan region with a 3D printer. As part of collaborative efforts and ecosystems of innovation, the on-campus technology business incubator also aided in visor creation with their 3D printers. To distribute units, the collection was arranged with key stakeholders. For fewer than 2 months, over a thousand units were produced and distributed.

When factoring in methods and materials, limitations and dangers in using PPE were noted. With the potential for mechanical blockage of viral materials, 3D printing materials have varying levels of specifications and reproducibility based on varying factors. This includes the material itself, the printers used and settings, and ambient temperature, moisture, lighting, and wind. The designed standard tessellation (STL) files provide a virtual model, but slight variances in the G-code to optimize the printing of thermoplastics did present a problem with exact replication. Despite these challenges, the aim was to provide needed equipment quickly until such a time that mass-produced products [Clifton *et al.* (2020)].

4.7. *Print, build, and quality control*

Once design and materials were selected, the rendering to the G-code for each machine needed to be completed. When rendering the CAD files, it must be noted that there can be limited adhesion, which causes failures and density variations when compared to subtractive methods such as CNC. The challenge was finding the most efficient means of production while minimizing risk and optimizing resource usage. The goal was to create parameters that optimized printing while considering the time sensitivity. Therefore, printing setting alterations allowed for optimized throughput and was achieved with specific configurations as well as print times set to time the most optimal methods. These were then rendered for production. The unit's components can be seen in Fig. 6, with a completed version shown alongside it. With the adhesion methods, though, several issues were experienced, which caused failed prints, excessive stringing, and lowered quality. In the latter cases, this impacted postproduction processes.

The building of shields was done with the help of available staff, following a production-like process of cutting Perspex and elastic string before assembling everything together. Disinfection played a key role, and stakeholders from the medical

Fig. 6. Completed prints with the final product.

faculty were directly inclined to identify the possible treatments, including chemical treatment, chemical vapor, or irradiation. For the context of SA, the chemical bath appeared most viable. This was done after the shields were completed and before distribution to workers. In terms of sterilization of the plastic, it is considered sterile as it leaves the extruder between 210°C and 220°C. This surpasses the required 121°C. However, contamination of the airflow in the environment, build plate, and packaging remains present. The use of conventional sterilization of the object as well as packaging was used. For PLA, a common biomaterial would melt if the five-minute sterilization cycle is used with steam. This also depends on the form of the polymer used in terms of PLA, which is composed of l-lactide and d-lactide chains. The specific properties relating to PLA, such as thermal and mechanical, depend on the distribution ratio of these chains. Thus, the melting temperatures could vary from one brand to another, especially when factoring in Super PLA [Oth *et al.* (2019)]. It is interesting to note that thermal sterilization across the European Union is prohibited in hospitals at the time of writing. A reason presented was the inactivity of prions. Although other forms of sterilization such as radiation and ethylene oxide are used in other areas such as food, these could not be used in this instance as they can potentially create toxicity on the surface of these objects. As a result, a safer technique is low-temperature sterilization with hydrogen peroxide as residues are not formed [Oth *et al.* (2019)].

4.8. *Distribution and review*

At the time of writing, manufacturers were able to create these visors on a massive scale. However, further services have been expanded within the makerspace to produce other PPE for other departments. Examples include social distancing flags, door opening mechanisms, and investigations into potential models for further PPE needs. External organizations were manufacturing ventilator parts. In the meantime, further mandates such as ear savers were requested.

5. Discussion

This study expanded on how I4.0 technology such as AM was used during the pandemic [Singh *et al.* (2020)] and the role of an innovation environment. It was found that the pandemic accelerated the need for innovation in several areas including the need to produce PPE. The case study showed that a makerspace can be an innovation environment under certain conditions, where the process to create needed PPE was shown. Several practices that align with needed CSF were identified that supported early-stage adoption of AM to achieve this even in a developing country context [Armani *et al.* (2020); Choong *et al.* (2020)]. Furthermore, it was shown that there is a need to maintain and support innovation through technology adoption [Coronado-Medina *et al.* (2020); Das (2020)], where this is an expansion of a mechanism to achieve this [George *et al.* (2020)] including that of SA [Ayentimi and Burgess (2019)].

With the activities and documents reviewed, the makerspace assessed showed a strong association with innovation by creating conducive facilitating conductions of the UTUAT model. A reason for this could be the practices identified in Table 1 that are applied in various scopes and disciplines, where some of which align with CSFs [Pozzi *et al.* (2021)]. The makerspace as an innovation environment was shown to also support facilitating conditions by sharing infrastructure and pooling resources distributed over geographical locations towards rapid and targeted efforts [Sharma (2021)]. This includes the effective adoption of AM advancing its maturity within the academic space [Hajoary (2021)]. Moreover, due to the capabilities of such an environment, there are some key similarities with DIHs that could account for the innovation development, such as the channeling of expertise and partnership development, demonstrating that core services of DIHs can be applied within developing regions as well [Crupi *et al.* (2020)].

From this space, as with similar studies, the usefulness of AM was shown as an agile production technology that can be adapted to address various situations and associated needs [Armani *et al.* (2020); Chong *et al.* (2018); Corsini *et al.* (2021); Manero *et al.* (2020)]. AM perceived usefulness can be said to have been enhanced due to the support of a larger innovation ecosystem, as key designs to create several components eased PEoU [Verma and Prakash (2021)]. Furthermore, it was found that AM as a technology adoption paradigm was increased rapidly due to the pandemic, not only for PPE but also for other facets in rapidly prototyping solutions within the 4IR [Schumacher *et al.* (2016)]. It was also shown how such technology integrates into larger ecosystems with the support of innovation environments to enable rapid strategic responses [Lu (2017)]. It is worthwhile to note that, after time, these efforts would later be replaced by injection molding, which is a production process significantly more efficient than AM. This is noted as one of the barriers of AM, where much more robust production outputs are required, especially for medical equipment [François *et al.* (2020)].

Theoretically, various constructs impact technology adoption, including societies' perceptions of technological capabilities [Singh *et al.* (2020)]. In this case, there was rapid dissemination of prototypes as a key deliverable, further proving a case for

AM. However, several risks and considerations are present. This includes reproducible methods [Clifton *et al.* (2020)] and integration within existing systems [Tino *et al.* (2020)], which places innovation environments as key pillars to support established CSF for I4.0 technology adoption. However, further research is required to address other aspects and applications of models such as TAM and UTAUT when considering these new technologies' rapid pace and impact [Masood and Sonntag (2020)]. Further theoretical considerations include the following:

- Many studies consider the nature and adoption of technology, although what constitutes a novel, disruptive, state of the art, smart or high technology is unclear and warrants further investigation.
- Usefulness perceptions can change due to accelerated needs, as with those faced with the context of the pandemic. This should be noted when adopting theory and the potential risks when pushing new technology adoptions.
- Low levels of trust can hinder new incumbents from entering innovation ecosystems, limiting the usage of novel technologies.
- Constant feedback loops and communication between the different users such as designers, procurement of raw materials, supply chain managers, and engineers are key variables that could be expanded under the UTAUT model that impacts perceptions. As such, collaboration needs to be factored into analysis points and noted as a CSF.

From a practical point, innovation environments have been shown to facilitate improvements for academia by channeling needed resources and leveraging technology. This paper adds that newer novel technologies in conjunction with key theoretical principles can address real-world problems. The constructs of theory such as user perception are vital, and innovation environments could potentially aid in this regard. However, due to the limited nature of the studies' focus, generalization is not possible. Nevertheless, a few thoughts are present from a practical standpoint.

5.1. *Innovation environments can form a key part of infrastructure towards innovation*

Having the capacity to access such environments can allow users (or employees) to evaluate and test parts, capacities, and technologies. They could also alleviate supply chain disruptions in the short term, such as those caused by the pandemic [Luthra *et al.* (2020)]. If in place, they can be used as central points in leveraging existing communities of practice and support true collaboration to enhance innovation capacity. This means that they can act as key areas to positively impact facilitating conditions that affect technology adoption [Venkatesh *et al.* (2003)]. Moreover, there can be a drive to develop digital hubs such as the DIHs at a country-wide level to support needed skill development. Skills are considered a CSF to effectively adopt I4.0 technologies for large organizations but also SMEs [Crupi *et al.* (2020)] to grasp opportunities of this paradigm [Moeuf *et al.* (2020)].

However, the failure rates of accelerators and incubators within both business and academic constructs cannot be overlooked. This is one example where an innovation mechanism has continually delivered, but this relies on well-skilled task forces. Finally, the inequity between communities can be disproportional without access to such infrastructure, leading to skewed technology adoption rates [Sharma (2021)].

5.2. *Universities can broaden technology adoption through innovation environments*

Universities are often considered drivers and developers of the knowledge economy. As a result, they are looked to as sources of innovation [Chang (2017)]. This has been shown through successful initiatives such as the commercialization of research through various aspects [Cunningham *et al.* (2019); Kruger and Steyn (2019)]. By facilitating this through an innovation environment such as a makerspace, faculties can broaden technology adoption to develop further innovations in research and generate viable commercial outcomes. This case showed an innovative approach towards tools and equipment for hospitals, such as surgical equipment of use-specific tools. This demonstrates an innovation environment's role to enable CSF towards smart technology integration [de Sousa Jabbour *et al.* (2018)].

5.3. *Managing advancing technologies such as AM*

AM as a technology of I4.0 can adapt to change and react to needs to enable agility in various fields [Schumacher *et al.* (2016)]. The usefulness of these technologies in a developing country can be promoted and aid in supporting innovation with project management as a CSF [de Sousa Jabbour *et al.* (2018)]. There are, however, limitations and challenges with AM. Raw materials usages and recycling need to be considered as well as quality control management. This requires maintenance of machines and key knowledge in their usages such as bed adhesion, temperature, warping of plastics due to ambient temperatures, clearing of blocked nozzles, lubrication of moving parts, broken fans, and upgrading of firmware [Steenhuis and Pretorius (2017)]. In addition, several issues can occur during printing requiring constant monitoring if the settings are not optimized with these variables.

Going forward, actors on all fronts need to effectively manage changes and navigate novel technologies based on practical constructs of theory such as PEoU, owners' characteristics, and the owners' consent. The main contribution, based on the findings and existing literature, is a design model to guide developing countries to strengthen innovation capabilities with novel technologies of I4.0 [Asplund *et al.* (2021)]. The model is shown in Fig. 7. In these activities, though, reckless developments and oversight of ethics remain a concern despite the novelties and capabilities brought on by the 4IR. When rendering and designing them, terms and conditions of open source content should be considered, especially where the purpose would be towards profiteering [Tarfaoui *et al.* (2020)]. This adds to the literature by showing how state of the art technologies can be channeled through such environments, strengthening innovation ecosystems in even developing regions, to achieve several of the benefits of the 4IR paradigm [Xu *et al.* (2018)].

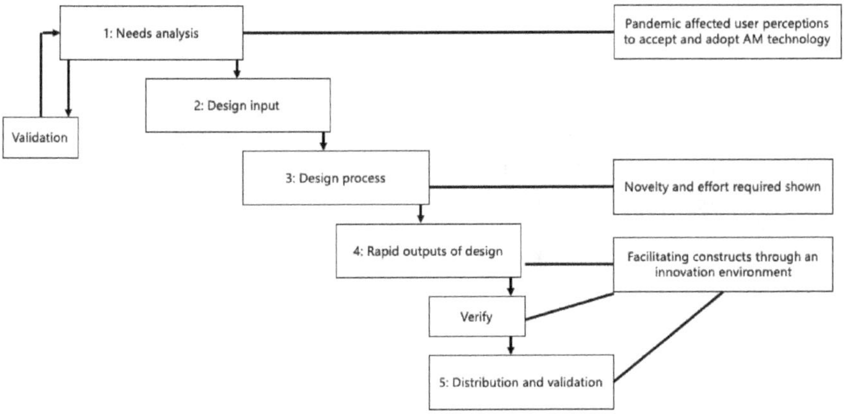

Fig. 7. Design model to adopt and apply innovative technology.

6. Conclusion

Large-scale adoption of technology in the present context was shown to enable innovation across economies to address the challenges of the COVID-19 pandemic. This was achieved through a global community movement that leveraged rapid advances in I4.0 technology, specifically AM, towards the next generation of manufacturing. Part of which was a makerspace, which from the findings was shown to be an innovation environment given certain parameters. Furthermore, certain practices that support adoption were identified, which included the usage of community systems. By using these principles, it was shown how this central space was able to develop PPE and address supply chain shortages by channeling expertise and resources. In this sense, the case demonstrated how early-stage adoption could be channeled quickly through such an environment to streamline adoption even in a developing country. The adoption of this depends on certain constructs as specified in the TAM and UTUAT models, which were shown to have applications in the field of I4.0 and by extension, the 4IR.

Based on these findings, a model was developed and presented to provide a starting point for using innovation environments as infrastructure to support innovation by driving technology adoption for rapid and targeted solutions development.

6.1. *Limitations and suggestions for future research*

This study although striving for academic rigor has several limitations. First and foremost is that the study took place in a narrowly defined area. Due to this context, the study provides limited insights and generalization of the model.

Based on this, it would be interesting to see how other developing countries used AM and other I4.0 technologies, but more importantly, where they originated. For example, did they originate within academic environments, R&D labs, or business spin-offs that are associated with being agile in technology adoption.

The model and analysis assumed that the constructs of the TAM and UTUAT models, especially facilitating conditions, are applicable to I4.0. It would be interesting to note what other models are used and compare their usefulness and effectiveness in current studies.

It was noted that by reverse engineering solutions, medical testing of the equipment's effectiveness and standardization raises several concerns. As a result, regulation presents a significant gap for future research in that standardization; testing and intellectual properties are vague when using novel technologies such as AM, which can replicate existing products.

Finally, the specific skills contained not only in this makerspace, but also in other similar environments that can enhance technology were not especially noted, although they do play an important role. The skill set required then in this regard requires future investigation.

Acknowledgements

To the authors' knowledge, there is no conflict of interest and no funding was received for this research. We would like to thank the founders of the makerspace, Isak and Heila, who envisioned a space that could act as a hub to support innovation even in a developing country. We would also like to thank the accelerator manager Anea and the technician, Lauric, who aided in developing and identifying areas of collaboration. Also, the ICT contact person who aided in sponsorship and distribution, Herman. Finally, Chantal who reviewed all efforts.

References

Adams, S., Brown, M., Dahlstrom, , Davis, A., DePaul, K., Diaz, V. and Pomerantz, J. (2018). *NMC Horizon Report: 2018 Higher Education Edition.* EDUCASE, Louisville.

Antonites, A. and Van Vuuren, J. (2014). Inducing entrepreneurial creativity, innovation and opportunity-finding skills. *South African Journal of Economic and Management Sciences*, **8**, 3: 255–271.

Armani, A. M. *et al.* (2020). Low-tech solutions for the COVID-19 supply chain crisis. *Nature Reviews Materials*, **5**, 6: 403–406.

Armijo, P. R., Markin, N. W., Nguyen, S., Ho, D., Horseman, T., Lisco, S. and Schiller, A. H. D. (2020). 3D printing of face shields to meet the immediate need for PPE in an anesthesiology department during the COVID-19 pandemic. *American Journal of Infection Control*, **49**, 302–308.

Asplund, F., Björk, J., Magnusson, M. and Patrick, A. J. (2021). The genesis of public-private innovation ecosystems: Bias and challenges. *Technological Forecasting and Social Change*, **162**, 1–14.

Ayentimi, D. T. and Burgess, J. (2019). Is the fourth industrial revolution relevant to sub-Sahara Africa? *Technology Analysis and Strategic Management*, **31**, 6: 641–652.

Belhouideg, S. (2020). Impact of 3D printed medical equipment on the management of the Covid19 pandemic. *International Journal of Health Planning and Management*, **35**, 1014–1022.

Brem, A., Viardot, E. and Nylund, P. A. (2021). Implications of the coronavirus (COVID-19) outbreak for innovation: Which technologies will improve our lives? *Technological Forecasting and Social Change*, **163**, 120451.

Chang, S. H. (2017). The technology networks and development trends of university-industry collaborative patents. *Technological Forecasting and Social Change*, **118**, 107–113.

Chong, S., Pan, G. T., Chin, J., Show, P., Yang, T. and Huang, C. (2018). Integration of 3D printing and industry 4.0 into engineering teaching. *Sustainability*, **10**, 11: 3960.

Choong, Y., Tan, H., Patel, D., Choong, W., Chen, C., Low, H., Tan, M., Patel, C. and Chua, C. (2020). The global rise of 3D printing during the COVID-19 pandemic. *Nature Reviews Materials*, **5**, 9: 637–639.

Clifton, W., Damon, A. and Martin, A. K. (2020). Considerations and cautions for three-dimensional-printed personal protective equipment in the COVID-19 crisis. *3D Printing and Additive Manufacturing*, **7**, 3: 97–99.

Coronado-Medina, A., Arias-Pérez, J. and Perdomo-Charry, G. (2020). Fostering product innovation through digital transformation and absorptive capacity. *International Journal of Innovation and Technology Management*, **17**, 6: 2050040.

Corsini, L., Dammicco, V. and Moultrie, J. (2021). Frugal innovation in a crisis: The digital fabrication maker response to COVID-19. *R&D Management*, **51**, 2: 195–210.

Crupi, A., del Sarto, N., di Minin, A., Gregori, G. L., Lepore, D., Marinelli, L. and Spigarelli, F. (2020). The digital transformation of SMEs — A new knowledge broker called the digital innovation hub. *Journal of Knowledge Management*, **24**, 6: 1263–1288.

Cunningham, J. A., Audretsch, D., Kuratko, D., Lehmann, E. and Menter, M. (2019). Entrepreneurial ecosystems: Economic, technological, and societal impacts. *The Journal of Technology Transfer*, **44**, 2: 313–325.

Dalmarco, G., Ramalho, F. R., Barros, A. C. and Soares, A. (2019). Providing industry 4.0 technologies: The case of a production technology cluster. *Journal of High Technology Management Research*, **30**, 2.

Das, R. C. (2020). Interplays among R&D spending, patent and income growth: New empirical evidence from the panel of countries and groups. *Journal of Innovation and Entrepreneurship*, **9**, 1.

Davis, F. (1985). *A Technology Acceptance Model for Empirically Testing New End-User Information Systems: Theory and Results.* Massachusetts Institute Technology, Cambridge.

de Sousa Jabbour, A. B. L., Jabbour, C. J. C., Foropon, C. and Filho, M. G. (2018). When titans meet-Can industry 4.0 revolutionise the environmentally-sustainable manufacturing wave? The role of critical success factors. *Technological Forecasting and Social Change*, **2018**, 132: 18–25.

European Commission. (2018). *Smart Anything Everywhere — Digital Innovation Hubs — Accelerators for the Broad Digital Transformation of the European Industry.* European Commission, Brussels.

European Commission. (2020). *European Digital Innovation Hubs in Digital Europe Programme — Draft Working Document.* European Commission, Brussels.

Ferrás-Hernández, X., Armisen-Morell, A., Sabata-Alberich, A. and Tarrats-Pons, E. and Arimany-Serrat, N. (2019). The new manufacturing: In search of the origins of the next generation manufacturing start-ups. *International Journal of Innovation and Technology Management*, **16**, 2: 1–18.

Fram, S. (2013). The constant comparative analysis method outside of grounded theory. *Qualitative Report*, **18**, 1: 1–25.

François, P. M., Bonnet, X., Kosior, J., Adam, J. and Khonsari, R. (2020). 3D-printed contact-free devices designed and dispatched against the COVID-19 pandemic: The 3D COVID initiative. *Journal of Stomatology, Oral and Maxillofacial Surgery*, **122**, 4: 381–385.

Gangwar, H., Date, H. and Ramaswamy, R. (2015). Understanding determinants of cloud computing adoption using an integrated TAM-TOE model. *Journal of Enterprise Information Management*, **28**, 1: 107–130.

George, G., Lakhani, K. R. and Puranam, P. (2020). What has changed? The impact of COVID pandemic on the technology and innovation management research agenda. *The Journal of Management Studies*, **57**, 8: 1754–1758.

Guinan, P. J., Parise, S. and Langowitz, N. (2019). Creating an innovative digital project team: Levers to enable digital transformation. *Business Horizons*, **62**, 6: 717–727.

Hajoary, P. K. (2021). Industry 4.0 maturity and readiness models: A systematic literature review and future framework. *International Journal of Innovation and Technology Management*, **2030005**, 2020.

Hooton, C. A. (2018). Defining tech: An examination of how the 'technology' economy is measured. *Nordic and Baltic Journal of Information and Communications Technologies*, **2018**, 1: 101–120.

Koven, S. (2020). Critical supply shortages-the need for ventilators and personal protective equipment during the covid-19 pandemic. *New England Journal of Medicine*, **41**, 1: 1–2.

Kruger, S. (2018). Industry 4.0 value creation with the internet of things: Application and cybersecurity risks. In *SFSA Conference*, 12–14 December, CSIR, Pretoria.

Kruger, S. (2019). Innovative approaches in teaching and learning for the fourth industrial revolution. In *AISSAC Conference 2019*, 16 September, Skukuza Conference Centre, Kruger National Park.

Kruger, S. and Steyn, A. A. (2019). Enhancing technology transfer through entrepreneurial development: Practices from innovation spaces. *Journal of Technology Transfer*, **45**, 6: 1655–1689.

Kruger, S. and Steyn, A. A. (2020). A conceptual model of entrepreneurial competencies needed to utilise technologies of Industry 4.0. *International Journal of Entrepreneurship and Innovation Management*, **22**, 1: 56–67.

Lee, M., Yun, J., Pyka, A., Won, D., Kodama, F., Schiuma, G., Park, H., Jeon, J., Park, K., Jung, K., Yan, M., Lee, S. and Zhao, X. (2018). How to respond to the fourth industrial revolution, or the second information technology revolution? Dynamic new combinations between technology, market, and society through open innovation. *Journal of Open Innovation: Technology, Market, and Complexity*, **4**, 3: 21.

Lindsley, W. G., Noti, J. D., Blachere, F. M., Szalajda, J. and Beehold, D. (2014). Efficacy of face shields against cough aerosol droplets from a cough simulator. *Journal of Occupational and Environmental Hygiene*, **11**, 8: 509–518, doi: 10.1080/15459624.2013.877591.

Lu, Y. (2017). Industry 4.0: A survey on technologies, applications and open research issues. *Journal of Industrial Information Integration*, **6**, 1–10.

Luthra, S., Kumar, A., Zavadskas, E., Mangla, S. and Garza-Reyes, J. (2020). Industry 4.0 as an enabler of sustainability diffusion in supply chain: An analysis of influential strength of drivers in an emerging economy. *International Journal of Production Research*, **58**, 5: 1505–1521.

Macedo, H. D., Sassanelli, C., Larsen, P. G. and Terzi, S. (2021). Facilitating model-based design of cyber-manufacturing systems. *Proceedings of CIRP*, **104**, 1936–1941.

Manero, A., Smith, P., Koontz, A., Dombrowski, M., Sparkman, J., Courbin, D. and Chi, A. (2020). Leveraging 3D printing capacity in times of crisis: Recommendations for COVID-19 distributed manufacturing for medical equipment rapid response. *International Journal of Environmental Research and Public Health*, **17**, 13: 1–17.

Masood, T. and Sonntag, P. (2020). Industry 4.0: Adoption challenges and benefits for SMEs. *Computers in Industry*, **121**, 103261.

Matos, F. and Jacinto, C. (2019). Additive manufacturing technology: Mapping social impacts. *Journal of Manufacturing Technology Management*, **30**, 1: 70–97.

Moeuf, A., Lamouri, S., Pellerin, R., Tamayo-Giraldo, S., Tobon-Valencia, E. and Eburdy, R. (2020). Identification of critical success factors, risks and opportunities of industry 4.0 in SMEs. *International Journal of Production Research*, **58**, 5: 1384–1400.

Mueller, T., Elkaseer, A., Charles, A., Fauth, J., Rabasch, D., Scholz, A., Marquardt, C., Nau, K. and Scholz, S. (2020). Eight weeks later-the unprecedented rise of 3D printing during the COVID-19 pandemic-A case study, lessons learned, and implications on the future of global decentralized manufacturing. *Appled Science*, **10**, 12: 1–14.

NICD. (2020). National Institutue for Communicable Diseases, https://www.nicd.ac.za.

Nikou, S. (2019). Factors driving the adoption of smart home technology: An empirical assessment. *Telematics and Informatics*, **45**, 101283.

Oth, O., Dauchot, C., Orellana, M. and Glineur, R. (2019). How to sterilize 3D printed objects for surgical use? An evaluation of the volumetric deformation of 3D-printed genioplasty guide in PLA and PETG after sterilization by low-temperature hydrogen peroxide gas plasma. *Open Dentistry Journal*, **13**, 1: 410–417.

Peffers, K., Tuunanen, T. and Niehaves, B. (2018). Design science research genres: Introduction to the special issue on exemplars and criteria for applicable design science research. *European Journal of Information Systems*, **27**, 2: 129–139.

Pozzi, R., Rossi, T. and Secchi, R. (2021). Industry 4.0 technologies: Critical success factors for implementation and improvements in manufacturing companies. *Production Planning and Control*, 1–21, doi:10.1080/09537287.2021.1891481.

Prince, J. D. (2017). 3D Printing: An industrial revolution. *Journal of Electronic Resources in Medical Libraries*, **9**, 1: 5–6.

Punchoo, R., Kruger, S. and Wolvaardt, L. (2018). The development of 3-D prints to support teaching and assessment in undergraduate human physiology in the visually impaired. In *SAAHE Conference*, 27–30 June, Gateway Hotel, Durban.

Rahman, M. M., Lesch, M. F., Horrey, W. J. and Strawderman, L. (2017). Assessing the utility of TAM, TPB, and UTAUT for advanced driver assistance systems. *Accident Analysis and Prevention*, **108**, 361–373.

Rayna, T., Striukova, L. and Darlington, J. (2015). Co-creation and user innovation: The role of online 3D printing platforms. *Journal of Engineering and Technology Management*, **37**, 90–102.

Rüßmann, M. *et al.* (2015). Future of productivity and growth in manufacturing. *Bost. Consult.*, April, https://www.bcg.com/publications/2015/engineered_products_project_business_industry_4_future_productivity_growth_manufacturing_industries.

Santos, M. Y., Oliveira e Sá, J., Andrade, C. Lima, F. V., Costa, E. Costa, C. Martinho, B. and Galvão, J. (2017). A Big Data system supporting Bosch Braga Industry 4.0 strategy. *International Journal of Information Management*, **37**, 6: 750–760, https://doi.org/10.1016/j.ijinfomgt.2017.07.012.

Sassanelli, C., Gusmeroli, S. and Terzi, S. (2021). The D-BEST based digital innovation hub customer journeys analysis method: A pilot case. In *IFIP International Federation for Information Processing 2021, PRO-VE 2021, IFIP AICT 598*, pp. 460–470.

Sassanelli, C., Rossi, M., and Terzi, S. (2020). Evaluating the smart maturity of manufacturing companies along the product development process to set a PLM project roadmap. *International Journal of Product Lifecycle Management*, **12**, 3: 185–209.

Schumacher, A., Erol, S. and Sihn, W. (2016). A maturity model for assessing Industry 4.0 readiness and maturity of manufacturing enterprises. *Procedia CIRP*, **52**, 161–166.

Schwab, K. (2017). *The Fourth Industrial Revolution.* Crown Publishing, New York.

Seo-Zindy, R. and Heeks, R. (2014). Researching the emergence of 3D printing, makerspaces, hackerspaces and fablabs in the global south: A scoping review and research agenda on digital innovation and fabrication networks. *Electronic Journal of Information Systems in Developing Countries*, **23**, 5: 54–71.

Sharma, G. (2021). The makerspace phenomenon: A bibliometric review of literature (2012–2020). *International Journal of Innovation and Technology Management*, **18**, 3: 2150006-1–16.

Shin, J., Park, Y. and Lee, D. (2018). Who will be smart home users? An analysis of adoption and diffusion of smart homes. *Technological Forecasting and Social Change*, **134**, 246–253.

Singh, S., Prakash, C. and Ramakrishna, S. (2020). Three-dimensional printing in the fight against novel virus COVID-19: Technology helping society during an infectious disease pandemic. *Technology in Society*, **62**, 101305.

Sony, M. and Naik, S. (2020). Critical factors for the successful implementation of Industry 4.0: A review and future research direction. *Production Planning and Control*, **31**, 10: 799–815.

Steenhuis, H. J. and Pretorius, L. (2017). The additive manufacturing innovation: A range of implications. *Journal of Manufacturing Technology Management*, **28**, 1: 122–143.

Steenhuis, H. J., Fang, X. and Ulusemre, T. (2020). Global diffusion of innovation during the fourth industrial revolution: The case of additive manufacturing or 3D printing. *International Journal of Innovation and Technology Management*, **17**, 1: 1–34.

Tarfaoui, M., Nachtane, M., Goda, I., Qureshi, Y. and Benyahia, H. (2020). 3D printing to support the shortage in personal protective equipment caused by COVID-19 pandemic. *Materials (Basel)*, **13**, 15: 3339.

Tino, R., Moore, R., Antoline, S., Ravi, P., Wake, N., Ionita, C., Morris, J., Decker, S., Sheikh, A., Rybicki, F. and Chepelev, L. (2020). COVID-19 and the role of 3D printing in medicine. *3D Printing in Medicine*, **6**, 1: 1–8.

Turpin, M., Matthee, M., Kruger, S. and van Belle, J. (2020). Assisting information systems students to engage with the internet of things (IoT). In *2020 10th International Conference on Cloud Computing, Data Science & Engineering (Confluence)*, India, 2020, pp. 552–558.

Van Der Schaaf, H. and Daim, T. (2020). Critical factors related to student success technology. *International Journal of Innovation and Technology Management*, **17**, 6: 2050045.

Venkatesh, V., Morris, M. G., Davis, G. B. and Davis, F. (2003). User acceptance of information technology: Toward a unified view. *MIS Quarterly*, **27**, 3: 425–478.

Venkatesh, V., Thong, Y. L. and Xin, X. (2012). Consumer acceptance and use of information technology: Extending theory of acceptance and use of technology. *MIS Quarterly*, **36**, 1: 157–178.

Verma, A. K. and Prakash, S. (2021). Technology adoption: A solution for SMEs to overcome problems during COVID-19. *Journal of the Academy of Marketing Science*, **25**, 1: 7352–7363.

Walsh, G. S., Przychodzen, J. and Przychodzen, W. (2017). Supporting the SME commercialization process: The case of 3D printing platforms. *Small Enterprise Research*, **24**, 3: 257–273.

Wegmann, R. M. and Schärrer, L. (2020). Outpacing the pandemic? A factorial survey on decision speed of COVID-19 task forces. *Journal of Organizational Effectiveness*, **7**, 2: 191–202.

Wesemann, C., Pieralli, S., Fretwurst, T., Nold, J., Nelson, K., Schmelzeisen, R., Hellwig, E. and Spies, B. (2020). 3-D printed protective equipment during COVID-19 pandemic. *Materials (Basel)*, **13**, 8: 1–9.

World Health Organization. (2021a), websites accessible: https://www.who.int.

World Health Organisation. (2021b). Coronavirus disease (COVID-19), websites accessible: https://www.who.int.

Xu, L., Da Xu, E. L. and Li, L. (2018). Industry 4.0: State of the art and future trends. *International Journal of Production Research*, **56**, 8: 2941–2962.

Yin, R. K. (2017). *Designing Case Studies.* Sage, Thousand Oaks.

Younes, G. A., Ayoubi, C., Ballester, O., Rassenfosse, D., Fory, D., Cristelli, G., Pellegrino, G., Heuvel, M., Webster, E. and Zhou, L. (2020). COVID-19: Insights from innovation economists. *Science and Public Policy*, 1–13, https://www.ncbi.nlm.nih.gov/pmc/articles/PMC7337780/.

Biography

Sean Kruger is an experienced team leader and manager in Research and Development (R&D) as well as Information and Communication Technology (ICT). He has a Masters in both IT and financial management. At the University of Pretoria, has worked on multiple projects to deliver strategic outcomes and drive research outputs for the past 10 years. Part of which is business model reinvention to deliver new forms of value. His PhD research focuses on strategic innovation in an ever-digitised world using advanced technologies of the 4IR alongside ICT and Information systems. Consequently, he has published and presented several relevant works towards developing leaders and entrepreneurs for the future of work.

Adriana A. Steyn has been with the University of Pretoria for the last thirteen years after she returned to academia from industry. She is currently a full-time senior lecturer in the Department of Informatics. Throughout the years, Riana has engaged numerous students by presenting both undergraduate and postgraduate modules. She has published various articles based on her entrepreneurial and educational experiences over the last few years. She has supervised many students and has delivered numerous PhD students. Her research focuses mainly on technology in Education within the business analysis and design space, and how she can engage students more effectively whilst still delivering good quality content. Her different approach to teaching was born from her own Entrepreneurial research which she is also passionate about. Her PhD focused specifically on entrepreneurs. Here she developed a framework for SMEs to engage more effectively with technology as well as developed an e-skills for entrepreneurs course which focuses on effective technology engagement to create sustainable businesses. She is still actively involved in entrepreneurial research in the South African context. She is also a National research fund (NRF) y-Rated researcher since 2020. She is also a UP teaching excellence Laureates recipient (2019) as well as an Association of Information Systems' Award for Innovation in Teaching recipient (2018) (International award).

Impact of the COVID-19 Outbreak on Engineers' Mobility: Evidence From Patent Data in the Semiconductor Industry*

Ayano Fujiwara
Japan University of Economics, Nihon Keizai Daigaku,
Shibuya-ku Tokyo, Japan
ayanokaayano@gmail.com

This study examines how the mobility of engineers in the semiconductor industry changed after COVID-19. Through the analysis of patent data, differences in the impact on the probability of engineers moving across borders before and after the outbreak were compared. The analysis reveals that before the outbreak, the probability of engineers moving internationally was higher for top-ranked engineers, who accounted for 1% of all engineers, than that for second-, third-, and lowest-ranked engineers. However, after the outbreak, behavioral changes were observed only in top-ranked engineers, so they had a lower probability of mobility than any other rank of engineers.

Keywords: COVID-19; knowledge worker mobility; semiconductor industry.

1. Introduction

Since the outbreak of the COVID-19 pandemic around the end of 2019, our lives have changed dramatically. Telecommuting and online classes are on the rise [Champeaux *et al.* (2020); Sebastian (2021)], people are less likely to go out, and when they do, they prefer private cars to public transportation [Bauer *et al.* (2020)]. As a result, the demand for electronic devices and automobiles needed for remote work and other purposes has skyrocketed, causing an imbalance between the supply and demand for semiconductors, which are some of the most important parts and components of such products [Bauer *et al.* (2020)]. Such emergencies tend to isolate companies that can survive and thrive from those that cannot [Amis and Janz (2020)]. In the past, there have been frequent catch-up cycles in the semiconductor industry, with latecomer firms and countries catching up with the leading firms and leading firms subsequently losing their leadership positions in the industry [Landini *et al.* (2017); Lee and Malerba (2017)]. In 1971, the American company, Intel, invented the microprocessor (CPU) and became the world's largest chipmaker [WiCht (2021)]. However, in the 1980s, Japanese semiconductor manufacturers

*This chapter was originally published in International Journal of Innovation and Technology Management, Vol. 19, No. 6, March 2018, published by World Scientific Publishing, Singapore. Reprinted with permission.

overtook the United States to become the world's largest chip manufacturers [Endo (2018)]. Since the 1990s, Asia has gained an important position as a production base for semiconductors [Kondo (2017)]. Although the manufacturing base of electronics shifted to East Asia, it was the U.S., Western European, and Japanese companies that took the lead in technology and product development [Yeung (2022)]. In the 2010s, however, advanced companies from South Korea, Taiwan, and China gradually developed their technological capabilities and became dominant in semiconductor manufacturing [Yeung (2022)]. Consequently, now American semiconductor manufacturers are no longer in a leadership position, having ceded that position to Taiwan's TSMC in terms of technology and to South Korea's Samsung in terms of sales volume [WiCht (2021)].

For latecomers to catch up with advanced firms, it is important to effectively incorporate external knowledge [Lee and Malerba (2017)], as it is very difficult for a company to create all the technologies alone from scratch. Thus, if there are already existing technologies and knowledge outside the company, it will save both time and money to use them effectively [Mansfield (1998)]. [Lee (2013)] specified that the channels for accessing knowledge from advanced foreign firms vary according to the stage of research and development (R&D) capability of the country or firm. Specifically, in the early stages of technological progress, the process begins with "learning-by-doing" [Arrow (1971)], which occurs naturally through the use of imported machinery and equipment in production activities and then moves on to technology licensing, establishing overseas R&D bases, and international mergers and acquisitions (M&A) [Lee (2013)]. In recent years, more complex and difficult to learn technology has been acquired through "learning-by-hiring" [Fujiwara and Watanabe (2017); Kim (1997)]. Kim [1997] indicated that Samsung was successful in its semiconductor business because of hiring scientists and engineers from U.S. companies. Moreover, [Fujiwara and Watanabe (2017)] examined the mobility of Japanese engineers to South Korean, Taiwanese, and Chinese companies in the electronics industry using patent data and found that latecomers in these countries are hiring more engineers from developed Japanese companies.

In discussing "learning-by-hiring," the excellence of scientists is also an important factor to consider. Zucker and Darby [1996] pointed out that the mobility of productive scientists between universities and firms leads to knowledge spillover. Lacetera *et al.* [2004] showed that when an organization hires productive scientists, the productivity of existing scientists increases due to peer effects. Kim [1997] proved that the mobility of experienced scientists brings about a lasting, rather than transient, effect on knowledge transfer. Almeida and Kogut [1997] showed that knowledge expands rapidly across firms as star scientists move between firms. These studies suggest that more knowledge spillover takes place when more talented engineers move between firms. Therefore, there exists an international competition for talent, with countries and companies trying to acquire brains and talents, by hiring distinguished scientists and engineers [Carr *et al.* (2005); Chambers *et al.* (1998); Giannoccolo (2009); Saxenian (2002)]. Since the ability to attract highly skilled personnel creates winners and losers [Milio *et al.* (2012)], better personnel are considered worth competing for [Chambers *et al.* (1998)]. Meanwhile, [Borjas *et al.*

(1992)] showed that better educated and more highly skilled scientists are more likely to move to locations that offer better conditions. The reason for this, Marx *et al.* [2015] explained, is that elite inventors undertaking high-impact research are more likely to choose better conditions because more companies are willing to hire them. Therefore, the phenomenon of talented engineers moving across company boundaries or national borders and its impact has been of concern to many scholars [Almeida and Kogut (1999); Lacetera *et al.* (2004); Rosenkopf and Almeida (2003); Tzabbar (2009); Zander and Kogut (1995)].

These studies however presuppose a normal situation, where people are free to move to any country or region they want to. However, since the first case of the coronavirus was reported in around December 2019, lockdowns and travel restrictions have been implemented in many countries and regions. Since then, various studies have reported the impact of COVID-19 on the economy and innovation. For example, Chen *et al.*; Chen *et al.* [2021a; 2021b] showed that the number of people moving in to a country was related to the number of infected people there. Brem *et al.* [2021] showed that innovations to tackle the virus have dramatically increased. Nevertheless, there has been little research on whether the mobility patterns of inventors have changed after COVID-19 spread globally. In particular, the semiconductor industry has seen a surge in demand due to COVID-19, which has accelerated competition for semiconductor engineers, and major changes are expected in the international movement of engineers, especially with the United States and Japan attracting factories of Taiwanese companies [Sekiguchi and Okada (2021)]. The impact of COVID-19 is expected to stagnate the international mobility of talent. Meanwhile, how top-class semiconductor engineers behave in such an environment will have an impact on the future of the semiconductor industry.

This study analyzes the factors affecting the international mobility of engineers before and after COVID-19. Specifically, it examines whether top-class engineers are more mobile and whether this is altered by the outbreak. Next, the impact of infection rates, mortality rates, and gross domestic product (GDP) loss rates in the destination countries on the international mobility of engineers after the outbreak is examined.

The remainder of this paper is organized as follows. Section 2 examines the impact of skilled worker mobility (in particular, elite skilled workers) on knowledge spillover. Section 3 describes the sample of the study and a proposed econometric model, and Section 4 discusses the results. Section 5 provides the concluding remarks.

2. Mobility of Knowledge Workers

2.1. *Mobility*

Previous research has shown that scientist mobility facilitates knowledge flows [Almeida and Kogut (1999); Feldman (2000); Fujiwara and Watanabe (2017); Rosenkopf and Almeida (2003); Zucker *et al.* (1994)]. For example, Almeida and Kogut [1999] analyzed patents in the semiconductor industry, finding that the inter-firm transfer of scientists significantly affects local knowledge spillovers. The mobility of individuals is believed to have a positive impact on those moving to the hiring firm, as well as the incumbent employees of the destination firm. Mobile workers contribute to the hiring firm by sharing previously developed inventions and knowledge from their prior employers [Rosenkopf and Almeida (2003); Singh and Agrawal (2011)]. Firms acquire knowledge embedded in individuals by hiring experts from other firms [Kogut and Zander (1993)] even if their knowledge is technologically or geographically distant [Song *et al.* (2003)]. Slavova *et al.* [2016] pointed out that incumbent researchers in destination firms may enjoy peer effects with the arrival of new scientists. Thus, scientist mobility appears to be an effective channel for firms and individuals to acquire external knowledge and technology [Fujiwara and Watanabe (2017); Palomeras and Melero (2010); Song *et al.* (2003)].

2.2. *Elite inventors*

The relationship between worker mobility and knowledge flows depends on whether the considered knowledge worker is perceived to have a high level of excellence. The criteria for measuring the excellence of an inventor can be broadly classified into three categories: productivity, length of experience, and impact of the research involved. Regarding productivity, Zucker and Darby [1996] suggested that the mobility of productive scientists between universities and companies generates knowledge spillovers. Lacetera *et al.* [2004] showed that when productive scientists are newly hired by an organization, the productivity of incumbent scientists increases due to peer effects. Regarding the length of experience, Kim [1997] demonstrated that the mobility of experienced scientists makes knowledge transfer permanent, at least for a certain period. Regarding the impact of the research involved, Almeida and Kogut [1997] showed that knowledge expands rapidly across firms as star scientists move between companies. Further, Tzabbar [2009] empirically showed that star scientists' mobility affects the capabilities of incumbent scientists in the destination firm.

The excellence of a scientist also influences the ease of mobility. For example, Borjas *et al.* [1992] found that better-educated and highly skilled scientists are more likely to move to better locations. Similarly, Marx *et al.* [2015] demonstrated that elite inventors, that is, inventors who are more collaborative and whose work has greater impact, are more likely to move to firms with better conditions, as more firms are willing to hire them. Mobility opportunities are disproportionately broader for elite inventors, suggesting that they may decide whether to move depending on the conditions at the preferred destination firm.

3. Materials and Methods

3.1. *Data*

This study used the U.S. patent and Patent Cooperation Treaty (PCT) databases to analyze the international mobility of knowledge workers in the semiconductor industry. Since the pioneering work of Schmookler [1966] and Scherer [1965], patent data have been commonly used to examine innovation and to assess its relationship with technological and economic development. This study heuristically identified patents filed by the same person and constructed the career history of 158,599 patent inventors from the 135,869 patents filed between January 1, 2018 and December 31, 2020. In determining whether each name corresponds to the same person or a different person with the same name, inventors for whom it was certain their name corresponded to the same person were extracted first. The Dice coefficient on the degree of overlap of their International Patent Classification (IPC) numbers was calculated. The Dice coefficient is used to measure the similarity between two sets of data. The average of the Dice coefficients obtained for the same person (0.26) was used as the threshold value to determine whether inventors were the same persons who had moved to a different firm. The addresses of the employers and the inventors were then used to track the geographic location of the inventors' successive patents to identify cases of cross-border, inter-firm mobility. Intercompany migration in 2020 was identified by comparing employers in patents from January–December, 2020 to employers from January–December, 2019; similarly, intercompany migration in 2019 was identified by comparing employers in 2019 to employers in 2018.

In this study, the analysis was performed by dividing the data into four categories: countries with high and low ratings of control over the spread of infection and of control over the economy after an outbreak. Specifically, the ranking called "Evaluation of Corona Response in Each Country" [Takayama (2020)], created by the Nissay Research Institute using data from Johns Hopkins University, Eurostat, and Datastream, was used. Based on this ranking, a novel dataset was constructed and divided into two groups: one with a high evaluation index of six points or more and the other with a low evaluation index of five points or less, in relation to infection control and economic damage. Regarding infection control, the dataset was divided into two groups: countries rated highly for controlling the spread of infection (e.g. New Zealand, Australia, Singapore, China, and Taiwan) and countries that controlled the infection less effectively (e.g. the Netherlands, Malaysia, Poland, the UK, and France). Regarding economic damage, the dataset was divided into countries that successfully prevented GDP loss (e.g. Taiwan, South Korea, China, the United States, and Japan) and countries that experienced significant GDP loss (e.g. India, the UK, France, and Spain).

Table 1 summarizes the percentages of inventors with confirmed cross-border, inter-firm transfers in their countries of origin and arrival before and after the COVID-19 outbreak. This table shows the top 15 countries with the most patent applications related to semiconductors. For example, among the inventors who moved internationally before the COVID-19 outbreak, the percentage of inventors who moved to Chinese companies after the outbreak clearly decreased. In addition, the percentage of inventors moving to the Netherlands has also decreased after the outbreak. On the other hand, it can be observed that the proportion of inventers moving to the United States and Germany increased after the outbreak.

3.2. *Variables*

3.2.1. *Mobility*

This study aimed to identify cases of cross-border inventor mobility with respect to the previous year. To track worker mobility, each firm's semiconductor patents were

Table 1. Inventors who moved internationally by country of origin and country of arrival.

	Evaluation of corona response in each country		Departure country		Destination country	
	Spread of infection	Economic damage	Before (%)	After (%)	Before (%)	After (%)
United States	9	6	30.0	32.5	51.5	55.9
Japan	9	7	12.7	5.9	5.0	3.7
Taiwan	10	8	8.5	9.1	9.5	9.9
China	10	10	7.6	4.5	7.5	3.7
Belgium	4	2	6.6	7.6	3.0	1.7
Germany	7	5	5.7	4.7	4.5	8.6
United Kingdom	2	2	4.3	2.8	4.5	3.6
Korea	10	8	3.4	1.8	3.1	1.7
Austria	5	2	2.5	1.4	0.9	0.4
Netherlands	7	1	2.3	5.2	4.2	2.6
Singapore	7	10	2.1	3.6	2.3	2.9
Hong Kong	4	9	2.0	0.7	0.5	0.1
India	1	5	1.9	3.6	0.0	0.1
Italy	2	4	1.8	1.9	0.6	0.0
Ireland	8	3	1.6	2.3	0.7	2.9

examined for the period between 2018 and 2020. All inventors listed in these patents were tracked, and cases in which an inventor was employed by more than one firm were identified. In addition, all the cases in which the worker moved to another country were identified using the addresses of the employer and the inventor. In the estimation, a dummy variable was used, which took a value of one for inventors with confirmed cross-border, inter-firm mobility, and zero otherwise.

3.2.2. *Elite inventors*

First, an elite-inventor dummy variable was created by measuring inventor excellence in terms of productivity and research impact. The elite-inventor dummy was divided into three levels: "top-ranked inventors," "second-ranked inventors," and "third-ranked inventors." Inventor productivity was measured by counting the number of patents an inventor was involved in during the previous year. For all inventors in the semiconductor industry, the number of patents in a year was examined. The top 1% of inventors in the sector were ranked as "top-ranked inventors," those between 1% and 5% in terms of number of patents were ranked as "second-ranked inventors," and those between 5% and 10% were ranked as "third-ranked inventors." Inventors with less than 10% in terms of number of patents were classified as "non-elite inventors." Second, to assess research impact, previous studies typically used the number of citations in patents [Albert *et al.* (1991); Carpenter *et al.* (1981)]. However, in this study, as little time has passed since the patent applications were filed, it is reasonable to assume that the number of citations may not be indicative of research impact. Therefore, following previous studies, research impact was measured by the number of claims in patents [Squicciarini *et al.* (2013)]. A ranking was created by calculating the average number of claims in patents in which inventors were involved in the previous year. Inventors whose average number of claims in the patents was in the top 1% of the total number of patents were ranked as "top-ranked inventors," those between the top 1% and 3% were ranked as "second-ranked inventors," and those between the top 3% and 5% were ranked as "third-ranked inventors." Researchers whose research impact was below 5% in the researcher rankings were ranked as "non-elite inventors."

3.2.3. *Control variable*

A firm's location is likely to affect whether workers move across borders. Since the concentration of semiconductor companies greatly varies across geographical areas, three regions were controlled for in this study: North America, Asia, and the rest of the world. Table 2 displays descriptive statistics for the key variables.

3.3. *Analytical methods*

To accurately assess the impact of COVID-19 on the international mobility trend of inventors, their mobility was compared before and after the COVID-19 outbreak. To this end, this study used historical data on migration before the COVID-19 outbreak (2018–2019). To analyze how the mobility pattern of inventors changed before and after the COVID-19 outbreak, a placebo test was conducted by estimating the international mobility of inventors before the pandemic. Therefore, this study addressed the pre- and post-COVID-19 outbreak periods as well as the post-Coronavirus shock period.

3.4. *Regression models*

A probit model was estimated for assessing the likelihood that an inventor j appearing in patent i migrates to another country. Assuming that Eij indicates international migration, Xij is a dummy variable for inventor excellence, and Zij is a dummy for the inventor's region of residence in the previous year, the proposed model can be expressed as follows:

$$\Pr(E_{ij} = 1) = e(\beta X_{ij} + \gamma Z_{ij})/(1 + e(\beta X_{ij} + \gamma Z_{ij})). \quad (1)$$

Each patent corresponds to an observation, and all models were estimated using Stata 15. Probit estimation was performed using either the inventor's international mobility dummy variable or the inventor's excellence dummy variable as the explanatory variable. This probit estimation was performed on the pooled data of the

Table 2. Descriptive statistics.

Variable	Obs	Mean	Std. Dev.	Min	Max
International migration dummy variable	227,090	0.009	0.092	0	1
Excellence as measured by productivity	227,090	1.548	0.934	1	4
Excellence as measured by research impact	227,090	1.056	0.360	1	4
Reputation for infection control policies	225,379	6.883	1.815	0	10
Evaluation of economic policy	225,379	8.930	1.622	0	10
Region of residence in the previous year	226,949	2.514	0.668	1	3

international mobile inventors and non-mobile inventors in 2020 and 2019 (as a placebo test). These placebo tests were conducted to identify variations in international mobility during the placebo testing period (January–December 2019) and the post-corona shock period (January–December 2020). Furthermore, similar estimations were performed on a dataset divided into countries with high and low ratings of infection control, depending on the impact of the pandemic on the destination country. Finally, probit estimation was performed on a dataset divided into countries with high and low economic losses due to the COVID-19 outbreak.

4. Results

Table 3 reports the baseline estimation results before and after the COVID-19 outbreak. The international mobility of inventors was regressed on the elite-inventor dummy variable. The results confirmed that elite inventors had a significantly higher mobility probability than non-elite inventors. Their excellence was measured by their patent productivity and research impact.

Table 4 shows the results of the probit estimation obtained using observations for countries with a low reputation for infection control measures.[a] The results of the placebo test showed that elite inventors, superior in terms of productivity and research impact, had a higher probability of international mobility than non-elite inventors, as expected. In line with the main results regarding the tendency of inventors to move after the COVID-19 outbreak, the coefficients on top-, second-, and third-ranked inventors were 0.193, 0.578, and 0.403, respectively. Their excellence was measured by productivity. These results showed that only top-ranked elite inventors had a lower propensity for international mobility. In particular, it should be noted that for top-ranked elite inventors, the placebo test showed a statistically significant positive effect on international mobility. In contrast, no significant differences were found in the baseline analysis. When excellence was measured by research impact, the coefficients on top-, second-, and third-ranked inventors were −0.178, 0.771, and 0.719, respectively. These results indicate that top-ranked elite inventors had a lower mobility probability than non-elite inventors. Thus, top-ranked inventors tended to avoid moving to countries where the infection control measures were ineffective.

Table 5 shows the results of the probit estimation for inventors from countries with a high reputation for infection control.[b] The results of the placebo test showed that elite inventors had a higher probability of international mobility than non-elite inventors, as expected. The main results confirmed that elite inventors, top-ranked in terms of excellence measured by productivity, had the highest probability of international mobility. In addition, the probability of international mobility was significantly higher for top-ranked elite inventors in terms of research impact. These

[a] AE, AI, AT, BB, BE, BM, CA, CH, CY, CZ, DE, DK, ES, FI, FK, FR, GB, GR, HU, IE, IL, IN, IR, IT, JE, KW, KY, KZ, LI, LT, LU, LV, MA, MK, MT, MY, NC, NL, OM, PL, PT, RO, RU, SD, SI, SK, UA, UY, VG, WS.

[b] AU, BR, CN, CO, EG, HK, JP, KR, MX, NO, NZ, PE, PH, QA, SA, SE, SG, TH, TR, TW, US, VN, ZA.

Table 3. Baseline estimation results.

	Before COVID-19 outbreak						After COVID-19 outbreak					
	Coef.	Std. Err.		Coef.	Std. Err.		Coef.	Std. Err.		Coef.	Std. Err.	
Excellence as measured by productivity												
Top-ranked	0.332	0.029	***				0.309	0.042	***			
Second-ranked	0.292	0.031	***				0.308	0.044	***			
Third-ranked	0.352	0.043	***				0.297	0.042	***			
Excellence as measured by the impact of research results												
Top-ranked				0.303	0.078	***				0.582	0.090	***
Second-ranked				0.413	0.069	***				0.401	0.087	***
Third-ranked				0.414	0.075	***				0.326	0.093	***
Region of residence the previous year												
North America	−0.485	0.030	***	−0.407	0.029	***	−0.397	0.038	***	−0.289	0.038	***
Asia	−0.659	0.028	***	−0.585	0.028	***	−0.790	0.038	***	−0.662	0.038	***
Constant	−2.035	0.023	***	−2.002	0.023	***	−1.946	0.030	***	−1.942	0.031	***
Number of obs.	154,098			154,098			72,851			72,851		

Note: $^{***}P < 0.01$, $^{**}P < 0.05$, $^{*}P < 0.1$.

Table 4. Probability of international migration of inventors to countries with low ratings of infection control.

	Countries with low ratings of infection control policies											
	Placebo			*Main*			*Placebo*			*Main*		
	Coef.	Std. Err.		Coef.	Std. Err.		Coef.	Std. Err.		Coef.	Std. Err.	
Excellence as measured by productivity												
Top-ranked	0.431	0.086	***	0.193	0.154							
Second-ranked	0.506	0.071	***	0.578	0.101	***						
Third-ranked	0.590	0.098	***	0.403	0.093	***						
Excellence as measured by research impact												
Top-ranked							0.217	0.136		−0.178	0.261	
Second-ranked							0.215	0.135		0.771	0.117	***
Third-ranked							0.479	0.158	***	0.719	0.142	***
Region of residence the previous year												
North America	0.122	0.060	**	0.261	0.077	***	0.169	0.060	***	0.367	0.077	***
Asia	−0.074	0.093		−0.260	0.148	*	−0.018	0.090		−0.135	0.147	
Constant	−2.309	0.035	***	−2.237	0.045	***	−2.216	0.032	***	−2.232	0.045	***
Number of obs.		16,494			8,365			16,494			8,365	

Note: ***$P < 0.01$, **$P < 0.05$, *$P < 0.1$.

Table 5. Probability of international migration of inventors to countries with high ratings of infection control.

	Countries with high ratings of infection control policies											
	Placebo			*Main*			*Placebo*			*Main*		
	Coef.	Std. Err.		Coef.	Std. Err.		Coef.	Std. Err.		Coef.	Std. Err.	
Excellence as measured by productivity												
Top-ranked	0.324	0.031	***	0.309	0.044	***						
Second-ranked	0.247	0.035	***	0.232	0.050	***						
Third-ranked	0.284	0.050	***	0.262	0.047	***						
Excellence as measured by research impact												
Top-ranked							0.455	0.097	***	0.867	0.111	***
Second-ranked							0.567	0.082	***	0.150	0.149	
Third-ranked							0.369	0.089	***	0.117	0.134	
Region of residence the previous year												
North America	−0.976	0.042	***	−0.993	0.054	***	−0.914	0.041	***	−0.902	0.055	***
Asia	−1.114	0.040	***	−1.345	0.054	***	−1.058	0.039	***	−1.239	0.054	***
Constant	−1.577	0.036	***	−1.381	0.049	***	−1.544	0.036	***	−1.369	0.049	***
Number of obs.	137,604			64,486			137,604			64,486		

Note: $^{***}P < 0.01$, $^{**}P < 0.05$, $^{*}P < 0.1$.

Table 6. Probability of international migration of inventors to countries with high GDP loss.

	Countries with high GDP loss											
	Placebo			*Main*			*Placebo*			*Main*		
	Coef.	Std. Err.		Coef.	Std. Err.		Coef.	Std. Err.		Coef.	Std. Err.	
Excellence as measured by productivity												
Top-ranked	0.349	0.118	***	0.092	0.245							
Second-ranked	0.614	0.093	***	0.797	0.150	***						
Third-ranked	0.474	0.144	***	0.184	0.171							
Excellence as measured by research impact												
Top-ranked							0.582	0.184	***	0.940	0.307	***
Second-ranked							1.149	0.175	***	0.195	0.445	
Third-ranked							0.954	0.193	***	0.591	0.233	*
Region of residence the previous year												
North America	0.321	0.078	***	0.480	0.127	***	0.447	0.078	***	0.587	0.125	***
Asia	−0.366	0.132	***	−0.186	0.184		−0.370	0.146	***	−0.060	0.182	
Constant	−2.300	0.053	***	−2.402	0.087	***	−2.267	0.050	***	−2.365	0.083	***
Number of obs.	7,856			3,462			7,856			3,462		

Note: $^{***}P < 0.01$, $^{**}P < 0.05$, $^{*}P < 0.1$.

Table 7. Probability of international migration of inventors to countries with low GDP loss.

	Countries with low GDP loss											
	Placebo			*Main*			*Placebo*			*Main*		
	Coef.	Std. Err.		Coef.	Std. Err.		Coef.	Std. Err.		Coef.	Std. Err.	
Excellence as measured by productivity												
Top-ranked	0.331	0.030	***	0.316	0.043	***						
Second-ranked	0.258	0.033	***	0.262	0.047	***						
Third-ranked	0.336	0.046	***	0.310	0.043	***						
Excellence as measured by research impact												
Top-ranked							0.268	0.087	***	0.515	0.095	***
Second-ranked							0.290	0.078	***	0.374	0.090	***
Third-ranked							0.328	0.085	***	0.270	0.104	***
Region of residence the previous year												
North America	−0.606	0.033	***	−0.530	0.041	***	−0.534	0.033	***	−0.420	0.041	***
Asia	−0.735	0.031	***	−0.905	0.041	***	−0.667	0.030	***	−0.774	0.041	***
Constant	−1.954	0.026	***	−1.833	0.033	***	−1.918	0.026	***	−1.830	0.034	***
Number of obs.	146,242			69,389			146,242			69,389		

Note: $^{***}P < 0.01$, $^{**}P < 0.05$, $^{*}P < 0.1$.

results suggest that top-ranked inventors tended to choose countries with adequate infection control measures as their international destinations.

Table 6 shows the estimation results for inventors in countries that suffered large GDP losses and significant economic damage.[c] Table 7 shows the estimation results for inventors in countries with small GDP losses and high evaluations of economic measures.[d] The results of the placebo test indicated that elite inventors had a higher probability of international mobility than non-elite inventors both in countries with high and low GDP losses. The primary results confirmed that the probability of international migration was higher for elite inventors than for non-elite inventors in both cases. These results suggest that the economic measures of the destination country did not affect the mobility of elite inventors after the COVID-19 outbreak.

5. Conclusion

This study examined how the cross-border mobility of inventors in the semiconductor industry was affected by the infection control performance and economic performance of countries following the COVID-19 outbreak. The estimation results suggest that the international mobility of inventors significantly changed following the COVID-19 outbreak. Top-ranked elite inventors, characterized by high productivity and research impact, who constitute the top 1% of all inventors, tended to avoid countries with high infection rates and low reputation for infection control measures and only move to countries with low infection spread rates. This result is consistent with the findings of Marx *et al.* [2015], which suggested that top-ranked elite inventors can afford to choose the environment to which they want to move. Countries that were rated highly as having controlled the spread of infection include China, Taiwan, and South Korea. It is presumed that inventors who have been producing high impact patents with high patent productivity have moved to these countries after the outbreak. On the other hand, second- and third-rank inventors, rather than top-rank ones, tend to move to the Netherlands and the United Kingdom, whose reputation for controlling the spread of infection is low.

Regarding the economic situation after the outbreak, it was confirmed that the top-ranked patent-productive inventors did not move to countries with poor economic conditions, while those who had been engaged in high-impact research tended to move to countries with poor economic conditions. Although economic conditions were expected to be advantageous in hiring foreign investees, the results suggest that infection status may be a more important indicator than economic conditions for investees who have engaged in high impact research.

Looking at the top 15 countries with the largest number of patent applications in the semiconductor field, the results suggest that after the outbreak, top-ranked inventors with both high patent productivity and high quality of patents involved are increasingly moving to China, Taiwan, and Korea. On the other hand, there is a

[c] AE, AI, AT, BB, BE, BM, BR, CO, CY, CZ, ES, FK, FR, GB, GR, HK, HU, IL, IN, IR, IT, JE, KW, KY, KZ, LI, LT, LU, LV, MA, MK, MT, MX, MY, NC, NZ, OM, PE, PH, PT, RO, RU, SD, SI, SK, TH, UA, UY, VG, WS, ZA.

[d] AU, CA, CH, CN, DE, DK, EG, FI, IE, JP, KR, NL, NO, PL, QA, SA, SE, SG, TR, TW, US, VN.

tendency for inventors who are highly productive but not top-ranked in terms of patent quality to move to U.S. firms.

As highlighted by Bauer *et al.* [2020], leaders of semiconductor companies are probably considering restructuring their business strategies for when the pandemic is over and for the next normal. Competition for talented inventors, the key to success at such a time, has already begun, and it seems that companies and countries that have been able to secure talented people have been divided into two groups: companies and countries that have been able to secure talented people and companies and countries that have not. In a pandemic disaster, one way to hire new employees may be to conduct networking activities in new ways, such as communicating online [Giones *et al.* (2020)]. In the semiconductor industry, there is a catch-up cycle in which leaders are being replaced among companies and countries [Lee and Malerba (2017)], and a gradual shift from the leadership of the United States, Western Europe, and Japan to advanced companies in Korea, Taiwan, and China has been noted [Yeung (2022)]. China and South Korea have achieved innovation catch-up and aim to go beyond catch-up [Chen *et al.* (2021a,b); Lee (2013)]. Indeed, China and Korea have succeeded in attracting top-ranked innovators even after the outbreak, while the United States, UK, and other countries have not. Taking this into account, we can speculate that the potential for China and other East Asian countries to assume leadership of the semiconductor industry in the next era will be even greater.

The study findings provide important insights into how semiconductor industry leadership will change in the next normal era. For planners of national and corporate strategies, it is suggested that controlling the infection is more important than economic policy in order to attract talented investors. However, it is also clear that if the economic situation is good, it will be successful in attracting patent-productive inventors. On the other hand, the academic contribution of this study is that the "learning-by-hiring" investigated in previous studies assumed a normal era with no obstacles to cross-border mobility. However, this study was able to compare international migration in normal times with international migration in non-normal times. In other words, during the normal period, the more talented inventers tended to move across national borders, but after the outbreak, behavioral changes were clearly observed in the top-ranked inventers, and they tended to decide whether to move based on the infection status, regardless of the economic status of the destination.

The above results suggest that the more elite the engineers are, the more likely they are to be able to choose the organization for which they work and the country to which they move, and the more likely they are to move to a place where the infection is more controlled or to remain in a safe place. Considering that top-ranked engineers will play a major role in the important semiconductor patents that will be invented over the next few years, the pandemic will have more than a small impact on the future power structure of the semiconductor industry. Thus, countries that successfully control the pandemic will be able to secure more top-ranked engineers by either retaining them or recruiting them from other countries, which is expected to promote further innovation. However, since the pandemic is still ongoing, it will be a few years before we start noticing how the power structure of the semiconductor industry will change.

Finally, several issues could not be fully addressed in this study. First, this study analyzed the international mobility of inventors using current patent data. However, as the possibility that inventors may apply for patents long after moving cannot be denied, mobility data measured over a longer period should be utilized. If long-term mobility data become available, economic information, such as changes in the sales of destination companies, should also be considered. Second, when measuring inventors' level of excellence, this study used their patent productivity and research impact of the previous year. Using research performance data for the past several years would allow for the effects of both short- and long-term inventor mobility and innovation to be examined. Existing research on the effects of individual mobility and travel restrictions has mostly focused on the epidemiological effects. Thus, this study makes a significant contribution by quantitatively assessing the current impact of COVID-19 on the international migration of knowledge workers in the semiconductor field. Newly available data will further deepen the analysis of the impact of the COVID-19 pandemic on innovation in the future.

References

Albert, M. B. *et al.* (1991). Direct validation of citation counts as indicators of industrially important patents. *Research Policy*, **20**: 251–259.

Almeida, P. and Kogut, B. (1997). The exploration of technological diversity and geographic localization in innovation: Start-up firms in the semiconductor industry. *Small Business Economics*, **9**: 21–31.

Almeida, P. and Kogut, B. (1999). Localization of knowledge and the mobility of engineers in regional networks. *Management Science*, **45**: 905–917.

Amis, J. M. and Janz, B. D. (2020). Leading change in response to COVID-19. *Journal of Applied Behavioral Science*, **56**: 272–278.

Arrow, K. J. (1971). The economic implications of learning by doing. In *Readings in the Theory of Growth*. Palgrave Macmillan, London, pp. 131–149.

Bauer, H. *et al.* (2020). *How the semiconductor industry can emerge stronger after the COVID-19 crisis*. McKinsey & Company.

Borjas, G. J., Bronars, S. G. and Trejo, S. J. (1992). Self-selection and internal migration in the United States. *Journal of Urban Economics*, **32**: 159–185.

Brem, A., Viardot, E. and Nylund, P. A. (2021). Implications of the coronavirus (COVID-19) outbreak for innovation: Which technologies will improve our lives? *Technological Forecasting and Social Change*, **163**: 120451.

Carpenter, M. P., Narin, F. and Woolf, P. (1981). Citation rates to technologically important patents. *World Patent Information*, **3**: 160–163.

Carr, S. C., Inkson, K. and Thorn, K. (2005). From global careers to talent flow: Reinterpreting 'brain drain'. *Journal of World Business*, **40**: 386–398.

Chambers, E. G. *et al.* (1998). The war for talent. *McKinsey Quarterly*, **3**: 44.

Champeaux, H. *et al.* (2020). Learning at home: Distance learning solutions and child development during the COVID-19 lockdown (No. 13819). IZA Discussion Papers.

Chen, F. *et al.* (2021a). Customized bus passenger boarding and deboarding planning optimization model with the least number of contacts between passengers during COVID-19. *Physica A: Statistical Mechanics and Its Applications*, **582**: 126244.

Chen, J. *et al.* (2021b). Beyond catch-up: Could China become the global innovation powerhouse? China's innovation progress and challenges from a holistic innovation perspective. *Industrial and Corporate Change*, **30**: 1037–1064.

Endo, H. (2018). Why Have Japanese Semiconductors Sunk? Yahoo Column. Available at https://news.yahoo.co.jp/byline/endohomare/20181224-00108787.

Feldman, M. S. (2000). Organizational routines as a source of continuous change. *Organization Science*, **11**: 611–629.

Fujiwara, A. and Watanabe, T. (2017). Knowledge management using external knowledge. *International Journal of Innovation Management*, **21**: 1750031.

Giannoccolo, P. (2009). The brain drain: A survey of the literature. Università degli Studi di Milano-Bicocca, Department of Statistics, Working Paper, (2006-03), 2.

Giones, F. *et al.* (2020). Revising entrepreneurial action in response to exogenous shocks: Considering the COVID-19 pandemic. *Journal of Business Venturing Insights*, **14**: e00186.

Kim, L. (1997). The dynamics of Samsung's technological learning in semiconductors. *California Management Review*, **39**: 86–100.

Kogut, B. and Zander, U. (1993). Knowledge of the firm and the evolutionary theory of multinational corporations. *Journal of International Business Studies*, **24**: 625–645.

Kondo, A. (2017). Japan's semiconductor industry from an industrial location perspective. A study on the inferiority of competition. *Journal of Economics, Kumamoto Gakuen University*, **23**, 1: 247–262.

Lacetera, N., Cockburn, I. M. and Henderson, R. (2004). Do firms change their capabilities by hiring new people? A study on the adoption of science-based drug discovery. *Business Strategy over the Industry Lifecycle*, eds. J. A. C. Baum and A. M. McGahan. Emerald Group Publishing, Bingley, UK.

Landini, F., Lee, K. and Malerba, F. (2017). A history-friendly model of the successive changes in industrial leadership and the catch-up by latecomers. *Research Policy*, **46**: 431–446.

Lee, K. and Malerba, F. (2017). Catch-up cycles and changes in industrial leadership: Windows of opportunity and responses of firms and countries in the evolution of sectoral systems. *Research Policy*, **46**: 338–351.

Lee, K. (2013). How can Korea be a role model for catch-up development? A 'capability-based view'. *Achieving Development Success: Strategies and Lessons from the Developing World*, ed. A. K. Fosu. Oxford University Press, Oxford.

Mansfield, E. (1998). Academic research and industrial innovation: An update of empirical findings. *Research Policy*, **26**: 773–776.

Marx, M., Singh, J. and Fleming, L. (2015). Regional disadvantage? Employee non-compete agreements and brain drain. *Research Policy*, **44**: 394–404.

Milio, S., Lattanzi, R., Casadio, F., Crosta, N., Raviglione, M., Ricci, P. and Scano, F. (2012). Brain drain, brain exchange and brain circulation. The case of Italy viewed from a global perspective. *National Interest*, 1–50

Palomeras, N. and Melero, E. (2010). Markets for inventors: Learning-by-hiring as a driver of mobility. *Management Science*, **56**: 881–895.

Rosenkopf, L. and Almeida, P. (2003). Overcoming local searches through alliances and mobility. *Management Science*, **49**: 751–766.

Saxenian, A. (2002). Brain circulation. How high-skill immigration makes everyone better off. *Brookings Review*, **20**: 28–31.

Sekiguchi, K. and Okada, K. (2021). Lessons learned from reflection on project management initiatives in a semiconductor firm — importance of perspectives on program management and business ecosystem. *Journal of International Association of P2M*, **15**: 23–46.

Scherer, F. M. (1965). Firm size, market structure, opportunity, and output of patented inventions. *American Economic Review*, **55**: 1097–1125.

Schmookler, J. (1966). *Invention and Economic Growth.* Harvard University Press, Cambridge, MA.

Sebastian, S. (2021). A comparative study on the perception of school and college teachers towards work from home during the Covid-19 pandemic. *Turkish Journal of Computer and Mathematics Education*, **12**: 3715–3727.

Singh, J. and Agrawal, A. (2011). Recruiting for ideas: How do firms exploit the prior inventions of new hires? *Management Science*, **57**: 129–150.

Slavova, K., Fosfuri, A. and De Castro, J. O. (2016). Learning by hiring: The effects of scientists' inbound mobility on research performance in academia. *Organization Science*, **27**: 72–89.

Song, J., Almeida, P. and Wu, G. (2003). Learning-by-hiring: When is mobility more likely to facilitate inter-firm knowledge transfer? *Management Science*, **49**: 351–365.

Squicciarini, M., Dernis, H. and Criscuolo, C. (2013). Measuring patent quality: Indicators of technological and economic value. OECD Science, Technology and Industry Working Papers, No. 2013/03. OECD Publishing.

Takanori, S. (2022). *TSMC is coming, but semiconductor shortage still continues.* Nikkei Crosstech.

Takayama, T. (2020). Which countries are surviving the corona disaster well? A ranking of 50 countries. Nissay Research Institute.

Tzabbar, D. (2009). When does scientist recruitment affect technological repositioning? *Academy of Management Journal*, **52**: 873–896.

WiCht, F. X. (2021). Semiconductor industry and power play.

Yeung, H. W. C. (2022). Interconnected worlds: Global electronics and production networks in East Asia. *Innovation and Technology in the World Economy Series*, ed. M. Kenney. Stanford University Press, Stanford.

Zander, U. and Kogut, B. (1995). Knowledge and the speed of the transfer and imitation of organizational capabilities: An empirical test. *Organization Science*, **6**: 76–92.

Zucker, L. G. and Darby, M. R. (1996). Star scientists and institutional transformation: Patterns of invention and innovation in the formation of the biotechnology industry. *Proceedings of the National Academy of Sciences*, **93**: 12709–12716.

Zucker, L. G., Darby, M. R. and Brewer, M. B. (1994). Intellectual capital and the birth of U.S. biotechnology enterprises. National Bureau of Economic Research (No. w4653).

Biography

Ayano Fujiwara is an associate professor at Japan University of Economics. She received her PhD from The University of Tokyo in Japan. Prior to taking her present position, she worked as an assistant professor at Osaka University in Japan and a senior research fellow at the Ministry of Education, Culture, Sports, Science and Technology (MEXT), National Institute of Science and Technology Policy (NISTEP) in Japan. Her research interests lie in innovation and strategy, human resource management, and mobility of researchers. She is currently investigating the effect of mobility of researchers on their performance. She has published a book on innovation management called "Migration of Engineers: New Norm in Globalization" (Hakuto Shobo, 2016.02).

Emerging Digital Technologies to Combat Future Crises: Learnings From COVID-19 to be Prepared for the Future*

Tobias Guggenberger

Project Group Business & Information Systems Engineering of the Fraunhofer FIT
95444 Bayreuth, Germany

Jannik Lockl

FIM Research Center
University of Bayreuth
95444 Bayreuth, Germany

Maximilian Röglinger

FIM Research Center
Project Group Business & Information Systems Engineering of the Fraunhofer FIT
University of Bayreuth
95444 Bayreuth, Germany

Vincent Schlatt*

Project Group Business & Information Systems Engineering of the Fraunhofer FIT
95444 Bayreuth, Germany
Vincent.schlatt@fit.fraunhofer.de

Johannes Sedlmeir

Project Group Business & Information Systems Engineering of the Fraunhofer FIT
95444 Bayreuth, Germany

Jens-Christian Stoetzer

FIM Research Center
University of Bayreuth
95444 Bayreuth, Germany

Nils Urbach

FIM Research Center
Project Group Business & Information Systems Engineering of the Fraunhofer FIT
Frankfurt University of Applied Sciences
60138 Frankfurt am Main, Germany

Fabiane Völter

Project Group Business & Information Systems Engineering of the Fraunhofer FIT
University of Bayreuth
95444 Bayreuth, Germany

*Corresponding author.

*This chapter was originally published in International Journal of Innovation and Technology Management, Vol. 18, No. 4, March 2018, published by World Scientific Publishing, Singapore. Reprinted with permission.

In 2020, the world has witnessed an unprecedented global pandemic with COVID-19. It has led nations to take measures that have an enormous impact on individuals, society, and the economy. Researchers and practitioners responded rapidly, evaluating the opportunities to capitalize on technology for tackling the associated challenges. We investigate the innovative potentials of three emerging digital technologies — namely, the Internet of Things, artificial intelligence, and distributed ledgers — to tackle pandemic-related challenges. We present our findings on the most effective means of leveraging each technology's potential, the implications for use in crises, and the convergence of the three technologies.

Keywords: Artificial intelligence; blockchain; COVID-19; distributed ledger technology; open innovation; emerging digital technology; Internet of Things.

1. Introduction

The world is in a state of disruption. The spread of SARS-CoV-2[a] has affected countries across the globe. In January 2021, the number of global deaths related to COVID-19[b] exceeded 2,700,000 [Johns Hopkins University (2021)]. The first wave of exponentially increasing infection rates has been successfully overcome by governmental countermeasures [Cyranoski (2020)]. Nonetheless, infection rates across Europe and the US again increased exponentially at the beginning of autumn, resulting in a second wave of infections [Cohen (2020)]. The continuous governmental measures have severely impacted national economies. After more than 10 years of prosperity, a global recession has begun [Ayittey *et al.* (2020)]. Illustrating the scale of economic decline, between the beginning of the COVID-19 pandemic and the end of May 2020, more than 40 million residents of the United States lost their jobs [Aratani (2020)]. By the end of September 2020, half of the affected employees were still unemployed [Parker *et al.* (2020)]. Further, surveys in Europe show that approximately 20% of employees feared they would lose their job in the next three months [Eurofound (2020)].

The main measures employed to tackle the COVID-19 pandemic have been restrictions on business activities, daily life, and the provision of governmental aid packages [Chinazzi *et al.* (2020)]. The restrictions have left companies facing unprecedented challenges [Mandviwalla and Flanagan (2021)]: Societal lockdowns meant they had to instruct their employees to stay at home, yet, companies were nevertheless under pressure to maintain productivity and stave off the looming recession [Fernandes (2020); Waizenegger *et al.* (2020)]. Many organizations responded by furthering their engagement with digitalization initiatives, such as participating in digital sales channels [Alt (2020b)], intensified usage of video conferencing tools, and also more advanced opportunities for personal exchange [Giones *et al.* (2020)]. A substantial number of enterprises have accelerated their involvement in novel forms

[a] SARS-CoV-2 is among the most common abbreviations of the severe acute respiratory syndrome coronavirus 2.

[b] COVID-19 is among the most common abbreviations of the viral pneumonia coronavirus disease 2019.

of digital collaboration [Naidoo (2020); Watson *et al.* (2020); Hacker *et al.* (2020)], opening up to emerging digital technologies (EDTs) best suited to the requirements of their use-cases [Chan *et al.* (2019); Abdel-Basset *et al.* (2021)].

Research and practice have already suggested a broader application of EDTs to mitigate the spread of the COVID-19 pandemic and its effect on the population [Wang *et al.* (2020a); Keesara *et al.* (2020); Ting *et al.* (2020)]. In recent years, researchers and practitioners have analyzed various EDTs. Many of these EDTs are referred to by well-known acronyms, such as SMAC (social media, mobile, analytics, and cloud) for the EDTs that have already found a lot of applications [Fitzgerald *et al.* (2014)] and DARQ for the EDTs that are — or will soon be — on the verge of adoption, such as distributed ledger technology (DLT), artificial intelligence (AI), extended reality, and quantum computing [Daugherty (2019)]. To date, however, the insufficient practical applications of extended reality and quantum computing imply that we cannot observe their practical use on a larger scale and derive specific recommendations on how they might be used in the face of the COVID-19 pandemic. Concurrently, we observe that combining the Internet of Things (IoT) with AI and DLT covers SMAC's core aspects and provides a trio that is particularly suitable for implementing the solutions previously suggested elsewhere. Bai *et al.* [2020], for example, capitalized on the IoT when implementing a program for diagnosing COVID-19 and improving the disease's treatment. In another response incorporating diagnostic features, Mashamba-Thompson and Crayton [2020] propose a low-cost, self-testing, and tracking system for COVID-19, which involves both DLT and AI. The design of this system is purposefully not specific to COVID-19, and it can be used in the case of other infectious diseases. The World Economic Forum (WEF) has also repeatedly suggested leveraging DLTs in global supply chains to maintain the provision of critical pharmaceuticals and medical equipment [AlMuhairi (2020)].

Our focus is further supported by recent works suggesting it is likely that the impact of IoT, AI, and DLT on our daily lives will increase substantially in the near future [Schweizer *et al.* (2020); Brem *et al.* (2020)]. Accordingly, we pose the following research questions:

(1) What role do IoT, AI, and DLT and their convergence play in combatting the COVID-19 pandemic or future crises?
(2) Which resulting implications for research, practice, and policy can be identified?

In this paper, we want to offer valuable insights on these questions and provide guidance for the current pandemic, as well as in preparing for future pandemics or similar crises [Craven *et al.* (2020)]. Furthermore, we intend to contribute to the theory on the convergence of emerging digital technologies as well as open and convergence innovation.

2. The COVID-19 Pandemic and its Socio-Economic Effects

SARS-CoV-2 is the third highly pathogenic coronavirus to emerge in the human population in the 21st century [Zhu *et al.* (2020)]. An infection with SARS-CoV-2 causes COVID-19, with symptoms including non-productive cough, fever, dyspnea, myalgia, fatigue, normal or decreased leukocyte counts, and radiographic evidence of pneumonia [Huang *et al.* (2020)]. Immune system factors of individuals are relevant to the probability of infection or reinfection and the duration and severity of the disease. These factors include genetics, age, physical and nutritional condition, and neuroendocrine-immune regulation. Many aspects of the virus remain unexplored, and a better understanding could help curtail COVID-19 [Li *et al.* (2020a)]. Early data about the spread of SARS-CoV-2 have suggested much higher transmission and case-fatality rates than other common influenza viruses. These high rates forced governments to implement drastic measures to tackle the spread of the virus [Craven *et al.* (2020); Financial Times (2020)]. Further research on COVID-19 is, thus, urgently needed to enable governments to fine-tune countermeasures appropriately.

On 11 March 2020, the World Health Organization (WHO) declared COVID-19 a worldwide pandemic. The pandemic represented an instant stress test for healthcare systems and caught them flatfooted. To restrict the spread of the virus, many countries imposed curfews. These usually included school closings, restrictions on cross-border travel, suspensions of public transport, and the prohibition of public gatherings [Craven *et al.* (2020)]. The United Nations (UN) declared the united response to the COVID-19 pandemic to be the greatest global challenge since World War 2.

In contrast to this portentous comparison, countries' reactions to the crisis were quite diverse [Atkinson (2020)]. While China's government initially reacted very slowly to the situation, it soon took drastic countermeasures to gain control over the spread of the virus. Other South-Asian states like Hong Kong, Singapore, and Taiwan acted quickly, with the implementation of mass testing, fever scans, and contact-tracing to lower the number of cases in their territories [Craven *et al.* (2020)].

To grasp the impact of diseases like COVID-19, research regularly analyzes the impact on individuals, societies, and economies [e.g. Jason *et al.* (2008); Szucs (1999)]. In the case of the COVID-19 pandemic, it is apparent that individuals face novel interaction patterns, such as social distancing. On a societal level, we can observe the effect that political measures have on daily routines. Economically, we tentatively look at the effects on international trade and the gross domestic product (GDP). All these effects need to be considered when analyzing the potential and actual impact of the use of EDTs. In the following, we review those most apparent effects during the crisis.

2.1. *Individual level*

The countermeasures employed by most governments severely restricted social interaction. International travel became practically impossible, with both vacations and family visits to foreign countries limited by destination countries' regulations [World Health Organization (2020)]. Social relations were also affected at a national level. In many cases, visiting relatives and friends at home, in hospitals, or at nursing homes was forbidden, even in severe illness. For the first time in history, church services stopped, and funerals took place only in the narrowest family circles [Craven *et al.* (2020)]. The impact the crisis has so far had on people's mental health is immense, with many individuals suffering from feelings of fear and helplessness during phases of isolation and uncertainty [van Bavel *et al.* (2020)]. Social isolation can lead to a dramatic deterioration of mental health and, ultimately, result in severe psychological disorders such as depression, anxiety, or post-traumatic stress disorder [Qiu *et al.* (2020)]. For vulnerable social groups, such as children and the elderly, isolation in a lockdown can be particularly challenging and have long-term negative consequences on physical and mental health [Wang *et al.* (2020b)]. However, isolation and uncertainty during a crisis can affect not only the lives of individuals but also society [Marabelli *et al.* (2021)].

2.2. *Societal level*

Adding to the high levels of uncertainty among the population, valid and reliable information is often hard to come by despite — or, perhaps, even because of — non-stop media reports on the pandemic. False claims and conspiracy theories circulate via social media and other channels, making it difficult to assess the reliability of information [Boberg *et al.* (2020); Laato *et al.* (2020)]. However, the timely spread of accurate information is vital for controlling the pandemic and preventing panic among citizens [Lin *et al.* (2020); Laato *et al.* (2020); Mirbabaie *et al.* (2020)]. The rapid global spread of the COVID-19 pandemic has also led to unprecedented challenges in international collaboration. For example, the Chinese government was criticized heavily for its inadequate information policies, particularly at the beginning of the pandemic [Peeri *et al.* (2020)]. In concurrence with national foreclosures, such assignments of guilt could lead to discrimination and injustice toward foreigners [Sorokowski *et al.* (2020)]. Outbreaks worldwide also revealed a fundamental lack of resources in hospitals, as could be observed in Northern Italy. Studies found adequate medical supplies (e.g. educated personnel, beds, and personal protective equipment) to be a significant indicator of public health system resilience.

Nevertheless, even industrialized nations with well-developed healthcare systems struggled to provide adequate supplies to their hospitals and physicians [Craven *et al.* (2020)]. In the context of developing countries, healthcare systems are usually less established, which could lead to even more severe outbreaks of COVID-19 in the future [Loayza and Pennings (2020)]. An overstrained healthcare system is likely to raise discussions about affordability, accessibility, and privileges regarding medical care in society and can further increase uncertainty and distrust toward the government.

2.3. *Economic level*

With the ongoing limitations on daily life, the virus's economic impact and aftermath are of global discourse. In recent years, inclusive globalization has led to the development of highly optimized global supply chains serving manufacturing companies. These highly interrelated chains provide competitive advantages for companies but leave them vulnerable to exogenous effects. In this case, the COVID-19 pandemic has had a significant effect on the global economy's supply-side [Gruszczynski (2020)]. The worldwide GDP declined by 4.36% in 2020 [International Monetary Fund (2021)]. This number exceeds the impact of any shock to the global economy since World War 2. Nevertheless, researchers also observe positive outcomes from the pandemic. For example, Chesbrough [2020] highlights that organizations may use the crisis to explore the concept of *open innovation.* Open innovation is defined as "a distributed innovation process involving purposive knowledge flows across organizational boundaries for monetary or non-monetary reasons" [Chesbrough and Bogers (2014)]. The concept may support organizations in overcoming the effects of the pandemic and building long-term competitive advantages. In specific, Chesbrough [2020] suggests that organizations can benefit from knowledge flows both inside and outside as more collective knowledge is created and creative ways to apply this knowledge can be explored, which can speed up the innovation processes. In turn, speeding up innovation processes can result in improved products [Chesbrough (2020)]. However, the findings imply that organizations should carry on the practice of open innovation even after resolving the current crisis.

Besides open innovation, a further strategy for coping with the challenges of COVID-19 represents *convergence innovation* (CI). Following convergence innovation involves uniting objects and ideas from different sources. While the objects and ideas may be unrelated at first, the sources' stakeholders must share similar goals [Lee and Olson (2010)]. In order to facilitate the latter, an ecosystem for enabling CI should be established. It must be designed to autonomously decide or act on the basis of smart sensors, AI, IoT, big data analytics, machine learning, and ambient computing, which scan and analyze the environment. The extracted relevant information then may be used for evaluating the innovation ideas [Lee and Lim (2018)]. Lee and Trimi [2021] argue that convergence innovation may be applicable both for managing the pandemic as well as for preparing for the post-pandemic future. This is mainly due to the reason that activities related to agility and adaptability, which are highly important organizational skills during the pandemic, are at the core of the concept [Lee and Trimi (2021)]. The authors also highlight that the power of convergence can unfold if different objects, including technologies, are united. For this reason, we will observe three emerging digital technologies in the following section, before we assess their potential for convergence over the latter course of this paper.

3. Emerging Digital Technologies and their Potentials

IoT, AI, and DLTs are EDTs. Since they are very different technologies at varying degrees of adoption, they may complement each other well. However, before discussing the potential of their convergence, we outline the most essential characteristics of each of the three technologies in Table 1 and present relevant use-cases in the following to provide a common understanding.

The *Internet of Things* represents the connection of physical objects with the digital world by means of digital logic, sensors, and networking capabilities. As a result, a network of smart interconnected objects emerges [Borgia (2014); Fleisch *et al.* (2009)]. IoT-related actions appear in private as well as business contexts and among humans as well as among machines. In the shape of smart things, people today are connected to various sensors, which set the scene for an interconnected

Table 1. Definition and key characteristics of IoT, AI, and DLT.

Technology	Definition	Key characteristics
IoT	Connection of physical objects utilizing digital logic, sensors, and networking capabilities and the resulting network of smart, interconnected objects	• Connection of the physical and the digital world • Increasingly self-dependent action of physical things • Development from individual smart things to systems of systems
AI	Umbrella term for the study of machines able to perform cognitive functions usually associated with human minds	• Enables machines to perceive, reason, learn, solve problems, make decisions, and interact with the environment • Dependent on human input, quality, and quantity of data
DLT	Append-only distributed databases with high tamper-resistance and without distinct operator	• Transparent and practically immutable history of transactions allows for auditability • Neutrality helps establish collaboration between competitors on a joint DLT platform

world [Allam and Jones (2020)]. IoT devices thoroughly helped to improve processes [Shoukry *et al.* (2019)] and enable novel business models [Paukstadt and Becker (2019)]. In this sense, smart things represent objects from the real world in the digital world, building a cyberphysical system of systems. In the widespread, prevailing understanding, the IoT is conceptualized as a paradigm as well as a technology [Oberländer *et al.* (2018); Huber *et al.* (2019); Athanasopoulou *et al.* (2018)]. In recent years, features of the IoT have led to a wide range of different applications that allow users to record every aspect of their activities [Püschel *et al.* (2020)]. These records include, for example, their location, current heart rate, and the number of steps they take each day. Monitoring such records helps detect potential health issues before symptoms appear [Turakhia *et al.* (2019)]. Applications of the IoT are already widespread, not only among the general population but also in industrial applications, where the IoT provides countless solutions for consumers, businesses, and production [Rosemann (2013); Porter and Heppelmann (2014)]. However, ongoing research and — in particular — the variety of new ideas developed during the COVID-19 pandemic regarding applications of the IoT suggest that its full potential is yet only partially utilized [Noura *et al.* (2019); Brem *et al.* (2020)].

Artificial intelligence serves as an umbrella term for the study of machines that perform cognitive functions usually associated with human minds [Maedche *et al.* (2019); Rai *et al.* (2019)], thereby classified as intelligent agents [Russell and Norvig (1995)]. As the term is often connotated by the perception that artificial intelligence may replace human intelligence, researchers introduced the alternative term of "Augmented Intelligence" to address the observation that artificial intelligence may also enhance human intelligence [Selz (2020)]. Furthermore, researchers and practitioners often distinguish between so-called "weak" and "strong" AI. While the former denotes (algorithmic) solutions to specific problems, the latter describes the imitation of human brain activity and perception [Goertzel and Pennachin (2007)].

Most applications of AI incorporate weak AI, also referred to as Machine Learning (ML). Methods of AI or ML are applicable in both predictive and descriptive settings [Khandani *et al.* (2010)]. While predictive AI denotes the prediction of future developments based on historical data, descriptive AI denotes the interpretation of existing data. In a medical context, current application areas include radiographic image processing, medication, and diagnosis [Wang and Summers (2012); Tucker *et al.* (2015); Kononenko (2001); Vaishya *et al.* (2020)].

In predictive settings, AI is used in a variety of applications. For instance, a predictive analytic model uses hospitalized patients' data to identify those likely to need intensive care in the future. This allows doctors to prevent a critical deterioration of the patients' health. Hence, researchers apply pattern-recognition algorithms onto large datasets to determine relevant factors for developing patients' health status [Pearl (2018)]. Descriptive methods have been used in medical contexts long before the outbreak of the pandemic. While support in cancer detection is probably the most widely known use-case for artificial neural networks, there are many possibilities for further application [Brem *et al.* (2020)]. Classifiers, such as naive Bayesian models, can be used for veracity assessment as they monitor verbal indicators of the quality of information. However, methods for detecting other problematic material such as fake news are still in development [Shirish *et al.* (2021)].

Distributed Ledger Technologies, of which blockchains are the probably most popular subset, describe distributed, append-only databases that serve as a physically decentralized but logically centralized source of truth for information and asset ownership [Rossi *et al.* (2019); Alt (2020a)]. In the decade since their successful first implementation — the cryptocurrency Bitcoin — DLTs have developed rapidly, resulting in extended functionality, such as support for arbitrary logic, so-called smart contracts (e.g. in Ethereum), privacy (e.g. in Monero and Zcash), and implementations to address the performance and governance needs of specific organizations (e.g. Corda, Hyperledger Fabric, and Quorum). DLTs provide tamper-resistant, transparent, and, thus, auditable infrastructures for information-sharing and ownership tracking [Lockl *et al.* (2020); Rossi *et al.* (2019)]. The well-known drawbacks of DLTs — namely, performance and data privacy issues — are both a consequence of redundant operations and may soon be mitigated due to rapid advances in cryptography, notably Zero-Knowledge-Proofs (ZKPs) [Ben-Sasson *et al.* (2018)].

DLT is becoming the backbone of several cross-organizational digital platforms, for example, in public administration [Rieger *et al.* (2019)] and medical supply chain management [Mattke *et al.* (2019)]. In the latter context, MediLedger provides a digital supply chain to prove to the regulator that no fake medicines have been inserted as products have passed through the hands of multiple stakeholders [Mattke *et al.* (2019)]. To meet the privacy needs of all participating parties, MediLedger makes use of ZKPs to demonstrate supply chain integrity without the need to reveal critical business information to competitors. Another frequent application of DLT is the establishment of decentralized identity management or *Self-Sovereign Identities* (*SSIs*) [Mühle *et al.* (2018)]. SSIs build a privacy-preserving digital identity management system using ZKPs, allowing users to maintain full control over their identity [Hesse and Teubner (2020)]. SSIs' anonymous digital credentials [Camenisch and Lysyanskaya (2001)] do not rely on oligopolies of certificate authorities but, instead, build on DLT-based public registries that provide information about credential issuers [Stokkink and Pouwelse (2018)].

4. Observations from the COVID-19 Pandemic

The three EDTs in focus have been subject to a significant increase in attention and use during the past decade. Owing to their characteristics, several novel applications have emerged during the COVID-19 pandemic. Below, we synthesize proposals from research and practice on how DLT, AI, and the IoT can tackle problems arising from the COVID-19 pandemic. By doing so, we provide a foundation for further analysis.

4.1. *The internet of things*

In terms of existing, technology-driven measures against the COVID-19 pandemic, the wide distribution of smart things among the general population provides a broad range of benefits [Peeri *et al.* (2020); Urbaczewski and Lee (2020)]. For example, the Robert Koch Institute (RKI)[c] has developed an app for smartphones that uses Bluetooth technology to trace potential exposure to infectious persons. Smartphones with the installed app exchange temporary and encrypted random codes via Bluetooth and store the respective encounters.

Users with a positive test for SARS-CoV-2 can upload their test results to a central server, which then notifies users who are located nearby the infectious person [Robert Koch Institute (2020)]. This mechanism allows for privacy-preserving digital contact tracing to disclose infection chains [Ferretti *et al.* (2020)]. In contrast, other countries like South Korea utilize a centralized, less-privacy-oriented approach to trace down infection chains [Hsu (2020); Blasimme and Vayena (2020)].

While applications such as that developed by the RKI focus on the societal level, a specific person's health data might also help the individual [Riemer *et al.* (2020)]. For example, the Shanghai Public Health Clinical Center uses smart things to track patients' temperature levels. Nurses and physicians can hence monitor patients' health status without the need for personal contact, enhancing the efficiency of the process and reducing the chance of infection [Gupta *et al.* (2020)]. Fatima *et al.* [2020] further demonstrate that various IoT-provided data — such as recordings of patients' coughing, heart rate variance, and body temperature — can feed a fuzzy inference system, which then calculates the probability that the patient is infected.

The applications listed above are related to consumer IoT devices. However, various industrial IoT applications have also made an impact [Fahrni *et al.* (2020)]. In particular, additive manufacturing-enabled smart factories allow for higher flexibility and, thus, demand-oriented production of various medical supplies with short lead times [Pearce (2020); Javaid *et al.* (2020); Wang *et al.* (2016)]. At least, in the

[c] Robert Koch Institute is a federal government agency and research institute with responsibility for disease prevention and control in Germany.

short term, such production facilities show great potential to ease the pressure resulting from increasing numbers of patients and increasing demand for medical supplies. Unmanned aerial vehicles (UAVs) have also been used during the COVID-19 pandemic to maintain physical distance and reduce the time that specific countermeasures would take to carry out by hand or use traditional things. Equipped with cameras, sensors, and GPS receivers, modern UAVs can act autonomously and provide IoT services from high altitudes [Lagkas *et al.* (2018)]. For example, agricultural UAVs have been used to disinfect large areas of cities, to transport medical equipment, and for surveyance [Gupta *et al.* (2020)].

4.2. *Artificial intelligence*

AI is already in widespread use in the medical sector and shows the potential to support the fight against the COVID-19 pandemic in both predictive and descriptive settings. Proposed applications relate to both the individual level (e.g. effectively diagnosing the illness) and the societal or economic level (e.g. predicting the pandemic's course and its consequences for important metrics in the economy). While some of these applications are already being used to tackle different challenges in the context of the COVID-19 pandemic, research also proposes a variety of novel use-cases for AI to deal with emerging issues.

For example, in predictive settings, Jiang *et al.* [2020] propose a method for anticipating the clinical severity of the illness based on the individual patient's data. They rely on a set of distinct features of COVID-19, which they processed using different algorithms. Predictions reached an accuracy of up to 80%. Thus, applied AI supports medical decision-makers to allocate resources efficiently and better utilize scarce medical supplies, a phenomenon that we already observed during the current pandemic. Another example is provided by Rao and Vazquez [2020] who use AI to predict the location of potential future outbursts of COVID-19 based on data about interactions between infected and non-infected people. A suitable app installed on consumers' smart things (e.g. smartphones) could notify affected individuals. Allam and Jones [2020] note that an entire array of data generated in urban environments, such as flight data, should be included to enable predictions about the spread of COVID-19 to facilitate an adequate and timely response to future outbreaks [Hu *et al.* (2020)].

In descriptive settings, advances have already been made in detecting COVID-19. Several researchers develop learning algorithms for the classification of computer tomographic images to identify infections. For example, the classification network suggested by Xu *et al.* [2020] achieves an overall accuracy of 86% in detecting COVID-19. Also, Li *et al.* [2020b] suggest a learning model to differentiate COVID-19 from common cases of pneumonia. The widespread application of ML algorithms could, thus, support healthcare systems by balancing out the supply shortages currently hindering the extensive use of blood-based testing. Furthermore, descriptive methods can be used to prevent the spread of fake news about apparent treatments for the disease, causes of the outbreak, and countermeasures taken [Boberg *et al.* (2020); Cinelli *et al.* (2020)]. Had such tools been available during the

COVID-19 pandemic, their holistic integration into social networks could have impeded the spread of fake news and supported countermeasures.

4.3. *Distributed ledger technology*

Due to the pandemic's global nature and many of the related problems, digital collaboration is of particular importance. On the economic level, the WHO is establishing a digital infrastructure to share pandemic-related information on a DLT-based platform and foster collaboration [Anzalone (2020)]. Moreover, the evident problems in the supply of medicines and face masks have led the WEF to suggest wider utilization of DLTs in the hope that this will increase connectivity, collaboration, and the resilience of global supply chains [AlMuhairi (2020)].

The COVID-19 pandemic has also accelerated efforts to establish SSI-based systems for use by both members of the public and companies. First, digital credentials for proving immunity as a result of past infection or vaccination might make it easier for authorities to check permissions in daily life and for physicians to check individuals' medication. For example, Bill Gates already suggested that digital credentials might play a key role but emphasized that individuals' privacy must not be compromised. SSI is particularly suitable for this task [Gates (2020)]. An industry initiative for SSI-based credentials in COVID-19 use-cases is already operating [Ledger Insights (2020)]. Second, the relevance of digital and decentralized processes has increased due to higher levels of work from home during lockdowns and quarantines. This novel working environment requires secure and convenient methods for authentication and access management, which can be delivered through SSI. Third, a credentials-based reputation and proof-of-competence architecture might be a means to combat the flood of fake news and misleading information, which can, at times, be more dangerous to individuals than the crisis or the illness itself [Laato *et al.* (2020)].

5. Implications for Research and Practice

Drawing on prior research and applications of the three EDTs during the COVID-19 pandemic, we suggest ways in which academia and practice might effectively leverage their potential.

5.1. *Leverage the IoT for data creation and increased production capabilities*

Most of the applications emerging from the IoT and convergent innovations built on top of it are not yet as commercialized as, say, digital platforms like Amazon. However, the fact that smart homes could manage households of infected people [Chatterjee *et al.* (2018)] and smart factories could operate the production of medical aids autonomously [Borgia (2014)] means that the increased maturity of the IoT could support our daily lives and provide a clear route through these times of uncertainty. For example, they could be used for temperature checking in front of restaurants, keeping distance during events, or in place of human interaction. As a result, vivid markets for relevant health data could evolve as the need for quantitative data is rising.

The IoT brings about many opportunities, for example, for data generation and supporting operations in daily life. However, one must beware of the pitfalls associated with these opportunities. Discussions about the privacy implications of collecting citizens' data on a large scale instantly arose after it was announced that contact-tracking apps were in development. Data privacy considerations led to emotive discussions, and many concerns raised are yet to be addressed [Derikx *et al.* (2016)]. This consideration is particularly relevant when regarding IoT in conjunction with AI. While IoT devices are responsible for data creation, AI allows for additional insights into the vast amount of personal data, such as the medical data of smartwatch users. While this brings great opportunities, as stated in the examples given in this paper, we also want to emphasize that health data is highly critical regarding personal privacy [Shahmiri (2016)]. As such, a meaningful balance between data exploitation and privacy is needed [Bartoletti (2019)]. In this regard, governments should also acknowledge their role as data aggregators as well as providers and build related competencies in advance so that they can make sensible decisions in how to regulate data tracking.

5.2. *Focus on foundational research on AI and interdisciplinary practice*

First, we emphasize that the availability of reliable and comprehensive data to train AI algorithms is key for its successful application. Practitioners should leverage data from a variety of sources to ensure a solid basis for training, applying, and evaluating algorithms in COVID-19-related applications. Thanks to the widespread adoption of the IoT, numerous data sources are available for training AI algorithms, including, for example, healthcare sensors in hospitals and wearables such as smartwatches. The data generated can be used to predict the further progression of the disease or to classify clinical images. As the general infrastructure required to generate necessary data is available and in use, manufacturers of smart things and systems should provide data in a standardized, tidy format to make it universally applicable. This observation aligns with Lee and Trimi [2021] who highlight that data generated can be used as an ecosystem for enabling collaborative innovation. This suggestion also applies to official authorities that act as data providers. However, various legal and regulatory challenges relating to such data processing are yet to be resolved. Additionally, the IT-based ecosystems developing around AI applications should be carefully designed to tackle potentially evolving winner-takes-all-markets [Maedche *et al.* (2019)].

Second, we observe that the majority of AI algorithms are generic. Research from academia and practice should now develop a substantial knowledge base of general AI algorithms that apply to various use-cases. For example, different training sets adapt classifiers of conventional cases of pneumonia for the detection of cases of COVID-19 pneumonia. This knowledge allows the rapid implementation of AI applications in future crises and enhances the adoption of AI in normal circumstances. Research must, therefore, increase its foundational work and develop such a holistic base of knowledge.

Concomitantly, and third, more interdisciplinary research could lead to the development of even better algorithms. Our findings suggest that future investments and research in AI should focus on interdisciplinarity. Collaborations between different research disciplines and investigating different technologies can leverage future AI applications in various industries. In addition to the fundamental knowledge of IS and data science, domain-specific expertise is necessary to increase a variety of AI applications. This is in line with Nylund *et al.* [2020] who highlight the importance of collaboration for profitability. Also, Chesbrough [2020] suggests that inside and outside knowledge flows can foster the speed of innovation, specifically in times of crisis. Therefore, research should foster interdisciplinarity to support the implementation of AI in new use-cases against future crises.

5.3. *Utilize DLT and SSI to strengthen collaboration and privacy*

Although DLT has only recently emerged, many prototypes have already been developed. However, only a few productive use-cases, often with limited functionality or participants, have been implemented. This gap has possibly emerged because DLTs do not typically increase efficiency when used in isolation but, instead, deliver value in an ecosystem. This impact may be caused by the fact that platform ecosystems are dependent on externalities like network effects. Due to the neutral character of DLTs, open ecosystems can emerge and thereby, initiate meta-organizations without central intermediaries [Kretschmer *et al.* (2020)]. To enable this process, DLT-based use-cases must be accompanied by strong standardization and require tight cooperation from development to usage. Consequently, DLT-based technologies are not suitable for solving challenges in the short term but require long-term research and development, often among competitors. Existing successful solutions such as MediLedger could be used as models for improving medical supply chains and for extending collaboration on the political level since the requirements for independence and security of businesses and governments are similar.

To use DLT and SSI's full potential, academia should combine different fields and focus on projects that are not driven by business but, rather, developed to protect the individual (e.g. SSI). In general, global collaboration and collaborations aiming to combat COVID-19 can benefit from DLT, as organizations, institutions, and countries are often in competitive relationships and benefit from a neutral platform to work on. Moreover, due to its decentralized and privacy-preserving characteristics, SSI is a promising approach to fostering digital credentials by supporting the tracking of infected and non-infected citizens' social touchpoints. It may also provide comfortable and secure identity access management in organizational and private contexts.

5.4. *Consider the convergence of technologies when designing new solutions*

The convergence of technologies — such as data used for AI algorithms stemming from IoT, or smart things acting autonomously through AI and DLT applications — is important but requires an interdisciplinary mindset. The IoT and its

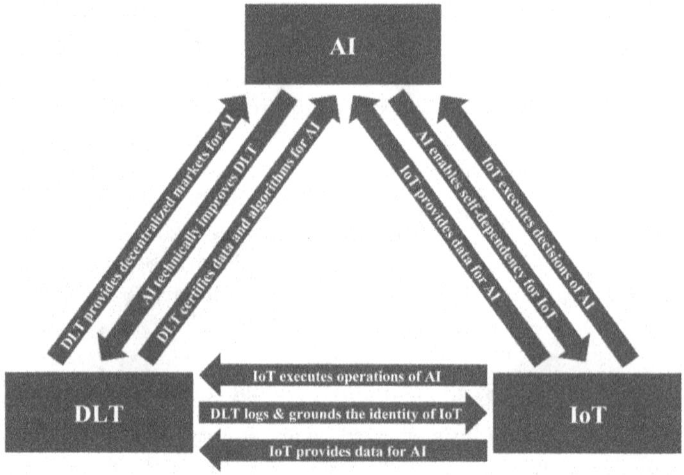

Fig. 1. Convergence of the IoT, AI, and DLT.

tremendous and autonomous data collectors bring plenty of privacy concerns that often outweigh their potential from an ethical perspective. Reconciling the hazard of privacy leaks with the opportunities at hand is a huge challenge. In their combination, EDTs could address these pitfalls and raise potentials through their mutual applicability. In specific, the approach of convergence innovation may support researchers and practitioners in identifying the potential of combining technologies that seem unrelated at first [Lee and Lim (2018)]. For example, while at first sight DLTs aggravate privacy issues in terms of medical data in almost every way, the technologies whose development is accelerated to address precisely these issues — such as ZKPs — may also help other technologies to overcome these hurdles. Figure 1 depicts the co-action of the EDTs presented. The observations during the COVID-19 pandemic motivated us to conceptualize the convergence of the three EDTs examined [Curran *et al.* (2010)]. The interplay of these technologies, grounding on their specific characteristics, is context-agnostic.

We summarize that researchers and practitioners should not just focus their efforts on one promising technology but, instead, investigate how their interplay addresses socio-economic challenges. In the light of recent observations, we suggest a visualization of the interplay of the three EDTs and invite future research to enhance our propositions, which we elucidate in the following.

Many cross-organizational processes include both physical assets and information. Hence, this relationship makes the IoT very suitable to improve processes, and accordingly, many initiatives exist in this area [Huh *et al.* (2017); Lockl *et al.* (2020)]. Smart things could thereby feed information into local databases or distributed ledgers. Furthermore, such things can ultimately execute operations that have been optimized with AI or triggered by smart contracts, allowing them to perform physical tasks. In parallel, the IoT benefits from AI applications, which increase the self-dependency of things, enabling material agency.

As a result, proactive services and systems of systems [Porter and Heppelmann (2014); Huber *et al.* (2019)] may soon become widely applicable.

Moreover, a DLT-enabled SSI reputation system might be particularly beneficial when combined with AI methods, which help distinguish fact from fiction or follow information paths through the Web. The IoT and AI could also capitalize on DLT-based documentation of the lifecycle of data, AI algorithms' evolution, and decentralized marketplaces for data and computing power. Pertinent marketplaces for health-related data implemented through DLT are already present in the field of genomics [Thiebes *et al.* (2020)]. Furthermore, DLT-based identities could provide verifiable credentials for humans and things, which can then be used to increase trust in data integrity. They could also be used as an anonymization layer to tackle data privacy issues.

AI can benefit from the integration of the IoT and DLT in various ways. Likewise, combining the three technologies offers ways to improve the security, reliability, and applicability of many applications. As AI algorithms require massive amounts of data, data generated and collected through things within the IoT can serve as a basis for improvements. In turn, AI applications for the IoT provide decision-making capabilities to things and thereby support autonomy. In the case of DLT, AI's role may be to provide technical improvements to DLTs themselves [Pandl *et al.* (2020)]. DLT can also provide the type of traceable data fundamental to the successful implementation of applications of AI.

Each of the three EDTs holds significant potential to combat both the spread and the socio-economic effects of a pandemic. In particular, the convergence of EDTs may accelerate the promises held by each EDT on its own [Dietzmann *et al.* (2020); Lee and Lim (2018)]. For example, large amounts of data can be collected using the IoT. AI algorithms can extract the most valuable information from this collected data. DLTs can enable collaboration on a joint digital platform and increase trust in data by ensuring its integrity. Consequently, practitioners are well advised to not only focus on technologies that promise immediate benefits with little effort.

5.5. *Capitalize on convergence innovation as core competence of organizations*

Following Lee and Trimi [2021], convergence innovation can be a new core competence in organizations. Core competencies are an established concept in management sciences [Prahalad and Hamel (1990)]. They provide the foundation of organizational success and are hence crucial to achieving economic success in a post-COVID-19 world. The power to innovate and, thus, the ability to adapt to changing conditions are crucial for any company. As such, also during the COVID-19 pandemic, we saw that many firms and researchers started to combine the IoT, AI, and DLT to bring forth innovations.

Consequently, we propose that the convergence of IoT, AI, and DLT is applicable in the current as well as prospective contexts. As such, we verify and expand the concept of convergence innovation of Lee and Trimi [2021]. In particular, we demonstrate how innovation can arise out of the convergence of EDTs. This demonstration again shows that the concept of convergence innovation is not static but develops over time and might also include other technologies in the future. It also holds true for the main findings of this study. While this paper shows how the three introduced technologies foster the development of new applications, we also like to point out that future emerging technologies should also be considered for convergence innovations. Furthermore, we introduce DLT as an important technology for convergence innovation. This again shows that the concept of convergence innovation is not static but develops over time and might also include other technologies in the future [Lee and Trimi (2021)]. This also holds true for the main findings of this study.

6. Suggestions for Policy

We identified the potential use of EDTs to combat the current COVID-19 pandemic and future crises. The IoT is already quite established, and AI is just on the verge of being leveraged. Utilizing DLTs is even more challenging due to the need for long-lasting collaboration, standardization, and improvements in terms of privacy and scalability. On the other hand, EDTs offer opportunities for immediate and long-term impact. In the hope of moving beyond theoretical discussions to stimulate implementation, we summarize some policy implications in the following.

6.1. *Sandbox projects*

Sandbox projects provide opportunities to develop the necessary regulatory frameworks through exploration. In a controlled environment, projects may be deployed to evaluate the need for adjustment or the introduction of regulations. This practice has proved appropriate in various instances. For example, an initiative by the German Federal Office of Refugees and Migration demonstrates how projects in a highly regulated environment can sound out EDT's potential; in the case in question, DLT. The project aims to foster consistent, cross-organizational processes that ensure data transparency and integrity [Rieger *et al.* (2019)]. All parties involved can, thereby, identify issues in their production systems. As the current crisis has shown, regulatory requirements can, in some instances, hinder the deployment of EDT. We expect that further sandbox projects will help to reveal challenges that need to be overcome before EDT is deployed to combat current and future crises.

6.2. *Fast-track amendments and revisions of statutes*

Legislators should use learnings from sandbox projects to amend policies and statutes. As sandbox projects usually deliver initial results within months, quick and unbureaucratic amendments can be enacted. Analogous to the current acceleration of processes and approvals for the development of a vaccine against COVID-19, amendments required for the use of EDT must be sped up. We identified several opportunities in the medical sector, but regulatory obstacles may inhibit efforts to put these to effective use. Hence, governments must support the application of EDT to maximize their potential. The European Payment Services Directive II, for example, aims to encourage innovation in the payment service market [Constantinides *et al.* (2018)]. Initiatives such as this allow for the emergence of innovation by non-established institutions, which policymakers should also foster in the current crisis.

6.3. *Long-term investments in fundamental and interdisciplinary research*

Currently, investment in research addressing the challenges of the pandemic is huge. However, we strongly urge that investment is maintained beyond the current crisis.

Policymakers must increase long-term investments in the research on EDT. While we identified EDT opportunities to provide ad-hoc support to medical staff, policymakers, and the wider public, more fundamental and interdisciplinary research is necessary. As those investments might not necessarily provide short-term returns, policymakers and governmental initiatives must incentivize and support such research [Laato *et al.* (2020)]. For example, several Canadian hospitals joined forces during the pandemic by launching an initiative to let teams worldwide develop cost-efficient and easily implementable designs for respiratory devices. In addition to initiatives like these, which support research unbureaucratically, larger research projects should be set up to gain long-term returns from EDT's effective use to tackle future crises. This approach should then lead to a self-sustaining market with ongoing investments.

6.4. *Fostering open innovation*

Knowledge of the application, possibilities, and limitations of EDT requires specialization and is highly scattered. Thus, using the knowledge and the skills of individuals and institutions around the world is necessary to leverage the full potential of EDT in the fight against COVID-19 in a short amount of time. The open innovation paradigm enables fast innovation [Chesbrough (2020)] and builds upon two mechanisms: inside–out and outside–in. The former refers to knowledge flows from inside organizations to external partners, while the latter addresses knowledge flows originating from individuals or other external parties to organizations. These concepts should also be leveraged in the context of COVID-19. Open innovation fostering inside–out knowledge flows could be enabled by data sharing initiatives backed by government funding, such as Zenodo, allowing researchers and practitioners to exchange data, e.g. to train AI models. Also, short-term pausing of patents may foster exploring further convergence initiatives as other parties can build upon existing inventions and innovations. In addition, outside–in innovation could be achieved through open initiatives like Kaggle competitions or hackathons. Challenges as such can allow exploring novel ideas on the convergence of the three technologies to utilize the technologies' full potential. We observe two options for fostering open innovation through policy, either through enforcement or through incentivization. Enforcement could be undertaken e.g. by state-ruled short-term suspension of patent rights. In contrast, incentivization represents less radical measures. For example, governments may subsidize open challenges and hackathons.

7. Outlook

In the long term, only the combination of multiple EDTs will address the future's unforeseen challenges. The IoT, AI, and DLT require interdisciplinary research by cryptographers, computer scientists, and engineers to develop and improve algorithms and things. Legal experts, social scientists, economists, and information systems researchers need to study the resulting implications and undesirable side-effects of applying the resultant technologies, building a decision-basis for politicians and business leaders who can push forward the implementation of initiatives.

Our observations show numerous opportunities for EDT in future crises and future research. These opportunities include, but are not limited to, the following:

- Utilize the facilities provided by the IoT for data generation and executing operations to ease daily life and keep productivity high during lockdowns.
- Closely collaborate with practice to collect and use various data sources to train and apply AI algorithms in the fight against the COVID-19 pandemic while ensuring generic applicability for future scenarios.
- Facilitate the development of data markets, allowing companies to monetize relevant health data, collected from different sources collaboratively.
- Leverage the trust-delivering nature of DLT and the privacy-preserving features of SSI to allow for the required collaboration on a global scale in difficult times and the processing of useful data without compromising the individual's privacy.
- Examine the convergence of the three EDTs to leverage potentials and solve challenges through the mutual application.

To identify further potentials for the technologies of the EDTs for future crises, researchers and practitioners should rely on paradigms like open innovation and convergence to speed up innovation processes.

Despite all adverse effects on the individual, society, and economy, the crisis also functions as a catalyst for digitalization: It provides not only a challenge but also unique opportunities. Many retailers discovered digital sales channels as a means of offering their products. Some forms of digital tools and collaboration that were hardly imaginable in the recent past are now a reality. The gained experience of digital collaboration will likely outlast this crisis and will drive future digital co-working initiatives [Giones *et al.* (2020)]. Managers and policymakers are responsible for retaining the progress made while leading us back to the new normal. In doing so, a reflected and balanced view of the potentials and risks of EDT is essential. Open innovation can support managers and policymakers in exploring these potentials and risks. In this commentary, we have provided an overview of the enormous potential that arises with these technologies' thoughtful use. At the same time, we must pay attention to the caveats and risks, especially concerning the data to be processed. To preserve citizens' privacy and autonomy, decisions about the use-cases and prerequisites are an overall societal question that must meet ethical standards. A detailed investigation of this aspect gives plenty of future research opportunities, to which IS scholars must contribute.

References

Abdel-Basset, M., Chang, V. and Nabeeh, N. A. (2021). An intelligent framework using disruptive technologies for COVID-19 analysis. *Technological Forecasting and Social Change*, **163**: 120431.

Allam, Z. and Jones, D. S. (2020). On the Coronavirus (COVID-19) outbreak and the smart city network: Universal data sharing standards coupled with artificial intelligence (AI) to benefit urban health monitoring and management. *Healthcare*, **8**, 1: 46.

AlMuhairi, M. O. (2020). Why COVID-19 makes a compelling case for the wider integration of blockchain. World Economic Forum, May 8. Available at https://www.weforum.org/agenda/2020/05/why-covid-19-makes-a-compelling-case-for-wider-integration-of-blockchain/ [accessed on 27 Mar 2021].

Alt, R. (2020a). Electronic Markets on blockchain markets. *Electronic Markets*, **30**, 2: 181–188.

Alt, R. (2020b). Evolution and perspectives of electronic markets. *Electronic Markets*, **30**, 1: 1–13.

Anzalone, R. (2020). IBM's Blockchain will support the MiPasa COVID-19 data project. *Forbes*, March 28. Available at https://www.forbes.com/sites/robertanzalone/2020/03/28/ibms-blockchain-will-support-the-mipasa-covid-19-data-project/#c316d27474f7 [accessed on 27 Mar 2021].

Aratani, L. (2020). US job losses pass 40m as coronavirus crisis sees claims rise 2.1m in a week. *The Guardian*, May 28. Available at https://www.theguardian.com/business/2020/may/28/us-job-losses-unemployment-coronavirus [accessed on 27 Mar 2021].

Athanasopoulou, A., Haaker, T. and de Reuver, M. (2018). Tooling for internet-of-things business model exploration: A design science research approach. In *Proceedings of the 26th European Conference on Information Systems*, pp. 1–11.

Atkinson, C. (2020). G20 leaders must answer to COVID-19. *Science*, **368**, 6487: 111.

Ayittey, F. K., Ayittey, M. K., Chiwero, N. B., Kamasah, J. S. and Dzuvor, C. (2020). Economic impacts of Wuhan 2019-nCoV on China and the world. *Journal of Medical Virology*, **92**, 5: 473–475.

Bai, L., Yang, D., Wang, X., Tong, L., Zhu, X., Zhong, N., Bai, C., Powell, C. A., Chen, R., Zhou, J., Song, Y., Zhou, X., Zhu, H., Han, B., Li, Q., Shi, G., Li, S., Wang, C., Qiu, Z., Zhang, Y., Xu, Y., Liu, J., Zhang, D., Wu, C., Li, J., Yu, J., Wang, J., Dong, C., Wang, Y., Wang, Q., Zhang, L., Zhang, M., Ma, X., Zhao, L., Yu, W., Xu, T., Jin, Y., Wang, X., Wang, Y., Jiang, Y., Chen, H., Xiao, K., Zhang, X., Song, Z., Zhang, Z., Wu, X., Sun, J., Shen, Y., Ye, M., Tu, C., Jiang, J., Yu, H. and Tan, F. (2020). Chinese experts' consensus on the Internet of Things-aided diagnosis and treatment of coronavirus disease 2019 (COVID-19). *Clinical eHealth*, **3**: 7–15.

Bartoletti, I. (2019). AI in healthcare: Ethical and privacy challenges. *AIME 2019: Artificial Intelligence in Medicine*, Lecture Notes in Computer Science, Vol. 11526. Springer, Cham, pp. 7–10.

Ben-Sasson, E., Bentov, I., Horesh, Y. and Riabzev, M. (2018). Scalable, transparent, and post-quantum secure computational integrity. Cryptology ePrint Archive: Report 2018/046. Available at https://eprint.iacr.org/2018/046.pdf [accessed on 27 Mar 2021].

Blasimme, A. and Vayena, E. (2020). What's next for COVID-19 apps? Governance and oversight. *Science (New York, N.Y.)*, **370**, 6518: 760–762.

Boberg, S., Quandt, T., Schatto-Eckrodt, T. and Frischlich, L. (2020). Pandemic populism: Facebook pages of alternative news media and the Corona crisis — A computational content analysis. Preprint, arXiv:2004.02566v3 [cs.SI]. Available at https://arxiv.org/abs/2004.02566 [accessed on 27 Mar 2021].

Borgia, E. (2014). The Internet of Things vision: Key features, applications and open issues. *Computer Communications*, **54**: 1–31.

Brem, A., Viardot, E. and Nylund, P. A. (2020). Implications of the Coronavirus (COVID-19) outbreak for innovation: Which technologies will improve our lives? *Technological Forecasting and Social Change*, **163**: 120451.

Camenisch, J. and Lysyanskaya, A. (2001). An efficient system for non-transferable anonymous credentials with optional anonymity revocation. *EUROCRYPT 2001: Advances in Cryptology*, ed. B.Pfitzmann, Lecture Notes in Computer Science, Vol. 2045. Springer, Berlin, pp. 93–118.

Chan, C. M., Teoh, S. Y., Yeow, A. and Pan, G. (2019). Agility in responding to disruptive digital innovation: Case study of an SME. *Information Systems Journal*, **29**, 2: 436–455.

Chatterjee, S., Byun, J., Dutta, K., Pedersen, R. U., Pottathil, A. and Xie, H. (2018). Designing an Internet-of-Things (IoT) and sensor-based in-home monitoring system for assisting diabetes patients: Iterative learning from two case studies. *European Journal of Information Systems*, **27**, 6: 670–685.

Chesbrough, H. (2020). To recover faster from Covid-19, open up: Managerial implications from an open innovation perspective. *Industrial Marketing Management*, **88**: 410–413.

Chesbrough, H. and Bogers, M. (2014). *Explicating Open Innovation: Clarifying an Emerging Paradigm for Understanding Innovation.* Oxford University Press, Oxford. Chinazzi, M., Davis, J. T., Ajelli, M., Gioannini, C., Litvinova, M., Merler, S., Piontti, A. P. y., Mu, K., Rossi, L., Sun, K., Viboud, C., Xiong, X., Yu, H., Halloran, M. E., Longini, Jr., I. M. and Vespignani, A. (2020). The effect of travel restrictions on the spread of the 2019 novel coronavirus (COVID-19) outbreak. *Science*, **368**, 6489: 395–400.

Chinazzi, Matteo, Davis, Jessica T., Ajelli, Marco, Gioannini, Corrado, Litvinova, Maria, Merler, Stefano *et al.* (2020). The effect of travel restrictions on the spread of the 2019 novel coronavirus (COVID-19) outbreak. *Science*, **368**, 395–400 (6489) DOI: 10.1126/science.aba9757.

Cinelli, M., Quattrociocchi, W., Galeazzi, A., Valensise, C. M., Brugnoli, E., Schmidt, A. L., Zola, P., Zollo, F. and Scala, A. (2020). The COVID-19 social media infodemic. Preprint, arXiv:2003.05004 [cs.SI]. Available at http://arxiv.org/pdf/2003.05004v1 [accessed on 27 Mar 2021].

Cohen, J. (2020). Second wave of coronavirus intensifies across Europe [update]. *Forbes*, October 19. Available at https://www.forbes.com/sites/joshuacohen/2020/10/19/second-wave-of-coronavirus-hits-europe-major-differences-in-impact-across-countries/?sh=3aba012f1542 [accessed on 27 Mar 2021].

Constantinides, P., Henfridsson, O. and Parker, G. G. (2018). Introduction — Platforms and infrastructures in the digital age. *Information Systems Research*, **29**, 2: 381–400.

Craven, M., Singhal, S. and Wilson, M. (2020). COVID-19: Implications for business. Executive Briefing, McKinsey & Company. Available at https://www.mckinsey.com/business-functions/risk/our-insights/covid-19-implications-for-business [accessed on 27 Mar 2021].

Curran, C.-S., Bröring, S. and Leker, J. (2010). Anticipating converging industries using publicly available data. *Technological Forecasting and Social Change*, **77**, 3: 385–395.

Cyranoski, D. (2020). 'We need to be alert': Scientists fear second coronavirus wave as China's lockdowns ease. *Nature*, March 30. doi:10.1038/d41586-020-00938-0.

Daugherty, P. (2019). Managing technology for the post-digital era. *MIT Sloan Management Review*, August 19. Available at https://sloanreview.mit.edu/article/managing-technology-for-the-post-digital-era/ [accessed on 27 Mar 2021].

Derikx, S., de Reuver, M. and Kroesen, M. (2016). Can privacy concerns for insurance of connected cars be compensated? *Electronic Markets*, **26**, 1: 73–81.

Dietzmann, C., Heines, R. and Alt, R. (2020). The convergence of distributed ledger technology and artificial intelligence: An end-to-end reference lending process for financial services. In *Proceedings of the 28th European Conference on Information Systems.*

Eurofound (2020). Living, working and COVID-19 dataset. Available at https://www.eurofound.europa.eu/data/covid-19 [accessed on 27 Mar 2021].

Fahrni, S., Jansen, C., John, M., Kasah, T., Körber, B. and Mohr, N. (2020). Coronavirus: Industrial IoT in challenging times. McKinsey & Company, April 22. Available at https://www.mckinsey.com/industries/advanced-electronics/our-insights/coronavirus-industrial-iot-in-challenging-times [accessed on 27 Mar 2021].

Fatima, S. A., Hussain, N., Balouch, A., Rustam, I., Saleem, M. and Asif, M. (2020). IoT enabled Smart Monitoring of Coronavirus empowered with Fuzzy Inference System. *International Journal of Advance Research, Ideas and Innovations in Technology*, **6**, 1: 188–194.

Fernandes, N. (2020). Economic effects of coronavirus outbreak (COVID-19) on the world economy. *SSRN Electronic Journal.* doi: 10.2139/ssrn.3557504.

Ferretti, L., Wymant, C., Kendall, M., Zhao, L., Nurtay, A., Abeler-Dörner, L., Parker, M., Bonsall, D. and Fraser, C. (2020). Quantifying SARS-CoV-2 transmission suggests epidemic control with digital contact tracing. *Science (New York, N.Y.)*, **368**, 6491: eabb6936.

Financial Times (2020). Coronavirus tracked: the latest figures as countries fight to contain the pandemic. Available at https://www.ft.com/content/a26fbf7e-48f8-11ea-aeb3-955839e06441 [accessed on 27 Mar 2021].

Fitzgerald, M., Kruschwitz, N., Bonnet, D. and Welch, M. (2014). Embracing digital technology: A new strategic imperative. *MIT Sloan Management Review*, **55**, 2: 1–12.

Fleisch, E., Sarma, S. and Thiesse, F. (2009). Preface to the focus theme section: 'Internet of things'. *Electronic Markets*, **19**, 2: 99–102.

Gates, B. (2020). 31 questions and answers about COVID-19. *GatesNotes*, March 19. Available at https://www.gatesnotes.com/Health/A-coronavirus-AMA [accessed on 27 Mar 2021].

Giones, F., Brem, A., Pollack, J. M., Michaelis, T. L., Klyver, K. and Brinckmann, J. (2020). Revising entrepreneurial action in response to exogenous shocks: Considering the COVID-19 pandemic. *Journal of Business Venturing Insights*, **14**: e00186.

Goertzel, B. and Pennachin, C. (eds.) (2007). *Artificial General Intelligence*, Cognitive Technologies. Springer-Verlag, Berlin.

Gruszczynski, L. (2020). The Covid-19 pandemic and international trade: Temporary turbulences or paradigm shift? *European Journal of Risk Regulation*, **11**, 2: 337–342.

Gupta, M., Abdelsalam, M. and Mittal, S. (2020). Enabling and enforcing social distancing measures using smart city and ITS infrastructures: A COVID-19 use case. Preprint, arXiv:2004.09246v1 [cs.CY]. Available at http://arxiv.org/pdf/2004.09246v1 [accessed on 27 Mar 2021].

Hacker, J., vom Brocke, J., Handali, J., Otto, M. and Schneider, J. (2020). Virtually in this together — how web-conferencing systems enabled a new virtual togetherness during the COVID-19 crisis. *European Journal of Information Systems*, **29**, 5: 563–584.

Hesse, M. and Teubner, T. (2020). Reputation portability — quo vadis?*Electronic Markets*, **30**, 2: 331–349.

Hsu, J. (2020). Contact tracing apps struggle to be both effective and private: Google, Apple, and governments are asking people to opt in to unproven technologies. *IEEE Spectrum: Technology, Engineering, and Science News*, September 24.

Hu, Z., Ge, Q., Li, S., Jin, L. and Xiong, M. (2020). Artificial intelligence forecasting of Covid-19 in China. Preprint, arXiv:2002.07112v2 [q-bio.OT]. Available at https://arxiv.org/pdf/2002.07112 [accessed on 27 Mar 2021].

Huang, C., *et al.*. (2020). Clinical features of patients infected with 2019 novel coronavirus in Wuhan, China. *The Lancet*, **395**, 10223: 497–506.

Huber, R. X. R., Püschel, L. C. and Röglinger, M. (2019). Capturing smart service systems: Development of a domain-specific modelling language. *Information Systems Journal*, **29**, 6: 1207–1255.

Huh, S., Cho, S. and Kim, S. (2017). Managing IoT devices using blockchain platform. In *Proceedings of the 2017 19th International Conference on Advanced Communication Technology (ICACT)*, PyeongChang, Korea, pp. 464–467.

International Monetary Fund (2021). Report for Selected Countries and Subjects. Available at https://www.imf.org/en/Publications/WEO/weo-database/2020/October/ [accessed on 27 Mar 2021].

Jason, L. A., Benton, M. C., Valentine, L., Johnson, A. and Torres-Harding, S. (2008). The economic impact of ME/CFS: Individual and societal costs. *Dynamic Medicine*, **7**: 6.

Javaid, M., Haleem, A., Vaishya, R., Bahl, S., Suman, R. and Vaish, A. (2020). Industry 4.0 technologies and their applications in fighting COVID-19 pandemic. *Diabetes & Metabolic Syndrome: Clinical Research & Reviews*, **14**, 4: 419–422.

Jiang, X., Coffee, M., Bari, A., Wang, J., Jiang, X., Huang, J., Shi, J., Dai, J., Cai, J., Zhang, T., Wu, Z., He, G. and Huang, Y. (2020). Towards an artificial intelligence framework for data-driven prediction of coronavirus clinical severity. *Computers, Materials & Continua*, **63**, 1: 537–551.

Johns Hopkins University (2021). Global cases of coronavirus COVID-19 (2019-nCoV). COVID-19 Dashboard by the Center for Systems Science and Engineering (CSSE), March 27. Available at https://gisanddata.maps.arcgis.com/apps/opsdashboard/index.html#/bda7594740fd40299423467b48e9ecf6 [accessed on 27 Mar 2021].

Keesara, S., Jonas, A. and Schulman, K. (2020). Covid-19 and health care's digital revolution. *The New England Journal of Medicine*, **382**: e82.

Khandani, A. E., Kim, A. J. and Lo, A. W. (2010). Consumer credit-risk models via machine-learning algorithms. *Journal of Banking & Finance*, **34**, 11: 2767–2787.

Kononenko, I. (2001). Machine learning for medical diagnosis: history, state of the art and perspective. *Artificial Intelligence in Medicine*, **23**, 1: 89–109.

Kretschmer, T., Leiponen, A., Schilling, M. and Vasudeva, G. (2020). Platform ecosystems as meta-organizations: Implications for platform strategies. *Strategic Management Journal*. doi: 10.1002/smj.3250.

Laato, S., Islam, A. K. M. N., Islam, M. N. and Whelan, E. (2020). What drives unverified information sharing and cyberchondria during the COVID-19 pandemic?*European Journal of Information Systems*, **29**, 3: 288–305.

Lagkas, T., Argyriou, V., Bibi, S. and Sarigiannidis, P. (2018). UAV IoT framework views and challenges: Towards protecting drones as "things". *Sensors (Basel, Switzerland)*, **18**, 11: 4015.

Ledger Insights (2020). 60 strong Self Sovereign Identity group targets COVID-19 immunity passports, credentials. April 14. Available at https://www.ledgerinsights.com/sovereign-identity-covid-19-immunity-passports-credentials/ [accessed on 27 Mar 2021].

Lee, S. M. and Lim, S. (2018). *Living Innovation: From Value Creation to the Greater Good.* Emerald Group Publishing, Bingley, UK.

Lee, S. M. and Olson, D. L. (2010). *Convergenomics: Strategic Innovation in the Convergence Era.*Gower Publishing, Ltd., Surrey, England and Burlington, VT, USA.

Lee, S. M. and Trimi, S. (2021). Convergence innovation in the digital age and in the COVID-19 pandemic crisis. *Journal of Business Research*, **123**: 14–22.

Li, X., Geng, M., Peng, Y., Meng, L. and Lu, S. (2020a). Molecular immune pathogenesis and diagnosis of COVID-19. *Journal of Pharmaceutical Analysis*, **10**, 2: 102–108.

Li, L., Qin, L., Xu, Z., Yin, Y., Wang, X., Kong, B., Bai, J., Lu, Y., Fang, Z., Song, Q., Cao, K., Liu, D., Wang, G., Xu, Q., Fang, X., Zhang, S., Xia, J. and Xia, J. (2020b). Artificial intelligence distinguishes COVID-19 from community acquired pneumonia on Chest CT. *Radiology*, **296**, 2: 200905.

Lin, S., Ma, C., Lin, R., Huang, J., Xu, R. and Yuan, A. (2020). Research on the influence of information diffusion on the transmission of the novel coronavirus (COVID-19). Preprint, medRxiv 2020.03.31.20048439. Available at https://www.medrxiv.org/content/10.1101/2020.03.31.20048439v1 [accessed on 27 Mar 2021].

Loayza, N. V. and Pennings, S. (2020). Macroeconomic policy in the time of COVID-19: A primer for developing countries. Research and Policy Briefs No. 28, World Bank, Washington, DC.

Lockl, J., Schlatt, V., Schweizer, A., Urbach, N. and Harth, N. (2020). Toward trust in Internet of Things ecosystems: Design principles for blockchain-based IoT applications. *IEEE Transactions on Engineering Management*, **67**, 4: 1256–1270.

Maedche, A., Legner, C., Benlian, A., Berger, B., Gimpel, H., Hess, T., Hinz, O., Morana, S. and Söllner, M. (2019). AI-based digital assistants. *Business & Information Systems Engineering*, **61**, 4: 535–544.

Mandviwalla, M. and Flanagan, R. (2021). Small business digital transformation in the context of the pandemic. *European Journal of Information Systems.* doi: 10.1080/0960085X.2021.1891004.

Marabelli, M., Vaast, E. and Li, J. L. (2021). Preventing the digital scars of COVID-19. *European Journal of Information Systems*, **30**, 2: 176–192.

Mashamba-Thompson, T. P. and Crayton, E. D. (2020). Blockchain and artificial intelligence technology for novel coronavirus disease-19 self-testing. *Diagnostics*, **10**, 4: 198.

Mattke, J., Hund, A., Maier, C. and Weitzel, T. (2019). How an enterprise blockchain application in the U.S. pharmaceuticals supply chain is saving lives. *MIS Quarterly Executive*, **18**, 4: 245–261.

Mirbabaie, M., Bunker, D., Stieglitz, S., Marx, J. and Ehnis, C. (2020). Social media in times of crisis: Learning from Hurricane Harvey for the coronavirus disease 2019 pandemic response. *Journal of Information Technology*, **35**, 3: 195–213.

Mühle, A., Grüner, A., Gayvoronskaya, T. and Meinel, C. (2018). A survey on essential components of a self-sovereign identity. *Computer Science Review*, **30**: 80–86.

Naidoo, R. (2020). A multi-level influence model of COVID-19 themed cybercrime. *European Journal of Information Systems*, **29**, 3: 306–321.

Noura, M., Atiquzzaman, M. and Gaedke, M. (2019). Interoperability in Internet of Things: Taxonomies and open challenges. *Mobile Networks and Applications*, **24**, 3: 796–809.

Nylund, P. A., Ferras-Hernandez, X. and Brem, A. (2020). Automating profitably together: Is there an impact of open innovation and automation on firm turnover?*Review of Managerial Science*, **14**, 1: 269–285.

Oberländer, A. M., Röglinger, M., Rosemann, M. and Kees, A. (2018). Conceptualizing business-to-thing interactions: A sociomaterial perspective on the Internet of Things. *European Journal of Information Systems*, **27**, 4: 486–502.

Pandl, K. D., Thiebes, S., Schmidt-Kraepelin, M. and Sunyaev, A. (2020). On the convergence of artificial intelligence and distributed ledger technology: A scoping review and future research agenda. *IEEE Access*, **8**: 57075–57095.

Parker, K., Minkin, R. and Bennett, J. (2020). Economic fallout from COVID-19 continues to hit lower-income Americans the hardest. Social & Demographic Trends, Pew Research Center, September 24. Available at https://www.pewsocialtrends.org/2020/09/24/economic-fallout-from-covid-19-continues-to-hit-lower-income-americans-the-hardest/ [accessed on 27 Mar 2021].

Paukstadt, U. and Becker, J. (2019). Uncovering the business value of the Internet of Things in the energy domain — a review of smart energy business models. *Electronic Markets.* doi: 10.1007/s12525-019-00381-8.

Pearce, J. M. (2020). A review of open source ventilators for COVID-19 and future pandemics. *F1000Research*, **9**: 218.

Pearl, R. (2018). Artificial intelligence in healthcare: Separating reality from hype. *Forbes*, March 13. Available at https://www.forbes.com/sites/robertpearl/2018/03/13/artificial-intelligence-in-healthcare/#697d4911d750 [accessed on 27 Mar 2021].

Peeri, N. C., Shrestha, N., Rahman, M. S., Zaki, R., Tan, Z., Bibi, S., Baghbanzadeh, M., Aghamohammadi, N., Zhang, W. and Haque, U. (2020). The SARS, MERS and novel coronavirus (COVID-19) epidemics, the newest and biggest global health threats: what lessons have we learned? *International Journal of Epidemiology*, **49**, 3: 717–726.

Porter, M. E. and Heppelmann, J. E. (2014). Spotlight on managing the Internet of Things. *Harvard Business Review*, **92**, 11: 64–88.

Prahalad, C. K. and Hamel, G. (1990). The core competence of the corporation. *Harvard Business Review*, **68**, 3: 79–91.

Püschel, L., Röglinger, M. and Brandt, R. (2020). Unblackboxing smart things: A multi-layer taxonomy and clusters of non-technical smart thing characteristics. *IEEE Transactions on Engineering Management*. doi: 10.1109/TEM.2020.2988981.

Qiu, J., Shen, B., Zhao, M., Wang, Z., Xie, B. and Xu, Y. (2020). A nationwide survey of psychological distress among Chinese people in the COVID-19 epidemic: implications and policy recommendations. *General Psychiatry*, **33**, 2: e100213.

Rai, A., Constantinides, P. and Sarker, S. (2019). Editor's comments: Next-generation digital platforms: Toward human-AI hybrids. *MIS Quarterly*, **43**, 1: iii–x.

Rao, A. S. R. S. and Vazquez, J. A. (2020). Identification of COVID-19 can be quicker through artificial intelligence framework using a mobile phone-based survey in the populations when cities/towns are under quarantine. *Infection Control and Hospital Epidemiology*, **41**, 7: 826–830.

Rieger, A., Guggenmos, F., Lockl, J., Fridgen, G. and Urbach, N. (2019). Building a blockchain application that complies with the EU general data protection regulation. *MIS Quarterly Executive*, **18**, 4: 263–279.

Riemer, K., Ciriello, R., Peter, S. and Schlagwein, D. (2020). Digital contact-tracing adoption in the COVID-19 pandemic: IT governance for collective action at the societal level. *European Journal of Information Systems*, **29**, 6: 731–745.

Robert Koch Institute (2020). Interrupt chains of infection digitally with the Corona-Warn-App. Available at https://www.rki.de/EN/Content/infections/epidemiology/outbreaks/COVID-19/CWA/CWA.html;jsessionid=D79F0CB3B98555638D28767C7F41474C.internet062 [accessed on 27 Mar 2021].

Rosemann, M. (2013). The Internet of Things: new digital capital in the hands of customers. *Business Transformation Journal*, **9**, 1: 6–15.

Rossi, M., Mueller-Bloch, C., Thatcher, J. B. and Beck, R. (2019). Blockchain research in information systems: Current trends and an inclusive future research agenda. *Journal of the Association for Information Systems*, **20**, 9: 1388–1403.

Russell, S. J. and Norvig, P. (1995). *Artificial Intelligence*. Prentice Hall, London, UK and Englewood Cliffs, NJ, USA.

Schweizer, A., Knoll, P., Urbach, N., von der Gracht, H. A. and Hardjono, T. (2020). To what extent will blockchain drive the machine economy? Perspectives from a prospective study. *IEEE Transactions on Engineering Management*, **67**, 4: 1169–1183.

Selz, D. (2020). From electronic markets to data driven insights. *Electronic Markets*, **30**, 1: 57–59.

Shahmiri, S. (2016). Wearing your data on your sleeve: Wearables, the FTC, and the privacy implications of this new technology. *Texas Review of Entertainment & Sports Law*, **18**: 25–48.

Shirish, A., Srivastava, S. C. and Chandra, S. (2021). Impact of mobile connectivity and freedom on fake news propensity during the COVID-19 pandemic: A cross-country empirical examination. *European Journal of Information Systems*. doi: 10.1080/0960085X.2021.1886614.

Shoukry, A., Khader, J. and Gani, S. (2019). Improving business process and functionality using IoT based E3-value business model. *Electronic Markets*. doi: 10.1007/s12525-019-00344-z.

Sorokowski, P., Groyecka, A., Kowal, M., Sorokowska, A., Białek, M., Lebuda, I., Dobrowolska, M., Zdybek, P. and Karwowski, M. (2020). Can information about pandemics increase negative attitudes toward foreign groups? A case of COVID-19 outbreak. *Sustainability*, **12**, 12: 4912.

Stokkink, Q. and Pouwelse, J. (2018). Deployment of a blockchain-based self-sovereign identity. In *Proceedings of the 2018 IEEE International Conference on Internet of Things (iThings), IEEE Green Computing and Communications (GreenCom), and IEEE Cyber, Physical and Social Computing (CPSCom), and IEEE Smart Data (SmartData)*. IEEE, Piscataway, pp. 1336–1342.

Szucs, T. (1999). The socio-economic burden of influenza. *The Journal of Antimicrobial Chemotherapy*, **44**, Suppl. B: 11–15.

Thiebes, S., Schlesner, M., Brors, B. and Sunyaev, A. (2020). Distributed ledger technology in genomics: A call for Europe. *European Journal of Human Genetics*, **28**, 2: 139–140.

Ting, D. S. W., Carin, L., Dzau, V. and Wong, T. Y. (2020). Digital technology and COVID-19. *Nature Medicine*, **26**, 4: 459–461.

Tucker, C. S., Behoora, I., Nembhard, H. B., Lewis, M., Sterling, N. W. and Huang, X. (2015). Machine learning classification of medication adherence in patients with movement disorders using non-wearable sensors. *Computers in Biology and Medicine*, **66**: 120–134.

Turakhia, M. P., Desai, M., Hedlin, H., Rajmane, A., Talati, N., Ferris, T., Desai, S., Nag, D., Patel, M., Kowey, P., Rumsfeld, J. S., Russo, A. M., Hills, M. T., Granger, C. B., Mahaffey, K. W. and Perez, M. V. (2019). Rationale and design of a large-scale, app-based study to identify cardiac arrhythmias using a smartwatch: The Apple Heart Study. *American Heart Journal*, **207**: 66–75.

Urbaczewski, A. and Lee, Y. J. (2020). Information technology and the pandemic: a preliminary multinational analysis of the impact of mobile tracking technology on the COVID-19 contagion control. *European Journal of Information Systems*, **29**, 4: 405–414.

Vaishya, R., Javaid, M., Khan, I. H. and Haleem, A. (2020). Artificial Intelligence (AI) applications for COVID-19 pandemic. *Diabetes & Metabolic Syndrome: Clinical Research & Reviews*, **14**, 4: 337–339.

van Bavel, J. J., Baicker, K., Boggio, P. S. and Willer, R. (2020). Using social and behavioural science to support COVID-19 pandemic response. *Nature Human Behaviour*, **4**: 460–471.

Waizenegger, L., McKenna, B., Cai, W. and Bendz, T. (2020). An affordance perspective of team collaboration and enforced working from home during COVID-19. *European Journal of Information Systems*, **29**, 4: 429–442.

Wang, C. J., Ng, C. Y. and Brook, R. H. (2020a). Response to COVID-19 in Taiwan: Big data analytics, new technology, and proactive testing. *JAMA*, **323**, 14: 1341–1342.

Wang, G., Zhang, Y., Zhao, J., Zhang, J. and Jiang, F. (2020b). Mitigate the effects of home confinement on children during the COVID-19 outbreak. *The Lancet*, **395**, 10228: 945–947.

Wang, S. and Summers, R. M. (2012). Machine learning and radiology. *Medical Image Analysis*, **16**, 5: 933–951.

Wang, S., Wan, J., Li, D. and Zhang, C. (2016). Implementing smart factory of Industrie 4.0: An outlook. *International Journal of Distributed Sensor Networks*, **12**, 1: 3159805.

Watson, R., Ives, B. and Piccoli, G. (2020). Practice-oriented research contributions in the COVID-19 forged new normal. *MIS Quarterly Executive*, **19**, 2: 5–8.

World Health Organization (2020). Coronavirus disease (COVID-19) travel advice. Available at https://www.who.int/emergencies/diseases/novel-coronavirus-2019/travel-advice [accessed on 27 Mar 2021].

Xu, X., Jiang, X., Ma, C., Du, P., Li, X., Lv, S., Yu, L., Chen, Y., Su, J. and Lang, G. (2020). Deep learning system to screen coronavirus disease 2019 pneumonia. Preprint, arXiv:2002.09334v1 [physics.med-ph]. Available at https://arxiv.org/abs/2002.09334 [accessed on 27 Mar 2021].

Zhu, N., Zhang, D., Wang, W., Li, X., Yang, B., Song, J., Zhao, X., Huang, B., Shi, W., Lu, R., Niu, P., Zhan, F., Ma, X., Wang, D., Xu, W., Wu, G., Gao, G. F. and Tan, W. (2020). A novel coronavirus from patients with pneumonia in China, 2019. *The New England Journal of Medicine*, **382**, 8: 727–733.

Biography

Tobias Guggenberger (tobias.guggenberger@fit.fraunhofer.de) is a researcher and pursuing his PhD at the Project Group Business & Information Systems Engineering of the Fraunhofer FIT. His research interest centers on distributed technologies, inter-organizational process management, and design science. He received his Master's degree in business administration.

Jannik Lockl (jannik.lockl@fim-rc.de) is a research associate and doctoral candidate at the Research Center FIM and the Fraunhofer Project Group for Business & Information Systems Engineering. His research focus is on the exploration of emerging digital technologies. Jannik is founder of several startups and is also working as a consultant on industry projects with companies like BMW, IBM, and the German Federal Office for Migration and Refugees.

Maximilian Röglinger (maximilian.roeglinger@fim-rc.de) is Professor of Information Systems and Business Process Management at the University of Bayreuth. Maximilian also serves as Deputy Academic Director of the Research Center Finance & Information Management (FIM). He works in a leading position with the Project Group Business & Information Systems Engineering of the Fraunhofer FIT. Maximilian's activities in research, teaching, and industry center around business process management, digital innovation, and customer orientation.

Vincent Schlatt (vincent.schlatt@fit.fraunhofer.de) is a researcher at the Project Group Business & Information Systems Engineering of the Fraunhofer FIT and currently pursuing his PhD in Information Systems at the FIM Research Center, University of Bayreuth. His research interests focus on decentralized technologies, such as blockchain and self-sovereign identity and design science research. He received his M.Sc. in Information Technology.

Johannes Sedlmeir (johannes.sedlmeir@fim-rc.de) is a researcher at the Project Group Business & Information Systems Engineering of the Fraunhofer FIT and currently pursuing his PhD in Information Systems at the FIM Research Center, University of Bayreuth. In his research, Mr. Sedlmeir works on the energy consumption and performance benchmarking of different blockchains, decentralized digital identities, and the application of cryptographic methods such as Zero-

Knowledge Proofs for scalability and privacy on blockchains. He received his M.Sc. in Theoretical and Mathematical Physics.

Jens-Christian Stoetzer (jens.stoetzer@uni-bayreuth.de) is a graduate student researcher at the Research Center FIM and the Fraunhofer Project Group for Business & Information Systems Engineering. His graduate studies at the University Bayreuth primarily focus on topics regarding the management and implications of emerging technologies. He has work experience in multi-national companies, inhouse consultancies of leading universal banks, and management consulting.

Nils Urbach (nils.urbach@fim-rc.de) is a Professor of Information Systems, Digital Business and Mobility at the Frankfurt University of Applied Sciences, Germany. He is also the Deputy Director of the Finance & Information Management (FIM) Research Center and the Project Group Business & Information Systems Engineering of Fraunhofer FIT. His works have been published in several international renowned journals such as the Journal of Information Technology, Journal of Strategic Information Systems, and MIS Quarterly Executive as well as in the proceedings of key international conferences.

Fabiane Völter (fabiane.voelter@fit.fraunhofer.de) is a researcher at the Project Group Business & Information Systems Engineering of the Fraunhofer FIT and currently pursuing her PhD in Information Systems at University of Bayreuth. In her research, Fabiane Völter is focusing on user-centric aspects of emergent technologies. She received her M.Sc. in Computer Science.

A Framework to Manage University–Industry Technology Transfer*

Priyanka Sharma
Department of Marketing
Indian Institute of Management Lucknow
Lucknow, Uttar Pradesh, India
priyanka@iiml.ac.in

This paper focuses on university–industry relationships, and the value in such linkages that motivates firms to choose a particular mode to acquire university-generated research output. We combined insights from literature review and 15 exploratory interviews of multiple stakeholders, and developed a framework to examine university–industry linkages. We grounded our framework on the social exchange theory (SET) and quadruple helix concept. It proposes university climate readiness (e.g. incentive system), firm climate readiness (e.g. managers' attitude toward academic research), and exchange readiness (e.g. a firm's absorptive capacity) as antecedents to science-business collaboration, coupled with environmental readiness factors (e.g. unique socio-cultural setting in developing economies) as moderating variables. The framework highlights (1) functional value (i.e. technology pricing, quality, and applicability) and (2) relational value (i.e. trust between academia and industry) in the said relationship. The framework further provides a basis for practitioners to arrive at a suitable university-developed technology transfer mode (e.g. patent licensing, research services, and research partnerships).

Keywords: Technology transfer; technology acquisition; university–industry; university climate readiness; firm climate readiness.

1. Introduction

Although the role of universities as a partner in business value creation is not a new phenomenon, the emergence of a global knowledge economy has indeed transformed university–industry (UI) partnerships into strategic alliances, going on to build strong state economies [Etzkowitz (2008); Fischer *et al.* (2021)]. In the process, it has captured increased managerial interest, as well as scholarly attention [Wallin *et al.* (2014); Kumar (2017); Moraes Silva *et al.* (2020); Perkmann *et al.* (2021)]. Largely, the industry can benefit from university research output in several ways; however, systemic issues do pose a challenge in selecting the appropriate mode of university–industry technology transfer (UITT) [Perkmann and Walsh (2007); Muscio and Vallanti (2014); Albats *et al.* (2020); Melnychuk *et al.* (2021)].

*This chapter was originally published in International Journal of Innovation and Technology Management, Vol. 19, No. 8, March 2018, published by World Scientific Publishing, Singapore. Reprinted with permission.

Although UI partnership has received significant attention from researchers in the past, there have been several gaps in terms of understanding the various modes of UI interactions [Siegel *et al.* (2003); Palmatier (2017); Compagnucci and Spigarelli (2020); Nsanzumuhire and Groot (2020); Perkmann *et al.* (2021)]. *First*, there has been a lack of a comprehensive study of technology transfer (TT) networks that encompasses all entities, along with their inter-relationships. Such a study would help in understanding the modes of acquiring new technology, which in fact, is possibly one of the most critical issues for firms [Cowan and Daim (2011); Lopes and Lussuamo (2021)]. Herein, it may be noted that extant literature has looked to address the same, albeit from the stakeholders' perspective, using the triple helix model [Etzkowitz (2008); Dalmarco *et al.* (2018)], encompassing a university [Thursby *et al.* (2001); Friedman and Silberman (2003)], the industry [Santoro and Chakrabarti (2002)], and/or the state [Mowery *et al.* (2001)]. Furthermore, most of the articles in these lines have been centered on "academic capitalism" that includes university spin-offs, its patenting policies, and revenue streams. It is important to reiterate here that any entity (e.g. university) generally operates under multiple internal and external influences (e.g. university policies, faculty orientation and state policies). Therefore, an all-inclusive framework does create a more practical value for both administrators and policymakers. Additionally, while some authors have used the prism of "academic capitalism", some others [see Geisler and Rubenstein (1989)] have examined it from "dyadic perspective". *Second*, most of the extant literature has chosen to follow the traditional triple helix model, failing thereby to encompass and amalgamate from a larger environment, which possibly would have shed light on independent existence as well as interactions between universities and industry [Etzkowitz (2008); Lopes and Lussuamo (2021)]. However, a few contemporary researchers have looked to address this issue by proposing a transition to a quadruple helix model that encompasses the government, the university, and the industry, as well as the civil society [Miller *et al.* (2016); Carayannis *et al.* (2017)]. *Third*, it may be noted that much of our understanding in this area is possibly based on the knowledge accumulated from developed economies, and thereby, the UI theory may not be universally valid. Based on this backdrop, an intriguing and relevant question does arise: how much of the existing UI theory is actually "transferable" to the context of "developing economies" without adaptation? Unfortunately, there does not seem to be any straight answer. Nevertheless, prior research has indicated that the economic status *vis-a-vis* the level of industrialization do go on to affect the formation of a UI network [Ponomariov and Toivanen (2014)]. Furthermore, by now, it has been well acknowledged both within the research community, academia, and possibly to some extent even the industry that developing economies do need to focus on state policies, sufficient university resources, and have further clarity on IP rights [Schiller (2006); Nezu (2007); Bhattacharjee (2008); Quiñones *et al.* (2020); Kanojia *et al.* (2021)]. India, being one of the fastest growing developing economies for instance, while choosing to capitalize on its mettle of academic research, has been focusing on being an emerging leader in biotech, medical equipment, and ICT. But, unfortunately it has not been able to translate the same into widespread success [Watkins *et al.* (2015)], primarily owing to laxities in both policymaking and implementation. To be fair, there has been a steady increase in the number of articles on TT in the context of emerging economies [see Wong and Salmin (2016); Wickramasinghe and Malik (2018); Puffal *et al.* (2020). However, most of these studies have failed at capturing their unique socio-cultural setting. Thus, there is a dire necessity to re-assess and enhance the existing theories to envisage TT initiatives [Yadav (2010)].

To address the gaps above, this study looks to present a comprehensive model of university-based technology acquisition mode choice of industrial firms. Specifically, (1) it extends the SET to account for various participating entities, and elaborates upon both the relational and functional values in such linkages [Emerson (1976)]. (2) It proposes a typology of factors (i.e. university climate readiness, firm climate readiness, and exchange readiness) that affect linkage characteristics. (3) It highlights the moderating role of environmental readiness on UI interactions (factors attributed to developing economies) and (4) identifies a classification scheme of UITT mode choice, based on contingent linkage characteristics. In brief, this paper attempts at going beyond existing literature by providing a blueprint for actors to align their resources, management practices, and organizational structures to foster strong science-business collaboration [Hsu *et al.* (2015); Compagnucci and Spigarelli (2020)].

2. Methodology

2.1. *Literature review*

Following Webster and Watson's [2002] study, we begin with a systematic literature review of university-originated TT as a prominent research mode in this domain [Pattnaik and Pandey (2016); Figueiredo and Fernandes (2021)]. Adopting the methodology of Tranfield *et al.* [2003], while using relevant keywords (i.e. TT, UI linkages, barriers to technology commercialization, etc.), we searched for relevant articles in four databases that include Emerald Insight, EBSCO, JSTOR, and ScienceDirect. We analyzed 155 research papers (from 1966 to 2021) that discussed the mechanisms and barriers/drivers of UITT. Figure 1 shows a distribution pattern of the key journals that were referenced.

2.2. *In-depth interviews*

Since the primary aim of this research includes "theory development", we also conducted a purposive or theoretical sampling [Glaser and Strauss (1967)] of 15 respondents who have been associated with a premier national-level technology institute in India. We adopted this procedure, because a small sample of well-informed subjects is better than larger ones covering minimally involved subjects [Harper (2001)]. The premier public institute (established in the late 1950s) was chosen due to: first, its innovation and incubation center, which helped in commercializing various technologies, since its inception in 2000. Second, we considered the accessibility and willingness of the respondents to participate in this study. The profile of the 15 respondents are as follows: the dean of research and development (R&D), one senior office-bearer and TTO consultant, followed by the TTO head, five faculty

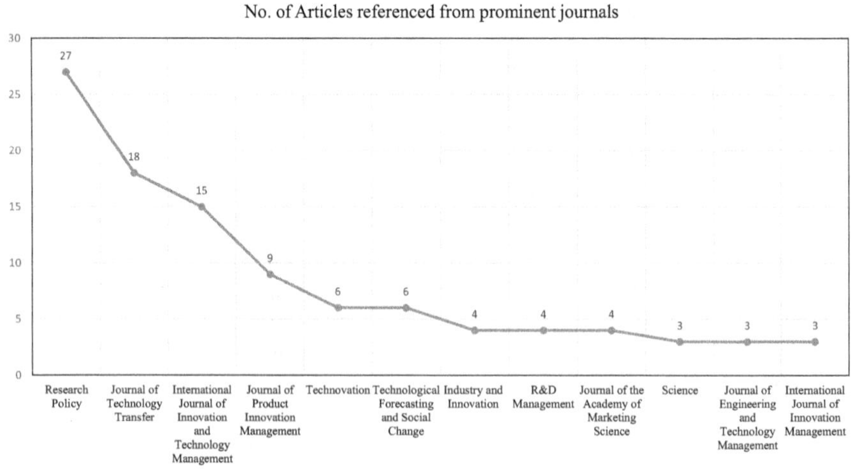

Fig. 1. Distribution of key journals referenced in the study.

scientists, four entrepreneurs, and two senior directors from the industry. We believe that this composition does contain a balanced representation of both the academia and the industry. Notably, the five faculty scientists that were chosen belong to the R&D office; they had the most patents under them and also had commercialization experience. From the incubation center, we selected the four most successful entrepreneurs. The two senior directors belong to the public sector unit (PSU) and have intensively promoted research collaboration with Indian universities. Notably, the interviews with these 15 participants included open-ended questions (see Appendix A) as prescribed for such research [Miles and Huberman (1994)]. In fact, the questions were modified to suit the specific roles of the respondents. Additionally, in order to ensure quality, we informed all the respondents about the aim of our study and assured them of complete anonymity and confidentiality. Each interview lasted for about 1–1.5 hours and was audio-recorded and manually transcribed verbatim. Post-transcription, we sent back the content to the respondents to avoid any biases. Inspired by the method by Kohli and Jaworski [1990] to understand market orientation, three of us analyzed the results of both literature review and expert surveys to construct a holistic framework, encompassing the research propositions on science-industry links.

3. Conceptual Framework

Four possible flows may be visualized between the universities and the industry (Fig. 2). Herein, it is relevant to reiterate that we dealt with "cell 3" that includes the transfer of university-developed intellectual property (IP, e.g. knowledge, inventions, and prototypes) to private firms or publicly-owned commercialization agencies for both business and social benefits [Markman *et al.* (2005)]. It may also be added that technology sourcing could be a strategic decision considering firm

		Origin of Technology (i.e., transferor)	
		University	**Industry**
Recipient of Technology (i.e., transferee)	**University**	**Cell #1**: University to University (Bozeman and Corley 2004)	**Cell #2**: Industry to University (Thurston and Eckelman 2011)
	Industry	**Cell #3**: University to Industry (Etzkowitz 2008)	**Cell #4**: Industry to Industry (Hagedoorn 2002)

Fig. 2. Possible combinations of TT between the university and the industry.

performance and market timing [Brem *et al.* (2014)]. Additionally, commercialization of university-developed technologies to native industries promotes regional economic development and leveraging domestic capabilities in science and technology is the key for development of emerging economies [Ponomariov and Toivanen (2014)]. Therefore, an inquiry in this domain becomes critical for multiple reasons.

The industry at large can and does collaborate with universities through various modes [Perkmann and Walsh (2007); D'Este *et al.* (2019)]. However, different institutional norms governing public/private knowledge and organizational structures, do lead to divergent research goals and orientation toward commercialization of technology *per se* [Bruneel *et al.* (2010); Hamadi *et al.* (2018); Hou *et al.* (2019); Schaeffer *et al.* (2021)]. Table 1 summarizes some prominent prior studies.

As identified earlier, most previous works in extant literature did seem to be devoid of a clear and concise taxonomy of factors looking to assess the maturity of stakeholders and develop UI linkages, whereby a sound theoretical underpinning and an ability to predict different modes are needed to acquire university-developed technology. Thus, to advance research in this domain, this study bases itself on the quadruple helix concept, coupled with the SET [Lawler and Thye (1999)]. SET in effect, states that for any exchange/interaction, two or more actors must offer something of value to another, while being free. Importantly, they must have the capacity to engage with one another [Lawler (2001)]. Importantly, SET has been used for decades to explain UI relationships [Santoro and Bierly (2006); Plewa *et al.* (2013)], and thus, is extremely pertinent for this study.

The triple helix model involving relationships among the university, the industry, and the government has gained prominence for both academia and policymakers to fuel local collaborations and regional development [Etzkowitz and Leydesdorff (1995, 2000); Carayannis and Campbell (2010); Leydesdorff *et al.* (2014)]. Such networks specifically focus on "tri-lateral networks and hybrid organizations" at the intersection of those helices [Carayannis *et al.* (2018), p. 150]. Triple helix is a prominent model for innovation as a result of knowledge produced through the universities (higher education), the industries (economy), and the governments (multilevel). It has been conceptualized within a broader quadruple helix innovation model (i.e. government, university, industry, and civil society)

Table 1. Prominent studies on UIT.

Authors	Sample	Method	Perspective				Context		Main focus/Results	Theoretical underpinning
			Uni.	Ind.	State	Society	Developed economy	Developing economy		
Lincoln [1966]	Health Division, Oak Ridge National Laboratory	Empirical	X	X			X		UI cooperative research to give technical consultancy to in-plant personnel	—
Roy [1972]	US university administrators	Conceptual	X				X		Mixed responses from universities on UITT. Funding for universities with proven track record and favorable administrative and reward structure	—
Blumenthal *et al.* [1986]	1200 faculty, 40 US universities	Empirical	X				X		University challenge: to preserve benefits and minimize risks	—
Geisler and Rubenstein [1989]	Literature review	Conceptual	X	X					Barriers: differences in mission/objectives, organizational structure, researcher orientation, costs	—
Gerwin *et al.* [1992]	16 professors, 7 administrators, US universities	Conceptual	X	X	X		X		Identified professors, liaison office, firms barriers	—
Meyer-Krahmer and Schmoch. [1998]	433 professors, German universities	Empirical	X				X		UITT driver: funding. Different technological fields, different interaction pattern	National systems of innovation and leap-frogging model.
Mora Valentin [2000]	Literature review	Conceptual	X	X					Barriers: research topic, knowledge appropriation, communication, culture and contract terms.	—
Siegel *et al.* [2003]	98 stakeholders, 5 US universities	Conceptual	X				X		Barriers: Different stakeholder perspectives, culture, bureaucracy, inflexible reward systems, and ineffective TTOs	—
Siegel *et al.* [2004]	98 stakeholders, 5 US universities	Conceptual	X				X		Barriers: cultural and informational divide, inadequate TTO and faculty rewards	—
Link and Siegel [2005]	TTO directors, 113 US universities	Empirical	X				X		Universities with higher royalty paid to faculty have efficient UITT	—
Santoro and Bierly [2006]	Senior executives, 173 US firms	Empirical	X				X		Drivers: social connectedness, trust, IP policies, technological relatedness	Knowledge-based view of firm
D'Este and Patel [2007]	Large-scale survey of UK researchers	Empirical	X				X		Individual researcher characteristics more important than department characteristics	"Technology integration" in knowledge management
Perkmann and Walsh [2007]	Literature review	Conceptual	X						Framework of UITT channels with differences across industries and scientific disciplines	—
Sherwood and Covin [2008]	104 industry managers	Empirical		X			X		Driver: partner trust, familiarity and communications	Situated learning theory
Breznitz *et al.* [2008]	MIT and Yale University's spin-offs	Conceptual	X				X		Low support-low selectivity policies suit entrepreneurially developed environments	—
Van Burg *et al.* [2008]	Dutch university spin-offs	Conceptual	X				X		Guidelines to build capacity to create spin-offs	Science-based design

Table 1. (*Continued*)

Authors	Sample	Method	Perspective				Context		Main focus/Results	Theoretical underpinning
			Uni.	Ind.	State	Society	Developed economy	Developing economy		
Bekkers and Freitas [2008]	575 Dutch university, 454 industry researchers	Empirical	X				X		Importance of UITT depends on discipline and characteristics of knowledge/researcher/institution	—
Barbolla and Corredera [2009]	30 Spain university researchers	Conceptual		X			X		Drivers: company's interest, absorptive capacity, attitude towards university	—
Leahy and Lane [2010]	Literature review/author's experience	Conceptual	X	X					Identified barriers according to product life cycle	Product development process
Bruneel *et al.* [2010]	3431 individuals, UK firms	Empirical	X	X			X		Orientation and Transaction related barriers	—
Perkmann *et al.* [2011]	Literature review	Conceptual	X						UITT performance measurement system	—
Ahrweiler *et al.* [2011]	European pharmaceutical industry	Empirical		X			X		UI links facilitate innovation diffusion networks	Innovation economics and economic sociology
Tartari *et al.* [2012]	1544 individuals, 70 UK universities	Empirical	X				X		Orientation and transactional barriers	—
Perkmann *et al.* [2013]	Literature review	Conceptual	X						Suggests antecedents and consequences of academic engagement and commercialization	—
Schofield [2013]	33 stakholders	Empirical	X	X	X			X	7 groups of UITT barriers	—
Burg *et al.* [2013]	26 entrepreneurs exploiting university inventions	Conceptual		X			X		Discusses established and specific fairness entrepreneurial rules	—
Audretsch *et al.* [2014]	Special issue on TT	Conceptual	X	X	X				Summarizes key themes of Technology Transfer Society, 2011 annual conference	—
Schoen *et al.* [2014]	16 European universities	Conceptual	X				X		A typology of 4 TTO models	—
Libaers [2014]	Scientists, 150 US universities	Empirical	X				X		Lower odds for firms to approach foreign-born scientists	Status characteristics theory
Hsu *et al.* [2015]	12 specialists, 12 directors, Taiwan university technology units	Empirical	X				X		Drivers: human capital, institutional, cultural resources	—
Bstieler *et al.* [2015]	105 projects, US biotechnology industry	Empirical	X	X			X		Barrier: IP rights	—
De Fuentes and Dutrénit [2016]	325 innovative firms, Mexico	Empirical		X				X	Driver: firm's absorptive capacity; dependence on non-local universities for codified knowledge	—
Wirsich *et al.* [2016]	318 technology-companies	Empirical		X				X	UI collaboration affects technological newness	—
Kumar [2017]	2 centers of excellence, University of Connecticut, Georgia State University	Conceptual	X					X	Successful research center drivers: structure, people, process, dashboard metrics, financial support	—
Lilien [2017]	Institute for the Study of Business Markets	Conceptual	X	X			—	—	Academics and practitioners have differing assets and needs	—

Table 1. (*Continued*)

Authors	Sample	Method	Perspective: Uni.	Ind.	State	Society	Context: Developed economy	Developing economy	Main focus/Results	Theoretical underpinning
Villani *et al.* [2017]	9 intermediary firms facilitating UITT in Italy	Conceptual	X	X			X		TTOs aim to improve cognitive and organizational proximity	—
Rajalo and Vadi [2017]	12 cases having R&D contracts between enterprises and University of Tartu	Empirical	X	X			X		Appropriate partner selection means matching the levels of institutional motivation and absorptive capacity between partners	Semiotic model of interaction and the boundary-crossing concept from organizational theory.
Crescenzi *et al.* [2017]	Italian inventors over the 1978–2007 period	Empirical	X	X			X		Geographical proximity is an important facilitator in UI collaboration	—
Gulbrandsen and Thune [2017]	4400 survey responses from academic employees in Norwegian universities	Empirical	X				X		External interaction is positively influenced by non-academic work experience, in line with prior research	—
Sengupta and Ray [2017]	Higher Education Business and Community Interaction surveys in UK	Empirical	X				X		Effect of organizational size and reputation on the link between past research and knowledge transfer. Contract research provides maximum benefit to universities.	Ambidexterity involving exploration and exploitation
Albats *et al.* [2018]	UI collaborative projects in Finland and Russia	Conceptual	X	X			X		KPIs: e.g. resources allocated by partners to collaboration; efficiency of collaboration management and role clarity	Collaboration lifecycle given by Brown *et al.* [1988] and Perkmann *et al.* [2011]
Fischer *et al.* [2018]	462 knowledge-intensive entrepreneurial projects in Brazil and patenting of 126 universities	Empirical	X					X	Divide UIC according to openness, UIC levels and objects of collaboration	—
Ryan *et al.* [2018]	Centres for Science, Engineering and Technology, Ireland	Conceptual	X				X		University collaboration spawns firm-level capabilities for exploratory innovation	Triple Helix Model
Dalmarco *et al.* [2018]	Managers of business incubators and incubated entrepreneurs in Brazil	Conceptual	X					X	A framework to study academic entrepreneurship in Brazil	Triple Helix Model
D'Este *et al.* [2019]	Survey of scientists in CSIC in Spain	Empirical	X				X		Identify four modes of UI interaction. Interdisciplinarity is prominent for to market-based interaction mechanisms	—
Skute *et al.* [2019]	Papers published from 2011 to 2016	Conceptual							Bibliometric analysis	
Suh *et al.* [2019]	Korea	Empirical	X	X			X		Framework to analyze satisfaction with UI cooperation programs.	KANO model
Bellini *et al.* [2019]	SMEs in Italy in ICT sector	Empirical		X			X		Importance of trust and collaborative know-how	—
Sheriff and Muffatto [2019]	Literature review	Conceptual	X						Factors affecting university spin-offs, e.g. national IP, local entrepreneurship ecosystems	—

Table 1. *(Continued)*

Authors	Sample	Method	Perspective				Context		Main focus/Results	Theoretical underpinning
			Uni.	Ind.	State	Society	Developed economy	Developing economy		
Mõttus *et al.* [2019]	Academic staff in Estonian public universities	Empirical	X				X		Science as primary field, large number of publications affect entrepreneurship	
Albats *et al.* [2020]	Firms of different sizes, in different regions and industries, and engaged in UI collaboration for innovation	Conceptual		X					Companies require specific human capital. Effect of university operational characteristics and identifying barriers	—
Tang *et al.* [2020]	Chinese firms	Empirical	X	X			X		Relationships of university proximity and research quality with the product innovation performance	—
Compagnucci and Spigarelli [2020]	144 journal articles	Conceptual	X	X	X				Systematic literature review	—
Nsanzumuhire and Groot [2020]	68 publications	Conceptual	X						Systematic literature review	—
Quiñones *et al.* [2020]	Public university in Philippines	Empirical	X					X	Identify barriers to UITT, e.g. time constraints, theoretical research, high costs of managing research projects, bureaucracy	—
Tavella and Bogers [2020]	Scandinavian university faculty	Conceptual	X				X		Identify individual-level barriers to UITT among faculty	—
Perkmann *et al.* [2021]	Publications from 2011 to 2019.	Conceptual	X	X					Systematic literature review	—
Melnychuk *et al.* [2021]	Panel data set of 56 global pharmaceutical firms	Empirical		X					Studies the role of firm's capabilities in university knowledge integration in a firm's internal R&D	Knowledge-based view and absorptive capacity
Fischer *et al.* [2021]	University in Brazil	Conceptual	X					X	Internal capabilities of universities to foster frugal innovations	—
Schaeffer *et al.* [2021]	Universities in Brazil	Conceptual	X	X	X			X	Explains interrelation between universities and eco-system actors	—
Kanojia *et al.* [2021]	318 respondents from India	Empirical	X	X				X	Identify critical factors for UITT	—
Abd Rahim *et al.* [2021]	115 academic entrepreneurs in Malaysia	Empirical	X	X				X	Academics' opportunity recognition and social capital are critical for academic entrepreneurship performance	Self-regulated learning and social capital theory
This research	Literature review of 152 papers, 15 in-depth expert interviews	Conceptual	X	X	X	X		X	A comprehensive typology of factors to develop UI linkages and predict UITT mode choice of firms	SET and quadruple helix

[Carayannis and Campbell (2010); Carayannis and Rakhmatullin (2014)]. There are two types of relationships that support various mechanisms in the triple helix model. They include collaboration and conflict moderation (e.g. R&D, consulting, developing new markets, TT, incubation, and financing) and substitution (taking on the role of each other when the other sphere is weak) [Carayannis and Rakhmatullin (2014); Carayannis *et al.* (2018)]. Further, the triple helix model conceptualizes two approaches to knowledge production; "Mode 1" considers university-based knowledge production as a linear model of innovation. "Mode 2" emphasizes upon non-linear knowledge application and knowledge-based problem solving [Carayannis *et al.* (2017)]. In fact, Carayannis and Campbell [2009] even proposed "Mode 3", which should incorporate the civil society into the framework to form a quadruple helix innovation system framework. Galvao *et al.* [2019] stated that the triple helix model helps in understanding how the linkages between the university, the industry, and the government go on to develop "a dynamic of self-reinforcement for innovation, knowledge, and economic development". Some of the concepts associated with the triple helix model include academic entrepreneurship, TT and university profits, UI collaboration, and innovation [Meyer (2003); Frenken *et al.* (2005); De Fuentes and Dutrénit (2016)]. Although, greater participation from multiple triple helix agents increases the likelihood of business innovation [Hernández-Trasobares and Murillo-Luna (2020)], there are several challenges to such participation. Galvao *et al.* [2019, p. 828] stated: "few studies have examined the barriers to cooperation between universities and industries from the academic researchers" which needs further elaboration from the perspective of various stakeholders in the TT process. Furthermore, Zhang *et al.* [2020] have called for studies to take into account (1) the situational conditions, especially the institutional context in emerging economies and (2) the implications of quadruple helix linkages in managing industry–university research alliances. We look to address these literature gaps and build on the triple/quadruple helix model by considering specificities of all stakeholders that include the university, the industry, the government, and the larger society to foster robust knowledge economies.

4. Description of Variables

4.1. *Dependent variables*

4.1.1. *Linkage characteristics*

Researchers in the past have defined UI linkages as bi-directional linkages between university and industry to create mutual value over time [Plewa and Quester (2007); Ryan *et al.* (2018)]. Thus, grounded on SET, the linkage characteristics entail both social and structural aspects, measured as: (1) functional value, comprising of economic, strategic, and technological benefits derived by exchange parties. (2) Relational value, including empathy, liking, structural ties, governance, and institutionalization of norms [Smith (1998)]. Notably, existing literature thus far has primarily focused on the relational involvement [Perkmann and Walsh (2007); Villani *et al.* (2017)]. However, in contrast, our interviews with the 15 participants revealed that both relational and functional merits are required for UI collaboration. Importantly, while relational values allow managers to lower their overall research costs by developing long-term partnerships with academia, functional values help in ascertaining both the viability and utility of academic research output with respect to cost estimations [Sheriff and Muffatto (2019); Quiñones *et al.* (2020)]. For example, an overestimated value of university-generated IP does lead to payment and licensing issues [Bruneel *et al.* (2010)].

4.1.2. *Modes of UITT*

Based on our literature review, the four broad modes include patent licensing, research services, collaborative research venture, and research papers [Perkmann and Walsh (2007); Perkmann *et al.* (2013); D'Este *et al.* (2019)]. Specifically, "*patent licensing*" for instance, involves licensing a university-developed technology to industry [Fischer *et al.* (2018)]. The Bayh-Dole Act in 1980 empowered US universities to retain their title and license inventions resulting from federal-sponsored research [Thursby *et al.* (2001)]. Generally, once TTO becomes aware of an invention *per se*, it evaluates the commercial value of the invention, and files for a global/domestic patent [Friedman and Silberman (2003)]. Once patented, the technology is appropriately marketed and licensed to the industry. *Research services*, on the other hand, include contract research or consulting. Contract research is done by universities under the direction of clients from the industry, while academic consulting refers to advice and expertise provided by individuals or a small group of industry professionals for personal compensation in order to commercialize inventions and/or generate additional research opportunities [Meyer-Krahmer and Schmoch. (1998); Sengupta and Ray (2017); Rajalo and Vadi (2017)]. For instance, in the steel industry, the former mode (i.e. contract research) is more important. Under a *collaborative research venture*, both universities and industries collaborate to pursue joint research objectives [Hall *et al.* (2001)]. However, this is not as widely adopted as IP, as ownership issues do arise, often going on to become intense, especially when the research is of relatively short duration and is expected to end in less appropriable results. Lastly, *papers and conferences* are channels of open science that include reports, publications, public forums, conferences, and informal interactions [Cohen *et al.* (2002)]. Importantly, they are the least resource intensive, as compared to the other modes.

4.2. *Independent Variables*

4.2.1. *University climate readiness*

Organizational climate represents the perception of work situations, organizational characteristics, and the nature of relationships among employees. It shapes an individual's innovative behavior in effect [Churchill *et al.* (1976); Sengupta and Ray (2017); Quiñones *et al.* (2020)]. Thus, we define "university climate" as policies, characteristics, and routines that go on to shape its orientation toward technology commercialization. While we define "university climate readiness" as the degree to which a university is effectively prepared to carry out TT from labs to the industry at large. Notably, the general use of "readiness" does indicate a state of being that is both psychologically and behaviorally prepared to take action [Weiner (2009)]. Researchers in the past have suggested two dimensions of university climate readiness that include structural support and transferor attitude. Structural support refers to strategy, reward systems, organizational structure, business processes, and lateral links within the university [Galbraith (1995); Rao and Mulloth (2017); Albats *et al.* (2018)]. Transferor attitude focuses on the actors, specifically referring to their motivation and interest, informal networks, and the availability of a knowledge pool to conduct research that is commercially viable [Gulbrandsen and Thune (2017); Tavella and Bogers (2020)]. Interestingly, the respondents of our study stated that the faculty sees patent licensing as futile, negating thereby the interest of the industry clients.

4.2.2. *Firm climate readiness*

Extending the theory of organizational climate, "firm climate readiness" alludes to the degree to which a firm is prepared to support collaboration and acquisition of university-developed technology. Our in-depth interviews set two major dimensions of this factor: structural support and transferee attitude. Importantly, while the former relates to structural aspects (e.g. bureaucracy, long turnaround time, and reward system for innovation), the latter (as highlighted in discussions with the faculty and the TTO head) refers to managers' attitudes toward the faculty, *vis-a-vis* its applicability in academic research [van Den Berghe and Guild (2007); Albats *et al.* (2020); Melnychuk *et al.* (2021)].

4.2.3. *Exchange readiness*

Exchange readiness is a dyadic concept and encompasses: (1) the appropriateness of university technology, prototypes, skills, procedures, and documents and (2) the learning capability of the recipient firm. Importantly, TT is successful only if the manager receiving the knowledge can effectively reproduce the same/similar results and/or builds a lab-scale prototype at the level of quality agreed upon. It may also be noted that the universities' market orientation essentially drives them to conduct valuable research for the industry [Kohli and Jaworski (1990)], whereby "absorptive capacity" is critical to acquire the technology *per se* [Cohen and Levinthal (1990); Rajalo and Vadi (2017)]. Thus, based on our in-depth interviews and literature review, we posit that exchange readiness includes university-market orientation, along with a firm's absorptive capacity.

4.3. *Moderating Variables*

4.3.1. *Economic infrastructure*

Importantly, both political and economic infrastructures do influence technological developments of a region [Leydesdorff and Etzkowitz (1996); Sheriff and Muffatto

(2019); Compagnucci and Spigarelli (2020)]. One should note herein that national innovation systems are generally centered on knowledge infrastructure, which in turn, forms a key component of an economic infrastructure [Smith (1997)]. Needless to say that poor infrastructure is detrimental to technological competitiveness and the firms' capabilities, as it limits their access to information and hampers their ability to absorb and assimilate technologies. Thus, we posit that analysis of UI linkages should focus primarily on economic infrastructure.

4.3.2. *Societal mindset*

Societal mindset refers to the common mental attitude or disposition of a society that predetermines the understanding of and responses toward a given situation. For instance, while explaining the failure of the US administration to turn invention into innovation, Smil [2013] stressed upon a societal mindset, besides investments, institutional frameworks, and policies. Under the Indian context for instance, the cultural dimensions do suggest that Indians generally do not seem to be motivated to take action-initiatives, and tend to be content thereby with long-established rules and routines [Hofstede (2001)]. However, technology commercialization does involve risks for both faculty and the industry at large. Thus, under the aegis of an equilibrium framework under uncertainty, "risk aversion" goes on to explain who would effectively become entrepreneurs, vis-a-vis work as laborers, assuming that all potential entrepreneurs are equally able and competent [Kihlstrom and Laffont (1979)]. Briefly, this alludes to the fact that less risk-averse individuals are more likely to engage in TT as compared to others.

4.3.3. *State policy relevance*

Government programs do encourage closer links between public sector research and private sector expectations [Dezhina (2018); Chen *et al.* (2019)]. In transition economies, it helps to create breakthroughs in UI collaboration networks toward more sophisticated types of alliances [Inzelt (2004); Kanojia *et al.* (2021)]. Whether Bayh-Dole in the United States or the federal policies in Canada [Rasmussen (2008)], the state policies almost always have encouraged universities to exercise IP rights on their research and appropriate its value for a greater cause by partnering with the industry. Thus, under the triple helix model, the state, the academia, and the industry work are in an inter-woven fashion to build strong state economies [Mowery *et al.* (2001)].

5. Development of Propositions

5.1. *University climate readiness and UI linkage characteristics*

5.1.1. *Structural support*

Different work cultures from corporations and institutional bureaucracy negatively affect the development of external linkages in universities [Fontana *et al.* (2006)].

As stated by the dean of R&D: "*We live in a paradigm where one research paper in leading journal is valued more than a commercially successful product... Having patents is not a yardstick to appraise faculty...*".

Further, the respondents revealed that the existing incentive structure in India (way of promotions and increments in salary) encourages a faculty to set up research labs. However, there is no mechanism to measure their utilization. So, most labs fail to meet the intended objectives in the long run. Our field study also confirms that TTO has no clear policy guidelines and metrics to evaluate staff performance. Thus, a lack of accountability does discourage the faculty from discussing commercialization possibilities because TTOs aim to improve cognitive and organizational proximities [Villani *et al.* (2017)].

Although strong structural support is needed to develop UI engagement, some scholars in the past argued that too much incentive for commercialization would promote solving only industrial problems and would hurt basic research thereof. However, it would lay the foundation for applied research [Gluck *et al.* (1987)]. Industry–university research centers affect teaching and restrict the dissemination of research findings with an aim to improve industrial products and processes [Adams *et al.* (2001)]. The following are some quotes from our participants highlighting the points as discussed thus far.

P1: *The greater the structural support in a university, the higher the relational value in UI linkages.*

P2: *The relationship between the structural support in a university and the functional value in UI linkages will be curvilinear such that the slope will be positive for lower levels of structural support and then become negative at higher levels of structural support.*

5.1.2. *Transferor attitude toward TT*

Further, from our interviews, the TTO consultant reaffirmed that the faculty are not motivated to commit time for an entrepreneurial step, and therefore, they are pretty reluctant to train licensees [Yusuf (2008); Tavella and Bogers (2020)]. They'd rather prefer to publish papers in leading international journals, while working on research trends that are followed in the United States/Europe, which in turn are naturally isolated from local issues. But UITT scientists must know the local industry needs and regulatory compliances, and must thereby proactively search for existing technologies and patents, while leveraging upon them to develop marketable products [Leahy and Lane (2010)].

Additionally, even if a faculty knows the industrial setup, firms believe that the scientific knowledge is often too generic, and universities carry a small patent portfolio [Lipinski *et al.* (2008); Gilsing *et al.* (2011); Quiñones *et al.* (2020)]. One of our interviewees stated that a few faculty members showed antipathy toward commercialization: "*There is little focus by faculty to develop saleable technologies. People mostly contribute to theoretical development of their field and if one develops something in the lab he stops at that stage.*"

Furthermore, the industry at large looks for full research/product documentation. However, a common theme across our interviews with TTO consultants, directors, and entrepreneurs revealed that faculties do tend to show little discipline in documenting such details. Also, due to varying domain expertise, a faculty works as a standalone unit, which essentially negates prototype development that could possibly be commercially viable. Moreover, it may be noted that except in the case of individual consulting, the administration/TTO staff of an institute is effectively responsible for maintaining industry relations. Hence, an inventor attitude would not actually affect the relational value, but rather the research output. The observations from our participants summarize these points (as below).

P3: *The greater the positive attitude of transferor toward TT, the higher the functional value in UI linkages.*

5.2. *Firm climate readiness and UI linkage characteristics*

5.2.1. *Structural support*

Hierarchical structure and organizational processes affect technology investments [Hitt *et al.* (1998); Leahy and Lane (2010); Rajalo and Vadi (2017); Suh *et al.* (2019)]. In India, partnering with PSUs is a major concern for faculties, as PSUs are highly bureaucratic (compared to private firms), lack consistent vision, and have long approval cycles. An interviewee (faculty member) summarized the same: "*We finished the project on time and sent several review requests to the PSU, but every time they replied that they were busy. Finally, they visited after 4 years and just asked to ship it without any demonstration/discussion. This de-motivates us to collaborate further.*"

Industrial funding provides for the remuneration of research staff and the purchase of equipment, raw materials, etc. However, often there are unpredictable changes in funding procedures that effectively delay the projects [Bogler (1999)]. This was highlighted by a faculty member: "*Industries do not reveal their financial strength, and the payment terms are strictly based on their turnover/profits. This blocks the money and places the financial burden on the faculty.*"

Further, inappropriate legal and strategic regulations for firms' R&D efforts deter them from acquiring external technology [Arbussa and Coenders (2007)]. Our participants noted:

P4: *The greater the structural support in a firm, the higher the relational value in UI linkages.*
P5: *The greater the structural support in a firm, the higher the functional value in UI linkages.*

5.2.2. *Transferee attitude toward TT*

Our field studies reinforced the managers' belief that faculty members do take long to publish their research results, and do not possess the necessary practical insights

[Matthyssens *et al.* (2005); Bruneel *et al.* (2010)]. Although Indian universities do work on global technology trends, the industry considers their research as not applicable. The faculty respondents stated that firms' managers often pressurize them for immediate or short-term results, and ask them not to share knowledge with other colleagues [Bogler (1999)]. Thus, we may affirm that managers, especially in larger firms are: (1) less inclined to invest in novel technologies, fearing cannibalization. (2) They are not interested in projects with significant inventor involvement to transfer tacit knowledge and (3) tend to prefer small incremental technologies; importantly, if something does go wrong, the faculty is to be blamed [Yusuf (2008); Tellis (2013)]. Herein, it may also be noted that at times adoption is difficult, owing to "not-invented here" syndrome or "pride of ownership" disputes with academicians [Cohen and Levinthal (1990); Lipinski *et al.* (2008)].

The other issue of salience includes information leakage [Gilsing *et al.* (2011)]. Managers worry that universities may use the same knowledge for further research and publish papers, making it thereby public. To ensure competitive advantage, managers tend to choose to include a non-disclosure clause, categorically stating that the technology was actually developed by the university. However, the faculty being an integral party to it, often wishes to share ownership rights, which effectively delays further "deal-signing" with industry partners. Thus, unless the industry is willing to learn from and value knowledge resting in universities' labs, weak UI linkages would continue to affect the socio-economic development of this region (i.e. India).

P6: *The greater the positive attitude of transferee toward TT, the higher the relational value in UI linkages.*

5.3. *Exchange readiness and UI linkage characteristics*

5.3.1. *University market orientation*

In general, most scientists have insufficient skills to build a business case for industrial clients [Leahy and Lane (2010)]. This focal issue has been raised by the TTO consultant, who stated: "*Researchers should fetch relevant details/samples requested by industry in a definite time frame but mostly they don't, and if we ask about the stage of technology (embryonic or ready to use) they take it casually. Unfortunately, they don't understand how the market works and bypass transparency in information disclosure which creates issues.*"

Additionally, the absence of or the low profile of industrial liaison offices and product features do have a significant impact on the functional value derived from partnering with academic institutions [Rogers (2003); Leahy and Lane (2010)]. Interestingly, as mentioned by the TTO consultant, the area of research also plays a major role: "*Usually a technology takes 6–12 months to commercialize and yield returns. There is no guarantee that even after waiting for 1–2 years it will fetch the expected returns. So, firms are hesitant to invest in certain domains (e.g. biotechnology/mechanical engineering).*"

Our field study shows that industry partners are not interested in a standalone technology, but a complete solution to cover all possible patent infringement. Although university-market orientation increases exchange readiness of the university, it has a dark side as well [Hong and Walsh (2009)]. For instance, too much focus on industry needs can actually narrow the university's outlook toward selected disciplines and easy to commercialize technologies. But then, what will happen to social sciences, management, or mathematics? Since only a limited number of firms are motivated to partner with universities, a high market orientation of faculty or TTO staff can create role conflicts in leading negotiations with the industry. Efficiency of collaboration management and role clarity is thereby highly crucial to effective partnerships [Albats *et al.* (2018)]. Extant literature has shown that entrepreneurial orientation does have a positive impact on new product development performance, but the effects are reduced when firms simultaneously adopt market orientation philosophy [Morgan *et al.* (2015)]. This is summarized by our participants in the following manner:

P7: *The relationship between the market orientation of the university and the relational value in UI linkages will be curvilinear such that the slope will be positive for lower levels of market orientation and then become negative at higher levels of market orientation.*
P8: *The greater the market orientation of university, the higher the functional value in UI linkages.*

5.3.2. *Firm absorptive capacity*

Absorptive capacity is critical to acquire new knowledge [Cohen and Levinthal (1990)]. Lack of training (skills and knowledge), fewer employees with scientific background, and low awareness about external knowledge sources are characteristics of technology laggards [Bishop *et al.* (2011)]. According to the respondents, a negative TT experience also makes a firm wary of future initiatives. In fact, the TTO consultant noted that Indian firms have poor knowledge management practices; they tend to prefer mature technologies from developed countries and are late adopters.

P9: *The greater the absorptive capacity of a firm, the higher the functional value in UI linkages.*

5.4. *The moderating role of environmental readiness in developing UI linkages*

5.4.1. *Economic infrastructure*

Financial crisis and government policies affect UI collaboration [Davey *et al.* (2011)]. Product development involves risk at every stage, and there are insufficient fall back options for scientists in case of a failure, which in turn, effectively incurs higher exit costs; the same was echoed by a faculty member:

> *"Due to economic downturn, a client's firm could not pay and the project was terminated. But I cannot give the same reason to my project staff. I paid their salaries from my pocket."*

Geographic proximity of transacting parties lowers maintenance costs, but the current institute lacked in this aspect [Bishop *et al.* (2011); Crescenzi *et al.* (2017); Tang *et al.* (2020)].

P10: *Economic infrastructure moderates the link between structural support in university and relational value in UI linkages; thus, the stronger the economic infrastructure, the stronger the link between the structural support in the university and the relational value in UI linkages.*
P11: *Economic infrastructure moderates the link between structural support in firms and relational value in UI linkages; thus, the stronger the economic infrastructure, the stronger the link between the structural support in the firm and the relational value in UI linkages.*

5.4.2. *Societal mindset*

The socio-cultural dimension consists of customs, lifestyles, and values that characterize a society [William (2002)]. Society, in general, does not take failure positively; it compels people to opt for a secure and stable source of earning. One of the participants (an entrepreneur) highlighted the same by stating:

> *"The US market is value driven and the Indian market is cost driven. Cultural and historical differences explain why our companies avoid risking money on developing technologies."*

In similar lines, a faculty member stated:

> *"Philosophically speaking, many people in academia feel that intellect and material wealth are separate, and business is the means to only make money. So the faculty should gain knowledge, publish papers and teach but not get involved in taking it to market."*

P12: *Societal mindset moderates the link between structural support in the university and relational value in UI linkages; thus, the broader the societal mindset, the stronger the link between the structural support in the university and the relational value in UI linkages.*

5.4.3. *State policy relevance*

Funding has a profound influence on the development and commercialization of university-based research [Swamidass and Vulasa (2009); Davey *et al.* (2011)]. According to faculty responses, although both government and the industry support universities in conducting R&D activities, government grants are predominantly directed for basic/fundamental research [Shapiro and Taylor (2013)]. Ironically, government policies are often criticized for a lack of clear vision and disbursement plans, extending project deadlines thereby [Yusuf (2008)]. The dean of R&D stated in this regard:

> "*The government should launch certain tax laws and give rebates on new technology adoption so companies are motivated to partner with academia.*"

P13: *State policy relevance moderates the link between structural support in the university and relational value in UI linkages; thus, the more relevant the state policies, the stronger the link between the structural support in the university and the relational value in UI linkages.*
P14: *State policy relevance moderates the link between structural support in the firm and relational value in UI linkages; thus, the more relevant the state policies, the stronger the link between the structural support in the firm and the relational value in UI linkages.*

5.5. *Linkage characteristics and mode of UITT*

Prior research has shown that a lack of inter-organizational trust and collaboration experience are some of the key factors that defer the pace of UITT [Bruneel *et al.* (2010); Bellini *et al.* (2019)]. The in-depth interviews that we conducted suggest that both flexibility and transparency of university IP policies and shared governance by UI partners are positively related to trust formation. On the other hand, trust in itself is positively related to knowledge transfer and innovation performance [Bstieler *et al.* (2015)]. Thus, relational value would in all possibility, influence managers of firm in choosing a particular mode of UITT.

Furthermore, universities value IP as a tool to both advance and disseminate knowledge. However, the industry does look to protect the value of their R&D investments. The industry, at its end, assesses the functional value associated with the university's research output in order to choose UITT modes, and thereby maximize the technological gains in the process.

P15: *The choice of the UITT mode depends on the combination of relational value and functional value as perceived by the firm.*

As Table 2 shows, in cases where both relational and functional values are low, the industry chooses to opt for research papers and conferences for collaboration. In the process, it keeps the product development costs to a minimum. On the other hand, if both relational and functional values are high, the industry chooses a research joint venture as maturity, whereby the appropriate technical capabilities enable them to conduct exploratory research. In between, if a firm does look for higher functional or relational value, it chooses patent licensing or consulting.

Table 2. UITT Mode choice of firms based on relational and functional value.

Characteristics of modes of university industry technology transfer		
Mode	Relational value	Functional value
Research papers, conferences	Low	Low
Patent licensing	Low	High
Consulting/research services	High	Low
Research joint venture	High	High

Figure 3 presents the overall conceptual framework. To advance the theory on UI relationships, it amalgamates various elements that have been described in both Tables 1 and 2. Appendix B provides a summary of all possible indicators to measure each variable included in the present conceptual framework.

6. Discussion

6.1. *Theoretical contributions*

In line with the recommendations of earlier researchers [MacInnis (2011); Compagnucci and Spigarelli (2020); Nsanzumuhire and Groot (2020)], this paper offered several key to theoretical contributions. (1) It clearly "*identified*" what value a firm derives by partnering with the academia. (2) It "*delineated*" a comprehensive typology of factors to promote UI linkages. (3) It "*summarized*" state-of-the-art by providing a systematic literature review. (4) It "*differentiated*" available UITT mode choice of firms, based on perceived relational and functional value. Finally, (5) it "*integrated*" SET, the quadruple helix model, along with other concepts in the

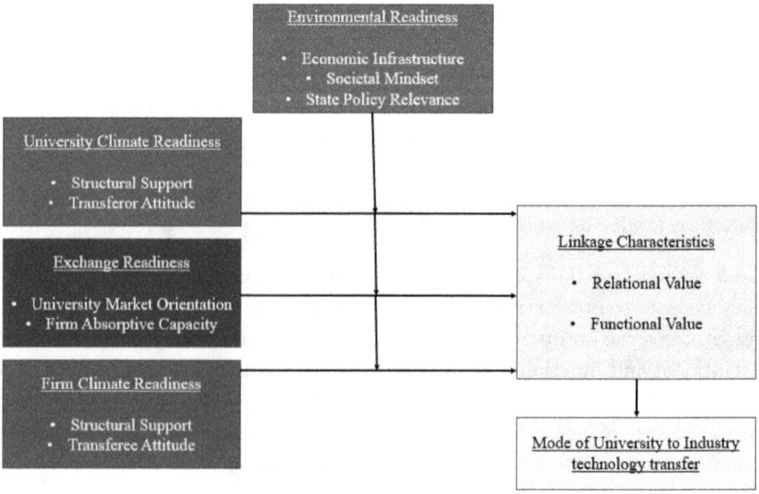

Fig. 3. Proposed framework to manage UITT.

typology. Including the unique socio-cultural factors of a developing economy, the model can be employed to examine UITT in a more general context.

Inter-firm collaboration for innovation and technology development is not a new phenomenon. Increased competition, shorter technology lifecycle, and market uncertainties lead firms to adopt a broader horizon in terms of innovation objectives and knowledge sources [Leiponen and Helfat (2010)]. In that respect, sourcing university-developed technologies come under the domain of inter-organizational/inter-firm relationships which serve as vehicles to spur economic growth [Mueller (2006); Klofsten *et al.* (2019)]. However, for success of UITT, the agents need conducive environment and capabilities to manage such relationships. This study used the quadruple helix model to develop a framework for UITT [Carayannis *et al.* (2018)]. The typology (i.e. university climate readiness, firm climate readiness, exchange readiness, and environmental readiness) assesses the maturity of the transacting organizations, the exchange flows, the government/state bodies, and the society at large. Grounded in SET, the study further postulates two dimensions of UI linkage characteristics, i.e. relational value and functional value, where each can assume high/low values independent of the other to decide the mode choice for university to industry TT.

6.2. *Managerial implications*

Table 3 provides implications of the study for university, industry, and environment. Easy TT policies and error-free processes ensure that both transferors and transferees can interact seamlessly for a win–win situation. Today, US universities for instance, have assumed a vital role in shaping vibrant economies [Cohen *et al.* (2002)]. However, even then, only a small fraction of technologies produced (less than 100 universities) is really utilized by firms [Atkinson and Blanpied (2008)]. In developing countries like India on the other hand, this ratio is further skewed due to lack of a supportive ecosystem for both managers and faculties. Thus, it requires careful deliberation to identify factors to promote UITT, and thereby account for complex interactions among researchers, university administrators, TTO staff, firm managers, governments, and society [Colombelli *et al.* (2021); Lopes and Lussuamo (2021)].

Suitable data collection and monitoring mechanisms (information systems and analytics) would possibly enable better resource allocation within both universities and firms; identify and track faculty experts, check the progress, and manage project funding. Herein, one may want to use the indicators from Appendix B to calculate both the university's and firms' readiness scores, along with environmental readiness to assess possibilities of academia-industry-state interactions. In fact, firms could also choose to use these scores to segment universities, and decide upon partnership regimes with research institutes and public laboratories.

6.3. *Future research directions*

Table 4 summarizes our recommendations: (1) vertically, to delve deeper into structure, stakeholders, and UITT characteristics and (2) horizontally, to examine UITT from a broader context.

Table 3. Illustrative implications of the proposed typology for theory and practice.

Entity	Factor	Examples	Implications to manage UITT
University	Climate readiness	• Low awareness of IPR policies and technology commercialization	• Sensitize faculty and university officials (INTV) • Provide incentives to motivate faculty and students (INTV) • Establish audit strategy for UITT projects (INTV) • Bring business leaders on board (INTV)
	Exchange readiness	• Not enough platforms to connect with industry	• Maintain web portal of faculty and their expertise (INTV) • Join technology open houses and trade shows (INTV) • Train TTO staff [Lockett and Wright (2005)]
Industry	Climate readiness	• Bureaucracy	• In case of failed TT both entities should share the loss (INTV) • Flatter and more horizontal structures [Hitt *et al.* (1998)]
	Exchange readiness	• Technologically laggard industry	• Regard universities as a partner in value chain (INTV) • Nurture UITT champions in the company (INTV) • Adequate sustained budget for faculty [Gulbrandsen and Smeby (2005)]
Environment	Environmental readiness	• Knowledge creation versus knowledge commercialization • Lack of policies to motivate industry to adopt university-generated research	• Provide benefits to firms if open offices near universities (INTV) • Quick loans to indigenous industry at low interest rates (INTV) • Structural reforms in university system, pay scale and institutional capabilities to facilitate UITT [Rasmussen (2008)]

Table 4. Future research agenda derived from our proposed typology.

Themes	Future research avenues
Vertical	• Empirical assessment of university, TT office, industry, government, and context-specific factors for successful UITT.
	• Interaction effect of climate readiness and exchange readiness for university and industry. Is it synergistic or contradictory?
	• Does relational value influence the perception of functional value and vice versa?
	• How do climate readiness and exchange readiness factors behave over different stages of UITT?
	• Does UITT mode choice affect a firm's performance?
	• How do past experiences moderate the relationship between antecedents and linkage characteristics? Are there systematic differences in: (i) university/industry assessment and (ii) actual impact from when the past engagement exceeds expectations or falls below expectations?
Horizontal	• Do strategic learning orientation, articulated learning intent, JV commitment, and relationship age affect UI linkages?
	• Does the 2 × 2 typology of mode choice of firms apply to partnerships between firms or firm and government labs (e.g. "Defence Research and Development Organization")?
	• How do UITT barriers/drivers behave in one-to-many kinds of UI relationships?
	• How can university and industry contribute to the betterment of society (undergraduate/graduate/executive education)?
	• How does the phenomenon relate to management principles (e.g. faculty entrepreneurship, change management, TTO management, and human resource management)?
	• How can one leverage information systems to manage research projects?
	• How can research on big data and internet of things (IOT) be used to solve industry problems?
	• Does open innovation/crowdsourcing change the relative necessities of UI partnerships and/or their impact?

Future researchers could also (1) use this study to discern the effect of university/firm participation on relational outcome (quality/satisfaction/commitment) and/or (2) use simulation models to capture possible interactions among the players (academia, firms, states, and society), as within this ecosystem, uncertainty can be reduced when their functions become synergistic. Importantly, this comprehensive framework may also be applicable for each entity being considered separately; e.g. identify which structural reforms can effectively increase the rate of technology commercialization in universities. Additionally, future research could also explore the below points.

6.3.1. *Gaining deep insights into science-business collaboration*

Some possibilities could be to address how faculty gender and tenure, industry sector, and state policies effectively drive scientist entrepreneurship. Second, whether the barriers/drivers and governance modes actually differ for customer management/sales consulting [Bekkers and Freitas (2008); Gaughan and Corley (2010); Aldridge and Audretsch (2011); Ahearne (2017)].

6.3.2. *Widening the breadth of science-business collaboration*

As the next stage of this research, one could examine the connection between UITT, along with other theoretical constructs, theories, and research fields. For example, both ambiguity and knowledge transfer challenges in strategic alliances [Simonin (1999)]; or how corporate social responsibility relates to university technology commercialization; or whether Big Data may be used as a new frontier to develop UI relationships [Park (2014)]; or whether open innovation could be a suitable substitute to UI partnerships [Bianchi *et al.* (2011); Moretti (2019)]; or possibly extending the aspects of social network analysis.

Acknowledgments

I wish to profusely thank the journal editor and the anonymous reviewers for their pertinent feedback and suggestions to improve this work. We also thank the editorial team for processing this manuscript and the seamless communication.

Appendix A. Sample Questionnaire for Entrepreneurs

- Discuss about your role in the current firm?
- Do you have a history of research collaboration with this institute? Any other institute?
- What drives you to partner with this academic institution for technology adoption?
- How is your experience with the licensing process followed at this institute?
- What are possible reasons that prevent TT from university to industry?
- What are your suggestions for a university to build a TTO?
- Any suggestions for firms interested in licensing a university developed technology?
- Anything else you wish to share regarding scope and challenges for TT from university to industry in India?

Appendix B. Synthesis of the Variables in the Proposed Model

Variable	Salient indicators
University structural support	• Bureaucracy [Davey *et al.* (2011)] • Hierarchical structure [Friedman and Silberman (2003)] • Insufficient and scattered funding [Swamidass and Vulasa (2009)] • Role conflict of TTO [O'Kane *et al.* (2015)] • Lack of institutional mechanism to check quality of its research output (INTV) • Lack of mechanisms to proactively evaluate IP produced therein for patenting and commercialization potential (INTV) • Lack of institutional mechanisms to maintain industry relations (INTV) • Lack of inter and intra departmental collaboration to craft a commercially viable product (INTV) • Misaligned incentive policy (INTV) • Lack of objective evaluation and accountability of TTO staff (INTV) • Failure to hire suitable talent in TTO (INTV)

(*Continued*)

Variable	Salient indicators
	• Lack of clearly stated policies to access labs/research facilities and monitor their performance (INTV) • Failure to assess financial and technical merit of prospective firms (INTV) • Lack of clarity on technology commercialization policies (INTV)
Transferor attitude towards technology transfer	• Slack and relaxed attitude of TTO staff [Leahy and Lane (2010)] • Perceived futility of patenting and its utilization (INTV) • Lack of documentation (INTV) • Low awareness about patenting and commercialization process (INTV)
Firm Structural support	• Lack of management support for innovative ideas [Hsu *et al.* (2015)] • Weak legal regulations for internal R&D activities [Arbussa and Coenders (2007)] • Inflexible incentive and reward system for innovation [Lipinski *et al.* (2008)] • Compartmentalization in PSUs (INTV) • Bureaucracy and long turnaround time in PSUs (INTV) • Lack of communication from firms to university on the real world problems and their expectations from academic world (INTV) • Lack of consistent vision (INTV)
Transferee attitude towards technology transfer	• Negative attitude toward applicability of university research [Bruneel *et al.* (2010)] • Turn blame on university for failed TT [Matthyssens *et al.* (2005)] • Perception of risk of information leakage if partnering with universities [Gilsing *et al.* (2011)] • "Not invented here" syndrome [Cohen and Levinthal (1990)] • Inertia toward technology acquisition [Yusuf (2008)] • Short term orientation, need quick results, time bound work (INTV)
University Market orientation	• Market reputation of university as below average principal [Lipinski *et al.* (2008)] • Lack of prospecting, negotiation, and communication skills of TTO staff [Siegel *et al.* (2004)] • Prototype not meeting industry expectations [Rogers (2003)] • Lack of communication from university to industry [Leahy and Lane (2010)] • Technology not presented properly in a given time frame [Leahy and Lane (2010)] • Small patent portfolios [Abramo and Pugini (2012)] • No relative process improvement for firm to adopt university technology [Rogers (2003)] • Scientific knowledge being too generic [Gilsing *et al.* (2011)] • Early stage invention (INTV) • Area of research (biosciences vs. computer science) (INTV) • Failure to offer complete solution instead of a single technology or patent (INTV) • Not enough platforms to find and connect with potential industry partners (INTV)
Firm absorptive capacity	• Low awareness about research conducted in universities and other research labs [Davey *et al.* (2011)] • Negative experience from previous UI collaboration [Lipinski *et al.* (2008)] • Lack of expertise to assimilate and transform new technology into commercial applications (INTV) • Technologically laggard (INTV) • Inability to quickly and correctly recognize value in new technology (INTV)
Societal mindset	• Societal attitude of risk aversion (INTV) • A general belief that knowledge shouldn't be exchanged for materialistic benefits (INTV)
Economic infrastructure	• Economic cycle [Davey *et al.* (2011)] • No fall back options or infrastructural support to combat failure (INTV) • Lack of nearby industry corridors to universities (INTV)

(*Continued*)

Variable	Salient indicators
State policy relevance	• Lack of business regulation framework to motivate industry to adopt university generated research and invest in joint R&D (INTV) • Lack of policies for tax rebate on investment in new R&D (INTV) • Challenges for inventors/researchers to get outside ethical committee clearances for commercialization, e.g. in biotechnology-related products (INTV)
Linkage characteristics	• Overinflated value of university generated IP [Bruneel *et al.* (2010)] • Lack of trust on the other party [Santoro and Saparito (2003)] • Ownership of IPR [Hall *et al.* (2001)] • High exit cost (INTV) • High gestation period for new technology commercialization, e.g. pharma (INTV) • Disagreement on payment terms (INTV)

References

Abd Rahim, N., Mohamed, Z., Amrin, A. and Masrom, M. (2021). Impact of self-regulated learning on entrepreneurial opportunity recognition and academic entrepreneurship performance. *International Journal of Innovation and Technology Management*, **18**, 4: 2150016.

Abramo, G. and Pugini, F. (2012). Assessing the relative technology transfer performance of universities and public research laboratories: The case of Italy. *International Journal of Technology Transfer and Commercialisation*, **11**, 1–2: 51–69.

Adams, J. D., Chiang, E. P. and Starkey, K. (2001). Industry-university cooperative research centers. *Journal of Technology Transfer*, **26**: 73–86.

Ahearne, M. (2017). Research centers, business schools, and the world of sales. *Journal of the Academy of Marketing Science*, **45**, 4: 461–464.

Ahrweiler, P., Pyka, A. and Gilbert, N. (2011). A new model for university-industry links in knowledge-based economies. *Journal of Product Innovation Management*, **28**, 2: 218–235.

Albats, E., Bogers, M. and Podmetina, D. (2020). Companies' human capital for university partnerships: A micro-foundational perspective. *Technological Forecasting and Social Change*, **157**: 120085.

Albats, E., Fiegenbaum, I. and Cunningham, J. A. (2018). A micro level study of university industry collaborative lifecycle key performance indicators. *The Journal of Technology Transfer*, **43**, 2: 389–431.

Aldridge, T. T. and Audretsch, D. (2011). The Bayh-Dole act and scientist entrepreneurship. *Research Policy*, **40**, 8: 1058–1067.

Arbussa, A. and Coenders, G. (2007). Innovation activities, use of appropriation instruments and absorptive capacity: Evidence from Spanish firms. *Research Policy*, **36**, 1: 1545–1558.

Atkinson, R. C. and Blanpied, W. A. (2008). Research universities: Core of the US science and technology system. *Technology in Society*, **30**, 1: 30–48.

Audretsch, D. B., Lehmann, E. E. and Wright, M. (2014). Technology transfer in a global economy. *Journal of Technology Transfer*, **39**, 3: 301–312.

Barbolla, A. M. B. and Corredera, J. R. C. (2009). Critical factors for success in university-industry research projects. *Technology Analysis & Strategic Management*, **21**, 5: 599–616.

Bekkers, R. and Freitas, I. M. B. (2008). Analysing knowledge transfer channels between universities and industry: To what degree do sectors also matter? *Research Policy*, **37**, 10: 1837–1853.

Bellini, E., Piroli, G. and Pennacchio, I. (2019). Collaborative know-how and trust in university–industry collaborations: Empirical evidence from ICT firms. *The Journal of Technology Transfer*, **44**, 6: 1939–1963.

Bhattacharjee, Y. (2008). Indian government hopes bill will stimulate innovation. *Science*, **319**, 5863: 556–556.

Bianchi, M., Cavaliere, A., Chiaroni, D., Frattini, F. and Chiesa, V. (2011). Organisational modes for open innovation in the bio-pharmaceutical industry: An exploratory analysis. *Technovation*, **31**, 1: 22–33.

Bishop, K., D'Este, P. and Neely, A. (2011). Gaining from interactions with universities: Multiple methods for nurturing absorptive capacity. *Research Policy*, **40**, 1: 30–40.

Blumenthal, D., Gluck, M., Louis, K. S., Stoto, M. A. and Wise, D. (1986). University-industry research relationships in biotechnology: Implications for the university. *Science*, **232**: 1361–1367.

Bogler, R. (1999). Rewards and costs: How do they affect the choice by university researchers of the preferred funding source in the USA? *Higher Education Policy*, **12**, 2: 159–175.

Brem, A., Gerhard, D. A. and Voigt, K. I. (2014). Strategic technological sourcing decisions in the context of timing and market strategies: An empirical analysis. *International Journal of Innovation and Technology Management*, **11**, 3: 1450016.

Breznitz, S. M., O'Shea, R. P. and Allen, T. J. (2008). University commercialization strategies in the development of regional bioclusters. *Journal of Product Innovation Management*, **25**, 2: 129–142.

Brown, M. G. and Svenson, R. A. (1988). Measuring R&D productivity. *Research-Technology Management*, **31**, 4: 11–15.

Bruneel, J., d'Este, P. and Salter, A. (2010). Investigating the factors that diminish the barriers to university-industry collaboration. *Research Policy*, **39**, 7: 858–868.

Bstieler, L., Hemmert, M. and Barczak, G. (2015). Trust formation in university-industry collaborations in the US biotechnology industry: IP policies, shared governance, and champions. *Journal of Product Innovation Management*, **32**, 1: 111–121.

Burg, E., Gilsing, V. A., Reymen, I. M. and Romme, A. G. L. (2013). The formation of fairness perceptions in the cooperation between entrepreneurs and universities. *Journal of Product Innovation Management*, **30**, 4: 677–694.

Carayannis, E. G. and Campbell, D. F. J. (2009). "Mode 3" and "quadruple helix": Toward a 21st century fractal innovation ecosystem. *International Journal of Technology Management*, **46**: 201–234.

Carayannis, E. G. and Campbell, D. F. J. (2010). Triple helix, quadruple helix and quintuple helix and how do knowledge, innovation and the environment relate to each other? A proposed framework for a trans-disciplinary analysis of sustainable development and social ecology. *International Journal of Social Ecology and Sustainable Development (IJSESD)*, **1**, 1: 41–69.

Carayannis, E. G., Campbell, D. F. J., Grigoroudis, E., Meissner, D. and Stamati, D. (2017). "Mode 3" universities and academic firms: Thinking beyond the box trans-disciplinarity and non-linear innovation dynamics within co-opetitive entrepreneurial ecosystems. *International Journal of Technology Management*, **77**: 145–185.

Carayannis, E. G., Grigoroudis, E., Campbell, D. F., Meissner, D. and Stamati, D. (2018). The ecosystem as helix: An exploratory theory-building study of regional co-opetitive entrepreneurial ecosystems as quadruple/quintuple helix innovation models. *R&D Management*, **48**, 1: 148–162.

Carayannis, E. G. and Rakhmatullin, R. (2014). The quadruple/quintuple innovation helixes and smart specialisation strategies for sustainable and inclusive growth in Europe and beyond. *Journal of the Knowledge Economy*, **5**: 212–239.

Chen, G., Yang, G., He, F. and Chen, K. (2019). Exploring the effect of political borders on university-industry collaborative research performance: Evidence from China's Guangdong Province. *Technovation*, **82**: 58–69.

Churchill, G. A., Jr., Ford, N. M. and Walker, O. C., Jr. (1976). Organizational climate and job satisfaction in the salesforce. *Journal of Marketing Research*, **13**: 323–332.

Cohen, W. M. and Levinthal, D. A. (1990). Absorptive capacity: A new perspective on learning and innovation. *Administrative Science Quarterly*, **35**, 1: 128–152.

Cohen, W. M., Nelson, R. R. and Walsh, J. P. (2002). Links and impacts: Survey results on the influence of public research on industrial R&D. *Management Science*, **48**, 1: 1–23.

Colombelli, A., De Marco, A., Paolucci, E., Ricci, R. and Scellato, G. (2021). University technology transfer and the evolution of regional specialization: The case of Turin. *The Journal of Technology Transfer*, **46**, 4: 933–960.

Compagnucci, L. and Spigarelli, F. (2020). The third mission of the university: A systematic literature review on potentials and constraints. *Technological Forecasting and Social Change*, **161**: 120284.

Cowan, K. R. and Daim, T. U. (2011). Review of technology acquisition and adoption research in the energy sector. *Technology in Society*, **33**: 183–199.

Crescenzi, R., Filippetti, A. and Iammarino, S. (2017). Academic inventors: Collaboration and proximity with industry. *The Journal of Technology Transfer*, **42**, 4: 730–762.

Dalmarco, G., Hulsink, W. and Blois, G. V. (2018). Creating entrepreneurial universities in an emerging economy: Evidence from Brazil. *Technological Forecasting and Social Change*, **135**: 99–111.

Davey, T., Baaken, T., Muros, V. G. and Meerman, A. (2011). *The State of European University-Business Cooperation. Study on the Cooperation between Higher Education Institutions and Public and Private Organisations in Europe.* Science-to-Business Marketing Research Centre, Muenster, Germany. Available at http://ec.europa.eu/dgs/education_culture/repository/education/tools/docs/uni-business-cooperation_en.pdf.

Dezhina, I. (2018). Innovation policy in Russia and the development of university–industry linkages. *Industry and Higher Education*, **32**, 4: 245–252.

De Fuentes, C. and Dutrénit, G. (2016). Geographic proximity and university-industry interaction: The case of Mexico. *Journal of Technology Transfer*, **41**, 2: 329–348.

D'Este, P., Llopis, O., Rentocchini, F. and Yegros, A. (2019). The relationship between interdisciplinarity and distinct modes of university-industry interaction. *Research Policy*, **48**, 9: 103799.

D'Este, P. and Patel, P. (2007). University-industry linkages in the UK: What are the factors underlying the variety of interactions with industry? *Research Policy*, **36**, 9: 1295–1313.

Emerson, R. M. (1976). Social exchange theory. *Annual Review of Sociology*, **2**, 1: 335–362.

Etzkowitz, H. (2008). *The Triple Helix: University-Industry-Government Innovation in Action.* Routledge, New York.

Etzkowitz, H. and Leydesdorff, L. (1995). The triple helix–University-industry-government relations: A laboratory for knowledge based economic development. *EASST Review*, **14**, 1: 14–19.

Etzkowitz, H. and Leydesdorff, L. (2000). The dynamics of innovation: From national systems and "Mode 2" to a triple helix of university–industry–government relations. *Research Policy*, **29**, 2: 109–123.

Figueiredo, N. and Fernandes, C. (2021). Cooperation university-industry: A systematic literature review. *International Journal of Innovation and Technology Management*, **17**, 8: 2130001.

Fischer, B. B., Schaeffer, P. R., Vonortas, N. S. and Queiroz, S. (2018). Quality comes first: University-industry collaboration as a source of academic entrepreneurship in a developing country. *The Journal of Technology Transfer*, **43**, 2: 263–284.

Fischer, B., Guerrero, M., Guimón, J. and Schaeffer, P. R. (2021). Knowledge transfer for frugal innovation: Where do entrepreneurial universities stand? *Journal of Knowledge Management*, **25**, 2: 360–379.

Fontana, R., Geuna, A. and Matt, M. (2006). Factors affecting university-industry R&D projects: The importance of searching, screening and signalling. *Research Policy*, **35**, 2: 309–323.

Frenken, K., Hölzl, W. and De Vor, F. (2005). The citation impact of research collaborations: The case of European biotechnology and applied microbiology (1988–2002). *Journal of Engineering and Technology Management*, **22**, 1–2: 9–30.

Friedman, J. and Silberman, J. (2003). University technology transfer: Do incentives, management, and location matter? *Journal of Technology Transfer*, **28**, 1: 17–30.

Galbraith, J. R. (1995). *Designing Organizations: An Executive Briefing on Strategy, Structure, and Process.* Jossey-Bass, San Francisco, CA.

Galvao, A., Mascarenhas, C., Marques, C., Ferreira, J. and Ratten, V. (2019). Triple helix and its evolution: A systematic literature review. *Journal of Science and Technology Policy Management*, **10**, 3: 812–833.

Gaughan, M. and Corley, E. A. (2010). Science faculty at US research universities: The impacts of university research center-affiliation and gender on industrial activities. *Technovation*, **30**, 3: 215–222.

Geisler, E. and Rubenstein, A. H. (1989). University-industry relations: A review of major issues. *Cooperative Research and Development: The Industry-University-Government Relationship*, eds. A. Link and G. Tassey. Springer, Dordrecht in Netherlands, pp. 43–62.

Gerwin, D., Kumar, V. and Pal, S. (1992). Transfer of advanced manufacturing technology from Canadian universities to industry. *Journal of Technology Transfer*, **17**, 2–3: 57–67.

Gilsing, V., Bekkers, R., Freitas, I. M. B. and Van Der Steen, M. (2011). Differences in technology transfer between science-based and development-based industries: Transfer mechanisms and barriers. *Technovation*, **31**, 12: 638–647.

Glaser, B. and Strauss, A. (1967). *The Discovery of Grounded Theory: Strategies for Qualitative Research.* Wledenfeld and Nicholson, London.

Gluck, M. E., Blumenthal, D. and Stoto, M. A. (1987). University-industry relationships in the life sciences: Implications for students and post-doctoral fellows. *Research Policy*, **16**, 6: 327–336.

Gulbrandsen, M. and Smeby, J. C. (2005). Industry funding and university professors' research performance. *Research Policy*, **34**, 6: 932–950.

Gulbrandsen, M. and Thune, T. (2017). The effects of non-academic work experience on external interaction and research performance. *The Journal of Technology Transfer*, **42**, 4: 795–813.

Hall, B. H., Link, A. N. and Scott, J. T. (2001). Barriers inhibiting industry from partnering with universities: Evidence from the advanced technology program. *Journal of Technology Transfer*, **26**, 1: 87–98.

Hamadi, T., Leker, J. and Meerholz, K. (2018). Emergence of innovation champions: Differences in the R&D collaboration process between science and industry. *International Journal of Innovation Management*, **22**, 8: 1840008.

Harper, D. (2001). *Changing Works: Visions of a Lost Agriculture.* University of Chicago Press, Chicago.

Hernández-Trasobares, A. and Murillo-Luna, J. L. (2020). The effect of triple helix cooperation on business innovation: The case of Spain. *Technological Forecasting and Social Change*, **161**: 120296.

Hitt, M. A., Keats, B. W. and DeMarie, S. M. (1998). Navigating in the new competitive landscape: Building strategic flexibility and competitive advantage in the 21st century. *The Academy of Management Executive*, **12**, 4: 22–42.

Hofstede, G. (2001). *Culture's Consequences: Comparing Values, Behaviors, Institutions, and Organizations Across Nations.* Sage Publications, Thousand Oaks, CA.

Hong, W. and Walsh, P. (2009). For money or glory? Commercialization, competition, and secrecy in the entrepreneurial university. *The Sociological Quarterly*, **50**, 1: 145–171.

Hou, B., Hong, J. and Shi, X. (2019). Efficiency of university–industry collaboration and its determinants: Evidence from Chinese leading universities. *Industry and Innovation*, **28**, 4: 456–485.

Hsu, D. W. L., Shen, Y. C., Yuan, B. J. C. and Chou, C. J. (2015). Toward successful commercialization of university technology: Performance drivers of university technology transfer in Taiwan. *Technological Forecasting and Social Change*, **92**: 25–39.

Inzelt, A. (2004). The evolution of university-industry-government relationships during transition. *Research Policy*, **33**, 6: 975–995.

Kanojia, M., Shukla, B., Wali, A. and Joshi, M. (2021). Critical success factors for leveraging technology transfer from higher education institutions to industry: Indian context. *International Journal of Innovation and Technology Management*, **18**, 4: 2150018.

Kihlstrom, R. E. and Laffont, J. J. (1979). A general equilibrium entrepreneurial theory of firm formation based on risk aversion. *Journal of Political Economy*, **87**, 4: 719–748.

Klofsten, M., Fayolle, A., Guerrero, M., Mian, S., Urbano, D. and Wright, M. (2019). The entrepreneurial university as driver for economic growth and social change — Key strategic challenges. *Technological Forecasting and Social Change*, **141**: 149–158.

Kohli, A. K. and Jaworski, B. J. (1990). Market orientation: The construct, research propositions, and managerial implications. *Journal of Marketing*, **54**, 2: 1–18.

Kumar, V. (2017). The role of university research centers in promoting research. *Journal of the Academy of Marketing Science*, **45**, 4: 453–458.

Lawler, E. J. (2001). An affect theory of social exchange. *American Journal of Sociology*, **107**, 2: 321–352.

Lawler, E. J. and Thye, S. R. (1999). Bringing emotions into social exchange theory. *Annual Review of Sociology*, **25**, 1: 217–244.

Leahy, J. A. and Lane, J. P. (2010). Knowledge from research and practice on the barriers and carriers to successful technology transfer for assistive technology devices. *Assistive Technology Outcomes and Benefits*, **6**, 1: 73–86.

Leiponen, A. and Helfat, C. E. (2010). Innovation objectives, knowledge sources, and the benefits of breadth. *Strategic Management Journal*, **31**, 2: 224–236.

Leydesdorff, L. and Etzkowitz, H. (1996). Emergence of a triple helix of university-industry-government relations. *Science and Public Policy*, **23**, 5: 279–286.

Leydesdorff, L., Park, H. W. and Lengyel, B. (2014). A routine for measuring synergy in university–industry–government relations: Mutual information as a triple-helix and quadruple-helix indicator. *Scientometrics*, **99**, 1: 27–35.

Libaers, D. (2014). Foreign-born academic scientists and their interactions with industry: Implications for University Technology Commercialization and Corporate Innovation Management. *Journal of Product Innovation Management*, **31**, 2: 346–360.

Lipinski, J., Minutolo, M. C. and Crothers, L. M. (2008). The complex relationship driving technology transfer: The potential opportunities missed by universities. *Journal of Behavioral and Applied Management*, **9**, 2: 112–133.

Lilien, G. L. (2017). Perspectives on university research centers: Lessons from the ISBM. *Journal of the Academy of Marketing Science*, **45**, 4: 459–460.

Lincoln, T. A. (1966). Problems and rewards in university-industry cooperative research. *Archives of Environmental Health: An International Journal*, **12**, 4: 452–456.

Link, A. N. and Siegel, D. S. (2005). Generating science-based growth: An econometric analysis of the impact of organizational incentives on university-industry technology transfer. *European Journal of Finance*, **11**, 3: 169–181.

Lockett, A. and Wright, M. (2005). Resources, capabilities, risk capital and the creation of university spin-out companies. *Research Policy*, **34**, 7: 1043–1057.

Lopes, J. and Lussuamo, J. (2021). Barriers to university-industry cooperation in a developing region. *Journal of the Knowledge Economy*, **12**, 3: 1019–1035.

Lopez-Rubio, P., Roig-Tierno, N. and Mas-Tur, A. (2021). A research journey from national systems of innovation to national systems of entrepreneurship: Introducing the sextuple helix. *International Journal of Innovation and Technology Management*, **18**, 8: 2130008.

MacInnis, D. J. (2011). A framework for conceptual contributions in marketing. *Journal of Marketing*, **75**, 4: 136–154.

Markman, G. D., Gianiodis, P. T., Phan, P. H. and Balkin, D. B. (2005). Innovation speed: Transferring university technology to market. *Research Policy*, **34**, 7: 1058–1075.

Matthyssens, P., Pauwels, P. and Vandenbempt, K. (2005). Strategic flexibility, rigidity and barriers to the development of absorptive capacity in business markets: Themes and research perspectives. *Industrial Marketing Management*, **34**, 6: 547–554.

Melnychuk, T., Schultz, C. and Wirsich, A. (2021). The effects of university–industry collaboration in preclinical research on pharmaceutical firms' R&D performance: Absorptive capacity's role. *Journal of Product Innovation Management*, **38**, 3: 355–378.

Meyer, M. (2003). Academic entrepreneurs or entrepreneurial academics? Research–based ventures and public support mechanisms. *R&D Management*, **33**, 2: 107–115.

Meyer-Krahmer, F. and Schmoch, U. (1998). Science-based technologies: University-industry interactions in four fields. *Research Policy*, **27**, 8: 835–851.

Miles, M. B. and Huberman, A. M. (1994). *Qualitative Data Analysis*. Sage Publications, Thousand Oaks, California.

Miller, K., McAdam, R., Moffett, S., Alexander, A. and Puthusserry, P. (2016). Knowledge transfer in university quadruple helix ecosystems: An absorptive capacity perspective. *R&D Management*, **46**, 2: 383–399.

Mora Valentin, E. M. (2000). University-industry cooperation: A framework of benefits and obstacles. *Industry and Higher Education*, **14**, 3: 165–172.

Moraes Silva, D. R. D., Lucas, L. O. and Vonortas, N. S. (2020). Internal barriers to innovation and university-industry cooperation among technology-based SMEs in Brazil. *Industry and Innovation*, **27**, 3: 235–263.

Moretti, F. (2019). "Open" lab? Studying the implementation of open innovation practices in a university laboratory. *International Journal of Innovation and Technology Management*, **16**, 1: 1950012.

Morgan, T., Anokhin, S., Kretinin, A. and Frishammar, J. (2015). The dark side of the entrepreneurial orientation and market orientation interplay: A new product development perspective. *International Small Business Journal*, **33**, 7: 731–751.

Mõttus, M., Lukason, O. and Varblane, U. (2019). Which individual characteristics are associated with academic entrepreneurship? Evidence from Estonia. *International Journal of Innovation and Technology Management*, **16**, 2: 1950018.

Mowery, D. C., Nelson, R. R., Sampat, B. N. and Ziedonis, A. A. (2001). The growth of patenting and licensing by US universities: An assessment of the effects of the Bayh-Dole act of 1980. *Research Policy*, **30**, 1: 99–119.

Mueller, P. (2006). Exploring the knowledge filter: How entrepreneurship and university-industry relationships drive economic growth. *Research Policy*, **35**, 10: 1499–1508.

Muscio, A. and Vallanti, G. (2014). Perceived obstacles to university–industry collaboration: Results from a qualitative survey of Italian academic departments. *Industry and Innovation*, **21**, 5: 410–429.

Nezu, R. (2007). *Technology Transfer, Intellectual Property and Effective University-Industry Partnerships. The experience of China, India, Japan, Philippines, the Republic of Korea, Singapore and Thailand.* WIPO Publication No. 928(E). World Intellectual Property Organization, Switzerland. Available at http://www.wipo.int/edocs/pubdocs/en/intproperty/928/wipo_pub_928.pdf.

Nsanzumuhire, S. U. and Groot, W. (2020). Context perspective on university-industry collaboration processes: A systematic review of literature. *Journal of Cleaner Production*, **258**: 120861.

O'Kane, C., Mangematin, V., Geoghegan, W. and Fitzgerald, C. (2015). University technology transfer offices: The search for identity to build legitimacy. *Research Policy*, **44**, 2: 421–437.

Palmatier, R. W. (2017). Marketing research centers: Community, productivity, and relevance. *Journal of the Academy of Marketing Science*, **45**, 4: 465–466.

Park, H. W. (2014). An interview with Loet Leydesdorff: the past, present, and future of the triple helix in the age of big data. *Scientometrics*, **99**, 1: 199–202.

Pattnaik, P. N. and Pandey, S. C. (2016). Revisiting university spinoffs: Conceptual advancements and theoretical underpinnings. *International Journal of Innovation and Technology Management*, **13**, 1: 1650005.

Perkmann, M., Neely, A. and Walsh, K. (2011). How should firms evaluate success in university-industry alliances? A performance measurement system. *R&D Management*, **41**, 2: 202–216.

Perkmann, M., Tartari, V., McKelvey, M., Autio, E., Broström, A., D'Este, P., Fini, R., Geuna, A., Grimaldi, R., Hughes, A., Krabel, S., Kitson, M., Llerena, P., Lissoni, F., Salter, A. and Sobrero, M. (2013). Academic engagement and commercialisation: A review of the literature on university-industry relations. *Research Policy*, **42**, 2: 423–442.

Perkmann, M., Salandra, R., Tartari, V., McKelvey, M. and Hughes, A. (2021). Academic engagement: A review of the literature 2011–2019. *Research Policy*, **50**, 1: 104114.

Perkmann, M. and Walsh, K. (2007). University-industry relationships and open innovation: Towards a research agenda. *International Journal of Management Reviews*, **9**, 4: 259–280.

Plewa, C., Korff, N., Johnson, C., Macpherson, G., Baaken, T. and Rampersad, G. C. (2013). The evolution of university-industry linkages — A framework. *Journal of Engineering and Technology Management*, **30**, 1: 21–44.

Plewa, C. and Quester, P. (2007). Key drivers of university-industry relationships: The role of organisational compatibility and personal experience. *Journal of Services Marketing*, **21**, 5: 370–382.

Ponomariov, B. and Toivanen, H. (2014). Knowledge flows and bases in emerging economy innovation systems: Brazilian research 2005–2009. *Research Policy*, **43**, 3: 588–596.

Puffal, D. P., Ruffoni, J. and Spricigo, G. (2020). Empirical evidence for Brazilian firms in terms of university–industry interaction, public funding and innovation outcome. *International Journal of Innovation Management*, **25**, 4: 2150040.

Quiñones, R. S., Caladcad, J. A. A., Quiñones, H. G., Castro, C. J., Caballes, S. A. A., Abellana, D. P. M. and Ocampo, L. A. (2020). Priority challenges of university technology transfer with interpretative structural modeling and MICMAC analysis. *International Journal of Innovation and Technology Management*, **17**, 5: 2050038.

Rajalo, S. and Vadi, M. (2017). University-industry innovation collaboration: Reconceptualization. *Technovation*, **62**: 42–54.

Rao, B. and Mulloth, B. (2017). The role of universities in encouraging growth of technology-based new ventures. *International Journal of Innovation and Technology Management*, **14**, 4: 1750014.

Rasmussen, E. (2008). Government instruments to support the commercialization of university research: Lessons from Canada. *Technovation*, **28**, 8: 506–517.

Rogers, E. M. (2003). *Diffusion of Innovations*. Free Press, New York.

Roy, R. (1972). University-industry interaction patterns. *Science*, **178**, 4064: 955–960.

Ryan, P., Geoghegan, W. and Hilliard, R. (2018). The microfoundations of firms' explorative innovation capabilities within the triple helix framework. *Technovation*, **76**: 15–27.

Santoro, M. D. and Bierly, P. E. (2006). Facilitators of knowledge transfer in university-industry collaborations: A knowledge-based perspective. *IEEE Transactions on Engineering Management*, **53**, 4: 495–507.

Santoro, M. D. and Chakrabarti, A. K. (2002). Firm size and technology centrality in industry-university interactions. *Research Policy*, **31**, 7: 1163–1180.

Santoro, M. D. and Saparito, P. A. (2003). The firm's trust in its university partner as a key mediator in advancing knowledge and new technologies. *IEEE Transactions on Engineering Management*, **50**, 3: 362–373.

Schaeffer, P. R., Guerrero, M. and Fischer, B. B. (2021). Mutualism in ecosystems of innovation and entrepreneurship: A bidirectional perspective on universities' linkages. *Journal of Business Research*, **134**, 184–197.

Schiller, D. (2006). Nascent innovation systems in developing countries: University responses to regional needs in Thailand. *Industry and Innovation*, **13**, 4: 481–504.

Schoen, A., de la Potterie, B. V. P. and Henkel, J. (2014). Governance typology of universities' technology transfer processes. *Journal of Technology Transfer*, **39**, 3: 435–453.

Schofield, T. (2013). Critical success factors for knowledge transfer collaborations between university and industry. *Journal of Research Administration*, **44**, 2: 38.

Sengupta, A. and Ray, A. S. (2017). University research and knowledge transfer: A dynamic view of ambidexterity in British universities. *Research Policy*, **46**, 5: 881–897.

Shapiro, S. and Taylor, J. (2013). Federal R&D: Analyzing the Shift from Basic and Applied Research Toward Development. Department of Economics, Stanford University. Accessed May 12, 2018. http://citeseerx.ist.psu.edu/viewdoc/download?doi=10.1.1.462.5446&rep=rep1&type=pdf.

Sheriff, M. and Muffatto, M. (2019). University spin-offs: A new framework integrating enablers, stakeholders and results. *International Journal of Innovation and Technology Management*, **16**, 2: 1950020.

Sherwood, A. L. and Covin, J. G. (2008). Knowledge acquisition in university-industry alliances: An empirical investigation from a learning theory perspective. *Journal of Product Innovation Management*, **25**, 2: 162–179.

Siegel, D. S., Waldman, D. A., Atwater, L. E. and Link, A. N. (2003). Commercial knowledge transfers from universities to firms: Improving the effectiveness of university-industry collaboration. *Journal of High Technology Management Research*, **14**, 1: 111–133.

Siegel, D. S., Waldman, D. A., Atwater, L. E. and Link, A. N. (2004). Toward a model of the effective transfer of scientific knowledge from academicians to practitioners: Qualitative evidence from the commercialization of university technologies. *Journal of Engineering and Technology Management*, **21**, 1: 115–142.

Simonin, B. L. (1999). Ambiguity and the process of knowledge transfer in strategic alliances. *Strategic Management Journal*, **20**, 7: 595–623.

Skute, I., Zalewska-Kurek, K., Hatak, I. and de Weerd-Nederhof, P. (2019). Mapping the field: A bibliometric analysis of the literature on university–industry collaborations. *The Journal of Technology Transfer*, **44**, 3: 916–947.

Smil, V. (2013). *Made in the USA: The Rise and Retreat of American Manufacturing.* MIT Press, Cambridge, MA.

Smith, B. (1998). Buyer-seller relationships: Bonds, relationship management, and sex-type. *Canadian Journal of Administrative Sciences*, **15**, 1: 76–92.

Smith, K. (1997). Economic infrastructures and innovation systems. *Systems of Innovation, Technologies, Institutions and Organizations*, ed. C. Edquist. Routledge, Ottawa, Canada, pp. 86–106.

Suh, Y., Woo, C., Koh, J. and Jeon, J. (2019). Analysing the satisfaction of university–industry cooperation efforts based on the Kano model: A Korean case. *Technological Forecasting and Social Change*, **148**: 119740.

Swamidass, P. M. and Vulasa, V. (2009). Why university inventions rarely produce income? Bottlenecks in university technology transfer. *Journal of Technology Transfer*, **34**, 4: 343–363.

Tang, Y., Motohashi, K., Hu, X. and Montoro-Sanchez, A. (2020). University-industry interaction and product innovation performance of Guangdong manufacturing firms: The roles of regional proximity and research quality of universities. *The Journal of Technology Transfer*, **45**, 2: 578–618.

Tartari, V., Salter, A. and D'Este, P. (2012). Crossing the Rubicon: Exploring the factors that shape academics' perceptions of the barriers to working with industry. *Cambridge Journal of Economics*, **36**, 3: 655–677.

Tavella, E. and Bogers, M. (2020). Leadership at an entrepreneurial university: How department heads manage multiple logics at a Scandinavian University. *International Journal of Innovation and Technology Management*, **17**, 5: 2050035.

Tellis, G. J. (2013). *Unrelenting Innovation: How to Build a Culture for Market Dominance.* Jossey-Bass, San Francisco, CA.

Thursby, J. G., Jensen, R. and Thursby, M. C. (2001). Objectives, characteristics and outcomes of university licensing: A survey of major US universities. *Journal of Technology Transfer*, **26**, 1–2: 59–72.

Thurston, M. and Eckelman, M. J. (2011). Assessing greenhouse gas emissions from university purchases. *International Journal of Sustainability in Higher Education*, **12**, 3: 225–235.

Tranfield, D., Denyer, D. and Smart, P. (2003). Towards a methodology for developing evidence-informed management knowledge by means of systematic review. *British Journal of Management*, **14**, 3: 207–222.

Van Burg, E., Romme, A. G. L., Gilsing, V. A. and Reymen, I. M. (2008). Creating university spin-offs: A science-based design perspective. *Journal of Product Innovation Management*, **25**, 2: 114–128.

van Den Berghe, L. and Guild, P. D. (2007). Firm perceptions of competitive advantage of new university technology and their impact on exclusivity of licensing transactions. *International Journal of Innovation and Technology Management*, **4**, 4: 479–494.

Villani, E., Rasmussen, E. and Grimaldi, R. (2017). How intermediary organizations facilitate university–industry technology transfer: A proximity approach. *Technological Forecasting and Social Change*, **114**: 86–102.

Wallin, J., Isaksson, O., Larsson, A. and Elfström, B. O. (2014). Bridging the gap between university and industry: Three mechanisms for innovation efficiency. *International Journal of Innovation and Technology Management*, **11**, 1: 1440005.

Watkins, A., Papaioannou, T., Mugwagwa, J. and Kale, D. (2015). National innovation systems and the intermediary role of industry associations in building institutional capacities for innovation in developing countries: A critical review of the literature. *Research Policy*, **44**, 8: 1407–1418.

Webster, J. and Watson, R. T. (2002). Analyzing the past to prepare for the future: Writing a literature review. *MIS Quarterly*, **26**, 2: 13–23.

Weiner, B. J. (2009). A theory of organizational readiness for change. *Implementation Science*, **4**, 1: 67.

Wickramasinghe, V. and Malik, K. (2018). University–industry collaboration in Sri Lanka — A developing country perspective. *International Journal of Innovation and Technology Management*, **15**, 4: 1850032.

William, W. (2002). Citizenship questions and environmental crisis in the Niger Delta: A critical reflection. *Nordic Journal of African Studies*, **11**, 3: 377–392.

Wirsich, A., Kock, A., Strumann, C. and Schultz, C. (2016). Effects of university-industry collaboration on technological newness of firms. *Journal of Product Innovation Management*, **33**, 6: 708–725.

Wong, C. Y. and Salmin, M. M. (2016). Attaining a productive structure for technology: The Bayh-Dole effect on university-industry-government relations in developing economy. *Science and Public Policy*, **43**, 29–45.

Yadav, M. S. (2010). The decline of conceptual articles and implications for knowledge development. *Journal of Marketing*, **74**, 1: 1–19.

Yusuf, S. (2008). Intermediating knowledge exchange between universities and businesses. *Research Policy*, **37**, 8: 1167–1174.

Zhang, S., Yuan, C. and Han, C. (2020). Industry–university–research alliance portfolio size and firm performance: The contingent role of political connections. *Journal of Technology Transfer*, **45**, 5: 1505–1534.

Biography

Priyanka Sharma is an assistant professor in the Marketing area at Indian Institute of Management (IIM) Lucknow, India, where she investigates Business-to-Business (B2B) relationships and university-industry linkages. Her works have appeared in Marketing Intelligence and Planning, Benchmarking: An International Journal, The Journal of High Technology Management Research, and Journal of Business-to-Business Marketing.

Index